# How to Do *just about* Everything

**Simon & Schuster**
1230 Avenue of the Americas
New York, NY 10020

## eHow, Inc.

**Editor-in-Chief:** William R. Marken
**Book Editor:** Sharon Rose Beaulaurier
**Editors:** Dale Conour, Julie Jares, Jason Jensen,
Roberta Kramer, Deborah McCaskey, Jill Metzler,
Sonya Mukherjee, Mimi Towle
**Editorial Assistants:** Shawn Asim, Linette Kim,
Alison Goldberg, Matt Holohan
**Creative Director:** Patrick Barrett

**Founder & CEO:** Courtney Rosen
**CFO:** Mark Murray
**VP of Engineering:** Gladys Barnes
**Director of Business Development:** Jose Guerrero
**General Counsel:** James M. Hackett
**VP of Commerce:** Josh Prince
**VP of Marketing:** Kristen Sager
**VP of Operations:** Jeff Tinker
**VP of Product Strategy:** Joseph A. Vause
**VP of Sales:** Kevin Walsh

Courtney Rosen and other contributors to this book
appear on behalf of eHow, Inc.

## .com press

**CEO:** John Owen
**President:** Terry Newell
**COO:** Larry Partington
**VP, International Sales:** Stuart Laurence
**VP, Publisher:** Roger Shaw
**Creative Director:** Gaye Allen
**Production Director:** Stephanie Sherman

**Managing Editor:** Janet Goldenberg
**Art Director:** Diane Dempsey
**Studio Manager:** Brynn Breuner
**Production & Layout:** Joan Olson, Lorna Strutt
**Production Manager:** Chris Hemesath

**Project Coordinators:** Margaret Garrou, Lorna Strutt
**Contributing Editors:** Mandy Erickson, Norman Kolpas
**Copy Chief:** Elissa Rabellino
**Copy Editors:** Linda Bouchard, Claire Breen,
Kathy Kaiser, Gail Nelson, Cynthia Rubin,
David Sweet
**Proofreader:** Ruth Jacobson
**Indexer:** Ken DellaPenta

●com|**press**

Designed and produced by .com press
.com press is a division of Weldon Owen Inc.,
814 Montgomery Street, San Francisco,
California 94133

Printed in the United States by Phoenix Color

10 9 8 7 6 5 4 3 2

Library of Congress Cataloging-in-Publication Data
is available.

ISBN 0-7432-1110-3

# How To Do *just about* Everything

**Courtney Rosen & the eHow Editors**

**Simon & Schuster**

New York • London • Toronto • Sydney • Singapore

# Contents

# Contents

## PERSONAL FINANCE, BUSINESS AND REAL ESTATE

# Contents

## HOME MAINTENANCE AND IMPROVEMENT

### Plumbing

## GARDENING

# Contents

## FOOD

# Contents

## PASTIMES AND CRAFTS

# Contents

# Contents

## PETS

# Contents

## STYLE, ETIQUETTE AND PERSONAL CARE

## HEALTH AND FITNESS

# Contents

## SPORTS AND RECREATION

# Contents

# AUTOMOBILES

## TRAVEL

## A NOTE TO READERS

When attempting any of the described activities in this book, please note the following:

Risky activities  Certain activities described in this book are inherently dangerous or risky. Before attempting any new activity, you should always know your own limitations and consider all applicable risks (whether listed or not).

Professional advice  While we strive to provide complete and accurate information, it is not intended as a substitute for professional advice. You should always consult a professional whenever appropriate, or if you have any questions or concerns regarding medical, legal or financial advice.

Physical or health-related activities  Be sure to consult a physician before attempting any health- or diet-related activity, or any activity involving physical exertion, particularly if you have any condition that could impair or limit your ability to engage in such an activity.

Adult supervision  The activities described in this book are intended for adults only, and they should not be performed by children without responsible adult supervision.

Violations of law  The information provided in this book should not be used to violate any applicable law or regulation.

All of the information in this book is obtained from sources that we believe are accurate and reliable. However, we make no warranty, express or implied, that the information is sufficient or appropriate for every individual, situation or purpose. Further, the information may become outdated over time. You assume the risk and full responsibility for all of your actions, and eHow, Inc., and the publishers will not be liable for any loss or damage of any sort, whether consequential, incidental, special or otherwise, that may result from the information presented. Some states do not allow the exclusion of implied warranties or the exclusion of incidental or consequential damages, so the above exclusions may not apply. The descriptions of third-party products and services in this book are for informational purposes only and are not intended as an endorsement by eHow, Inc., of any particular product or service.

# Foreword

We created eHow with one clear and ambitious goal: to help people discover how to do just about everything. It's a concept that stemmed from my own personal experience.

It all began when I found myself surfing the Web for hours one afternoon, trying to find out how to rotate the wheels on my inline skates. No site could give me the information I needed. *What if?* I wondered. What if there were one place on the Web where I could look up just about anything I wanted to do—and get easy, step-by-step instructions?

Less than a year later, we launched eHow.com—the world's most useful Web site— which now provides millions of people, including me, with more than 15,000 concise sets of instructions (or "eHows," as we call them). In addition, our company has built one of the Web's largest stores, where you can buy the things you need to complete any project or task.

For this book we have selected 1,001 of our favorite and most requested eHows to help you tackle life's basics during those times when you aren't online. Like our site, they provide the essential steps along with useful tips and warnings. Skill-level icons— ⌄ — indicate the ease or difficulty of each undertaking on a scale of one to five, with one being the easiest. In the last few pages you'll also find a keyword index to help you quickly locate instructions for every task.

Keep this book handy so you can refer to it whenever you need to accomplish things like removing red wine from your carpet, jump-starting your car or setting a formal table. Or enjoy browsing through these pages just for fun. Who knows? Someday you may need to know how to waltz, care for a ferret or shuck oysters—and you'll find the instructions right here.

This book and the eHow.com site were made possible by the knowledge and hard work of our talented writers and editors. Our team has created answers to more than 90 percent of the big and little questions eHow's visitors ask day after day. Thanks to these fabulous individuals, I at last know the proper way to introduce people, boil an egg, remove the skunk odor from my dog, and much more. I hope you'll find this knowledge as useful and rewarding as I do.

Have fun getting things done!

Courtney Rosen
Founder and CEO

*P.S. Next time you're online, visit our ever-expanding universe of how-to solutions at www.ehow.com. You'll find instructions, shopping, links to related sites, tips from other users and more. And please, feel free to contribute a tip or two yourself!*

...NE TICKETS • CHOOSE A LAWN GRASS • ... OF A LIGHT ... ONLINE • ...
...FER STICKERS • USE A COMPUTER TO TRANSFER CASSETTES TO CDS • GROW ANNUALS • RESEARCH STOCKS TO BUY • REPAIR SCRATC...
...MS • AVOID GETTING BLISTERS WHILE HIKING • MAKE A SNOWMAN • DRESS BUSINESS CASUAL—WOMEN • BUY A COMPUTER • PACK F...
...E • PLAY TOUCH FOOTBALL • MAKE A GREAT FIRST IMPRESSION ON A DATE • REFUSE A DATE TO ENSURE ANOTHER REQUEST • MAKE ...
...H • PAY BILLS DURING AN EXTENDED ABSENCE • ASK FOR FORGIVENESS • SHELL A HARD-BOILED EGG • MAKE A LAYUP • MAKE A BED ...
...RVIVE DOWNSIZING • RID YOUR HOME OF COCKROACHES • GET YOUR NAME OFF MAILING LISTS • BUY A VACATION HOME • USE CRUTCH...
...IN MENSA • FLIRT • PLANT A BARE-ROOT TREE OR SHRUB • CHECK A WOUND FOR INFECTION • FIND A GOOD MECHANIC • FLY A KITE • S...
...THLY BILLS ON TIME • DO PREVENTIVE HOME MAINTENANCE • LEARN TO TYPE • DEEP-CLEAN YOUR CARPET • GET INTERNET ACCESS • ...
...WERHEADS • CREATE YOUR OWN READING LIST • PAN FOR GOLD • GET RID OF UNWANTED HAIR • BUY A CONDO OR CO-OP APARTMENT ...
...D A SAND CASTLE • HIT A BASEBALL • TALK TO YOUR CHILD ABOUT SEX • SOOTHE A BURNT TONGUE • REPAIR A DRIPPING SHOWERHEA...
...ER • BE A PROPER GUEST AT A PARTY • MAKE A BASIC MARINADE • PLAN A FAMILY REUNION • MIX A FROZEN MARGARITA • REPAIR STUC...
...A LUNAR ECLIPSE • BLOW-DRY HAIR STRAIGHT • APPLY EYELINER • REPAIR A CARTRIDGE FAUCET • TAKE READING NOTES • CHOOSE A ...
...R • BREW A POT OF COFFEE • SURVIVE AN ENCOUNTER WITH A BEAR • CREATE AN EMERGENCY ROAD KIT • BUY A NEW CARPET • BOIL ...
...E MASHED POTATOES • CARE FOR A MATTRESS • PREPARE YOUR CLOTHES FOR DRY CLEANING • DELIVER KITTENS • TREAT HEAD LICE • ...
...ER • CHOOSE A HAIRSTYLIST • CHOOSE A TRAVELING COMPANION • CARE FOR JOCK ITCH • FINGER PAINT • BE A MAID OF HONOR • LEA...
...SEPLANTS • INSPECT A USED CAR BEFORE BUYING • GET FULLY EQUIPPED FOR ICE HOCKEY • ESTIMATE YOUR MORTGAGE PAYMENT • P...
...VE A PUMPKIN • CARE FOR HEMORRHOIDS • FIGHT INSOMNIA • INCORPORATE A BUSINESS • BECOME A PHOTOGRAPHER • INCREASE TH...
...URE NO MORE REQUESTS • PLANT BULBS IN FALL • STORE LEFTOVERS • BRING YOUR BUSINESS ONLINE • MAKE COLOR LAST BETWEEN ...
...ERS • TRAVEL WRINKLE-FREE • TREAT DIARRHEA • CLEAN GUTTERS • TEACH YOUR CHILD MANNERS • RESOLVE CONFLICT IN A MARRIAG...
...R NEW DOG TO YOUR HOME • REPAIR A BAD CREDIT HISTORY • BUY PEARLS • CLEAN JEWELRY • BROIL MEAT • SELL YOUR HOME WITHO...
...VENT YOUR DOG FROM CHEWING ON FURNITURE • GET THE BEST PRICE ON MUSIC CDS • WATER FLOWERS • MAKE HOT CHOCOLATE • C...
...ANGE BEDROOM FURNITURE • MAKE PUMPKIN PIE • MOW, EDGE AND TRIM A LAWN • CHOOSE A MAJOR IN COLLEGE • BREAK IN A LEATH...
...RUISE • HOUSE-TRAIN YOUR PUPPY • OPEN A WINE BOTTLE • BUY CAR TIRES • HELP A TEEN FIND A JOB • EXERCISE AT YOUR OFFICE • FI...
...E SCARY SPIDERS • SET UP A STEREO SYSTEM • CAST A LINE IN FLY-FISHING • FIND A JOB ONLINE • CLEAN A BARBECUE GRILL • TREAT ...
...K) OR 403(B) • GET A JOB • CARE FOR A MIGRAINE • STORE BREAST MILK • CHOOSE A HIGH-QUALITY GARMENT • HIT A FOREHAND IN TE...
...TE AN OFFER ON A HOME • MOVE TO A NEW HOME WITH YOUR CAT OR DOG • CHOOSE A DOCTOR • CARE FOR SILVER • USE A SNORKEL...
...R DEFAULT PRINTER • CLEAN AND CARE FOR MARBLE • RESEARCH A SUBJECT ON THE INTERNET • STOP A NOSEBLEED • SPEND LESS O...
...RCOME YOUR FEAR OF FLYING • CLEAN YOUR DOG'S EARS • MAKE A COSMOPOLITAN • REMOVE MAKEUP THOROUGHLY • SWIM THE FRE...
...A HOME-IMPROVEMENT PROJECT • WINTERIZE YOUR GARDEN • FIND THE BEST PLACES TO MEET PEOPLE • SEPARATE EGG WHITES FROM ...
...IR PET • PADDLE A RIVER RAFT • THROW A FOOTBALL • PROPAGATE HOUSEPLANTS FROM CUTTINGS • AVOID A COLD • SCRAMBLE EGGS ...
...ISTER • GRILL VEGETABLES • GET A FREE E-MAIL ACCOUNT • BE A BEST MAN • REPLACE A LIGHT SWITCH • MAKE EGGNOG • CREATE YO...
...CH TROUT • HANDLE FAMILY TENSION AT YOUR WEDDING • CHOOSE A DOMAIN NAME FOR A WEB SITE • CHOOSE A CABERNET • KNOW W...
...OKIES • MAKE A GIANT BUBBLE WAND • CHANGE A FLAT TIRE ON A BIKE • PREVENT THE FLU • SLOW THE AGING OF YOUR DOG • CONDUC...
...KE • SELECT A BASIC SET OF KITCHEN EQUIPMENT • TRAIN A VINE • BUY AN INK-JET PRINTER • PROTECT YOUR TEETH IN YOUTH SPORTS ...
...E HASH BROWNS • SELECT A MATTRESS • STAY MOTIVATED TO EXERCISE • UNCLOG A SINK • EVALUATE FREE INTERNET SERVICE PROVID...
...M SCRATCHING FURNITURE • CLEAN A COFFEEMAKER • EXAMINE A MOLE • MAKE OATMEAL • CANCEL A DATE AT THE LAST MINUTE • TA...
...ON • CLEAN WINDOWS • BOIL PASTA • SELECT A CAT BREED • CLEAN A CRYSTAL CHANDELIER • CREATE AN INVESTMENT PORTFOLIO • P...
...EPTION • INTRODUCE YOUR NEW BABY TO YOUR CAT • REINFORCE YOUR CHILD'S LEARNING AT HOME • DEAL WITH A BAD REPAIR • PER...
...DITIONS • BREW A POT OF TEA • UTILIZE THE LEMON LAW • MAKE BUBBLE MIX • SHAKE HANDS • GET RID OF FLEAS • CHOOSE THE RIGH...
...M A CONTAINER • GIVE A NEGATIVE EMPLOYEE REFERENCE • INTRODUCE PEOPLE • ALLEVIATE PUFFY EYES • TRIM A MUSTACHE • WRITE ...
...AY • MARINATE MEAT • CHOOSE A LIPSTICK COLOR • TIE A TIE • PAINT WOOD MOLDING • MAKE A JUMP SHOT • BECOME A STOCKBROKE...
...VE A EULOGY • FIND FREE STUFF ON THE WEB • CLEAN A POLYURETHANE-COATED HARDWOOD FLOOR • CALCULATE YOUR GOLF HANDIC...
...RKET FOR YOUR PRODUCT OR SERVICE • IMPRESS YOUR IN-LAWS • CARE FOR YOUR GARDEN SEASON BY SEASON • DEAL WITH STRANG...
...T ALLERGIES • MAKE HOLLANDAISE SAUCE • SHUCK OYSTERS • POLISH BRASS AND COPPER • LOSE WEIGHT • MAKE BROWNIES • PLA...
...ME OR MICE • TIME YOUR TRIP TO LONDON • DRESS BUSINESS CASUAL—MEN • HELP YOUR CHILD PREPARE FOR THE FIRST DAY OF SCHO...
...ST AID KIT FOR YOUR PET • WASH A CAR • MEASURE YOUR WINDOW FOR CURTAINS • CALCULATE YOUR DEBT-TO-INCOME RATIO • GARGL...
...A FLUID LEAK • USE A COMPUTER SCANNER EFFICIENTLY • CHOOSE FLATTERING EYEGLASS FRAMES • OVERCOME A PHOBIA • MAKE ...
...SHELLED SHRIMP • PREVENT HANGNAILS • MAKE A BASIC VINAIGRETTE • USE ESSENTIAL PHRASES IN FOREIGN LANGUAGES • MAKE TUR...
...RODUCE YOUR NEW BABY TO YOUR DOG • BUY A SOFA • PEEL AND MINCE GARLIC • CHOOSE A GOOD SEAT ON AN AIRPLANE • SEND AN ...
...TE ANYTHING • MAKE A DRY MARTINI • SECURE VENTURE CAPITAL MONEY • FIT EXERCISE INTO YOUR BUSY SCHEDULE • WEAN YOUR BA...
...A BUSINESS LOAN • MAKE A CORNUCOPIA • NEGOTIATE AN EMPLOYMENT CONTRACT • PLAY DARTS • STOP ON INLINE SKATES • PLAY B...
...VENT IDENTITY THEFT • USE CHOPSTICKS • REPLACE THE GRIP ON A GOLF CLUB • SEASON A CAST-IRON SKILLET • INVEST FOR YOUR C...
...A WINDOWS COMPUTER • TREAT ATHLETE'S FOOT • TEACH YOUR DOG NOT TO BEG AT THE TABLE • CHOOSE A CELLULAR PHONE SERVIC...
...I NOTE • COPE WITH MENOPAUSE • STOP WORRYING • CHANGE YOUR MOTOR OIL • SHOOT A FREE THROW IN BASKETBALL • PREVENT ...
...SKIN • SELECT A FUTON • KEEP A DOZEN RED ROSES FRESH • MONITOR STOCKS • LEARN HTML • PREVENT SHOE ODOR • FLY WITH ...
... • GRILL HAMBURGERS AND HOT DOGS • WHITEN YOUR TEETH • BLOW YOUR NOSE • CHOOSE A HIGH-SPEED INTERNET ACCESS P...

# How to...

## 1 Help Your Child Prepare for the First Day of School

Is it that time again already? Follow these simple steps to help your child face those first-day fears.

### ⊙ Steps

1 Begin preparing your child a few weeks before the big day (sooner, if this is his first school experience or a new school). If your household has relaxed bedtime and morning routines over the summer months, start to wake your child a little earlier each morning, and move bedtime up 15 minutes every few nights to re-establish "school hours."

2 Plan a back-to-school shopping day with each child individually, and make it a special event. Leave room in your budget for one or two small extravagances (reuse last year's backpack, but buy this year's hottest cartoon-character notebook).

3 Before the big clothes-shopping trip, spend some time with each child sorting through last year's things and deciding together what goes into which pile (keeper, hand-me-down or donate). Insist that your child try on every keeper.

4 For a new year in a new school, visit there a week or so before the first day. Walk through the buildings, locating the classrooms, the bathrooms and the lunchroom.

5 If your child will be riding the bus, find out the route he will take and drive it together a few times. If he is a walker, plan the route and walk it together both ways.

6 Help your child deal with first-day jitters by focusing on some special advantage of, for example, being a fourth-grader. Perhaps your child is now old enough for his own house key, an increase in allowance or some other new privilege.

7 Celebrate the big day. Go out for dinner or plan a special meal the night before, or present your child with a small gift.

### ✳ Tips

Unless your child's school sends out a detailed list of required supplies for his specific grade and classes, it's best to buy just the general stuff in August. Middle school and high school teachers in particular are likely to provide lists of exactly what your child will need for each subject a few days into the school year.

Don't wait too long to make that back-to-school shopping trip. By mid-August, local sources may be sold out of hot items.

Review important safety rules with your child, such as using established walking routes to and from school, what to do if approached by a stranger, and what to do if he misses the bus or loses the house key.

## 2 Help Your Child Make Friends at a New School

It's hard to be the new kid, but here's how you can help your child survive and thrive in a new school.

### ⊙ Steps

1 Contact the new school as soon as you know your child will be attending. Ask for whatever suggestions or support the staff can offer to help your child connect with classmates.

2 Address your child's practical concerns with specifics. Brainstorm ways to handle particular situations, such as whom to sit with on the bus, whom to eat lunch with and how to remember all those names.

3 With a younger child, rehearse conversations she might have with a potential new friend. Suggest that your child approach a potential friend with a question or remark that will engage the person in an ongoing dialogue, which might lead to a conversation about a shared interest.

### ✳ Tip

As the saying goes, make new friends, but keep the old. Encourage your child to keep in touch with friends from the old school or neighborhood by supplying her with stationery and stamps or an e-mail account.

4 Encourage your child to join whatever clubs, teams or other groups relate to her interests.

5 Emphasize that making friends takes time. Celebrate small successes such as learning the names of all the girls in chemistry class or getting invited to someone's sleepover.

6 Be a good role model. Share with your child your own feelings about the family's recent move and how you are going about making your own new friends.

7 Be a good friend. Recognize that your child will need some extra support and understanding from you to make a successful transition.

⚠ **Warning**

Most new friendships take time to develop. If, however, your child seems to have made no progress toward establishing new relationships after a few months, consider talking with a family counselor.

## Reinforce Your Child's Learning at Home   ·3

Show your child that learning can be fun. Here are a few real-life ways to do it.

### ⊙ Steps

1 Teach reading and writing by using vacations as a learning experience. Have younger children read road signs, and encourage older children to keep a travel journal.

2 Enlist your child's help in writing cards and greetings during holidays.

3 Ask your child to read at least 30 minutes a day, and encourage him to keep a daily diary or journal.

4 Sharpen your child's math skills while you shop—teach him to compare values and bargains and to add up prices.

5 Take your child to a baseball game and teach him about batting averages and other statistics.

6 Bring your child into the kitchen and ask him to help you measure ingredients for cooking.

7 Use items around the house—cans, boxes, books—to teach younger children about geometry.

8 Expand your child's horizons with history and geography—for instance, construct a family tree with him, using your family history as an example of how history connects us with the past. Read about historical events in an encyclopedia.

9 Give your child a puzzle map of the United States to work on at home, or have him follow a map on family trips.

10 Introduce your child to the world of science by having him observe and record details about the environment, such as the variety of plants and insects in the front yard, and by buying science kits.

11 Take your child to a science museum, especially one that offers lots of hands-on activities.

12 Have your child observe the properties of water: freezing, melting, boiling, evaporating and condensing.

✱ **Tip**

Stimulating a child's curiosity and love of learning can help him develop critical mental habits that will last a lifetime.

**Things You'll Need**

❑ books

❑ notebooks

❑ encyclopedia

❑ educational puzzles

## 4 | Write a Book Report

Writing a good book report requires summarizing a lot of information in a very small space. Follow these steps to make the task easier.

### ⊙ Steps

1 Take thorough and careful notes as you read the book (see 14 "Take Reading Notes").

2 Gather your reading notes and the book and have them by your side as you write your report.

3 Ask yourself, What would I want to know about this book?

4 Look through your notes and decide, based on the assigned length of the book report and your answers to the above question, what is essential to include and what can be excluded.

5 State the book's main point: Why did the author write the book? Or for fiction, give a brief plot summary.

6 Outline the plot or main ideas in the book (see 15 "Outline a Paper"), or for fiction describe the story and key dramatic points.

7 Follow your outline as you write the report, making sure to balance the general and the specific. A good book report will both give an overview of the book's significance and convey enough details to avoid abstraction.

8 Summarize the overall significance of the book: What has this book contributed to the knowledge of the world? For fiction: What does this story tell us about the author's views on life's big questions?

**✳ Tip**

Make sure to proofread your book report carefully before turning it in.

## 5 | Learn to Type

Mastering the keyboard isn't difficult if you go about it methodically and practice a little every day. Here are the basic strokes to get you started.

### ⊙ Steps

1 Put your fingers on "home row": left pinkie on *a*, left ring finger on *s*, left middle finger on *d*, and left index finger on *f*. For the right hand, put the pinkie on the semicolon, the ring finger on *l*, the middle finger on *k*, and the index finger on *j*.

2 Type the following—looking anywhere but the keyboard—saying the names of the letters out loud and using either thumb for the space bar: *f f space j j space d d space k k space s s space l l space a a space semicolon semicolon space.*

3 Repeat this as many times as you need to in order to feel that you're getting an intuitive sense of these letters.

4 Bring in *g* and *h* by reaching with the appropriate index finger.

**✳ Tips**

Take a typing class or use instructional software if you need external structure to help you practice regularly.

Some find the number keys too far away to type accurately. If you experience this, watch the keys as you type, since errors with numbers can be costly.

If you use word-processing software, check the program's reference manual or Help menu to learn formatting techniques, such as changing the type style and setting new margins.

5 Use this same saying-it-out-loud technique to learn the rows above and below home row: the left pinkie for *q* and *z*, the right pinkie for *p* and the slash. Again, the index fingers do double duty: *r, t, v* and *b* for the left index finger; *u, y, m* and *n* for the right index finger.

6 Use your pinkies for the shift key: the left pinkie if the right hand is typing the letter and vice versa.

7 Learn the numbers: left pinkie for *1,* left index finger for *4* and *5,* right pinkie for *0,* and right index finger for *6* and *7.*

8 Move to actual texts as soon as you can, since they'll make your learning real.

9 Master other keys as you see fit—such as the Control key and the arrow keys—but be aware that these differ from keyboard to keyboard and may not be worth learning.

10 Practice for at least 15 to 30 minutes every day.

## ⚠ Warnings

Avoid looking at the keyboard, however tempted. It's the only way to really learn to type.

Keys on computer keyboards vary slightly by model.

---

## Study for the SAT | 6

Though many colleges place less emphasis on SAT scores than applicants realize, the exam is still an important measure of a student's academic potential.

### ◎ Steps

1 Decide when you'll take the test, and register by the appropriate deadline—leave plenty of time to study.

2 Focus on learning the test as much as the content. The SAT is a multiple-choice exam in which each correct answer adds to your score and each incorrect answer subtracts from it.

3 Obtain copies of earlier tests from the College Board, a test-preparation company or a bookstore. Practice taking the test to become comfortable with it.

4 Review class notes in language arts and math. Within those subject areas, concentrate on reading comprehension, vocabulary, grammar and usage, geometry, algebra and arithmetic.

5 Practice by giving yourself timed mini-tests. Don't spend too much time on any one question, since each is worth an equal amount. If you finish before the time is up, go back and work on any questions you skipped the first time around, or review your answers if you completed the test.

6 Study all you want until the night before the test. Then knock off and get a good night's rest.

### ✳ Tips

Leaving a question blank neither adds nor subtracts anything. If you can eliminate two answers as definitely wrong, guess between the remaining two choices. If you are completely lost on a question, skip it.

If you are unhappy with your practice scores, consider an SAT preparatory course such as those offered by Kaplan or Princeton Review.

## 7 | Write a College Application Essay

A good college application essay sets its author apart from thousands of other applicants. Here are some steps you can take to make your essay stand out.

### ⊙ Steps

1   Start early. Give yourself enough time to think about your essay and revise it as needed.

2   Write about something you're familiar with.

3   Be yourself. The admissions team is interested in who you are—not someone you think they want you to be.

4   Be original. Though many college applications will have standardized essay questions, try to put an original, creative spin on your response. Make the essay your own.

5   Write an essay that shows how you're unique. For example, one student who wrote about her distinctive laugh got accepted on early decision to Columbia University. Include any experiences or jobs that might set you apart from other applicants.

6   Be authentic. There's no need to embellish your experiences.

7   Use a relaxed, comfortable tone of voice, but avoid being too familiar, sarcastic or comic.

8   Check to make sure your essay answers the questions asked. Avoid wandering too far from your subject matter.

9   Proofread your essay for spelling, punctuation and grammar.

10  Mail your application early to avoid any postal mishaps.

### ✳ Tips

Keep in mind that your audience will probably be a group of people very much like your high school teachers, but with slightly higher standards.

Try not to play it overly safe when writing your essay. You want to write an essay that is memorable.

Make sure the essay is well organized (see 15 "Outline a Paper").

## 8 | Choose a Major in College

The major you choose in college doesn't set the course for the rest of your life; it's merely a starting point. What's important is following your interests and discovering what you love to do.

### ⊙ Steps

#### Practical Aspects

1   Consider which courses you've done well in previously and decide which major they have prepared you for.

2   Investigate the quality of the professors and courses. Ask your academic adviser which departments are well-regarded in their fields. Get a list of these departments' courses to see if they interest you. Also ask students who are majoring in these subjects if they are satisfied with their respective programs and professors.

3   Do internships to get a feel for the kinds of jobs you could get with different majors.

### ✳ Tips

If you are having trouble deciding, consult your adviser about creating your own major.

Try a double major or a minor if you are having trouble narrowing down your fields of interest.

4   Consider the requirements for any potential majors. Find out whether they can be completed in four years or if they require graduate studies; also consider whether you would be willing to spend the necessary time and money.

5   Look at the different fields to which your major can be applied. Try to find a major that will offer flexibility when you are looking for a job.

6   Think about the growth of the field that interests you. Is the field expand-ing? Are graduates with your major being hired right out of college, or do they need additional training?

7   Contemplate the earning potential and base salary of jobs that are relat-ed to certain majors. Think of the lifestyle you would like to maintain and how certain salaries may affect it.

## Personal Aspects

1   Figure out what it is you love to do. Are there fields of study that spark your interest, or have you taken courses that you particularly enjoyed?

2   Ask yourself whether you have what it takes to succeed in your major.

3   Think about whether you would be happier having a job you love with little pay or having a job you can tolerate with substantial pay. Choose a career course accordingly.

4   Be flexible; there's time to change your major if you're unhappy with it.

## Take Lecture Notes                                        9

There are many ways to take lecture notes. This "trigger" method is time-tested and widely practiced.

### ◉ Steps

1   Write down the date.

2   Draw a vertical line down the lined portion of the page, about one-third of the way over from the left margin.

3   Write down categories and questions on the left side of the line as the lecture proceeds—for instance, "What to do if you catch fire."

4   Put specifics and answers on the right side of the line—for instance, "1. Stop; 2. Drop; 3. Roll."

5   Use abbreviations to keep up with your professors. Simple symbols include an up arrow (↑) for "increase" and a right arrow (→) for "led to" or "resulted in."

6   Note anything you're unclear about at the top of the page, and ask about it during the question period.

### ✳ Tips

Number your lists for easier structuring and recall.

Review your lecture notes the evening of the day you took them. This will help the knowl-edge stick in your mind.

Consider studying for exams by covering the right side of your notes and using the left side as a trigger to help you recall details.

## 10 | Research a Subject on the Internet

If you know where to look and what sources to trust, the Internet can be a great tool for conducting research.

### ⊙ Steps

1 Begin your search with a Web search engine. Enter keywords or phrases related to the subject matter you're interested in, and click Search.

2 In the results list, click on a site's name to go to it. Even if the site doesn't have great information, check to see if it has links to other sites that might be more useful. Use the Back button on your browser to return to the original results list.

3 If the first list had too many or too few results, tinker with your keywords to produce more focused search results.

4 Go to some of the many online encyclopedias for information about your subject. You'll find them under the Reference heading at a subject-indexed search site such as Yahoo. From the encyclopedia's search page, enter keywords and phrases related to your subject.

5 Go to sites that specialize in Internet research. These sites offer links to research materials and will sometimes do your research for you.

6 Look for online library catalogs. Some provide online access to the full text of certain articles and books.

7 Check out Internet newsgroups on your subject. You can even post a request for information.

8 Visit chat rooms that are related to your subject matter.

### ✳ Tips

Use multiple search engines to get a variety of search results.

Consider the source of information: university Web sites and government sources tend to be more reliable than individuals' personal Web sites.

### ⚠ Warning

Use caution when gathering information from the Internet. Is the information coming from a trustworthy source? Is a corporation endorsing the information?

## 11 | Do Research in the Library

The library is a great place to begin research for a term paper. Works are cataloged either in a computer database or on cards in drawers (the "card catalog").

### ⊙ Steps

1 Check the computer database, if that's what your library uses. Go to a computer terminal and enter a keyword or phrase from the subject matter you wish to research. Most systems will allow you to enter a specific author, title or subject. If you are searching for newspaper, magazine or journal articles, look in an online periodical index. Note that there are indexes for specialized subject areas, such as medicine.

2 Jot down the item's call number (it indicates where the item can be found, and will read something like "RUG 1.732"), as well as the availability status (whether or not it's checked out) and a listing of related items. At some libraries you can print out this information or e-mail it.

3 Or find your library's card catalog, if your library still uses this older system. A card catalog is a stack of drawers containing a large number of alphabetized note cards. Every item in the library will have three note

### ✳ Tips

When you find an item in the nonfiction stacks, it will probably be surrounded by many other works on the same subject. Browse the surrounding works for extra research material.

Most modern libraries offer not only books and periodicals but also films, videos, audio resources and possibly Internet connections. Ask a librarian for details.

cards: an author card, a title card and a subject-heading card. These are often filed in separate sets of drawers. For newspaper, magazine and journal articles, especially older ones that may not be indexed in computer databases, ask a librarian to recommend the appropriate periodical index to use. Older periodical indexes are usually in book form.

4   When you find the appropriate item, look for the call number.

5   Make a list of as many call numbers on your topic as you can find before going to the stacks. Try rephrasing your keywords and subjects to find a broad range of books you can narrow down after some browsing. To consolidate your search, make note of the call numbers on your list that are close to each other.

6   Find the section in the library that corresponds to the call number of your item. Some books and periodicals may be in closed stacks or storage, and you may have to page them.

7   Remember that librarians are paid to help library patrons. If you need help, ask someone.

Most libraries have photocopiers. Rather than check out a large number of books, make copies of just the pages with the material you need. Note which books they're from.

If your library doesn't have the material you need, ask a librarian about arranging for an interlibrary loan.

## Create Your Own Reading List | 12

So little time, so much to read. Making a list of books to read for pleasure is a lifelong process.

### ◎ Steps

1   Buy a journal, notebook or electronic assistant and use it for your list.

2   Join the public library, even if you go there just to browse.

3   Subscribe to book-review magazines or newsletters. Scan them for books and authors that interest you.

4   Read the best-seller lists to glean even more suggestions.

5   Investigate award-winning authors and books. Prestigious awards such as the Nobel Prize in Literature, the Pulitzer Prize, the National Book Award and the Booker Prize signify worthy literary accomplishments.

6   Read up on favorite topics and peruse the books' bibliographies (usually found in nonfiction works), adding titles to your list.

7   Discover your favorite authors and note their other works.

8   Join a book group and get referrals from other readers.

9   Audit or take a class at the local college or adult education program, or visit an Internet chat room or newsgroup. All can offer good pointers to worthwhile reading.

### ✱ Tips

You will find out about more books than you can possibly read in one lifetime, so focus your list from time to time, according to your interests.

Going on a trip? Read guidebooks, historical novels, cookbooks or whatever interests you most about your destination.

Take suggestions from people whose opinions and taste you trust.

## 13 Read Quickly and Effectively

**Sail through the barrage of information out there by using some key reading and skimming skills.**

### ⊙ Steps

1 Read different materials at different speeds: Skim or speed-read less important items, and save critical or difficult works for when you are most alert and have time.

2 Pick out the main ideas of a book by reading its cover flaps and scanning the table of contents. Use the index to quickly locate key words.

3 Survey the layout of your reading material. Look at the title and the bold-face section headings, and piece together the logical flow. This framework will guide you in reading the piece more carefully.

4 If you need to skim, try reading the first sentence of each paragraph (which usually is the topic sentence) to get a general idea of its content.

5 Practice reading more quickly by moving your index finger down a row of text at a speed slightly faster than your normal reading speed.

6 Underline sparingly so the truly useful information doesn't get lost.

7 Jot down quick notes, questions or thoughts that will make it easier to refer to the material later. Taking notes also makes for active reading and better retention of important points (see 14 "Take Reading Notes").

### ✳ Tips

Increasing your vocabulary will help you improve your reading speed.

Sign up for a speed-reading course—many are available.

## 14 Take Reading Notes

**Remembering what you read will help your schoolwork, and taking good reading notes will help you retain what you've read.**

### ⊙ Steps

1 Budget enough time for taking notes. The time you spend now will pay off with less review time and increased retention.

2 Date your notes, and write full bibliographic information next to the date, including author, title, publication, date of publication, city, publisher, and volume number for journal articles.

3 Take notes in outline form to structure the material, and break it into related chunks and subchunks.

4 Use the structure of the book (or article) as the structure of your notes. For instance, chapters correspond to major headings, chapter sections to subheadings.

5 Note anything that is pertinent to the author's argument; try to avoid trivial minutiae. Important points tend to be contained in introductory and concluding paragraphs.

6 Distinguish facts from opinions, and quotations from summaries, in a way that will make it clear which is which when you review your notes.

7 Review your reading notes the next day, and do it again a few days later. This is a time-efficient way of retaining the material.

### ✳ Tips

Consider using index cards if you're taking notes for a research paper. Be sure to list the bibliographic information on a separate, numbered card.

One way of deciding what is relevant is to "cheat" by reading the conclusion first so that you'll know what's important as soon as you come across it in the text.

Use abbreviations in your notes—for instance, an up arrow (↑) for "increase" and a delta (Δ) for "change."

## Outline a Paper 15

An outline helps you organize a paper's content in a logical and sequential way. Here is a basic guide.

### ⊙ Steps

1 Write your composition's working title at the top of a blank sheet of paper. It does not need to be the one you use for your final paper; something like "Midterm Paper" or "History Paper" will suffice.

2 Beneath the working title, write a few lines about the goal of the paper and the steps you will take to achieve that goal. For example: "In this paper, I will show the secrets of a successful and happy life, using scholarly journals from psychologists and veterinarians."

3 Follow the summary with a statement of your paper's thesis—for example, "Owning a dog can make one's life healthier and happier."

4 Begin to lay down the basic framework for your paper by dividing its content into sections.

5 Start by writing either an Arabic or Roman numeral 1—depending on your style of outline—followed by a period, then the title of the section (a "section heading"). In an informal outline use Arabic numerals; in a formal outline use Roman numerals.

6 Write a few lines describing what you wish to accomplish in the section.

7 Use subsections to list specific examples or topics that you wish to discuss under each heading. Mark them with a lowercase letter (a, b, c and so on)

8 Follow this format for each section heading, then put the sections in the following general order: introduction, body, conclusion.

### ✱ Tips

You may want to write each section heading on a separate sheet of paper to allow yourself room to take notes and brainstorm.

Remember that a paper outline is merely a tool in the paper-writing process and does not bind you to anything. Feel free to change its format to suit your needs.

As you write your paper, refer back to your outline to make sure you're on track.

## Write a Paper 16

Writing a good research paper is a tough challenge, but breaking it down into smaller pieces helps a lot.

### ⊙ Steps

1 Choose a topic that is broad enough to be interesting but narrow enough to be manageable.

2 Find your sources. Start with three or four, check their bibliographies for additional sources, and repeat the process until you have enough material to work with.

3 Reserve one index card for each source. Record the bibliographic information for the source on its index card, and number each card for ease of future reference.

4 Take reading notes on index cards, writing down only the material that is most relevant to your project. Write the source number on each card.

5 Organize your index cards by topic and subtopic.

6 Use the cards as a basis for an outline (see 15 "Outline a Paper").

### ✱ Tips

Avoid letting the size of the project daunt you. Stay focused on each subtask, and remember that if you do those well, you'll end up with an excellent research paper.

Use bibliography software to help manage your sources. Consult a style guide, such as the MLA (Modern Language Association) style manual, for details on citation of sources.

Consider taking a class on writing research papers.

7 Write an introduction that grabs the reader and plots out the trajectory of your argument.

8 Write the body of the paper, following the structure you created in your outline. Be sure to cite sources.

9 Write the conclusion, reviewing how you've made your points.

10 Come up with a title after you've written the paper, not before: You don't want the content of the paper to be hamstrung by an inappropriate title.

11 Read your paper at least twice to be sure your argument makes sense and is presented logically.

12 Proofread carefully; teachers hate typographical errors. Use your word processor's spelling checker, but don't rely on it utterly.

Don't leave such a difficult task to the last minute. Start early, and work gradually.

### ⚠ Warning

Be sure to cite your sources whenever you make use of an idea from someone else.

---

## 17 Write a Bibliography

**A bibliography or reference section is necessary for any research paper. Here is the standard method of writing one.**

### ⊙ Steps

1 List, alphabetically by author, each source used in writing the paper. Write the last name of the author, followed by a comma, and then his or her first name, followed by a period.

2 Include the full title of the work, if it is a book. Underline the title and follow it with a period.

3 Write the name of the city in which the work was published, followed by a colon.

4 Include the name of the publisher, followed by a comma.

5 Conclude the entry with the date of publication, followed by a period.

6 If you are citing an article from a periodical, list the author's name as you would when citing a book. Cite the article's name, followed by a period, enclosed in quotation marks. Then write and underline the name of the journal or magazine it came from. Include the date of publication, followed by a colon and the relevant page numbers; close the entry with a period. Volume and issue numbers are not included for newspapers and magazines. For trade or academic journals, include the volume and issue number after the underlined journal title. Follow with the date of the publication in parentheses, then a colon and the relevant page numbers.

### ✱ Tips

Buy a good writers handbook that gives examples of research writing for your area of study: Each academic discipline has its own format for publication.

Cite material from the Web by first giving the author's name; the title of the document followed by a period, in quotation marks; the title of the scholarly project, periodical, or professional or personal Web site, underlined; the names of the editors, if given, followed by a period; the name and location of the associated institution or organization, followed by a period; the date of access of the source; and the full URL in angle brackets (<and>), beginning with the protocol (e.g., "http"). Close the entry with a period.

---

## 18 Improve Your Memory

**Scores of books, videos, Web sites and seminars are devoted to memory enhancement. The steps below summarize the main points of most techniques.**

### ⊙ Steps

1 Make sure you're alert and attentive before trying to memorize anything.

### ✱ Tips

Review what you have memorized right before going to sleep; this might help you recall it better in the morning.

2   Understand the material rather than merely memorizing it, if it's the type that requires deeper comprehension.

3   Look for larger patterns or ideas, and organize pieces of information into meaningful groups.

4   Link the new bits of knowledge with what you already know. Place what you learn into context with the rest of your knowledge, looking for relationships between ideas.

5   Engage your visual and auditory senses by using drawings, charts or music to aid memory. Creating a memorable mental picture can also help.

6   Use mnemonics—devices such as formulas or rhymes that serve as memory aids. For example, use the acronym "HOMES" to memorize the Great Lakes (Huron, Ontario, Michigan, Erie and Superior).

7   Repeat and review what you've learned as many times as you can. Apply it or use it in conversation, as continual practice is the key to remembering things in the long term.

Things that interest you are easier to remember. Try to develop an interest in what you're memorizing.

Your memory and thinking will function much better if you're in good health, well-rested and properly hydrated.

Try writing down or reciting aloud what you've memorized—this can help etch it into your mind.

## Cram for a Test                                                    19

Cramming, while not an ideal style of study, is an inevitable part of student life. Focus on general concepts, memory techniques and relaxation.

### ⊙ Steps

1   Compose yourself. Relax and take several deep breaths to clear your mind of clutter and stress.

2   Cover the most difficult information first.

3   Review the main points, general ideas and broad, sweeping concepts. These are essential to understanding the more detailed points on which you will be tested.

4   Skim lecture notes and assigned reading materials (see 13 "Read Quickly and Effectively").

5   Take breaks to stretch, relax, eat or exercise. As a general rule, you should take a break for 10 minutes out of every hour.

6   Review the main points and concepts one more time and then get some sleep before the big exam.

### ✱ Tips

Go easy on the caffeine and sugar. The initial boost from these substances will inevitably be followed by a crash.

Nourish yourself. Eat a good meal with a balanced carbohydrate-to-protein ratio. Avoid overeating, which tends to cause sluggishness.

### ⚠ Warning

Avoid staying up all night before a test. Depriving yourself of sleep may hurt more than it helps.

## Break the Procrastination Habit                                    20

There's an old joke that the members of Procrastinators Anonymous plan to meet ... but keep putting it off.

### ⊙ Steps

1   Think about why you procrastinate: Are you afraid of failing at the task? Are you a perfectionist and only willing to begin working after every little element is in place? Are you easily distracted?

### ✱ Tip

Remember that progress, not perfection, is your goal.

2   Break up a large, difficult project into several smaller pieces.

3   Set deadlines for completion. Try assigning yourself small-scale deadlines—for example, commit to reading a certain number of pages in the next hour.

4   Work in small blocks of time instead of in long stretches. Try studying in one- to two-hour spurts, allowing yourself a small break after each stint.

5   Start with the easiest aspect of a large, complex project. For example, if you're writing an academic paper and find that the introduction is turning out to be difficult to write, start with the paper's body instead.

6   Enlist others to help. Make a bet with your family, friends or co-workers that you will finish a particular project by a specified time, or find other ways to make yourself accountable.

7   Eliminate distractions or move to a place where you can concentrate. Turn off the television, the phone ringer, the radio and anything else that might keep you from your task.

## 21   Find Out Your IQ

Though IQ (intelligence quotient) has come under scrutiny as a measure of intelligence, finding out your IQ can help you join certain organizations and can open other doors for you.

### ⊙ Steps

1   Find an appropriate IQ test—there are a great many out there. On the Web, consider visiting www.iqtest.com to take an IQ test and to get general information about the process.

2   Take the test and score it.

3   Take several more tests and average the scores, dropping the lowest and highest. The result will give a good approximation of your IQ.

4   Understand the results. Generally, an IQ of 100 places you in the 50th percentile (exactly average); 110 puts you in the 75th percentile; 120 in the 93rd; and 130 in the 98th, which is high enough to join Mensa.

5   Remember that no single number can measure something as complex and nuanced as intelligence. Instead, IQ is intended to measure your chances of academic success in schools.

**✴ Tip**

Be aware that high-IQ societies such as Mensa usually accept the results of only certain IQ tests. Contact the individual society to find out its requirements (see 22 "Join Mensa").

**⚠ Warning**

Keep in mind that there are many important human abilities that IQ tests can't measure, such as musical or artistic talent, physical coordination, social ability, ambition and sense of humor.

## 22   Join Mensa

Mensa is an international organization of people in the top 2 percent of the intelligence range. Founded in England in 1946, it now has more than 100,000 members. Here's how to join.

### ⊙ Steps

1   Keep in mind that testing in the top 2 percent on an accepted IQ test or standardized test is the only membership criterion.

**✴ Tips**

Visit Mensa's Web site (see step 2) to get more detailed information for your specific situation.

2 Visit the Mensa Web site (www.mensa.org) to get the information you'll need to complete the steps below. Alternatively, call (817) 607-0060 or (800) 66MENSA, or send a letter to American Mensa, 1229 Corporate Drive West, Arlington, TX 76006-6103.

3 Find out if Mensa will accept the results of an intelligence test you've already taken. Mensa also accepts scores from approximately 200 standardized tests (such as the LSAT or GMAT).

4 Order official test results from the appropriate testing company and send them to Mensa.

5 Contact your nearest Mensa office to take the official Mensa test, if you haven't qualified through another test.

6 Be prepared to pay annual dues if you're admitted.

As a Mensa member, you'll be able to interact with other Mensa members at social events, through publications and during various activities.

## Get a Job                                                          23

Good timing plays a role in finding a job, but that's only part of the picture. Here's how to find the job you want.

### ⊙ Steps

1 Assess your skills, experience and goals, and select appropriate employment fields that interest you.

2 Spread the word. Tell everyone you know and meet that you are looking for a job—you will be surprised at the number of opportunities you'll discover this way.

3 Network, network, network. Attend professional-association meetings in your industry, scour the associations' membership directories for contacts, and schedule informational interviews with people in the field. Always get more names of people to contact at the end of the informational interview. Volunteer for something.

4 Contact your local or state employment office, or your college career center, for resources and leads.

5 Get out and about. The most direct way to learn about job openings is to contact employers themselves. Target an area downtown, dress the part, and stop in at every appropriate business establishment, including employment agencies, to fill out an application.

6 Remember that many job openings are not listed in the newspaper help-wanted section. However, Internet job boards are often used by employers for their ease and immediacy.

7 Pick up the phone. Yes, it's scary, and yes, you'll hear "No" a lot, but you only need a handful of "Yeses" to land a job.

8 Follow up on written contacts. Send out résumés if you must, and you'll certainly fill out applications, but these alone won't get your face in the place. Follow up with a phone call within five to seven days of every written communication.

9 Ask for interviews. If you find yourself interviewing for a position that's not for you (or with an interviewer who obviously doesn't think you're

### ✳ Tips

When you're interviewing, make it a dialogue. Asking questions will make you appear knowledgeable and eager, as well as help to calm your nerves.

Review the Sunday help-wanted section to get a feel for the hiring marketplace.

Drop in on your local chamber of commerce breakfast or after-dinner meeting. These are usually open to nonmembers for a small fee and offer the opportunity to make valuable contacts.

See 27 "Speed Up a Job Hunt" for additional pointers.

### ⚠ Warning

Avoid making the mistake of turning down additional interviews once you've had a good one. Keep your job search in high gear right up until your first day on the new job.

right for the opening), ask for interviews with other department heads or even with other companies that the interviewer may know are hiring.

10 Prepare. Do some research on the hiring company and its industry so that you'll have a stock of relevant questions to ask the person across the desk.

11 Give the impression that you're ready to be part of the team.

12 Send a thank-you note after the interview. E-mail is acceptable.

13 Call your interviewer three days later and ask if there is any more information you can provide.

---

## 24 Find a Job Online

The Internet is rewriting the rules of the job-search game. Make sure you know all the ways to find a job online.

### ◎ Steps

1 Peruse the Web sites of any companies that interest you. Most companies will post job openings on their sites.

2 Go to a Web site specifically geared toward finding jobs. You can search for jobs on these sites by career field, location and even potential salary.

3 Search on your school's career-center Web site, if you're a student. These Web sites have job listings, guidance for writing résumés and advice on interviewing.

4 Visit an online newspaper and search the classifieds section for help-wanted ads and job opportunities. Many national as well as local newspapers have Web sites.

5 Check out search engines, as these also feature classified sections. Browse according to your location and interests.

### ✱ Tips

Search frequently—new job listings are posted every day.

Many sites offer services that will allow you to e-mail your résumé directly to a potential employer.

### ⚠ Warning

Some sites made specifically for finding jobs may require a membership fee. Read the fine print before signing up.

---

## 25 Network Effectively

Networking can get you a job or otherwise expand your business horizons. The key to networking is taking the initiative—and refining your conversational skills.

### ◎ Steps

1 Talk to people you don't know, everywhere you go. Cocktail parties and weddings are just the tip of the iceberg; don't forget about airplanes, supermarket lines, sports events, festivals, bookstores and so on.

2 Learn to ask "What do you do?" with comfort, sincerity and interest.

3 Become a better listener. Ask a question and then be quiet until you hear the answer.

### ✱ Tips

Make news so you can get your name out there. Be the dog walker who gets on the evening news for organizing the Doggy Olympics.

Stay in touch with people you like and respect even if they can't help you immediately. You don't want to go to someone only when you are desperate.

4   Practice your own presentation of your skills. Learn more than one approach, whether frank or subtle.

5   Keep a great updated brochure, business card or some other form of information about yourself on you at all times. Get comfortable with handing out your card.

6   Take classes to improve your public speaking, body language and writing skills.

7   Join every networking club and association in your field.

8   Follow up on any lead, no matter how minor.

## Prepare a Basic Résumé                              26

There are as many kinds of résumés as there are jobs. Use a style that matches your personality and career objectives.

### ⊙ Steps

1   Choose one or two fonts at most, and avoid underlined, boldfaced and italic text. Many companies use automated recruiting systems that have difficulty with special formatting.

2   Opt for the active voice rather than the passive voice (say "met the goal" rather than "the goal was met").

3   Provide contact information such as your home address, phone number and e-mail address at the top of your résumé.

4   Include an objectives statement, in which you use clear, simple language to indicate what kind of job you're looking for. This should appear below your contact information.

5   List your most recent and relevant experience first. Include time frames, company names and job titles, followed by major responsibilities.

6   In a second section, outline your education, awards, accomplishments and anything else you wish prospective employers to know about you.

7   Hire a proofreader or have someone you trust proofread your résumé. Mistakes in spelling, grammar or syntax can land it in the circular file.

8   Limit your résumé to one page unless it is scientific or highly technical. Less is definitely more when it comes to résumés.

9   Write a cover letter to submit with your résumé (see 29 "Write an Effective Cover Letter").

### ✱ Tips

Refrain from using "I" in your résumé.

Leave out personal information, particularly as it relates to your age, race, religious background and sexual orientation.

Avoid obscure fonts, clip art and other unnecessary visuals.

checklist

## ✓ 27 Speed Up a Job Hunt

When you're looking for a job, it's all too easy to let yourself be lulled by the familiar rhythms of home or work life. Before you know it, another month has gone by and you're still out of work or unhappily employed. Here are some ways to jump-start your job search and get your career in gear.

### Know yourself

- ❏ Make a list of your skills. Note which ones you're most interested in using, and which are most likely to interest employers.

- ❏ Identify the skills that you haven't gotten a chance to use in your current or most recent job. Which ones are most important to you?

- ❏ Think about how you can use your favorite skills in a new job. Set specific short-term and long-term goals to guide your job search.

- ❏ Decide which of your short-term goals are negotiable and which are not.

- ❏ Write a 2-minute speech describing your experience, skills and goals. Rehearse it.

### Get organized

- ❏ Make a list of leads: people you know, people they've referred you to and companies that interest you.

- ❏ Set goals—for example, to send out 10 résumés this week, make five cold calls or conduct two informational interviews.

- ❏ Make weekly and daily to-do lists, and check off each item as it's completed.

- ❏ Keep files or notebooks noting everyone you've written to, called or interviewed with, and anything you want to remember. Include job listings and contacts' business cards.

- ❏ Keep your files handy and well-organized so you can refer to them quickly in case of a phone call.

### Brush up job-seeking skills

- ❏ Hire a proofreader to catch any errors in your résumé.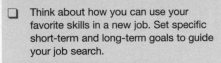

- ❏ Ask a friend or colleague to grill you about your experience so you can practice your answers.

- ❏ Videotape yourself in a mock interview to see how you come across.

- ❏ Hire a consultant to look over your résumé and teach you some interviewing techniques.

- ❏ Make sure you have clean, wrinkle-free professional attire ready to wear for job interviews.

### Research and target employers

- ❏ Read trade publications to learn about companies in your field and determine which ones may be hiring.

- ❏ Talk to friends or acquaintances in the field for the inside scoop on companies.

- ❏ Set up informational interviews or ask to spend a day with someone who has the type of job you're seeking.

- ❏ Target your cover letters to individuals who may be in a position to hire you— send a copy to the HR department as well.

- ❏ After scheduling an interview, search the Web for more facts about the company.

- ❏ Ask the company for a press kit or annual report if it's not available on the Web.

- ❏ Make a list of questions that show your knowledge and interest in the company.

## Write a Résumé When Changing Careers | 28

Your résumé should change along with your career goals. Here are some ways to restructure and polish your résumé as you move toward a new profession or career.

### ⊙ Steps

1 Read up on the skills and requirements for the new career or job you are seeking. Look at job listings in the newspaper or online to get an idea of what skills you'll need to break in.

2 Make a list of the skills and requirements you discovered in step 1. Your new résumé will need to focus on them.

3 Compare the skills and requirements on that list with those listed on your current résumé, underlining the qualifications both have in common. These are the skills that will carry over to your new résumé.

4 Rewrite the résumé to highlight the skills that apply to your new career. Focus on your strengths, experience and education in these areas.

5 Change the focus of your résumé. If you are a pharmacologist trying to break into pharmaceutical sales, for example, focus on your experience with different vendors and other tasks that relate to sales.

6 Think of any other experiences relevant to the skills on your list, including volunteer work, internships, hobbies and travel. Work all of these experiences into your résumé.

### ✳ Tips

Consider volunteering, interning or taking a second job within your new area of interest to gain experience.

If you don't feel you can write an effective résumé, specialized services can do it for you. Look in the yellow pages or on the Internet under "Résumé" or "Résumé Service."

### ⚠ Warning

You may have to settle for a lower-paying job until you can build up your experience—and hence your résumé—when changing careers.

## Write an Effective Cover Letter | 29

A résumé is an essential tool for any job search, but it's not the only tool. Your cover letter is equally important.

### ⊙ Steps

1 Find a job posting, job tip or advertisement that interests you, and make sure you are truly qualified for the position. Busy employers sometimes receive hundreds of letters, so don't waste their time or yours.

2 Match the letterhead style and paper you will use for your cover letter to that of your résumé. This helps to establish a solid first impression.

3 Skip the salutation if you do not know the name of the person who will be reviewing your résumé. It's best to address the letter to a specific person; call the company and see if the receptionist can give you a name and title.

4 Grab the reader's attention right away—make him or her want to keep reading. You need to distinguish yourself early from the rest of the pack.

5 Mention in the first paragraph where you learned about the job opportunity and why you're interested.

6 Establish a professional image in the second and third paragraphs by highlighting your most significant accomplishments and qualifications. Be careful not to quote your résumé verbatim.

### ✳ Tips

Before writing your cover letter, research the company to which you're applying. Then your letter can refer to specifics about the employer's business as reasons for your interest in working there.

Keep it short. Most cover letters are one page and use a standard business-letter format (see 36 "Write a Formal Business Letter").

Consider using bullet points in your middle paragraphs to further highlight accomplishments.

Avoid getting too personal or wordy. Save stories and relevant anecdotes for the interview.

Don't brag. Confidence is important, but don't overdo it.

7   Clarify what you can contribute to the employer's organization rather than what you hope to gain from this potential relationship. You can discuss the latter in the interview.

8   Remind the reader, in the last paragraph, that your résumé will further explain your qualifications, experience and education. Request a personal interview, and indicate the times you will be available.

9   Close your letter by telling the reader that you look forward to hearing from the company, and restate your enthusiasm for learning more about the opportunity.

10  Double-check your document for spelling and grammar; refer to a stylebook if necessary. Carelessness makes a bad impression on employers.

11  Print your letter using a good ink-jet or laser printer.

## ⚠ Warning

Never send a photocopied letter or use a form letter. This tells the prospective employer that you are not interested enough to write an original letter.

---

## 30 | Succeed at a Job Interview

**Most interviewers form their opinion of you in the first few minutes of a meeting. Here's how to make a good impression.**

### ◉ Steps

1   In the days before your interview, talk to people who have worked at the company. If it's practical, hang around outside the building while employees are arriving and note how they dress and behave.

2   Learn the name and title of the person you'll be meeting with. Arrive at least 10 minutes early to collect your thoughts.

3   Take time to greet and acknowledge the secretary or administrative assistant; it's good old-fashioned courtesy, and besides, this person may have a lot of influence.

4   Bring along an extra résumé and letters of recommendation in case the interviewer doesn't have them handy.

5   Be open and upbeat. Face your interviewer with arms and legs uncrossed, head up, and hands and face at ease. Smile and look the interviewer in the eye.

6   Know the company's business, target clients, market and direction cold.

7   Walk in prepared with a few relevant questions and listen carefully.

8   Subtly give the impression that you're already part of the team by using "we" when asking how something is done. For example, say, "How do we deal with the press?"

9   Conclude with a positive statement and a quick, firm handshake. Ask when you might follow up, and get a business card from the interviewer.

10  Send a thank-you note.

### ✱ Tip

Avoid asking about money at the start of the interview.

## Request a Reference From a Former Employer 31

A good employment reference can cinch that sweet job offer you've worked so hard for.

### ⊙ Steps

1   Get references before you need them. Managers make job changes, too, and time can erase the memory of even the most outstanding employee.

2   Offer to write the reference letter for your former employer to review and sign. This saves him or her valuable time, and it allows you to highlight the accomplishments you consider most valuable to future employers.

3   Contact former employers and other references before offering their names to potential employers. Beyond simple courtesy, this gives you the chance to supply these people with important information such as who might be calling, the type of job you're applying for, and which of your skills you would like your reference to emphasize.

4   Acknowledge a reference with a thank-you note, even if you didn't get the job. If you did, offer a celebratory lunch.

### ✱ Tips

If you encounter an unhelpful policy, such as one that restricts managers from giving reference information beyond confirming job title and dates of employment, ask the manager if he or she will give you a personal (rather than professional) reference.

Consider co-workers and department heads with whom you've had significant interaction—they can be good references, too.

---

## Negotiate an Employment Contract 32

Be confident and careful when negotiating a new contract.

### ⊙ Steps

1   Research your market value before your first interview: Talk to friends and acquaintances in the business, contact headhunters, and consult career Web sites that include information such as salary ranges and benefits packages.

2   Assess the company's approach, noting whether it invites negotiations or makes an offer first.

3   Listen to the way an offer is presented. A negotiation-minded manager will ask what figure you had in mind to get the process moving.

4   Delineate the different aspects of the job offer: money, benefits, responsibilities, stock options, schedules.

5   If the offer appears set, be creative in negotiating for alternative perks such as time off, relocation expenses or a transportation allowance.

6   Repeat the offer out loud after you hear it, then don't say anything until the employer does. Often, your silence will be misinterpreted as hesitation and the employer will sweeten the pot.

7   Speak your mind if you have any concerns.

### ✱ Tips

Clearly demonstrate your sincere excitement and interest in the job as well as in the compensation.

Focus on being an ally—not an adversary—throughout the negotiations. This will keep things amiable and show that you are a team player.

## 33 | Work Efficiently

We'll keep this short so you can get back to work.

### ⊙ Steps

1 Keep your desk and your files organized to avoid wasting time shuffling through piles of paper.

2 Go through your inbox at the beginning of each workday. Either throw away, file or follow up on each item.

3 Prioritize a list of the tasks you need to accomplish that day.

4 Delegate tasks to co-workers and assistants if possible.

5 Finish one task before you go on to the next.

6 Reduce paperwork by storing important information on your computer or electronic organizer.

7 Communicate effectively and plan carefully to make sure a job is done properly the first time around.

8 Schedule time when you'll be available and let colleagues know, to avoid constant interruptions. Close the door if you need to.

9 Take breaks. A short walk or quick lunch away from the office will increase your overall productivity.

10 Before leaving for the day, tidy up your desk and make a short list of projects you will need to do the next day.

11 Try not to take work home. You need the break.

### ✳ Tips

Recognize when you have the most energy in a day and do the important or harder tasks then.

Note that certain days (usually Monday or Friday) are more hectic, and schedule accordingly.

Have someone else answer your phone if possible. Give instructions about calls you wish to take and those that can be returned later.

### ⚠ Warnings

Avoid regularly going out for long business lunches—big meals make for unproductive afternoons.

Avoid procrastination (see 20 "Break the Procrastination Habit").

## 34 | Make a To-Do List

Invest just a little time planning your day, and accomplish more things smoothly.

### ⊙ Steps

1 Set aside 10 to 15 minutes before you go to bed or as soon as you wake up in the morning to jot down a to-do list for the day.

2 Use any format that is comfortable for you—try writing in your daily planner. Make sure your list is on one page and can be carried with you wherever you go.

3 Try assigning tasks to hourly time slots, even if exact timing isn't crucial.

4 Fill in preset, mandatory appointments such as business meetings or child-pickup times.

5 Prioritize tasks in order of urgency, and write those down before less important ones.

6 Figure out when, during the day, you are most productive and alert. Schedule the more demanding tasks during these times.

7 Schedule an easy job after a difficult one or a long task after a short one to keep yourself stimulated.

### ✳ Tips

Schedule things comfortably, allowing time for unexpected delays or mishaps; avoid an impossibly tight timetable.

Be sure to list everything you need to accomplish—the more you can account for, the more smoothly your day will run and the less you need to remember.

Break down large projects into specific tasks before writing them down on your list.

Feel free to revise your list as necessary, as the day goes on.

8   Indicate time for breaks and time to spend with family and friends.

9   In addition to your daily schedule, keep an ongoing list of projects that you need to accomplish but haven't penciled into your daily list—things to fix around the house, bills to mail, people to call. Update this list at least once a week.

10  Try keeping a list of long-term goals. For example, you might be planning to remodel your home or return to school for an advanced degree.

11  Make a running list for leisure or entertainment goals—books to read, videos to rent, restaurants/bars/clubs to try. Write down names as you hear or read about them.

## Delegate Responsibility    35

**Many people delegate less than they should. Divvy up your assignments and hand out tasks for others to do—this will increase your overall productivity and efficiency.**

### ⊙ Steps

1   Decide whether you want to delegate.

2   Decide to whom you want to delegate responsibility. Does this person have the requisite skills and background knowledge? How quickly will your helper learn?

3   Brief the person on the task: Define exactly what he is responsible for. Explain how the task fits into the larger project. Clarify objectives and decide on deadlines.

4   Encourage your delegate to act independently and to make his own decisions by emphasizing the results. Say, "I want to see such-and-such. Don't tell me the details."

5   Allow the person to perform the task. Offer help as needed, but don't be intrusive—if he has a different way of doing things than you do, be flexible and open-minded about it.

6   Periodically check the standard of work. Provide helpful feedback.

7   Recognize the person who does the job—give him credit for it. Public recognition for a job well done will encourage effort in the future.

### ✴ Tips

Delegate tasks at times when productivity is likely to be high—try earlier in the week as opposed to Friday.

Be available to answer questions and discuss progress.

Be generous with praise for jobs that are well-executed.

### ⚠ Warnings

Avoid thinking that it is too much trouble to delegate responsibility—delegating will pay off over time if the task needs to be done again and again.

Delegating a task doesn't mean you are no longer responsible for seeing that it's completed.

## Write a Formal Business Letter    36

**The business-letter format is very important for communicating formally with a company. These steps describe the full block format, in which all lines start at the left.**

### ⊙ Steps

1   Type the letter using a word processor. Formal letters should not be written by hand.

### ✴ Tips

Some people prefer to center the date and closing section instead of aligning them at the left.

2   Use your own letterhead. If you don't have letterhead, use formal 8½-by-11-inch stationery with a matching envelope. Avoid store-bought note cards.

3   If you don't have preprinted letterhead, type your name, title and return address four to six lines down from the top of the page.

4   Type the date two to six lines down from the letterhead or return address. Three lines below is the standard.

5   Choose your alignment: left aligned or justified on both sides.

6   Skip two lines and type the recipient's full name, business title and address, aligned at the left margin. Precede the name with Mr., Ms. or Dr. as appropriate.

7   Skip two to four lines and follow with your greeting, again using the formal name and closing with a colon—"Dear Mr. Jones:" for example.

8   Skip two more lines and begin your letter. Introduce yourself in the first paragraph, if the recipient does not already know you. Examples: "We recently met at a seminar at the Biltmore" or "I recently purchased an insurance plan from your company."

9   Continue with the body of the letter, stating your main purpose for writing. This may be to lodge a complaint, compliment the business on its products or services, or request information. Be as brief and concise as possible.

10  Skip two lines and conclude the letter with "Sincerely," "Thank you" or "Best wishes," followed by a comma.

11  Leave at least four blank lines for your signature, then type your name and title. Sign the letter in ink in the space created.

Try to keep the letter to one page. Generally, a short letter will get a quicker response than a long, rambling composition that takes several pages to come to the point.

Make certain your punctuation, spelling and grammar are letter-perfect. Use your computer's spelling-check program and proofread the letter before you send it.

## ⚠ Warning

No matter how upset you are with the recipient, try not to show your anger in your letter. You are much more likely to get the response you desire if you remain courteous.

---

## 37 | Write a Speech

Writing a speech is in many ways like writing a paper, except that there is no penalty for spelling and punctuation errors.

### ⊙ Steps

1   Assess how much time your speech should take. If you don't have a time limit, try to keep your speech brief yet informative.

2   Think about your audience and let your perception of the audience shape the tone of your speech as you write it.

3   Begin with an introduction that establishes who you are, what your purpose is, what you'll be talking about and how long you're going to take. You may want to include a joke, anecdote or interesting fact to grab the audience's attention.

4   Organize your information into three to seven main points and prioritize them according to importance and effectiveness.

5   Delete points that aren't crucial to your speech if you have too many for your time frame.

6   Start with your most important point, then go to your least important point and move slowly back toward the most important. For example, if

### ✱ Tips

The introduction should make up about 10 to 15 percent of the total speech. The conclusion should make up 5 to 10 percent.

When preparing your speech, make your notes easy to read by writing or printing them in large, clear letters.

Rehearse and time your speech before delivering it. Prune it if necessary.

If you'll be presenting a great deal of information, consider using handouts or visual aids to help your audience remember your points.

you have five points, with No. 5 being the most important and No. 1 being the least important, your presentation order would be 5-1-2-3-4.

7   Add support to each point using statistics, facts, examples, anecdotes, quotations or other supporting material.

8   Link your introduction, points and conclusions with smooth transitions.

9   Write a conclusion that summarizes each of your points, restates your main purpose and leaves the audience with a lasting impression.

## Deliver a Speech                                                    38

Mastering your tone and body language is the formula for a successful delivery.

### ⊙ Steps

1   Approach the podium confidently and put your notes in a place where you can see them easily.

2   Stand up straight with your feet shoulder-width apart. Look at the audience, pause and begin speaking. If there is no microphone, project from your diaphragm, not your throat.

3   Set the tone in your introduction with appropriate facial expressions and diction, and a specific mood (such as folksy or hard-hitting).

4   Make eye contact with people in different parts of the audience, including the back row.

5   Pause briefly after you state key points to allow the audience time to absorb the information. Also, use natural and relaxed hand gestures and facial expressions to emphasize certain points.

6   Pronounce your words clearly and vary your rate, pitch and volume to keep the delivery lively.

7   Refresh your memory by periodically glancing at your notes, but avoid reading from your notes directly unless you are reading a long quotation.

8   Close your speech by thanking the audience and then confidently exiting the stage.

### ✱ Tips

Practice! Videotape yourself to discover distracting habits such as swaying back and forth, saying "uh" and "um" too often, or making nervous gestures.

If you stumble on a word, it's a sign you should slow down.

## Lead Effective Business Meetings                                    39

Too many business meetings are ill-directed, digressive and drawn out. Call a meeting only when it's absolutely critical, and structure it firmly so that it achieves its purpose.

### ⊙ Steps

1   Decide whether you really need to call a meeting. Can the issue be resolved by an individual or a conference call?

2   Determine who needs to attend. Try keeping the number of attendees small, as large meetings get unwieldy. Suggest that people attend only

### ✱ Tips

Schedule a meeting before lunch, at the end of the day or immediately before another one to prevent it from going on too long.

the parts of the meeting that involve them. This way you can keep the discussion more focused.

3   Set definite starting and stopping times.

4   Prepare an agenda. Explain the goal of the meeting; if there are many goals, decide which ones command priority and make this clear.

5   Circulate the agenda in advance to allow attendees to prepare.

6   Assemble visual aids such as charts, handouts or slides.

7   Start the meeting at the designated time, regardless of whether everyone is present. Avoid taking too much time to summarize for latecomers.

8   Start off the meeting with straightforward, easily resolved issues before heading into thornier ones.

9   Allocate a specific amount of time for each issue. Move through issues, allowing for discussion but discouraging digression or repetition. Use a timer to help monitor the time.

10   Postpone discussion until the end of the meeting if debate on an issue runs overtime. Make sure to cover the other issues on the agenda.

11   Follow up: Circulate copies of the minutes after the meeting to remind everyone of conclusions and action plans.

Try removing the chairs from the meeting room and conducting a stand-up meeting to make it shorter and more efficient.

## Things You'll Need

❑ written agenda

❑ visual aids (optional)

❑ timer

---

## 40   Take Minutes at a Business Meeting

Business meetings may be conducted formally or informally, depending on the company and the circumstances. The following guidelines are based on Robert's Rules of Order.

### ⊙ Steps

#### Taking Minutes

1   Obtain the meeting agenda, minutes from the last meeting, and any background documents to be discussed. Consider using a tape recorder to ensure accuracy.

2   Sit beside the chairperson for convenient clarification or help as the meeting proceeds.

3   Write "Minutes of the meeting of [exact association name]."

4   Record the date, time and place of the meeting.

5   Circulate a sheet of paper for attendees to sign. (This sheet can also help identify speakers by seating arrangement later in the meeting.) If the meeting is an open one, write down only the names of the attendees who have voting rights.

6   Note who arrives late or leaves early so that these people can be briefed on what they missed.

7   Write down items in the order in which they are discussed. If item 8 on the agenda is discussed before item 2, keep the old item number but write item 8 in second place.

8   Record the motions made and the names of people who originate them.

### ✳ Tips

You do not need to record topics irrelevant to the business at hand. Taking minutes is not the same as taking dictation.

Consult only the chairperson or executive officer, not the attendees, if you have questions.

The person taking minutes does not participate in the meeting.

Write in a concise, accurate manner, taking care not to include any sort of subjective opinion.

Some of these guidelines may not apply, because regular business meetings tend to be more casual (e.g., formal voting rarely occurs).

No matter what type of minutes you take, focus on capturing and communicating all important actions that took place.

9 Record whether motions are adopted or rejected, how the vote is taken (by show of hands, voice or other method) and whether the vote is unanimous. For small meetings, write the names of the attendees who approve, oppose and abstain from each motion.

10 Focus on recording actions taken by the group. Avoid writing down the details of each discussion.

## Transcribing Minutes

1 Transcribe minutes soon after the meeting, when your memory is fresh.

2 Follow the format used in previous minutes.

3 Preface resolutions with "RESOLVED, THAT ..."

4 Consider attaching long resolutions, reports or other supplementary material to the minutes as an appendix.

5 Write "Submitted by" and then sign your name and the date.

6 Place minutes chronologically in a record book.

---

## Negotiate an Agreement　　41

**Whether you are negotiating a business contract or the use of a cubicle, it takes tact and understanding to come to a fair agreement. Here are some ways to take the sting out of negotiating.**

### ⊙ Steps

1 Ask questions to learn what the other side wants. Try to step into the other person's shoes to see the problem from his or her point of view.

2 Communicate what you want. When you speak, make a point instead of just arguing. Focus on understanding and addressing everyone's needs.

3 Summarize conflicts of interest and obstacles to solutions.

4 Break down what you want into specific detail so you can search for areas of agreement.

5 Keep talking until you find a solution that meets your mutual interests.

6 If you reach an impasse, end the meeting and reschedule it for another time. A few days' rest might spark some new ideas.

### ✳ Tips

See yourself and the other person as two team members searching for a solution, rather than as opponents.

Stay calm. Nothing is negotiated well when both parties are agitated.

### ⚠ Warning

Avoid taking it personally. When someone is attacking you, he or she is usually just attacking your position.

---

## Resolve Conflicts at Work　　42

**Friction in the workplace can be stressful and counterproductive for everyone involved. Learn to approach the person with whom you are struggling and resolve the situation.**

### ⊙ Steps

1 Decide whether you want to confront the person who is bothering you. It is usually better to air grievances in the open than to let them fester.

### ✳ Tips

Deal with problematic personalities by trying to understand what motivates their behavior, then tailoring your actions to work with

2 Speak to the other person calmly, politely and rationally. Focus on the situation and facts, avoiding gossip and personal attacks.

3 Be careful not to express hostility in your posture, facial expression or tone. Be assertive without being aggressive.

4 Listen to the other person carefully: What is she trying to say? Be sure you understand her position.

5 Express interest in what the other person is saying. You can acknowledge her ideas without necessarily agreeing or submitting. Saying "I understand that you feel this way. Here's how I feel ..." acknowledges both positions.

6 Communicate clearly what you want, offering positive suggestions and recommendations. Be willing to be flexible.

7 Speak to your supervisor if a problem with a difficult co-worker seriously threatens your work, but avoid whining.

the personality type. Once you grasp why people behave as they do, you will be able to interact with them more effectively.

For example, be firm with bullies at work—don't let them pressure you into doing anything unwanted. Be forceful in your opinions, but act with a bit of caution.

Around complainers, avoid acting too sympathetic if you feel their complaints are ill-founded; instead, ask what sorts of actions they plan to take to change the situation. Squarely ask them what they want.

## 43 | Give a Negative Employee Reference

While it is easy to provide a glowing reference for former top-notch employees, it is much more challenging to give a negative reference. Here are some simple steps to guide you.

### ⊙ Steps

1 Confirm to the employer who contacts you that the job candidate worked for your company.

2 State the time period during which the person was employed, and his or her job title. Let your human resources department confirm the former employee's compensation.

3 Offer no additional information. Derogatory remarks could land you in a costly and lengthy lawsuit.

4 Give the former employee a written letter stating the dates of employment and his or her pay level at the time of discharge. The ex-employee could present that to prospective employers instead of asking them to call you.

5 Inform the ex-employee, if he or she wants to know what you have been saying, that as a matter of policy you will provide only confirmation of employment dates, job title and pay levels.

6 Tell your former employee exactly what you said, if he or she asks you.

### ✱ Tip

If the person inquiring about the ex-employee is your close friend, you might be willing to risk making a few general comments about the ex-employee's merits or performance on the job.

### ⚠ Warning

Remember that anything you say to a prospective employer—even a close friend—could get back to the employee and land you in court.

## Negotiate for More Vacation Time     44

If your company is typical, you get just a few short weeks of vacation a year. Here's how to wrangle for more.

### ⊙ Steps

1   Choose an appropriate time to ask for more vacation. The best time is usually during a solid performance review, but other choice times include the end of a profitable fiscal year, after a successful presentation or simply when you find your manager in a good mood.

2   Make sure you're able to give your manager a good reason why you should get more vacation time.

3   Prepare a list of reasons why you feel you deserve to be rewarded this way. Perhaps you put in extra hours on a weekly basis, or you just saved the company a lot of money on a large purchase.

4   Decide what you're willing to give up in order to get more vacation time. This may mean sacrificing some or all of your upcoming raise or agreeing to work an extra half-hour each day, for example.

5   Make sure to point out any benefits your employer will reap from this arrangement. These reasons may include your greater job satisfaction, or a way for your employer to keep payroll increases down.

### ✱ Tip

Be willing to bend. Agreeing not to take three weeks off in a row or agreeing to split up time in some other manner may help your case.

### ⚠ Warning

Ask for what you want, but don't demand. You may risk offending the boss.

## Ask for a Raise     45

Consider whether you merit a raise and whether your company is in a position to give you one. Then choose your moment and your methods carefully.

### ⊙ Steps

1   Evaluate your worth. List your achievements, skills and contributions.

2   Arm yourself with information. Know what a normal raise is for someone of your experience and occupation.

3   Assess your supervisor's mood and outlook. Is he or she ready to consider your request?

4   Choose an appropriate time of day. Make an appointment or ask if there are a few minutes to spare. Plan for an end-of-business-day meeting.

5   Consider asking for a specific amount that's a little higher than what you want. Say 8 percent when you would be happy with 6 percent.

6   Be realistic. If your company is going through tough times but you still feel deserving, decide how you'll respond if a lower amount is offered.

7   Be flexible. Would you consider a supplement in perks, time off, flextime or vacation time in lieu of a raise? Negotiate.

8   If your supervisor turns you down, have a plan ready and regroup.

### ✱ Tip

If you can, print out an outline showing that you're paid less than others in your position—but are producing more and better results.

### ⚠ Warning

Avoid losing your temper or your sense of humor.

## 46 Resign From a Job

Regardless of your reasons for leaving a job, you can do so in a professional manner.

### ⊙ Steps

1 Consider all your options before resigning. Could your employer offer you something that would make you want to stay? Perhaps you should discuss with your employer your dissatisfaction or the better offer that you have received before making a permanent decision.

2 Write a letter of resignation and sign your name. If you were unhappy at the time of leaving, the letter might be a simple sentence conveying the effective date of your resignation. If you were genuinely happy, it could express your regret at leaving and the fact that you'll miss everyone.

3 Refrain from explaining why you are resigning, where you will be working, or how much more money you will be making. Do say that you are willing to help with the transition that your resignation will cause.

4 Request a sit-down conversation with your manager, ideally at the end of the day, so that you can deliver the news in person in addition to turning in the letter. Be sure to close the door.

5 Remember that you can be specific or vague if your supervisor asks for a reason. It's best not to use this time as a venting session.

6 Stick with the "better opportunity" angle if your tenure was unhappy. If you feel you must tell the truth, try not to be too personal. For example, "I would have preferred more training" is better than "You were terrible at training me."

7 Keep in mind that you may have to get a recommendation from your supervisor, so don't burn bridges.

### ✳ Tips

If you would like a letter of recommendation, request one. Have it mailed to you.

If you prefer not to say where you're headed, a simple "taking time off" will do.

Note that in most cases, some notice is expected if you want to leave on good terms. In general, the amount of proper notice is equal to the number of weeks of vacation you received.

Understand that your employer may be angry that you are leaving. Try not to become involved in a dispute about the situation.

### ⚠ Warning

Be as positive as possible. You might return, or you may later need to ask for a reference. Keep your departure neutral.

## 47 Survive Downsizing

Losing a job is one of life's most stressful experiences. As more and more companies get "lean and mean," you may find yourself laid off—but you will survive.

### ⊙ Steps

1 Leave your place of work immediately. Even if you saw it coming, you are likely to be too upset to answer co-workers' questions. You can come back later for your coffee mug.

2 Discuss your situation with your spouse and other family members who will be affected. Will your partner have to work overtime for a while? Can your son or daughter get a part-time job to help with college tuition?

3 Review your financial situation. You may have set aside what seemed like a reasonable amount for a "rainy day," but if your unemployment goes beyond a month or two, you may need to make some lifestyle adjustments.

### ✳ Tips

Get references in writing from your supervisor, co-workers and company personnel representative. Be sure the latter states clearly that your termination was due to a workforce reduction.

Handle the paperwork to continue your benefits and roll over your retirement-plan money. There are strict time limits for these things; you snooze, you lose.

4 Request a meeting with your company's human resources representative. Find out if you're entitled to severance pay or compensation for unused vacation or personal days, and how to continue your benefits and roll over your 401(k). Find out how vested you are in the company's pension plan, if applicable.

5 Take advantage of any outplacement services your employer offers. Many companies now provide career assessment and counseling as well as use of company facilities such as personal computers, copiers and fax machines to aid laid-off employees in their job searches.

6 File for unemployment compensation if you qualify. This may be a blow to your self-esteem, but you and your family are entitled to such benefits, and meeting basic needs must come before pride.

## ⚠ Warning

Losing a job, even through no fault of your own, can be devastating. If your feelings of anger, sadness or helplessness persist beyond a few weeks, consider getting short-term therapy for depression.

## Become an Astronaut | 48

Only the most highly skilled applicants enter NASA's space program, and fewer still make it into space. Depending on their background, astronauts train as pilots or mission specialists.

### ◉ Steps

1 Know that you must be between 5 feet 4 inches and 6 feet 4 inches tall to be a pilot and between 4 feet 10½ inches and 6 feet 4 inches to be a mission specialist. You also need to be in top physical condition, and have great stamina.

2 Maintain an excellent academic record in your undergraduate and graduate studies. Many astronauts have doctoral degrees.

3 Choose a scientific field for your bachelor's degree that you can use if you become an astronaut. Possibilities include medicine, biology, chemistry, physics, aerospace engineering and mathematics.

4 Make certain you have at least three years' work experience in your field before applying as a mission specialist. An acceptable substitution might be a two-year graduate degree with one year of experience.

5 Have at least 1,000 hours of pilot-in-command time in jet aircraft, preferably with flight-test experience, if you wish to be a mission pilot.

6 Send for an application package (see Tips for the address). You'll have to pass the strict NASA physical as a basic qualification.

7 Realize that if you're accepted as an astronaut candidate, you're committing yourself to a training period of one to two years in Houston without a guarantee that you'll ever go into space. Training will be intense and often in low-gravity conditions. It will include land and sea survival training and scuba diving.

8 Prepare to remain with NASA for at least five years if you pass the training period and are accepted as an astronaut.

### ✱ Tips

You can obtain an application package by writing to the Astronaut Selection Office, Mail Code AHX, Johnson Space Center, Houston, TX 77058 or call (281) 483 5907.

If you're claustrophobic, don't apply to be an astronaut. Your problem will definitely be discovered.

Consult the NASA Web site (www.nasa.gov) for more specific information about appropriate degrees.

### ⚠ Warning

You must be a team player at all times. Lives will depend on you.

---

## 49 | Become a Veterinarian

Competition for veterinary jobs is tight, so training and grades are of utmost importance.

### ⊙ Steps

1 Volunteer at a local veterinary office, SPCA, farm or animal hospital during high school to gain experience working with animals.

2 Attend college, perhaps in a preveterinary program if your school offers one; otherwise, consider biology, biochemistry or another science.

3 Find out which college courses are required by the American Veterinary Medical Association and by each veterinary school that interests you.

4 Maintain a very high grade point average in college. This is a must.

5 Find out which standardized tests are required by each veterinary school that interests you, since this varies from school to school.

6 Apply to any of the 27 accredited veterinary schools in the United States that offer the four-year Doctor of Veterinary Medicine (D.V.M.) degree.

7 Graduate from veterinary school and take the North American Veterinary Licensing Exam for your veterinary license.

8 Be prepared to take a state exam covering state laws and regulations.

### ✱ Tips

Some veterinary schools don't require a bachelor's degree for admission, but they all require some college courses, and a bachelor's degree can be an advantage.

A license in one state does not automatically permit the licensee to practice veterinary medicine in another state.

### ⚠ Warnings

Be prepared to deal with matters such as incurable illness and euthanasia on a regular basis.

You will often be on call during nonworking hours, just like a medical doctor.

---

## 50 | Become a Movie Director

There are many paths to a career in directing films.

### ⊙ Steps

1 Brainstorm to come up with any potential contacts in the film industry. Work as an apprentice under anyone currently directing student films, TV commercials, music videos or feature films.

2 Consider applying to film school to gain both knowledge and industry contacts. Some top film schools can be found at New York University, the University of Southern California, the American Film Institute in Los Angeles, California Institute of the Arts and the University of California at Los Angeles.

3 Apply for work on movie sets, in entry-level jobs such as production assistant or as anyone's assistant. If you work hard and make friends, you can move up the ladder.

4 Target jobs directing TV commercials or music videos, where many film directors get their start.

5 Develop a reel (a tape of the work you've directed).

6 Shoot films on your own; to start, they can be short (10 minutes long) and in black and white. If necessary, cast and write your films yourself to build your experience and résumé.

7 Send postcards and updates regularly to industry contacts you have made, including directors, producers and actors. Constant networking leads to opportunities.

### ✱ Tips

Be creative and persistent, and understand that there isn't one right way to become a film director.

Read *The Hollywood Reporter* and *Variety* to find out about upcoming productions and possible job openings.

Network, network, network.

### ⚠ Warning

As with most jobs in the entertainment field, directors work long and irregular hours.

---

## Become a Photographer 51

To be successful in this satisfying career, you need an artistic eye, technical skills, a knack for marketing yourself and a passion for your work.

### ☉ Steps

1 Take pictures for your high school yearbook or student newspaper after you have taken a workshop in the basics. You will get an idea of how deep your passion is for the medium.

2 Decide which type of photography—such as news, advertising or fine-art photography—best suits your interests and talents.

3 Understand that a four-year college degree is increasingly necessary if you want to be a photojournalist or a photographic specialist in medicine or other sciences. The contacts you make and the experience you receive from required college internships will be invaluable.

4 Develop an outstanding portfolio. Include excellent photographs you have taken on your own—in particular, those focusing on a given theme.

5 Be willing to work as a photographer's assistant once you have some experience. You are not going to be competing with experienced photographers for a while.

6 Realize that more than 50 percent of photographers work on a freelance basis. Many magazines and organizations that use photographers do not keep them on staff.

7 Attend workshops and seminars to remain up-to-date on technical advances in photography.

### ❋ Tips

Use the best camera equipment you can afford.

Take business and public relations classes if you eventually want to set up your own studio.

Ask a studio photographer for an internship if you are not enrolled in a college. But realize that if internships are available, photography students in college may be your competition.

Consider using stock photo agencies to sell your photos. They are listed in the annual *Photographer's Market*.

### ⚠ Warning

Be willing to travel at a moment's notice if you become a photojournalist; also be prepared for irregular hours.

## Become an Interior Designer 52

Professionals in this field design and furnish the interiors of commercial, industrial and residential buildings. They must be up on federal, state and local codes and able to wear many hats.

### ☉ Steps

1 Understand that as an interior designer you will need to know more than how to decorate a space. For example, you will need to fully understand flammability and toxicity standards, be able to easily read a blueprint and know how to communicate with engineers, architects and clients.

2 Obtain a bachelor's degree in interior design from a college whose design program has been accredited by the Foundation for Interior Design Education Research (FIDER). Peruse FIDER's Web site (www.fider.org) for a list of approved programs.

3 Include computer-aided design (CAD) courses in your electives. As a designer you will be expected to know how to use a computer to create your space designs.

4 Apply for internships through your school. Your contacts might lead to a job in the future.

### ❋ Tip

Subscribe to interior design and architecture magazines to learn about the latest trends.

### ⚠ Warning

Designers work irregular schedules, at the convenience of their clients.

5   Contact your state's regulatory agency to confirm its licensing requirements for interior designers. State-by-state information is located on the
National Council for Interior Design Qualification (NCIDQ) Web site
(www.ncidq.org).

6   Spend a year or two working in the field after graduation, prior to taking
and passing the NCIDQ exam. This is a prerequisite to receiving a
license. Take the exam even if your state does not require licensure. You
will need to pass it to be accepted in professional organizations that are
key to the success of designers.

## 53   Become a Private Investigator

Private investigators work for attorneys, insurance companies,
businesses and the general public; they may be on staff at a
large corporation or be self-employed.

### ◎ Steps

1   Realize that many people in this field have a military or law enforcement
background. Others have a college degree in business, criminal justice
or political science. They are your competition for jobs.

2   Enroll in a detective school if you don't have any of the experience listed
above. You'll be taught the skills that a private investigator needs to
have, including how to fingerprint, take samples of evidence, write
reports and use firearms.

3   Polish your writing skills. This is one of the most important things you
can do to ensure success. You'll need to write reports frequently, and
they must be of professional quality.

4   Become proficient at using credit checks and computer searching
resources, such as Lexis-Nexis. They'll be a large part of your work,
and this skill can be your entry into working for a firm.

5   Apply for your private investigator's license if one is required in your
state. Your local police department or a local detective agency can tell
you which government division handles this.

### ✳ Tips

Honestly assess your qualifications. You need to be mature,
assertive, persistent and logical.

Be sure you meet your state's
requirements. You may have to
take an exam and post a bond.

### ⚠ Warning

Be prepared for long, irregular,
solitary work hours, especially
during surveillance work.

## 54   Become a Stockbroker

If you thrive on action, bloom in a fast-paced environment and
dream of a career with rewards as great as the risks, consider
becoming a stockbroker.

### ◎ Steps

1   Begin to prepare for your career in high school by taking courses in
math, economics and business. And with even a small starting sum, you
can manage your own stock portfolio (in a parent's name if you are
under 18) to learn about different investments and their return.

### ✳ Tips

The brokerage business boils
down to sales. It can be a
rewarding second career for
someone moving over from a
sales position in real estate or
insurance, for example.

2  Join an investment club, which compares different investment opportunities, analyzes results and jointly invests its funds.

3  Go to college. Most brokers are college graduates with a degree in finance, economics or business.

4  Pass the General Securities Registered Representative Examination (Series 7 exam), administered by the National Association of Securities Dealers. Most states also require the Uniform Securities Agents State Law Examination (Series 63 exam) and the Uniform Investment Advisor Law Exam (Series 65 exam).

5  Take advantage of on-the-job training, offered by most brokerage firms, to prepare for the above exams—a process that takes four to six months. Upon passing the required exams, a broker becomes a registered representative of his or her sponsoring firm.

6  Expect a competitive work environment after being hired. Firms often hire a plethora of recent college graduates with the expectation that a large percentage will "wash out" during the grueling early months of training and building a clientele.

7  Emphasize your studies and work experience (if any) in finance, economics and/or business when writing your résumé. A professional, aggressive image is crucial at the interview, where prospective employers will be evaluating your tenacity along with your business savvy.

View firsthand the products you'd be brokering by visiting any brokerage firm or mutual-fund Web site. Also visit job fairs where securities firms are recruiting and talk to a real live stockbroker.

Ambitious individuals can take the Uniform Combined State Law Exam (Series 66 exam) in lieu of the 63 and 65 exams.

## ⚠ Warnings

As with any sales job, you need thick skin to succeed, and especially to survive those lean early years as you build up a clientele.

Again, as with other sales careers, income can be high but can fluctuate dramatically from month to month.

# Become a Chef                                    55

A chef is a highly skilled and inventive cook who can turn a delicious meal into an artistic presentation. It takes years to become accomplished and known in this field.

## ⊙ Steps

1  Work in a restaurant during high school for the experience, even if it is in a noncooking position. You will learn what it is like to be on your feet for long hours.

2  Ask your guidance counselor if there is a training program in your community for chefs.

3  Understand that to be a successful chef in an urban area you must have years of hands-on experience and formal training. Schooling can take four years. See the American Culinary Federation Web site (www.acfchefs.org) for information on accredited culinary schools, apprenticeships, certification, jobs and related organizations.

4  Decide what type of cooking you would like to do and in what type of kitchen you would like to work.

5  Realize that an apprenticeship may require you to first work the least-skilled jobs in the kitchen. As you develop skills and further your education, you can advance up the culinary ladder in a larger restaurant by becoming a line chef, sous-chef, head chef, executive chef and, finally, master chef. Pastry chefs follow their own distinct ladder.

6  Make certain you will possess the education, experience and skills necessary for your certification as a chef by the American Culinary

## ✳ Tips

Be certain that this is the career to which you want to devote your time. Initially, consider taking a short course at a culinary school while working in a restaurant kitchen.

Stay up-to-date on food trends and kitchen equipment. Read as many culinary magazines and journals as possible.

Choose an area of specialization if you want to work in upscale restaurants.

## ⚠ Warning

If the head chef leaves, his or her entire staff may be asked to do the same.

Federation or other membership organizations. Certification is not always required but greatly increases your chances of landing a job.

7   Take appropriate business courses if you think you would like to open your own restaurant eventually, or if you plan to advance to a managerial or executive position.

---

## 56   Become a Radio Disc Jockey

You need a pleasant speaking voice and excellent verbal skills for this job. On the air, you may introduce music, conduct interviews, and read commercials and even the weather forecast.

### ◉ Steps

1   Take speech, drama and English courses in high school and college. Make tapes of your speaking voice and ask your speech and drama teachers for their opinion of your vocal projection.

2   Consider working part-time while you are in high school as a mobile disc jockey at parties. Observe experienced mobile DJs and you'll learn what's good vs. what's unprofessional. Find out from them what equipment you need. If you're really good, you can eventually advance to more formal affairs, such as weddings. The experience will be priceless.

3   Ask your guidance counselor for a list of colleges and universities that specialize in broadcasting.

4   Apply to several schools that offer a broadcasting degree with a radio emphasis. Although it's not always necessary for a DJ to have a degree, it will give you a major advantage within the broadcasting industry.

5   Gain experience at your college radio station by doing any work that will teach you about radio broadcasting, a station's equipment and the problems associated with airtime. Offer to be the DJ or radio announcer at the station during unusual hours. Then make a tape of the show and include the experience on your résumé.

6   Get an internship of any kind at a local radio station while you're in college. It can sometimes lead to a permanent position. Realize that you will most likely be doing office work initially, not talking into a microphone or running the board. But you need this experience.

7   Consult your broadcasting adviser about the availability of entry-level radio jobs through the college.

8   Consider a radio job at a small community station after graduation if the opportunity presents itself. You'll probably begin with an entry-level position to learn the ropes, but your chances of speaking on the air in the near future will be far greater than in a larger market. The large markets want you to have had several years of on-air experience.

### ✱ Tips

Become an expert on a variety of interesting topics. Prepare demo tapes that demonstrate your knowledge and your excellent speaking voice.

Time management during a show and the ability to connect with your audience are key skills to have in this field.

### ⚠ Warning

Be prepared for the possibility of unusual working hours if you become a DJ.

## Become a Firefighter 57

Many little boys and girls have dreamed of growing up to be a firefighter. Here's how to make those dreams come true.

### ⊙ Steps

1 Be at least 18 years old, with a high school diploma or general equivalency diploma (GED).

2 Pass a rigorous test of physical strength and stamina, a medical exam and a drug screening.

3 Find out what real firefighters do. This isn't *Backdraft;* it's alternately dirty, dangerous and dull. If this is still your dream, read on.

4 Keep yourself in top physical condition. The fire-fighting exam is very demanding, as is the work itself.

5 Take basic CPR and whatever other emergency medical procedure training is available to you. A growing percentage of calls to fire departments are in response to medical emergencies.

6 Apply to take the fire-fighting exams. You can get all the necessary information from your state or local fire department.

7 Complete your local fire department's training program. Many municipal fire departments have a two- to four-month program of classroom instruction and practical training covering fire-fighting techniques, fire prevention, hazardous materials and emergency medical procedures.

8 Successfully complete your department's probationary period of employment, which can last from three to six months.

### ✱ Tip

Some fire departments have formal apprenticeship programs that last up to five years. These can be a great way to earn while you learn.

---

## Become a Lifeguard 58

Lifeguarding is a favorite summer job. Here's how to qualify. Certification is almost always required.

### ⊙ Steps

1 Decide where you want to work. You could be a pool, water park or beach lifeguard. Age and certification requirements vary for each job.

2 Take a lifeguard training course, such as the American Red Cross Lifeguard Training class. This class will give you basic certification as a lifeguard and will teach you surveillance and rescue skills, CPR and first aid. Also, take other classes as required including general first aid and CPR courses.

3 Brush up on your people skills. Lifeguards with the Red Cross Water Safety Instructor (WSI) certification can teach swimming and aquatic safety classes and will need to interact with other staff members, children and adults.

4 Fill out an application. You may be required to take written and physical tests.

5 Increase your credentials with advanced training, such as the Red Cross Head Lifeguard and Professional Rescuer courses.

### ✱ Tips

You must be at least 15 years old to take the American Red Cross Lifeguard Training class, although there is also a GuardStart class for kids ages 11 to 14. Call your local American Red Cross office to find out about classes.

For some beach lifeguard jobs, such as those in Los Angeles County and San Diego County, you are required to try out to enroll in their training academies.

## 59 | Buy a Computer

Buying a computer means investigating many features: RAM (random-access memory), processor speed, graphics capability, hard disk space and so on. Here's how to start.

### ⊙ Steps

1 Choose a specialty store, consumer electronics store, retail chain, limited-service discount chain, local computer builder or mail-order/Internet vendor based on your hardware and service needs.

2 Buy when you need to buy. No matter how long you wait for the best deal, the same configuration will cost less in six months.

3 Decide which features you'll need based on what you're going to do with the computer. For example, if you're going to be creating graphics, sound and video, you'll want plenty of RAM. If you're going to be doing heavy computational tasks (searching large databases, watching video), you'll want a super processor.

4 Decide if you want a laptop, which you can carry around with you, or a desktop model.

5 Choose a computer brand based on quality, price and technical support.

6 Figure out the core configuration you need, including processor and speed, amount of RAM and hard disk capacity.

7 Determine which additional drives you need, such as CD-ROM, DVD-ROM, CD recorder or Zip.

8 Select peripherals and additional hardware such as modems, sound cards, video cards and speakers.

9 Decide how many extra internal card slots and disk-drive bays you'll need in order to allow room for future expansion.

10 Determine what preinstalled software you want or need. Get at least an operating system, such as Windows or the Mac OS, an antivirus program and programs for word processing, spreadsheets, databases and keeping your checkbook.

11 Choose the warranty or service coverage appropriate to your needs.

### ✳ Tips

Keep abreast of the latest technology by reading the new-product reviews in magazines and on the Web.

Find out what hardware and software are included with the models you're considering, and use that as a basis for comparing prices. Ask "What's the catch?" if a price seems too low.

Understand that RAM is where your computer temporarily stores data to be processed. Although more RAM is better, you don't need much if you restrict your computer use to simple tasks (word processing, check balancing). Games, however, can require lots of RAM; graphics and sound are other space hogs.

Today's processors are usually fast enough for all but the most demanding applications, such as streaming video.

## 60 | Install RAM

If your computer slows down when you're working with large files, try installing extra RAM. These instructions will work for most machines built since the mid-1990s.

### ⊙ Steps

1 Determine what kind of RAM you need—and whether your computer has enough open slots to hold it. The new RAM should match the existing RAM's specifications and configuration.

2 Shut down the computer and leave it plugged into the surge suppressor.

### ✳ Tips

Your computer will accept either SIMMs or DIMMs. Check your manual to find out which.

If you have an older machine, you may need to adjust DIP switches or jumpers. Consult your manual.

3  Disconnect all peripherals, such as the monitor, from the computer.

4  Remove the computer cover.

5  Ground yourself to the computer with professional grounding equipment, or by touching a metal part of the chassis.

6  Remove any cards or internal components necessary to give yourself unobstructed access to RAM sockets.

7  Pick up your SIMM (single in-line memory module) or DIMM (dual in-line memory module) by the ends without touching pins or chips.

8  If adding a SIMM, find the notched end and turn the SIMM so that it is parallel to the existing RAM card(s). Insert the SIMM into the socket at a 30-degree angle. If adding a DIMM, insert the DIMM straight in so that it is perpendicular to the motherboard.

9  Use slight pressure to keep a SIMM from backing out while rotating the module to an upright position perpendicular to the motherboard.

10  Make sure the small holes on each side of a SIMM fit into holders.

11  Feel or hear retaining clips lock a SIMM into the socket; close the side clips on a DIMM.

12  Gently try to pull the module out to ensure that it is locked in position.

13  Replace all internal components.

14  Leave the cover off and reconnect the monitor, keyboard and mouse.

15  Turn on the computer.

16  Check the amount of RAM by right-clicking the My Computer icon in Windows and choosing Properties. On a Mac, use the About This Macintosh command in the Apple menu.

17  If you don't see the right amount of RAM, turn off the computer, remove and replace the RAM, and reboot. If that doesn't work, call a technician.

18  Shut down the computer and disconnect the peripherals again.

19  Replace the cover and reconnect all peripherals.

## ⚠ Warnings

Stand on uncarpeted flooring to reduce static electricity. Touch as little as possible inside your machine and especially avoid touching chips. Static damage, and even oil from fingertips, may cause a failure months later.

Label any cards or internal components you remove to access RAM sockets so that you'll replace them in their proper places when you are finished.

Some recent stub-chassis computers built by Compaq, Hewlett-Packard and others have little or no work space inside. Some units require removing the hard drive and power supply to access the RAM. Do not attempt to do this yourself.

If your computer is under the manufacturer's warranty, modifying the product usually voids that warranty.

## Back Up a Hard Drive                    61

It's important to back up your critical files on at least a weekly basis. The following explains how to run Microsoft's built-in Backup utility in Windows 95/98.

### ⊙ Steps

1  Connect a drive (such as a Zip drive or other removable media, a tape drive or a second hard disk drive) that can hold the information you want to back up.

2  Open the Start menu and select Programs.

3  In the submenu that appears, click Accessories, then System Tools.

4  Click Backup to run Microsoft's Backup program.

### ✳ Tips

If you don't have a large-capacity backup drive, it may be more convenient to save a limited number of critical files, not your entire hard disk. You can also back up files to a network drive.

To restore a disk from a backup, open the Tools menu in the Backup utility. Select Restore Wizard.

5   For the easiest backup, answer the questions presented to you by the Backup Wizard. (The wizard will ask you what you want to back up, where you want to store the backup, if you want the data to be verified and/or compressed, and what you want to name the backup.)

6   Click Next after you answer each question.

7   Click Start to commence the backup.

**⚠ Warning**

Microsoft Backup cannot be used to write to CD-R/CD-RW. This can be done with add-on software.

---

## 62  Buy Peripherals for a Computer

You need a monitor, keyboard and mouse to use a computer. What other peripherals are worth considering?

### ⊙ Steps

1   Buy a printer unless you have access to one at work or will use your computer only to surf the Internet. Ink-jet printers cost less and can print colors. Laser printers are more expensive (only very expensive ones can print in color) but have better text quality and are more likely to print PostScript fonts and files. Laser printers also cost less per use, as ink-jet cartridges run out quickly and are expensive. (See 66 "Buy a Laser Printer" and 67 "Buy an Ink-Jet Printer.")

2   Buy a scanner if you wish to "photocopy" text, documents or pictures into your computer (see 68 "Buy a Scanner").

3   Buy a backup storage device, such as an external hard drive, Zip drive or CD-RW drive, if you need to back up large amounts of data and your computer doesn't have a built-in Zip drive or CD-RW drive.

4   Buy powered stand-alone speakers for better sound quality if your system came with unpowered speakers.

5   Buy a microphone to use computer telephony, voice activation and various educational programs, or to record your own simple sounds.

6   Buy a digital camera for the easiest way of transferring photographs into your computer (see 64 "Choose a Digital Camera").

7   Buy other peripherals to meet specific wants and needs. For example, buy a joystick to increase your speed and flexibility when playing action games, or a digital video camera for teleconferencing (see 65 "Choose a Web Camera").

**✻ Tip**

Manufacturers continually introduce new types of peripherals. Something not yet invented when you buy your computer may increase its capability later on.

**⚠ Warning**

Your computer must meet the system requirements of any peripherals you buy.

---

## 63  Buy a Computer Monitor

The main criteria for selecting a monitor are size and resolution (the ability to render detail). If you work with graphics or play computer games, you need a monitor with higher resolution.

### ⊙ Steps

1   Determine how big a monitor will fit on your desk. If desk space is limited, consider buying a flat-screen monitor.

**✻ Tips**

For gaming or graphics, look for a refresh rate of at least 75 Hz at 1,024 by 768 resolution.

2 Even if you eventually buy from a mail-order or Web retailer, go to computer stores and check out different monitors in person.

3 Compare features such as antiglare coating, digital controls, built-in microphone, built-in speakers or speaker mounts, USB ports and ease of adjustment.

4 Compare limited warranties.

5 Make your buying decision based on display clarity in the size you want, for the price you want to pay.

You'll need a graphics card that meets the monitor's maximum specs for refresh rate and resolution.

### ⚠ Warning

The tube size and viewable area of a monitor are not the same. Read system specs carefully.

## Choose a Digital Camera                    64

Digital cameras cost more than regular cameras, but they offer the convenience of immediate viewing, multiple-image storage and computer connectivity—and there's no film to develop.

### ◉ Steps

1 Buy the camera with the highest resolution you can afford, at least 2 to 3 megapixels (2 million to 3 million pixels), if possible.

2 Look for a 100 percent glass lens as opposed to a plastic one.

3 Buy a camera with as much RAM as you can afford. More RAM means the camera can store more pictures, so you won't need to download or erase them as often.

4 Expect zoom to be the feature you will use most. Compare optical, as opposed to digital, zoom capabilities.

5 Compare flash modes, if any.

6 Investigate viewfinders: Look for an optical (through-the-lens) viewfinder as well as an LCD display.

7 Consider autofocus and macro features, shutter-release lag times, and bundled software.

8 Compare additional features you might want: interchangeable lenses, steady-shot, burst mode, auto exposure, automatic white balance, voice memo, variable shutter speeds, manual focus and self-timer.

9 Compare removable media of various types (if you need more storage space for your photos).

10 Investigate batteries, chargers and battery-saving features.

11 Look for additional features you might need, such as USB or IEEE 1394 (FireWire) connectivity (to connect the camera to the appropriate port on your computer), a battery-time-remaining indicator, an AC adapter or video-out connections for outputting to a television.

### ✳ Tips

If you will only output pictures to a computer monitor (for viewing, Web-page use or e-mail), an inexpensive digital camera with a 640-by-480-pixel resolution will provide very satisfactory results.

If you plan to print photographs on a good (at least 720 dots per inch) color printer, look for a high-resolution camera.

A 1-megapixel camera can provide photo-quality output for 5-by-7-inch prints.

### ⚠ Warnings

Beware of high-resolution cameras with low prices. The specified resolution may only apply to software interpolation, rather than true optical resolution.

If you do buy a low-priced camera, make sure it has a charge-coupled device (CCD).

To compensate for low profit margins and high return rates, some vendors have restrictive return policies, which may include "restocking" fees. Check these out before you buy.

## 65 | Choose a Web Camera

Web cams stream live video or frequently changing still images onto Web pages. The most popular type, a videoconferencing camera, is discussed here.

### ⊙ Steps

1   Try to get the highest frame-per-second rate, highest resolution and best fidelity you can.

2   Compare lens types and focus controls.

3   Consider camera sizes and mounting options. Most cameras will sit on top of a monitor, but not all rotate both horizontally and vertically.

4   Compare bundled software and the manufacturers' limited warranties (most run for one year).

5   Check for additional features, such as a zoom or telephoto lens, video still-capture quality and a built-in microphone.

### ❋ Tips

You can also use a digital still camera or a digital camcorder to set up a Web cam.

Make sure your computer has an appropriate port for connecting the camera. USB is the most common interface standard.

### ⚠ Warning

Windows NT does not support USB.

## 66 | Buy a Laser Printer

Laser printers provide better quality than ink-jet printers but cost more. Consider print quality, speed, reliability and price.

### ⊙ Steps

1   Decide what types of documents you will be printing (text, graphics, odd paper sizes, etc.).

2   Make a list of specific features you need, such as the ability to handle large files, the ability to print on various media (labels, envelopes) without jamming, a size to fit a particular desk space, two or more paper trays, and compatibility with specific software.

3   Compare the print quality of different printers. Compare the resolution, or dpi (dots per inch). Use a magnifying glass if print quality is critical.

4   Compare speed specifications. Although you probably won't get the rated speed at home, the ratings are useful for comparing printers.

5   Learn how much RAM the printers have, and whether it's expandable.

6   Realize that the printer's paper path needs to be no sharper than 90 degrees to consistently handle envelopes, labels, transparencies or card stock. If you plan to use special media often, avoid printers with 180-degree U-turn paper paths.

7   Compare prices of consumable items such as toner cartridges and replacement drums.

8   Compare warranties and service contracts.

### ❋ Tips

Look for at least 600-by-600 dpi (dots per inch) resolution.

If you want to print PostScript fonts or PostScript graphics, you'll need a PostScript printer. Many, but not all, laser printers can handle PostScript; most ink-jet printers can't.

Printer RAM will affect the printer's speed and ability to handle large files. If the printer includes many built-in fonts, that may also improve speed.

You may need to purchase the printer cable separately.

### ⚠ Warning

Be wary of terms such as "laser-class printer." These inexpensive printers use toner cartridges, but use LEDs instead of lasers and produce inferior text quality.

## Buy an Ink-Jet Printer 67

While most people think that ink-jet printers are just cheap substitutes for laser printers, they're actually better for some things, such as photographs.

### ⊙ Steps

1 Prioritize among price, versatility, print quality, speed and reliability.

2 Add specific capabilities such as photo printing, compatibility with operating systems other than Windows, ease of use, cost of use, ability to handle large files quickly, USB connectivity and ability to print on various media without jamming.

3 Choose a specialty photo printer if you plan to print a lot of photos.

4 Choose a higher-end model with a small dot size (and thus higher resolution) if printing presentation-quality text, graphics and photos.

5 Choose a printer whose paper path is no sharper than 90 degrees if you want to print on envelopes, labels, transparencies or card stock.

6 Spend $250 or less unless speed is the most important consideration.

### ✱ Tips

Buy a model with at least 600-by-600-dpi resolution.

Avoid single-cartridge printers, which only come with a color cartridge—they can't print true color.

Most ink-jet printers are not PostScript-compatible. If you need to print PostScript graphics or fonts, consider a laser printer.

Color ink-jet cartridges can be expensive, offsetting the low cost of the printer. Special coated papers can also add to the cost of color printing.

## Buy a Scanner 68

Use a scanner to transfer printed materials—photos, drawings, even text—into your computer.

### ⊙ Steps

1 Buy a low-resolution scanner only if you will use it just to scan text.

2 If you don't plan to scan from books or magazines, consider a sheet-fed unit, which takes up far less desk space than a flatbed scanner.

3 Purchase a low-resolution or medium-resolution scanner if you plan to scan photographs to use on the Internet, as the resolution of Web graphics is low anyway.

4 Buy a high-resolution scanner if you plan to scan photographs to print and you have a high-resolution printer (greater than 600-by-600 dots per inch, or dpi).

5 Buy a model with 36-bit color depth if you plan to scan photographs or color graphics.

6 Purchase a parallel-port scanner if you don't expect to use the scanner often or work with large files.

7 Remember that even scanners that cost less than $100 will provide a good picture—600-by-1,200-dpi resolution. Scanners priced between $150 and $250 usually provide 1,200-by-1,200-dpi resolution.

8 Know that speed is the biggest factor in pricing. Parallel-port scanners, which use your existing printer port, are the cheapest and slowest. USB scanners, which require that your computer have a USB port, are faster and cost more. SCSI-card scanners are the fastest and most expensive. You need to install a SCSI card in your computer if it does not have one.

### ✱ Tips

Your computer will need at least 32 (ideally 64) MB of RAM to scan.

Don't buy a scanner that has greater resolution than your printer or display device. The extra money will be wasted.

Make sure the scanner includes scanning software, an image-editing program and an OCR program (to translate scanned text into text you can actually edit).

### ⚠ Warnings

Some manufacturers mislead consumers with resolution claims. Optical resolution is the primary determining factor of quality.

Be wary of small flatbed scanners that use a CIS (contact image sensor) instead of a CCD (charge-coupled device). They are more reliable but produce inferior image quality and color.

## 69 | Use a Computer Scanner Efficiently

Here are a few tricks to help you make the best possible scans.

### ◉ Steps

1 Pre-scan; then drag diagonally to select the area for the final scan.

2 Avoid scanning anything at a greater resolution than you can display or print.

3 Adjust scanning software settings to match the type of document: text document, line art, black-and-white photograph or color photograph.

4 Scan at 72 dpi (dots per inch) if you are scanning photographs or documents to use on the Web, because this is a suitable resolution for most Web viewing.

5 Scan at no more than 200 dpi if you are scanning text documents or documents to archive.

6 Scan at the scanner's maximum optical resolution if you are scanning photographs to print on a high-resolution printer (greater than 600 dpi).

### ✳ Tips

Images scanned at a lower resolution produce smaller files, which load faster, are easier to edit and conserve disk space.

Scanning software designed to improve your scanner's resolution is useful for graphics and for photographs lacking detail.

## 70 | Update Any Device Driver

Driver software tells a computer how to work with peripheral devices, such as scanners and printers. Upgrading to a new operating system or other software may cause conflicts with existing drivers. Sometimes device manufacturers upgrade drivers, which can fix known problems when installed.

### ◉ Steps

1 Figure out which driver version you currently have. On a Windows computer, right-click My Computer and click Properties; select the Device Manager tab. Click the plus sign to the left of a specific device to find the drivers that are currently installed for it. On a Macintosh, use the Apple System Profiler program to check driver versions. (If the Profiler doesn't list a device, check the Extensions Manager control panel.)

2 Find out whether a newer driver exists by visiting the Web site for the manufacturer of your device. A newer driver will have a later creation date than the one you have.

3 Follow instructions to download a newer driver.

4 Make sure you have the original drivers. If there are problems with the new driver, you want to be able to restore the old one.

5 Double-click the icon for the downloaded driver.

6 Follow installation instructions that appear. Look for a file named readme.txt or readme.doc.

7 If the installation didn't remove the old driver, remove it. On a Windows computer, right-click the driver in the Device Manager and select

### ✳ Tip

If upgrading the driver doesn't solve problems with the device, replace the device or remove the new software from your system.

### ⚠ Warnings

Attempting to change video drivers could make your computer inoperable. Get professional help if you need it.

These instructions are intended for Windows 95/98 and do not apply to Windows NT or Windows 2000.

Remove. On a Macintosh, drag the old driver file out of the Extensions folder in your System Folder, and either save it elsewhere or delete it.

8 Restart the computer.

## Buy a Laptop Computer 71

Laptop computers can't really substitute for desktop computers, but a good laptop can be a solid and convenient supplement to a desktop model.

### ◉ Steps

1 Check the periodic surveys in top computer magazines for comprehensive information about the reliability of specific laptop brands and customer satisfaction with them. Choose a brand based on quality, price and limited warranty.

2 Determine the core configuration you need, including processor and speed, amount of RAM, and hard disk size.

3 Decide on the type of display. Choose a dual-scan display if your budget is extremely limited. Select an active-matrix display for the quickest response and best visual quality (especially under challenging conditions), though at the cost of shorter battery life. Choose an HPA (High-Performance Addressing) display if your budget rules out an active-matrix display but you need to use the laptop under challenging lighting and wish to maximize battery life.

4 Compare weights of units you're considering. Think about how often and how far you'll need to carry the computer and its peripherals.

5 Determine the size of display you want. Remember that bigger screens add to the unit's price, weight and bulk.

6 Choose an ultraportable unit if weight is more important than price, reliability, battery life and ease of use.

7 Buy a unit with built-in CD-ROM and floppy drives if convenience is more important than portability or reliability. Consider a model with removable internal drives for the most flexibility.

8 Test the comfort and feel of the input device and keyboard. Choose between a touch pad, used by most manufacturers, and the pointing stick (also called the "command point") used by IBM and Toshiba.

9 Make sure the laptop comes with a lithium-ion battery. Be skeptical of manufacturers' battery-life claims.

10 Decide what preinstalled software you want or need.

11 Choose the length of warranty or service coverage you need.

### ✻ Tips

Touch pads are more reliable than pointing sticks.

Get a laptop with a DVD-ROM drive if you would like to watch movies while traveling.

Consider leasing a computer if you need to upgrade often or spread out payments over two or more years. Keep in mind that leasing is, overall, more expensive than buying.

## 72 | Get the Best Battery Life From a Laptop Computer

A rechargeable battery will last an average of two years. You can take steps to get better total battery life and longer battery life per charge.

### ⊙ Steps

1 Charge the battery for 12 hours before use.

2 Let the battery drain completely before recharging if you have a nickel-cadmium (NiCad) battery. Upgrade to a nickel-metal-hydride (NiMH) battery—or better, a lithium-ion battery—if one is made for your machine.

3 Let the battery drain as much as possible before recharging if you have an NiMH battery.

4 Recharge an NiMH battery between long periods of inactivity.

5 Travel with an extra battery. Use the two batteries equally.

6 Avoid running the floppy and CD drives off the battery, if possible.

7 Reduce the display's brightness when possible.

### ✱ Tips

As time goes by, you will need to recharge any rechargeable battery more often. When the battery life is about 25 percent of its original level, get a new battery.

With normal use, expect about half the per-charge life claimed by the manufacturer.

Use the laptop manufacturer's power-management software only in those rare instances when you can sacrifice performance for battery life.

If you're buying a laptop, get one with a lithium-ion battery.

## 73 | Travel With a Laptop

Protecting your laptop from theft and damage, and ensuring that it will be usable in foreign countries, requires preparation and care.

### ⊙ Steps

1 Get a heavily padded carrying case that fits the peripherals and accessories you need to carry.

2 Use a case that isn't obviously for a laptop, to deter theft.

3 Take the components, peripherals and accessories you might need, but leave the CD-ROM drive or other parts you won't. Take an extra battery if you will use the laptop on an airplane.

4 Remove disks from disk drives.

5 Get power and telephone-jack adapters if you will need them for international travel. Find out the power requirements and plug shapes for your destination before you leave.

6 Find out what communication facilities will be available. Learn how you can connect to your ISP if necessary.

7 Back up all important documents before you leave.

8 Check your insurance and warranty coverage.

9 Make sure your laptop has enough battery power to boot if required by customs or security personnel.

10 Avoid leaving your computer unattended in the airport.

### ✱ Tip

An X-ray machine won't erase your data, but a metal detector can.

### ⚠ Warning

Do not plug your laptop directly into a foreign outlet, even if you have an adapter plug, or you may fry your computer. Always use a power converter that claims it can handle the voltage at your destination. (Make sure it can handle your computer's current draw as well.)

### Things You'll Need

☐ carrying case

☐ extra battery (optional)

☐ adapter plug(s) and power converter (optional)

☐ telephone-jack adapters (optional)

11  Deter theft and breakage by monitoring your laptop closely as it travels through the x-ray machine. Better yet, ask for manual inspection.

12  Keep your laptop out of overhead bins and in plain sight when flying.

13  Once you arrive, change the date and time settings and the modem settings, if necessary.

## Exit a "Frozen" Windows Program          74

When a program freezes, you can't work in it or exit it. You're trapped! But not if you follow these instructions, which work for Windows 95/98.

### ⊙ Steps

1  Use the keyboard command Control+Alt+Delete, pressing the keys simultaneously. A box labeled Close Programs appears.

2  Scroll through the list of open programs until you come to the one that has frozen.

3  Select the frozen program.

4  Click on End Task.

5  A message will appear saying, "Program is not responding. End task?" Click on End Task. The program will shut down, and you'll be able to reopen it in the usual way.

**✳ Tips**

Using the command Control-Alt-Delete twice in a row will shut down the computer.

If your programs keep freezing, restart the computer.

**⚠ Warning**

When a program freezes, any unsaved material may be lost. Some software applications may allow you to recover some material lost in a crash.

## Uninstall a Windows Program Safely          75

When you install a program on a PC, it invariably includes ancillary files scattered through your Windows folder. To remove a program completely, use the Add/Remove Programs utility.

### ⊙ Steps

1  Check your documentation to see if the application has its own custom uninstall program, and use it if it's available.

2  If not, open the Start menu and select Settings, then Control Panel.

3  Double-click on Add/Remove Programs.

4  Find the program you want, then click Add/Remove.

5  In the box that appears, confirm to remove the program and click through the Wizard that follows.

6  Consider using a third-party utility, such as Clean Sweep or Norton Utilities, to uninstall remnants of programs from your system.

**✳ Tips**

Usually the Add/Remove Programs utility will alert you to the presence of shared programs and let you leave them on your system.

Only delete an application folder as a last resort. The program could have added programs or files to additional folders. To be safe, rename the application folder and reboot your PC. If it restarts without a problem, delete the folder. If it does not, rename the folder with its original name and do not delete it.

## 76 | Troubleshoot a Computer

Is your computer functioning strangely or not at all? Before paying for technical support, take a look at your system. A little common sense may help you solve simple problems.

### ⊙ Steps

1 Restart the computer. Many software problems will correct themselves when you do.

2 Check your cables. Keyboard not working? Make sure it's plugged in. Mouse not responding? Make sure it's plugged in.

3 Check the electric power. Test the outlet by plugging a lamp into the same power source as your computer's.

4 Disconnect peripheral devices (such as a printer or external Zip drive) and restart the computer.

5 Consider the possibility of a computer virus. Run an antivirus program (see 85 "Protect a Computer From Viruses").

6 Run a utility program (such as Norton Disk Doctor) to defragment your hard drive or to identify and fix certain problems.

### ✳ Tips

If you do decide to call technical support, write down the exact problem and what you were doing when it occurred. Also note any error messages.

Be as specific as possible when talking to the support person.

Computers tend to crash or hang when their hard disks become too full. Free up space by deleting unnecessary files and emptying the Trash or Recycle Bin.

## 77 | Start Your Windows Computer in DOS

Installation instructions for some DOS games and other applications require you to boot to MS-DOS. Troubleshooting in Windows 95/98 may also require this.

### ⊙ Steps

1 Click Start.

2 Click Shut Down.

3 In the box that appears, click Restart in MS-DOS mode.

4 Click OK.

### ✳ Tips

Type "exit" and press Enter to return to Windows from MS-DOS.

You can also open DOS by opening the Start menu and selecting Programs, then MS-DOS Prompt.

## 78 | Change Your Default Printer

You can change the default printer to any other printer that is connected to your computer. These instructions are for Windows 95/98/NT.

### ⊙ Steps

1 Click on the Start menu and click on Settings, then Printers.

2 A window will appear showing the icons of all the printers that are installed on your system. Right-click on the icon for the printer you want to use as the default. A menu will appear.

### ✳ Tip

Once you have set a printer as the default, you can still print from other installed printers. The Print dialog box offers you a selection each time you print, but the default printer will be the one that appears automatically.

3   Click on Set as Default.

4   To make sure the correct printer is now set as the default, right-click on the printer icon again. When the menu opens, a check mark should appear before Set as Default.

## Find a File on Your PC's Hard Drive | 79

Use your computer's Find function when you have forgotten the name or location of a file. These instructions are for Windows 95/98/NT.

### ⊙ Steps

1   Click on the Start menu, then on Find, and then on Files or Folders.

2   Enter the filename in the box labeled Named. If you remember only key words or phrases used in the document, enter them in the box labeled Containing Text. Try to choose a unique word or phrase to help narrow the search.

3   If you have an idea where the file is stored, use the Browse function to start the search in a particular folder.

4   Place a check mark in the box labeled Include Subfolders.

5   Click on Find Now. Within a few moments, you will receive a list of every file in the folder or drive that you selected whose name (or contents) includes the words you typed. (For example, if you entered "apples," you would get files called "Red apples" and "Golden delicious apples" in addition to "Apples.")

6   Double-click on the file to open it, or note the location so you can open the file later.

### ✱ Tips

Click on the Date tab to search for a file created or last used within a certain time frame.

Click on the Advanced tab to search for files created by a certain application.

You can also perform file searches from within many software applications, such as Microsoft Word.

## Find a File on a Mac | 80

Mac OS 8.5 and later versions include Sherlock, a vast improvement over the older Find File command.

### ⊙ Steps

1   Click on the Apple menu and select Sherlock. Or, from the Finder, press the keys Command-F.

2   Choose your search criteria. You can search by one or more attributes of the file (name, size, type, date modified, creator and so forth).

3   Choose a location to search. You can search locally or on a network.

4   To search the actual contents of a file for specific phrases, click on the Find by Content tab, then specify the phrase and a location in which to search. If the Find button is dimmed, click Index Volumes (indexing may take a while).

5   Search the Internet by keyword by selecting the Search Internet tab.

6   Click Find to run the search.

### ✱ Tips

When you search by name, the search finds all filenames that include the phrase you typed. So a search for "apple" would find files named "Aunt Mary's apple pie recipe" and "Apple Computer stock prices."

In the Sherlock results list, if you click once on the icon of a file, Sherlock will give you its location, no matter how embedded within folders it may be. If you double-click on the icon, the application will launch.

www.ehow.com

## 81 | Use Mac Files on a Windows Computer

If you save Mac files on a PC-formatted disk, you can open them on a PC, but you may lose some formatting. Here are tips for saving your Mac files so they transfer as well as possible.

**⊙ Steps**

1  If you can, save the file on your Mac using the same program (such as Microsoft Word or Excel, or WordPerfect) as you'll be using on the PC. Make sure to add the three-letter file extension (such as ".doc") when saving the file. You should be able to open the file on a PC just by double-clicking it, and your formatting should be retained.

2  If you don't have the same program in Mac and PC versions, try saving your file in a common format, such as Rich Text Format (RTF), which most word processors can read, or JPEG, if saving images. To open these, you might need to open the program you want on the PC, then use the Open command in the File menu.

3  If the first two options don't work, buy a conversion program for your PC to translate Mac file formats.

**✽ Tip**

You can always save a text document as Plain Text; you'll lose all the document's formatting, but the file will always open in any word processor.

## 82 | Use Windows Files and Disks on a Mac

Today's Macintosh systems can read floppy disks, Zip disks and other removable media formatted for the PC. They contain translators that can open Windows documents if you have the same application type on your Mac.

**⊙ Steps**

1  Make sure Automatic Document Translation is turned on in the Macintosh Easy Open or File Exchange control panel.

2  Put the PC disk in the Macintosh disk drive.

3  Double-click the PC disk icon.

4  Double-click the icon of the document you wish to open.

5  If the document doesn't open immediately, the Mac's Easy Open or File Exchange control panel may give you a list of applications to try. Choose the same type of application (graphics, word processing, spreadsheet) as the document.

6  If this method doesn't work, open the Mac version of the PC application that created the document. (For example, if it is a Microsoft Word for Windows file, open Word on the Macintosh.) If you lack that application, try a similar one (for example, the word processor in AppleWorks). Open the File menu and choose Open, then browse your disks for the PC file. If the file you're looking for doesn't appear in the Open box, make sure that All Files is selected, if possible, in the File Type menu. If that doesn't work, try another program.

**✽ Tips**

If your system software includes the PC Exchange control panel, make sure it is turned on.

If you can't open the file, or if its formatting is messed up, ask the person who gave you the document to resave it in a widely translatable format, such as RTF (Rich Text Format) for word processing documents. Many programs can also save files in the formats of earlier versions.

**⚠ Warning**

You can't run or install Windows application programs on a Mac; you can only open documents.

## Increase the Memory for a Macintosh Application · 83

If you work with large documents, you may see a message complaining about insufficient memory (RAM). A document might not even open, or a program might run very slowly. You can assign more RAM to the application to see if that helps.

### ⊙ Steps

1 Single-click the icon for the application to which you want to allocate more memory. Be sure to exit the application first.

2 From the File menu choose Get Info, or press the keys Command-I.

3 In OS 8.5 and later versions, select Memory from the Show menu in the box that appears.

4 Type a new value into the Preferred Size box, perhaps 1.5 or 2 times the suggested size shown. You can decrease the memory in the same way.

5 Click the close box. Your change will take effect the next time you launch the application.

**✱ Tip**
If you attempt to increase the minimum size to a value larger than the preferred size, you will get an error message.

## Format a PC Disk on a Mac · 84

If you want to use Mac files on a PC, you need to make sure you use PC-formatted disks to transfer the files. (Macs read PC disks, but PCs don't read Mac disks.) But even if you have Mac disks, you can reformat them as PC disks using your Mac.

### ⊙ Steps

1 Insert a floppy disk (with write protection off) or Zip disk into its drive.

2 If a dialog box appears, telling you the disk is unreadable, you can format it by clicking on the appropriate button.

3 If a dialog box doesn't appear, select the disk by clicking on it, click on the Special menu option, and select Erase Disk.

4 Select the format you want from the menu in the dialog box that appears. Your Mac will format the disk and tell you when it's finished.

**✱ Tip**
Make sure there is nothing you want to keep on the disk before formatting it.

## Protect a Computer From Viruses · 85

If you think your computer may be infected, take all necessary steps to clear your system and avoid infecting other computers.

### ⊙ Steps

1 Be cautious about what disks and files you accept from other people. Don't reuse disks that have been in other computers, don't download files from insecure sites, and don't open e-mail attachments unless you are expecting them. Be wary of messages and attachments, even from

**✱ Tips**
Keep up-to-date on virus alerts and install any patches released by software publishers.

people you know, with vague subject lines and contents, such as "Check this" or "See these pics!!!"

2   Obtain an antivirus program to more safely share disks, download files from the Internet and open e-mail attachments.

3   If your system gets a virus, visit your virus-scan software manufacturer's Web site and install any virus updates that are available. Then run the software. The software may not be able to delete the virus, but it may be able to identify it.

4   Search the Web for information regarding your specific virus by typing the name of the virus or its associated file into a search engine, followed by the word "virus." For example, "Melissa virus," "BubbleBoy virus," and so on.

5   Download and install any software patches or other programs that will help you eliminate the virus. Or follow any instructions you find on deleting the virus manually.

6   Run another virus scan to make sure the virus was dealt with properly.

7   Employ extra caution when you receive attachments that end in the commonly used extensions .doc, .exe, .com, .xls or .ppt. Never open attachments that end in .vbs or .js, since a typical user would never have a reason to open these files.

If you think your computer was infected with an e-mail virus that mails itself to people in your e-mail address book, phone those people and tell them not to open the messages or attachments. Avoid sending out any e-mail messages until you have properly eliminated the virus; many viruses attach themselves to outgoing messages without your knowledge.

Generally, deleting the file that caused the virus isn't sufficient to eliminate the problem, since many viruses can create new files or corrupt existing files.

## 86 Get the Best Price on Computer Software

Price variations on software from retail stores and Internet retailers are small, but you can get legal-to-use programs free or find other ways to save. Here are some options to explore.

### ◉ Steps

1   Use Internet search engines that find the best price on specific products.

2   Get software free from your employer. Many businesses purchase multi-computer licenses and are only too happy to have you work from home.

3   If you will be using the software for a home-based business, ask a large retailer for a business price.

4   Buy a "works" program (one program with various functions) or an office suite (a set of related programs) instead of individual word processing, spreadsheet and database programs if you plan on using most or all of the programs.

5   Buy the upgrade version of Microsoft Office instead of the full version if you already have any of these programs: all office suites, Microsoft Works, WordPerfect, Lotus 1-2-3 or any Microsoft program included in the version of Office you want.

6   Consider shareware or freeware programs or buy a basic program instead of a professional program if you do not need sophisticated features. Search the Internet for programs of the type you want.

7   Buy an older version of a program at a deep discount after the newer version has been released if you don't need the new features. If you change your mind, you can often upgrade inexpensively.

### ✳ Tips

Be aware that most software manufacturers offer upgrade prices to users of competing software.

Most chain retailers will give you a price adjustment (usually between 100 and 150 percent of the difference) if the price on a product is reduced (by that store or a local competitor) within a week or two of purchase.

### ⚠ Warning

Remember to add shipping costs when comparing prices from Internet and other mail-order retailers.

**How to Do (Just About) Everything**

## Play Music CDs on the Computer 87

Recent versions of Windows have CD player software built in. These instructions are for the Windows CD Player.

### ⊙ Steps

1  With the computer turned on, put a music CD, label side up, in the CD-ROM drive. Close the drive.

2  If auto play is enabled, the CD will start playing the first track. If this is the case, skip to step 6.

3  If the CD does not start playing automatically, open the Start menu. Choose Programs, then Accessories, then Entertainment.

4  Click CD Player.

5  Click the Play button on the CD Player window (a single right-pointing arrow in the top row).

6  Use the Pause, Stop, Skip to Next Track, and Go Back to Last Track buttons to control what you listen to.

7  Choose Edit Playlist from the Disc menu to program a particular sequence of tracks.

8  Minimize the CD Player window if you plan to listen to the entire CD while working.

### ✳ Tips

Sound cards usually come with a more sophisticated CD program.

Adjust volume by clicking on the speaker icon on your desktop.

## Use a Computer to Transfer Cassettes to CDs 88

You can use a CD burner to make a complete transition from tape to CD, or to make compilation CDs. You'll need a sound card with a Line In jack (other than a microphone jack).

### ⊙ Steps

1  Plug in your tape deck or portable player near your computer.

2  Connect the tape deck or player to the Line In jack on the sound card.

3  Use the jacks labeled Tape Out, Line Out or Playback on the deck, or use a headphone jack. Proceed to step 4, 5 or 6, depending on what you will connect to the computer.

4  If you're using a tape deck with a Tape Out, Line Out, or Playback jack, connect a cable with two RCA plugs on one end to the back of the deck. Connect the stereo miniplug on the other end to the sound card.

5  If you're using a deck with a headphone jack, connect a cable with a ¼-inch plug on one end to the headphone jack. Connect the stereo mini-plug on the other end to the sound card.

6  If you're using a portable player, connect a cable with stereo miniplugs on each end from the unit to the sound card.

7  Open the CD recorder application.

8  Select Line In as the source or input.

### ✳ Tips

If you are planning to play your recorded CD on an old CD player, select the Close the Session option before you start recording the CD. Some old CD players will not read recorded CDs unless the session is closed.

### ⚠ Warnings

Any computer activities during recording can interfere with the process. Prevent your modem or screen saver from activating during recording.

It may be illegal to copy copyrighted materials without the copyright owner's permission (especially for commercial purposes).

9   Open the File menu and select New or whatever command is used for beginning a recording.

10  Sample a track to set a recording level. Set the level to peak at 0 dB, 80 VU, or as high as possible without going into the red portion of the meter display.

11  Put the tape deck in Play/Pause mode before starting the track. If your source unit lacks a pause button, click Play a few seconds before the end of the preceding track.

12  Look for the command that begins recording: probably Record, Save or Extract to File. Start the recording process before the song starts.

13  Click Stop at the end of the track or side.

14  Save the recording as a WAV file to the desktop. Save individual tracks as separate WAV files, or save the entire side of the tape if your software allows it.

15  Open the WAV file in your recorder program (drag it into the CD-R window in some applications).

16  Select the recording speed.

17  Find the command that will record the file to CD: probably Record, Create or Save.

### Things You'll Need

- ☐ tape player
- ☐ CD burner
- ☐ recordable CDs
- ☐ cables
- ☐ sound card

---

## 89   Use a Computer to Transfer LPs to CDs

You can use your CD burner to archive your record collection or to make compilation CDs. You will need a sound card with a Line In jack (other than a microphone jack).

### ◉ Steps

1  Clean the LP and the stylus.

2  Plug in your turntable and preamplifier or receiver near your computer.

3  Connect the preamplifier or receiver to the Line In jack on the sound card. Use jacks labeled Preamp Out or Tape Out or a headphone jack. Use a cable with two RCA plugs on one end and a stereo miniplug on the other end. (Use a ¼-inch plug-to-miniplug adapter for a headphone jack.)

4  Switch the preamplifier or receiver to Phono.

5  Open your CD-recorder application.

6  Select Line In as the source or input.

7  Open the File menu and select New or whatever command is used for beginning a recording.

8  Sample a track to set a recording level. Set the level to peak at 0 dB, 80 VU, or as high as possible without going into the red portion of the meter display.

9  Lower the stylus to the beginning of the LP to record the entire side. Or start a few seconds before the end of the preceding track.

### ✳ Tips

If you hear a hum, try grounding the turntable or preamp to the computer by connecting a wire to screws on the chassis of each component.

Many programs for cleaning up LP noise are available. Before recording the WAV files to CD, use software to remove noise before and after songs, clicks and pops, and unwanted songs or excerpts.

### ⚠ Warnings

Do not expect the CD to sound as good as the LP.

Your preamplifier or receiver must have a Phono section.

10 Look for the command that starts the recording process: probably Record, Save or Extract to File. Begin recording before the song starts.

11 Click Stop at the end of the track or side.

12 Save the recorded file to the desktop as a WAV file. Save individual tracks as separate WAV files, or save the entire LP side if your software allows.

13 Open the WAV file in the CD recorder software (drag it into the CD-R window in some applications).

14 Select the recording speed.

15 Look for the command that will record the file to a CD: probably Record, Create or Save.

Any computer activities during recording can interfere with the process. Prevent your modem or screen saver from activating during recording.

It may be illegal to copy copyrighted materials without the copyright owner's permission (especially for commercial purposes).

## Get Internet Access　　90

The following steps describe how to access the Internet using an Internet service provider (ISP) and a computer modem. Many new computers include software that lets you set up an ISP account and connect to the Internet immediately.

### ⊙ Steps

1 Buy a computer that has a modem or add a modem to your existing computer. Most Internet service providers require at least an Intel 386 processor (or a Macintosh of any vintage) and a 14.4-Kbps modem. Most new computers will easily satisfy these requirements.

2 Make sure your modem is properly installed, and connect it to the nearest phone jack using a phone cord.

3 Look on your computer's desktop for an icon that bears the name of an Internet service provider. If you find one, double-click on the icon and follow instructions to install the software and activate your account.

4 If you can't find an icon and you use Windows, open the Start menu and choose Settings, then Control Panel. In the window that appears, double-click the Internet Options control panel. Click the Connections tab, then click the Setup button at the top of the window.

5 On a Mac, look for the Internet Setup Assistant in the Apple menu.

6 If your computer doesn't come with Internet software, look in the yellow pages under "Internet" for Internet service providers in your area.

7 Look for special offers from large, commercial ISPs on television, in newspapers and in the mail.

8 Contact a provider and request installation software.

9 Once you've received the software, follow the instructions on the package to install the program and set up your account.

### ✹ Tips

There are a number of other ways to go online besides a dial-up modem, including cable modems and digital subscriber lines (DSL) (see 92 "Choose a High-Speed Internet Access Method").

Read your terms-of-service agreement carefully before signing on.

Consider rates and fees, e-mail and other features, technical support and system requirements when choosing an ISP.

### ⚠ Warning

Make sure your ISP offers connection speeds matching those of your modem—56 Kbps for a 56-Kbps modem, for example. Transferring data at 28.8 Kbps with a 56-Kbps modem is a waste of your modem's capacity.

## 91 | Evaluate Free Internet Service Providers

Some new ISPs don't charge for an account. Before you sign up, make sure that quality hasn't been sacrificed to cost.

### ⊙ Steps

1   Find out what features the ISP offers. At a bare minimum, these should include e-mail and access to the World Wide Web. Other good features include access to newsgroups, instant messaging, and chat. Odds are, a free ISP won't have Web hosting or other services, but check.

2   Ask the same questions you would of other ISPs: What modem speeds does the ISP support? What operating systems? How many users per ISP modem? Is technical support available by phone?

3   Make sure the ISP is actually free. Read the fine print to see if there are any hidden charges that may show up later.

4   Determine how the company supports itself. Many free ISPs depend on advertising and end up bombarding their customers with commercial e-mail messages. If you think this may irritate you, seek out another ISP.

5   Look for reviews to get a feel for user satisfaction and service.

6   Carefully review the ISP's terms of service and other fine print, keeping an eye out for any deceptive wording or other traps.

### ✳ Tip

There's nothing to lose if you sign up for a free ISP and end up not being satisfied—you haven't paid anything.

## 92 | Choose a High-Speed Internet Access Method

High-speed Internet access is becoming more available. Depending on where you live, you may be able to get a cable, DSL or satellite connection. Weigh the pros and cons carefully.

### ⊙ Steps

1   Find out what services are available in your area. For cable modems, call your local cable company. For a digital subscriber line (DSL), call your local telephone company, but other providers may also offer DSL packages. Contact your current ISP to see if it offers DSL, and also check the Web. Consider a satellite service if other high-speed services are unavailable in your area.

2   Compare prices and speeds for various services.

3   Compare all hardware and installation costs, if any, including satellite installation and setup.

4   After completing your basic research, decide whether the extra cost of increased speed is worth it. You may choose to wait until competition drives down prices.

5   Expect actual cable modem and DSL speeds to vary according to your location, neighborhood and usage at any given moment. Cable should be faster. Expect satellite to be slower than DSL or cable. Recognize that your connection may not ever achieve the maximum speed advertised by the provider.

### ✳ Tips

DSL service has two parts: the actual line, set up by the phone company, and an ISP to connect your DSL to the rest of the Internet. The phone company will offer ISP services in addition to the line, but you might wish to choose a different ISP (for better rates; different features, such as more Web space or more e-mail accounts; or for better technical support). ISPs that offer DSL services will typically interface with the phone company for you.

Telephone and cable companies often provide free or subsidized hardware and installation. A service-term contract is required with these deals.

6 Before choosing your current telephone or cable TV company as your Internet provider, consider your level of satisfaction with its service, especially its customer service.

7 Make sure your cable wiring can support two-way modem transmission before choosing cable. (Ask the cable company. Some cable modem services require a dial-up modem connection for Internet uploads.)

8 Find out how many other users will ultimately share your cable access before choosing cable.

9 Compare extras offered by high-speed ISPs, such as multiple accounts, domain aliasing and extra Web space, if you'll use them.

### ⚠ Warnings

If you live in the Northern Hemisphere, you must have unobstructed access to the south to use a satellite dish.

Regardless of whether you select your telephone company to be your ISP, you will be dependent on it for DSL service.

Satellite requires a phone line for uploads.

## Choose a Good Computer Password　　93

Whether it's for e-mail or for online banking, a good password should be easy to remember and difficult to figure out.

### ◎ Steps

1 Use numbers as well as letters. If possible, use symbols such as $ and *.

2 Randomly capitalize letters if the password is case-sensitive.

3 Use as many characters as possible, with a minimum of six.

4 Choose a string of characters that can be typed quickly without looking at the keyboard.

5 Avoid using your username, personal name, the personal names of friends or family members, your birthday or other things that people may know about you.

6 Avoid using an actual word from any language. If someone is serious about cracking your password, he or she can run dictionaries from multiple languages against your account. Also avoid slang and technical jargon. The word "password" is an obvious no-no.

7 Find an easy way to remember your password. Avoid writing it down.

8 Change your password every three to six months, especially if your account gives you access to restricted information.

9 If you have different accounts, it's wise to use a different password for each one, as long as you can remember them.

### ✱ Tips

Acronyms for a phrase work well because they're easy to remember. (For example, "EGBDF" for "Every good boy does fine," also the sequence of lines in the treble clef.)

For an even better password, add a number or symbol somewhere in the acronym. (For example, "MMNIS3" for "My mother's name is Susan," followed by the random number 3.)

## Avoid Giving Personal Information to Web Sites　　94

Protect your privacy and security and minimize junk mail by using caution when browsing the Web.

### ◎ Steps

1 Avoid giving your Social Security number to anyone online for any reason unless you are certain that the site is trustworthy and the browser connection is secure.

### ✱ Tips

To verify that a site is using SSL (Secured Socket Layer), click on

2  When shopping online, make sure the site is secure before providing your name and address.

3  Be selective when registering with Web sites. Read the company's privacy policy before providing personal information. Look for a little box somewhere in the registration form that grants your permission for the company to send you mail or, worse, sell your personal information. This box is often prechecked. Uncheck it if you do not wish to receive mail from the site.

4  If you don't see any privacy information in the registration process, look for a statement somewhere on the site that describes the company's policy. If you don't find one, send e-mail to the site's Webmaster. Ask that your information not be used.

5  If you get e-mail from a site where you registered or shopped, and you didn't request it, look for a way to "unsubscribe" described at the bottom of the e-mail message. If you don't find one, try writing back to the e-mail address and asking to be taken off the mailing list.

6  When posting to a Web-based discussion board, use only your first name or use a fake name. Avoid providing any contact information other than your e-mail address and the URL of your Web page.

7  Try setting your browser to reject cookies, but realize that many site features won't work without cookies. (Cookies are what makes it possible, for example, for a site to know that you've been there before.)

the Shop icon—the URL will change from "http" to "https." If the URL is not displayed, right-click anywhere on the site that is not a link and select Properties to view the URL.

You can optimize your browser to accept cookies only from specific Web sites.

---

## 95 | Find Free Stuff on the Web

It's often said nothing in life is free, but the Internet may be rewriting the rules.

### ⊙ Steps

1  Enter whatever you're looking for, preceded by the word "free," into a Web search engine. (If you're looking for free stuff in general, a good search string is "free stuff.")

2  Once you've found a site that offers the free stuff you're looking for, follow the instructions on how to get it.

3  Check software manufacturers' Web sites for free trial versions of their software. Sometimes you can get a complete program to try; it will expire after a certain date. The trial program may have limited features.

4  Visit the Web sites for your favorite products to see if the sites give away free samples.

### ✱ Tips

Some "free stuff" has a catch: you might have to view ads while using a free ISP, for example. Investigate before you download.

Free stuff includes screen savers, clip art, computer wallpaper, simple software and so on.

### ⚠ Warning

Computer "shareware" can be downloaded for free, but you generally have to pay later on to keep using it.

**How to Do** *(Just About)* **Everything**

## Download Files 96

Downloading files may open up your hard disk to computer viruses. Avoid downloading from Web sites that you think might be dangerous or insecure.

### ⊙ Steps

1 Visit the Web page that has the link to the file you wish to download.

2 Click on the download link (usually a link that says "Download" or the name of the file).

3 Indicate which language and operating system you use, if necessary.

4 Select the download site nearest to you geographically, if given a choice. A window will pop up asking whether you wish to open the file or save it to disk.

5 Select "Save to disk" to retain the file for future use. If you want to use it only once, select Open.

6 If you selected "Save to disk," choose where you want the file to go on your hard disk. Most browsers then open a window indicating download progress, including percentage downloaded and time remaining.

### ✳ Tips

Many browsers offer the option of downloading multiple files simultaneously. However, downloading multiple files at once takes just as long as downloading them one at a time.

You can still browse the Web while your file is downloading. Just click on the original browser window.

Many larger files are compressed, typically as Zip files. To open these, you'll need a file-compression/decompression program.

## Conduct an Advanced Internet Search 97

To conduct an advanced search on the Internet, use Boolean operators, such as "AND" and "OR," to make your search as specific as possible.

### ⊙ Steps

1 Go to a Web search engine.

2 To find documents containing an exact phrase, type the phrase, surrounded by quotation marks, into the search field. For example, typing "fish sticks" (with the quotation marks) will return documents that contain the phrase "fish sticks," but not Web pages that contain only "fish" or "sticks."

3 To find documents containing a pair of words, but not necessarily together, type the words separated by the word "AND" in all caps. For example, typing "fish AND sticks" (without the quotation marks) will return Web pages that contain "fish," "sticks" and "fish sticks."

4 To find documents containing either one word or the other, type the words separated by the word "OR" in all caps. For example, typing "fish OR sticks" (without the quotation marks) will return documents that contain "fish" or "sticks," or both.

5 To exclude a word from your search, type the word you wish to exclude into the search field, preceded by the word "NOT" in all caps. For example, typing "fish NOT salmon" (without the quotation marks) will return only documents that do contain the word "fish" and do not contain the word "salmon."

### ✳ Tips

Check the directions for the search engine you're using. Some require very specific syntax.

Some search engines allow the following symbolic substitutions for Boolean words: & for AND, | for OR, ! for NOT, and ~ for NEAR. But not all searches allow this, so if your query comes up blank, try using the words instead.

Some search engines don't support the Boolean words "NEAR" or "NOT."

6   To find documents that contain two words separated by 10 to 25 words, type the two words separated by the word "NEAR" in all caps, into the search field.

7   If your search expression is lengthy or complicated, use parentheses to separate the different parts. For example, typing "fish OR sticks NOT (salmon OR trout)" will get you entries that have the words "fish" or "sticks" or both, but do not have the words "salmon" or "trout."

## 98 | Shop Online

**You can now buy just about anything online. If you haven't yet tried e-shopping, here's a general outline.**

### ⊙ Steps

1   Use a search engine to find the product you're looking for if you don't know specifically which site to go to. Or try a product-comparison site to check different prices or product reviews.

2   Visit several sites to find the best products and prices.

3   Most sites use a shopping cart system. As you browse the site and find items you want, click Add to Cart (or a similar button).

4   Specify a quantity and other relevant specifics (color, size and so on) when you add an item to your shopping cart.

5   Click Continue Shopping (or a similar button) to keep browsing. Otherwise, click Proceed to Checkout (or something similar) to finalize your order.

6   For any kind of shopping site, provide your name, address, e-mail address, phone number and payment information when prompted during checkout. Once you've entered this information, you are usually presented with an order-confirmation page, including all your items, the total price, and the address and other information you've entered.

7   Make sure your order is accurate and then confirm it.

### ✳ Tips

Most traditional catalog retailers have Web sites now.

Shop from sites that use a secure server to process transactions. If you're uneasy about providing your credit card number online, you can usually pay by check or call in your credit card number by phone.

In most cases, the online store will send you an e-mail message to confirm the details of your order. Many online stores send you e-mail updates if any problems occur with your order.

Shipping times and costs vary among sites.

## 99 | Bid at Online Auctions

**Online auctions can be a great way to get deals on goods, from computers and electronics to antiques and collectibles.**

### ⊙ Steps

1   Register as a bidder by entering your credit card number and an e-mail address for communication purposes. Registered bidders will be asked to submit a username and password.

2   Search categories to find things you want to bid on.

3   Select an item; enter your username, your password and the bid amount.

### ✳ Tips

Before bidding, ask the seller questions about how the item was stored or cared for and whether it has a certificate of authenticity. Check out size and weight specifications to ensure that you know what you're purchasing.

4   Enter a bid that is within your budget but higher than the current high bid. High bids are displayed along with the description of the item.

5   Click the Submit Bid button to go to the Web site's confirmation page. The site will advise you immediately on the status of your bid (whether you've been outbid or currently have the highest bid).

6   Look for a Current Winner message on the page showing that your bid is currently the highest. If no one outbids you before the auction period ends, you "win" the auction.

7   Check your e-mail regularly during the auction. You will receive an e-mail message if you are outbid during the auction. Place another bid if you wish to bid higher.

8   Work out payment and shipping details directly with the seller when you win an auction. (The seller will most likely contact you via e-mail.) On some auction sites, you can submit payment through the site or a trusted third party. Payment is usually accomplished with a money order or personal check. Some sellers also accept credit cards.

If you have problems with a seller, complain to the site. Sites usually post negative feedback about a seller, and you can warn others who might have similar problems. Be a good buyer as well, as you may be rated by the seller.

⚠ **Warning**

Comparison shop before you bid. Just because something's up for auction doesn't mean it's a good deal. Shop carefully—you could end up paying more money than you would in a traditional store.

## Watch Video Clips on the Web                  100

You can watch anything from music videos to political debates on the Web, as long as you have the appropriate browser plug-ins and viewing software. With "streaming" video, you don't have to actually download the clip to view it; otherwise, you need to download the clip first.

◉ **Steps**

1   Visit the Web site that hosts the video clip you wish to view. The clip will probably have several different links according to viewing format—such as QuickTime or RealPlayer—and modem speed.

2   Select the link that matches your connection speed and offers a format that your software supports.

3   Try a different format if you cannot view the clip you chose and another is offered (not all sites offer a choice of formats and connection speeds).

4   Download and install the appropriate viewing software or plug-in if you cannot view the clip in any format. Many sites that host video clips also provide links to sites where you can download this software for free.

5   Note that technology in this area is advancing quickly. Update your player frequently to keep up.

✴ **Tips**

Newer PCs come equipped with the Windows Media Player. Macintoshes come with the QuickTime MoviePlayer. You can get the free, basic version for streaming video from the Real.com Web site.

If the clip is choppy or refuses to play, and you have the appropriate player software, try defragmenting your hard disk; also see if the site provides minimum requirements to view the video.

⚠ **Warning**

Video quality is often poor on a 56 Kbps or slower connection.

## 101 | Use the Internet to Locate People

Put the Internet to work to find your best friend from kindergarten, a long-lost relative or the roommate who skipped out without paying the phone bill.

### ⊙ Steps

1  The person you're looking for may have a personal home page. To find out, simply type the person's first and last names into a Web search engine and view the results.

2  If the person you're looking for is a college student, he or she may have an e-mail account through the school. Visit the school's Web site (usually in the form of www.schoolname.edu) and check the campus directory.

3  The person may have an e-mail account through his or her job. If you know where the person works, visit the company's Web site and use its directory. If the site has no directory, try sending an e-mail message to the person at firstname.lastname@company.com.

4  The person may use the same Internet service provider that you do. Try searching in your ISP's member directory.

5  If none of the above suggestions work, try an online directory Web site.

### ✱ Tips

Search services often turn up old addresses, if they turn up anything at all.

Some online search services find e-mail addresses, some find phone numbers and postal addresses, and some find both.

## 102 | Make Phone Calls Over the Internet

Using the Internet as an alternative to traditional telephone calls can be less expensive but slightly more complicated.

### ⊙ Steps

1  Make sure you can connect to the Internet at a minimum speed of 28.8 Kbps. Higher connection speeds will allow clearer conversations.

2  Make sure your computer is equipped with a sound card of at least 16 bits. The sound card should also allow recording.

3  Purchase compatible speakers and a microphone if you don't already have these components.

4  Buy or download Internet telephony software and install it on your computer. The software you choose must be the same as or compatible with the software of the people you wish to call.

5  Make arrangements with the person you wish to call establishing that you will be online at a specific time.

6  Follow the instructions of your specific telephony software for making a call. This usually involves accessing a server and selecting a name from a list of users who are currently online.

### ✱ Tips

In general, online telephone calls can only be made between two people who have computers, Internet access and compatible software, although some applications (such as Dialpad) allow you to call regular telephones.

For optimal clarity, use a full-duplex sound card.

Instant-messaging software will give you instant messages, but without the voice effects.

## Create Your First Web Site

These simple guidelines are for entry-level Web programmers. Better options are available for more sophisticated users.

### ⊙ Steps

### Getting Started

1  Choose an ISP or other Web hosting service to host your site.

2  Investigate several hosting services, considering maximum space, accessibility, reputation and terms of service.

3  Select and download a Web-page editor. Several simple editors are available for free; Netscape Composer is one. These editors let you see what your site will look like as you build it, so you won't have to learn HTML or other programming languages. Newer word processors, spreadsheets and other applications can also generate HTML files.

4  Your Web-page editor will give you specific instructions about options such as naming your site, creating different sections, creating backgrounds, adding links and inserting images.

### Using Images

5  Create images for your site by drawing them with your computer's paint program or by using a scanner for photographs and other hard-copy images. Or take photographs with a digital camera.

6  If you find an image on another Web page that you'd like to use, send an e-mail to the page's owner or administrator and request permission to download and post it. Download an image from a Web site by right-clicking on it (or on a Mac, click and hold down the mouse ) and select Save Picture.

### Publishing Your Site

7  Your Web host ISP may have its own system for uploading pages. Otherwise, obtain a File Transfer Protocol (FTP) program. Any will do.

8  Open your FTP program and log in to your host server by entering your login name and password.

9  Access the directory where your home page belongs. (Your Web ISP will give you this information.) The directory address is usually in the form of /pub/username, /pub/www/username, or /pub/username/www. Your FTP program and host server will have specific instructions on how to access your directory.

10  Upload each page and graphic of your site according to the specific instructions of the FTP program and your host server.

### ✱ Tips

Many Web hosts let you use your own "domain name" (such as www.me.com) if you have one, or will assign you a name.

Some Web sites, such as Homestead (www.homestead.com), provide both hosting and site-building services.

Many graphics software programs come with clip art—simple images in various categories— that you can use on your site.

Clip-art CD-ROMs can be purchased from software retailers.

You may want to limit the size of the images you include; larger images can make your page take a long time to view.

Your FTP program may give you a choice between ASCII and binary mode when uploading. Use ASCII mode for uploading pages, because pages are text files. Use binary mode for image files.

The above steps are a general strategy for uploading your site. Your FTP program and Web-page ISP will have more specific instructions.

### ⚠ Warning

To use content, clip art or images from someone else's site, you need permission from the creator, unless the site or clip-art collection specifically states that the content or art can be reused.

## 104 | Choose a Domain Name for a Web Site

A domain name reflects your business or personal identity.
Choose wisely.

### ◉ Steps

1 Write down the name of your business. Remembering that short and
sweet domain names are the easiest to remember, create a list of possible names using your business name (for example, smithauto.com,
smauto.com, smitheys.com).

2 Create a list of services your business provides and a list of possible
names from those services (for example, autorepair.com, fixcar.com,
brokedown.com).

3 Use catchphrases from your brochure and other promotional materials to
create additional possibilities.

4 For personal domain names, use your name, your pet's name, your hobbies, your surname or even your child's name.

5 Visit the Whois Web site (www.whois.org). Using Whois, you can type in
your favorite picks and see if they're taken and by whom. If they are
taken, keep trying with your alternate choices.

6 Use other organizational suffixes, such as .net or .org, if the .com name
is taken. However, since users randomly searching for your site may be
directed to the .com site first, .net and .org names are usually best for
personal rather than business domain names.

7 If you're really set on using a domain name that has been taken, contact
the owner of that domain name by checking the Administrative Contact
section on the Whois site. Domain-name owners sometimes sell domain
names they don't use.

### ✱ Tip

Ask family, friends and associates for their opinions of your
choices. What seems funny to
you might be incomprehensible
to someone else.

### ⚠ Warning

Don't use the name of a well-
known company or product, or
any variation of that name, in
hopes of attracting people to
your site. Not only is this unethi-
cal, but it may subject you to
legal action.

## 105 | Register a Domain Name

Setting up a Web site with your own domain name (www.me.com)
is a straightforward process, though finding a name you like
may prove difficult. Registration usually gives you exclusive use
of a domain name for two years.

### ◉ Steps

1 Go to the Network Solutions Web site (www.networksolutions.com),
Register.com or another official Internet registrar.

2 Enter the name or phrase of the domain name you would like to register.
Follow the rules regarding name length and format.

3 Search for the name.

4 If the name is already taken, enter a new name and search again until
you find one that is still available. If you tried .com as a suffix, try .org
or .net instead.

### ✱ Tips

Have a list of possible names
ready when you visit the site.

The more unusual the name, the
more likely it will be available.
Most common or well-known
corporate names are taken.

If the domain name is already
taken and you desperately want
it, you may contact the owner
and offer to buy it.

5 Register the domain name.

6 Pay the filing fee online or through the mail, following the instructions on the Web site.

Once you have the domain name, contact your ISP to see about using it as your Web site or e-mail address.

## Learn HTML                                             106

HTML, which stands for Hypertext Markup Language, is the formatting language used to create most Web pages.

### ◉ Steps

1 Call your local community college or university. Many schools give courses on HTML and Web design and have programs that offer a certificate of completion and/or course credits.

2 Purchase a book on HTML design. Book/CD-ROM combinations offer hands-on learning and Web development tools.

3 Go to the HTML Writers Guild Web site (www.hwg.org) and sign up for the trial membership. The HTML Writers Guild offers classes in HTML, Web design and Web graphics for members.

4 Learn HTML on your own by looking at a page's source code. With your browser, open a simple, easy-to-read page. Open the View menu, then select Source or Page Source, depending on your browser. Study how the source code translates into the page you see in the browser.

5 Purchase an HTML reference manual to help you decipher the tags and their roles. You can even copy a page's source code and insert your own elements to see what happens.

6 Visit the World Wide Web Consortium at www.w3c.org to find an HTML tutorial and learn more about HTML's history.

7 Ask a Web-page designer to teach you HTML as he or she designs a page for you. It costs a little more, but you will learn as you go and be able to update your own page.

### ✽ Tip

It is best to learn HTML before you use an HTML assistant or Web design application. You can use HTML code to make changes that many HTML assistants won't allow you to make.

### ⚠ Warning

Use another's source code only to learn. Using parts of someone else's Web page as your own is copyright infringement. Once you have learned HTML, you can create your own pages.

## Learn About Java                                        107

Java is a programming language created for the Internet. You can use Java to create scripts, animated text and other interesting objects.

### ◉ Steps

1 Contact a local university or community college. Many colleges offer programming packages that include Java and other programming languages, as well as Web design.

2 Log on to the Web site of Sun Microsystems, the company that created Java, to find tutorials and examples of Java programming.

3 Purchase a comprehensive book about Java. A good Java book will include an outline of Java history, an explanation of how it works, examples and worksheets; some even come with interactive CD-ROMs.

### ✽ Tips

Java applets are small applications written in Java. Applets are typically attached to Web pages.

One of Java's strengths is that it is platform-independent. Java programs can run on various operating systems, as long as the computer running the program has a Java virtual machine installed to interpret the standard Java byte code into code that will run on that system.

4   Sign up for an online Java course. The HTML Writer's Guild (www.hwg.org) is one potential source.

5   Search the Internet for some of the many user groups, forums and Web sites dedicated to Java.

6   Consider learning JavaScript, used in Web browsers. Unrelated to Java, JavaScript is an interpreted language. JavaScript is easier to learn but more limited than Java.

7   If you're serious about programming, read books or take classes on general skills such as developing algorithms and designing data structures.

Java is an object-oriented, or modular, programming language, like C++.

---

## 108 | Publicize Your Web Site

Get the word out! Help people from all over the world find your Web site.

### ◉ Steps

1   Register your site with your favorite Internet search engines. Most search-engine sites have links (toward the bottom of the engine's home page) that say "Add a site" or "Add URL." Click on these links and follow the sites' instructions.

2   Visit Web sites such as Submit It (www.submit-it.com), which help you submit your URL to multiple search engines simultaneously.

3   Visit sites that are related to or similar to your own, or maintained by your friends, and suggest linking to each other's pages.

4   Join a Web ring, a group of Web sites on a particular topic that link to each other in a chain. Or start your own Web ring. Visit the WebRing site (www.webring.org) for information.

5   Pay to place banner ads on well-trafficked Web sites; contact individual sites for their rates. Or join a free banner exchange, such as LinkExchange (www.linkexchange.com).

### ✳ Tip

Use META tags in your HTML pages to help your Web site come up in more search-engine results. To learn more about META tags, visit Web developer sites, such as WebDeveloper.com or InternetDay.com. For other tips about search-engine results, go to Search Engine Watch (www.searchenginewatch.com).

---

## 109 | Get a Free E-mail Account

Free e-mail is typically Web-based. It usually doesn't have as many features as Internet service provider or work-based e-mail, but you can access it anywhere.

### ◉ Steps

1   Decide what type of e-mail service would be best for you. Consider factors such as the volume of outgoing and incoming mail, message storing, the ability to send and receive attachments, frequency of use and security.

2   Do a search for "free e-mail" or "Web mail" using a Web search engine.

### ✳ Tips

If you travel a lot or often use other people's computers, a Web-based e-mail service will probably be best for you.

3   Visit various sites that offer free e-mail. Review their respective plans, features and terms of service.

4   Once you've found a free service that suits your e-mail needs, follow the site's instructions on how to set up your account.

Some free e-mail services operate by inundating you with advertising e-mail messages from their sponsors; others make you view ads on the screen.

## Send an E-mail Attachment                                        110

These instructions will give you the basics of how to send an e-mail attachment no matter which program you are using.

### ◉ Steps

1   Go to your e-mail program.

2   Click the New Mail, Write Message or similar button, depending on your application, to create a new e-mail message.

3   Enter the address of the recipient in the To field.

4   Type a subject in the Subject field.

5   Add a message to the body of the e-mail as usual.

6   Click the Attachments button. Many programs have an icon of a paperclip for it. Also look for an Insert File or Insert Attachment option in the File menu.

7   Browse your files to find the attachment you want to send. You may need to click on a Browse or Find button to see your directory.

8   Click on the filename. If your program allows you to attach more than one file at once, hold down the Control key (or Shift key on a Mac) as you select another one.

9   Click the Attach Insert or Open button, depending on your e-mail program.

10  To send another file from a different location, click the Attachments button again and repeat the steps.

11  Click the Send button when you're done.

### ❋ Tips

Change picture attachments to the JPEG format. They'll take up less space and send faster in that format.

Make sure the recipient can read your attachment. Most word processors can read RTF (Rich Text Format). Web browsers can all open JPEG and GIF image files.

If you're sending files to a person who uses a modem, be careful about sending large files (300K or more), because they can take a long time to download.

Consider compressing your files with a utility such as WinZip or StuffIt. Your recipient usually needs to have the compression software as well, but some programs are able to make "self-extracting" files that decompress automatically.

## Create Your Own E-mail Mailing List                              111

By creating your own e-mail mailing list, you can easily send copies of a message to a group of recipients.

### ◉ Steps

1   Collect the e-mail addresses of your recipients.

2   Open your e-mail program and save these names as a group. Look for a function that is called something like Address Book, Contacts or Nicknames. Name the group and enter your recipients' e-mail addresses separated by commas or semicolons. Click Save. Note that many e-mail programs require that you enter all of the individual addresses to your Address Book before you can add them to a group.

### ❋ Tips

Using the BCC field instead of the CC field allows the messages to be sent without showing each recipient the e-mail addresses of the other recipients. However, not all e-mail programs support the BCC feature.

3  Open a new message and address it to yourself.

4  Add the subject and body of the message.

5  Put the group e-mail addresses in the field marked BCC (blind carbon copy). Your e-mail software should allow you to do this automatically from the Address Book or from the Nickname function. If it doesn't, copy the list and paste it in the BCC field of your message.

6  Click Send. The original message will be sent to you, as you entered your own address in the To field.

7  Each member of the group will receive a copy of the message.

If you have a large mailing list (hundreds or thousands), you may want to consider one of the bulk e-mail programs that you can purchase for this purpose. To avoid being accused of spamming, include only addresses of people who have agreed to receive your messages.

## 112  Stop Unwanted E-mail

As anyone who's ever had an inbox cluttered with unwanted advertisements knows, spam, or unsolicited commercial e-mail, can be a big problem.

### ⊙ Steps

1  Contact your ISP and complain. ISPs don't like spam any more than you do; the mail clogs their servers. The ISP can filter out mail from a suspected spammer address.

2  Avoid displaying your e-mail address in Internet chat rooms and only give out your e-mail address on secure sites.

3  Avoid including your e-mail address when you post to newsgroups.

4  Send a complaint message to the postmaster at the spammer's ISP, if you can figure it out. Many spammers forge return addresses, but you can sometimes figure out the ISP from the full e-mail header. In some e-mail programs you can right-click on the e-mail message and choose Options or Properties to see this information.

5  Be careful when selecting a free ISP or e-mail account. Some of these services make their money by letting "sponsors" send e-mail messages to their subscribers.

6  If your e-mail provider doesn't have a built-in spam filter, search the Web for e-mail filters and other anti-spam software. Many of these programs are free and can be easily installed.

### ✱ Tip

To reduce spam in your e-mail account, open a second, free e-mail account to be used exclusively for Web-site registrations, chat rooms and mailing lists (see 109 "Get a Free E-mail Account").

### ⚠ Warning

Don't reply to spam unless the message includes clear instructions for removing yourself from a mailing list. In most cases, responding only verifies that your e-mail address is active. Sometimes the spammer has forged a return address, so by responding you're actually bothering an innocent person.

## 113  Read a Newsgroup on the Internet

Internet newsgroups are a great way to share information online. Once you have a news reader set up on your computer, reading and posting to newsgroups is relatively simple.

### ⊙ Steps

1  Get your news server name from your ISP or network administrator.

### ✱ Tips

Your ISP or network may not subscribe to all the newsgroups you want. If possible, use a separate

2   Determine whether your current ISP software, e-mail program or Web browser includes a news-reading utility (many do). If not, download and install one.

3   Configure your news reader by inputting your news server address and any other information it requests (it might ask for an e-mail address and mail server as well).

4   Use your reader to call up a list of available newsgroups. This list will probably pop up during setup the first time you use your reader.

5   Look through the hierarchical list of newsgroups to find any that sound interesting. Let the prefixes of each group (such as "comp" for computer-related topics and "rec" for recreational topics) guide your search. The other words in the name go from general to more specific keywords.

6   Subscribe to whichever newsgroups you want to read or post to. (Note that some readers allow you to read newsgroup messages without your having to subscribe.)

7   Select the newsgroup you want to read.

8   Select a message by double-clicking on the subject. (Note that different readers may have different ways of reading messages.)

reader to maximize your access to the Internet. Newsgroups that begin with "alt" (denoting "alternative" topics) may be especially hard to find on ISPs.

If you come across a newsgroup message that appears to be gibberish, it may be a message encrypted into "Rot13." This is an encryption code that replaces each letter with the letter that is 13 spots ahead of it in the alphabet. This coding is used mainly to protect people from possibly offensive postings. You can decode these messages by hand, or see if your reader has a Rot13 decoding utility.

## Use Online Forums 114

Forums, also called discussion boards, function in a similar way to newsgroups, except that they are available through ISPs and individual Web sites.

### ◉ Steps

1   Explore some of the forums and special-interest groups on your ISP or online service.

2   Use a search engine and look for Web sites that focus on your interests. Many of these will have forums or chats.

3   Read the "posts" (messages) and follow the current "threads" (comments related to a single topic) for several days. See if the group has a FAQ (frequently asked questions) document and read it.

4   Write a post of your own. Be prepared for a mixed response.

5   Explain yourself if someone takes exception to your comments, but do not get into a heated argument via posts.

6   Determine whether your forum companions get together for chat sessions. Join in if they do.

7   Send e-mail to your new friends and develop new relationships.

### ✳ Tips

Keep your initial posts short and noncontroversial.

Befriend a veteran or two and ask about the group's taboos.

Always represent yourself accurately; you may want to meet the forum regulars one day.

### ⚠ Warning

Generally, forums are open to all. That means you may run into angry, combative people who will "flame" you for posting ideas that run counter to their own. If you handle the attacks calmly without retaliating, others will respect you.

## 115 | Find an Internet Chat Room

Use these guidelines to communicate in real time with people all over the world.

### ⊙ Steps

1   Check for any chat utilities offered by your ISP, if you use one. Most large commercial ISPs offer a variety of chat rooms categorized by topic and demographic segment, as well as general chat rooms with no specific focus.

2   Find out about chat functions offered by any instant-message programs you use. Many of these programs let users participate in public chat rooms as well as create their own.

3   Search the World Wide Web, either directly or through a chat room data-base, for Web-based chat rooms on specific topics.

4   Check out IRC, or Internet Relay Chat, which requires IRC software and involves a set of networks and channels.

### ✱ Tips

Many Web-based chat rooms require you to download and install plug-in software before they can be accessed.

Many chat services let users preview a room by reading the profiles of any users who are currently in the room.

## 116 | Practice Chat Room Etiquette

Many chat rooms have sets of rules and guidelines, often unof-ficial, by which users are expected to abide.

### ⊙ Steps

1   Find out whether a particular chat room has its own FAQ (frequently asked questions) section before you enter. If it does, review the FAQ section for specific etiquette guidelines.

2   Introduce yourself when you enter a room by typing your age and gender. In some rooms, a general location, such as your state, is also appropriate to mention.

3   If you want to address an individual in the room without sending an instant message, introduce your statement or question with the person's screen name and a colon or hyphen (for example, "SportsFan: What's your favorite football team?").

4   Avoid referring to users by their real names.

5   Allow all users to make comments and ask questions. Don't try to take control of the room by flooding it with your own entries.

6   Avoid direct confrontations with rude users. Report disruptive users to the chat host if a host is available. Otherwise, leave the chat room.

7   Don't harass other users with threats, unwanted sexual comments or anything else that might make them uncomfortable.

### ✱ Tips

Some chat rooms offer you the option of blocking out messages and chat room entries from spe-cific users. This feature is a good alternative to abandoning the room or getting the chat host involved.

To get a feel for how a chat room operates, try "lurking"—observ-ing the room without making any entries—for a while before offer-ing your own comments.

### ⚠ Warning

Don't type the same sentence, word or phrase into the chat room over and over again. This is called "scrolling" and is heavily frowned on by users and hosts.

## Decide Whether to Repair an Electronics Product  117

While quality has declined over the years, performance and functionality have improved. Weigh the trade-offs to decide whether to replace a formerly reliable product.

### ⊙ Steps

1 Find out if the product is covered by the manufacturer's warranty or an extended service agreement.

2 Find out the cost of a replacement product.

3 Get a free estimate on repair, if repair shops in your area will provide one. If not, find out the hourly labor charge. Expect to pay $60 to $80 per hour for labor in U.S. cities, with a one-hour minimum charge.

4 Find out how long the repair is warranted. Most shops warrant repairs for 60 to 90 days.

5 Consider the resale value of the product if it is repaired.

6 Consider the portability of the broken product and how far you'll have to haul it to the repair shop.

7 Remember that you might have to spend time learning how to use a new product.

8 Ask a repair technician if any additional parts are likely to need replacement in the near future.

9 Learn about features on current products that your product lacks.

10 If applicable, make sure your software will work on new hardware before abandoning the broken product.

11 Repair the product if the category no longer exists (such as a Beta VCR or eight-track tape player) or you have an old software collection that is valuable to you.

12 Replace the product if you can benefit from upgrading to newer technology (such as from a VCR to a DVD player).

13 Remember that manufacturers must provide at least a 90-day limited warranty for new products sold in the United States.

### ✳ Tips

Expect a good repair shop to take several weeks to repair your product. Also, manufacturers can be slow to send proprietary parts or may no longer stock them.

Audio and video tape decks have minor variations in speed; if you replace one, your tapes are likely to sound "wrong" due to variations in pitch.

New tape decks lack microphone inputs and once-popular forms of noise reduction.

Most new turntables won't play 78-rpm records.

If you choose to replace the product, try to find a way to dispose of the old product that is kind to the environment.

## Set Up a Stereo System  118

While these instructions presume a basic stereo receiver, the connection process would be the same for higher-end components. You would just have additional connections to make.

### ⊙ Steps

#### Connect Turntable to Receiver

1 Connect the turntable to the input labeled "Phono."

2 Connect the green grounding wire to the grounding pin or screw on the receiver, or loosen a screw on the receiver chassis and connect the wire to the screw, then tighten securely with a scewdriver.

### ✳ Tips

RCA cables are normally supplied with mass-market components, but not with high-fidelity components. Use the supplied cables or upgraded cables.

3   Connect the RCA cables (usually hardwired to the turntable) to the receiver. Connect the red plug to the jack that either has a red band or is marked "Right." Connect the black plug to the other jack or the jack marked "Left."

## Connect Line-Level Signal Source Components to Receiver

4   Connect the RCA cables to the back of the CD player.

5   Connect the red plug to the jack with the red band or the jack marked "Right." Connect the black plug to the other jack or the jack marked "Left."

6   Connect the other ends of the cables to the jacks labeled "CD" or "CD Player" on the back of the receiver.

7   Repeat these steps for all other line-level playback components. (Find appropriately labeled inputs or use the "Aux" input.)

8   Connect the cassette deck (or other recorder) outputs to jacks on the receiver labeled "Tape In," "Tape 1," "Tape Play" or something similar. Outputs are usually labeled "Line Out" or "Playback."

9   Connect cassette deck inputs to jacks on the receiver labeled "Tape Out," "Record Out" or "Tape 1 Out." Inputs are usually labeled "Line In" or "Record."

## Connect Receiver to Speakers

10  If your receiver or speakers have "bare wire" connectors, strip the ends of the speaker wire with wire cutters, then twist the exposed ends. If your receiver or speakers accept connectors such as spades or banana plugs, add connectors to the speaker wire as needed.

11  Connect one pair of wires for the left speaker (meaning the speaker that is to your left as you face the speakers and receiver).

12  Connect the positive terminals of the receiver to the positive terminals of the speaker, and connect the negative terminals of the receiver to the negative terminals of the speaker. Speaker wire is labeled + or –, or each lead is a different color or has a color-coding strip. Outputs on the receiver and inputs on the speakers are labeled + and –.

13  Securely tighten the lugs or binding posts on the receiver and speakers.

14  Install the wires for the right speaker the same way.

15  Position the speakers. Place the two speakers away from the walls, at the corners of an equilateral triangle (with your listening position as the third corner). Start with the speakers about 6 to 8 feet apart and angled to face each other slightly. Experiment to achieve the ideal positioning.

Any line-level component can be connected to any line-level input (anything not labeled "Phono").

Plug components into a surge suppressor. Turn on your source components before your receiver.

## ⚠ Warnings

Most audio components need ventilation. Leave "breathing room" around vents.

You must have an input labeled "Phono" for your turntable to work. Otherwise, you will need to buy a phono preamplifier.

## Things You'll Need

☐ screwdriver

☐ wire cutters

# Improve AM Reception                                    119

AM radio reception can be noisy as a result of distance from the station's antenna, interference from other stations, the quality of your radio or conditions in your home.

## ⊙ Steps

1 Gradually rotate the radio 360 degrees. Leave it in the position where it sounds best.

2 Reverse the AC plug if it isn't polarized. (If you can flip the plug over, then it's nonpolarized.)

3 Plug the radio into a different AC outlet.

4 Move the radio closer to a window.

5 Experiment to learn if appliances and powered products In your home are causing interference: computer monitor, television, electric blanket, light dimmer, fluorescent light, hair dryer, air conditioner, smoke detector. If possible, turn off the offending item. Otherwise, move the radio to another room.

6 Upgrade to an external antenna if your receiver, tuner or radio has a place to connect one.

7 Buy a passive AM antenna that doesn't need to be connected to a radio or receiver.

**❋ Tip**

Passive (not AC or battery-powered) antennas don't boost signal as much as powered antennas, but powered antennas boost noise along with signal.

# Improve FM Reception                                   120

FM radio reception can be poor due to distance from the station's antenna, signal blockage, interference from other stations or the quality of your radio, but you can improve reception.

## ⊙ Steps

1 If you have a radio with a telescoping antenna, fully extend the antenna and rotate it to different angles.

2 If you live in a big city or mountainous area, move the radio to the place in your home that has the fewest large obstacles between you and the radio station's transmitter.

3 Switch from stereo to mono.

4 With a receiver or tuner, connect a wire-loop or T-shaped dipole FM antenna to the back of your unit. Move the antenna until you get the cleanest signal. Use a signal-strength meter or display to gauge signal strength if your unit has one.

5 Alternatively, upgrade to a third-party passive or powered antenna.

6 Install a rotatable roof antenna for the best possible reception. Connect your unit to an existing television roof antenna for the next-best alternative.

**❋ Tips**

If your unit didn't come with an antenna and you don't wish to buy one, run wires from the antenna terminals to the outside of your home.

Use a rotator to aim a roof antenna toward the radio-station transmitter.

Passive (not AC or battery-powered) antennas don't boost signal as much as powered antennas, but powered antennas boost noise along with signal. If you live near the station, a passive antenna is likely to provide better results. If you live far from the station, a powered antenna is likely to provide better results.

## 121 | Get the Best Price on Music CDs

CDs that sell at retail stores can often be found for up to 40 percent less on the Internet.

### ⊙ Steps

#### Individual CDs

1 Use Internet search engines called shopping bots, which find the lowest prices on specific products. You can find these by typing "shopping bots" in one or more Internet search engines.

2 Avoid CD merchants in shopping malls, as these have higher prices.

3 Find CDs at consumer electronics stores for 15 percent to 25 percent less than at CD specialty stores.

4 Check general-merchandise discount stores for popular titles.

5 Ask if a store offers frequent-buyer cards (for example, buy 10, get 1 free).

6 Check CD specialty stores for unadvertised sales, usually covering all titles on specific labels.

7 Consider used CDs. Ask the store if you can listen before you buy.

#### CD Clubs

1 Consider a record label's club only if you plan to limit your buying to popular titles from major artists.

2 Expect to pay up to $4 per CD for shipping and handling, including "free" selections.

3 Be prepared to make your selections and rejections (some clubs automatically send you a CD every month unless you instruct them not to) within the required periods.

4 Check the CD club's FAQ Web page for suggestions about getting the best value from CD club membership.

5 If a club offers wholesale prices, and you will buy enough CDs to justify the dues, membership may be a good deal.

### ✳ Tips

Remember to add shipping charges before comparing prices from Internet and other mail-order retailers.

Check several Internet price-comparison sites before deciding, and try to discern the comparison site's biases. Many such sites only include retailers who pay, or preferentially rank retailers who pay.

A club is a good value if you can find enough "free" selections you would buy anyway.

### ⚠ Warning

Major-label clubs often do not carry CDs made by their leading competitors.

## 122 | Buy Recordable CDs

Recordable CDs are a great way to archive your LP collection, make compilation albums and put your computer's audio software to good use.

### ⊙ Steps

1 Buy CD-R discs for your audio deck unless the manufacturer specifically claims the audio deck will recognize and record CD-RW discs.

2 Buy blank discs that can be used at your drive's fastest speed(s).

3 Only buy computer CD-R discs for your CD-R drive.

### ✳ Tips

Check whether the blank discs can record and play as fast as your equipment can.

Check your owner's manual for recommendations of disc brands.

4   Buy CD-RW discs for your CD-RW drive to back up your hard drive.

5   Buy CD-R discs for your CD-RW drive for archival use or for permanent recording of music.

6   Compare block error rates (BLER) of different discs to find the highest-quality discs.

7   Buy blank CDs in jewel boxes unless you use another type of protective case.

8   Ask about manufacturer's rebates before buying a quantity of discs; sometimes discs are almost free after rebates.

9   Make sure you test a brand carefully before you buy a lot of discs—some brands of recorders/burners and players have problems reading some brands of recordable discs.

If you experience problems when using a disc on other playback units, try rerecording at a different speed.

## ⚠ Warnings

You can alter an audio CD recorder to get it to use computer media, but doing so may be considered a violation of U.S. law.

Media sold on spindles may be scratched and unusable.

---

## Repair Scratched CDs                           `123`

For the cost of one CD, you can repair many with a CD-repair kit—these work on audio CDs, CD-ROM discs and DVDs.

### ◉ Steps

1   Buy a fluid-based CD scratch-repair kit.

2   Get a soft, lint-free cloth, such as one made for cleaning eyeglasses, if your kit doesn't come with cloths or swabs.

3   Follow the manufacturer's instructions. Wipe across the CD, working from the inside out in straight lines. Never wipe in a circular pattern.

4   Repeat the process, if necessary.

### ✱ Tips

Use a cleaner rather than a repair kit if the scratches are minor but cause skipping or stopping.

Avoid using alcohol, abrasive cleaners, petroleum-based products, ammonia, commercial plastic cleaners or toothpaste, and avoid scrubbing, polishing or buffing.

---

## Troubleshoot a CD Player                       `124`

Although you will rarely be able to repair your own CD player, you may be able to diagnose problems. That can help you decide whether to have it repaired.

### ◉ Steps

1   Check all connections—player to amplifier or receiver, receiver to speaker, and so on. Check and clean contacts on RCA jacks and cables and try a different input on the amplifier or receiver.

2   Clean the lens. Use only a special CD lens cleaner and follow the instructions carefully.

3   Check the traverse assembly (the metal rod that the laser travels along and the gear that drives it) if CDs aren't recognized or won't play, frequent skipping occurs at random, CDs randomly get stuck in one spot, the player can't find tracks correctly, or cleaning the lens doesn't work. Dust and lint may be interrupting its function.

### ✱ Tips

Check the manufacturer's Web site for a troubleshooting page or a way to e-mail questions. Make note of your serial number first.

Indications that you have removed screws or handled any internal components will void a manufacturer's limited warranty.

### ⚠ Warnings

Do not try to diagnose a unit that appears to have no power.

4   Have the laser-head assembly checked by a repair person if the traverse assembly seems intact and free of debris.

5   Check for a stuck CD if the drawer won't open or close or will only partially open or close. If there isn't one, have gears and belts replaced.

6   Lubricate the gears if the CD player will only play certain tracks or up to a particular point on a disc.

7   Look for broken plastic parts, such as gears and clips.

8   Look for loose or broken internal connections.

9   Have the power supply replaced if your CD player overheats.

10  If your player won't recognize a disc, make sure the CD is properly loaded and not scratched, and that the lens is clean.

Attempts to adjust the laser can result in eye injury.

Once you open the chassis, you may cause additional damage that increases the cost of repairs.

Avoid CD-cleaning discs with brushes attached. Some can damage the lens-suspension system.

---

## 125  Buy a VCR

Today's VCRs offer a variety of features. Do your homework before buying so you avoid paying for options you aren't going to use.

### ⊙ Steps

1   Decide how you're going to use the machine. Will you use it just to run video rentals or do you intend to tape television shows? Will you be taping sports events so you can break down the action later?

2   Determine if you want automatic features such as auto start, which turns on the VCR whenever a tape is inserted; auto rewind, which automatically rewinds a tape once it gets to the end; auto shutoff, which shuts off the VCR automatically; or auto eject, which ejects the cassette when the VCR shuts off.

3   Decide if you want index search, which marks the tape each time you record so that you can return to the exact spot either by number or by scanning forward or backward. Another feature, jog shuttle, lets you scan at various speeds, from frame by frame to warp speed.

4   Think about different playback options, such as still picture/frame-by-frame playback, slow motion/reverse slow motion, and variable-speed search/reverse-motion playback.

5   See if you want VCR Plus, a way to automatically tape shows easily.

6   Figure out if you want special features such as digital effects, including picture in picture, which lets you see two programs simultaneously; or flying erase head, which is used to edit tapes. Other features include manual tracking, editing from a camcorder, editing to or from another VCR and audio dubbing.

### ✱ Tips

If you ever tape shows, think about index search or high-speed searching methods.

If you watch or tape sports events and like to deconstruct the action, consider advanced playback options.

If you tape shows regularly, consider VCR Plus.

## Program a VCR

Programming a VCR is a notoriously complicated task. Here are some general strategies to try when the manual is not enough.

### ⊙ Steps

1 Read the instructions thoroughly. If you have lost the manual, contact the VCR manufacturer to order a new one. You may be charged a small fee.

2 Make sure your TV and VCR are connected properly to each other and to your cable system or antenna.

3 Keep in mind that if you have a cable box, you may need to set the VCR to channel 3 and then select the desired channel on the cable box. If you don't have a cable box but instead hook up your cable directly to the VCR, you may need to set the TV to channel 3 and the VCR to the channel you want to record.

4 You'll need to provide antenna reception for the VCR if you don't have cable. Usually the VCR and TV can share an antenna, but you may need a separate antenna for the VCR.

5 Check that the date and time (including the AM/PM setting) are set correctly on the VCR before you program it.

6 Put a blank tape into the VCR. If you are reusing an old tape, wind it back to the beginning and check that the erasure-prevention tab is still present. If it's been broken off, you can't record.

7 Schedule recording to start and end a few minutes before and after the show, just in case your VCR's clock is a few minutes off. If it's a sports event that might run into overtime, program even more time at the end.

### ✳ Tips

Many VCRs require the use of a remote control for programming. If you've lost yours and a universal remote won't work with your VCR, contact the VCR manufacturer or search the Web for sites that specialize in replacing remote controls. Be ready to provide the VCR make and model number.

Breathe a sigh of relief if you have a newer VCR with VCR Plus. With this feature, you punch in a numeric code for the program you wish to record. The code, which is included in most TV listings in newspapers and magazines, allows the VCR to automatically record the desired program.

Keep abreast of evolving technology. There are personal television services that let you record programs directly from the TV without using a VCR at all.

## Buy a DVD Player for Video

A DVD, or digital versatile disc, is a compact disc that holds movies instead of music. Because the format is digital, the picture and sound quality can rival that of a movie theater.

### ⊙ Steps

1 Consider your budget. DVD players are generally much more expensive than VCRs, though prices are coming down.

2 Read audio-video magazines to investigate reviews and features.

3 Check your television to determine what kind of video and audio inputs it has so that you can choose a DVD player that is compatible.

4 Choose a player that has a minimal number of controls on its face. A few players have a lot of buttons, switches and dials, which can make things confusing. All you really need are the Open/Close button and the Play button. You can do the rest with the remote control.

5 Consider what features you want. Most players support these standard features: language choice for automatic selection of video scenes; audio tracks; subtitle tracks and menus (this feature must be supported with additional content on the disc); special-effects playback, including

### ✳ Tips

A movie can be stored on just one side of the disc, so there is no need to turn the disc over as with the earlier laser discs.

DVD offers scanning and scene selection, which VHS cannot.

A DVD can be loaded with a foreign-language track, subtitles and other material.

freeze, step, slow, fast and scan; parental lock for denying playback of discs or scenes with objectionable material (this feature must be supported with additional content on the disc); programmability; playback of selected sections in a desired sequence; random play and repeat play; digital audio output; compatibility with audio CDs.

6 Choose a DVD player that has an A/V receiver with a built-in Dolby digital decoder to take full advantage of the digital sound. It will also allow you to upgrade your sound system to surround sound later.

7 Select a DVD player that has good video outputs. (Make sure the outputs are compatible with your TV, though.) All DVDs have both composite and S-video output jacks, and many higher-end models have component video outputs.

8 Choose the best of a variety of audio outputs that are compatible with your TV. Most lower-end models support analog stereo surround sound or Dolby Pro Logic surround sound only. Higher-end players can be connected to a Dolby digital receiver to produce multichannel surround sound using five or more speakers.

## 128 Buy a Fax Machine

When looking for a fax machine, consider quality, price and special features. If you need to send faxes but not receive them, consider a fax modem as an alternative.

### ⊙ Steps

1 Determine the type of machine you want. Choose a film-cartridge fax machine to get mediocre print quality. Look for an ink-jet fax machine to get better print quality for a slightly higher price but the highest cost of use. Buy a laser fax machine for good print quality if you can afford to pay more. If you'll receive a lot of faxes, the higher purchase price will quickly be offset by the lower cost of use.

2 Look for machines with four choices for image quality.

3 Make sure the machine can print 64 shades of gray if you'll be receiving and copying both text and images. Color-capable machines are also available, but they're expensive.

4 Figure out how many speed-dial numbers you'll need, if any.

5 Decide whether you need an integrated digital answering machine.

6 Compare each model's capacity for feeding multiple pages, storing received faxes when the machine is out of paper and "broadcast" faxing to a group of recipients.

7 Evaluate how easy the machine is to use.

8 Look for advanced business features, if necessary, such as delayed transmission, the ability to "poll" other fax machines, copy reduction and enlargement, and "shrink to fit" 8½-by-11-inch pages.

9 Budget for everything you'll need, such as paper, extra cartridges, a surge suppressor and a service contract.

### ✱ Tips

You typically don't need to get a separate phone line (the fax or an attached answering machine may be able to tell incoming faxes from voice calls, or the sender can input a fax-activation code), but an extra line is convenient if you're doing a lot of faxing.

Be sure to budget for consumable items, such as paper and cartridges or ink.

A film cartridge typically produces 357 pages. Divide cartridge price by number of pages to figure out the cost per page.

Toner cartridges for laser fax machines can produce up to several thousand pages, depending on the brand and model.

10  Consider service contracts offered by the dealer if they include maintenance and loaner privileges and cover normal wear.

11  Base your final decision on functionality and initial and ongoing costs.

## Choose a Cellular Phone   `129`

Can't bear to be away from the receiver for a single second? Join the legions just like you and get a cell phone.

### ⊙ Steps

1  Estimate how many calls per week you'll make on your cell phone and how many minutes you'll spend talking.

2  Determine how much you're willing to pay for your cell phone and for the monthly service.

3  Decide which features are important to you: size and weight, color options, number storage, messaging, customized settings, fax, paging and Web capabilities, and caller line identification (CLI), which displays the phone number of an incoming call.

4  Take accessories into account: You'll probably need an AC adapter for charging the phone, and you might also want a car adapter, a carrying case or fun goodies such as removable colored faceplates.

5  Consult consumer reports in magazines, newspapers, the Web and other news media for opinions on different phones and providers.

6  Decide on a service provider in concert with your choice of phone (see the next eHow), since certain plans require the use of specific phones.

**✳ Tip**

Service providers sometimes offer deals including free phones or great discounts when you sign up for their plans. Look around for those.

**⚠ Warning**

Review the terms of the contract to see if there are early-cancellation fees.

## Choose a Cellular Phone Service Provider   `130`

Try to estimate your calling needs before you start investigating plans, and then find one that most closely matches how you think you'll use the phone.

### ⊙ Steps

1  Estimate how much you're willing to pay (in both up-front fees and monthly fees) for wireless phone service.

2  Decide how much geographic coverage you need. Will you mostly be using your phone locally or will you also use it a lot when you travel?

3  Choose between digital and analog service. Digital service has more features (such as text paging and eavesdropping protection) than analog service, but it also usually costs more up front. However, digital could save you money if you use your phone extensively.

4  Search the yellow pages and Web listings for wireless-service providers. Review various pricing plans, paying particular attention to charges for "roaming" (use outside the local area) and calling during peak hours.

5  Once you've found a plan that suits your price and needs, contact the company and follow its instructions about activating your service.

**✳ Tip**

It is often helpful to purchase a cell phone and choose a service provider simultaneously. Sometimes service providers offer free phones or great deals on phones when you sign up for a plan.

**⚠ Warning**

Review the terms of the contract to see if there are early-cancellation fees.

## 131 | Select a Pager Service

A wide assortment of pager services is available. Be careful not to pay for features you don't want.

### ⊙ Steps

1 Decide where and when you want your pager to work. Pager services now offer plans that can cover you nationwide or even worldwide, within a multistate region, in specific areas or on a temporary basis.

2 Determine whether you want the capability to send messages from your pager.

3 Decide if you want callers to be able to leave a voice message or just a phone number. Voice mail can prove convenient if you are out of range of the pager or you have turned the pager off when a call comes in.

4 Consider whether you want sports, news and financial information paged to you.

5 Contact the major pager service providers. Most of them, such as SkyTel and PageNet, have Web sites.

6 Find out if the pager service offers customer service 24 hours a day, seven days a week.

7 Investigate whether it offers 800-number access and a live operator who can take messages.

8 Determine if each plan the service offers is flexible. Make certain that there is a means for you to get undelivered or stored messages when your pager is within the service area.

9 Find out if the pager service offers hardware—that is, a pager unit—that enables you to access all of the features in your chosen plan.

### ✳ Tip

Yearly plans are usually less expensive than month-to-month plans.

## 132 | Synchronize Your Palm Device With Your Computer

One of the greatest strengths of the palm computing platform is the ability to add information on either a PC or palm-held device, then synchronize the information between the two. This eHow assumes that the Palm desktop has been installed successfully on your computer.

### ⊙ Steps

1 Be sure HotSync Manager is running.

2 On a Macintosh, launch HotSync Manager from the Instant Palm Desktop and make certain HotSync is enabled.

3 In Windows, check to see that the HotSync icon appears in the Windows task bar.

4 Place the palm device in the cradle. Then press the HotSync button on the cradle.

### ✳ Tips

If you're having trouble performing a HotSync operation, try lowering the connection speed.

If you want to use a HotSync cable instead of a cradle, you must initiate the HotSync from the Palm device.

You can synchronize multiple Palm devices with one PC. You'll be prompted to select a user the first time you perform a HotSync.

5   If nothing happens, tap the HotSync icon on the palm screen, then tap Local Sync.

6   Wait for the synchronization to be complete, then launch Palm Desktop. You'll notice that items added to the palm device now appear on the Palm Desktop, and items added to the Palm Desktop now appear on the palm device.

## "Beam" a File to Another Palm Device     `133`

One of the high cool factors in using a palm-held device is the capability to "beam" information wirelessly from one device to another. To beam and receive beams, you must be using at least a Palm III, or an earlier device upgraded to a Palm III.

### ⊙ Steps

### Beam an Application Entry (Data)

1   Place the two palm devices facing each other, no more than 3 feet apart.

2   Select the file you want to beam.

3   Tap the menu icon, and then display the Record drop-down menu.

4   Choose Beam Memo if you are using the Memo Pad.

5   Choose Beam Event if you are using the Date Book.

6   Choose Beam Address if you are using the Address List. You must have a specific address entry selected to beam an address.

7   Choose Beam Item if you are using the To Do List.

### Beam an Application Program

1   Place the two palm devices facing each other, no more than 3 feet apart.

2   Tap the Applications icon (Palm III) or the House icon (above Palm III) to display the Applications list.

3   Tap the Menu icon, then choose Beam from the App drop-down menu.

4   Select an application from the Beam box, and then tap Beam.

5   Applications with a padlock symbol next to the size of the application are locked and cannot be beamed.

6   Tap Done to close the Beam box.

### ✳ Tips

It can be incredibly useful to beam an application entry, such as directions to a restaurant, from one device to another. It can also be fun to beam shareware games to all your friends.

You can beam entire categories of information from the Address Book, To Do list and Memo Pad.

If you are having trouble beaming, try placing both palm devices on a flat surface.

## 134 | Get Rich

It's easy to get to Easy Street: Buy hot stocks, start your own Internet company, hit it big in the lottery. Right? Wrong. Getting rich in America takes a sensible and sane approach.

### ◎ Steps

1   Decide what "rich" means to you. Does it mean money for everything you need? Money for everything you want? Enough to retire where you live now? Enough to retire and live in Costa Rica?

2   Start saving. Most experts agree that investing 10 to 15 percent of your gross monthly income creates a very comfortable nest egg for later years.

3   Take advantage of compound interest—earning interest on your interest by letting investment returns accumulate and build on themselves.

4   Resist temptation, whether that means a brand-new car right out of college or weekly dinners at nice restaurants. Invest the money you save by buying a used car or going out only twice a month, and you will have thousands of dollars more at retirement.

5   Take care of yourself. This will reduce medical costs later on in life, as well as extend the years you can work—and save.

6   Go to college. By one study, college graduates earn roughly $20,000 more per year than people with just a high school diploma, and a post-graduate degree nets $20,000 more than a bachelor's.

7   Get married. Married people are generally healthier than singles. Plus, they can economize on expenses, and they have more to invest. And because married people live longer, they can work and save longer.

8   Enjoy the ride. Don't be so concerned with amassing a fortune later on that you neglect to enjoy life now. Strive for balance.

### ✳ Tips

Use a planning calculator (available in personal-finance software or on financial Web sites) to learn how much you need to save per year to achieve a specific goal.

Little expenses add up. Switch to regular coffee each morning, rather than a double-shot, half-caf foamy latte. Put the extra $1 or $1.50 you save in a mutual fund, and you could have $90,000 more at retirement.

Figure out how much you'll need to maintain your current lifestyle. Ask a financial adviser for help if you need it.

### ⚠ Warning

Don't waste the money you do have on "get-rich-quick" schemes, lotteries or gambling.

## 135 | Create an Investment Portfolio

A high-performing portfolio is every investor's goal. First, you'll need to develop your own objectives and strategies.

### ◎ Steps

1   Determine what items or events you're saving for. These can be retirement, a new home, your children's education or anything else you choose.

2   Determine when you want to retire, purchase a home or send your children to college, to help you decide what percentage return you need to earn on your initial investment.

3   Decide how much money to invest. Invest what you can comfortably afford now, keeping in mind that you can change that amount later.

4   Determine how much risk you are willing to take. Many investments generate high returns and are riskier than others.

### ✳ Tips

With less than $25,000 to invest, consider mutual funds rather than individual stocks to diversify and balance risk.

Invest as much as you can afford in your company's 401(k) plan. Your contribution is invested before your salary is taxed.

Tax-free bond funds usually generate lower returns, but they also pose less of a risk.

5 Once you decide the amount you are willing to invest, the returns you want to achieve, when you need the money and how much risk you are willing to accept, put together your investment portfolio.

6 An investment counselor or stockbroker is a good source of advice. Tell these advisers your objectives and ask them to suggest how to allocate your money.

7 Reevaluate your portfolio at least annually. Analyze each investment.

## ⚠ Warning

Allocate only a portion of your savings to stocks, depending on your age and tolerance for risk. Invest the balance in other instruments—CDs, bonds, money market accounts.

## Make Good Investments                                    136

Whether you are a first-time investor or an investment guru, mistakes happen. The key to avoiding mishaps is to keep on top of investment rules, tax codes and annual reports.

### ◉ Steps

1 Study. Read financial news, personal-finance magazines, corporate annual and quarterly reports, proxy statements, registration statements and prospectuses for the financial products you're considering.

2 Develop goals and strategies to meet your goals. Use these to choose stocks and other investments. Ask for professional advice if you are uncomfortable investing on your own.

3 Diversify. Avoid putting large portions of your portfolio in a single stock or industry so that you're not so affected by its ups and downs.

4 Take advantage of tax breaks. Participate in the 401(k) plan at work. Set up an Individual Retirement Account if you qualify, or a SEP-IRA or Keogh plan if self-employed.

5 Buy stocks that you plan to keep for three to five years. Remember that "good" stocks at unrealistically high prices are a bad buy. Aim to buy at a low price, sell at a high price. See 138 "Research Stocks to Buy."

6 Invest in what you know, and avoid buying stocks in unfamiliar industries and companies.

7 Shop for total value. That means learning to calculate key financial figures, such as price-earnings ratios, so you can compare stocks.

8 Resist fads. If everyone is buying gold, variable annuities or some other investment, watch out. The herd soon will change direction.

9 Know when to fold. Your objective may be to hold a particular stock or mutual fund for three to five years, but if its track record looks like terminal descent, bail out.

### Things You'll Need

☐ financial newspapers and magazines

☐ corporate reports

☐ proxy and registration statements

☐ relevant prospectuses

## 137 Understand the Stock Market

Before you join the fray, here are some key steps to take toward building an understanding of the stock market.

### ⊙ Steps

1 Understand "equity securities." As an equity investor, when you buy stock you take an ownership stake in a company and assume a corresponding degree of risk.

2 Learn the language of the market, familiarizing yourself with such financial terms as "price-earnings [PE] ratio," "margin," "option," "earnings per share" and "leverage."

3 Analyze the holdings of several successful mutual-fund companies, noting which stocks they have held—and dumped—over the past three or four years.

4 Read the quarterly and annual reports that several large corporations have filed with the Securities and Exchange Commission (SEC).

5 Research companies that you have personal knowledge of and a high degree of confidence in. Evaluate their SEC filings, looking for trends that indicate growth and continuing profitability.

6 Get online. Dozens of companies offer financial news, advice and analysis online (see 138 "Research Stocks to Buy").

7 Take advantage of all the information your brokerage has to offer regarding individual stocks. Know what you are buying—and why—before you invest.

8 Invest on paper for a few weeks and carefully monitor the performance of your would-be portfolio before you actually start plunking down your money.

### ✱ Tips

Invest in reputable companies and stick with them for the long haul.

Some full-service brokerages charge as much as $150 per stock trade, while some discount brokerages charge as little as $8 per trade.

Set up an electronic portfolio of your stocks through an online service such as Yahoo Finance. This will allow you to monitor your stocks' performance throughout the day and to get the latest news about the companies you've invested in (see 140 "Monitor Stocks").

If you don't have the time to do your own research, invest in a no-load mutual fund that has had good returns for at least the past three years.

### ⚠ Warning

Be prepared for a roller-coaster ride. The market can be volatile.

## 138 Research Stocks to Buy

One of the most important parts of "playing the market" is researching companies.

### ⊙ Steps

1 Obtain corporate financial statements filed with the Securities and Exchange Commission. You can get such documents without charge via www.freeedgar.com.

2 Analyze quarterly statements covering two or three years, noting trends in earnings per share and revenue.

3 Look for a trend of consistent growth in earnings per share.

4 Calculate the company's price-earnings (PE) ratio, a measure of a stock's value. (Divide the stock price by annual earnings per share.)

5 Compare the PE ratio with industry norms and with the S&P 500's ratio. The lower the ratio, the less expensive the stock is relative to earnings.

### ✱ Tips

Make sure the company isn't giving short shrift to its research and development budget.

Calculate a sales-per-employee figure and compare the company with its competitors.

Assess management. Find out where managers worked before they joined the company by reading proxy statements, registration statements and annual reports.

6   Beware of debt. Check out the company's balance sheet, looking for the extent of its long-term debt.

7   Check cash flow—the movement of cash through the company. You'll want the company to have positive cash flow.

## Buy Stocks                                                    139

Buying stock in a company is relatively easy once you've researched the stocks you're interested in and have a broker or brokerage account to handle your purchase.

### ⊙ Steps

1   Educate yourself fully about stocks before purchasing them. You can find information about stocks and brokers on the Internet.

2   Determine what you want in a broker or brokerage account. Do you want to meet with someone face-to-face? Will you want to be able to reach someone by phone? Do you require Internet access? Is price your only consideration? Do you want to buy and sell only stocks, or would you also like to buy and sell mutual funds, bonds or foreign stocks?

3   Choose a broker or brokerage firm to purchase the stocks on your behalf based on your needs. Need a lot of advice? Start with a full-service brokerage. The least expensive brokers may not offer advice. Fairly confident and want low prices? Try an online brokerage.

4   Contact a broker or firm and request an application. Many firms offer online applications, although most require that you send a check or wire money to actually open the account.

5   Deliver a check in person if possible to speed up the process.

6   Begin buying and selling stocks once your account is open.

7   Review statements you receive and reevaluate your portfolio's performance. Are you moving toward your investment goals?

### ✳ Tips

Ask friends or colleagues for broker or brokerage-firm recommendations. If you don't have a personal recommendation, read ads in financial publications such as *The Wall Street Journal.*

An online brokerage account is convenient and fast but can be susceptible to computer glitches. Ask if you will be able to make trades by telephone if need be.

### ⚠ Warnings

Ask brokerage firms to list all fees. Watch out for hidden costs (account transfer, electronic transfer or handling fees).

It can take a few days to open a brokerage account, so don't expect to be able to trade on the same day you decide to open an account.

## Monitor Stocks                                                140

Monitoring the rising and falling prices of stocks is an essential part of being a successful investor or stock trader.

### ⊙ Steps

1   Monitor your stocks' prices on a daily basis, noting whether prices are heading up, down or fluctuating. Find your stocks in the newspaper or on the Internet.

2   Track performance by reading monthly statements from your broker. Use the Internet for up-to-the-minute tracking when needed. (You can create a portfolio of stocks on your personalized home page.)

### ✳ Tips

The stock market can be extremely volatile. It is advisable to keep a three-year horizon in mind. Day trading can be profitable, but requires sophistication and constant attention.

3  Closely monitor each stock you are interested in (not just those you own, but those you might buy). Monitoring can help you make an immediate decision on whether to buy, sell or hold.

4  Add to stocks you like or those that are growing nicely when you have additional income to invest. Remember to diversify your investments.

5  Contact your broker by phone or the Internet to buy or sell a stock.

6  Specify the action you want to take and at what price you want to take it. Your broker will do the rest and provide you with a confirmation of your transaction when your order is executed.

Read *The Wall Street Journal* or *Barron's*, and read or watch any daily news that informs you about your stocks and events that affect the stock market.

A stock's performance should be compared with others' in its group and evaluated over time— don't automatically sell your stock if you notice that it is declining in price.

---

## 141 | Trade Securities Online

**Online trading depends on the same principles and skills as off-line trading, so use them to guide your thinking and actions.**

### ⊙ Steps

1  Have a long, serious and brutally honest talk with yourself (and perhaps a trusted friend) about the kind of personality you have, making sure that you are disciplined and goal-oriented.

2  Be sure you have at least $5,000 in easily available funds.

3  Set limits to your trading activity, such as number of trades and/or dollar amount of commission, for an initial three-month period.

4  Research at least three online brokerage services and read all of the "terms and conditions" statements concerning trading accounts.

5  Open an account with the brokerage service you choose for the minimum amount necessary to trade.

6  Write down all of your trading (buys and sells) immediately after execution: date, time and price per share of the actual purchase; quantity; all security or position identification (symbol, CUSIP number). Use these records for tax preparation and save them in case you are audited.

7  Evaluate your performance at the end of the three months. What were your gains and losses? Emotional reaction to the process? Did you stick to your goals?

### ✱ Tip

Free research online is available from many of the big investment firms. Avoid fee-for-service features of your account unless they will directly improve your ability to trade intelligently.

### ⚠ Warnings

All laws regarding securities trading apply to trading online.

Technical service calls and broker advice over the phone are probably not free—check first.

Never trade on advice from chat rooms, message boards or any other questionable sources.

Trade only with your savings until you are experienced. Only then consider borrowing on margin.

---

## 142 | Invest for Your Child's College Education

**Using money you can put aside and your child's own contributions from allowance and birthday funds, you can create a tidy nest egg for your child's education.**

### ⊙ Steps

1  Start early and let compounding work for you—that is, earning interest on interest. The more you can save now, the less you will have to set aside later.

### ✱ Tips

In addition to using an education IRA, you may be able to take early withdrawals without penalty from your other IRAs to pay for college costs.

2   Buy a mix of investments such as mutual funds, savings bonds, individual stocks and corporate bonds.

3   Look into setting up an education IRA (Individual Retirement Account). Contributions are not tax-deductible, but your investments grow tax-free until you withdraw them.

4   Find out whether the state in which your child will likely attend college offers a state-backed tuition-savings plan.

5   Check out mutual funds that specialize in college-tuition savings. They won't ask for big monthly investments.

6   Ask relatives who regularly send birthday, Christmas or Hanukkah gifts to consider putting a part of the money into savings bonds or other investments for your child.

7   Encourage your child to contribute 10 percent of a weekly allowance or income from part-time work to the investment pool.

8   Give your child a role in making decisions about the investments to learn about and appreciate sound personal-finance habits.

9   Start searching for college grants, scholarships and work-study deals before your child completes his or her junior year of high school.

Your child should avoid taking out student loans unless there is no other way. It's a burden to begin paying back debt soon after graduation.

If it isn't out of the question, ask your child to look into the active-duty military or the guard or reserve component of the armed services. Enlistees receive the promise of a large college tuition subsidy.

## Determine the Type of Life Insurance You Need          143

The best life insurance to have is the kind that is in force when you die. But since most of us live a long time, some thought should go into the type of contract we choose.

### ⊙ Steps

1   Determine how long you want your life insurance coverage to be in effect—for example, from now until your children finish college, or throughout your life.

2   Buy a term (fixed-length) contract with an increasing premium (annually renewable term, or ART) if that length of time is less than four years.

3   Buy a term contract with a level premium if you need coverage for a longer time (5, 10, 15 or 20 years).

4   Buy a permanent (lifelong) contract if you wish to provide a death benefit for your beneficiary no matter how long you live.

### ✳ Tips

Most types of permanent insurance (often called whole-life) have a cash value. You may borrow against it at a low interest rate while keeping most of the death benefit in force.

If your employer offers term life insurance and that's what you need, buy all you can because group life is the least expensive term insurance available.

## Plan for Retirement          144

It may seem as if retirement is in the distant future, but it's never too early to start planning to enjoy it—and finance it.

### ⊙ Steps

1   Start planning for retirement early. Think about how you want to live— and where. Calculate how much money you think you will need.

### ✳ Tips

Allocate retirement investment money to a mixture of stocks,

2   Plan for the possibility of living longer than you now expect. Include the possibility of being on a fixed income for as long as 20 or 30 years.

3   Create a financial plan either with a certified financial planner or by using computer software like Intuit's Quicken. (Remember to include your Social Security benefits.) This will help you figure out how much money you should invest for retirement on a regular basis.

4   Contribute funds weekly, monthly or annually to your employer's 401(k) plan or your SEP-IRA. Be sure to consider a Roth IRA or a traditional IRA if you qualify. See 146 "Select a Retirement Account."

5   Pay off major debts, such as home mortgages, college loans and other significant cash-flow drains, as quickly as you can.

6   As you approach retirement, you may want to reduce your discretionary expenses and attempt to live on a fixed income. Adjust your asset allocation based on your spending patterns. If you are spending more than your assets are earning, you may have to lower spending and take more risks in the hope of increasing your returns. Ask for advice.

bonds and cash according to your research and the advice of investment counselors. Know your tolerance for risk taking and plan accordingly.

If you can't pay off your debt, try to put some toward the debt and some toward a savings plan. You may want to try reducing credit card and high-interest debt by taking out a low-interest loan or low-interest line of credit.

### ⚠ Warning

Consider purchasing long-term care insurance if you are concerned about losing your assets if you need nursing-home care.

## 145  Save and Invest in a 401(k) or 403(b)

Many companies offer 401(k) plans that let you increase your savings for retirement through payroll deduction (nonprofits offer a 403[b] plan). Your contributions can reduce your taxes now and grow tax-free until you retire.

### ⊙ Steps

1   Ask your employee benefits office to provide you with information on pension and retirement plans, or make an appointment to speak with a benefits representative. Many firms provide a 401(k) plan, but your employer may offer other arrangements.

2   Carefully read all the information, especially the terms and conditions of any agreement forms, disclosure statements or limited-liability contracts you must sign to participate.

3   Determine what percentage of your gross income you can afford to divert from your paycheck to the plan. Find out if your plan allows borrowing or penalty-free withdrawals in case of hardship.

4   Rank the savings and investment choices available to you from "least risky" to "most risky" and decide the level of risk you want to take.

5   Allocate your investment among savings and investment choices in the plan as a percentage (e.g., 50 percent money market, 30 percent mutual fund, 20 percent bond fund) according to your tolerance for risk and your investment goals.

6   Complete and sign all of the necessary paperwork authorizing the payroll department to redirect your chosen amount of gross salary to your retirement savings plan.

7   Review your investment plan and allocations quarterly, and know when you can make changes.

### ✱ Tips

Some employers match a percentage of your contribution.

Consider riskier investment choices with higher gains potential if you anticipate other sources of retirement income, including Social Security, company or military pension plans, or a family inheritance.

### ⚠ Warnings

If the plan requires you to invest a portion of your contribution in company stock, that portion of your account could be worthless if the company goes broke.

If you are not fully vested in the plan, you may not be able to transfer all of the funds in your account to a new employer.

# ✓ 146 Select a Retirement Account

The IRS recognizes six tax-sheltered retirement savings plans. Some are for individuals, others are for employees or the self-employed. Depending on your situation, you may be able to invest in more than one plan. Check with your financial adviser about the best plan(s) for you, and note that the regulations listed here may change.

| | IRA | ROTH IRA | 401(k) | 403(b) | SEP-IRA | KEOGH |
|---|---|---|---|---|---|---|
| Who can contribute | Anyone under 70$\frac{1}{2}$ | Anyone of any age who does not exceed income limits | Almost anyone under 70$\frac{1}{2}$ who works for a company with a 401(k) plan | Almost anyone under 70$\frac{1}{2}$ who works for a company that has a 403(b) plan (generally nonprofit organizations) | Almost anyone under 70$\frac{1}{2}$ who is self-employed; also employees of small companies that offer SEP-IRAs | Anyone under 70$\frac{1}{2}$ who is self-employed |
| Pretax or post-tax contributions | Pretax | Posttax | Pretax | Pretax | Pretax | Pretax |
| Income limits | None | $110,000 (single); $160,000 (couple). | None | None | None | None |
| Employer contribution | None | None | Possible—depends on employer policy | Possible—depends on employer policy | Possible—depends on employer policy | None |
| Annual contribution limit | $2,000 | $2,000 | Up to 15% of gross salary or $10,500, whichever is less* | Up to 15% of gross salary or $10,500, whichever is less* | Up to 15% of gross salary or $25,500, whichever is less* | Generally $30,000 or 25% of gross income, whichever is less |
| Borrowing allowed? | No | No | Yes; pay back through paycheck deductions | Yes; pay back through paycheck deductions | No | No |
| Penalty on withdrawal** | 10% penalty before age 59$\frac{1}{2}$ | 10% penalty before age 59$\frac{1}{2}$ | 10% penalty before age 59$\frac{1}{2}$, unless you are retired—in which case you may withdraw at 55 without penalty | 10% penalty before age 59$\frac{1}{2}$, unless you are retired—in which case you may withdraw at 55 without penalty | 10% penalty before age 59$\frac{1}{2}$ | 10% penalty before age 59$\frac{1}{2}$ |
| Taxes on withdrawal? | Yes | No if account has been open at least five years and one of the following applies: You are at least 59$\frac{1}{2}$, you are buying a first home, you are disabled or deceased | Yes | Yes | Yes | Yes |
| Mandatory distribution | Yes, at 70$\frac{1}{2}$ | No | Yes, at 70$\frac{1}{2}$ | Yes, at 70$\frac{1}{2}$ | Yes, at 70$\frac{1}{2}$ | Yes, at 70$\frac{1}{2}$ or upon full retirement from the business |

\* According to year 2000 IRS guidelines.
\*\* There are exceptions—for example, the purchase of your first home.

chart

---

## 147 | Save and Invest in an Individual Retirement Account

New tax laws have enhanced your ability to create a financially comfortable retirement through tax-deferred saving and investing. Make your IRA part of a comprehensive financial plan.

### ◎ Steps

1   Check IRS rules to make sure your salary qualifies you to open an Individual Retirement Account (IRA).

2   Research the different IRA types (such as traditional and Roth) thoroughly, making sure you understand their unique tax-favored features and how many of them apply to you.

3   Review your W-4 or other appropriate Internal Revenue Service tax-payment schedules and make adjustments if they are not current.

4   Calculate the maximum contribution you can make to an IRA.

5   Determine how much money you can afford to deposit annually in the IRA up to your limit.

6   Choose a reputable financial institution that provides the services and options you need at reasonable cost. You can hold stocks, bonds and mutual funds in your IRA, and it can be administered by a bank, mutual fund or brokerage firm.

7   Fund the IRA. You have until April 15, unless you file a tax return extension, to make IRA contributions for the previous tax year.

8   Allocate the money in your IRA into investment choices that accommodate your retirement goals and risk tolerance.

9   Consider purchasing a variable annuity within your IRA from a highly rated insurance company to protect the value of your account. Your investments may have a lower market value at the time of your death.

10  Consider having your employer make automatic electronic transfers to your IRA to keep you on target.

11  Review your financial situation at least annually to determine if you can contribute more or if your qualifications for contributing have changed.

12  Consider reallocating your IRA money to lower-risk investments as you get closer to retirement.

### ✳ Tips

Consult a qualified tax accountant or financial planner prior to opening your IRA if you don't have a financial plan or if you are not well informed of newer tax laws for IRAs.

Only deposit money that you know you won't need soon, because penalties may apply to withdrawal prior to age 59½. If certain types of emergencies arise, the IRS does permit access to IRA monies without penalty.

### ⚠ Warnings

If you're currently enrolled in an employer-sponsored retirement, pension or deferred-compensation plan, you may not be able to deduct your IRA contributions on your income tax return.

Avoid accounts with high account-transfer or closing fees, as you may want to move your IRA later.

Leaving all of your IRA in low-interest savings accounts, while safe, may cause you to miss out on significant market growth, which can exceed 10 percent.

Large allocations in high-risk investments could result in your retirement account's being greatly diminished or wiped out.

---

## 148 | Choose a Bank

There are more banking options than ever these days. With a little research and legwork, you can find the banking relationship that fits you and your finances.

### ◎ Steps

1   Consider a bank that is convenient to your everyday activities. Look for banks that are easily accessible as you drive to and from work or while you run your usual errands.

### ✳ Tips

Ask friends and family to recommend a bank.

2   Check out different banks' Web sites. There you can get a good idea of the types of accounts, available services and rates offered before you set foot inside a branch office.

3   Think about what is most important to you in a banking relationship. If you want to be able to develop a personal, long-term relationship with a bank, a smaller, local bank might best suit your needs. If you travel frequently and need access to branch offices while you are out of town, consider a regional or national bank.

4   Consider how you will be banking. If online banking and ATM banking interest you, select a bank that offers those services.

5   Visit the branch office where you would be conducting most of your banking business. Are the tellers professional and friendly? Are the account officers and/or managers accessible? Are the hours of operation compatible with the hours when you will do your banking?

6   Compare interest rates and service charges among banks to make sure you're getting the best deal.

Many banks will use the combined balance of all your accounts (checking, saving, money market, etc.) in calculating monthly account service charges, so consider moving all of your accounts to one bank.

Consider a "virtual bank." All banking is done online or by mail, and service charges, if any, are minimal. Some virtual banks will even reimburse you for fees you incur using their cards at another bank's ATM.

## Pay Monthly Bills on Time 149

**Paying your bills promptly will help you avoid late fees and interest charges. Follow these steps to ward off procrastination and keep your finances in good order.**

### ◎ Steps

1   Set aside a special place to put your bills when they arrive, such as a desk cubbyhole, a special section in a drawer or a bill inbox. As soon as you receive them, open your bills, then put them in this special place.

2   Set aside two times a month, two weeks apart, to pay bills. The middle and end of the month are good times.

3   Call the companies that send you bills and have them revise your payment due dates to correspond with one of the two times you plan to pay your bills each month.

4   Mark your calendar to remind you of bill-paying dates and to help you keep to your schedule.

5   Pay your bills with checks or money orders, then note the check number, the date and the amount paid on the receipt portion of each bill.

6   File these receipts away and keep them for seven years.

7   Place the envelopes containing your payments next to your keys so that you will remember to take them with you and mail them immediately.

### ✳ Tips

Some credit card companies, mortgage lenders and automobile financing companies change due dates. Check the due dates for such bills when they arrive.

Utility and phone companies are usually a little more flexible and will wait for a few days before they send you a reminder notice or charge you a late fee. Credit card companies, mortgage and automobile lenders, oil companies and landlords are stricter.

Many banks allow you to arrange for automatic bill payment from your checking account.

## 150 Live Within Your Budget

Living within your budget can be challenging. A few simple practices can help ensure that you are successful.

### Steps

1   List all of your expenses, savings and income from the past year. Use your checkbook register, credit card receipts and bills to do this. A computer-based financial program such as Intuit's Quicken may help.

2   Determine, as accurately as possible, what expenses you expect to have for the next year. You can project expenses for a shorter period, such as the next three months, then multiply by four for yearly expenses.

3   Enter this information into a ledger or computer-based financial program to accurately track your income and expenses.

4   Determine what you can reasonably afford to spend each month and then track how well you are doing by entering actual expenses into the ledger or computer program.

5   If you find that you are spending less than you had anticipated, you may want to put more money in your savings account to help out with unexpected expenses.

6   If you find that you are spending more than anticipated, try identifying the items you really don't need (new clothes, CDs, expensive dinners) and avoid purchasing them until you are back within your budget.

### ✱ Tips

Allocate a portion of your income for savings and retirement. Retirement funds are best placed in your company's 401(k), if it has one, so that you are not tempted to tap into the money.

You may want to set aside 10 to 20 percent of your take-home income for savings.

### ⚠ Warning

Avoid trying to forecast your expenses too far into the future. Doing so can result in inaccurate budgets and overspending.

## 151 Calculate Your Net Worth

Calculating your net worth can be very easy, provided all of the necessary information is readily available. Doing this will help you when deciding whether to make major purchases.

### Steps

1   List all of your fixed assets, such as real estate and cars, at their current value.

2   List all of your liquid assets: cash, certificates of deposit, stocks, bonds and bank accounts.

3   List all jewelry, furniture and household items at their current value.

4   Add together all of the above. These are your total assets.

5   Subtract all of your debts, such as your mortgage, car loan and credit card balances, from your total assets. The result is your net worth.

6   Reevaluate and update your net worth calculations on an annual basis.

### ✱ Tips

Be realistic when evaluating the current value of your assets. Such information can be useful in determining whether you are adequately insured. Share the information with your insurance company to help you decide.

It is advisable to use the after-tax value of your marketable securities (stocks and bonds) when calculating their value.

## Calculate Your Debt-to-Income Ratio 152

Lenders use your debt-to-income ratio (how much you owe on credit cards and loans compared with how much you earn) to help evaluate your creditworthiness.

### ⊙ Steps

1 Add up your total net monthly income. This includes your monthly wages and any overtime, commissions or bonuses that are guaranteed; plus alimony payment received, if applicable. If your income varies, figure the monthly average for the past two years. Include any monies earned from rentals or any other additional income.

2 Add up your monthly debt obligations. This includes all of your credit card bills, loan and mortgage payments. Make sure to include your monthly rent payments if you rent.

3 Divide your total monthly debt obligations by your total monthly income. This is your total debt-to-income ratio.

4 Take action if your ratio is higher than 0.36, which industry professionals would call a score of 36. The lower the better. Any score higher than 36 may cause an increase in the interest rate or the down payment on a loan you apply for.

**✱ Tip**

When you tally your total monthly debts, use the minimum payment on your statements.

**⚠ Warnings**

When calculating your income, a lender will only consider money from a job that you've been at for at least two years.

Unreported earned income cannot be used in the calculation.

## Establish Credit 153

Credit isn't established overnight. Prepare now for financial emergencies by securing a good credit rating.

### ⊙ Steps

1 Get checking and savings accounts in your own name.

2 Apply for a charge card in your own name from a retail store or financial institution. Make at least a minimum payment monthly to establish a record of managing debt.

3 Apply for a loan in your name to buy jewelry, furniture or another item that will be paid off in installments for at least a year. Make all payments on time.

4 Secure a small loan from a credit union or bank (an auto loan, for instance), and pay installments on time.

5 Check your credit rating by calling your creditors or ordering a copy of your credit report.

6 If you experience trouble getting a loan, ask a friend or family member to co-sign it.

**✱ Tips**

Although not a credit indicator, a checking or savings account shows how you manage money. Avoid bouncing checks and add to your savings monthly.

A spouse's death or a divorce could leave you without credit. Establish credit in your own name.

Secure a job for several months before applying for credit.

## 154 Obtain a Car Loan

Borrowing money to buy a car isn't hard if you have two things: sufficient income and a good credit rating.

### ⊙ Steps

1 Choose your new set of wheels and negotiate a price with the seller (see 923 "Buy a New Car").

2 Research interest rates. Several Web sites, such as Bankrate.com, publish surveys of loan rates across the United States. Compare the rates with those offered by your local bank, credit union or car dealer.

3 Find out what your current car is worth as a trade-in. Research values in the *Kelley Blue Book Used Car Guide,* available at the library, your bank or on the Internet.

4 Determine how much of a down payment you can make. Use your trade-in value and cash—or just cash—to come up with the standard 20 percent usually required. Talk with the car dealer that has the new car you want.

5 Apply where you find the best rates, and the length of the loan and monthly payment fit your budget.

6 Consider saving more for a down payment or choosing a less expensive car if you don't qualify.

7 Build a better credit rating if that's what causes you to be turned down. Try again after six months of paying your bills on time.

### ✳ Tips

If you lack adequate income or a good credit history, lenders won't approve your loan until you prove you can repay it while meeting your other obligations.

If a bad credit history prevents you from getting a loan, contact Consumer Credit Counseling Service or a similar group.

### ⚠ Warning

Beware of for-profit imitators that promise to cleanse your credit history for a fee.

## 155 Obtain a Copy of Your Credit Report

Getting a copy of your credit report is fairly simple and allows you to keep track of your credit history and check for errors.

### ⊙ Steps

1 Visit the Web site for one of these credit reporting agencies: Equifax (www.equifax.com), TransUnion (www.transunion.com) or Experian (www.experian.com).

2 Decide whether you want to order a report online, by phone or by mail.

3 Have a credit or debit card handy if ordering online or by phone.

4 Include your full name, current address and any other addresses you have had in the last two years, Social Security number, date of birth, current employer and phone number if ordering by mail. Sign your request and include a check for the applicable amount. You can expect to receive a paper copy of your credit report within 15 business days.

5 Review the report closely for errors. If you do find errors, inform the bureau in writing that you believe the information is in error. Include copies of any documentation to support your position.

6 Consider using one of the services that reports information from all of the major agencies—they can sometimes report information differently.

### ✳ Tip

You may qualify for a free copy of your credit report if you can verify one of the following: You are unemployed, on welfare or plan to seek employment within 60 days; you have recently been refused credit due to something in your credit report; you believe you are a victim of fraud; you live in Colorado, Georgia, Maryland, Vermont, Massachusetts or New Jersey.

## Repair a Bad Credit History

No matter how bad your credit is, you can take steps that will make it better.

### ⊙ Steps

1 Pay all of your bills on time. Late payments (payments that are 30 days late or more) have a negative effect on your credit rating.

2 Reduce the number of credit cards you carry. Write to your creditors to request that they close your accounts and report this status change to all three credit-reporting agencies.

3 Avoid bankruptcies, tax liens (a lien for not paying state or federal income taxes or property taxes) and collections. A bankruptcy stays on your credit report for up to 10 years. Collection accounts and paid tax liens stay on for seven years, and unpaid tax liens will haunt you forever.

4 Request in writing that your creditors reduce the credit limits on your accounts to lower your amount of available credit. The total amount of available credit is considered by lenders even if you owe nothing.

5 Ask a family member or friend to co-sign on a small loan or credit card to help you re-establish credit. Make your payments on time.

6 Get a secured credit card to help reestablish your credit. You will have to keep a designated amount of money in an account that will be sufficient to cover your charges. Make payments on time.

7 Get a yearly copy of your credit report to catch any errors (see 155 "Obtain a Copy of Your Credit Report").

### ✱ Tips

When you have a friend or relative co-sign on a loan or credit card, remember that that person's credit will be affected by the payment history as well.

Credit-repair clinics and consumer credit agencies arrange repayment plans and restructure payments to fit your budget. But even if the creditor agrees to the plan, smaller payments and skipped payments can still be reported against you. Some credit-repair clinics charge up to $2,000 up front to get the paperwork started and cover administrative fees. Some CCAs are free. You can call the creditors yourself and make these same arrangements for free.

## Prevent Identity Theft

Some simple precautions, as well as the ability to spot trouble when it starts, may help you keep someone else from cashing in on your identity.

### ⊙ Steps

1 Be extremely protective of your PIN numbers, especially at ATMs. Try to memorize your PIN number, but if you have to write it down, don't write it on your ATM card or leave it in your wallet or purse.

2 Change passwords often.

3 Remove mail from your mailbox promptly. If you suddenly stop receiving mail, call the post office immediately. Crooks can forge your signature to have your mail forwarded elsewhere, then obtain information that will allow them to apply for credit in your name.

4 Refuse to give your credit card number or other personal information to an unsolicited caller.

5 Tear up or shred credit card receipts, unused loan applications and any other items with personal information before throwing them into the trash. Thieves often go through garbage.

### ✱ Tips

If you find out that a forwarding order has been placed on your mail without your knowledge, go to the post office to check the signature and cancel the order. Ask the post office to track down the mail—it can remain in the postal system for up to 14 days.

Call the U.S. Postal Service Crime Hot Line (800/654-8896) if you are victimized by mail fraud.

To put a fraud alert on your credit file, contact the credit bureaus—Equifax, Experian and TransUnion. Any future credit applications will have to be confirmed with you over the phone.

6   Obtain a copy of your credit report regularly to check for fraudulent accounts and other information. Report all errors to the credit bureau.

7   Report stolen credit cards immediately.

8   Take the time to carefully review all of your bank and credit card statements and other bills. Report any inconsistencies at once.

### ⚠ Warning

If Grandma dies, do not toss out her unused checks or other personal documents. Thieves even steal the identities of dead people and wipe out accounts.

---

## 158  Get Out of Debt

**Getting out of debt is challenging, but it can be accomplished with dedication and perseverance.**

### ◎ Steps

1   Cut up your credit cards except for one or two to use for emergencies. Throw away the pieces.

2   Cancel all of your credit lines and request a lower interest rate on the debt you have left.

3   Transfer as much debt as possible to the credit card that has the lowest interest rate, or get a debt-consolidation loan from a bank at a lower rate.

4   Use cash for all your purchases, and only buy what you can afford.

5   Commit to start paying off your debts one at a time and do it. Pay off the credit card and loans with the highest interest rate first.

6   Double your payments on the next debt by taking the payment you made on the first debt and adding it to the current debt.

7   Triple your payments on the next debt by combining payment amounts. Continue until all your credit cards and other debts are paid off.

### ✳ Tips

If you have investments that are paying 6 to 10 percent but a credit card debt with an interest rate of 17 to 21 percent, cash out your investments and pay off your debt.

Ask your creditors how much repayment is needed before they are able to send a favorable report to credit agencies. Sometimes they will accept less than your total debt.

Use consumer credit agencies to arrange repayment of debt. Many are free.

---

## 159  Get Telemarketers to Stop Calling You

**You can curtail or eliminate annoying calls from telemarketers. All it takes is a little effort and the following information.**

### ◎ Steps

1   Contact your phone company about caller ID services. With caller ID, you'll be able to see who is calling before you answer, then block your number from callers who won't allow you to identify them.

2   Resist trying to reason with a telemarketer. Telemarketing companies have scripted responses for almost anything you say.

3   Prepare for those unwanted calls before they happen. Write the phrase, "Put my number on your don't-call list" on a memo by your phone.

4   Stay on the line when a telemarketer calls. You actually have to speak to telemarketers in order to get them to stop calling you.

5   Announce your prepared phrase, "Put my number on your don't-call list," to the telemarketer. Per FCC requirements, once you've said this sentence, the telemarketer is prohibited from calling you again for 10

### ✳ Tips

Get the name of the caller and the company's name and address, and ask the caller for a copy of the company's don't-call list. If the telemarketer doesn't know what that is or cannot supply you with one, take action by filing a formal complaint with the government agency. Contact Know Fraud at (877) 987-3728; www.consumer.gov/knowfraud.

Realize that making these annoying calls is the telemarketers' job. They are not trying to personally assault you over the phone.

years. (Make sure you say that exact sentence. Just saying "Take me off your list" or "Stop calling me" does not legally force the telemarketer to stop calling you.)

6   Write a letter to Telephone Preference Service, Direct Marketing Association at P.O. Box 9014, Farmingdale, NY 11735-9014. Provide your name, address and home telephone number and say that you do not want calls from any telemarketers. Be sure to sign the letter and keep a copy.

## Get Your Name Off Mailing Lists      **160**

**With some concentrated effort, you can eliminate or drastically cut down on the amount of unsolicited useless information that shows up in your mailbox.**

### ◉ Steps

1   Write a letter to the Direct Marketing Association at P.O. Box 9014, Farmingdale, NY 11735-9014, and register for the Mail Preference Service. Your name will be placed in a delete file, and you should notice a decrease in junk mail about three months after you register.

2   Call the customer service department of individual companies that send you junk mail. Ask to be removed from the company's mailing list. Have the mailing label with you when you call so you can relay exact names and codes from the label.

3   Tell mail-order companies from which you regularly order products not to give or sell your name to other companies. Do the same for any religious, political, professional and charitable organizations that you may contribute to, as well as for credit card companies, banks, schools and utility companies.

4   Avoid sending in warranty registration cards. You'll still be covered by the warranty, but the company won't use it as an invitation to send you more information on its products.

5   Buy a "stop junk mail" kit. For a price, you'll receive the materials you need to notify a limited number of the largest mailing list companies that are responsible for junk mail. Although this may be just the tip of the iceberg, it can protect you from future junk mail.

6   Get an unlisted phone number, or at least decline to list your address. Some mailing lists are formulated from names and addresses as they appear in telephone books.

7   Avoid filling out change-of-address forms when you move. The U.S. Postal Service sells these names and addresses to direct marketers. Instead, individually notify friends, family, creditors and so on.

8   Contact your nearest post office, as a last resort, for forms you can fill out to stop companies from sending you mail you don't want. If the mail continues, the companies may be subject to prosecution.

### ✳ Tips

Although stuffing business reply envelopes with nasty notes and sending them back at the company's expense might make you feel better, it won't help stop future mailings.

The Direct Marketing Association's Mail Preference Service won't eliminate all junk mail. You should contact individual companies doing the mailing if unsolicited mail doesn't stop.

It will generally take up to six months after your initial contact for you to stop receiving mail from a particular company.

**161 Choose a Business Structure**

Going into business for yourself isn't just a matter of opening a bank account and printing up some cards and stationery. When you set up on your own, you'll need to decide what type of business structure to establish for legal and tax purposes. The best structure for your business will depend on how large your company is, what sort of business you do and what your personal assets and income are. Use the chart below to compare the relative merits and drawbacks of different business structures and see which gives you the best protection and tax benefits. Check with legal and financial professionals, and note that these guidelines vary from state to state and that they may change.

| | OWNERSHIP RULES | LIABILITY OF OWNERS | CAPITAL | TAXES |
|---|---|---|---|---|
| Sole proprietorship | One owner. | Owner is personally liable for all of the business's obligations. | Owner contributes all capital required. | Business income, expenses and profit or loss are reported on the owner's personal tax return. |
| General partnership | May have an unlimited number of general partners. | Each general partner is personally liable for all of the business's obligations. | General partners contribute money or services for a portion of profits and losses. | The partnership itself is not taxed; profits or losses are reported by each general partner. |
| Limited partnership | May have an unlimited number of general and limited partners. | Each general partner is personally liable for all of the business's obligations. Limited partners usually have no personal liability. | General and limited partners contribute money or services for a portion of profits and losses. | The partnership itself is not taxed; profits or losses are reported by each general and limited partner. |
| C Corporation | May have an unlimited number of shareholders and classes of stock. | Generally, shareholders have no personal liability for the business's obligations. | Shareholders contribute capital by purchasing common or preferred stock. | The corporation is taxed on its earnings. The shareholders are taxed on any dividends they receive. |
| S Corporation | May have up to 75 shareholders, but only one class of stock. | Generally, shareholders have no personal liability for the business's obligations. | Shareholders contribute capital by purchasing stock. | The corporation itself is not taxed; profits or losses are reported individually by the shareholders. |
| LLC—Limited liability company | May have an unlimited number of company members. | Generally, company members have no personal liability for the business's obligations. | Members contribute money or services for a portion of profits and losses. | The LLC itself is not taxed (but a choice can be made to do so); profits or losses are reported by each member. |

chart

## Decide Whether to Go Into Business for Yourself | 162

If you want to satisfy your entrepreneurial urge, try owning a small business—but first consider whether your finances, personality and skills are up to the challenge.

### ⊙ Steps

1 Think about whether you want to work for yourself. Do you enjoy being the boss? Or do you feel more comfortable reporting to someone else?

2 Determine how much of a risk taker you are. You must be willing to be patient and give the business enough time to get established and grow.

3 Consider how much time and effort goes into running a small business. Many entrepreneurs work harder for themselves than they ever have for a former employer.

4 Find a business that suits you. Assess your skills, interests and personal values and seek a business that is in line with these attributes.

5 Decide whether you want to start a business or buy an existing one. Launching a business may involve fewer start-up costs and can proceed more slowly, but the business will take time to get established. An existing business usually requires more money up front.

6 Have enough money in the bank to get started. You'll need enough funds to pay for your everyday living expenses while sustaining the business until it turns a profit. Count on a minimum of three to six months.

### ✳ Tips

Talk to other entrepreneurs to get a perspective on what owning a small business entails.

Join a trade association, such as the National Association of Women Business Owners or the National Federation of Independent Business, for support information about issues facing small-business owners.

Visit your local U.S. Small Business Administration office or visit its Web site to learn about government loan programs and low-cost resources to help you get your business started.

## Form a Sole Proprietorship | 163

Setting up a sole proprietorship takes minimal effort. It's also the simplest type of business to structure and operate.

### ⊙ Steps

1 Find out which local, state and federal licenses and permits you need. Obtain them by contacting the Small Business Administration (SBA).

2 Make sure that you have the right to use your chosen business name by checking with the office of deeds or the appropriate city office in your area. Call the SBA if you don't know which office to call. This way you can verify that the name has not already been taken.

3 Get a Fictitious Business Name Statement by registering the name of your business in the county where you do business.

4 Apply for an employer ID number with the IRS using Form SS-4.

5 Apply for a state ID number with the Department of Revenue in the state in which you are forming your sole proprietorship. You need to have this number if you pay wages to employees, pay excise tax or have a Keogh retirement plan.

6 Consider getting business insurance to protect your personal assets.

### ✳ Tips

To protect your company name, register with state and federal agencies, and file with the county where you do business.

You can also do a preliminary trademark check via the U.S. Patent and Trademark Office Web site at www.uspto.gov.

### ⚠ Warning

Sole proprietors assume unlimited legal liability with no protection for personal assets if the business goes bankrupt.

## 164 | Form a Partnership

A partnership allows you to share the risks and rewards of a business venture with one or more partners.

### ⊙ Steps

1   Obtain all required local, state and federal licenses and permits. Contact the Small Business Administration (SBA) in your area to find out which ones you will need.

2   Register the name of the company in the county where the partnership does business, and obtain a Fictitious Business Name Certificate.

3   Get an Employer Identification Number from the IRS using Form SS-4.

4   In addition, get an ID number from the state Department of Revenue or the appropriate state office in your area. (Check with the SBA to find that office.)

5   Draft a written agreement between the partners determining a financial plan, management responsibilities, and the rights and obligations of individual partners. A written agreement is not required but can save a lot of headaches should a dispute arise. It's advisable to engage the services of an attorney in drafting this document.

6   Get help preparing tax returns, filing estimated taxes and preparing business statements until you understand them fully.

### ✱ Tip

Partners report profits and losses on their individual income tax returns and must pay self-employment tax.

### ⚠ Warnings

General partners assume unlimited legal liability with no protection for personal assets if the business goes bankrupt.

Responsibility for the business actions of each individual partner is shared by all partners.

## 165 | Incorporate a Business

Whether you have a small mom-and-pop establishment or a multinational company, the steps to incorporating are similar.

### ⊙ Steps

1   Determine if you want out-of-state, in-state or foreign incorporation. Most small and medium-sized businesses incorporate in the state where the majority of their business is conducted.

2   Enter into a preincorporation agreement with the co-founders of the business, establishing who will serve on the first board of directors, who will buy stock, how many shares and at what price.

3   File an application for registration of the name under which you wish to incorporate. Contact the Secretary of State's office to obtain the forms. After you file, the office will let you know if the name has been taken.

4   Prepare articles of incorporation for your business, following instructions from the Secretary of State's office. The office will send you a certificate of incorporation, which will include the name of the company, the purpose for which it is being formed, the location of the company and other basic information.

5   Sign the certificate. The number of legally qualified individuals required to sign varies from state to state.

6   Hold a stockholders' meeting after you receive your corporate charter from the state.

### ✱ Tips

Contact an attorney for help conducting the stockholders' meeting or drawing up the certificate of incorporation.

An attorney or other person may act as a "dummy" incorporator to help draw up the certificate of incorporation, then resign at the stockholders' meeting.

Use broad but clear language to describe the scope of the proposed corporation to give yourself the greatest possible latitude for future expansion.

You must have an office in the state in which you are forming your corporation.

7  Adopt corporate bylaws and elect the board of directors at the meeting. Send an agenda to shareholders before the meeting to let them know what issues (and board candidates) they will be voting on. Once the board is formally elected, any documents created in connection with the prein-corporation agreement need to be adopted.

## Research the Market for Your Product or Service    166

Before you start your business, test the market to make sure there will be demand for your product or service.

### ⊙ Steps

1  Learn about your market. Go to trade shows and network with other professionals in your line of business. Subscribe to trade publications.

2  Spend time with potential customers. Randomly ask people in the grocery store checkout line or at the bus stop what they'd like in the type of product or service you want to sell.

3  Set up a focus group to gather opinions about your product or service. This could be an informal gathering of your friends and family, or a more formal group assembled by a market research firm you hire. Be sure to get group members' reactions to your pricing model.

4  Send out a survey to potential customers. Make the form easy to fill out by asking multiple-choice questions. Ask the respondents if they would buy this product or service.

5  Analyze your findings to determine whether your idea is viable. How did people react to your product or service? What do people like or dislike about your product or service? Make adjustments, including the hardest one—letting go of your idea, if necessary, and finding another one.

### ✳ Tips

Make sure that the people you're surveying are indeed those who are potential customers.

Collect a large sample so that your findings will be accurate.

Create a well-designed survey. Ask very specific questions.

### ⚠ Warning

Avoid assuming that what you like is what others will like. You must meet the needs of the greatest number of customers.

## Write a Business Plan    167

Every business should have a business plan. It is your road map to the future and is usually essential if you want to get financing.

### ⊙ Steps

1  Organize the information for your business plan. Include information on your company, product or service, customers, market, competition and potential risk.

2  Write an executive summary. This is the first section of the plan—a two-page description of all the elements covered in more detail later.

3  Describe your company. Spell out the purpose of your business. Talk about the skills you and your management team have.

4  Explain your product or service. Detail how you will make or provide it. Analyze the costs associated with this process. List your supply sources.

5  Talk about the market you're entering. Discuss general trends in the industry. Include details about the market segment you are pursuing, the

### ✳ Tips

Be sure to gather all of the information for your business plan before you start writing it. Organize your research in outline form, then start writing.

Limit the plan to less than 50 pages. Investors and lenders get business plans every day. Most plans get a cursory look before they are either discarded or kept for further review.

niche you are targeting and your target customer; provide demographics on your potential customers and explain their buying habits. Analyze your competition.

6 Describe your marketing plan. Explain how you will generate sales through advertising, promotion and public relations. Estimate all costs conservatively.

7 Detail your yearly revenue projections and your expenses.

⚠ **Warning**

A business plan is a never-ending process. As your company grows, update your business plan projections.

## 168 Apply for a Business License

The types of licenses you'll need to run your business depend on your industry and the state in which you operate.

### ⊙ Steps

1 Go to the appropriate government agencies to see which licenses you need. Be aware that there are licensing requirements at all levels of government—federal, state, regional, county and city.

2 Acquire any necessary specialized licenses such as those needed to sell food and liquor or to handle hazardous materials.

3 Find out if your profession requires a license. Lawyers, dentists and doctors, mechanics and real estate agents all require a professional license before they open up shop. You may, too.

4 If you are buying an existing business, see if the licenses are transferable. Some expire once ownership changes hands. Licenses take time to be transferred, so find out how it works where you are.

**✱ Tip**

Check with the state chamber of commerce, local trade associations and professional groups for information on licenses and state registration.

## 169 Hire Employees

A business is only as good as the people it employs. Here are some steps to hiring an effective staff.

### ⊙ Steps

1 Determine what jobs you need done and what skills are needed.

2 Write precise job descriptions, including duties and skill requirements.

3 Conduct salary surveys among similar businesses in comparable locations to determine how much to budget for salaries.

4 Advertise in appropriate media. Ask friends, family and associates for recommendations. If you need generalists, place employment ads in local newspapers. If you need specialists, consider advertising in trade publications or other specialized media, including job fairs and the Internet.

5 Consider using an employment service. An agency can help you write job descriptions, put together an employee manual, devise a benefits package, and screen applicants.

**✱ Tips**

Create an annual employee budget to know how much you can afford.

Let current employees know about openings that might be of interest to them.

Make sure the job description is accurate, so people will know what they are applying for.

A job fair is a good way to meet prospective employees and talk face-to-face before the interview. Newspapers and trade groups

6   Interview carefully. Focus on the applicant's qualifications, track record, attitude and demeanor.

7   Bring others into the interview process. Ask the applicant to meet with several managers so that you can get others' impressions.

8   Check references and employment history. Many employers also ask that applicants agree to credit-history checks and drug screenings.

9   Put your offer in writing, spelling out the job description, hours, salary, benefits, vacation and sick time and other pertinent details.

often stage job fairs for industries such as services, high-tech or sales.

### ⚠ Warning

Remember that asking questions about an applicant's race, religion, marital status, age or disability is illegal.

## Write a Mission Statement    `170`

Writing a company mission statement will help you and your employees focus on a common goal and give everyone a benchmark to gauge performance.

### ⊙ Steps

1   Include everybody whose perception of your company matters. Collect as many ideas as you can.

2   Define your company. Think carefully about what role it plays in the industry and community.

3   State the things to which you're dedicated. Are you dedicated to quality, your customers, your success?

4   Assess the value of your product. Use written questionnaires to poll your customers, suppliers, strategic partners and other external parties about the benefits of and ideals behind your product.

5   Set up a small committee to go through the ideas you have collected and incorporate them into your company's mission statement.

6   Give the mission statement high visibility; post it in the lobby and halls. People will see it every day and be reminded of what their work means.

### ✱ Tip

Live your mission statement every day. In order to gain credibility with your employees, customers and vendors, you must practice what you preach.

### ⚠ Warning

Be realistic. Set standards that are reasonable and reachable by you and your employees.

## Apply for a Business Loan    `171`

Money to expand a business can come from a variety of sources. Most require you to provide a thorough financial profile.

### ⊙ Steps

1   Determine what the uses of a loan will be and the amount you need.

2   Decide on the type of loan you want and whether you want to obtain it from a bank, the Small Business Administration or another lender.

3   Update the company's balance sheet, indicating the current status of assets, liabilities and equity.

4   Update the profit-and-loss statement with a summary covering the company's expenses, revenues and costs for a particular accounting period.

### ✱ Tips

If two banks turn you down for a loan, you can apply to one of the Small Business Administration's many loan programs.

Apply for a line of credit at a bank well before you actually need the capital.

5   Develop cash flow projections for at least one year, showing how money will flow in and out of the company quarter by quarter.

6   Contact prospective lenders and ask them for an application. In many cases, the quickest way to accomplish this is in person, although it can also be done via e-mail, fax or mail.

7   Consider consulting with legal counsel to aid you in reviewing loan documents and their stipulations.

Business owners with few business assets can expect to put up personal assets to secure a loan.

⚠ **Warning**

Be wary of lenders that want to secure your intellectual property as collateral for your loan.

---

## 172 | Secure Venture Capital Money

Venture capitalists invest money in start-ups in exchange for an equity ownership in the company. VCs receive hundreds of pitches from entrepreneurs each year. Here's how to stand out.

### ◎ Steps

1   Prepare a business plan. VCs will expect you to clearly define the purpose of your business, disclose pertinent financial information (including revenue streams and projections) and provide information on your executive management team.

2   Do research on venture funds to find the appropriate fit for your company. Look in *Pratt's Guide to Venture Capital Sources,* available in many bookstores and libraries, to see what fields each firm is likely to fund. Some focus on retail and service companies, while others look specifically for technology start-ups.

3   Get an introduction to the venture capital firm. You'll have a much better chance if you've been personally introduced to the VC rather than blindly sending your business plan. These introductions can be made by executives of companies already being funded by the VC or by lawyers and accountants who work with the firm. Try to contact four to five VCs.

4   Arrange a meeting with the VC. Consider bringing key members of the management team to the meeting.

5   Follow up your visit with a thank-you note and additional information.

6   Be persistent and polite.

✳ **Tips**

Choose your timing carefully. VCs want to see that you've done the basic groundwork and are ready to springboard to the next level. Spell out what your next big step is, and what resources you will need to get there.

Think big. Investors want to see that you have a large-scale vision for your company and that you have plans to grow and expand.

Show off your top executive team. VCs want to see a solid management team that is knowledgeable as well as flexible, driven and committed.

⚠ **Warning**

Acquiring funding is a demanding process—have a thick skin, patience and determination.

---

## 173 | Bring Your Business Online

Bringing your business onto the Internet requires a strong business model and a sense of what you want to accomplish by having a Web site. Here's how to get started.

### ◎ Steps

1   Decide whether you want to provide information about your business or transact commerce. Answering such questions can help determine the amount of effort required to build the site.

✳ **Tips**

When registering for a domain name, think of alternative names in case your first choice is taken.

2   Decide if you are going to develop your own Web site or contract with a Web-site developer.

3   Gather information on Web publishing via books, magazines and other current periodicals if developing your own site.

4   Browse other Web sites for design and functionality ideas.

5   Apply for a domain name through the InterNIC Web site (rs.internic.net) You can search for the availability of a certain name and link to one of InterNIC's accredited registrars. Your ISP may be able to host your site. Ask for information.

6   Begin to develop the site. Install various checkpoints along the way to ensure that the project is progressing in the right direction.

7   Implement your marketing campaign before your site goes live, and step up your marketing efforts to bring traffic to your site after.

Create a Web site that is easy and logical to navigate.

If you have a smaller business, consider selling your products through online classifieds and/or online auctions. These are simpler and less expensive ways of transacting commerce online.

### ⚠ Warning

Developing a Web site, whether you do it yourself or have someone else do it, can be time-consuming. Begin planning as soon as you decide you want a site.

# File for a Patent                                                            174

A patent gives you the exclusive right to make, use or sell a product, device or process for a set period of time. Today utility patents (the most common kind) are good for at least 17 years.

### ⊙ Steps

1   Determine whether your idea warrants patent protection. The Patent and Trademark Office (PTO) has an online patent database at www.uspto.gov.

2   Compose a written patent application consisting of a number of subparts required by the PTO, which typically include a detailed description of the invention's structure and operation; a listing of the attributes that set the invention apart from previous related inventions (known as the "prior art"); a precise description of what aspects of the invention deserve the patent (the patent claims); and a signed oath or declaration.

3   Create a drawing of the invention that shows all the invention's parts or aspects. You can either submit formal drawings with your application or submit simple sketches until your patent is approved, at which point you'll be required to submit detailed drawings of your invention before the patent will issue.

4   Determine your filing fee by checking the fee schedule at the PTO Web site. For utility patents, the filing fee is $380 for independent inventors and companies with fewer than 500 employees and $760 for large companies. (Expect additional fees of more than $3,000 for getting the patent issued and maintaining it in force until its expiration date.)

5   File the application, drawings or sketches, and fee with the assistant commissioner for patents at the PTO.

6   Communicate with the patent examiner regarding the scope of your invention and its qualifications for a patent. Typically, this takes more than a year. Some self-help resources, such as www.nolo.com, provide detailed information for every step of this complicated process.

7   If a patent is issued, pay the issue fee of $605 for small entities and $1,210 for large entities.

### ✳ Tip

To get the earliest possible date for your invention, you may also file a Provisional Patent Application (PPA) for $75. A PPA must contain a detailed description of the invention but need not include most of what must go into a regular patent application. If you do file a PPA, you must file a regular patent application on the same invention within one year in order to preserve the PPA's filing date.

### ⚠ Warnings

To preserve your right to obtain a patent on your invention, you must file a regular or provisional patent application within one year of the date your invention is offered for sale in the United States, publicly used in the United States or described in a printed publication anywhere in the world (which almost certainly includes descriptions in electronic formats).

This information is not a substitute for professional legal counsel. Refer to legal references and consult an attorney for up-to-date, comprehensive guidance.

## 175 Decide if a Home-Based Business Is Right for You

Working from home sounds like the ideal way to work, but your personality, lifestyle and home life will dictate whether it is a viable alternative for you.

### ⊙ Steps

1 Ask yourself what you are trying to accomplish by starting a home-based business. Do you want more time to spend with your family? Do you want to have some flexibility in your work hours? Do you want to be your own boss? Do you want to make more money?

2 Consider your personality when making this decision. Are you the sort of person who enjoys the solitude of working alone?

3 Consider whether there are small children, pets or anything else that might distract you at home.

4 Decide what type of business you are interested in. Is it performing a service or creating a product? Is it best done at home, or will an office or additional workspace be required once you are successful?

5 Talk to other people who do the same or similar work from home. Ask what problems they run into.

6 Discover whether you can make enough money to meet your financial needs doing this sort of work.

7 Research what sort of resources will be required to get your business going—cash, equipment, marketing.

8 Identify whether you can do all the work yourself or if this business will require work from additional people. Can you use independent contractors or will you have to hire employees?

9 Decide on a business that suits your personal needs and meets your financial commitments.

### ✳ Tip

Ask yourself these lifestyle/work-style questions: Are you a self-starter? Are you able to meet deadlines without someone constantly reminding you? Do you require personal interaction throughout the day? Can you make decisions on your own? Do you enjoy having lunch with co-workers? Do you need a regimented workday? Do you prefer to leave your work behind when you leave the office? Do you prefer a flexible schedule that allows you to intersperse personal needs with work needs?

### ⚠ Warnings

Running a home-based business is not glamorous; it is hard work that requires great time management and dedication.

Although working from home makes it easier to do things around the house, you might very well find yourself caught in a vise when family and work demands conflict.

## 176 Set Up a Home Office

Once you're ready to set up shop in your home, it's time to turn your little corner into a real corner office.

### ⊙ Steps

1 Establish a permanent space within your home for your office. A separate room is ideal.

2 Decide on an office arrangement. The best is a U-shaped arrangement, which lets you use three surfaces to keep everything within reach.

3 Choose an L-shaped arrangement that provides a secondary surface if space is limited. A parallel arrangement can provide two full-sized working surfaces if they are placed opposite each other.

4 Consider a V-shaped arrangement, which consists of a small working area in front of you (generally used for a computer monitor) and two surfaces

### ✳ Tips

If you don't have a separate room available, use devices like screens, bookcases and directed lighting to create the necessary separation between home space and office space.

Consider getting a small headset for your phone, both to free your hands and to block out background noise.

angled to your left and right if your office area is very small. This is similar to a U-shape, except the central working area is much smaller.

5 Establish two business-only phone lines (one for voice and one for fax and/or Internet) for your office. If you'll need to forward calls to other offices, ask your phone company about related services.

6 Buy office furniture that suits the arrangement you've chosen. Include desks and tables, chairs and desk lamps.

7 Buy a phone with a built-in answering machine and a hold button. If you'll be transferring calls from within your home office, make sure your phone has a transfer button.

8 Buy a computer system, including a printer. Consider built-in fax software if you'll be sending and receiving files created on a PC.

9 Purchase a separate fax machine if you'll be sending and receiving photos or articles from newspapers or magazines by fax. To save money, consider buying a fax machine that can also serve as a photocopier.

10 Stock your office with standard office supplies. If you're self-employed, budget the cost of these items in your monthly business expenses; otherwise, your employer may provide these supplies for you.

### Things You'll Need

- ❏ desk
- ❏ desk chair
- ❏ desk lamp
- ❏ phone lines
- ❏ telephone
- ❏ answering machine
- ❏ Internet access
- ❏ computer with modem
- ❏ printer
- ❏ fax modem or fax machine/copier
- ❏ office supplies

---

## Reduce Expenses in a Home-Based Business          `177`

Working from home is less costly than renting office space. Once you've decided to skip the hassle and expense of commuting, there are additional ways to reduce your costs.

### ◎ Steps

1 Keep complete and accurate accounting records, and review your expenses at the end of each month to determine where you could cut back.

2 Join a purchasing alliance for small and home-based businesses to get discounts on everything from health insurance to office supplies.

3 Purchase multifunction office machines. For example, look for a fax machine that also copies and scans documents.

4 Take tax deductions for business use of your vehicle and home.

5 Earn supplier discounts. Often a supplier will offer a 2 percent discount if an invoice is paid within 10 days of the invoice date.

6 Give free Internet access services a try (see 91 "Evaluate Free Internet Service Providers").

7 Go over your insurance coverage with your agent and look for ways to cut your premiums. Consider adding an incidental business option to your existing homeowner's insurance at a much lower cost than a standard business liability policy. Shut off nonessential equipment at night.

8 Check garage sales and thrift stores for office furniture. You can get great bargains, and sometimes you can even find like-new used or reconditioned fax machines and typewriters.

### ✱ Tips

Consult an accountant before taking deductions for business use of your home and vehicle.

If your current suppliers don't offer discounts for early payment, try to find those that will. At the very least, pay your bills on time so that you won't have to pay late fees.

### ⚠ Warning

Don't get too budget-happy and stop buying items that are truly necessary to your operation, such as trade journals and required continuing education courses.

## 178 | Find an Apartment

Finding the right apartment for you—in the right price range, with the right amenities, in the right area of town—isn't hard if you know how to manage the process. Here's what to do.

### ☉ Steps

1   Figure out how much you can afford. Be sure to include utilities.

2   Think about what cities or neighborhoods you'd like to live in. Consider commute time and what you'd like your local neighborhood to offer.

3   Write down what features are important to you, such as parking, acceptable pet policies, proximity to public transportation, security, laundry facilities and number of bedrooms and bathrooms.

4   Scan the apartment listings in the local newspaper where you want to live; check online services such as Rent Net (www.rent.net); look for rental signs in targeted neighborhoods.

5   Keep a file of clipped newspaper ads, computer printouts and notes. Go through your file and call for appointments to see your choice. Make note of any additional information you get.

6   Sign up with an apartment-finder service if you are new to the area, can't get around, don't have time to go through the classifieds or want fewer choices to consider.

7   Inspect apartments carefully.

8   Fill out an application for the apartment you want. Submit it with a check for the amount you and the landlord agree on to cover a credit check and show good faith.

9   Establish a move-in date, sign a contract and arrange to pay any security deposit and rent required.

### ✱ Tips

Drive by prospective buildings to get a feel for the neighborhood.

Use the Internet to get information on prospective areas and as another source for listings.

### ⚠ Warnings

Apartment-finder services usually get commissions from landlords, so beware of a service that demands a hefty fee from prospective tenants.

Apartment-finder services usually have a limited number of units to offer, because they go by what is on their client list. They may also have limited information about their apartments and may offer little leeway in negotiating leases.

## 179 | Determine How Much You Can Pay in Rent

It takes just a few simple calculations to determine how much you can afford to pay in rent.

### ☉ Steps

1   Calculate your total monthly household net income after taxes, including your spouse's income if you're married, and any child-support or alimony payments.

2   Multiply your total monthly net income by .30. This number will give you a general idea of the amount of rent you can afford to pay.

3   Add up all of your other monthly expenses, such as car and credit card payments. Include estimates for food, entertainment and transportation.

4   Add together the rent amount from step 2 and the amount from step 3. Make sure this total does not exceed your monthly income. If it does, adjust the amount of rent you can afford.

### ✱ Tip

Housing in some areas costs much more, so set your target accordingly when you plan a move to another city or state.

### ⚠ Warning

Landlords look at the ratio of your debts (including estimated rent payments) to your income in considering your rental application—but your credit history is another important factor.

## Handle Housing Discrimination 180

Discrimination against particular groups of renters is illegal and wrong. If you can show you've been discriminated against, the law is on your side.

### ⊙ Steps

1  Contact the Better Business Bureau if the property is managed by a management company. There may be a record of previous complaints.

2  Follow your hunch if you get the feeling you've been unfairly denied a rental or given only a limited selection of properties to look at. (Spotting a "For Rent" ad in the paper for a property you looked at a month ago could be a red flag. A little investigation at this point will help you figure out whether your feeling is valid.)

3  Contact the Department of Housing and Urban Development (HUD) to find the nearest local office. HUD administers the Fair Housing Act. Visit www.hud.gov for a directory of contact information.

4  Ask the HUD office to send you a complaint form. You'll be asked to outline the specifics of your discrimination charge. You can file your complaint with HUD if you fall under one of the country's "protected classes." Federally protected groups include those based on race, color, religion, gender, national origin and disability status.

5  File a complaint with your state housing agency if you don't belong to one of the protected classes. Many state laws broaden the protection to include age, occupation, sexual orientation or military background.

6  Consider bypassing HUD and state housing agencies altogether and filing a claim directly in a state or federal court. This may prove more productive because government agencies often have excessive caseloads and limited resources. If government officials don't think you have a case after reviewing your complaint, you may be able to find a private attorney who's willing to represent the claim.

### ✱ Tips

Denying a rental to particular groups of people is the most obvious form of housing discrimination. Other overt forms include advertising or verbal statements that indicate a preference based on a group characteristic, falsely denying availability of a rental unit that is actually available, and refusing a guide dog, hearing dog or service dog.

If you have a poor credit or payment history, the landlord is within rights to deny you the property. A bad referral from a previous landlord is a valid reason to deny a rental applicant as long as that criterion is applied equally to all tenants.

Wait until you get the assessment of your case from HUD or state housing officials before you hire an attorney. It will help you ask the right questions.

## Negotiate an Apartment Lease 181

Make sure you get all the details written out and agreed to before you sign on the dotted line. You'll have to abide by that agreement for the term of the lease.

### ⊙ Steps

1  Make a list of what is important to you and what details you want to include in the agreement.

2  Study the lease agreement as it is written and highlight any areas you want to change or negotiate.

3  Explain to the landlord your reasons for wanting or needing the change.

4  Be willing to give something up in order to get something else.

5  Act responsibly and respectfully. You'll have more success if you are pleasant to deal with.

### ✱ Tips

Remember that your ability to bargain depends on whether the landlord is anxious to have you as a tenant or there are plenty of other great prospective tenants from whom to choose.

Negotiating the lease also involves such items as rent-due date, move-in date and things to be fixed or improved before the move-in date.

6  Provide documentation to support your worthiness as a renter, such as a good credit report and a recommendation from another landlord or rental-management company.

7  Get everything in writing once you agree.

**⚠ Warning**

Laws vary from state to state, so study your lease carefully to figure out what is negotiable.

---

## 182 | Get a Landlord to Accept Pets

**If you can present your case in a persuasive manner, you may be able to get your landlord to accept your pooch or cat.**

### ◉ Steps

1  Provide your landlord with written statements from former landlords that commend your pet's behavior and verify that your rental unit was well-maintained while you and your pet occupied the premises.

2  Invite your landlord to meet your pet and view the pet's behavior.

3  Offer the landlord a "pet deposit."

4  Inform your landlord in writing that you will pay for damages caused by your pet during your lease.

**✱ Tip**

Your state may have a law that allows tenants to keep pets under certain circumstances (such as a companion dog for a disabled tenant) even if the landlord has a no-pets policy.

---

## 183 | Get a Landlord to Respect Your Privacy

**Many states have laws regarding when and why a landlord may enter a tenant's home. If your landlord disregards your privacy rights, you should be able to address the problem easily.**

### ◉ Steps

1  Familiarize yourself with your state's privacy laws to find out what your landlord may and may not do.

2  Review your lease or rental agreement for clauses covering landlord entry to your home.

3  Ask your landlord not to enter your home without a good reason or notice.

4  Write a letter to your landlord confirming the mutual understanding and thanking your landlord for agreeing to respect your privacy. Keep a copy for your own records.

5  If your requests for privacy fall on deaf ears, follow up with a more serious letter that refers to your state's privacy laws as well as your lease or rental agreement. Again, keep a copy for your records.

6  Take legal action against your landlord or break your lease if your landlord continues to violate your privacy.

**✱ Tip**

In many states, a landlord is required to provide at least 24 hours' notice before entering a tenant's residence. Any un-announced visit should occur during normal business hours, 9 to 5 on weekdays and possibly Saturday afternoons.

**⚠ Warning**

Make sure you fully understand your rights and responsibilities before threatening your landlord with legal action.

# Get a Landlord to Make Repairs          184

In most states, landlords are legally required to maintain rental units in fit and habitable condition. But a landlord is typically responsible only for certain major repairs.

## ⊙ Steps

1   Assess your situation. Repairs needed to keep the residence habitable would be considered major, while minor repairs are matters of convenience. Examples of major repairs are a door that won't lock, a broken furnace, a toilet that won't flush and deteriorating lead paint.

2   Do your homework. Study up on local ordinances and state housing codes, and review your rental contract to see if your landlord is responsible for the specific repairs you need.

3   Make your request for a repair in writing, unless it's an emergency that requires immediate action. Detail the problem, how it affects you and what you want done and when.

4   If your landlord fails to remedy the problem, build your case. Take pictures. Have a professional assess the problem and estimate repair costs. Gather forces and present your request as a group if other tenants suffer from the same problems.

5   Consider calling state and local building or health inspectors if repeated requests are ignored. Be prepared to provide documentation of the problem and your attempts to have it fixed.

6   Consider the repair-and-deduct option. Have the repair work done professionally and deduct its cost from your monthly rent. View your specific rental agreement in detail before taking this route.

7   Take extreme caution before you decide to withhold monthly rent payments as a tactic. This is illegal in some states, and in states where it is permitted, it requires strict adherence to certain procedures. Mishandling this could get you kicked out of your residence.

### ✳ Tips

Keep records of all correspondence with your landlord and write down the date for everything. You'll need comprehensive evidence of your dealings should the case enter a courtroom.

Provide as much detail as you can when you write to your landlord. Also, point out that the problem may worsen over time and become a much more expensive repair.

### ⚠ Warning

Before you withhold rent, sue or adopt another drastic approach, make sure that such an approach is legal in your state, that the necessary repair is major, that you have given your landlord adequate notice and time to act, and that you are willing to end your tenancy should the landlord or judge successfully evict you.

# Tell Your Neighbor the Music's Too Loud          185

You don't want to rock the boat or tip the neighborhood canoe, but you do want to be able to sleep in on Saturdays. With a tactful approach, you can achieve your goal.

## ⊙ Steps

1   Start by smiling. Catch your neighbor's eye when he heads out in the morning or give him a friendly nod when he comes home.

2   Get to know this person if you don't already. What's his name? Where does he work? How long has he lived on your street?

3   Try to make pleasant chitchat and find a common interest—sports? gardening? movies?

### ✳ Tips

If you establish friendly relations with the people in your neighborhood at the outset, it's easier to make requests of them when the need arises.

In general, being friendly and direct will get you much better results than being hostile.

4 Mention, in an offhand way, that you can hear his music from your house. Tell him it sometimes wakes you up. For many people, this will be enough to let them know that their behavior needs to change.

5 Wait a week or two to see what happens.

6 Mention in a more direct way that you'd like the volume lower. Be clear and specific with your request—and don't forget to be friendly.

7 Find out if other neighbors are bothered, if no change happens, and ask them to mention it, too.

8 Consider soliciting the help of one of his friends on the block—he might be willing to heed the complaint from someone closer.

9 Wait a week or two to avoid creating a conflict that could become hostile.

10 Escalate if you must: Write a letter, solicit legal advice or call the police. These methods up the conflict ante, so use them with care.

## ⚠ Warning

This is your neighbor—someone you might see every day for a long time to come—so make sure you act tactfully and thoughtfully. You don't want to come home to a feud every day.

---

## 186 | Buy a Home

You'll do a lot of looking around, go through piles of paperwork, suffer through the loan process—and then hope the seller accepts your offer. Here are the broad steps you'll take.

### ◉ Steps

1 Figure out how much home you can afford. Consider a down payment, closing costs, mortgage, insurance and taxes.

2 Decide where you want to live. Think about your commute to work, area schools, and resale value of the homes in various neighborhoods.

3 Think about what kind of home you want. Do you want a newer home that requires little or no remodeling? Would you prefer an older home with character that might require some fix-up work? One story or two? Are you interested in a condo or townhouse?

4 Start going to open houses to see what the market is like. The more homes you look at, the better idea you will have of what you can afford and what you do and don't like.

5 Hire a real estate agent or attorney—depending on where you live—to represent you in buying a home. You can also choose to handle the transaction on your own.

6 Find a lender, and get prequalified or preapproved for a home loan.

7 Find the perfect home for you and make an offer.

8 Open an escrow account—or have your broker do it—after your offer is accepted. The escrow office will perform a title search and see if there are any outstanding liens on the property.

9 Hire an inspector to make sure the home is up to code and not in need of any repairs that the seller might be unwilling to pay for or that you could not afford.

## ✱ Tips

Be patient. Finding a home that fits your family's needs can take some time.

Home values fluctuate with the ups and downs of the economy.

Buying a home is likely to be the biggest single investment you'll ever make. Invest wisely.

10  Hire a termite inspector to make sure the property doesn't have any pest or water damage.

11  When you and the seller have come to an agreement on any repairs to be made and who will be responsible for paying for them, remove all inspection contingencies.

12  Close escrow when all loan documents are signed, the title insurance policy is issued, all money is received by the escrow agent and all fees are paid.

13  Move in!

## Determine How Big a Mortgage You Can Afford          187

Before you look for that dream house, you need to ask yourself what you can really afford to spend each month. These calculations are based on a typical down payment of 20 percent.

### ⊙ Steps

1  Collect some home guides or look at a few ads in the Sunday newspaper for houses you would consider buying. Look at the asking prices of a few selected homes and multiply these by 0.80 to give yourself a ballpark figure on the mortgage debt amount for those homes. (This assumes that you will be making a 20 percent down payment.)

2  Calculate what the mortgage payments for these homes would be. Use personal-finance software or an online mortgage calculator. To make a quick approximation of your monthly payments, see 195 "Estimate Your Mortgage Payment."

3  Add what you will have to pay monthly toward property taxes, insurance and private mortgage insurance (PMI).

4  Add to this number your monthly utility costs. (If you are renting and have no idea what utility costs are, ask friends and family what they pay. Or ask your real estate agent for typical figures.)

5  Add in your monthly budget for home maintenance. Budget about 1 percent of the cost of the home for maintenance each year. (If the house costs $150,000, budget $1,500 annually, or $125 per month.)

6  Add in the prorated monthly cost of any furnishings, landscaping and nonessential improvements to the house.

7  Compare this figure with your monthly net income to estimate affordability. Multiply your monthly income by 0.40 (40 percent is a common measure). If that figure is equal to or greater than your estimated monthly cost figures, the house of your dreams may well be in your price range.

### ✱ Tips

If you have consumer debt (credit cards, personal loans), try to eliminate or reduce it since it will drag on your ability to qualify for a mortgage and make the monthly payment.

If you have monthly payments (car, credit cards, personal loans, etc.), be sure to take these into account when determining that bottom-line affordability figure.

### ⚠ Warnings

Lenders can only tell you what you might be able to afford based on your salary and debt level. You also have to feel comfortable with the reality of the monthly payment.

Don't assume that you can cut back your expenses and stretch yourself into a house payment. You can only eat boxed macaroni and cheese so many times.

questions

## ✓ 188 Evaluate a Neighborhood

Real estate experts always say that the three most important things to consider when evaluating a property are location, location and location. That's because a home with convenient shopping, congenial neighbors and good schools nearby will hold its value far better than an identical home in a lesser neighborhood. Of course, it will also be much more pleasant to live in. Ask these questions to determine the quality of the neighborhood you're considering, and to evaluate other local factors that go into making a house a good home—and a good investment.

❑ How well do residents keep up their properties?

❑ Ask your real estate agent: How many neighbors rent vs. own?

❑ How far away is the nearest shopping area? Is it easy to get to at the times you'll need to go?

❑ Check with state or school watchdog organizations. What is the quality of the local schools?

❑ Are local sidewalks and streets well-maintained?

❑ How much traffic is there? Is it safe for children?

❑ Is public transportation nearby? Will it take you where you want to go?

❑ Is there a highway accessible from the neighborhood?

❑ How close are the nearest parks? Do they suit your family's needs?

❑ How close and accessible are cultural and entertainment facilities—theaters, museums and ballparks?

❑ Visit the neighborhood after nightfall. Does it feel safe? How noisy is it?

❑ Check with the local police station. How much crime is in the neighborhood?

❑ Check with any neighborhood organizations. Are crime-watch or special activities planned?

❑ Check a map. How far is the nearest fire station? police station?

❑ Is there emergency medical service in the area?

❑ How far away is the nearest medical center? Is it close enough for your needs?

❑ Are you in the flight path of an airport? Note that flight paths may change with weather conditions or at different times of day.

❑ Is a fire station or train station so close as to cause noise pollution?

❑ Check with the homeowners' association regarding any rules, regulations or covenants. How do these jibe with your own style of decorating or living?

❑ Visit the city or county offices. Are any new developments planned? What impact will these have on traffic, noise and school systems?

❑ Are the water and sewer systems adequate for all the homes in the area or for any future local development plans?

## Retain a Real Estate Agent to Buy a Home {189}

Most buyers don't realize that many real estate agents actually have a financial responsibility to the seller, not the buyer. Here's how to hire a buyer's agent whose first responsibility is to you.

### ◉ Steps

1 Locate buyers' agents in the area in which you want to buy. Call local real estate offices; ask friends and associates; and investigate associations such as the Real Estate Buyer's Agent Council.

2 Call three or four agents to discuss your needs.

3 Ask prospective agents about their views of a buyers' agency and what their fee structure is. Do they require a percentage of the sales price, do they work for a flat fee, or will they be paid by the seller?

4 Ask prospective agents about their "feel" for the local real estate market, and listen closely to see if they appear to be up on what's happening.

5 Meet face-to-face with the buyers' agents you like so you can learn more about them.

6 Ask for references and check them. Ask references tough questions such as, "What would you have changed about this agent?" and "Did this agent do anything you didn't like?"

### ✳ Tips

Look for designations in agents' titles. The designation for buyers' agents is ABR (accredited buyers' agent).

You generally don't need to pay an agent who is helping you buy a home. The seller's agent compensates a buyer's agent.

Get all agreements in writing.

### ⚠ Warning

If you have doubts about a pending relationship with an agent, talk to a real estate attorney.

## Shop for a House Online {190}

If you want to save some time and money, or you'd rather not look for homes under the watchful eyes of a real estate agent, then the Internet is your answer to house hunting.

### ◉ Steps

1 Determine your price range (see 187 "Determine How Big a Mortgage You Can Afford").

2 Decide on a location, which can be as specific as an address or as broad as your state of choice. A Web site may also ask you to search by ZIP code, region, city or neighborhood.

3 Decide on the property type and age of the home. For instance, do you want to live in a condominium, a co-op, or a single-family or multifamily home? Would you like to live in a home of a certain vintage, such as one built less than 5 years ago or more than 10 years ago?

4 Decide on a property size by number of rooms and bathrooms, as well as area in square feet.

5 Determine other features you want in your dream home, such as a swimming pool, fireplaces, a second story or a waterfront view.

6 Surf the Internet for sites that offer listings, such as Realtor.com—the site of the National Association of Realtors—and specific brokerages and agents in the area where you are hunting.

### ✳ Tips

Request e-mail updates on available homes and additional information about the community you're considering.

You can also find property listings at "For Sale By Owner" sites, such as the International Real Estate Digest (IRED), and local newspaper electronic classifieds.

7   Enter the information from steps 1 through 5 as requested by the site.

8   Look at the expanded information and photographs for the properties that come up in your search results.

9   Contact the agent listed if you see a home that fits your criteria. Ask for further information, such as more photographs and the home's history.

10  Set up an appointment to meet with the agent if you are still interested.

---

## 191 | Buy a Condo or Co-op Apartment

Buying a condominium or cooperative apartment is a lot like buying a single-family home, but there are things to consider that are unique to this type of property.

### ⊙ Steps

1   Look at the amenities of the development. Some developments are small while others are almost completely self-contained complexes.

2   Consider the homeowners' association dues.

3   Review the binding rules (known as Covenants, Conditions and Restrictions, or CC&Rs) of the homeowners' association. Make sure they won't affect your lifestyle. (Some places have many limitations, such as not allowing pets outside or parking outside—even in your own driveway.)

4   Review the recent repairs done to the unit you're considering. Will a major repair—such as a new roof—be necessary soon? Does the association have sufficient reserves to pay for the repairs? Speak with the secretary of the association and request a copy of the bookkeeping statements it provides to prospective buyers.

5   Notice the overall condition of the complex. Is it well-maintained?

6   Identify the number of units for sale compared with the overall number of units. At any time, there should only be 4 to 5 percent for sale. Anything higher might indicate an adverse condition.

7   Talk to owners in the complex or building. Often, disgruntled owners are more than happy to tell you what's really going on.

8   Look at the area surrounding the complex or building. Is it already developed, or could some undesirable neighbor, such as a factory or unacceptable business, move in?

9   Be aware of what is covered by homeowners' association insurance and what the association is responsible for, such as roofs, common areas and landscaping.

### ⚠ Warnings

Condos and co-op apartments often don't appreciate as quickly as single-family residences and often don't sell as quickly.

In order to buy into some co-ops, you have to be interviewed and approved by the co-op board.

## Buy a Vacation Home 192

Buying a vacation home is exciting—but as with any other major purchase, it's important to think things through carefully. Here are some suggestions to help you make the best buy.

### ⊙ Steps

1  Decide whether this is a place where you'd like to spend every vacation. Base your decision on your lifestyle and recreational interests.

2  Select the type of vacation home that best suits your needs.

3  Visit desired locations and tour properties for sale.

4  Determine whether the vacation property you are considering buying is priced fairly. Check real estate ads and ask local real estate brokers for prices of comparable vacation properties in the area.

5  Hire professional inspectors to uncover any potential problems.

6  Consider how you will maintain the vacation property throughout the year. Get references of rental management firms that can take care of maintenance, upkeep and rentals when you are not there.

7  Ask an attorney or broker to review sales contracts and agreements.

8  Make an offer based on comparable prices in the area.

### ✱ Tips

You may get a better deal if you buy during the off-season.

If you're seeking a time-share, look on the Internet for people selling their weeks independently.

### ⚠ Warnings

Consult a tax professional about tax consequences. Most experts advise that you should buy a vacation home for pleasure—not as an investment.

If you rent out a vacation property most of the year, the IRS will only allow you to occupy the property for two weeks out of the year without affecting its investment-property status.

## Make an Offer on a Home 193

You've found your dream home and you're ready to make your offer. Remember, the offer you make could become legally binding. Here are the steps you'll need to take.

### ⊙ Steps

1  Consult a lender or mortgage broker to find out how much you can afford to spend on a home, or use a calculator on a financial Web site such as Quicken.com (see 187 "Determine How Big a Mortgage You Can Afford").

2  Decide what type of financing you want: a fixed-rate or adjustable-rate mortgage.

3  Know how much money you have for a down payment; typically 5 to 20 percent of the purchase price is required, depending on the loan terms.

4  Get prequalified for a loan by a lender or mortgage broker.

5  State what inspections you want to have done before you'll agree to buy the home. You can get general home inspections, as well as geological, roof, pool/spa, earthquake/flood and environmental inspections.

6  State whom you want to pay for inspections, the termite report, required work, title insurance and escrow fees, and warranties.

7  Decide how long you want the escrow period to be.

### ⚠ Warning

Consult a real estate attorney or broker before you sign anything. What you agree to could severely limit the remedies available to you by law.

8 Establish how long both parties should have to complete inspections, approvals and work.

9 Put a limit on the amount of time the seller has to respond.

10 Present your offer and a letter of prequalification for financing to the seller yourself or through your agent.

## 194 | Get a Home Loan

**Securing a home loan is the most important step in the home-buying process. Here are the basics for getting your financing.**

### ⊙ Steps

1 Find a lender. Ask friends, family or co-workers for referrals; speak with local real estate agents; search the Internet.

2 Fill out a loan application.

3 Get an estimate of closing costs from the lender you choose. By law, the lender is required to provide this statement to you within three days of receiving the loan application. Make sure to ask what type of loan program your lender has selected for you, including the rates, terms and any special information, such as prepayment penalties.

4 Compare costs, fees and terms of loans if you are working with more than one lender.

5 Negotiate fees. Sometimes you can negotiate the amount of fees or loan points (a point is 1 percent of the loan amount) the lender charges you.

6 Consider lowering your interest rate by paying more points. The relationship of interest rate to points paid is an inverse one; the more points you pay, the lower the interest rate.

7 Provide required documentation.

8 Pay any up-front fees. Sometimes the lender requires that the appraisal, credit report or processing fee be paid at the beginning.

9 Review loan papers. Approximately one week prior to closing, loan papers will be ready for your review. Make sure the loan matches the original quote you were given.

10 Sign your loan papers and deposit your down payment funds into your account four to six days prior to closing.

11 Bring a cashier's check for the down payment to the title company, escrow company or attorney handling the closing. The lender will send the title company a check for the loan amount.

12 Get ready to congratulate yourself. Once the transaction closes and you have signed off on all contingencies, and received a copy of the deed and a set of keys, you own the home.

### ✳ Tips

If you are a first-time home buyer, you may qualify for a lower down payment or interest rate. Check with mortgage brokers, online mortgage companies, your county housing department or your employer to see what programs are available.

Too many inquiries can make it look as if the applicant is shopping for credit—which is a red flag for some lenders. When you do select a lender, you may have to explain in writing why there are other inquiries on your credit report.

### ⚠ Warning

Lenders may impose limits on how much of your down payment can come from borrowing. Remember that money received from a lender will show up on your credit report, and your payments will factor into your debt-to-income ratio.

## ✓ 195 Estimate Your Mortgage Payment

A home is the single largest purchase most of us are ever likely to make. This chart can help you get a handle on the daunting cost of a home by helping you estimate the monthly payment on a 30-year fixed-rate loan. The figures in the lefthand column are annual interest rates. The headings across the top are loan amounts, which are typically 80 or 90 percent of the purchase price. For example, if you're putting down 20 percent on a $250,000 home, look in the $200,000 column at your interest rate to find your monthly payment. (Be aware that these figures don't include other required payments, such as for private mortgage insurance, property taxes or homeowner's insurance.)

**Note:** For loan amounts not listed, look in the $100,000 column at your interest rate and multiply by the appropriate factor—for example, for a $189,000 loan, multiply the mortgage payment by 1.89.

| RATE | $50,000 | $100,000 | $150,000 | $200,000 | $250,000 | $300,000 |
|---|---|---|---|---|---|---|
| 6% | $299.78 | $599.55 | $899.33 | $1,199.10 | $1,498.88 | $1,798.65 |
| 6.25% | $307.86 | $615.72 | $923.58 | $1,231.43 | $1,539.29 | $1,847.15 |
| 6.50% | $316.03 | $632.07 | $948.10 | $1,264.14 | $1,580.17 | $1,896.20 |
| 6.75% | $324.30 | $648.60 | $972.90 | $1,297.20 | $1,621.50 | $1,945.79 |
| 7% | $332.65 | $665.30 | $997.95 | $1,330.60 | $1,663.26 | $1,995.91 |
| 7.25% | $341.09 | $602.18 | $1,023.26 | $1,364.35 | $1,705.44 | $2,046.53 |
| 7.50% | $349.61 | $699.21 | $1,048.82 | $1,398.43 | $1,748.04 | $2,097.64 |
| 7.75% | $358.21 | $716.41 | $1,074.62 | $1,432.82 | $1,791.03 | $2,149.24 |
| 8% | $366.88 | $733.76 | $1,100.65 | $1,467.53 | $1,834.41 | $2,201.29 |
| 8.25% | $375.63 | $751.27 | $1,126.90 | $1,502.53 | $1,878.17 | $2,253.80 |
| 8.50% | $384.46 | $768.91 | $1,153.37 | $1,537.83 | $1,922.28 | $2,306.74 |
| 8.75% | $393.35 | $786.70 | $1,180.05 | $1,573.40 | $1,966.75 | $2,360.10 |
| 9% | $402.31 | $804.62 | $1,206.93 | $1,609.25 | $2,011.56 | $2,413.87 |
| 9.25% | $411.34 | $822.68 | $1,234.01 | $1,645.35 | $2,056.69 | $2,468.03 |
| 9.50% | $420.43 | $840.85 | $1,261.28 | $1,681.71 | $2,102.14 | $2,522.56 |
| 9.75% | $429.58 | $859.15 | $1,288.73 | $1,718.31 | $2,147.89 | $2,577.46 |
| 10% | $438.79 | $877.57 | $1,316.36 | $1,755.14 | $2,193.93 | $2,632.71 |
| 10.25% | $448.05 | $896.10 | $1,344.15 | $1,792.20 | $2,240.25 | $2,688.30 |
| 10.50% | $457.37 | $914.74 | $1,372.11 | $1,829.48 | $2,286.85 | $2,744.22 |
| 10.75% | $466.74 | $933.48 | $1,400.22 | $1,866.96 | $2,333.70 | $2,800.44 |
| 11% | $476.16 | $952.32 | $1,428.49 | $1,904.65 | $2,380.81 | $2,856.97 |
| 11.25% | $485.63 | $971.26 | $1,456.89 | $1,942.52 | $2,428.15 | $2,913.78 |
| 11.50% | $495.15 | $990.29 | $1,485.44 | $1,980.58 | $2,475.73 | $2,970.87 |
| 11.75% | $504.70 | $1,009.41 | $1,514.11 | $2,018.82 | $2,523.52 | $3,028.23 |
| 12% | $514.31 | $1,028.61 | $1,542.92 | $2,057.23 | $2,571.53 | $3,085.84 |

chart

## 196 | Buy a Home With Poor Credit

Poor credit will make buying a home more difficult—but not impossible. Here are some options you can consider.

### ⊙ Steps

1 Ask the seller to carry the loan. If the seller still owes money on the home, you may be able to get a wraparound mortgage, which allows you to pay the monthly payment on the existing mortgage and an additional payment to cover the balance.

2 Pursue a lease-option. This will allow you to set the purchase price now, then apply a portion of the rent each month toward your down payment. At the end of the lease period, typically 12 to 36 months, prices should have increased and you will have accrued equity. Realize that if the option is not exercised, none of the monies that have been paid to the seller will be returned.

3 Increase the purchase price you are willing to pay to the seller, then ask the seller to credit that money back to you to be used for a down payment or for closing costs.

4 Borrow money from friends, relatives, a pension plan or a retirement plan to increase your down payment or help defray closing costs.

### ✳ Tips

Money borrowed for a down payment must be disclosed to a lender. If any of your down payment was a gift, provide proof.

Be prepared for a higher down payment and higher interest rate.

### ⚠ Warning

Make sure that doing a wraparound will not trigger a due-on-sale clause, which requires the loan to be paid off if the home is sold. Wraparound mortgages are not legal in all states.

## 197 | Close on the Sale of a Home You Are Buying

Closing on a home refers to the point when all the terms of the contract have been met and you are ready to sign the final loan papers that will transfer ownership of the property.

### ⊙ Steps

1 Review all loan documents. Compare them with the estimates you were given, and make sure you are getting the loan you agreed to. Do this 5 to 10 days before closing.

2 Get a final estimate from the title or escrow company of the money required to cover the remainder of the down payment and closing costs. Funds are usually required to be paid by cashier's check.

3 Make sure all inspections have been satisfactorily performed, all work completed, and clearances for completed work provided. Do this prior to signing any loan documents.

4 Do a walkthrough of the property prior to signing loan documents. Make sure all agreed-on work has been completed to your satisfaction.

5 Contact the phone, water, garbage, gas and electric companies and establish service in your name. You should do this at least 14 days prior to close of escrow.

6 Sign all documents.

7 Arrange to get keys once the transaction is recorded.

### ✳ Tips

In some states, an attorney handles the closing.

Be sure to read all the paperwork you will be signing, and follow up to make sure that these steps have been taken.

Once the home is in your name, have the locks changed and get new keys made.

### ⚠ Warning

Do not sign loan documents until all necessary work has been completed or an arrangement has been made to hold funds in escrow to cover that work.

## Obtain Homeowner's Insurance 198

Homeowner's insurance protects your home and your posses-
sions, and provides liability coverage as well. Most lenders will
not fund a loan without it.

### ⊙ Steps

1   Call at least three different companies for rates. They should be able to
    give you a quote based on the replacement value of your home.

2   Ask the companies about bundled plans, such as homeowner's and auto
    insurance together, since these plans often provide a price break on
    both kinds of coverage.

3   Ask agents about including a replacement-cost endorsement in the
    policy. This acts as an inflation-guard clause in the policy, making sure
    your coverage keeps up with the cost of replacement. Be sure to ask
    insurers how they define replacement cost; the most liberal plans cover
    everything regardless of replacement cost, while others set limits.

4   Ask about content coverage, particularly if you have antiques, col-
    lectibles or a home office. Some of these may have to be covered under
    a special coverage clause, but it's worth it.

5   Ask what the deductible is. The standard deductible on homeowner's
    insurance is $250. As a rule, don't go any lower than that because it
    dramatically increases the cost of the policy.

6   Ask what liability limits are. The standard amount is $100,000, but
    $300,000 is much more desirable and doesn't cost much more.

### ✱ Tips

If you're in an area that the government has designated as
"flood-prone," you may be able
to purchase flood insurance
through the National Flood
Insurance Program (NFIP).

Though your premiums will rise
slightly every year with a replacement-cost endorsement, it will
help keep your house fully covered based on the inflation rate.

For items not covered by a standard policy, such as artwork or
antiques, you should be able to
buy add-on coverage.

If you discover that your home
can't be insured through regular
companies, you may be able to
purchase coverage under the
Fair Access to Insurance
Requirements (FAIR) plan.

## Get Your Home Ready to Sell 199

If your home makes a good impression on buyers, your chances
of selling it faster and for more money are greater.

### ⊙ Steps

1   Obtain a pest inspection. Make the required repairs and keep a copy of
    the clearance handy to share with buyers.

2   Choose little fixes that make a big difference. Replace old caulk in the
    kitchens and bathrooms; retouch paint, and repaint if necessary; get car-
    pets cleaned; get rid of clutter; use brighter lightbulbs and open curtains
    to make rooms look bigger; get rid of pet odors.

3   Decide on which upgrades to make—such as replacing old, worn carpet;
    or replacing old sink faucets and light fixtures.

4   Make the entrance grand. First impressions are important.

5   Make sure your yard and landscaping are in top shape.

### ✱ Tips

If you have an inspection, get a
one-year home-repair warranty
that transfers to the new buyer.
This relieves buyers' worries that
something may go wrong with
the property.

Really clean out those closets.

### ⚠ Warning

Don't spend too much money on
changes that won't enhance your
bottom line.

## 200 | Sell a Home

If selling a home were easy, nobody would use an agent. But there are things you can do to make the process easier.

### ◎ Steps

1 Choose an agent to help you sell your home, or decide to put it on the market as "For Sale By Owner" (FSBO).

2 Set the price for your home. Talk to an agent or study the sale prices of comparable homes in your neighborhood (usually listed in local newspapers) to get an idea of what your home is worth. Visit open homes to get an idea of value, and contact a title company or real estate company to learn about final selling prices.

3 Get inspections completed and make necessary repairs to your home.

4 Prepare your home to be shown. Clean it thoroughly, get rid of clutter and tidy up the yard (see 199 "Get Your Home Ready to Sell").

5 Show your home at an open house and make it available to be shown also by appointment.

6 Ask a mortgage broker to provide free financial flyers for potential buyers.

7 Consider offers and evaluate contracts.

8 Accept an offer.

### ✱ Tips

Be prepared to answer these questions from buyers: How long has the property been on the market? Have there been any price reductions? Have there been any previous offers? How long have you owned the house? What improvements have you made?

Never tip your hand to a buyer or a buyer's agent and admit the lowest price you will accept.

## 201 | Retain a Real Estate Agent to Sell a Home

Unless you relish the challenges of selling a home on your own, you'll want a professional real estate agent to represent and protect your interests, and to help you complete the sale.

### ◎ Steps

1 Ask friends and neighbors about agents they know or who have sold homes to them. Search the classifieds and check real estate sites online.

2 Invite two or three agents who specialize in your area of town (their "farm area") to come to your home and give a listing presentation.

3 Prepare specific questions for the agents in advance, such as whether your home will be listed on the Multiple Listing Service (MLS), whether the agents are members of the National Association of Realtors (NAR), and whether their commission is negotiable.

4 Discuss the marketing programs each agent offers. Find out whether the agents do open houses, buy newspaper ads or send out mailings.

5 Ask each agent to estimate the value of your home.

6 Make a decision and select an agent to market your home. Make certain your agent and you understand each other's expectations.

7 Tell the agent how often you expect to be given updates.

8 Get everything in writing.

### ✱ Tips

When interviewing prospective agents, look for title designations such as CRS (certified residential specialist), GRI (graduate, Realtor Institute), CRP (certified relocation professional), CRB (certified real estate broker) and CRE (counselor of real estate).

Consider a real estate firm that charges a flat rate to sell your home, instead of a percentage of the selling price.

### ⚠ Warning

Beware of agents who suggest they can get an unreasonably high sales price. An agent might use a high listing price to get your business, and then seek a lower price later.

## Sell Your Home Without an Agent | 202

With a little savvy and a lot of tenacity, you can sell your home yourself—and save those commission costs.

### ⊙ Steps

1 Set a fair price for your home. Study the sale prices of comparable homes in your neighborhood. (You can get this information from a local real estate office, local newspaper or the county courthouse.)

2 Complete all required inspections and make repairs on your home.

3 Clean your house thoroughly and get rid of all clutter. Pay particular attention to the front of your home and the entryway.

4 Advertise in local newspapers and put a sign in your yard.

5 Contact a mortgage broker who can provide home-loan information to potential buyers at no charge.

6 Hold an open house on a weekend to maximize the number of people who will see your home.

7 Consider hiring a real estate attorney to go over contracts and help with the negotiations.

### ⚠ Warnings

Take the time to thoroughly understand contracts and discuss anything you don't fully understand with a lawyer. One wrong move on a contract can cost you dearly.

Find out what laws you must adhere to as a seller. Contact your state's or county's real estate division or the local Board of Realtors.

## Sell a Condo or Co-op Apartment | 203

Selling a condominium or cooperative apartment is different from selling a home. Here are some pointers to help you reach the right buyer, whether you use a real estate agent or not.

### ⊙ Steps

1 Make a list of all the amenities of your condo or apartment complex.

2 Consider location as a major factor. If you are near mass transit or working areas, use that as a selling feature.

3 Write ads highlighting the features of your property on 3-by-5 cards. Get permission to place these ads in nearby transit stations or office complexes. Use catchy selling phrases such as "Minutes From Transportation," "Walk to Work" and "Forget the Commute."

4 Advertise in the local newspaper. Get attention with eye-catching phrases such as "Forget the Yardwork," "Athletic Center With Pool," "Golfers' Paradise," "Everything You Ever Wanted" and "Enjoy Life."

5 Don't forget senior citizens. Many are tired of the hassles associated with single-family residences but aren't ready for a retirement home. Find local senior newspapers and gathering areas. Place your ads there.

6 Let your neighbors know you want to sell. Often they have friends or co-workers who are potential buyers.

### ✱ Tip

Remember that you are selling a lifestyle. People who buy this type of property don't want to spend time on yardwork and gardening. They may be the sporty, active type or perhaps older people who don't want the head–ache of a detached house.

## 204 | Determine What Kind of Faucet You Have

Tired of seeing your money go down the drain? First figure out what kind of faucet you have so you can get replacement parts.

### ⊙ Steps

1 Notice whether your faucet is operated by a single handle. This kind of faucet is called a washerless (seat-and-spring) faucet, and includes an internal ball assembly that houses the seats and springs. (Seats consist of two small rubber cups with holes in the bottom; the springs underneath keep them in constant contact with the water-supply valves inside the faucet body.)

2 Notice whether you have separate handles for hot and cold water. If so, you'll have to look at the inner workings of the leaky faucet to determine whether it is a compression type (also called a stem type) or a cartridge type. Shut off the water supply and remove the faucet handle; virtually all handles are fixed with a screw, which may be hidden under a decorative cap that can be pried off with a small screwdriver. Remove the screw, then lift or jiggle the handle off.

3 Identify your faucet as a compression or stem type if it has a shaft going down into the body of the faucet. It will have a rubber washer or grommet at the bottom or a series of rubber washers along the side of the stem. (These faucets are likely to be older, and a lot of the parts are likely to be metal.)

4 Recognize your faucet as a cartridge type if the interior workings are encased in a plastic body that is easily lifted out.

### ✽ Tip

The easiest way to replace parts is to open up the faucet and take the interior parts to a plumbing supply or hardware store. Have a salesperson help you find replacement parts.

### ⚠ Warning

When working with chrome or brass fixtures, protect the surfaces from tools with a piece of leather, heavy cloth or duct tape.

### Things You'll Need

☐ screwdriver

## 205 | Repair a Washerless (Seat-and-Spring) Faucet

Stopping leaks in those supposedly "leakproof" single-handled faucets is no big deal—these faucets only have about four moving parts.

### ⊙ Steps

1 Turn off the water at the water-supply valve. These are usually under the sink (or in the wall behind the shower assembly—often in a closet behind a removable panel). If there are no localized shutoffs, use the main water shutoff for the building.

2 Open the faucet to relieve water pressure in the lines.

3 With a wrench, loosen the base of the handle, which usually also serves as the cover for the ball assembly (this houses the springs and seats). The cover screws down onto the faucet. Turn counterclockwise (you may need to use pliers), then lift the ball assembly out of the faucet by the handle.

4 Note that the seats and springs consist of two small rubber cups with holes in the bottom and a spring underneath that keeps them in constant contact with the water-supply valves inside the faucet body.

### ✽ Tip

As you take the unit apart, lay out the parts on a clean surface in the order in which they were removed.

### ⚠ Warning

When working with chrome or brass fixtures, protect the surfaces from tools with a piece of leather, heavy cloth or duct tape.

5   Take the ball assembly to a hardware or plumbing supply store. (The seats and springs generally sit pretty tightly in the ball, but it's still a good idea to wrap the assembly in a rag to keep from losing parts.)

6   Ask a salesperson to help you match the proper replacement springs and rubber seats. It's also a good idea to note the faucet brand and model number; you can find it stamped on the faucet.

7   Back at home, remove the seats by popping them loose with a small screwdriver. The springs should come out with them; otherwise, you can remove them the same way. Insert the new spring into the hole and then place the rubber seat over it and press it into place.

8   Return the ball assembly to the body of the faucet and tighten the cover. Don't overtighten, as this can cause the seat to wear excessively.

9   Turn on the water supply and test the faucet for leaks.

### Things You'll Need

- ☐ wrench or pliers
- ☐ rag
- ☐ replacement springs and rubber seats
- ☐ screwdriver

# Repair a Compression or Stem-Type Faucet | 206

These simple steps will help dry up the problem of a leaky compression or stem-type faucet.

## ◉ Steps

1   Turn off the water at the water-supply valve. These are usually under the sink (or in the wall behind the shower assembly—often in a closet behind a removable panel). If there are no localized shutoffs, use the main water shutoff for the building.

2   Open the faucets to let water in the lines drain before beginning disassembly of the faucet.

3   Remove the faucet handle; virtually all handles are fixed with a screw, which may be hidden under a decorative cap that can be pried off with a small screwdriver. Remove the screw, then lift or jiggle the handle off.

4   Loosen the locknut inside with a crescent wrench. Once the nut is loosened and removed, pull out the stem. (With some types of faucets, the stem itself may be threaded into the body of the faucet assembly. It may be a left-handed thread—which means you'll have to turn it counterclockwise to loosen and remove it.)

5   Find the rubber washer at the stem's bottom. The washer may be held in place with a small screw; if so, remove the screw.

6   Replace with a new washer. Take the stem to your local hardware or plumbing supply store to pick out the proper-fitting replacement washer.

7   Reassemble the stem and faucet assembly in reverse order.

8   Turn the water supply back on and test for drips.

## ✳ Tips

If the faucet still leaks after you've replaced the washer, you may have to replace the valve seat, which requires a special wrench. The valve seat is located below the stem and can be accessed when the stem is removed.

If one washer needs to be replaced, replace them all now.

## ⚠ Warning

When working with chrome or brass fixtures, protect the surfaces from tools with a piece of leather, heavy cloth or duct tape.

### Things You'll Need

- ☐ screwdriver
- ☐ crescent wrench
- ☐ replacement washer

## 207 | Repair a Cartridge Faucet

Modern cartridge faucets feature an easily replaceable interior cartridge that houses the faucet's moving parts. Drips and leaks can often be stopped by simply replacing the cartridge.

### ⊙ Steps

1   Turn off the water at the water-supply valve. These are usually under the sink (or in the wall behind the shower assembly—often in a closet behind a removable panel). If there are no localized shutoffs, use the main water shutoff for the building.

2   Open the faucets to let water in the lines drain before beginning disassembly of the faucet.

3   Remove the handle from the faucet; virtually all handles are fixed with a screw, which may be hidden under a decorative cap that can be pried off with a small screwdriver. Remove the screw, then lift or jiggle the handle off. Set the handle aside after you've removed it.

4   Carefully pull the cartridge out of the fixture with pliers. (Some brands of faucets may have a lock ring or lock nut that holds the cartridge in place. This must be removed—use a screwdriver or pliers—before you can remove the cartridge itself.)

5   Take the cartridge to your local hardware or plumbing supply store and purchase a replacement.

6   Install the new cartridge and reassemble the faucet.

7   Turn the water back on and check for leaks.

### ⚠ Warning

When working with chrome or brass fixtures, protect the surfaces from tools with a piece of leather, heavy cloth or duct tape.

### Things You'll Need

- ☐ screwdriver
- ☐ pliers
- ☐ replacement water-valve cartridges

## 208 | Repair a Dripping Showerhead

A constantly dripping showerhead doesn't just waste water—it can drive you crazy.

### ⊙ Steps

1   Unscrew the showerhead from the pipe coming out of the wall. This can be done by hand but sometimes requires a crescent wrench or large pliers. The head may be held on with a screw, which you'll have to remove.

2   Look at the threads inside the showerhead where it screws into the pipe. There should be a small washer made of plastic or a rubber O-ring. Replace it if it looks even a little damaged or brittle.

3   Wrap the showerhead stem with Teflon tape or pipe sealer (pipe dope) to seal the connection.

4   Remount the showerhead on the stem. Don't overtighten. Hand-tightening should suffice.

5   Turn the water on and off. Wait several minutes and check for drips or leaks. If the showerhead is still leaking, you may have problems with the shower's water-control valve and need to call an expert.

### ⚠ Warning

When working with chrome or brass fixtures, protect the surfaces from tools with a piece of leather, heavy cloth or duct tape.

### Things You'll Need

- ☐ crescent wrench or large pliers
- ☐ screwdriver
- ☐ replacement washer or O-ring
- ☐ Teflon tape or pipe sealer

# Fix a Running Toilet

So your toilet goes through more water than Niagara Falls? Most likely the problem is the ball cock's diaphragm or the tank flap, so stop jiggling the handle and roll up your sleeves.

## ◉ Steps

### Identifying the Source

1 Remove the toilet-tank lid and place it out of the way on the floor.

2 Investigate the ball cock. It's a valve attached to the float (which is either a metal or plastic ball on the end of a long rod or a plastic canister that slides up and down a vertical plastic pipe). If you can see or hear water coming from this valve, it may need to be cleaned or replaced.

3 Reach down into the bottom of the tank and press down on the edges of the tank flap (a black or red rubber cone that fits into the tank's hole). If the sound of water running into the bowl stops, you know that the flap may be deformed or worn from age and needs to be replaced.

4 Get ready to work. Turn off the water supply for the toilet (this valve is most often found coming out of the floor or wall near the toilet; turn the handle in a clockwise direction). Flush the toilet to drain some of the water and make the work easier.

5 If you need to replace the diaphragm or tank flap, take it with you to a hardware store or plumbing supply house to make sure you buy the correct replacement.

### Cleaning or Replacing the Ball-Cock Diaphragm

1 Snap off the cover of the ball cock and put it out of the way.

2 Remove the four screws holding down the top plate of the ball cock, using a screwdriver. The float-control arm is attached to this and may be spring-loaded. You'll see a rubber diaphragm.

3 Remove the diaphragm carefully, noting which side is up, and check its condition. Sometimes a piece of gravel or rust or a hard-water deposit can get lodged under the diaphragm and cause a leak, or the diaphragm can become misshapen or worn through with age.

4 Replace the diaphragm or clean it by rinsing it in the tank's water; flush the valve itself by turning on the water supply for the toilet just enough to get a flow of water for a couple of seconds.

5 Replace the top plate and secure it with its screws.

6 Turn the water supply back on, allowing the tank to fill, and replace the lid.

### Replacing the Tank Flap

1 Remove the tank flap. Some have a clamp-type assembly, while others hook to short posts that stick out from the overflow pipe; all attachments are fairly easy to remove by hand.

2 Install a new tank flap.

3 Turn on the water supply and replace the lid.

## ✱ Tip

If these strategies don't solve the problem, you may need to hire a professional who can disassemble the toilet to find cracks or a worn connecting gasket.

## Things You'll Need

☐ screwdriver

☐ replacement diaphragm

☐ replacement tank flap

## 210 | Unclog a Toilet

A clogged toilet often can be cleared in a few simple steps. Give these a try before you call in the pros.

### ◎ Steps

1   Use the toilet as little as possible once you notice there's a problem. This will help prevent overflow and water damage.

2   Insert a plunger into the toilet, making sure the rubber globe or cup is fully seated over the drain opening.

3   Push down on the plunger handle with firm but careful strokes. Rough, careless use can damage the toilet bowl. If the clog isn't too tight, these bursts of increased water pressure will probably clear the obstruction.

4   Attack tougher problems with a snake (see 213 "Use a Plumber's Snake").

5   Consider a drain cleaner only as a last resort. Make sure that any product used is specifically marked as safe for use with porcelain, and follow the manufacturer's directions carefully. Never mix any of these chemical agents, as dangerous reactions could occur.

6   Flush the toilet several times to remove the drain cleaner and to check the flow.

### ✱ Tip

Buy the highest-quality plunger you can.

### Things You'll Need

☐ plunger

☐ plumber's snake (optional)

☐ drain cleaner (optional)

## 211 | Retrieve a Valuable Dropped Down the Sink

Don't panic! Dropping something of value down the drain isn't always the nightmare it seems. Try this method to get it back.

### ◎ Steps

1   Turn off the water immediately to prevent the possibility of the item's being washed out of reach.

2   Open the cabinet below the sink.

3   Find the P-trap, which is the U-shaped piece of pipe that connects the vertical pipe running from the sink to the horizontal pipe that goes into the wall.

4   Place a bucket under the trap.

5   Loosen the large threaded nuts that attach the trap to the other pipes. Sometimes you can do this with your hands; otherwise, you may need to use large Channellock pliers or even a plumber's pipe wrench.

6   Pull the trap off with a good yank, letting it fall into the bucket as necessary. The trap will be full of dirty water.

7   Put on gloves. Empty the trap into your hand—over the bucket—and look for your valuable.

8   Reassemble the P-trap, being careful not to overtighten the nuts.

### ✱ Tips

There may be another trap or filter in the main plumbing system, and if your valuable has gotten past the sink trap, it may still be in the main trap. Call a plumber.

If you're afraid of stripping or marring the nuts holding the plumbing together, place a thin rag or tape around the nuts before grabbing them with the plumber's wrench.

### Things You'll Need

☐ bucket

☐ Channellock pliers

☐ rubber gloves

## Unclog a Sink 212

If your sink is stopped up, try these simple steps before calling in a plumber.

### ⊙ Steps

1 Remove the sink strainer or plug from the drain.

2 Fill the sink halfway with water, if it's not already full.

3 Place the plunger over the drain, making sure that the plunger's rubber globe or cup is full of water. Plunge a half dozen or so times using careful but forceful strokes.

4 Remove the plunger and give the sink a chance to drain.

5 After the sink is completely unclogged, run hot water down the drain for several minutes.

6 Remove the P-trap or use a snake if the above steps yield no results (see 211 "Retrieve a Valuable Dropped Down the Sink" and 213 "Use a Plumber's Snake").

7 Consider a drain cleaner only as a last resort and follow the manufacturer's directions carefully. Do not mix chemical agents, as dangerous reactions could occur.

8 Call in a plumber for problems you can't resolve on your own.

### Things You'll Need

☐ plunger

☐ plumber's snake (optional)

☐ drain cleaner (optional)

## Use a Plumber's Snake 213

A plumber's snake can be a helpful tool to have around the house. Use it with the proper care and you can avoid some major plumbing bills.

### ⊙ Steps

1 Put on gloves with a nonslip grip. The snake—essentially a long cable—can get slippery and dirty.

2 Start with the smallest snake you can, graduating to a larger size if the first one doesn't work.

3 Insert the business end of the plumber's snake—the end opposite the handle—into the drain or toilet. Use care to avoid damaging sinks, toilets and pipes.

4 Turn the handle slowly in a clockwise direction, gently pushing the snake. Let it find its own way through—it may take quite a few revolutions of the handle.

5 Fill the sink or toilet bowl about halfway with water to help lubricate and provide some pressure to wash the clog out once it begins to break up.

6 Pull out the snake when the snake crank becomes hard to turn, clean its end, and reinsert it into the drain.

7 Repeat this process until the drain is clear.

### ⚠ Warning

Some snakes are motorized. If you're using a motor-driven snake, don't spin it too quickly, and be careful when retrieving it from the drain—it may whip around and strike you as it comes out of the pipe.

### Things You'll Need

☐ nonslip gloves

☐ plumber's snake

## 214 | Thaw a Frozen Pipe

Frozen pipes can be a huge inconvenience, and can cause water damage if they burst. Here are a few quick cures.

### ⊙ Steps

1  Open the faucet nearest the pipe, if possible. Do not force it.

2  Wrap the pipe in a towel and secure it with duct tape.

3  Pour boiling water over the towel. Repeat until the water has thawed and runs through the faucet.

4  Alternatively, wrap the pipe in a heating pad or place a heat lamp next to it. If you lack one of these, try a handheld hair dryer or a small electric heater.

### ⚠ Warning

Don't use any electrical appliances if there is standing water.

### Things You'll Need

☐ duct tape

☐ heating pad, heat lamp, hair dryer or small electric heater

---

## 215 | Repair Leaky Pipes Quickly

You can stop—or at least slow down—a leak to prevent water damage until a plumber can do the complete repair. These steps are for a temporary fix, not a long-term cure.

### ⊙ Steps

1  Tighten a threaded joint with a pipe wrench if the leak is there. If that doesn't stop the leak, it may at least slow the leak until the joint can be replaced. (Note: Some older plumbing may require brazing—a kind of welding. If the pipe has no threads, or you see signs of welding, leave this technique to the professionals.)

2  Plug a very small hole by sticking the tip of a sharp pencil in it. Break off the tip in the hole and cover the hole with duct tape, wrapping it in several layers.

3  Alternatively, apply epoxy putty specially formulated for leaks caused by cracks or small holes.

4  Fix larger holes by clamping a piece of hose around the pipe. With a knife, cut a length of hose at least 2 inches longer than the hole. (Rubber hose or even an old piece of garden hose will do.) You will also need three hose clamps. Slit the hose lengthwise and fit it around the pipe, then clamp the hose in place using a hose clamp at each end and one in the middle.

5  Discontinue use of the leaking plumbing or catch the spillage with a bucket until proper repairs can be made.

### ⚠ Warning

Use caution—old joints and pipe can be fragile. Rough treatment could worsen the problem.

### Things You'll Need

☐ pipe wrench

☐ pencil

☐ duct tape

☐ epoxy putty

☐ hose

☐ knife

☐ hose clamps

## Maintain Your Septic Tank 216

If you live apart from a municipal sewer system, "out of sight, out of mind" probably applies to your septic tank. But it's important to keep up with routine maintenance.

### ⊙ Steps

1 Hire a licensed and bonded septic-pumping contractor to test the tank annually, and have the sludge pumped out as often as necessary. If you neglect to do this, the sludge will build up, reducing the capacity of the tank and eventually causing sludge to leak into the drain field, which is a serious problem.

2 Have the septic-pumping contractor also perform a visual inspection for damage or potential problems. Workers pumping the tank should check the alarm, baffles, compressor, motor, timer and pump.

3 Avoid driving over your tank or drain field.

4 If you're putting in a swimming pool, keep it at least 15 feet away from the drain field.

5 Don't put chemicals such as paint thinner, insecticides or gasoline down the drains. These will kill the bacteria that break down waste products in the tank.

6 Refrain from sending nondegradable items, such as sanitary pads, plastic or rubber, down the drain.

7 Plant only grass and flowers above the tank and drain field—not trees, whose roots could interfere with the system.

### ✴ Tip

Contact a plumbing company to help you identify where the septic tank and drain field are if you don't know.

### ⚠ Warning

Call a plumber immediately if more than one toilet in your home backs up simultaneously. This could be an indication of a serious problem with your septic tank.

## Test Water Purity 217

The average person uses 72.5 gallons of water a day. But is that water safe? Water testing is expensive, so make sure you know what to test for and when to do it.

### ⊙ Steps

1 Request a Consumer Confidence Report (CCR) from your water district. Municipalities are now required to send these to homeowners yearly. This report will tell you about the water that is coming to your house.

2 Run some tap water into a clear glass and look closely at it in good lighting. Is it clear or discolored? Do you see sediment in the water? Smell the water; expect a faint smell of chlorine (like a swimming pool) if you are on a city water supply, but any other smell—particularly that of rotten eggs—indicates that your water should be tested.

3 Check drains, fixtures and porcelain items such as toilets and tubs for red, green, blue or brown staining.

4 Ask the local health department or Cooperative Extension Service (part of the U.S. Department of Agriculture) for the name of a reputable local water-quality testing facility. If you live in a municipality, your water will be of a consistent quality; you won't need to have it tested every year.

### ✴ Tips

Sometimes just-poured tap water is cloudy from air bubbles. This cloudiness should clear within a minute or two and isn't anything to be concerned about.

If you use well water, be aware of agricultural activity in your area, which affects the quality of your water. Test as you feel necessary after your first year on the property.

5   Alternatively, buy a home water test from a hardware store. While less accurate than a lab test, it's a less expensive alternative.

6   Be especially conscious of your water quality if you have a private water supply, such as a well. You alone are responsible for your water. Test well water for herbicides and insecticides when you first move in, and then at least twice that first year (early spring and late fall) for coliforms (bacteria) and nitrates, and once a year for lead, pH and total dissolved solids (TDS). If you do any work on your well, notice chemical use on or near your property, or see any of the above-mentioned indicators, have your water checked.

7   Have the water tested when you move into a new home so that you will have a baseline guide for future water testing. Check for coliforms, calcium, copper, iron, lead, magnesium, nitrates, pH, sodium, sulfate, zinc and TDS.

## 218 | Eliminate Hard Water

If your dishes have spots, your soap doesn't lather well and your white clothes look gray, you could have hard water—water with a high mineral-salt content. Here's what to do.

### ◉ Steps

1   Get a water test done to determine how hard your water is. Many water-softener retailers will do the test for free. Or call a water-conditioning specialist in your area. These people are familiar with the quality of the water in your area and can best recommend how to treat it.

2   Ask for and review the information from the softener performance data sheet. If the water is only moderately hard, consider buying a simple water softener (low cost). If there are additional minerals and iron, consider a higher-end softener (high cost).

3   Buy or rent a water conditioner. There are systems to fit every budget, from basic units that cycle regularly to on-demand units with computer controls. Some systems require a lot of attention; you may want to have a service company perform the required maintenance.

4   Check to see if you need a filtration system in addition to a water softener. Remember that a water softener only removes hardness from your water, not toxins.

### ⚠ Warning

People who are monitoring their sodium intake may want to consult a physician before installing an ion-exchange water softener, because it will add salt to your water.

### Things You'll Need

☐ water softener

☐ water conditioner

☐ filtration system

## 219 | Choose a Water-Filtration System

Filtration systems remove impurities from tap water. The most common use carbon or reverse-osmosis filtration. Look for certification by NSF International, which establishes the standards.

### ◉ Steps

1   Have your water tested so you know how much and what kind of filtration you need (see 217 "Test Water Purity").

### ✱ Tips

Install a sediment filter ahead of the carbon filter to remove solids that will clog the carbon.

2   Decide whether you want a faucet-mounted system, which is inexpensive and easy to install but requires frequent filter changes, or an in-line system, which mounts directly to your plumbing system. The latter is more costly but more comprehensive, and requires only occasional filter changes.

3   Look into an NSF-certified carbon filter for either system if your test comes back with chlorine, chloroform, pesticides or organic chemicals. Carbon filters are not effective against lead or other heavy metals, flouride, chloroform, or some microbial contaminants.

4   Think about getting an in-line reverse-osmosis filtering system if your water test shows sodium, ferrous iron, nitrates, lead, fluoride or organic contaminants. Be aware that a reverse-osmosis system puts out a limited amount of drinking water and wastes a lot of water (about 4 gallons of wasted water per gallon of clear water). If your water's calcium count is high, you'll need to use a water softener with this system (see 218 "Eliminate Hard Water").

5   Consider a system with a cutoff meter (also known as a performance indication device) that lets you know when it's time to change the filter.

Read product claims for removal and choose a system designed to treat your water conditions.

To obtain further information on water filtration, contact NSF International at www.nsf.org or call (800) NSF-MARK.

## ⚠ Warning

None of these filter types will solve hard-water problems.

---

# Replace a Light Switch                                220

You can replace a nonfunctional light switch in a few minutes. But as with any electrical repairs, be sure to make safety your first concern.

↖ ↖ ↖

## ◉ Steps

1   Turn off the power to the switch at the main circuit breaker or fuse box. Test by flipping the switch on to make sure the power is off. Tag the circuit box "Man at Work" or something similar so no one mistakenly turns the power back on while you're working.

2   With a screwdriver, remove the two screws holding the cover plate and take the plate off. (The cover plate is the piece of metal or plastic covering the switch.)

3   Remove the two mounting screws holding the switch in place inside the electrical box.

4   Pull the switch out of the wall. The switch should come out a few inches, exposing the wires.

5   Remove the screws holding the two wires coming out of the wall to the switch, making sure to tag which wire came from which screw (they are usually color coded) with colored pens and tape.

6   Take the switch to the hardware store and get another one exactly like it. Ask a salesperson for help if necessary.

7   Take the new switch home and hold it up to the wall, right side up, so that the word "off" appears when the switch is in the off position.

8   Attach the wires to the screws on the switch's back according to the tags you made earlier.

## ⚠ Warnings

Working with electrical systems is potentially dangerous. If you're unsure of your abilities or of any aspect of the project, call an electrician (see 256 "Hire an Electrician").

Whenever you turn the circuit breaker off or on, use only one hand and look away from the breaker to reduce the risk of injury should the breaker blow.

## Things You'll Need

☐ screwdriver

☐ replacement light switch

☐ colored pens and tape

9   Secure the new switch in the box with mounting screws.

10  Replace the switch cover.

11  Turn the main power back on and test your work.

---

## 221 | Replace a Lamp Cord

Replacing a lamp's electrical cord is often easier and safer than repairing it. Repaired cords are more likely to have loose connections or bad splices, which can cause fires or shocks.

### ◉ Steps

1   Unplug the lamp. Remove the lamp shade and unscrew the lightbulb from the socket.

2   Unscrew or snap the socket from the lamp, using a screwdriver if necessary, to gently pry the socket-shell base from the socket shell.

3   Unscrew the two wires from the socket's bottom.

4   Pull the wires off the screws, and then pull the cord out of the lamp from the bottom.

5   Push the new electrical cord into the lamp from the bottom up. Push slowly and evenly to avoid getting the wire stuck, particularly if the lamp is long.

6   Pull through a section of the new cord once it appears at the top of the lamp; it should be long enough to work with comfortably, a foot or two.

7   Separate the cord's two wires with a razor blade or utility knife, cutting 2 to 4 inches down the cord's center.

8   Strip about 1 inch of insulation from the separated wire ends with a wire stripper. (Do not cut toward yourself, and take care not to pinch the palm of your hand.) Make sure there are no other nicks or cuts elsewhere on the cord.

9   Twist the ends of each exposed wire clockwise so they don't fray, then curl each into a small hook.

10  Place one hook over each screw in the socket, wrapping the wire in a clockwise direction (this will help ensure a snug fit under the screw).

11  Make sure the wires won't come into contact with each other, then tighten the screws.

12  Reassemble the lamp by first screwing in the socket. Then replace the bulb and shade.

### ✳ Tip

When replacing a defective cord, also replace the plug (see 222 "Replace a Plug").

### ⚠ Warning

It is potentially dangerous to work with electrical systems. If you are unsure about your abilities or about any aspect of the project, call an electrician (see 256 "Hire an Electrician").

### Things You'll Need

- ☐ screwdriver
- ☐ replacement electrical cord
- ☐ razor blade or utility knife
- ☐ wire stripper

## Replace a Plug — 222

Instead of tossing out a lamp, appliance or extension cord with a damaged plug, follow these steps to replace the plug.

### ⊙ Steps

1. Decide whether you need a two-pronged plug (ungrounded) or a three-pronged plug (grounded). Replacement plugs can be purchased at hardware stores, lumberyards and home-improvement centers. If you have doubts about the exact plug you need, cut the old one off and take it and a short portion of the cord with you.

2. Select a heavy-duty plug; it may cost a little extra, but the plug will last much longer.

3. Open up the outside cover of the replacement plug. (Most have a screw or two that hold them closed, or feature a snap-lock system that can be pried open with a thin-bladed screwdriver.)

4. Cut off the old plug, if you haven't done so already. With a wire stripper, strip each wire in the cord to which you're attaching the new plug with a wire stripper. About $1/2$ to $3/4$ inch of bare wire is all that's needed.

5. Attach one wire under the screws at the end of each plug prong. If it's a two-pronged plug, it doesn't matter which wire is hooked to which prong. The cord will work either way. If it's a three-wire grounded plug, you'll need to be sure that the ground wire (with green insulation) is attached to the ground prong, which is the round prong. The other two can be attached either way.

6. Put the cover back on and snap or screw it into place. Your cord is ready to be plugged in.

### ⚠ Warning

Make sure that no bare wires are touching anything other than the attachment they're supposed to be touching.

### Things You'll Need

- ☐ replacement plug
- ☐ screwdriver
- ☐ wire stripper

---

## Replace an Electrical Outlet — 223

You can fix a faulty electrical outlet with a minimum of worry and cost. Just make sure you put safety first.

### ⊙ Steps

1. Turn off the power to the outlet at the fuse box or circuit breakers. Tag the circuit breaker box "Man at Work" or something similar so no one mistakenly turns the power back on while you're working.

2. Test the outlet with a circuit tester or an electrical appliance to make sure the power is off. Place the tester's probes inside the plug. If the tester's light goes on, recheck the main power and retest until there's no power in the outlet.

3. Unscrew the cover plate and remove it.

4. Unscrew the outlet and pull it out of the wall. It should come out a few inches. Set the screws aside.

5. Using colored pens or tape, mark where each wire was attached to the outlet. The wires and screws will be different colors; note the places where they attach.

### ✱ Tip

Don't overtighten the cover plate, or you may cause it to crack.

### ⚠ Warnings

Working with electrical systems is potentially dangerous. If you're unsure of your abilities or about any aspect of the project, call an electrician (see 256 "Hire an Electrician")

Whenever you turn the circuit breaker off or on, use only one hand and look away from the breaker to reduce the risk of injury should the breaker blow.

6    Loosen the screws holding the wires and remove the outlet.

7    Take the old outlet with you to a hardware or electrical-supply store. A salesperson can help you find the correct outlet to replace the old one. Keep the old outlet as a guide to installing the new one.

8    Using the marks on the old outlet as guides, attach the wires to the new outlet. Wrap the wires around the terminals with needle-nose pliers or your fingers.

9    Tighten the screws around the wires.

10   Screw the outlet back into the wall.

11   Screw the cover plate back on.

12   Reactivate the proper circuits at the fuse box and test your work.

### Things You'll Need

- ❑ circuit tester
- ❑ screwdriver
- ❑ colored pens and tape
- ❑ replacement electrical outlet
- ❑ needle-nose pliers

---

## 224   Lubricate Door Hinges

**If your door gives you a squeaky greeting each time you open or close it, apply a bit of oil to the hinge.**

### ◎ Steps

1    Buy some penetrating oil. It will come in either a small can with a thin spout, or a spray can with a thin plastic tube that attaches to the nozzle for very accurate spraying.

2    Have a rag or paper towel handy to wipe off excess oil.

3    Apply oil to the round pin located between the flat plates of a hinge. (When the door is open, the pin is halfway between the door itself and the jamb. The pin holds the plates together.) It's best to open the door and pull the pin halfway out of the hinge. Apply the oil into the exposed hole and onto the pin itself.

4    Open and close the door until the hinge stops squeaking. Apply small amounts of oil at first, increasing the amount if squeaking persists.

5    Push the hinge pin back into its original position.

6    Wipe away any excess or dripped oil with your rag or paper towel.

### ✲ Tip
Rusty hinges should be replaced.

### Things You'll Need

- ❑ penetrating oil
- ❑ rag or paper towel

---

## 225   Maintain Windows

**Maintaining the windows in your home is relatively painless and can save you money on heating, cooling and repair work later on.**

### ◎ Steps

### Maintaining Wood-Frame Windows

1    Start with a visual inspection of the windowpanes and the glazing (the putty that holds the glass in place). Cracked panes and missing glaze allow drafts, which raise heating and cooling bills. Replace broken panes or repair the glazing (see 226 "Replace a Broken Windowpane").

### ✲ Tip
You can now purchase window-glazing caulk in a tube that fits a caulking gun. It comes with a tip that properly forms the bead of glaze as you work.

2 Look over the paint. If it is badly chipped, spiderwebbed with cracks or chalky to the touch, you will need to paint the exterior woodwork. A poor paint job allows moisture to penetrate the wood, causing rot and swelling—which causes more paint damage.

3 Inspect where the window casing meets the wall. Use a high-quality paintable latex caulk to fill any gaps or cracks between the window frame and the siding or brick.

4 Make sure that the windows seal tightly when closed. If they are loose, you may need to add weather stripping around the window channels.

## Maintaining Metal- or Vinyl-Frame Windows

1 Start with a visual inspection of the window and frames. Rubber seals hold the glass in place. If the seals deteriorate over time, you'll have an air or water leak. The window sash will have to be removed from the unit and taken to a glass-repair shop to have the rubber replaced. You may need to call a professional to remove the window.

2 Check for cracked or broken glass, which should also be replaced by professionals at a glass shop.

3 Look for moisture between panes of glass if you have double- or triple-pane windows. Moisture indicates that the seal between the panes has failed. The space between the panes is usually filled with gas to help provide insulation; if the seal is broken, the insulation value of the window goes down.

4 Check around the window casing where it meets the wall; fill any gaps with a paintable latex caulk.

5 Make sure that any weather stripping is in good condition. (You can usually find it seated in a groove in the window frame; it's easy to replace.) Remove a short section of it from the window to take with you to the repair shop to find the right replacement. Remember to take measurements so that you get enough to do all the repairs needed.

## Maintaining Add-on Storm Windows

1 Check aluminum-frame, add-on storm windows for cracked or broken glass. Rubber seals hold these windows in place and most often will require specialized equipment to reinstall properly. Remove the pane of glass (with its individual frame) from the window unit and take it to a repair shop.

2 Look for broken frame corners on the individual panes. Take any windows with this problem to a repair shop.

3 Make sure that any weather stripping is in good condition. (You can usually find it seated in a groove in the window frame, and it can be easily replaced.) Remove a short section of it from the window to take with you to the repair shop to find the right replacement. Remember to take measurements so that you can get enough to do all the repairs needed.

4 Make certain that the unit's frame is well-seated and sealed with a bead of caulk against the window casing. (Don't seal the factory-provided weep holes near the bottom of the window frame—these allow drainage of any moisture that accumulates inside the framework.)

## ⚠ Warnings

When working with broken glass, wear leather gloves and eye protection.

If your house is two or more stories tall, work carefully on ladders.

## Things You'll Need

☐ latex caulk and caulking gun

☐ weather stripping

## 226 | Replace a Broken Windowpane

Do you have windows that are letting in more air than they should? With a little patience and care you can repair a broken windowpane—it's easier than you might think.

### ⊙ Steps

1 Remove the old glass carefully, wearing gloves and safety goggles. If the pane isn't broken, carefully chip out old glazing (putty used to seal each pane of glass to the frame) and glazing points (small metal anchors used to hold the glass in place until it's glazed) with a small chisel until you can remove the glass. Soften the glazing with a heat gun or even a blow dryer on a high heat setting to help ease this process.

2 Measure the opening, then subtract $1/8$ to $3/16$ inch from the vertical and horizontal measurements. You don't want the glass to be jammed tightly in the opening.

3 Purchase new glass with the appropriate dimensions. Any glass shop and many hardware stores and lumberyards can cut the glass to the size you need.

4 Set your new glass in place, and use at least two glazing points on each side (more if the opening is larger than 12 inches square). Don't press too hard against the glass, or you may break it.

5 Work the glazing against the glass and the window frame. Smooth it down with a putty knife or a glazing knife, which looks like a putty knife with a bent end.

6 Let the window set for 24 hours before opening it.

7 Paint the glazing to protect it, following the directions the glazing came with. Some manufacturers suggest waiting for several days or even longer before painting.

### ✱ Tip

Large windowpanes, or broken or cracked windowpanes in metal or vinyl frames, should be left to the pros.

### ⚠ Warning

Be careful with broken glass, and dispose of it properly.

### Things You'll Need

- ☐ gloves
- ☐ safety goggles
- ☐ small chisel
- ☐ heat gun or blow dryer
- ☐ replacement glass
- ☐ glazing points
- ☐ window glazing
- ☐ putty knife or glazing knife
- ☐ paint

## 227 | Use a Caulking Gun

Caulking is the easiest way to seal against air and water. Use caulk to fill cracks between wood trim and your walls, inside the house and outside.

### ⊙ Steps

1 Clean the area to be caulked, removing dirt, loose paint and old caulk. Be sure the area is dry before you begin.

2 Load a tube of caulk into a caulking gun, making sure it's well seated at both ends.

3 Use a utility knife to cut the tip of the spout. Cut off as little as possible, taking into consideration the size of the "bead" of caulk you need. Some people like to cut the spout at an angle, while others cut it straight; it doesn't make a big difference.

4 If using caulk that comes in a cardboard tube, look for a second seal at the base of the spout. Insert a nail or awl through the spout to puncture

### ✱ Tips

Many types of caulk are available, including silicone, acrylic and latex. Silicone caulk is probably the longest-lasting, but does not take paint well.

Keep a bowl of water at hand. Dip your finger in the water before running it down the bead of caulk.

the seal. Many caulking guns come with such a puncturing device. (Plastic tubes usually don't have a second, inner seal.)

5  Hold the gun at a slight angle. If you're filling a crack, insert the spout if you can; otherwise, run it at the surface.

6  Pull away from the bead slightly as you squeeze out the caulk, rather than push into it, which can be very messy.

7  Use just enough caulk to do the job. (Experiment in an out-of-the-way area. You may find that you'll need less of a bead than you think.)

8  Use your finger to gently press the caulk into the corner or crack.

9  Use a damp towel or rag to clean off most of the excess caulk, then use a dry one to clean off the rest.

## Things You'll Need

- [ ] caulk and caulking gun
- [ ] utility knife
- [ ] nail or awl
- [ ] towels or rags

---

# Regrout and Reseal Ceramic Tile                    228

Is the grout on your tile floor, countertop or backsplash badly stained, cracked or missing altogether? You can have it looking like new in no time.

## ◎ Steps

1  Buy a grout to match the existing grout color along with grout sealer. You'll find the best selection of colors at home centers, lumberyards or tile-supply stores. Some come premixed, but with most you just follow the manufacturer's mixing instructions. Choose a mildew-resistant grout.

2  Pry out old grout with a utility knife. Work carefully to avoid chipping or dislodging tiles, and wear safety goggles; grout can pop loose.

3  Vacuum or brush dust and dirt from grout lines (also known as joints). The grout lines can be dressed up even more with a cleaner if need be.

4  Mix your grout according to the manufacturer's instructions and work it into joints with a grout float, or if you are only repairing a small area, use your finger.

5  Wipe excess grout from the joint with a damp sponge, smoothing the grout to match existing joints.

6  Clean any grout from the tops of the tiles with the sponge.

7  Rinse your sponge often to speed the cleaning process.

8  Allow the grout to dry (this usually takes several hours at least, but overnight may be best). Follow the manufacturer's instructions.

9  Brush grout sealer onto the new dry grout. Sealing grout prevents it from absorbing water.

## ✱ Tip

If grout lines have cracked in wet areas, water may have seeped through to the drywall or to the substrate below.

## Things You'll Need

- [ ] grout
- [ ] grout sealer
- [ ] utility knife
- [ ] vacuum cleaner or dust brush
- [ ] grout float
- [ ] sponge
- [ ] brush

**229 Do Preventive Home Maintenance**

The best way to reduce home-repair costs and headaches is to perform preventive tasks on a regular basis. If you inspect your home regularly and keep everything in working condition, you'll cut down on repairs and nip emerging problems in the bud. Use this schedule to stay on top of home maintenance.

### Once a month

- Clear leaves and other debris from the walkway in front of your home.
- Scrub off any algae or moss from the walkway.
- Test the batteries in your smoke and carbon monoxide detectors.
- Pour ¼ c. baking soda down all the drains, then pour in 1 c. of vinegar. Let it stand overnight, then flush with hot water.
- Clean or change furnace filters if you have pets.
- Check fire extinguishers to see that they are still fully charged.
- If you have a steam boiler, check valves and inspect for rust; if they're rusty, replace the boiler.

### Every three months

- Check for cracks in any masonry or stucco on the outside of your home. Seal cracks immediately.
- Check washing machine and dishwasher areas for leaks.
- Clean or change furnace filters.
- Clean the filter in the stove hood.
- Make sure attic louvers are open to allow air to escape.
- Drain an electric water heater.

### Every six months

- Scrub off any mildew on the exterior of your home.
- Check for water and air leaks in the attic, basement and garage.
- Check the caulking in tubs, showers and sinks, and replace it if necessary.
- Check for wood decay.
- Check that the TV antenna is secure.
- Look for any signs of termites.
- Nail down any loose shingles or siding.
- Touch up the paint on the exterior of the house.

### Once a year

- Hire someone to inspect your chimney and clean it if necessary.
- Clean out gutters and downspouts; clear any debris from the roof.
- Inspect the roof for damage.
- Check the seals on windows and doors, and weather-strip if needed.
- Have someone service your heating and cooling systems.
- Replace batteries in smoke and carbon monoxide detectors.
- Inspect flooring for wear; refinish or replace if needed.

**calendar**

## Choose the Right Adhesive for a Job 230

Sticky, tacky, gooey. What is the best way to fasten this thing?

### ⊙ Steps

1 Consider the work surface. Is it porous or smooth? Wood, drywall, paper and cloth are porous; glass, metal, ceramic and plastic are not. Cyanoacrylate (superglue) and white glue adhere to smooth, nonporous surfaces; hot glue and carpenter's (wood) glue are better for porous surfaces. Contact cement is suitable for both porous and nonporous work surfaces.

2 Decide how quickly you want the adhesive to dry. Superglue bonds instantly, hot glue is quick, water-based contact cement sticks immediately and is dry within 30 minutes, white and carpenter's (wood) glues take a few hours, and silicone sealant requires about 24 hours to cure. Epoxies (heat-solidifying resins) vary.

3 Determine whether the adhesive needs to be water and/or heat resistant. Two-part epoxy, superglue, water-based contact cement and silicone sealant are resistant to both. Hot glue doesn't hold up well under extreme heat, but is waterproof. Carpenter's glue holds up under moisture and heat, whereas white glue doesn't fare well when exposed to either.

4 Think about cleanup. Silicone sealant, superglue and two-part epoxy are cleaned up with acetone—which is flammable and toxic. Water-based contact cement, new water-based silicone sealers, carpenter's glues and white glues clean up with water.

5 Read the labels. Make sure that the brand you choose is compatible with your purpose.

### ✳ Tip

Latex-based products are non-flammable and far less toxic than solvent-based ones.

### ⚠ Warning

Always read all warning labels, and glue in well-ventilated areas.

## Patch a Vinyl Floor 231

You can repair or replace vinyl sheet flooring and vinyl tiles with excellent results if you know the proper technique.

### ⊙ Steps

1 Measure the damaged area.

2 Find a lumberyard, home-improvement center or floor-covering supply house that carries the pattern of vinyl flooring you need. Purchase enough sheeting or tile squares to repair the damaged area. (Always keep any scraps for future repairs.)

3 Use a sharp utility knife to cut a piece of new vinyl flooring that is larger than the damaged area if you're repairing sheet vinyl flooring. Use a straightedge to keep the blade vertical. Replace whole squares if you're using 12-by-12-inch square tiles.

4 Line up the pattern of the new piece with the pattern along the edges of the damaged area.

5 Tape the replacement piece of vinyl over the damaged area with masking tape. (Make sure the new piece is secure and will not slip when cutting.)

### ✳ Tip

The cleaner the floor under the patch, the smoother the finished job will be. Any raised areas will wear faster than the rest of the floor.

### ⚠ Warnings

Some adhesives can have potentially harmful vapor—provide proper ventilation in your work area.

Always make sure to cut away from your body when cutting vinyl flooring.

6   Use a sharp utility knife to cut through both layers of vinyl. Cut an area just larger than the damaged spot. (This way the hole and replacement piece will be the same size.)

7   Remove both pieces of vinyl. Heat the old vinyl with a blow dryer to soften the adhesive before prying it up.

8   Clean debris and old adhesive from the floor with a putty knife. You can soften the old adhesive with a heat gun or blow dryer. Use a broom or vacuum cleaner for final cleaning.

9   Apply adhesive to the floor with a notched trowel or putty knife.

10  Press the new patch firmly in place starting at the center and working toward the edges to get all the air bubbles out from under the patch.

11  Wipe excess glue from the edges with a damp sponge.

12  Roll the patch firmly with a rolling pin or hand roller. Wipe the edges one more time to remove any excess glue.

13  Let the adhesive dry well before allowing heavy traffic back in the repaired area.

## Things You'll Need

- ☐ measuring tape
- ☐ replacement vinyl flooring
- ☐ utility knife
- ☐ masking tape
- ☐ putty knife
- ☐ heat gun or blow dryer (optional)
- ☐ adhesive
- ☐ notched trowel (optional)
- ☐ sponge
- ☐ rolling pin or hand roller

---

## 232 | Replace Asphalt Shingles

You may not need a new roof, but replacing a few bad or missing shingles to avoid water damage can save you money later on.

### ◉ Steps

1   Make sure the roof is dry before you climb on to it and that any ladder you use is sturdy and well-secured.

2   Check your roof at least twice a year and after bad storms, and look for loose, damaged or missing shingles.

3   Count the damaged pieces so that a salesperson can help you purchase the right number for the job.

4   Take one of the damaged shingles with you to a lumberyard or home-improvement center to match color and style.

5   Climb up to the rooftop.

6   Bend back the shingles above the damaged shingle. Use a gentle motion to avoid damaging nearby good shingles.

7   Remove nails and any remaining pieces of damaged shingle with the claw head of a hammer or a flat nail bar.

8   Use a sharp utility knife to cut the new shingle to match the size of the old one if necessary.

9   Slide the new shingle into place and nail it.

10  Glue down the raised shingles with roofing cement. This can be applied either from a tube with a caulking gun or from a can with a paint-stirring stick or old putty knife.

11  Make sure to remove any debris from the roof and gutters.

### ✱ Tip
This job is easier if the weather is warm: The shingles are much more pliable and less likely to get damaged. The new shingles will seal down more quickly as well.

### ⚠ Warning
If the roof is steep or you have a fear of heights, call in professionals. They have equipment and experience to handle tough jobs.

### Things You'll Need
- ☐ ladder
- ☐ hammer
- ☐ nail bar
- ☐ shingles
- ☐ utility knife
- ☐ nails
- ☐ roofing cement
- ☐ caulking gun, stick or putty knife

**How to Do (Just About) Everything**

## Clean Gutters 233

**Water trapped in gutters can cause major damage to your roof and walls. Maintaining clean gutters helps keep your home in good shape.**

### Steps

1. Gain access to the roof with a ladder. Don't lean the ladder against a downspout or gutter, which can easily bend or break.
2. Remove leaves and twigs from gutters by hand or with a large spoon, a gutter scoop or a small garden trowel.
3. Wet down caked-on dirt, which can be difficult to remove without damaging the gutter itself, then remove it with the gutter scoop or trowel.
4. Put debris in a bucket or plastic trash bag placed on the roof or ladder. If you use a bag, you can just drop it when it's full.
5. Check that the downspouts aren't clogged. Use water to unclog your downspouts by placing a garden hose in the opening. But be gentle at first; downspouts aren't designed to withstand the same pressure as a house drain. If a plugged downspout can't be cleared with a hose, use a small plumber's snake or an unbent clothes hanger. Again, be gentle. Gutters are not as strong as house pipes.
6. Alternatively, use a leaf blower to clean the gutters; however, remember that you'll be high up, often in awkward postures, and carrying a good-sized machine that not only is awkward to use but also can blind you with dust.
7. Use the hose to flush the gutters with water after cleaning. (This is also the best time to find out if there are any leaks in the system.)

### Tip

Consider covering your gutters with wire or plastic mesh. This will drastically cut down on debris.

### Warnings

Never hold on to the gutter or downspout for support. They're not meant to support your weight.

Make sure the ladder is sturdy and well-secured.

### Things You'll Need

- ❑ ladder
- ❑ large spoon, gutter scoop or small garden trowel
- ❑ bucket or trash bag
- ❑ garden hose
- ❑ leaf blower (optional)

## Repair a Leaky Gutter 234

**You can fix minor gutter leaks with roofing cement. Leaks in the downspout, often caused by leaky joints, require resealing.**

### Steps

#### Repairing Leaks in Gutter Railings

1. Clean the leaking area with a wire brush and water.
2. Dry the area and rub with coarse sandpaper.
3. Cover the hole with plastic roofing cement. Spread the cement at least 2 to 3 inches around the hole.
4. Cover with a piece of flashing (sheet metal) if you're dealing with a large hole; press the flashing into the cement and feather the edges of the cement to hold the flashing in place.

#### Repairing Leaks in Downspouts

1. Remove the leaking portion of the downspout.

### Things You'll Need

- ❑ wire brush
- ❑ coarse sandpaper
- ❑ plastic roofing cement
- ❑ flashing
- ❑ rubber gaskets
- ❑ silicone caulk
- ❑ gutter fasteners or connectors

2    Clean old caulk or adhesive from the joint with a wire brush.

3    Replace rubber gaskets if you're dealing with vinyl or PVC gutters.

4    Apply a bead of silicone caulk on one joint and then put the gutter back together.

5    Reattach the gutter with new fasteners or connectors if needed.

---

## 235 | Repair Wallpaper

Torn or damaged wallpaper can be repaired if you have extra wallpaper that matches the pattern. Here's how to make and apply a patch.

### ⊙ Steps

1    With a utility knife, cut a piece of wallpaper a few inches larger than the damaged section.

2    Place it over the damaged section and hold it in place with blue "safety" masking tape, being sure to match the pattern.

3    Use a sharp razor blade to trace the area to be removed, cutting right through both pieces of wallpaper at the same time. Try to make your cuts follow the pattern as best you can. (If possible, align your repairs along a seam.)

4    Carefully remove the top piece of paper and set it aside.

5    Use the razor to lightly score the wallpaper to be removed and apply water to loosen the adhesive (see 262 "Remove Wallpaper").

6    Use a putty knife to remove what you can't lift off with your fingers.

7    Clean or sand the area underneath the paper until it's smooth; use spackling compound to fill any dents. Apply primer (sizing) if you're down to a raw surface on the wall.

8    Apply wall-covering adhesive to the new wallpaper and place it on the wall.

9    Wipe away any adhesive on the surface with a damp sponge, then use a seam roller (see 263 "Hang Wallpaper") to press down the edges of the patch. Wipe the paper clean again.

### ✱ Tip

Repair a small tear by brushing on some wallpaper adhesive (or even white glue) and pressing the wallpaper back down. Repair a wrinkle or blister by slitting it with a razor and treating it as you would a tear.

### Things You'll Need

- ☐ utility knife
- ☐ replacement wallpaper
- ☐ blue "safety" masking tape
- ☐ sharp razor blade
- ☐ putty knife
- ☐ sandpaper
- ☐ spackling compound or primer
- ☐ wall-covering adhesive
- ☐ sponge
- ☐ seam roller

---

## 236 | Patch a Hole in Drywall

Oops, you knocked a hole in the wall. Don't worry, it's not hard to fix. Small holes (such as nail holes) can be filled with white tooth-paste or spackling paste. For something a bit larger, read on.

### ⊙ Steps

#### Patching Smaller Holes

1    Strip away any raised portions of the drywall paper around the edge of the hole.

### Things You'll Need

- ☐ sandpaper
- ☐ self-adhesive plastic mesh tape
- ☐ putty knife

2 Sandpaper all around the edges of the hole enough to scrape and roughen the paint.

3 For holes roughly 1 to 3 inches wide, apply self-adhesive plastic mesh tape. (Skip this step for smaller holes.)

4 Use a putty knife to apply spackling compound or a hard-setting, fast-drying patching compound. Smooth it out.

5 Repeat step 4 after the spackling shrinks, if necessary.

6 Allow the spackling to dry. Sand the area smooth, prime it and paint.

## Patching Larger Holes

1 Find the stud that is closest to the hole and use a drywall knife or saw to cut out a rectangle of drywall around the hole, including half of the width of the stud.

2 Roughen up the paint several inches all around the cut with sandpaper.

3 Cut a new piece of drywall the same size as the one you removed. Use the cutout as a patch.

4 Attach your new drywall patch to the stud using drywall screws or drywall nails, being careful to set the heads just below the surface, but not too deep—you don't want to break the paper.

5 Using a wide putty knife, apply a thin spread of joint compound along the seams. Gently press paper joint tape into the joint compound with your putty knife. Be sure that the edges of the tape are embedded in the compound, but scrape any excess compound from the tape.

6 After the joint compound Is dry, spread two or three additional thin coats of compound over the tape, extending 4 to 8 inches on each side of the seam to blend in with the surrounding wall. Sand lightly between coats.

7 Paint primer over the new patch. If the seams are still visible after it dries, apply more joint compound before final painting.

☐ spackling compound or patching compound

☐ drywall knife or saw

☐ drywall screws or nails

☐ joint compound

☐ paper joint tape

☐ primer

☐ paint

# Prepare a Room for Painting          **237**

It's all in the preparation. Take the time (probably more time than the actual painting will take) and you'll get the best result possible.

## ⦿ Steps

1 Remove what furniture you can; move what's left into the center of the room and cover with drop cloths. Use removable (usually blue) "safety" masking tape around moldings, doors and windows, and drop cloths to protect floors and furnishings.

2 Cover the smoke detector with a plastic bag and turn off air conditioning or heating while sanding or painting.

3 Sand or scrape loose and flaky paint with sandpaper and paint scrapers—down to bare surfaces if necessary.

⚠ **Warning**

Determine whether your home was built before 1980. If it was, it may contain lead paint, which is especially toxic to children and pregnant women. If you're going to sand, scrape or otherwise expose this paint, contact the National Safety Council's Lead Information Center at (800) LEADFYI for information on how to do so safely.

4   Using a putty knife, fill all nail and screw holes with spackling compound; fill cracks with caulk.

5   For more serious repairs, use drywall-taping techniques (see 236 "Patch a Hole in Drywall"). On woodwork, use epoxy filler (like that used on car bodies). Whatever you use, sand it down until it matches the area around it.

6   Wash all surfaces with TSP (trisodium phosphate) to remove grease and dirt. Use paint deglosser on glossy surfaces such as trim.

7   Rinse everything well with water to remove the TSP. Allow surfaces to dry thoroughly, and then dust and vacuum as needed.

8   Turn off the power to the room, then remove the cover plates from all electrical fixtures, outlets and switches. Place small bits of masking tape over switch handles and outlets to protect them from paint. It's safest to leave the power off as you paint the room—if you decide to turn the power back on, work carefully around electrical areas.

9   Loosen or remove cover plates from light fixtures; cover what remains with plastic bags. Remember not to turn on the lights—melting plastic really stinks. Paint during the day to get maximum lighting in the room, or use an extension cord to bring in a light source from another room.

10  Remove heating and air-conditioning vent covers.

## Things You'll Need

- ☐ drop cloths
- ☐ blue "safety" masking tape
- ☐ plastic bags
- ☐ sandpaper
- ☐ paint scraper
- ☐ spackling compound
- ☐ putty knife
- ☐ caulk and caulking gun
- ☐ epoxy filler
- ☐ TSP and paint deglosser

## 238 | Paint a Room

To paint a room, start with the ceiling and then paint the walls. Finish with the trim.

### ⊙ Steps

1   Prepare the walls and ceiling (see 237 "Prepare a Room for Painting"). Use a stain-blocking primer to cover any dark mark you can't remove (stains, knots, ink, dark paint); otherwise, that area will bleed through. Never paint on wallpaper (see 262 "Remove Wallpaper").

2   Make sure there is adequate ventilation in the room.

3   Plan on three coats: one coat of primer and two coats of finish. Always use primer on patched and unpainted surfaces; raw surfaces suck up paint like a sponge—or reject it.

4   Paint into all the corners with a 2-inch or 3-inch brush. Use the same brush to outline where the ceiling meets the wall (and vice versa), around doors and windows, above the baseboard and around any other trim or detailing—and wherever a roller won't fit.

5   Pour some paint into the roller pan and roll away on the ceiling and then the walls. Pour only a small amount of paint in your roller pan—this will keep the paint from drying out before you can use it. Try to start rolling before the brushed-on paint has had time to dry, so that the rolled-on paint will blend in rather than become a second coat. Rolling out a W, about 3 feet wide, and then filling it in, assures an even application of paint. Get as close into the corners as you can without making a messy paint line.

### ✱ Tip

If you have mildew, consider adding a specially designed primer or an additive to your paint.

### ⚠ Warning

If you use anything other than water-based latex paint, never put paint-soaked or cleaner-soaked tools or rags in an enclosed area of any kind—even a trash can with a lid. This is a recipe for spontaneous combustion.

### Things You'll Need

- ☐ stain-blocking primer
- ☐ primer
- ☐ paint or finish
- ☐ 2- or 3-inch brush
- ☐ paint roller

6   Paint from dry areas into wet. This will help reduce any paint ridges. Feather (thin out) all edges as you go, whether using a brush or a roller; this will also help reduce ridges.

7   Cover cans or buckets when you're not using them. Keep a rag and brush handy to deal with drips, spills and the general messiness of the process. If a drip becomes too dry to spread out, let it dry. Come back later, sand it and paint over it.

☐ roller pan

☐ rags

☐ sandpaper

## Paint Around Windows                                           239

As with all painting jobs, the more preparation you do now, the less work you'll have to do later. And of course the window will look nicer, too.

### ◉ Steps

1   Look for loose, flaky paint and remove it with a paint scraper and/or sander—all the way down to the wood if necessary. Sand down the areas you plan to paint.

2   If you're going to paint the outside of the window also, check the glazing between the glass and the frame. (Glazing is the putty that seals the window and holds the glass in place.) If it's cracked or crumbling, replace it.

3   Check the outside for other areas where water could enter between the window frame and the house—or even within the window itself—and caulk as necessary.

4   Remove or tape over all the hardware you can, such as locks, handles, latches or hinges.

5   Put blue "safety" masking tape on the glass next to the surface you're going to paint. It makes cleanup easier.

6   Use primer if you've exposed any raw surfaces. Choose primer appropriate for your surface (wood or metal).

7   Follow up with a coat of semigloss or glossy paint. It's durable and easy to clean.

8   Use an angled paintbrush and work from the top down. Paint the window frame first, then the trim on the wall around it. Make sure you don't paint windows shut (see Tips).

9   Scrape off any paint that has gotten on the glass with a razor blade made for this purpose after the paint has dried at least enough to be tacky. Gently run the razorblade, edge first, between the painted surface and the glass, then lay it flat (like a spatula) to scrape the rest of the paint off the glass.

### ✱ Tips

If the window is double-hung (windows slide up and down behind each other), paint each window separately, allowing one to dry before painting the other, and leave them open a bit while drying so they don't stick to each other or the frames. Don't paint the vertical grooves on the side where the windows actually slide.

Vinyl-covered windows cannot be painted with anything at all.

### Things You'll Need

☐ paint scraper or sander

☐ glazing

☐ caulk and caulking gun

☐ blue "safety" masking tape

☐ primer

☐ semigloss or glossy paint

☐ angled paintbrush

☐ razor blade

## 240 | Paint the Exterior of a House

This may be the most important painting (and preparation) you do. Paint and preparation vary with the type of surface: wood, stucco, metal, masonry. Check with your paint store.

### ⊙ Steps

1 Consider the weather: You'll want to avoid extreme temperatures, wind and wet weather. Never paint right after it rains, as surfaces will be too wet. Always try to paint in the shade, as direct sunlight can cause the paint to blister. The temperate conditions of fall and spring are usually best for painting outside.

2 Repair or replace any damaged surfaces, whether wood, stucco, masonry or metal.

3 Wash all surfaces with TSP (trisodium phosphate) and rinse thoroughly with water. Or use a pressure washer (available to rent) to reduce labor. Make sure that surfaces dry thoroughly.

4 Use sandpaper or a paint scraper to remove any loose, cracked, chipping or blistered paint—down to raw surfaces if necessary. Use a small drop cloth as you go to catch loose bits of paint and debris. If you decide the exterior needs to be sandblasted, hire a licensed professional.

5 Patch all nail or screw holes, gouges and cracks.

6 Caulk such places as seams and corners, above door and window trim, and where trim meets siding—or where any material meets a different kind of material, such as trim over masonry. (Exception: Don't use caulk where siding or shingles overlap or between shingles.) Use high-grade exterior caulk. Better caulks (such as silicone) actually bond to surfaces like glue and resist breaking down.

7 Use epoxy filler (the material used for car bodies) to repair serious problems in woodwork.

8 Cover dark stains—a wood knot, old paint, a wood stain—with a stain-blocking primer. The same goes for mildewed areas; you can find primers and additives made especially for mildew.

9 Sand all patched, raw and glossy surfaces; paint needs a slightly roughened surface to stick to. You can also use paint deglosser on all glossy surfaces. Remove sanding dust and debris.

10 Remove or cover all light fixtures, plumbing outlets, electrical covers and house numbers.

11 Remove all screens. You don't want to get paint on them; it's difficult (or impossible) to remove.

12 Use drop cloths to cover everything you don't want to paint, such as plants, walkways, cars and your neighbors' property.

13 Apply primer over all raw surfaces. Note that different surfaces—paint, metal, wood, stucco—require different primers.

14 Allow the primer to dry, then apply at least two coats of exterior paint. Let each coat dry between applications according to the manufacturer's instructions. Use a brush on all woodwork and a paint roller or spray machine for everything else.

### ✱ Tip

You can't paint vinyl or plastic. If there's a problem with any of these surfaces, you'll probably have to replace them.

### ⚠ Warnings

If the exterior was painted before the 1980s, you may be dealing with lead-based paint, which is extremely hazardous, especially for kids and pregnant women. Call the National Safety Council's Lead Information Center at (800) LEADFYI for instructions on how to deal with it safely.

If you're using anything other than water-based latex, never put paint-soaked or cleaner-soaked tools or rags in an enclosed area of any kind—even a trash can with a lid. This is a recipe for spontaneous combustion.

### Things You'll Need

- ☐ sandpaper
- ☐ paint scraper
- ☐ caulk and caulking gun
- ☐ epoxy filler
- ☐ stain-blocking primer
- ☐ paint deglosser
- ☐ drop cloths
- ☐ primer
- ☐ paintbrushes
- ☐ exterior paint
- ☐ paint roller or sprayer

## Repair Concrete
241

Other than earth movement, moisture is the main cause of cracks in concrete. Here's how to deal with moisture damage.

### ◉ Steps

1 Clean out cracks of any size as best you can, using a wire brush or even a strong spray of water.

2 Fill small cracks (less than 1/8 inch) with caulk specially made for concrete. (Be sure cracks are dry before caulking.)

3 Fill larger cracks or small holes (less than a few inches) using patching products designed for concrete. These usually are in the form of a powder that is mixed with water. They typically expand as they dry and become very hard.

4 Apply sealant or paint to the concrete.

### ✱ Tip

Patching compounds generally work better if the crack is damp or wet.

### Things You'll Need

☐ wire brush

☐ concrete caulk

☐ concrete patch product

☐ sealant

## Repair Masonry
242

Before you attempt to fix a crack in a brick, block or stone wall, determine the cause of the crack. This may be a job for a pro.

### ◉ Steps

1 Look closely where you see cracks forming.

2 Suspect moisture as the culprit if the cracks appear in the mortar along the joints of the bricks, blocks or stonework.

3 See if you can find out where the moisture is coming from and investigate ways to stop it. Remember that unless you treat the cause, the repair will only be temporary.

4 Consult a foundation professional if the bricks themselves are cracked— this could be a sign of foundation problems. If it's just one brick, it may be defective, and you can replace it.

5 Contact a foundation professional if the crack is long and continuous. This type of crack indicates movement of the wall.

6 Plan to replace the mortar ("re-point") if the cracks appear along the joints of the bricks. If the repair is fairly small, you may be able to do it yourself without having to call in a professional.

7 Use a cold chisel and mallet to knock out the mortar to a depth of about 1/2 inch.

8 Wet the area thoroughly with a hose. The brick should be soaked so that it won't leach the water from the mortar and cause it to crumble.

9 Mix your mortar in a shallow bucket: one part cement, one part lime, six parts builders' sand. Alternatively, consider buying premixed mortar if the repair is small.

### ✱ Tip

Be careful not to get mortar on the brick faces.

### Things You'll Need

☐ cold chisel

☐ mallet

☐ garden hose

☐ shallow bucket

☐ cement

☐ lime

☐ builders' sand

☐ pointing trowel

☐ masonry hawk

10 Scoop a little bit of mortar with a pointing trowel and create a small cylindrical shape with it.

11 Press this cylinder into the area between the bricks. Hold a masonry hawk or piece of cardboard under the area where you're working to catch falling mortar—it takes some practice to keep the mortar in the groove.

## 243 | Repair Stucco

Stucco looks great—unless it has a long, ugly crack running through it. Here's how to get it back into tip-top shape.

### ◉ Steps

1 Note the direction of the crack. Vertical cracks from base to window or roof to door sometimes indicate a problem with the foundation. Before fixing the crack, call a foundation specialist to determine the condition of the foundation.

2 Fix very small cracks by filling them with a high-quality caulk—preferably one that can be painted over. Use your fingers to press it in well, and a damp cloth to clean up.

3 Use a cold chisel or an old screwdriver to clean out wider cracks.

4 Soak the area thoroughly with a hose so that the stucco won't leach the water from the new mortar and cause it to crumble.

5 Mix your mortar in a shallow bucket: one part portland cement, four parts builders' sand and a little bit of water to make the mortar workable but not runny.

6 Cover the area to be patched with a polyvinyl acetate (PVA) bonding agent made for masonry.

7 When the bond is slightly sticky, fill the crack with the mortar mix.

8 Cover the patched area with a piece of bitumen-coated fiberglass. (Bitumen is a tarlike substance.)

9 Use a paint roller to press it into place, and apply a coat of bitumen over the patch.

10 Let the bitumen dry and then apply another coat, stippling it with a soft-bristled brush to match the rest of the wall.

11 Paint over the area with a primer made for stucco or bitumen patching. Allow the primer to dry.

12 Repaint the area—but be aware that you may have to repaint the entire wall so that the patch won't stand out.

### Things You'll Need

- ☐ caulk
- ☐ damp cloth
- ☐ cold chisel
- ☐ garden hose
- ☐ shallow bucket
- ☐ portland cement
- ☐ builders' sand
- ☐ PVA bonding agent
- ☐ fiberglass cloth
- ☐ bitumen
- ☐ paint roller
- ☐ soft-bristled brush
- ☐ primer
- ☐ paint

## Remove Corrosion From Aluminum | 244

Aluminum patio furniture, window frames and other fixtures are not completely safe from corrosion. If a piece turns a dull gray and has globs of white crystals on it, it's corroded.

### ◉ Steps

1 Remove the crystals and gray discoloration with fine wet/dry sandpaper dipped in mineral spirits. Don't try to polish the aluminum; simply rub it until it's bright again.

2 Wipe down the metal with a clean rag and some mineral spirits to remove grime and debris left from the sandpaper.

3 Allow the aluminum to dry.

4 Apply a chromate primer and allow it to dry completely.

5 Paint the aluminum or leave it with just the primer coating on it.

### Things You'll Need

- ☐ fine sandpaper
- ☐ mineral spirits
- ☐ rags
- ☐ chromate primer
- ☐ aluminum paint

## Help Keep a Basement Dry | 245

Most basements can be kept free of flooding, and you can take many preventive actions yourself.

### ◉ Steps

1 Make sure the ground alongside the foundation is sloped away from the house. Your yard should be graded to direct water to an appropriate drainage area.

2 Keep the gutters clean and free of obstructions so that water is directed away from the house's foundation (see 233 "Clean Gutters").

3 Caulk any openings around basement windows or doors.

4 Paint the basement walls with waterproof paint.

5 Install a sump pump that has an automatic switch. (Also consider installing a generator for your sump pump in case there is a power failure during a storm.)

6 Consult an established waterproofing or landscape contractor if there is a need for more serious remediation projects, such as installing underground drainage or regrading your yard.

### Things You'll Need

- ☐ caulk and caulking gun
- ☐ waterproof paint
- ☐ paintbrushes
- ☐ sump pump

## ✓ 246 Prepare Your Home for Natural Disasters

The forces of nature can be unpredictable and overwhelming, so it's wise to be ready to deal with disaster before it strikes. Here are some general precautions and specific recommendations to help safeguard your home and family.

### General preparedness

❑ Store drinking water, flashlights, batteries, a portable radio, a first aid kit, storable food (with manual can opener), essential medications, sturdy shoes, sleeping bags or blankets, and cash in a sturdy, accessible container.

❑ Take an emergency first aid course.

❑ Make sure all family members know how to shut off the gas and electricity.

❑ Compile a list of emergency contacts, including an out-of-state friend or family member.

❑ Locate the nearest emergency shelter.

❑ Practice an evacuation plan. If you have pets, make plans to take them with you.

### Earthquakes

❑ Brace your water heater.

❑ Fasten bookcases to walls.

❑ Hang heavy pictures away from couches, chairs and beds.

❑ Install latches in cupboards.

❑ Put large or heavy objects on bottom shelves.

❑ Identify a safe place in each room: away from glass and under sturdy furniture.

### Floods

❑ Have check valves installed in sewer traps to prevent backups.

❑ Seal basement walls with waterproof compounds.

❑ Store important documents in a waterproof box.

### Hurricanes

❑ Keep trees and shrubbery trimmed.

❑ Clean out roof gutters regularly.

❑ Install hurricane shutters on windows.

### Tornadoes

❑ Learn the tornado warning signs from your local emergency agency.

❑ Identify a safe place in your house: Basements are best, but stay away from windows.

### Heat waves

❑ Seal cracks around window- and wall-mounted air conditioners.

❑ Keep curtains and blinds drawn.

### Ice storms

❑ Buy portable propane or kerosene space heaters, and provide ventilation.

❑ Trim dead limbs from trees.

❑ Stock up on rock salt and sand.

**How to Do** *(Just About)* **Everything**

## Prepare Your Home for Winter 247

Some of these steps require professional help—call early, as calendars get full in the weeks leading up to winter.

◉ **Steps**

1 Add a second layer of insulation to your attic. R-30 insulation is considered the minimum. If your house is relatively new, it probably conforms. If not, consider adding insulation.

2 Caulk around window and door glass and trim, and all exterior trim. Install or replace weather stripping on all doors and windows. Check for cracks around pipes and electrical outlets entering or exiting the walls.

3 Install storm windows and doors if you have them. Consider purchasing storm windows if you have older windows that are not made from modern insulated glass.

4 Have your heating system checked by a licensed heating/air-conditioning professional. Most furnace manufacturers recommend at least annual inspections.

5 Check gutters and clean them if necessary. Clogged gutters can result in basement flooding when the snow melts (see 233 "Clean Gutters").

6 Replace any roof shingles that are missing or damaged (see 232 "Replace Asphalt Shingles").

7 Have your chimneys inspected by a chimney service and, if necessary, cleaned (see 306 "Clean Out a Fireplace and Chimney").

8 Check the foundation for areas where water may puddle.

9 Trim trees away from the house. Have dead trees and branches removed by professional tree trimmers, or do it yourself.

10 Drain and shut off outdoor water faucets.

11 Insulate any water pipes that are exposed to freezing cold.

12 Replace the batteries in carbon monoxide and smoke detectors, and check to make sure these are all in working order.

13 Check fire extinguishers and charge and replace as necessary.

14 Make sure you are stocked with rock salt, sand, snow shovels and any other items you will need during the winter.

### Things You'll Need

- ☐ insulation
- ☐ caulk
- ☐ replacement weather stripping
- ☐ storm windows
- ☐ batteries
- ☐ rock salt
- ☐ sand
- ☐ snow shovels

## Burglarproof Your Home 248

Having your home burglarized is a wrenching experience. Take these precautions to help prevent a burglary.

◉ **Steps**

1 Keep windows closed and doors locked—don't take chances for even a few minutes. Use a 1-inch dead bolt for each exterior door. Secure sliding glass doors by inserting a broomstick or dowel in the inside track.

⚠ **Warning**

If you install an alarm system, learn how to use it properly to avoid false alarms.

2   Consider installing an alarm system or motion-detecting lights.

3   Suggest that someone is home by using electric timers to turn on the radio and house lights at certain hours. Vary the lights that you turn on.

4   Make sure that outside doors are made of metal or a sturdy wood.

5   Check to ensure that doors fit tightly in their frames. If they don't, install weather-stripping around them.

6   Etch valuables with your driver's license number and state abbreviation in visible places. If you don't want to ruin valuables by marking them, photograph them instead. Keep an inventory of your property.

7   Keep jewelry and other valuables in a safe.

8   Consider getting a dog—many kinds of dogs will make enough noise to discourage burglars (see 618 "Select a Dog Breed").

9   Leave spare keys with a neighbor rather than hidden outside your house.

10  Keep shrubs and bushes trimmed so that they can't conceal prowlers.

## 249 | Replace a Dead Bolt

Replacing an existing dead bolt, whether for security or mechanical reasons, is a relatively easy job. Once you buy the lock, you can complete the task with a few simple steps.

### ⊙ Steps

1   Take the old dead bolt out of the door by using a screwdriver to remove the screws on the inside panel of the lock. Be sure to note how the lock comes apart.

2   Grasp the inside and outside pieces of the lock face.

3   Pull them away from the door.

4   Remove the screws from the lock-mechanism plate, which is on the edge of the door.

5   Measure the diameter of the hole in the door, or take the old dead bolt to the hardware store or lock shop to ensure that you purchase the proper-size replacement.

6   Place the new locking mechanism in the hole on the edge of the door.

7   Use the screws provided to attach the plate to the door edge.

8   Work the inside and outside halves of the lock cylinder into proper alignment. Secure them to the door with the screws provided.

9   Be sure that the bolt plate on the edge of the door is flush-mounted with the surface of the wood. Sometimes the hole for the plate will need to be enlarged slightly with a wood chisel.

10  Test the lock a few times from both the inside and the outside to ensure that it has been assembled properly.

### Things You'll Need

- ☐ screwdriver
- ☐ tape measure
- ☐ replacement dead bolt lock
- ☐ wood chisel

# Choose a Home Alarm System

Alarm systems for the home can be complicated and expensive, so it's crucial to determine your security needs before you begin consulting with alarm companies.

## ⊙ Steps

### Conducting Preliminary Research

1   Survey your home and determine how many windows and doors you want to be "switched," or integrated into the system.

2   Determine possible locations for the control panel and keypads. You might find it convenient to place a keypad close to the front door. You might also want a keypad close to the bedrooms. The control panel commands the system, and the keypads allow you to program the system and turn it, or its components, on and off.

3   Determine how far away windows and doors are from the control panel so that you know how far wires will be routed if you choose a wired alarm system or how far a wireless system needs to communicate with sensors. Keep in mind that it is difficult to install a hard-wired security system unless your house is still under construction.

4   Decide whether you want a security system that will be monitored 24 hours a day. The central monitoring station "watches" your home for a monthly fee. A less expensive alternative is a basic sensor system with a dialer accessory that connects the system to your phone lines and dials preselected numbers if the house's security is breached.

5   Consider your lifestyle. Does anyone in the family often get up in the middle of the night for a snack? Do you have a large pet that roams the house at night? Such circumstances will influence the type of motion sensor you select and how it is installed. It may also call for you or members of your family to take trips to the keypad to prevent false alarms.

### Choosing the System

1   Consult with a reputable home security system adviser.

2   Choose a system with a control panel that can monitor all the zones you have in your home. Each window or door integrated into the system is considered a zone. A basic system is capable of controlling eight zones. However, many panels permit the addition of expansion modules that allow the system to watch up to 32 zones.

3   Determine if the routing of the wires for a hard-wired security system might be too long. With a wired system, you will have to drill holes in walls where wires will have to be routed. If the wire run appears too long to you, choose a wireless system.

4   Make certain that a wireless system can perform up to the distance of the farthest zone.

5   Be certain that the system you choose can accept fire-protection sensors, carbon monoxide sensors and combustible-gas detectors, anti-freeze-up low-temperature switches (especially in cold climates) and water detectors. Make sure that panic buttons are or can be included.

6   Choose a system that is user-friendly. Make certain that inputting codes into the keypad is not a complicated process and is one that everyone in

## ✱ Tips

You may want to include some kind of alarm noisemaker. A blast of a siren or alarm bell not only alerts neighbors that an intruder is in your home, but also can scare the trespasser away.

A motion sensor outside the home can provide an early warning and, when used with a noisemaker, can discourage an intruder from entering your home.

the family can learn quickly. You don't want to have to refer to the owner's manual as you input or try to interpret codes.

7 Work the keypad of the system you select to assure yourself that it is easy to use. Encourage all family members to work the keypad so that you will select one that everyone can use comfortably.

## 251 Save Money on a Home-Improvement Project

With good planning and an honest assessment of your skills—and amount of free time—you can probably save some money on your next big project.

### ⊙ Steps

1 Consider what portion of the work you can realistically do yourself. For example, if adding a room, maybe you can paint it when it's done.

2 Consider less expensive alternatives when designing an addition, such as a prefabricated fireplace unit vs. traditional masonry.

3 Plan everything so you don't need to make changes once the contractor is working. Changes often entail additional charges.

4 Get several prices for the work from recommended contractors. Price quotes vary enormously due to such factors as the contractor's schedule, the time of year and the distance from the job.

5 Try to schedule your project for an "off" time of year. For example, install central air conditioning in winter, not in June.

6 Shop for materials that are on sale. Building-supply stores often have various items (such as tile or wood flooring) on sale due to overstocks or other factors.

7 Make sure that your initial contract for the work is comprehensive and that the initial price covers all work to be done.

### ✱ Tip

Most people can handle light demolition, painting, landscaping and garbage removal themselves, assuming that they have the time.

### ⚠ Warnings

If you have any doubts that the contract for the work is correct and complete, consult an attorney before signing.

Always attempt to minimize the amount you're required to pay ahead of work being completed. You probably won't be able to negotiate a contract without a deposit. Plan to pay up to 10 percent.

## 252 Hire a Builder

Finding the right builder is essential to the success of your project.

### ⊙ Steps

1 Interview several builders. Ask an architect for recommendations. If a real estate agent assisted you when you purchased your lot, ask the agent for several recommendations. Also consult friends and neighbors.

2 Review your completed plans with each builder, or ask the builders about designing plans for you.

3 Make sure that all the builders see the building site and are quoting to build the house on that site, including excavation and any other site-specific costs.

### ✱ Tips

Remember that you'll be working closely with the builder—be sure to select someone with whom you can establish a comfortable relationship.

Don't assume that the most expensive builder is the best, or the least expensive the worst. Price quotes vary based on a

4   Get price quotes from the builders and compare them, making sure that they each bid on the same items.

5   Ask for references—particularly previous customers—from each party. Check the references. Be sure to speak with them when the builder is not present. Look at some of the houses the builder has constructed.

6   Retain an attorney with experience in construction cases to draft or review the contract. Be sure that the payment schedule for the builder is clear and understandable.

7   Make sure that the contract specifies the start and completion dates. Insist on some type of late fee or penalty if the completion is delayed past a certain grace period (notwithstanding circumstances beyond the builder's control, such as inclement weather).

8   Execute the approved contract.

9   Make any required deposit payment, and be sure to write your checks as per the schedule (not earlier and not later).

builder's schedule, efficiency, overhead and distance from the job.

## ⚠ Warnings

Though recommendations from a real estate agent can be a good way to find a builder, be advised that the agent may have a prior business relationship with the builder and that it may factor into the recommendation.

You'll probably be unable to negotiate a contract without a deposit, but attempt to minimize the amount you're required to pay in advance—certainly no more than 10 percent.

---

## Hire a Roofing Contractor                     253

Roofing material ranges from standard asphalt shingles to more "upscale" materials like wood and slate. It's important to hire a contractor who specializes in your type of roof.

### ⊙ Steps

1   Decide what type of roofing you want. Are you looking for asphalt shingles or wood? Or is slate more your style? Your decision will depend largely on the style of your home and your budget.

2   Contact several roofing contractors. Ask the builder, as well as friends and neighbors, for recommendations. If you're having difficulty locating contractors, try contacting the local builders association to see if it can suggest someone.

3   Have the contractors come out and quote prices on the project. Provide access to the property and make sure all the contractors are bidding on the same type of roofing (such as a specific grade of asphalt shingles).

4   Make sure the roofers are including the removal of old roofing in their bids. (Note that it's not always necessary to remove the existing roof when installing a new one.)

5   Find out if each roofer has experience with the type of roofing you're installing. Most roofers have asphalt-shingle experience, but wood and slate roofing are specialties. If you're installing an expensive wood or slate roof, you'll want a contractor who has experience in this area. Ask to see pictures of prior projects.

6   Ask for references and check them out. Are the previous customers happy with the work that was done for them?

7   Execute a contract for the work specifying cost, payment schedule, material to be used, start date and completion date. Try to minimize the deposit you pay to the contractor prior to the start of the work or delivery of materials.

### ✳ Tips

Roofing is typically measured and sold by the "square." A square of roofing covers 100 square feet of surface area. Labor costs are also generally priced by the square.

Asphalt shingles are the most common roofing material and are available in many grades, with warranties of up to 40 years.

Wood shingles cost two to three times as much as asphalt. Slate roofing is by far the most expensive and most durable. Most "slate" roofs are now made of a manufactured material, but real slate is still used at the top end of the market.

Roofing is outside work, and your project may be subject to weather-related delays.

## 254 | Hire a Painter

Hiring a professional painter is more costly than doing it your-self, but it's a quick and easy way to get the job done right. Here's how to hire a top-quality painter for the best results.

### ⊙ Steps

1 Determine which areas of your home need to be painted.

2 Consider any work you want to have done before painting. For example, do you want to replace or repair moldings, patch damaged drywall or hang new doors?

3 Decide what colors and paints you want to use. You can get paint charts for all major brands at general home centers or paint stores. The painter you hire may also have suggestions—take these seriously.

4 Contact several painters. Ask friends, neighbors, builders and designers for recommendations. If you're having difficulty locating house painters, check the yellow pages.

5 Have the painting contractors inspect the site and quote a price for the job. Make sure the contractors are quoting on the same specifications—areas to be painted, number of coats and so forth.

6 Ask the painters for references and contact them. Were the customers happy with the job? Did the painter complete the project in a timely and professional manner?

7 Select a painter based on price, track record and your impressions.

8 Execute a contract specifying the work to be done, total cost, payment schedule, start date and estimated completion date.

9 Make sure the contract includes the paint brands and colors to be used in each location, as well as the number of coats.

10 Make sure the contract specifies that the painter is responsible for cleanup and the removal of paint from all surfaces (windows, floors).

11 Remove all furniture and other movable items before the painter is scheduled to begin. Anything not removed should be piled together in the center of the room and thoroughly covered with drop cloths.

### ✱ Tips

A good-quality paint job typically consists of one coat of primer and two finish coats of the color.

If you intend to have highly cus-tomized painting done (such as sponging or other decorator techniques), make sure that your painter has experience doing this type of work.

### ⚠ Warning

Always try to negotiate a con-tract with the smallest possible up-front or deposit payment. Try to make your payment schedule match the pace of work and material deliveries.

## 255 | Hire a Hardwood-Floor Contractor

Hardwood is a popular flooring choice. Whether you're installing new hardwood floors or having older floors refinished, find a contractor who can do the best job.

### ⊙ Steps

1 Determine the areas where you want the hardwood flooring to be installed or refinished.

2 Learn about the differences in material costs for various flooring prod-ucts if you're having new floors installed, and decide which type of floor-

### ✱ Tips

Many types of wood-flooring products are available. The most common type of hardwood floor-ing is unfinished oak, typically in 2¼- or 3-inch-wide strips (¾ inches thick), nailed into place.

ing you want to use. (See Tips for details about different options.) You can shop for flooring at a building-supply store.

3 Ask friends and relatives for recommendations to help find a contractor, or look in the yellow pages under "Floors."

4 Have contractors come to your home to measure and give estimates. Get several price quotes from competing contractors.

5 Discuss the finishing/coating options with the contractor. Do you have children or pets who make greater protection a must?

6 Ask to see pictures of past jobs if you're looking for a contractor to do specialty work, such as elaborate parquet or inlays.

7 Learn whether each contractor is experienced in the specific work you want done. For example, a contractor may install very high-quality standard oak floors, but may not be sufficiently skilled to handle a complex project with inlays or difficult cuts.

8 Ask the contractors for references and check them. Are previous customers happy with the work that was done?

9 Select the contractor who provides the best combination of satisfied references and price.

10 Make arrangements with the contractor to cover damage to painted trim and other items that may be damaged when refinishing or adding a floor. (You may have to accept the fact that you'll have to repaint or touch up base moldings in a room that's being worked on.)

11 Execute a contract specifying the work to be done, price, payment schedule, start date and estimated completion date. Try to pay the mini mum possible deposit, and arrange a payment schedule that matches the completion of work and delivery of materials to the site.

These floors are sanded and coated with polyurethane on-site.

Many engineered wood products are also available that offer thicknesses significantly less than $3/4$ inch. These $5/16$-, $3/8$- and $1/2$-inch thick products are particularly useful in renovations where a subfloor is already in place.

New unfinished flooring has to arrive at the house a week or two before it is laid in order to adjust to the environment. For the same reason, it will have to sit unsanded for another week or two after installation.

## ⚠ Warning

The process for finishing wood floors requires several coats, laid down over two to three days (or more), during which you can't use the floors and may even have to vacate the house due to strong fumes.

---

## Hire an Electrician `256`

Your home's electrical system is complicated and can be hazardous with improperly handled renovations. Always look for an experienced and reliable professional when hiring an electrician.

### ⊙ Steps

1 Evaluate what work needs to be done. Are you renovating or adding a room or rooms? Or do you need a repair to an existing system?

2 Consider your expansion needs realistically—with the number of electronic devices typically used today, additional outlets are often required. It is easy and inexpensive to add outlets at the time of a renovation.

3 Ask friends and neighbors for recommendations, and then contact several electricians. If you are having difficulty locating an electrician, check the yellow pages.

4 Have the electricians inspect the site and bid on the job. Provide them with written specifications listing all aspects of the project.

5 Check to make sure that the electricians are properly licensed and have proper insurance coverage.

**Tip**

Many electrical-system enhancements have been introduced in recent years. Discuss these with your electrician to determine if you want to add them to your project. Examples include whole-house surge protectors (to safeguard computers, VCRs and other electronics) as well as the entire range of "smart house" devices. It is much cheaper and easier to install these items when conducting a renovation.

6   Inquire about the length of time each electrician has been in business.

7   Ask for past customers as references and contact them. Ask customers if they were satisfied with the work. Did the contractor come back promptly to address any problems?

8   Select an electrician, basing your choice on a combination of price, experience and your impressions.

9   Review your specifications with the electrician and discuss any necessary items you may have missed. For example, will you require an additional or upgraded power connection to support your renovation?

10  Execute a contract specifying the work to be done, cost, payment schedule, start date and estimated completion date.

## ⚠ Warnings

Make sure that the contractor provides you with a proper certificate of insurance before any payment is made or work commences.

Always try to minimize any up-front or deposit payments, and try to negotiate a payment schedule that matches the pace of work and material deliveries.

---

## 257 | Hire a Plumber When Building or Remodeling

When hiring a plumber for a big project, find someone who will do a quality job at a good price—and who will also be available for emergencies.

### ⊙ Steps

1   Evaluate what you need to have done.

2   Ask friends and family for recommendations and then contact several plumbers. For more possibilities, check the yellow pages.

3   Have all the plumbers give you price quotes on the project. Give the plumbers access to the site and provide them with written specifications (including detailed descriptions of materials—for example, "Kohler 'Vintage' sink in white").

4   Confirm that the plumbers are including the removal of existing fixtures (such as an old tub) in their bids.

5   Make sure the plumbers are properly licensed and properly insured.

6   Ask how long each plumber has been in business. Look for one who has been in business for several years.

7   Ask for references and contact them. Were they satisfied with the work? Did the plumber return promptly to correct any problems?

8   Select a plumber based on price, experience and your impressions.

9   Execute a contract specifying the work to be done, cost, payment schedule, materials to be used for the project, start date and estimated completion date.

### ✳ Tips

When selecting a plumber, consider the firm's ability to provide someone on short notice for emergencies. Many plumbers have 24-hour emergency service available.

If your project is large, consider supplying the plumbing fixtures yourself (with the plumber supplying other material, such as pipe). Expensive tubs and other fixtures are often marked up considerably by plumbers.

### ⚠ Warnings

Make sure the plumber provides you with a certificate of insurance before you make any payments or work begins.

Always try to limit any deposits or up-front payments as much as possible. Try to keep your payment schedule closely aligned with the pace of work and material deliveries.

## Buy Replacement Windows | 258

New windows can really improve the look of an older home while also improving energy efficiency.

### ⊙ Steps

1  Consider which windows you want to replace. Do you want to replace them all or just certain ones?

2  Consider the time of year. In all probability the project will take at least several days, during which time your home may be somewhat exposed to the elements.

3  Contact several replacement-window vendors/installers.

4  Discuss the various window types the vendors offer (wood, vinyl-clad, aluminum-clad) and the merits and costs of each. Vinyl- and aluminum-clad windows do not require painting, so they are low-maintenance.

5  Discuss the energy-efficiency options (standard insulated glass, low-e glass and so forth) offered by the vendors. Consider low-e and other high-tech energy-saving options in the context of the estimated savings on your heating and cooling bills. Do the expected savings justify the extra cost?

6  Ask the vendor/installers for references and check them: Were past customers happy with the work done? Was the work completed in a timely manner? Have they had any problems since the installation? Did the contractor leave the site in a clean and undamaged condition?

7  Select a vendor/installer based upon price, window type, references and your impressions.

8  Make sure that the vendor/installer offers guarantee(s). Sign a contract for the work. If ordering the windows separately from a vendor, make sure that the installer has signed off on the list to verify that the windows specified are correct.

9  Make sure that the installer is properly insured. Get a valid certificate of insurance from the contractor before you pay any money or before the work begins.

### ✱ Tips

The two most common types of windows are double-hung and casement. Double-hung windows have bottom and top sashes that slide up and down to open or close the window. Casement windows are typically operated with a crank and open like a door.

Most windows consist of a single pane of glass per sash (two for insulated glass), over which a wood or plastic grille is placed. A true "divided lite" window has a built-in frame (instead of the grille) with separate panes of glass in each segment. True divided lite windows are typically two to four times the cost of standard windows.

### ⚠ Warning

Your window installer will undoubtedly insist on a substantial deposit. Always try to negotiate the smallest possible up-front payment and a schedule that matches the pace of work and material deliveries.

## Decorate a Room So It Seems Bigger | 259

Decorating sleight-of-hand can stretch the perceived dimensions of a room. Here are some ways to help a small room live large.

### ⊙ Steps

1  Open up the room by maximizing views of the outdoors or of an adjoining, more spacious room.

2  Keep the walls light in color, as light colors recede.

3  Provide good illumination, which will enhance the sense of space.

### ✱ Tip

Floor-to-ceiling mirrors definitely increase the sense of volume in a room. Keep in mind, however, that this is a look that comes and goes in popularity.

4   Paint moldings, doors and the like in the same color as the walls. Strongly contrasting elements chop up the space.

5   Put away some of the tabletop bric-a-brac. It makes the room seem cluttered, busy and crowded.

6   Paint the ceiling white. Rooms have a greater sense of space with high ceilings, and white ceilings seem higher than darker ones.

7   Run linear flooring such as wood strips and ceramic tile on the diagonal. This creates the longest straight lines possible in the room, and the eye will follow them.

8   Use the same flooring material throughout the space to unify it and make it seem more expansive.

9   Select ceramic tile that's oversized—even in small bathrooms.

10  Use furniture that is scaled appropriately to the room. For example, an oversize sofa will eat up too much space in a small room.

11  Decorate windows simply. Besides being the wrong scale for a small room, show-stopping treatments such as billowy draperies encroach into the space of the room.

## 260 | Select the Best Paint Color for a Room

Choosing a paint color can be a little tricky because lighting and shadows affect it dramatically. Here are some tips for getting the color just right.

### ⊙ Steps

1   Study color schemes you admire in home-decorating magazines and tear out any particularly appealing examples. Take them with you when shopping for paint.

2   Remember that color usually seems more intense on walls than it does on a sample card. When it doubt, go a shade or two lighter.

3   Keep in mind that yellow and rosy tones give a room a warm feeling. Greens, blues and grays are cooler colors.

4   Avoid snow-white except in ultramodern, minimalist environments, because it will seem too harsh, giving a sterile, operating-room effect. It's better to go with a white that contains a hint of peach, beige or pink.

5   Save bold color schemes for rooms where you don't spend long stretches of time, such as bathrooms and dining rooms. You may tire of these schemes if they're in the home office, kitchen, family room or other rooms in which you stay for hours.

6   Take fabric with you if you're matching it. If you don't have a swatch, grab a sofa cushion, bedspread or curtain panel, for example.

7   Start small, buying just a quart or so of paint, and then painting a section of wall with a paintbrush or roller. Or test the color on a good-size (perhaps 3 feet square) plywood or wallboard scrap, or on a piece of cardboard; set it against the walls in the room as the light changes (including artificial light) and evaluate it for a few days.

**✱ Tip**

If you plan to sell your house soon, stick with mainstream colors. These are more likely to appeal to prospective buyers.

8  Test a two-tone scheme, such as wainscoting in one color and walls in another, by painting two boards or painting one board in both colors.

9  Repeat the test, tinkering with more pink, less peach or whatever seems appropriate, in small cans of paint until you're satisfied. Yes, the cost for sampling various paints can add up, but it can prevent the disaster of applying, say, three gallons of the wrong color and being forced to repaint.

## Paint Wood Molding                                          261

Excellent prep work and patience are the secrets to successfully painting varnished wood molding, such as baseboards and door frames.

### ⊙ Steps

1  Clean the molding thoroughly with a cleaner like TSP (trisodium phosphate), which doesn't leave a film that could interfere with the adhesion of the paint.

2  Let the molding dry.

3  Mask off the area around the molding carefully with professional-quality blue "safety" masking tape, pressing down very firmly on the tape edges you will apply paint to. Try mashing down the edges with a spoon.

4  Place drop cloths as needed.

5  Have one or more paintbrushes on hand in widths appropriate to the molding you are painting. Purchase a high-quality brush or brushes with the type of bristles appropriate to the product you are using, either oil based or water based.

6  Apply a deglossing product (liquid-sanding solvent) according to the directions, which will specify a waiting period before applying primer.

7  Apply primer; oil-based primer is best. Note that there's often a window of only 30 to 60 minutes in which primer can be applied successfully over deglosser.

8  Sand rough areas after priming.

9  Let the molding dry; this may take a day or more.

10  Apply oil-based (alkyd) or water-based (latex or acrylic) paint.

11  Let the paint dry. Oil-based paint usually takes much longer to dry—a day or more—but many paint experts feel it gives a more durable finish.

12  Apply the second coat of paint.

13  Let the second coat dry, and remove the masking tape. Oil-based paint should be thoroughly dry before you remove the tape, but some paint experts advise removing tape when water-based paint is still slightly tacky; do what your paint-can directions or paint store advises.

### ✱ Tips

High-quality paints and brushes will yield better results. Quality brushes provide a more even coat of paint and will last through many paint jobs.

Clean brushes thoroughly. Do not rest brushes with their weight on the bristles—it will deform the bristles and ruin the brushes.

Avoid painting on hot, humid days or immediately following rain to avoid getting bubbles in the paint.

### ⚠ Warning

When using solvent (oil-based) products, ventilate the work area thoroughly. Don't smoke or have any type of open flame (even a gas water heater) in the area.

### Things You'll Need

❑ TSP and rags

❑ blue "safety" masking tape

❑ spoon

❑ drop cloths

❑ paintbrushes

❑ deglossing product

❑ primer and paint

❑ sandpaper

## 262 | Remove Wallpaper

You won't know how hard—or easy—removing that old wallpaper will be until you try. Here are a few guidelines to help you tackle the job.

### ⊙ Steps

1 Move furniture away from the walls and cover the floor with drop cloths.

2 Pick a corner or an edge of the wallpaper and try to peel it off using your hands, a putty knife or a wallpaper scraper. Some papers are designed to simply peel off.

3 If the paper doesn't peel off, or if the pattern comes away but the backing remains, score the paper lightly using a razor blade or a wallpaper-scoring tool. Be careful not to cut into the drywall or plaster underneath.

4 Apply plain water, water mixed with a mild household soap, or a commercial wallpaper remover to the wall using a paint roller, squirt gun or large sponge. Saturate the wall several times if necessary; the paper will absorb the water until the glue begins to loosen.

5 Alternatively, rent or buy a wallpaper steamer. Take care—steamers get very hot.

6 Try again to pull the paper off with your hands. You might still have to use a scraper or putty knife, however.

7 Wash away as much of the glue as possible, until you are down to the original painted or primed wall. You might have to use a heavy-duty scouring pad. Wait until the wall is dry and use sandpaper to sand off what remains of the paper, backing or glue.

### ✱ Tip

If the wallpaper resists your efforts, sand it with very coarse sandpaper (50, 60 or 80 grit).

### ⚠ Warning

Wallpaper removers can be caustic and the fumes can irritate your lungs. Wear gloves, long pants and sleeves, safety goggles, and a hat, and ventilate the room well.

### Things You'll Need

- ☐ drop cloths
- ☐ putty knife or scraper
- ☐ razor blade or scoring tool
- ☐ wallpaper remover
- ☐ paint roller, squirt gun or sponge
- ☐ scouring pad
- ☐ sandpaper

## 263 | Hang Wallpaper

Hanging your own wallpaper can be an experience you'll never forget. These steps are for drywall or plaster walls that are primed and painted and don't yet have wallpaper on them.

### ⊙ Steps

#### Preparing the Walls

1 Look for cracks, nail holes and loose paint or plaster on the walls. Fix them first (see 236 "Patch a Hole in Drywall").

2 Be sure that the walls are clean and dry and that every surface is either painted or primed. You don't want to apply paste to a surface that will just absorb it—the paper might not stick.

3 Remove all the electrical plates after you've washed the walls.

4 Plan to start papering in a place that is inconspicuous, and remember that your starting point will also be your ending point. (Corners and the areas behind opening doors are good places to start.)

5 Beginning at a doorway or corner, measure a distance that's an inch or two shorter than the width of your paper. Make a mark at this distance—

### ✱ Tips

Razor blades get dull amazingly quickly, so replace them often. You'll be glad you did.

Avoid sliding the paper around. Even if you don't tear it, the paper might stretch.

### ⚠ Warnings

After removing electrical cover plates, you'll be wallpapering right over exposed electrical outlets and switches. Be sure to turn off the electricity to the room before cutting around these fixtures. Water, electricity and metal are a dangerous combination.

be sure to make the mark as light as possible so that it won't show through the paper's background.

6  Using a carpenter's level and a pencil, draw a vertical line from the floor to the ceiling through this mark. If you start at a corner, be sure to use the level, not the corner, as your guide. You will align your paper to this line—again, be sure to make the mark as light as possible.

## Hanging the Paper

1  With a utility knife, cut a length of paper that's about 4 inches longer than the wall, from ceiling to baseboard. (With a large repeating pattern, you might have to cut the strips longer to make sure the pattern matches up from piece to piece.)

2  Apply paste to the paper (see 264 "Apply Paste to Wallpaper"). Or, if using prepasted wallpaper, follow the manufacturer's instructions. (Most professional installers apply paste even to prepasted wallpapers, but be aware that this voids some manufacturers' warranties.)

3  Start at the ceiling, aligning the paper with the plumb line you drew on the wall. Roughly 2 extra inches should flop against the ceiling, and 2 more inches should flop below the top of the baseboard.

4  Smooth the paper using a smoothing brush or a plastic smoother (which looks like a wide spatula without the handle). Remove wrinkles by pulling a section of the paper away from the wall until you reach the wrinkle. Smooth out the paper as you lay it back against the wall.

5  Smooth from the middle out, applying enough pressure to push out the bubbles but not pressing so hard that you stretch or tear the paper. If you have an air bubble that just won't budge, poke it with a pin and press down on the paper before the adhesive dries.

6  Trim the paper. Using a wide putty knife, press the paper against the ceiling, baseboard, or corner and trim it with a sharp razor blade. (The putty knife provides a straight edge to guide the blade.)

7  Continue with the next piece, aligning it with the one you just laid down. If a pattern just won't line up between two strips, match it at the most obvious spot—eye level.

8  Roll each seam with a seam roller, but don't press so hard that you squeeze out all the adhesive. Go back 10 or 15 minutes later and roll each seam again.

9  When you reach the end—the place where you started—you'll want to create a clean final seam. Lap the final strip of paper over the first strip and trim both simultaneously.

10  Be sure to wipe any excess adhesive off the paper, ceiling, baseboards and adjoining strips. Use a wet sponge, following with a dry rag.

Place pieces of tape over the outlets and switches to minimize their exposure to paste and water. But remember, the tape won't in any way protect you if the electricity is still on.

## Things You'll Need

- [ ] drywall-patching tools
- [ ] cleaning supplies
- [ ] tape measure
- [ ] carpenter's level
- [ ] pencil
- [ ] utility knife
- [ ] wallpaper
- [ ] wallpaper paste
- [ ] smoothing brush or plastic smoother
- [ ] pin
- [ ] wide putty knife
- [ ] seam roller

## 264 | Apply Paste to Wallpaper

Pasting wallpaper can be a sticky, gooey job. Here's how to apply paste well and (relatively) neatly.

### ⊙ Steps

1 Be sure that you have the correct adhesive paste for the job. Some papers, such as vinyl backed or lightweight, require a specific paste.

2 Mix wallpaper paste that comes as a powder in a separate bucket before pouring it into the bucket or roller tray you will use for the job. Stir well with a stirring stick to remove all the lumps, but not so well that you put a lot of air into the mix.

3 Pour liquid adhesive directly into a bucket or roller tray.

4 Lay a strip of wallpaper—already cut to size, pattern side down—on a long, flat, dry table (the table won't stay dry for long). Let one end of the paper flop over the edge of the table.

5 Use a paste brush or a paint roller to apply the paste to the half of the paper that remains flat on the table, being sure to cover every inch.

6 Fold the section you just pasted over onto itself, and slide the dry section of the paper onto the table. Apply the paste.

7 Fold the next section onto itself, then fold the two halves against each other, being very careful not to crease the paper. This process is called "booking." Booking keeps the paper moist, the paste from dribbling onto the floor and the pasted surface clean.

8 Set the paper aside in a clean spot for no more than 5 minutes before hanging it.

9 Be a clean freak: As soon as each strip of wallpaper is booked and set aside, use a clean, wet sponge to clean the table—but don't bother to dry the surface. Do this even if you're going to paste several pieces before you hang them; you'll want to get the adhesive off the table before it has dried.

### ✳ Tips

You're going to get paste on the table, the pattern face of the paper and yourself. Don't be overly concerned—it's water-soluble.

Let the paper set after applying paste. This allows the paper to expand or shrink before you lay it on the wall. It also takes a few minutes for the paste to activate the dry adhesive on prepasted wallpapers.

### Things You'll Need

☐ wallpaper paste

☐ buckets

☐ roller tray

☐ stirring stick

☐ paste brush or paint roller

☐ sponge

## 265 | Locate Wall Studs

A stud is a wooden 2-by-4 or 2-by-6. Studs make up the inside frame of a wall. Heavy shelves or pictures are most secure when mounted to wall studs.

### ⊙ Steps

1 Rap on the wall with your knuckle.

2 Move sideways along the wall, still rapping, and listen for a solid sound. Remember that studs are usually placed 16 or 24 inches apart—but you can't count on this. Studs may be located somewhat randomly, especially in older houses that have been remodeled.

### ✳ Tip

You don't have to knock hard for this to work.

### ⚠ Warning

Stud finders are not always reliable Drill a hole or pound in a nail to be sure you've found the stud.

3   If you don't trust your ear, use an electronic stud finder, available at most hardware stores. It beeps or flashes when it passes over wall studs or ceiling joists.

4   Try to locate the center of the stud. (This will be halfway between the edges detected by an electronic stud finder.)

## Hang a Picture 266

You've finally gotten that fantastic print or photograph framed. Now, how to hang it on the wall? Just follow these instructions.

### ⊙ Steps

1   Decide where to hang the picture. Avoid hanging one small picture on a huge expanse of wall—art looks better when it seems to extend the lines of furniture, windows or doorways or when several small pieces are grouped together.

2   Check that you are not hanging a heavy picture on wallboard only. Hang heavy objects only from a wall stud or beam.

3   Hold the picture up and make a small pencil mark on the wall where the top edge of the frame will be.

4   Choose an appropriate hook. You might want a two-piece nail-and-hook, or a hollow-wall anchor for heavier objects (see 268 "Install Screws and Anchors in Walls").

5   Holding the picture's wire taut, measure from the wire (or from the hanging tab if that's what the picture has) to the frame's top edge. Measure down that distance from the pencil mark you made on the wall and mark that spot—that's where the hook will go.

6   Nail the picture hook into the wall where you've just made a mark.

7   Hang the picture and adjust it so it's straight.

### ✴ Tips

You can hang wide frames using two hooks spaced about a third of the way in from each side. Use a level to make sure that the two hooks are correctly aligned.

Very lightweight pictures can hang from hooks that stick with adhesive to the wall.

Picture-hook packages usually indicate how much weight the hooks can bear.

### Things You'll Need

☐ two-piece nail-and-hook or hollow-wall anchor

☐ measuring tape

☐ nail

☐ hammer

## Hang a Shelf on a Wall 267

Adding storage or display space in your home can be a snap. Here's how to mount a simple wooden shelf and two brackets to a wall.

### ⊙ Steps

1   Buy a wooden shelf from a home-improvement store. Buy two shelf brackets—simple L shapes or something more decorative—making sure that the top leg of the bracket is no longer than the shelf is deep.

2   Buy screws if you don't have a supply at home or if they don't come with the brackets (see Tips).

3   Find the wall studs; you'll fasten the brackets to them (see 265 "Locate Wall Studs").

### ✴ Tip

Choose screws that will penetrate the wallboard and go into the stud about 1 inch. Choose shorter screws for mounting the shelf on the bracket, so they won't penetrate the top of the shelf.

4   Determine where you want the bottom edge of the shelf to sit, then mark the position in pencil, using a carpenter's level as a guide.

5   Line up the top of each bracket with the pencil line and mark the attachment holes on the wall. Set the bracket aside.

6   Test-drill the holes to make sure they are going into wood rather than wallboard. If there is no stud in a convenient place and the shelf is not going to carry more than a few pounds, you may be able to settle for using hollow-wall anchors (see 268 "Install Screws and Anchors in Walls").

7   Attach the brackets to the wall, lay your shelf on top, and screw the bracket into the shelf.

**Things You'll Need**

☐  wooden shelf

☐  shelf brackets

☐  screws

☐  carpenter's level

☐  drill

---

## 268 | Install Screws and Anchors in Walls

You must tie a heavy object into a wall stud, or it will tear a hole in your wall as it comes crashing down. However, you can hang lighter objects between studs using a hollow-wall anchor.

### ◉ Steps

#### Installing Screws in Solid Wood

1   Make sure that the threads are long enough to reach a joist or stud if you are installing a weight-bearing screw through Sheetrock.

2   Locate the stud and mark it with a pencil (see 265 "Locate Wall Studs").

3   Drill a pilot hole smaller than the hardware. Usually a ⅛-inch bit works well for this.

4   Turn the screw into the pilot hole, starting by hand. Use pliers if this becomes too difficult.

#### Installing Hollow-Wall Anchors

1   Choose a hollow-wall anchor such as a molly bolt, toggle bolt or plastic hollow-wall insert for a hollow wall or door.

2   Mark the position for the anchor or insert. Drill a hole in the wall just large enough to fit the anchor or insert.

3   Thread a screw through a molly bolt or toggle bolt before you push it through the wallboard into the hollow space in the wall. If using a plastic hollow-wall insert, place the insert into the hole before driving the screw or attaching the hook. Do not overtighten.

4   Alternatively, consider a relatively new type of anchor that looks like a giant screw with huge threads. You can simply thread these anchors directly into wallboard using a power screwdriver or a hand screwdriver; they bury themselves so they are flush with the wall and have a threaded opening to put a screw into.

### ✳ Tips

Remember that the more fasteners you use to support an object, the less stress is put on each fastener.

Hollow-wall anchors and other inserts are not strong enough to hold items from the ceiling. Screw directly into the wooden ceiling joists.

**Things You'll Need**

☐  hollow-wall anchor

☐  drill

☐  screws

☐  screwdriver

☐  power screwdriver (optional)

☐  pliers (optional)

## Install Curtain Rods · 269

Before you dress up your windows with curtains or draperies, make sure that you properly install rods and brackets for your window coverings.

### ⊙ Steps

1 Determine if you want to mount your curtain rods on the window casing or on the wall. You'll need hollow-wall anchors if you're not attaching the bracket to wood casing, a stud or a nailing block behind the wallboard (see 268 "Install Screws and Anchors in Walls").

2 Hold up the rod to the wall or casing to determine proper positioning. Place a carpenter's level over the rod to make sure the position is level.

3 Place the brackets 3 to 6 inches beyond the edge of the window, depending on your preference. Mark the placement for the top of the brackets on the wall or casing in light pencil.

4 Indicate the position of the bracket holes on the wall or casing with a light pencil mark.

5 Drill pilot holes—shallow holes that will help you start the screws or anchors—into the pencil marks on the wall or casing.

6 Insert screws (usually provided by the manufacturer) or anchors through the bracket and into the wall.

7 Position the curtain rod into the brackets.

### ✳ Tips

If your curtain rod is longer than 48 inches, consider installing a center bracket to support the weight of the rod and curtains.

Use wall fasteners that will properly support the weight of your rod and curtains.

### Things You'll Need

☐ carpenter's level

☐ curtain rods

☐ brackets

☐ pencil

☐ screws

☐ drill

---

## Measure Your Window for Curtains · 270

Whether you make your own curtains, buy off the shelf or order custom made, knowing the right measurements for your window is key.

### ⊙ Steps

1 Decide what kind of curtains you want: floor-length formal drapes, informal tab-tops or café curtains.

2 Decide where the curtain rod will go. You'll probably want it about 6 inches above the window frame, but you might want it higher or lower or—for a dramatic look on a tall, deep window—inside the frame.

3 Decide how much coverage you want. Curtains usually extend about 6 inches above the window frame, 2 to 3 inches on each side, and 2 to 3 inches on the bottom. Consider how much light you want to block— probably a lot if the window faces east and you like to sleep in—and how much privacy you want the curtains to provide.

4 Use a tape measure to measure from the curtain rod to the desired bottom point, and from side to side. Multiply the side-to-side measurement by 2 to allow for generously full curtains.

### ✳ Tip

Make sure the salesperson or decorator understands that these are desired finished dimensions of your curtains, not the dimensions of your window. (It is of course helpful to provide window dimensions as well.)

## 271 | Buy a New Carpet

Whatever your style or budget, you can find carpeting to fit your needs and tastes.

### ⊙ Steps

1 Decide which areas of your home you want to carpet.

2 Measure the rooms that you want to carpet.

3 Go to several vendors. Try both carpet-only showrooms and general home centers. Ask about installation costs unless you plan to lay the carpet yourself.

4 Consider the various grades of carpeting available. Are you carpeting a high-traffic location or a less frequented area of your home?

5 Consider your long-term needs. Is it worth paying more for carpeting that will last 10 years instead of 5? Do you expect to move or remodel within that time?

6 Take samples of any carpet you are considering so you can view them with your walls and furniture.

7 Expect carpet prices to vary considerably with quality and style. Typically sold by the square yard, carpeting can cost from $10 to $15 per square yard for basic carpet and upward of $30 per square yard for luxury carpeting (not including installation).

8 Make your selection after considering cost, style, color and durability.

9 Decide what type of padding you want under the carpeting. Often, a certain level of padding will be included in the installation price, and you will have the option to upgrade.

10 Have the vendor send someone to your home to measure the area to be carpeted.

11 Clean and empty the room before the installers arrive.

12 Check the carpet to make sure that it is clean and properly installed before signing an invoice.

### ✳ Tip

Extra padding is an effective way to improve the feel of less expensive carpeting and is well worth the extra cost.

### ⚠ Warning

Be extremely careful cutting and measuring carpet if installing it yourself.

## 272 | Buy a Sofa

Finding the right sofa is crucial to your living room's decor—and to the room's relaxation factor. Here are some tips that will help you rise to the challenge.

### ⊙ Steps

1 Determine potential size restrictions for your sofa. For example, if it will be moved up a flight of stairs or placed in a small room, determine the maximum measurements—depth and height as well as length.

2 Consider the color carefully because a sofa will last many years, during which various colors will become hot and then passé. A neutral sofa can be updated simply by swapping out the pillows.

### ✳ Tip

If the legs screw in (a mark of quality), this can be a help when moving the sofa. You'll be able to remove the legs to help the sofa turn a stairwell corner.

3  Have an idea about upholstery before you shop. A tough leather may be ideal for a rough-and-tumble household with pets and toddlers; Navajo-white cotton could be fine for careful adults who don't snack while sitting on the sofa.

4  Be aware that patterned, two-tone, tweedy and other multicolor fabrics will camouflage soil and stains more effectively than will solids.

5  Try out the sofa in the store. You and other family members should sit on it for several minutes, trying out both an outside cushion and a center cushion to be sure they're comfortable.

6  Check the fabric for comfort. If it's scratchy or itchy, pass it by.

7  Examine whether the fabric's pattern is aligned where edges meet. If it's a stripe, plaid or big print, the pattern on the back of the sofa should align with the pattern on the cushion and then on down to the front of the seating base.

8  Look at the workmanship of the cushion cording. Does it snake around or is it straight?

9  Remove the sofa cushions and see what's under them. You shouldn't see any wood— just smooth, upholstered surfaces.

10  Ask the salesperson about interior construction. The frame should be wood with corner blocks and glue; don't buy a sofa with nailed, stapled or unbraced joints, as these will loosen and wobble.

## Arrange Living Room Furniture | 273

If your present furniture arrangement seems stale, put some pizzazz into your living room.

### ⊙ Steps

1  With a tape measure, find the dimensions of the room. Draw the outline to scale on graph paper. A typical scale is 1/4 inch equals 1 foot.

2  Mark anything that would affect your arrangement: outlets for electricity, telephone and cable; light switches; windows; doors that open into the room; space between windows; and sill height.

3  Make scale paper cutouts of your living room furniture and shift them on the room drawing as needed until a likely arrangement emerges.

4  Select a focal point for your room and subtly orient other furnishings and some lighting toward it. If there's a fireplace, it will nearly always be the focal point; other focal points might be bookcases or built-in shelving to house lovely collectibles, or a sofa with a striking painting on the wall above it.

5  Arrange the furniture in such a way that pieces viewed as a unit don't show dramatic variance in height and mass as the eye sweeps the room. When a high-backed chair is next to a low table, boost the visual height of the table by hanging a piece of art above it.

6  Set up cozy conversation areas so that when you entertain, people can be seated and chat rather than having to stand. Examples would include two chairs separated by a low table, or two love seats facing each other.

### ✳ Tip

If you're comfortable using a computer, you might find home design software to be useful.

### Things You'll Need

☐ tape measure

☐ graph paper

☐ pencil and eraser

☐ ruler

☐ scissors

7   Pull furniture away from the walls for more flexibility in creating conversation areas. For example, use a sofa to divide space in a room.

8   Position the sofa so it's at a nonperpendicular angle to any walls to create drama. Perhaps put an area rug and coffee table parallel to the sofa.

9   Allow a minimum of 18 inches (24 is better) for traffic lanes through the room. Lanes will probably meander if you have two or three conversation areas in the room.

10  Freshen the room occasionally by shifting the furniture and accessories for a new look. Switch tabletop bric-a-brac around, add fresh flowers, change potpourri, move pictures.

## 274 | Select a Mattress

**Since the average mattress lasts about 10 years, buy the best you can afford. Here are guidelines.**

### ◎ Steps

1   Try out several mattresses before you make your decision.

2   Look at the warranty. Most premium mattresses come with at least a 10-year warranty. Note that many warranties are voided if the mattress has been stained or soiled in any way.

3   Wear loose, comfortable clothing when shopping for a mattress so you'll be comfortable lying down.

4   Think about whether you'll be sharing your mattress and how much room you need before you decide on a size.

5   Read labels to see what the ticking is made of. Quality ticking will be a cotton blend or damask, but ticking can also be a synthetic such as polyester or even vinyl.

6   Take off your shoes and rest on the mattress. This is the only way to tell if the padding is going to be comfortable.

7   Roll from the center of the mattress to the edges to see if the support is the same at all points, and check to see if the mattress has extra support around the edges where you would sit.

8   Buy a mattress with handles that are attached to the inner springs. They'll be less likely to break off.

9   Check the coil count. Coil construction and quality varies from company to company, but coils should start at 300 for a full, 375 for a queen and 450 for a king. Ask about the diameter of the coils. The wider, the sturdier.

10  Purchase a mattress and box spring (the foundation for the mattress) in one set, as they work together as a unit. (Low-profile box springs are also available for those who prefer a lower bed placement. These are roughly 3 to 4 inches lower than traditional spring sets.)

### ✳ Tips

Beds come in six different sizes: king (sometimes called eastern king), 76 inches wide by 80 inches long; California king, 72 inches wide by 84 inches long; queen, 60 inches wide by 80 inches long; full (or double), 54 inches wide by 75 inches long; twin (or single), 39 inches wide by 75 inches long; and twin extra-long, 39 inches wide by 80 inches long.

Try to bargain for the best price. Shopping for a mattress is similar to buying a car in that there is often room for negotiation.

### ⚠ Warnings

Pillow tops add an extra layer of padding to the top of the mattress but tend to sag more quickly than thinner padding on mattresses.

Hard mattresses don't necessarily offer the best support. If a mattress is too hard, it may add uncomfortable pressure to your hips and shoulders.

## Select a Futon

**275**

Originating in Asia, futons are flexible and foldable cotton or foam mattresses that double as couches. The style you buy will depend on whether it will be used as a couch, a bed or both.

### ⊙ Steps

1   Find out if the frame has at least a five-year warranty, especially if you're buying one that operates as both a bed and a couch.

2   Buy a futon with a mattress that's at least 6 inches thick. If the mattress is thinner than 6 inches, you'll probably be uncomfortable.

3   See what the futon is made of—usually either cotton, a cotton-foam combination, a cotton-polyester blend or a cotton-wool combination.

4   Purchase the heaviest mattress available—either an all-cotton mattress or a cotton/foam/springs mattress—if you're not going to move or roll up the futon very often.

5   Get a futon made of cotton and foam if you're looking for a mattress that weighs less. This combination also holds its shape and doesn't sag.

6   Try a cotton-polyester blend if you're looking for an even lighter mattress. It's flexible and soft and holds its shape.

7   Think about buying a cotton-wool combination if you want a supersoft mattress. But keep in mind that cotton-wool is not very flexible.

8   Consider an innerspring mattress made of a spring unit that sits between layers of foam and cotton. It's flexible and gives the feel of a traditional mattress. However, it does weigh more than the cotton and cotton-combination futon mattresses.

9   Lie down on the futon and spread your weight out evenly to check for comfort and support. Make sure the futon isn't lumpy.

10   Choose between a trifold and bifold frame. A trifold is folded twice and uses the width of the mattress as the couch. A bifold is folded once and uses the length of the mattress as the couch, providing more seat room.

11   Ask the manufacturer if the frame is made from southern yellow pine, which is ideal for futon frames because it's very heavy and durable. Most other types of pine and wood are too brittle to withstand the daily wear and tear a futon endures, and they don't hold up as well.

### ✱ Tips

Futon mattress sizes are as follows: king, 76 inches by 80 inches; California king, 72 inches by 84 inches; queen, 60 inches by 80 inches; full/double, 54 inches by 75 inches; twin/single, 39 inches by 75 inches.

Futon mattresses last from 2 to 10 years, depending on the quality.

Cotton-foam and cotton-polyester are the best mattresses for everyday use because they weigh less and hold their shape well.

Check the wall clearance on a frame before buying it. Some futons need to be pulled away from the wall before they can be converted into a bed. Others simply rest against the wall and don't need to be pulled out.

Buy a futon cover for your mattress to protect it from stains and dust.

## Arrange Bedroom Furniture

**276**

Bedrooms should be arranged for comfort and relaxation. Following are some tips to make your bedroom a cozy and welcoming retreat.

### ⊙ Steps

1   Acknowledge that every room needs a focal point and that the focal point in a bedroom is nearly always the bed. Give it center stage.

### ✱ Tips

Be bold in the planning stage—after all, there's no heavy lifting at this point. For instance, you might turn the bed cutout diago-

2   With a tape measure, measure the room. Draw the bedroom to scale on graph paper. A scale of ¼ inch equals 1 foot is a common choice.

3   Be sure to measure short wall spaces—the distance between windows, the distance between the edge of a radiator to the corner and such— and include the measurement in the drawing. That way, you'll know whether your triple dresser (or other big, heavy furnishing) can squeeze into the space.

4   Mark all of the room's fixed features on the scale drawing. These include heating ducts; windows (and the height of the sill from the floor); the drapery (or shutter) stack-up to the left and right sides of windows; radiators; outlets (especially ones for a central vacuum and cable television); phone jacks; light switches; doors (mark the swing width and direction); wall sconces; fireplaces; built-ins (bookcases, desks, dressing tables); and ceiling fan.

5   Measure your furnishings and make cutouts of their footprints according to your scale.

6   Arrange and rearrange the furniture cutouts on the room drawing to your heart's content. Allow at least 18 inches for traffic lanes, and set aside space for a bedside table (or pair of tables for a shared bed) as a perch for lighting, a glass of water, medication, eyeglasses, lotion, books or the remote control.

7   Place the bed so it doesn't impede the entry, closet or bathroom doors.

8   Decide on your final scheme and move the furnishings.

9   Tweak here and there as needed.

10  Position lamps and other accessories, including pictures on the walls. Note that most pictures should be visually anchored with a piece of furniture underneath.

nally into the corner (plan to put a tall plant, floor lamp or corner shelf behind the bed if the space looks empty).

Two heads are better than one. Enlist a friend or family member if you have doubts. And if the room is for a child, get his or her input for a happier result.

## Things You'll Need

- ☐ metal tape measure
- ☐ graph paper
- ☐ pencil and eraser
- ☐ ruler
- ☐ scissors

---

## 277 | Strip Wood Furniture

Anyone who's ever found cherry or tiger oak underneath layers of old paint knows that while some pieces are not worth stripping, others are.

### ◉ Steps

1   Make sure there's no chance your piece of furniture is an antique whose value could be destroyed by stripping the finish.

2   Set up your work area in a well-ventilated place with nothing around that could produce flames or sparks.

3   Remove drawer pulls and other hardware and place the furniture on a layer of newspaper or a disposable drop cloth (such as an old sheet). You may want to set the piece on scrap wood or bricks, especially if you're stripping the legs, to keep them from sticking.

4   Paint on a thick layer of stripper. Wear gloves and safety goggles.

### ✱ Tip

When you're finished, dispose of all brushes and remaining stripper as instructed by the paint stripper's manufacturer.

### ⚠ Warning

Even the new "safe" strippers are caustic. If any stripper gets on your skin, wash it off immediately with soap and warm water.

5   Allow enough time for the stripper to work. (It usually takes 5 to 10 minutes).

6   Scrape the bubbled paint (or varnish) and stripper off in strips, using a paint and varnish scraper, an old spatula, or a putty knife; use an old toothbrush or cotton swabs for crevices. Take care not to scratch or mar softwood or gouge through thin veneers.

7   Repeat if necessary. Two applications are often required, especially if it's an old piece with several layers of stubborn paint or varnish.

8   Wipe down the piece of furniture with clean rags and mineral spirits, and allow to dry. Don't skimp on the mineral spirits—you want the piece to be as clean as possible.

### Things You'll Need

- ☐ newspapers or drop cloth
- ☐ stripper and brush
- ☐ gloves and safety goggles
- ☐ scraper
- ☐ toothbrush or cotton swabs
- ☐ clean rags and mineral spirits

## Paint Wood Furniture                                                      278

Painting furniture involves sanding, priming and painting. Have the patience to apply that second coat of paint, and you'll be rewarded with a better-looking, longer-lasting finish.

### ◉ Steps

1   Make sure there's no chance that your piece of furniture is an antique whose value could be destroyed by changing the finish.

2   Set up your work area in a well-ventilated place with nothing around that could produce flames or sparks.

3   Remove drawer pulls and other hardware. Place the furniture on a layer of newspaper or a disposable drop cloth.

4   Sand the piece of furniture until smooth with fine-grit sandpaper or liquid sander. Wear gloves, safety goggles and a dust mask.

5   Remove any residual sawdust with a hand vacuum, brush or barely damp rag—you don't want to wet the wood.

6   Apply a coat of either white brush-on or gray spray-on water-based primer, depending on the size and area of the piece of furniture you intend to cover.

7   Allow the primer to become dry to the touch; this usually takes 1 to 2 hours. If you're not sure, read the recommended drying time on your can of primer.

8   If the primer coat looks spotty or thin, apply a second coat and allow it to dry.

9   Sand any rough areas.

10  Add a coat of water-based paint. Brush it on with even strokes, going in the direction of the wood grain. With spray paint, make slow passes with the can 8 to 12 inches from the wood surface. Allow the first coat to dry.

11  Add a second coat and allow it to dry overnight.

### ✱ Tips

Wash paintbrushes well immediately after use. Rinse under fast-running water until the water runs clear from the bristles.

When using spray paint, cover a wide area with newspaper to protect adjacent surfaces.

### ⚠ Warning

Always work in a well-ventilated area.

### Things You'll Need

- ☐ newspaper or drop cloth
- ☐ fine-grit sandpaper or liquid sander
- ☐ gloves
- ☐ safety goggles
- ☐ dust mask
- ☐ hand vacuum, brush or rag
- ☐ paintbrushes or spray gun
- ☐ water-based primer
- ☐ water-based paint

## 279 | Apply Wood Stain

Stains are designed to enhance the natural color of wood. The key is to put a stain on evenly and to keep your work area free of dust and other contaminants.

### ⊙ Steps

1 Set out a layer of newspapers to protect the work area.

2 Set the temperature in the room between 70 and 75 degrees F. If it's too cold or too hot, the stain's drying time will be affected.

3 Sand the wood smooth and vacuum or brush off debris. Oil-based stains in particular will look patchy if the wood isn't smooth.

4 Wet the wood slightly with a wide, clean paintbrush. This helps the stain spread more evenly.

5 Make sure that you have enough stain on hand for the job. If you have to buy more, it may come from a slightly different color lot.

6 Apply stain with a clean rag or paintbrush. Brushes are better for staining ornate carvings, molding and other irregularly shaped areas. Rags hold more stain and are easier to use on flat surfaces.

7 Use a spray gun to apply quick-drying alcohol-based stains (or dip the object in a stain bath for 5 minutes if a sprayer is too big or unable to reach fine details).

8 Wipe off excess stain with a paper towel.

9 Let the stain dry and then apply another coat if there are patchy areas.

10 Finish the project with varnish, shellac or wood polish to preserve the stain (see 280 "Apply Varnish").

11 Dispose of rags per instructions on the stain can.

### ✱ Tip

Use the stain liberally. Don't pour it onto the wood's surface, but don't be stingy with it.

### ⚠ Warning

Be cautious with stains—they can be flammable. Use them in well-ventilated areas, and wear gloves and a face mask when applying them.

### Things You'll Need

- ☐ newspapers
- ☐ sandpaper
- ☐ vacuum cleaner or brush
- ☐ wide paintbrush
- ☐ rags
- ☐ spray gun
- ☐ wood stain
- ☐ paper towels
- ☐ varnish, shellac or wood polish

## 280 | Apply Varnish

Varnishes protect wood from scratches and stains with a durable coating. These instructions apply specifically to oil-based varnishes, which are easiest to work with.

### ⊙ Steps

1 Set out a layer of newspapers to protect the work area. Make sure the area is well-ventilated.

2 Set the room temperature between 70 and 75 degrees F, which helps the varnish dry quicker without causing air bubbles and streaking.

3 Gather your disposable foam brushes, clean rags, steel wool pads and mineral spirits so that they are nearby when needed.

4 Strip any pre-existing finishes with a paint stripper. Wear gloves and a face mask while you work.

5 Clean the wood to be treated with a steel wool pad dipped in about 1 c. mineral spirits mixed with 2 tsp. linseed oil.

### ✱ Tips

Keep everything as clean as possible. A piece of lint or dust stuck in the varnish can ruin its smooth look. If you discover dust in the varnish, let it dry and then sand it with very fine sandpaper before applying the next coat.

Dragging the brush across the rim of the can will cause bubbles. Dab it instead. If you keep getting too many bubbles, thin the varnish with a little bit of mineral spirits.

6  Use a clean rag to dry the wood.

7  Pour enough varnish into a separate container to do the first coat, and dilute it with 20 percent mineral spirits (one part mineral spirits to four parts varnish). This coat seals the wood. (Read the label before use and follow the manufacturer's warnings and suggestions carefully.)

8  Use the foam brush to apply this diluted varnish into the wood. Work with the grain.

9  Let that coat dry at least 6 hours, but not more than 20.

10  Apply the second coat (nondiluted) with a new foam brush.

11  Put on up to five coats, depending on how much wear you anticipate the surface to receive. Use a new brush for each coat.

12  Dispose of rags, brushes and remaining stripper as advised by the stripper's manufacturer.

## Things You'll Need

- ☐ newspapers
- ☐ disposable foam brushes
- ☐ clean rags
- ☐ steel wool pads
- ☐ mineral spirits
- ☐ paint stripper
- ☐ gloves and face mask
- ☐ linseed oil
- ☐ varnish

## Upgrade Secondhand Furniture                    281

Secondhand furniture is inexpensive and can easily be upgraded. Here are some ways to update used furnishings.

### ⊙ Steps

1  Sand lightly, or use a liquid sanding product, and then paint wooden pieces (chairs, shelves, tables, sideboards) where the clear-coated finish has seen better days. Painted "antique" and faux finishes are popular; checkerboard and squiggle designs also are fun; or you may want to embellish that painted piece with decoupage.

2  Disguise a bad tabletop by having a mirror cut to cover the entire table, edge to edge. This works for dining tables and side tables, too.

3  Or you can hide a bad tabletop with a layer of ceramic tile. Use molding or sanded, varnished wood strips at the edges of the tile to fill to the perimeter of the table.

4  Reupholster a dining-table chair that has a pop-out seat. It's easy: Remove the old fabric and then cover with new fabric, using a staple gun to fasten it on the seat bottom. Make it taut but don't stretch it.

5  Cover up soiled or worn upholstery fabric on a dining chair by purchasing or sewing a new chair pad that ties onto the back of the chair. A chair pad with a ruffle on the front and sides usually hides the old upholstery completely.

6  Camouflage the blemished upholstery on a sofa or easy chair with a quilt (even an inexpensive moving-company quilt). Tuck it down deeply behind the back of the cushions.

7  Cover up the soiled arms of an upholstered chair or sofa by draping a pretty table runner over each arm.

8  Apply decorative brass-nailhead trim to hide nicked edges on wood furnishings such as tabletop edges and shelving.

### ✱ Tip

Altering the finish on any piece of furniture that might be a fine antique could reduce its value tremendously. Have a qualified person examine and appraise the piece for you first.

### ⚠ Warning

Be especially cautious about upgrading old baby furniture. Crib slats on older furniture may be so far apart that they pose a strangulation hazard for the baby; old painted finishes may contain lead.

9   Upgrade file cabinets, bookcases or Parsons tables by covering them with textured wallpaper (the type that mimics plaster friezes or pressed-tin ceilings). Then paint and glaze the piece—aged metallic finishes look spectacular on furniture.

10  Renew dull clear-coat finishes—varnishes, lacquer and the like—by cleaning with mineral spirits and possibly ultrafine steel wool; then apply a new coat of finish over the old (test first in an inconspicuous spot). This is a great way to save a picture frame or tabletop.

11  Revive an old trunk or cedar chest by scrubbing the exterior and lining the inside with wallpaper or by stapling in a tightly woven fabric, such as a new bed sheet. A flat braid can hide seams and corner imperfections.

12  Wrap a badly damaged lamp table or nightstand with fabric. The fabric can be fitted, almost like a slipcover, in a box shape for a rectangular table or draped over a round table; have glass cut for the top so that a nonwashable fabric won't be easily soiled.

13  Replace ugly, dated drawer pulls and knobs on a classically shaped chest of drawers, sideboard or similar piece.

14  Touch up small nicks and scratches on stained wooden pieces with special crayons (sold at paint and hardware stores)—or even an eyebrow pencil or shoe polish.

---

## 282 | Apply Wax to Wood

**Wax can make an old finish look new again while protecting the wood underneath. Good waxes contain carnauba and beeswax, and some have a silicone element to add shine.**

### ⊙ Steps

1   Seal new wood with a coat of clear varnish before waxing.

2   Clean old wood along the grain with a mixture of ¼ c. linseed oil and ¾ c. mineral spirits on a piece of fine steel wool. Go over the surface again with mineral spirits on a rag and let it dry. Make sure you have adequate ventilation when working with mineral spirits.

3   Apply liquid wood wax with a soft cloth. Pour wax on the cloth, not directly onto the wood.

4   Use circular motions and cover the entire surface.

5   Wait an hour or so and buff the first coat of wax with a clean, soft cloth.

6   Apply another coat, working with the grain.

7   Buff it again after an hour, and then once more after 6 or more hours.

8   Dispose of rags soaked with mineral spirits according to the instructions on the manufacturer's label.

### ✳ Tip

Wax polish should be used only on indoor woods, as it lacks durability.

### Things You'll Need

- ❏ clear varnish
- ❏ linseed oil
- ❏ mineral spirits
- ❏ steel wool
- ❏ rags
- ❏ liquid wood wax
- ❏ soft cloth

## Clean Painted Walls                              283

They may be vertical surfaces, but your walls get dirty, too. When you get the notion, get your wall cleaning in motion.

### ⊙ Steps

1   Protect your floors with newspapers or towels.

2   Brush cobwebs and dust from the wall with a soft-bristled brush.

3   Remove any remaining dirt with a dry-sponge—a rubber sponge available at most hardware stores. Rub the dry-sponge along the wall to lift dirt from it.

4   Fill a bucket about three-quarters full with warm water.

5   Add a small amount of dish soap—about as much as it takes to clean a sink full of dishes—to the bucket. This will be the cleaning bucket.

6   Place a second, empty bucket near the cleaning bucket. (You'll use this when you wring out the cleaning sponge.)

7   Dip a small portion of the flat face of a sponge into the cleaning bucket until it is damp.

8   Spread the cleaning solution on the wall with the sponge, beginning at the top and working toward the bottom. Use a ladder to reach the high spots on the wall.

9   Squeeze—but do not wring out—the sponge over the empty bucket after wetting the entire surface of the wall.

10  Blot the surface of the wall you've just cleaned to lift any further dirt from its surface.

11  Repeat this process until you have covered the wall.

12  Dry the wall using a terry cloth towel.

### ✳ Tip

Commercial products are available to remove oil-based or grease stains.

### Things You'll Need

- ☐ newspapers or towels
- ☐ soft-bristled brush
- ☐ dry-sponge
- ☐ buckets
- ☐ dish soap
- ☐ sponge
- ☐ ladder
- ☐ terry cloth towel

## Clean a Polyurethane-Coated Hardwood Floor      284

Polyurethane-finished hardwood floors are tough and will last for years with the proper care. Fortunately, caring for these floors is a snap.

### ⊙ Steps

1   Clear the room of rugs and as much furniture as possible. This helps to ensure that the entire floor gets equal treatment.

2   Sweep and/or vacuum the floor carefully. Dirt left on the floor during mopping can act as an abrasive.

3   Mix about 1 tsp. grease-cutting dish soap or oil soap into a large bucket full of warm water. The exact mixture isn't crucial; just keep the amount of soap to a bare minimum.

### ⚠ Warnings

Be very careful with water; you may need to spot-clean around any unsealed gaps between slats. Always buff the floor dry.

Don't use cleaning oils or furniture polishes on polyurethane-coated floors, as these can leave a residue that will cause refinishing problems later. Certain chemical-based strippers can damage the finish as well.

4  Start mopping in a corner along the wall farthest from the door, and mop the entire floor with firm strokes. Make sure the mop is well wrung out and not drippy. Both foam and string mop heads will work.

5  Use new solution when the water begins to grow cloudy or dirty.

6  Repeat the process with fresh water (no soap) once the entire surface has been thoroughly mopped with the cleaning solution. This will pick up the soapy residue and leave your floor clean and shiny.

7  Buff dry with clean, dry towels.

### Things You'll Need

- ☐ dish soap or oil soap
- ☐ bucket
- ☐ mop
- ☐ towels

---

## 285 | Deep-Clean Your Carpet

For heavily soiled carpets, shampooing is recommended, rather than spot-cleaning. Wet-cleaner machines spray and remove hot detergent solution while cleaning the carpet.

### ◉ Steps

1  Purchase or rent a wet-cleaner machine, also known as a steamer, at a hardware or grocery store. When you rent a machine, the necessary cleaning products are usually included or can be purchased at the rental store.

2  Vacuum the floor thoroughly.

3  Spray heavily soiled areas with prespray or traffic-lane cleaner. For really dirty areas, increase the amount of prespray used instead of increasing the amount of carpet shampoo.

4  Fill the machine's hose or reservoir with hot tap water.

5  Use the machine and carpet shampoo according to the steamer manufacturer's instructions.

6  Maximize the amount of water removed from the carpet by making a water-extraction pass with the water spray on, and then again with the spray off. Test the carpet with your hand. If your hand comes away with water droplets, extract again with the spray off; if your hand comes away damp and the carpet feels wrung out, you have extracted correctly.

7  Wait overnight for the carpet to dry before walking on it. To dry thoroughly, open windows and use fans.

### ✳ Tips

Special solutions are available to treat pet stains and odors.

To help your cleaning last longer, neutralize detergent residue left on the carpet by steaming with a vinegar-water rinse made up of 1 c. vinegar and 1 gallon water.

### ⚠ Warning

Oversaturating the carpet can cause water to soak through and damage the floor underneath.

### Things You'll Need

- ☐ wet-cleaner machine (steamer)
- ☐ prespray or traffic-lane cleaner
- ☐ carpet shampoo

---

## 286 | Clean Vinyl and Plastic Blinds

Don't go blindly into cleaning your window dressings. Follow these easy steps.

### ◉ Steps

#### Cleaning Monthly

1  Lower the blinds and close the slats.

2  Wipe with a damp rag. Avoid applying too much pressure to the blinds when scrubbing, as most are prone to denting and bending.

### ✳ Tips

Cloth-covered blinds should be vacuumed regularly and professionally cleaned every two years.

Most blinds can be professionally cleaned.

3   Close the slats in the opposite direction and wipe the other side.

## Cleaning Deeply

1   Remove the blinds from the window.

2   Release the blinds completely and lay them outside, on a drop cloth.

3   Spray the blinds with an all-purpose cleaner. Allow the cleaner to sit for a few minutes.

4   Scrub the blinds gently with a soft-bristled brush in a motion parallel to the slats.

5   Turn the blinds over and repeat this process.

6   Hang or hold up the blinds and rinse with a hose.

7   Shake as much moisture from the blinds as possible.

8   Hang the blinds outside and allow them to dry.

### Things You'll Need

❏ damp rag

❏ drop cloth

❏ all-purpose cleaner

❏ soft-bristled brush

❏ hose

# Clean Windows                                      287

**Brighten up your outlook by stripping off those layers of grime. Here's how to get your windows squeaky clean and streak free.**

## ◉ Steps

1   Prepare a cleaning solution of either a capful of ammonia or four to six drops of liquid dish soap in 2 gallons of water or 1 c. of vinegar in 1 quart of water. If using soap, use as little as possible to avoid streaking.

2   Dip a sponge into the solution, allowing the sponge to absorb just enough water to cover the window without flooding it.

3   Wash the surface of the window with the sponge, paying special attention to the sides and corners of the window frame, where dirt and grime tend to build up.

4   Dip a squeegee into a bucket of clean water.

5   Press the squeegee lightly into the surface of the window, starting at the top and pulling down vertically, stopping a few inches before the bottom of the window.

6   Wipe off the squeegee with a paper towel.

7   Press the squeegee down the area of the window directly beside the one you just cleaned, stopping at the same place.

8   Wipe off the squeegee with a paper towel.

9   Continue this process until the entire surface of the window except the final few inches at the bottom has been cleaned.

10  Pull the squeegee horizontally across the bottom section of the window and wipe the squeegee off with a paper towel.

11  Wipe off the water at the bottom of the window frame—where a great deal of moisture has by now collected—with a paper towel.

## ✳ Tip

For hard-to-reach windows, you can purchase squeegee extension poles at a hardware store that are specifically made for washing windows.

### Things You'll Need

❏ ammonia, dish soap or vinegar

❏ sponge

❏ squeegee

❏ bucket

❏ paper towels

## 288 | Clean Wood Walls and Paneling

Some people hesitate to clean wood paneling for fear of damaging it. Here's how to clean those walls and panels safely.

### ⊙ Steps

1 Dust wood walls and paneling with a soft rag, or vacuum with a vacuum cleaner brush about every two weeks.

2 Use a soft cloth to apply oil soap to particularly dirty wood according to the oil soap manufacturer's directions.

3 For tough stains, clean the wood with mineral spirits as a last resort. To test for staining, use a soft cloth to apply the spirits to an inconspicuous area of the wall. If the spirits do not stain, moisten the cloth with mineral spirits and lightly dab the spot or stain. Allow to dry.

### ⚠ Warning

Don't use mineral spirits near heat or flame. Always allow proper ventilation.

### Things You'll Need

☐ soft rags or vacuum cleaner

☐ oil soap and soft cloth

☐ mineral spirits (optional)

## 289 | Clean and Care for Marble

Marble isn't as tough as you may think; it's a comparatively soft stone that is easily scratched and marred. Chances are you paid a lot for it, so keep it clean and take good care of it.

### ⊙ Steps

1 Wipe down marble surfaces with a damp rag and buff dry with a chamois for routine weekly cleaning.

2 Use a neutral, nonabrasive cleaner (such as acetone, hydrogen peroxide or clear ammonia) for tough stains.

3 Apply the cleaner with a cloth and buff dry.

4 After cleaning, polish marble surfaces using a marble polish containing tin oxide.

5 Protect marble floors with a stone sealer, and use standard nonabrasive floor cleaners to clean them.

6 Place coasters under glasses and put plastic under cosmetics on marble surfaces. Use rugs to cover marble floors.

7 Refer scratches of any depth to a professional.

### ⚠ Warnings

Powdered cleansers will scratch or damage marble.

Even weak acids—vinegar, wine, orange juice, cola—can damage marble. Mop up spills immediately and rinse with water.

### Things You'll Need

☐ rags and chamois

☐ cleaner

☐ marble polish

☐ stone sealer

☐ floor cleaner

## 290 | Organize Your Kitchen

You've got three half-full bottles of vinegar in your cupboard and your utensil drawer is a minefield of knife tips and mangled wire whisks. Time to get organized!

### ⊙ Steps

1 Go through your kitchen and discard anything you don't use, along with any food, spices or medicines that are beyond their expiration dates.

2 Take everything out of your cupboards and drawers, and wash the insides with warm soapy water. Rinse, let dry and replace cupboard and drawer liners.

3 Store pots, pans and cooking utensils near the stove, nesting the pots and pans together to conserve space.

4 Store dishes and silverware near your eating area and/or dishwasher. Use racks and silverware holders to maximize use of space.

5 Be sure that children are able to reach items they use. Put things they should not use—such as sharp tools, alcohol and cleaning chemicals—well out of reach.

6 Alphabetize your spices and keep them near the stove on a spice rack or in a nearby cupboard on a revolving rack.

7 Remove large and seldom-used items from countertops and store them in a cupboard. For appliances that you use often, consider adding an "appliance barn," which can store toasters, blenders, juicers and other appliances on the countertop without clutter.

8 Store food items that you use on a daily basis in accessible spots, and store all like food items together—for example, tea and sugar.

9 Put food that may become infested with insects into sturdy plastic containers and seal them.

10 Use drawer dividers to organize utensils.

**Things You'll Need**

☐ racks and silverware holders

☐ spice rack

☐ appliance barn

☐ plastic containers

☐ drawer dividers

---

## Care for Silver 291

**Extended exposure to air can tarnish your precious silver. Here's how to keep your silver flatware looking clean and new.**

### ◉ Steps

1 Handling helps keep silver free of tarnish, so use it regularly.

2 Avoid exposing silver for long periods of time to foods such as eggs, mustard and mayonnaise, which are high in sulfur and can corrode silver.

3 Avoid leaving silver on rubber mats to dry, as rubber also contains sulfur.

4 Wash and dry silver by hand.

5 Use a soft dish towel when drying silver.

6 Apply silver polish according to label instructions.

7 Rub the polish in thoroughly.

8 Buff the surface of polished silver with a fresh, dry polishing cloth until the silver has a bright sheen.

9 Thoroughly remove the polish from the silver before use; silver polish tastes terrible.

10 If silver is to be stored for a long time, pretreat it with a tarnish-retardant polish before storing.

**✳ Tip**

Frequent polishing of silver-coated or -plated items may wear down their silver finish, leaving the base metal exposed. Rather than polishing such items, use them as often as possible and wash them by hand to prevent tarnishing.

**Things You'll Need**

☐ silver polish

☐ soft dish towel

☐ soft polishing cloths

☐ tarnish-retardant polish

## 292 | Polish Brass and Copper

Taking care of your brass objects and accessories is simple, and you may already have the necessary products.

### ⊙ Steps

1   Dust brass and copper regularly.

2   Wash in warm, soapy water; rinse and dry.

3   Use a commercial brass or copper cleaner as directed. A combination of toothpaste and Worcestershire sauce also works, although it is not as powerful as a commercial cleaner.

4   Apply with a soft cloth, wipe off, and buff with a clean, dry cloth.

5   Avoid using harsh chemicals, abrasive cleaners or scouring pads.

### ⚠ Warning

Do not polish lacquered brass or copper items.

### Things You'll Need

☐ brass or copper cleaner

☐ soft cloth

## 293 | Clean a Coffeemaker

One way to make your coffee taste better is to keep your drip coffeemaker clean and free of hard-water deposits.

### ⊙ Steps

1   Put the filter basket in place.

2   Combine one part white vinegar with one part water in the pot; pour it into the coffeemaker and replace the pot. Turn the machine on.

3   Allow the solution to empty completely into the pot.

4   Turn the coffeemaker off and rinse the pot and filter basket with warm water.

5   Pour clean water into the coffeemaker and turn it on.

6   Allow the water to empty completely into the pot.

7   Rinse the pot.

8   Wipe the outside of the coffeemaker with a soapy sponge and polish it dry.

### ✱ Tips

Clean your coffeemaker weekly if you make a lot of coffee.

Consider purchasing a special coffeemaker cleaner. Follow the manufacturer's directions.

Rinse the pot and basket every day with warm water and once a week with mild soap and warm water.

### Things You'll Need

☐ white vinegar

☐ sponge

## 294 | Clean a Refrigerator

That joke about the moldy produce being a science experiment has gotten pretty stale. It's time to clean out the fridge and freshen things up. Here's how to do this weekly chore right.

### ⊙ Steps

1   Turn the temperature-control knob inside the refrigerator to "Off." If you have a refrigerator with a drip pan underneath, remove it to clean.

2   Take everything out of the refrigerator.

### ✱ Tip

Condenser coils, usually located in the front of the refrigerator behind a metal plate near the floor, should be vacuumed several times a year to prevent dust buildup.

3 Throw away any food that is moldy, outdated or otherwise spoiled.

4 Take all removable parts out of the refrigerator, including shelves, wire racks and drawers.

5 Fill the sink with warm, soapy water (use a mild dish soap).

6 Wipe any food matter out of the drawers.

7 Hand-wash the shelves, wire racks and drawers, then rinse them in warm water.

8 Let the shelves, wire racks and drawers drain in a dish rack, on paper towels or on newspapers.

9 Remove any food matter from the bottom of the refrigerator.

10 Wash the inside of the refrigerator using a sponge or dishcloth and the warm, soapy water. Remember the compartments and door racks.

11 Rinse the inside of the refrigerator with a sponge or dishcloth and clean warm water.

12 For odor control, use a solution of 2 tbsp. baking soda to 1 quart warm water to wash the inside of the refrigerator. A solution of 1 c. vinegar and 1 gallon warm water is also effective; apply and rinse. A box of baking soda placed in the refrigerator will also cut down on odors.

13 Replace all shelves, wire racks and drawers.

14 Wash the outside of the refrigerator and the gasket (rubber molding around the door) with warm, soapy water; rinse and wipe dry.

15 Turn the temperature control knob inside the refrigerator back to the recommended setting.

16 Return the food to the refrigerator, first wiping off any bottles or jars that are sticky.

## ⚠ Warning

Never use harsh cleaners or scouring pads in or on the refrigerator.

## Things You'll Need

- ☐ mild dish soap
- ☐ sponge or dishcloths
- ☐ baking soda or vinegar

---

## Clean a Toilet                                           295

This will probably never be your favorite household chore, but you have to admit, it's one of the most important!

### ◉ Steps

1 Open the bathroom windows and door, or turn on the fan. You need good ventilation when working with household cleaners.

2 Put on rubber gloves and lift the toilet seat. Flush the toilet to wet the sides of the bowl.

3 Apply a generous amount of powder or liquid toilet cleaner to the bowl, focusing on getting it along the sides, not just in the water. Be sure to follow the directions for your type of toilet bowl cleaner.

4 Let the cleaner stand for a minute.

5 Using the toilet brush, swab all around the interior of the bowl, paying special attention to the area immediately beneath the rim, and to the water line.

## ⚠ Warning

Never mix cleaners. The fumes could be deadly.

## Things You'll Need

- ☐ rubber gloves
- ☐ toilet cleaner
- ☐ toilet brush
- ☐ pumice stone
- ☐ disinfectant

6   Flush the toilet to rinse. As the water in the bowl is replaced, thoroughly rinse the toilet brush in the incoming water.

7   Notice if the toilet bowl has developed a ring. If it has, scrub the stain with a wet pumice stone. Be sure the pumice remains wet throughout the process.

8   Spray the seat, the underside of the seat and the rim with disinfectant.

9   Wipe down the base, lid and tank top with disinfectant.

10  Allow the disinfectant to dry before using the toilet.

---

## 296 | Clean a Bathtub

Scrub-a-dub-dub, there's soap scum in your tub; now how do you get it clean? With brushes and gloves you'll clean out that tub and give it a sparkling sheen.

### ⊙ Steps

#### Cleaning the Walls and Above the Tub

1   Put on rubber gloves.

2   Spray all-purpose cleaner on the walls above the tub.

3   Allow the cleaner to sit a few minutes, then rinse or wipe it off.

4   Remove mildew from grout by using a tile cleaner.

5   Apply the tile cleaner to the grout with a grout brush and scrub thoroughly.

6   Rinse well.

#### Cleaning the Tub

1   Apply a heavy-duty bathtub or all-purpose cleaner to a tub coated in enamel, the most durable of bathtub materials. Allow it to sit for 5 minutes, and scrub with a scrub brush using gentle pressure. Rinse well.

2   Scrub away the remaining soap scum with a scrub brush or an old toothbrush. When scrubbing, pay special attention to the corners of the tub and the area around the drain, where soap scum and dirt tend to build up. Also, look for evidence of a bathtub ring, the ring of dirt and stains that forms around the edges of the tub, which will require extra time and scrubbing.

3   Rinse again.

4   Apply a nonabrasive bathroom or bathtub cleaner if the tub is acrylic, which can scratch easily. Gently scrub with a soft-bristled brush. Rinse the tub well.

5   Apply a specialized fiberglass cleaner or a nonabrasive bathtub cleaner to a fiberglass tub. Scrub gently with a sponge. Rinse well.

### ✱ Tip

Wipe down the tub with a washcloth or sponge after each use to avoid getting a bathtub ring.

### ⚠ Warning

Never mix cleaners. The fumes could be deadly.

### Things You'll Need

☐ rubber gloves

☐ all-purpose cleaner

☐ scrub brush

☐ tile cleaner

☐ grout brush

☐ nonabrasive bathroom or bathtub cleaner

☐ soft-bristled brush

☐ fiberglass cleaner

☐ sponge

# ✓ 297 Schedule Housekeeping Tasks

Keeping the house clean is an everyday chore, but you don't need to do it all every day. Some tasks you'll want to take care of daily; others you can put off for a week; still others you need to perform only once a year. To keep on top of the work, follow this schedule.

### Once a day

- Make beds.
- Pick up clutter.
- Throw dirty clothes in a hamper.
- Clean out bathtub and shower drains.
- Wipe off shower or tub.
- Wash dishes.
- Rinse kitchen sink.
- Empty kitchen garbage.
- Wipe off kitchen counter.
- Wipe stove.
- Sweep floor.

### Once a week

- Change bed linens.
- Vacuum carpets.
- Dust furniture.
- Clean shower or bathtub.
- Clean toilets.
- Throw out spoiled food in refrigerator.
- Empty all trash and gather recycling for pickup.
- Disinfect countertops.
- Flush sink disposal unit with cold water.
- Mop floor.

### Once a month

- Clean toothbrush and soap holders.
- Clean telephones.
- Clean the undersides of tables and chairs.
- Clean refrigerator shelves.
- Clean fridge exterior.
- Clean items on kitchen countertop.
- Disinfect trash cans.
- Clean stove, including range and backsplash.
- Check for cobwebs on ceilings, and vacuum.

### Every three months

- Wash or dry-clean quilts, duvets and bedspreads.
- Launder throw rugs and shower curtains.
- Wash blinds, shades, and curtains.
- Wash windows.
- Wash walls, moldings and baseboards.
- Wipe cabinets, wood-work and any smudges off walls.
- Clean refrigerator coils.
- Defrost freezer.
- Polish silver.

### Every six months

- Vacuum and turn mattresses.
- Empty bathroom cabinets and responsibly dispose of outdated medicines.
- Shampoo carpets.
- Wax or polish furniture.
- Empty kitchen cabinets and clean inside; throw away all outdated food.
- Clean tops of kitchen and bathroom cabinets.
- Vacuum behind large appliances.

### Once a year

- Empty dresser drawers and vacuum inside.
- Roll up area rugs and vacuum underneath.
- Clean ceiling fixtures.
- Reseal wood floors.
- Go through all paperwork (bills, statements, notices) and recycle everything you don't need.
- Organize remaining papers in a filing system.

calendar

## 298 | Clean Grout Without Scrubbing

Because sometimes it's OK to take the easy way out.

### ⊙ Steps

1   Put on rubber gloves.

2   Fill a spray bottle with a solution consisting of half liquid chlorine bleach and half warm water.

3   Turn the bottle nozzle to get a stream instead of a mist.

4   Spray the grout, saturating it with long, sweeping strokes.

5   Allow the saturated grout to sit for 10 to 15 minutes.

6   Repeat if needed.

7   Rinse or wipe off with a sponge.

### ⚠ Warning

Chlorine bleach is caustic at this concentration; wear safety goggles and a shower cap.

### Things You'll Need

☐ rubber gloves

☐ spray bottle

☐ chlorine bleach

☐ sponge

## 299 | Remove Hard-Water Deposits From Showerheads

Hard water left on plastic surfaces causes lime and mineral deposits that can ruin your showerhead. Here's how to tackle these deposit problems on plastic showerheads.

### ⊙ Steps

1   Combine 1 pint white vinegar and 1 pint hot water in a small bowl.

2   Remove the showerhead from the pipe.

3   Submerge the showerhead in the vinegar-water solution for 1 hour.

4   Rinse and replace the showerhead.

### Things You'll Need

☐ white vinegar

☐ bowl

## 300 | Make a Bed

These steps are for the traditional blanket and bedspread. If you use a comforter or thick quilt, you can simply place it on top of the sheets without tucking it in. Pillows go on top.

### ⊙ Steps

1   Put the bottom sheet on the mattress. If it is a fitted sheet, it will have sewn-in corners and you can fit it snugly over the mattress. If it's a flat sheet, follow step 2 to make hospital corners.

2   Lay the top sheet on the mattress so there's enough to tuck under the mattress on all four sides. Tuck the sheet snugly under the mattress at the foot of the bed and the head of the bed. Tuck the corners under the mattress on the long sides, making sure that the folds are flat. Tuck in the sides, pulling the sheet taut.

### ✱ Tip

A bed is a highly personal thing—choose bedding that will please the person sleeping there.

3   Place the top sheet over the fitted or bottom sheet, and again make hospital corners, but this time only at the foot of the bed.

4   Add blankets, repeating step 3.

5   Fold the top sheet back over the blankets at the head of the bed, pulling the sheet back about half a foot, and tuck under the side flaps.

6   Slip pillowcases over the pillows.

7   Place the pillows on top of the blanket and sheets at the head of the bed. Lay them flat, or prop them up against the headboard or wall.

8   Place the bedspread, quilt or comforter on the bed.

9   If you have a bedspread or thin quilt, fold the top of the spread down, lay the pillows on top, then fold the spread back over them, leaving part of the spread tucked under the pillows.

10  Place any remaining decorator pillows over the bed covering.

## Care for Down Pillows and Comforters    **301**

Down pillows and comforters are luxurious on cold winter nights, but they require special care. The rule of thumb is: The less often you clean your comforter or pillow, the longer it will last.

### ⊙ Steps

#### Caring for a Down Pillow

1   Cover your pillow with a pillow case at all times. This will keep your pillow free from dust, dirt and body oils.

2   Buy a pillow cover with a zipper for an extra layer of protection under your pillow case. This will also help those who have allergies.

3   Clean the pillow cover and case regularly to keep your pillow fresh.

4   Launder or dry-clean your pillow yearly.

5   Spot-treat any stains before you wash your pillow if you're going to machine wash it.

6   Wash the pillow in cold water using a detergent that has a degreaser so that oils are removed. Follow the pillow manufacturer's instructions for specific detergents to use.

7   Very gently squeeze out any excess water from the pillow after washing.

8   Dry the pillow with the dryer set on its lowest setting; put a tennis ball in with the pillow so that the fill moves as it dries.

9   Store your pillow in a dry and well-ventilated closet or room when you are not using it, in order to avoid mildew.

#### Caring for a Down Comforter

1   Place a cover over your down comforter to protect it from dust, dirt and body oils.

**✴ Tip**

Thoroughly dry your pillow and comforter so that they will not mildew.

**⚠ Warning**

Do not use fabric softener when you wash, as it will leave a coating on the down.

2   Shake out your comforter weekly to prevent the down from bunching up.

3   Air out your comforter occasionally to keep it fresh. Hang it on a clothes-line or shake it out a window.

4   Take your comforter to a dry cleaner every three to five years if you decide not to launder it at home.

5   Use a Laundromat with oversized washing machines if you have an oversized comforter, should you decide to machine-wash it.

6   Spot-treat any stains before you wash.

7   Wash your comforter in cold water using a detergent that has a degreas-er so that oils are removed.

8   Very gently squeeze out any excess water from the comforter.

9   Dry the comforter in the dryer on low heat setting with a tennis ball so that the fill moves as it dries.

10  Store the comforter in a dry and well-ventilated closet or room when you are not using it, in order to avoid mildew.

## 302 | Care for a Mattress

**Your mattress may be hidden under blankets and sheets, but it still needs special attention from time to time. If well cared for, it will last about 10 years.**

### ⊙ Steps

1   Cover your mattress with a cotton mattress pad, which will absorb per-spiration and can be removed and washed to keep the mattress clean.

2   Rotate your mattress twice a year, or more often if instructed by the manufacturer. Flip it over completely after the first six months. Then, after another six months, flip it over and turn it so that the head is at the foot of the bed. Some new mattresses don't need flipping. Check with the manufacturer.

3   Use the handles on the sides of the mattress for positioning only—not for carrying. Lifting by the handles can damage your mattress.

4   Air out your mattress each morning by folding back the covers to the bottom of the bed for half an hour before you make it. This will also prevent moisture buildup.

5   Try not to sit on the edge of the bed in the same place every day, because this can lead to sagging.

**✳ Tip**

Leave the "do not remove" tag attached to the mattress. You will need this for filing warranty claims.

**⚠ Warning**

Avoid spill and stain damage to your mattress. Many manufactur-ers void their warranties if there are stains.

## ✓ 303 Recycle Discards

Many cities have recycling programs that pick up cans, bottles and newspapers. Some also have programs for collecting motor oil and other hazardous waste. But did you know that still other common materials can be safely recycled? Here's how to help find a few of these items a happy second home.

### Printer cartridges

- Before you throw a cartridge away, be aware that printer cartridges can be recycled about six times without any loss of quality.

- Read the instructions on the box the cartridge came in. It may tell you how to send back the cartridge free of charge so it can be refilled.

- Contact Laser-Tone International at (800) 327-8458; this organization will pick up your cartridges at no charge. It will also deliver refilled cartridges.

- Go to the Eco-Office Web site at www.eco-office.com. It will provide a list of companies in your area that purchase used cartridges.

- Get in touch with Environmental Laser at (800) 442-8391 for more information.

### Packing peanuts

- Determine whether the peanuts are made from a vegetable derivative by running water on a few. If they disintegrate, they will decompose. Put them in a compost bin.

- Check with your local department of public works to see if it will pick up the peanuts.

- Look under packaging or shipping in the yellow pages for a store that will accept the peanuts. Many stores, such as Mail Boxes Etc., will let you drop them off.

- Call the Plastic Loosefill Council at (800) 828-2214 for a list of drop-off centers in your area.

- If you have a large quantity, seek advice from the Alliance of Foam Packaging Recyclers at (800) 944-8448 or www.epspackaging.org.

### Computers

- Write down all the information about the old computer, such as its brand, type and model number, and which peripherals you wish to recycle.

- Contact local schools or charities that might be able to make use of your equipment.

- Contact Back Thru the Future Micro Computers Inc. at (973) 884-2282. This outfit recycles computers and other office equipment for schools, government institutions, corporations and individuals.

- If you want to donate your computer to organizations that help people with disabilities, contact the Cristina Foundation at (800) 274-7846.

### Batteries

- Contact the Rechargeable Battery Recycling Corp. (RBRC) at (800) 8-BATTERY to learn how and where to recycle nickel-cadmium rechargeable batteries.

- Check with your local curbside recycling program about including household batteries with your other recyclables, and find out about special household hazardous-waste collection days.

- Try returning household batteries to stores that sell them. Several large houseware chains have battery-recycling programs.

- Take your old car battery to the garage, auto-parts store or retailer where you buy a new battery. Many recycling centers also take old car batteries.

reference

## 304 | Clean Out a Closet

So you're a pack rat? Set aside a couple of hours to clean out your closet. All it takes is a little organization to bring order to the chaos.

### ⊙ Steps

1   Start with a clean room, or you'll make an even bigger and more intimidating mess as you clean out the closet.

2   Choose one area of the closet to focus on, such as a shelf or the floor, and begin there. It will make the task seem less daunting if you break it up into manageable parts.

3   Get three boxes and mark them "Garbage," "Out of Place" and "Charity" or "Garage Sale."

4   Buy some stackable plastic bins with lids.

5   Evaluate each item you remove from the closet. Ask yourself if you have used the item in the past 12 months. If not, it's time to think seriously about getting rid of it.

6   Put things for Goodwill, the Salvation Army or another charity in the Charity box. Or if you have enough stuff to warrant a garage sale, set it aside in your Garage Sale box.

7   Stash things that belong in other rooms in the Out of Place box. (Give these things the 12-month test, too.)

8   Put as much as possible into the Garbage box. It's cathartic!

9   Sort the items you want to keep into categories, such as "High School Memorabilia," "Johnny's Artwork" or "Winter Accessories," and store them in the bins. Be sure to label the bins.

10  Label one bin "Odds & Ends." In it store found parts, orphaned gloves and other things that may eventually be reunited with their counterparts.

11  Stack the labeled bins neatly on the shelves and floor of the closet, making sure the ones you need to get into regularly are accessible.

### ✱ Tips

Give yourself a time limit. If you plan to spend 1½ hours cleaning, don't do more than that. It will still be there later.

Some charitable organizations will come to your house to pick up unused items.

### ⚠ Warning

Get permission to throw away things that do not belong to you personally.

### Things You'll Need

☐ boxes

☐ plastic bins with lids

☐ labels

## 305 | Clean Brick Surfaces

Brick is an excellent and timeless building material for walls, home exteriors and other outdoor structures. However, it can get just as grimy as anything else. Here's how to clean it up.

### ⊙ Steps

1   Attack mold, mildew and lichens aggressively. They can change the color of the masonry as well as affect its integrity. Prevent them from growing by keeping moisture to a minimum. Let as much air and sun reach the surface as possible.

2   Wear a dust mask and goggles when cleaning organic matter from brickwork. You'll create a lot of dust that you don't want to breathe.

### ⚠ Warning

Avoid using a wire brush, which will scratch brick surfaces.

3   Remove the crusties with a stiff scrub brush. To kill the spores, use a sponge to apply a solution of 3/4 c. chlorine bleach in 4 c. water. Or use a commercial fungicide, available at garden centers.

4   Look for a white salt residue (efflorescence) on brickwork.

5   Remove it with the scrub brush—don't use water, which will simply dissolve it, allowing it to soak into the brick.

6   Remove stains caused by mortar or cement by rubbing the area with a brick of the same color.

### Things You'll Need

☐ dust mask and goggles

☐ stiff scrub brush

☐ sponge

☐ chlorine bleach

---

## Clean Out a Fireplace and Chimney | 306

A clean fireplace and chimney is your best defense against a dangerous chimney fire.

### ⊙ Steps

1   Buy a set of chimney rods and brushes at the hardware store.

2   Change into old clothes and don safety goggles and a dust mask. Lay out a clean tarp in front of the fireplace. Cover the fireplace opening with a plastic tarp held on with duct tape.

3   Open the fireplace's damper. This is the metal door up inside the fireplace, located just above the firebox; it prevents cold air from entering your home when you don't have a fire burning.

4   Carefully climb up on your roof, taking the rods and brushes with you.

5   Remove the chimney cap—sometimes called a spark arrestor—and check it for weather damage. The purpose of the chimney cap is to keep sparks from escaping your chimney. It also serves to keep out rain, small animals and debris.

6   Assemble the chimney rods and brushes according to the equipment manufacturer's directions.

7   Run the brush down the chimney, using a short up-and-down plunging motion. Some brushes are designed to twist as well.

8   Go back inside the house and use a short chimney brush to clean the flue, which is the pipe that runs between the fireplace and the chimney.

9   Use a vacuum cleaner or small broom and dustpan to remove the cold ashes and creosote from the fireplace and the damper.

10  Brush the floor and walls of the fireplace with a stiff, dry scrub brush.

11  Use the brush to clean the creosote built up behind the damper.

12  Reach through the damper with a vacuum hose and vacuum the creosote out of the "smoke shelf," a cavity behind the fireplace.

13  Vacuum up all of the dust and debris.

### ✳ Tip

Many fire departments recommend a yearly chimney inspection. Consider hiring a chimney service to inspect your chimney and fireplace for possible dangers, and to clean them out. This should cost less than $100.

### ⚠ Warning

Don't use water to clean the fire brick or cement blocks. It could affect heat retention.

### Things You'll Need

☐ chimney rods and brushes

☐ dust mask and goggles

☐ plastic tarps

☐ duct tape

☐ vacuum cleaner

☐ stiff scrub brush

## 307 | Clean a Barbecue Grill

To make cleanup easier, try spraying the grill with nonstick spray before you barbecue. These directions are for kettle-type grills.

⊙ **Steps**

1   Put on rubber gloves.

2   Remove ash from the collector pan beneath the grill. (Make sure the charcoal is completely cool.)

3   Remove the grill's cooking and charcoal grates from inside the bowl.

4   Coat the bowl of the grill with spray-on oven cleaner.

5   Replace the grates and coat them with spray-on oven cleaner as well.

6   Wait as directed in the oven cleaner's directions.

7   Remove the grates again, and set them on newspaper. Scrub residue off the grates with a rag, steel wool or a wire brush, as needed. (If the grates have a nonstick coating, use a plastic scrubbing pad.)

8   Wipe out the bowl of the grill with wadded newspapers.

9   Use a high-pressure hose to rinse off the bowl and the grates.

10  Dry the grates and put a very light coating of cooking oil on each one.

11  Remove stains from the lid using warm, soapy water and a fine steel wool pad.

⚠ **Warning**

Avoid using harsh cleansers on any part of your barbecue grill.

**Things You'll Need**

☐ rubber gloves

☐ oven cleaner

☐ newspaper

☐ rags, steel wool or wire brush

☐ plastic scrubbing pad

☐ hose

☐ cooking oil

## 308 | Clean a Crystal Chandelier

Your delicate chandelier will glow more brightly without all that dust and grime. Here's how to make it sparkle again.

⊙ **Steps**

1   Set up alternative lighting nearby (since you won't be able to use the chandelier for lighting while you're cleaning it).

2   Turn off the chandelier's power at the wall switch. Place a piece of tape over the wall switch so that no one can accidentally turn it on while you're working.

3   Cover any upward-pointing bulbs with sandwich bags. Secure the bags with rubber bands.

4   Place a drop cloth below the chandelier.

5   Mix a solution of one part isopropyl alcohol or ammonia in three parts distilled water. Or, if you don't want to mix your own cleaner, buy a special chandelier cleaner from a lighting retailer. Put some solution in a spray bottle.

6   Spray every part of the fixture with the cleanser, avoiding wires and other electrical components.

**Things You'll Need**

☐ tape

☐ sandwich bags

☐ rubber bands

☐ drop cloth

☐ isopropyl alcohol or ammonia

☐ distilled water

☐ chandelier cleaner (optional)

☐ spray bottle

7  Allow the crystals to drip-dry. If your chandelier is too dirty for this drip-cleaning method, you'll have to hand-wash each individual crystal with the cleaning solution.

8  Remove the plastic bags from the lights once the crystals have dried, and wipe down light wells and other noncrystal parts with a soft cloth dipped in the cleanser.

9  Allow the entire fixture to dry overnight before turning its power back on.

## Remove Rust — 309

Rust is tough, but you can get rid of it on most surfaces. Here's an overview of your options for treating and preventing rust on common objects.

### Things You'll Need

- ☐ rubber gloves
- ☐ rust remover
- ☐ pumice scouring pad
- ☐ wire brush, sandpaper or sand blaster
- ☐ rust-inhibiting primer
- ☐ rust-resistant metal paint

### ⊙ Steps

1  Put on rubber gloves.

2  Treat the affected material (metal or otherwise) with a rust-removing agent that contains oxalic acid, taking care to follow instructions on the product label.

3  Treat severe rust stains (especially in toilet bowls) with a pumice scouring pad along with the rust-removing agent.

4  Prevent indoor metal items from rusting by keeping their surfaces dry, dusting regularly and wiping down occasionally with a damp cloth. Dry immediately after wiping down.

5  Keep outdoor wrought-iron structures rust-free by removing existing rust with a wire brush, some sandpaper or a sandblaster. Then go over bare spots with rust-inhibiting primer and paint the surface with rust-resistant metal paint.

## Remove Stickers — 310

Many common household items will help you remove stickers and adhesive-backed price tags from a variety of surfaces. You can also purchase products made especially for this purpose.

### ✱ Tips

Remove as much of a laminated sticker as you can before applying a liquid or solvent. Most products will not be able to penetrate the plastic coating.

Heat the sticker with a blow dryer before treating. (Do not use this method on plastics.)

### ⊙ Steps

1  Remove stickers from glass, plastic or metal with alcohol-based products such as nail polish remover or 91 percent rubbing alcohol. Oil-based products such as cooking oil, mineral oil and baby oil can also be used. Apply the liquid to a clean cloth and saturate the sticker; allow it to sit for a minute or so and peel the sticker from the surface.

2  Remove stickers from cardboard and other paper products with an alcohol-based product or with a commercial solvent. Apply the liquid to the sticker with a cotton swab until the sticker is saturated. Avoid getting too much liquid on the surrounding surface. Peel the sticker away.

3   Remove stickers from wood with furniture polish or any of the products listed in step 1. Again, saturate the sticker with the liquid and allow it to sit for 1 to 2 minutes. Peel the sticker away.

4   Saturate stickers that are on hard plastic surfaces (plastic tubs or food storage containers) with cooking oil. Allow the sticker to soften, then immerse it in water. Wipe the sticker away.

5   Repeat the sticker-removal process if any gummy residue remains after the first treatment. Scrape residue with a paint scraper or razor blade.

Avoid unnecessary stains. Test the liquid or solvent on an inconspicuous area of the surface before you proceed with the sticker-removal process. Do not use oil-based products on paper or cardboard.

## 311 | Rid Your Home of Ants

Ants enter homes looking for food, water and shelter. Controlling them usually requires a combination of methods.

### ◎ Steps

1   Keep ants out. Caulk and seal all cracks and crevices around your home's foundation; inside, pay special attention to areas where food is prepared.

2   Fix plumbing leaks. Remove food sources. Store food in clean, closed containers. Store garbage outdoors in sealed containers.

3   Use bait to destroy nests. For an entire colony to be destroyed, ant bait must be slow-acting. Some of the chemicals that are effective in baits are hydramethylnon, boric acid and fipronil. Baits will work only if there is no other food source nearby.

4   If ants are inside, wash them away with warm, soapy water. This removes the chemical trail and is as effective as most of the insecticides.

5   Do not allow any wood—firewood, yard debris or foundations—to remain in contact with the soil. Damp wood provides a habitat for carpenter ants. Trim tree branches and shrubs away from buildings.

**✳ Tip**

For extreme ant infestations, seek the help of a professional exterminator.

**⚠ Warning**

Be sure to keep ant baits away from children and pets.

## 312 | Rid Your Home of Flies

Flies spread disease, contaminate food and can place human health at risk.

### ◎ Steps

1   Keep flies out with barriers, your first and best line of defense. Screen all windows and doors. Seal and caulk all cracks and crevices.

2   Remove all outside organic-waste piles, which can be used as breeding sites: dog feces, animal manures, piles of grass clippings. (Hot compost piles are inhospitable to breeding flies.) Keep garbage in a container with a tightly fitting lid.

3   Put out traps—flypaper or sticky tape will catch a few flies. Use inverted cone traps to attract more flies with food bait.

**✳ Tips**

Egg-to-adult development in flies can take place in as little as 7 to 10 days.

The best time to control fly populations is at their juvenile or larval stage, by eliminating breeding areas such as organic garbage and dog feces.

Flies rapidly develop resistance to insecticides, so use them only as a last resort.

4   Remember that bait only works well if flies do not have access to other food sources. Place baits well away from eating areas.

5   Cover and refrigerate leftovers.

6   Use a flyswatter against the occasional fly that strays into the house.

## Rid Your Home of Clothing Moths | 313

The wormlike larvae of clothing moths feed on fabrics, clothing, carpets, rugs, furs, blankets, wool products, upholstery, piano felts and brushes—any materials of animal origin.

### ⊙ Steps

1   Keep your house clean. Vacuum under furniture, along baseboards, in corners, in closets and around heater vents and draperies. Get rid of full vacuum cleaner bags promptly, as they may contain eggs, larvae or adult insects.

2   Remove empty bird, rodent and insect nests from your home's perimeter, as they can also harbor moths.

3   Store out-of-season clothes properly. Dry-clean or wash them in hot water (above 120 degrees F for 20 to 30 minutes) before storing. Brush out any pockets, along the seams and under collars. Store clothes in airtight containers.

4   Place mothballs, flakes or crystals in airtight containers, and include a layer of paper to keep clothing from coming in contact with the insecticides. (These products contain naphthalene or paradichlorobenzene, which can fuse plastic, including plastic buttons, into fabric.) Vapors from the insecticides will build up in the container and slowly kill the moths.

### ✱ Tips

Clothing moths are not attracted to light.

Clothing moths flutter close by the area of infestation.

### ⚠ Warning

The chemicals in mothballs can cause skin, throat and eye irritation, and are toxic if swallowed or inhaled. Follow directions for use on the package.

## Rid Your Home of Pantry Moths or Weevils | 314

Bugs in your flour and cornmeal? Suspect pantry moths or weevils. The first line of defense is good housekeeping.

### ⊙ Steps

1   Check for infestation. Examine all food packages for telltale signs of moth or weevil infestation: webbing in corners, grains clumped together with sticky secretions, or small holes in containers. Also look for small bugs in the food or little moths flying around the kitchen. If you find them, read on.

2   Clean infested areas. Vacuum cupboards, then thoroughly scrub all shelves with soapy water, paying close attention to cracks and corners. Dry the cleaned area thoroughly. Keep cupboard and food-storage areas dry.

3   Discard infested food.

4   Store food properly. Clean containers with hot, soapy water, then rinse and dry them thoroughly before refilling. Use tightly sealed metal, glass

### ✱ Tips

Pantry moth larvae eat a wide assortment of foods, ranging from flour to dried chiles and candy.

It takes six to eight weeks for the pantry moth to complete its life cycle.

### ⚠ Warning

Do not use pesticides in or around any area where food is prepared, or on food itself.

or hard plastic containers to store food; plastic bags are inadequate, as insects can get through them. Keep old and new food separate, and keep infrequently used items in the freezer.

5 Eliminate the pests' food sources (such as improperly stored food) and breeding grounds (such as rodent nests).

## 315 Rid Your Home of Cockroaches

Cockroaches can transmit bacterial diseases and hepatitis virus, and have been known to spread dysentery and typhoid fever. Many people are allergic to them.

### ◉ Steps

1 Eliminate sources of food and water. Store food in tightly sealed metal, glass or hard plastic containers. Remove trash from kitchens promptly, and place in containers with tight-fitting lids. Repair any plumbing leaks in or under your home. Place pet water bowls in a pan of soapy water at night.

2 Vacuum all corners to remove tiny food crumbs. If anyone in the house is allergic to roaches, be sure that your vacuum cleaner has a HEPA filter.

3 Prune plants away from vents near your home's foundation where roaches can creep in. Remove piles of debris.

4 Caulk cracks and crevices wherever possible, both inside and outside.

5 Check furniture and appliances that have been in storage for egg cases.

6 Consider insecticide only if you must; cockroaches learn very quickly to avoid fast-acting insecticides such as insecticide spray. If you must use an insecticide indoors, dust a slow-acting one such as boric acid under cupboards and into cracks and corners. Remember that boric acid is permanently ineffective once it becomes damp.

7 Use baits and sticky traps as effective alternatives to spraying indoors. Add insect-growth regulators to baits to increase their effectiveness. Look for them where insecticides are sold.

**✳ Tip**

Tropical in origin, cockroaches require humidity and warmth as well as a food source. They prefer to live in cracks and tight crevices, and are nocturnal. Bathrooms and kitchens are favorite haunts.

**⚠ Warning**

Avoid the use of aerosol foggers. These can make the problem worse by dispersing the cockroaches over a wider area.

## 316 Rid Your Home of Spiders

Most spiders are beneficial, keeping many insect pests under control. Instead of killing spiders, take them outside and release them into your garden. Here's how to keep them outdoors.

### ◉ Steps

1 Practice good sanitation for control. Vacuum and clear away all webs, being sure to remove any egg cases. Move and dust frequently behind furniture, stored boxes and appliances.

2 Eliminate the spiders' food sources—including flies, cockroaches and moths—and they will be less likely to return. Check and repair all screens, and seal cracks.

**✳ Tip**

If you're determined to use a chemical control against spiders, keep in mind that these are only effective if the chemical lands directly on the spider. A flyswatter works as quickly.

3   Remove piles of wood, trash and debris from around the foundation of your home. Be sure to wear protective clothing: long-sleeved shirts, long pants, gloves and boots.

4   Hose off the outside of your home to destroy webs and egg cases.

5   Replace outdoor lights with yellow or sodium-vapor lightbulbs, which are less likely to attract insects and then spiders.

6   Shake out clothing that has been stored before putting it on.

⚠ **Warning**

Two kinds of poisonous spiders inhabit North America: the black widow and the brown recluse. Watch for black widows in piles of wood, trash or stones, and in sheds, garages and barns. Watch for brown recluse spiders in old hanging clothing, behind pictures or in dark corners.

## Rid Your Home of Mice                                      317

As with most pests, keeping mice out of your home in the first place is the best way to avoid infestation.

### ⊙ Steps

**Protecting Your Home**

1   Keep your lawn mowed. Mice do not like to travel through short grass.

2   Remove wood piles, trash and debris from your home's perimeter. Elevate wood piles 18 inches above ground level. To protect yourself when cleaning out wood piles, trash or debris, be sure to wear protective clothing: long-sleeved shirts, long pants, gloves and boots.

3   Check all vents and repair damaged screening with 16- to 20-gauge ¼-inch hardware cloth. Check the crawl-space doors to ensure that they fit tightly. Check where pipes enter the building. In wooden walls, place sheet-metal collars around those entrances. In stucco, stone or brick walls, use cement fill.

4   Fill cracks and crevices around the foundation and eaves with caulk or foam. Steel wool can be used, although it rusts.

5   Remove food sources by placing all food items, including pet food and bird seed, in tightly sealed containers. Clean up fallen bird seed. Keep trash in containers with tight-fitting lids.

6   Avoid vacuuming or sweeping mouse droppings, due to the dangers of hantavirus, a deadly virus spread to humans through contact with rodents and rodent urine and droppings. Droppings should be misted with a strong household disinfectant (chlorine bleach) and wiped up with paper towels.

### Trapping and Baiting

1   Place traps or poison pellets near holes and in places where you've seen mice. The trigger should be as near to the hole as possible.

2   Use fruit, candy or peanut butter if your traps require bait.

3   Check traps daily.

4   Put on thick gloves and remove the carcass from the trap once a mouse has been caught.

5   Wrap the carcass in newspaper or a plastic bag and place it in an outside garbage can.

✱ **Tip**

Mice are prolific breeders and can have as many as 13 litters per year. They can squeeze through a hole as small as a pencil eraser and are excellent climbers.

⚠ **Warning**

Mice can carry diseases. Some of them—such as hantavirus—are potentially fatal.

## 318 | Select Basic Gardening Tools

You don't need to spend a lot to start a garden, but you do need some basic tools. You can get started for under $100—less if you can find tools at yard sales or flea markets.

### ◎ Steps

1. Select a spading fork as your first tool. Before you plant anything, you will need to open and improve the soil. A spading fork looks like a pitchfork but has a shorter handle and wider tines. It is used to dig down into hard soil and break up the ground.

2. Next, choose a hoe. A hoe is useful for weeding and cultivating the surface of the soil to allow for penetration of nutrients and water.

3. Choose a watering can. Long nozzles allow the water to come out at a very gentle flow rate and are useful for reaching across long distances. Select a watering can that has a detachable spray head—this type of watering can is perfect for watering young seedlings.

4. Select a round-ended shovel for larger digging projects, such as planting shrubs and trees.

5. Buy a good bow rake, which has short tines on one side attached to a metal frame or "bow." It's used for leveling the soil after it has been turned and prior to planting, or for removing large clods of earth or rocks from the soil. You can also turn a bow rake over and use the flat side to smooth soil in preparation for planting.

6. Select a pair of garden shears that fits comfortably in your hand. Shears, sometimes called clippers, are used for pruning, shaping and removing foliage or branches. Don't buy the most expensive shears until you decide you like gardening.

**✻ Tip**

These are the basic garden tools. Anything else is frosting.

**⚠ Warning**

Don't buy the most expensive tools when you are just starting out. You may find that you don't really like gardening—and if that is indeed the case, you will not have lost a large investment.

**Things You'll Need**

- ❑ spading fork
- ❑ hoe
- ❑ watering can
- ❑ shovel
- ❑ bow rake
- ❑ garden shears

---

## 319 | Begin a Compost Pile

Make the greatest organic matter you can ever add to your soil—start a compost pile. Recycle your yard and kitchen waste and watch nature's most basic process unfold in your garden.

### ◎ Steps

1. Start a very basic compost simply by piling up leaves and grass clippings. If you do nothing else, you can dig out compost after about six months of warm weather.

2. For something a little more thought-out, start by finding a good place for your pile—somewhere that is handy to the garden and kitchen, yet out of plain sight.

3. Corral that compost with a simple frame—loosely roll 6 feet of stiff wire-mesh fencing (4 feet tall with ½-inch mesh, called hardware cloth) to make a ring. Leave three cut ends of wire exposed to secure the ring to itself and stand it up.

**✻ Tips**

Healthy compost smells pleasantly earthy—turn it more often and add more dry brown matter if yours smells funky.

Use liquid compost starters—called inoculants—if you have no healthy soil to add at first.

Water your compost pile only during extended dry weather, and then only enough to moisten it, not drench the contents.

Many excellent compost systems of varying sizes are available at different price levels.

4  Build a more permanent compost bin from slatted wood or recycled pallets. Leave it open on one side for access—adding, turning and digging out compost from the bottom—and do not cover the top.

5  Understand the two basic elements that make compost: green (grass clippings, old annuals) and brown (dry leaves, soil) garden debris. Try for a balance of one part green to one to two parts brown, until the mix is damp but not wet.

6  Put a layer of leaves 4 inches thick in the bottom of your pile, then 1 inch of your good garden soil. Next add 2 inches of grass clippings or old plants, then more brown and green in alternate layers.

7  Turn with a manure or spading fork one week after building your pile. Begin burying coffee grounds, eggshells and green kitchen waste into the pile and turn it weekly. You'll have compost in about two months.

8  Make another ring or bin and turn the compost from one into the other to neatly mix it up and aerate the pile for fastest results. (Start another pile after yours has grown to 3 feet cubed.)

9  Begin digging out compost from the bottom of the pile when you turn it over and cannot recognize the component parts any longer. Dig out shovelfuls of crumbly brown compost to use in your garden, and use the partially composted matter for mulch or to start another pile.

## ⚠ Warning

Do not compost animal waste, meats, oils, diseased plants or plants treated with weed killers.

## Things You'll Need

❏ garden and kitchen waste

❏ wire mesh or wood

❏ manure or spading fork

## Choose a Lawn Grass 320

Choosing the right grass for your new lawn ensures that it will be beautiful, healthy and easy to take care of for years to come.

### ◉ Steps

1  Select cool-season grasses such as bluegrass, tall fescue or perennial ryegrass if you live in an area that has cold winters and mild summers. Cool-season grasses are hardy and grow vigorously in the cool months of spring and fall.

2  Select warm-season grasses such as Bermudagrass, St. Augustinegrass or zoysiagrass if you live in an area where summers are hot and winters are mild. Warm-season grasses are less hardy, grow vigorously during the hot months of summer and turn brown in winter.

3  Choose locally adapted pest-resistant varieties, blends of varieties or mixtures of grass types. Your local nursery can help you choose.

4  Select cool-season fescues or warm-season St. Augustinegrass or zoysiagrass for shady spots.

5  Plant Bermudagrass, buffalograss or tall fescue in dry-summer areas.

### ✳ Tips

Most warm-season grasses are stiff and wiry, requiring a power-driven reel lawn mower to keep them looking their best.

Overseed warm-season grasses in fall with cool-season grasses to keep the lawn green in winter.

Zoysiagrass and buffalograss are the hardiest warm-season grasses.

## 321 Plant a Lawn

Plant a healthy lawn as the centerpiece of your landscape and reap more rewards than beauty alone. You'll enjoy cleaner air and cooler temperatures around the house.

### ◎ Steps

1   Choose the right type of grass for your climate (see 320 "Choose a Lawn Grass"). Decide whether you will start with grass seed, stolons or sod.

2   Plant cool-season grasses in early spring or fall. Plant warm-season grasses in late spring to early summer.

3   Test your soil—send a sample to your local cooperative extension service or a private lab, or test it yourself with a home kit. Find out what nutrients you have and lack, what the pH is, and whether or not you need lime or sulphur. (Or just check with neighbors or a nursery that knows local conditions.)

4   Improve the soil by spreading 2 to 3 inches of organic matter, such as compost or ground bark, over the planting area. Also spread a starter fertilizer, which is usually high in potassium and phosphorous, if it's called for after a soil test.

5   Till the soil to incorporate the organic matter to a depth of 6 to 8 inches. Make two or three passes with a rotary tiller in crossing directions.

6   In dry-summer areas, consider an irrigation system to simplify watering. Place enough sprinklers or hoses and pipes around to irrigate, or have an in-ground system installed.

7   Smooth the planting area with a leveling rake.

8   Sow seed, plant stolons or lay sod over the planting area.

9   Keep areas moist until grass is firmly established (six to eight weeks on average).

### ✱ Tips

Much of the equipment needed to plant a lawn can be borrowed or rented from your local nursery.

To make tilling easier, water the area thoroughly three or four days before planting.

### ⚠ Warnings

Keep kids and dogs off the grass until it's at least 1½ inches tall and ready for mowing.

Avoid letting your newly planted lawn dry out. You may need to water more than once a day for at least a week after planting.

### Things You'll Need

❑ grass seed, stolons or sod

❑ soil test kit

❑ organic matter

❑ fertilizer

❑ tiller

❑ leveling rake

## 322 Plant a Lawn From Seed

Planting grass from seed is an inexpensive way to grow a beautiful new lawn, but you need to prepare the soil carefully and watch over the sprouting seeds. Here are the basics.

### ◎ Steps

1   Select the right type of grass for your area (see 320 "Choose a Lawn Grass").

2   Measure the square footage of your planting area to determine how much seed you'll need. Purchase the seed at a local nursery or garden center. Information on the package will tell you how much to buy.

3   Prepare and level the soil, as described in 321 "Plant a Lawn."

4   Set your seed spreader (a drop spreader used for fertilizer works best for most lawns) at the appropriate setting and fill it with half the seeds.

### ✱ Tips

Once you have thoroughly wet the seedbed after planting, you only need to water enough to keep the top inch moist. Germination will take 5 to 14 days, depending on weather and grass type.

When the grass is 1 to 2 inches high, you can begin to water less often, but avoid letting the planting area go completely dry.

5   Walking at a steady pace, sow the seed over the planting area, moving back and forth in opposite directions. Repeat the process using the rest of the seeds, walking at a 90-degree angle to your original paths. This will ensure that the seed is sown evenly.

6   Fill a cage roller with fine-textured organic mulch, such as peat moss or ground bark. Walking quickly, push the roller over the planting area so a thin layer (1/8 to 1/4 inch) of organic matter covers all the seeds. This will help keep the seeds from drying out.

7   Push a water-filled roller (about a third full) over the entire area to make sure the seeds and soil are in good contact.

8   Water the seedbed thoroughly so the soil is moist to a depth of 6 to 8 inches. Apply the water slowly so that the seeds do not wash away.

9   Keep the seedbed moist (but not soggy) until the seed germinates and the new grass is a few inches high. In hot weather you may have to water more than once a day.

## ⚠ Warning

Heavy watering may wash away the seeds, and watering too frequently may rot the seedlings.

## Things You'll Need

☐ grass seed

☐ seed spreader

☐ cage roller

☐ mulch

☐ water-filled roller

---

# Plant a Lawn From Sod                                                323

Planting sod (living green grass) turns a patch of dirt into a beautiful lawn instantly. Here are the basic steps.

## ◎ Steps

1   Select the right type of grass for your area (see 320 "Choose a Lawn Grass").

2   Measure the square footage of your planting area to determine how much sod you'll need. Purchase fresh sod at a local nursery or garden center, or have it delivered from a local sod farm.

3   Prepare and level the soil, as described in 321 "Plant a Lawn." The final level should be an inch or two lower than grade to accommodate the thickness of the sod.

4   Pick up the sod or arrange to have it delivered on the day you are ready to lay it. Inspect the sod carefully to make sure it hasn't dried out. Reject it if it has dried, curled or cracked edges, or yellowing foliage

5   Start laying the sod along a straight edge, such as a driveway or walk. To create a straight edge, stretch a string across the center of the lawn.

6   Position the sod pieces so the ends butt up tightly against an edge or previously laid piece. Unroll the sod. Place edges as close as possible, but don't overlap them.

7   Stagger pieces as you move from row to row (as if you were laying brick) so the ends don't all line up.

8   Use an old kitchen knife to cut sod to fit around sprinklers or in odd-shaped areas.

9   Fill in any large spaces between pieces of sod with soil.

10  Push a water-filled roller (about a third full) over the entire area to make sure that sod and soil are in good contact and to help level the area.

## ✱ Tips

Lay the sod on dry soil to avoid a muddy mess.

When laying sod, kneel on a piece of plywood so you don't disturb soil or damage sod, and use kneepads to keep your knees from getting sore.

Laying sod is hard work. Enlist help, and use a wheelbarrow to cart pieces around.

Keep pets and kids off your new lawn by enclosing it with stakes and string.

## ⚠ Warning

Avoid letting sod dry out. Occasionally sprinkle it with water from a handheld hose, and store pallets of sod in the shade.

## Things You'll Need

☐ sod

☐ string ➤

11  Water thoroughly so the soil is moist to a depth of 6 to 8 inches.

12  Keep the planting bed moist (but not soggy) until sod roots knit with soil below. In hot weather, you may have to water more than once a day.

☐ old kitchen knife

☐ water-filled roller

---

## 324 | Plant a Lawn From Stolons

Buy or root your own stolons (foot-long sprigs of grass with stems and roots attached) to grow a quality lawn for less money than sod. Warm-season grasses are often planted from stolons.

### ◉ Steps

1  Prepare the soil where you'll introduce your stolons—till, toss out the rocks and weeds, and rake smooth. ("Stolon" is the formal name for runners; they're also called "sprigs" in various parts of the country.) With a hoe, make a series of furrows (or trenches) 3 inches deep, running the length of the area to plant, and 10 inches apart.

2  Buy enough stolons to plant. (You'll need about three stolons per linear foot of furrow.) Select stolons of vigorous grasses like Bermudagrass and centipedegrass already rooted. Keep them damp in plastic bags or wet burlap until planting.

3  Or root those grass runners that invade your flower bed and stretch across the driveway. Here's how: Cut or dig up enough foot-long pieces to plant your area and lay them in a shallow flat of moist potting soil or quarry sand until they root—in about 10 warm days.

4  Broadcast compost in a ½-inch layer across the planting area the day before you want to plant. Then soak the area thoroughly with water and let it dry only overnight.

5  Lay the stolons 6 inches apart in the furrow—put each on an angle with one end at the bottom. Be sure at least one piece of green leaf rises above soil level.

6  Wear gloves and use your hands to cover all but the top sprout of the stolons with soil. Press the grass and soil together firmly, then smooth it out so the whole area is level with sprouts only showing.

7  Water immediately and often. Keep the grass very moist for the entire growing season, and don't let it dry out over the winter, either.

8  Fertilize with a slow-release lawn formula after the lawn greens up the following year. Expect a thick lawn one year after planting.

### ✱ Tips

You'll need three runners per linear foot of furrow.

Keep foot traffic off the new lawn until it grows together.

Pull weeds by hand for the first year.

Don't use fertilizers containing only nitrogen.

### Things You'll Need

☐ rotary tiller

☐ leveling rake

☐ hoe

☐ stolons

☐ lawn sprinklers

☐ fertilizer

# ✓ 325 Care for Your Garden, Season by Season

Your garden follows an annual cycle of growth and dormancy. And you, the caretaker, must keep up with this cycle. Use this guide to help remind you of the tasks that need to be completed every spring, summer, fall and winter. Keep in mind that this is a general guide; adjust the tasks to your climate.

### Spring

- Sow annuals in containers indoors.
- Transplant seedlings into the garden when chance of frost damage is past.
- Fertilize shrubs, trees, vines and ground covers.
- Stake climbing and tall plants if needed.
- Deadhead spring-blooming annuals and perennials.
- Prune shrubs that flower on new growth.
- Prune shrubs that have finished flowering.
- Prune climbers to shape them.
- Lay sod or sow seeds for a lawn.

### Summer

- Transplant annuals for summer and fall bloom.
- Fertilize fruit-bearing plants.
- Continue to deadhead flowering plants.
- Remove dead branches from evergreens.
- Prune vines that flower on old wood after they're done blooming.
- Mulch to save water and control weeds.
- Dig, divide and store spring-blooming bulbs.
- Fertilize roses after each bloom cycle.
- Prepare soil in areas where you plan to plant in the fall.
- Keep summer flowers and vegetables constantly moist.

### Fall

- Plant spring-flowering bulbs.
- Plant lettuce and other cool-season vegetables.
- Lay sod or seed for a lawn if climate allows.
- Plant cool-season annuals in mild climates.
- Plant hardy perennials.
- Rake and dispose of fallen leaves and other debris.
- Divide perennials.
- Remove dead and diseased wood from shrubs in late fall.
- Move frost-intolerant container plants to a protected spot.

### Winter

- Plant bare-root trees, roses and other shrubs before spring growth.
- Protect plants from severe cold with plastic sheeting, burlap or other material.
- Prune dormant fruit trees and berries before spring growth.
- Sharpen lawn mower blades and shears.
- Dormant-spray fruit trees.
- Prune roses in winter to early spring, depending on climate.
- Start seeds of cool-season flowers and vegetables indoors.

calendar

www.ehow.com

## 326 Water a Lawn

Proper watering is key to keeping a lawn healthy and beautiful. It's best to water infrequently and deeply rather than often and lightly.

### ⊙ Steps

1 Purchase hose-end sprinklers or install a below-ground automated system.

2 Test your sprinkler output and consistency of coverage: Place flat-bottom cups or cans within the sprinkler pattern and measure the water over a given time. Make adjustments as necessary so the entire lawn is watered evenly.

3 Water early in the morning, or when winds are calm and enough daylight is left to dry the leaves before nightfall.

4 Apply enough water to wet the root zone to 6 to 8 inches deep with each irrigation, and let the soil dry partially between irrigations. To avoid producing runoff, run the sprinklers in cycles, turning sprinklers on for 10 minutes, turning them off to let the water soak in, then repeating.

5 Adjust the watering schedule depending on weather, seasons and rainfall. Grasses generally require more water during their active growing season than when they're dormant, though all grasses need an average of 1 to 2 inches of water per week in summer; cool-season grasses can take more than this in winter.

6 Set automated timers so you don't have to worry about turning the water off.

7 Maintain sprinkler systems so they operate efficiently. Watch them run, and make adjustments and fix clogs or leaks as necessary.

### ❋ Tips

Your lawn will tell you when it needs water—two signs are when the grass changes from bright green to dull gray-green and when footprints remain when you walk across the lawn.

To check how deeply water is penetrating, probe the soil with a stiff wire or screwdriver. It will move easily through moist soil and be harder to push when it reaches dry soil.

### Things You'll Need

❑ garden hose

❑ lawn sprinklers

❑ automated sprinkler timer

## 327 Mow, Edge and Trim a Lawn

Conscientious mowing, followed by edging and trimming, reduces weeds, thickens turf and improves the lawn's appearance and vitality.

### ⊙ Steps

#### Mowing

1 Choose the proper mower for your type of lawn. Use a rotary mower for taller, soft grasses such as bluegrass, fescue or ryegrass; use a reel mower on wiry or low-cut grasses such as Bermudagrass, bentgrass or St. Augustinegrass.

2 Set mower blades to the proper height according to grass type. Set blade height by placing the mower on a flat, paved surface. Use a ruler to measure between blades and pavement. Adjust according to the manufacturer's instructions.

3 Mow the lawn when it is about a third higher than the recommended mowing height.

### ❋ Tips

Mow bentgrass to a height of 1/4 to 1 inch; hybrid Bermudagrass, 1/2 to 1 inch; tall fescue, 2 to 3 inches; bluegrass, 1 3/4 to 2 1/2 inches; ryegrass, 1 1/2 to 2 inches; St. Augustinegrass, 1 1/2 to 2 1/2 inches; and zoysiagrass, 1 to 2 inches.

Mow at the upper end of the height range during hot weather or periods of drought. Taller grasses have deeper roots and survive heat and drought better than shorter grasses.

4 Leave grass clippings on the lawn, unless the grass has grown very tall between mowings. They will contribute organic matter and nutrients as they break down.

## Edging and Trimming

1 Use a handheld edger between pavement and grass. Place the wheel on the pavement with the blade over the edge and push and pull. For large lawns, use a power-driven model.

2 Use grass shears around trees, around the edges of beds or in places that are hard to reach.

3 Use a string trimmer to trim and edge large lawns or to cut grass too tall to mow.

4 Create a tailored, "English garden" look by using an edging tool (a shovel with a small blade shaped like a half moon) between beds and lawn. Push the blade in with your foot so that it slices off a thin piece of turf, leaving a clean, straight edge of soil between lawn and bed.

5 If you use an edging tool, return slices of soil to the garden beds to break down; chop slightly and bury them under the mulch for a neat, nourishing edge.

## ⚠ Warning

Wear protective footwear and eye protection and follow manufacturers' safety instructions. Remove young children and pets from the area being mowed.

## Things You'll Need

❏ lawn mower

❏ lawn edger

❏ grass shears

❏ string trimmer

❏ edging tool

---

# Remove Crabgrass From a Lawn                  328

Crabgrass is a thick-bladed, flat annual weed that invades lawns, vegetable gardens and flower beds. It is easy to get rid of if you pull it before it sets seed.

## ◉ Steps

1 Prevent crabgrass from becoming established by fertilizing to keep your lawn healthy and lush. Healthy turf grass will crowd out noxious weed seeds before they can germinate and grow.

2 Pull crabgrass as soon as it appears, in the early spring. Use a weed knife to pull out all of the roots.

3 Water your lawn deeply on a less frequent basis to encourage the roots to grow deep into the soil. Crabgrass has a shallow root system that will dry out faster than deep-rooted turf grasses.

4 Use chemical controls only if the crabgrass has become a pest. Use a nonselective herbicide to spot-treat weedy patches in the lawn. Avoid letting nonselective herbicides drift onto desirable plants or the rest of the lawn. If herbicide leaves large bare patches, see 329 "Reseed Bare Patches in a Lawn."

## ⚠ Warning

If using chemical sprays, wear protective clothing including goggles, respirator, neoprene gloves, long sleeves and long pants. And avoid spraying on a windy day.

## Things You'll Need

❏ lawn fertilizer

❏ weed knife

❏ nonselective herbicide

## 329 | Reseed Bare Patches in a Lawn

Whether they're caused by pests, weeds, dog urine or a bad golf swing, those little bare spots in your lawn are easy to repair. The trick is to keep on top of them.

### ◉ Steps

1. Rake and remove the dead grass and debris from the bare patch.

2. Use a spading fork or cultivating tool to loosen the soil in the bare area.

3. Incorporate 2 to 3 inches of compost into the prepared area.

4. Smooth the area with the back of a rake until the new soil is level with the surrounding area.

5. Seed thickly and evenly (taking care not to overcrowd the seeds or jumble them on top of each other). Incorporate the seeds into the soil gently, using the back side of the rake.

6. Cover the seeded area with a thin layer of fine compost or other organic matter to act as a protective mulch.

7. Water gently with a fan nozzle so you don't wash the seeds away.

8. Protect the area from birds if they are a problem. Insert 1-foot-long wooden stakes into the ground surrounding the perimeter of the patch, keeping the stakes 10 to 12 inches apart. Tie red Mylar flash tape to the stakes. This will frighten birds away from the seeded area.

9. Keep the repaired area moist until the seed germinates. Once the new grass is established, resume regular watering.

### ✳ Tip

If the bare patch is due to a gasoline spill or dog urine, flood the area with water to dilute the problem fluid. Other measures may be needed in order to control lawn disease or insects.

### Things You'll Need

❑ rake

❑ spading fork

❑ compost

❑ grass seeds

❑ garden hose and fan nozzle

❑ wooden stakes

❑ red Mylar flash tape

## 330 | Shop for Flowering Bulbs

Local nurseries and garden centers are convenient places to buy standard flowering bulbs like tulips and daffodils. Generally, though, you'll find a wider selection in catalogs and online.

### ◉ Steps

1. Select bulb varieties and types based on color, bloom time, height, ability to grow in sun or shade, and climate adaptation. Much of this information will be on the packaging or in catalog descriptions.

2. Choose healthy, firm bulbs, free of blemishes, bruises or soft spots. Usually bigger is better.

3. Choose the highest grade of bulb (if the bulbs are graded) unless cost is a major factor, as when purchasing large quantities. Higher-quality bulbs generally produce more flowers.

4. Make sure to note how closely the bulbs can be planted (the descriptions may say, but you might have to double-check in a book on bulbs or ask the nursery salesperson). Spacing helps determine the quantity of bulbs needed for each planting area.

### ✳ Tip

If you buy bulbs like tulips and hyacinths, which usually need chilling in mild climates, make sure you get them early enough to store in your refrigerator six to eight weeks before planting. Or purchase prechilled bulbs.

### ⚠ Warning

Bargain bulbs are not always as good a deal as they may seem. They're often smaller or lower-quality bulbs that don't bloom as well as more expensive choices.

5  Select hardy spring-flowering bulbs, such as daffodils, tulips, crocus and hyacinths, for fall planting.

6  Choose tender summer-flowering bulbs, such as begonias and gladiolus, for spring planting.

## Plant Bulbs in Fall                                                           331

Spring-flowering bulbs such as daffodils, tulips and hyacinths are generally planted in fall. Here's how to do it right and ensure a wonderfully colorful spring.

### ◎ Steps

1  Select bulb types as described in 330 "Shop for Flowering Bulbs."

2  Arrange for delivery, or make your purchase, so you can plant in fall. If necessary, chill bulbs such as tulips and hyacinths (which need a certain amount of cold weather to bloom properly) by storing them in the refrigerator for six to eight weeks before planting.

3  Improve the soil, if necessary, by incorporating ample organic matter. Soil preparation is not always necessary as long as drainage is good.

4  With a shovel or trowel, dig holes the appropriate depth for your bulb type. Consult packaging, catalogs or a book on bulbs for planting depth. A depth of two to three times the width of the bulb is a good rule of thumb.

5  Add bulb fertilizer to the bottom of the hole and roughly mix it into the soil.

6  Place the bulb in the hole. Make sure you have the right side up (usually point up, roots down). The bottom of the bulb should rest firmly on the bottom of the hole.

7  Refill the planting hole, tamping the soil lightly.

8  Water the bulbs thoroughly.

### ✽ Tips

Many spring-flowering bulbs can be planted under deciduous trees. They will bloom before the tree leafs out and shades the planting area.

There are many tools to help you when planting a lot of bulbs. Some make perfect holes by removing small cylinders of soil. Others are augerlike and can be attached to electric drills.

Alternatively, dig a long trench instead of individual holes.

### Things You'll Need

❑ spring-flowering bulbs

❑ shovel or trowel

❑ bulb fertilizer

## Do Basic Dormant-Season Pruning                                              332

Deciduous trees and shrubs shed their leaves and go dormant over the winter. This is the perfect time to prune them without fear of shocking them.

### ◎ Steps

1  Remove any growth that comes from below the graft (where the top of the plant was originally joined to rootstock). Cut the growth as close to the main body of the plant as possible.

2  Look for and remove any dead, diseased or injured wood. Branches that are different in color from the main body of the plant are suspect. Injuries may look like splits or blisters. Diseases may show up as black patches along the branch.

### ✽ Tips

Sharpen and oil your pruning tools before you start cutting.

3   Cut into the tip of a suspect branch to make sure that it is dead. If it is green on the inside, it is still alive. If the branch is brown on the inside, it is probably dead. Keep cutting back from the tip until you reach green wood.

4   Remove any branches that cross through the center of the plant; this will improve air circulation and discourage fungus disease.

5   Cut out any competing leaders—the upright growing limbs that will eventually turn into the main trunk. Most trees should have only one main branch headed in the "up" direction; multiple trunks sap the energy from a tree and weaken it over time.

6   Prune for shape and size. In the case of fruit trees, keep the branches low so that you can reach the fruit. Most maples look best with a rounded crown, and most roses should be pruned in a low vase shape. Know the basic shape of the plant you are working on.

7   Remove any water sprouts from fruit trees. Nonproductive water sprouts are light in color and grow straight up, as opposed to fruiting wood, which is crooked and dark.

8   Rake up and remove all prunings and fallen leaves. Insects overwinter in fallen plant debris.

## ⚠ Warning

Once the plants begin to grow leaves, sap is flowing through the branches. If you prune then, you take the chance of causing excessive bleeding or loss of vital fluids.

## Things You'll Need

❑ garden shears

❑ lopping shears

❑ pole pruner

❑ rake

---

## 333   Plant a Bare-Root Tree or Shrub

Many kinds of shrubs and trees are sold while leafless and dormant, with roots bare of soil. A bare-root plant may look pathetic, but if you start it out properly and care for it well, it will thrive.

### ⊙ Steps

1   Plant bare-root trees and shrubs in late fall, winter or early spring (from mid-November to April in most parts of the country) when the plants are dormant and the ground isn't frozen solid. They'll have a chance to put out new roots before they have to cope with hot sun, drying winds and the added stress of producing leaves.

2   Remove any packing material carefully, and rinse off or gently pull off any clumps of earth clinging to the roots; clip off any dead or damaged roots.

3   Immerse the roots in a bucket of water to soak for at least one to four hours, but no longer than overnight. Supplying enough moisture is key to the success of bare-root planting.

4   Dig a hole that's at least 2 feet wider than the root system and about as deep as the point where the roots flare from the trunk (or stems in the case of a shrub). Using your shovel, loosen the soil on the sides of the hole so it doesn't solidify around the plant's roots.

5   Mound soil in the bottom of the hole so that the peak reaches just about ground level.

6   Place stakes in the hole if you're planting a tree that will need support.

7   Set the tree or shrub on top of the mound so the roots cascade down over the sides. Spread them gently with your hands if you need to, and add or remove soil so that the crown of the root system is just at the surface of the ground.

### ✱ Tips

Unless you're planting a small shrub or a street or patio tree in a small, confined space, avoid amending (improving) the soil in the planting hole. The "good" soil will encourage the roots to confine themselves within that small area rather than spread out as they need to.

Deep, thorough watering is the key to healthy shrubs and trees. Give new trees at least an inch of water a week all around the root zone. (The roots of a woody plant extend about the same distance as its branches.)

### ⚠ Warning

Use the bare-root method only for deciduous trees and shrubs of the standard size sold in nurseries. Larger deciduous plants and all evergreens will suffer too much stress without an extra cushion of soil around their roots.

8  Fill the hole about halfway with soil and tamp it lightly with your foot to remove large air pockets.

9  Make sure the tree or shrub is standing straight up, then water slowly to saturate the soil and remove any remaining air pockets.

10  Finish filling the hole with soil. Use any extra soil to build a temporary berm above the perimeter of the roots, and water again.

11  Keep the soil moist for the first year after planting. Mulch to retain moisture, but keep at least 6 inches bare around the trunk. Check frequently; if you see yellow leaves or the soil feels dry, water immediately.

### Things You'll Need

❏ garden shears

❏ bucket

❏ shovel

❏ stakes (optional)

❏ mulch

## Plant a B-and-B Tree or Shrub    334

A balled-and-burlapped (also known as "B-and-B") tree or shrub comes with a burlap-wrapped clump of soil around its roots. Many evergreens are traditionally sold this way.

### ⊙ Steps

1  Buy balled-and-burlapped trees or shrubs for planting mainly in autumn or spring. Plants can also be set out during mild spells in winter if ground conditions allow.

2  Keep your tree or shrub in a cool, shady place until planting; cover the rootball with mulch; and keep the roots moist.

3  Calculate your hole dimensions carefully: A B-and-B plant is heavy, but the roots are easily damaged. The less you have to move it, the better. You'll want to set the plant into the hole so that the bottom of the trunk (or trunks) is just above the soil surface.

4  Measure the rootball, then dig a hole that's about 6 inches wider all around and roughly as deep. Lay a flat stake across the hole, measure the distance from the stake to the bottom of the hole and adjust the depth as needed.

5  Loosen up the sides of the hole with your shovel, and if your plant is too large to lift and lower without strain, cut down one side of the hole so that it forms a slope. You'll be able to simply slide the plant down the ramp and into the hole. Place stakes in the hole if you're planting a tree that will need support.

6  Move the plant to the hole very carefully. Ease the plant onto a plastic tarpaulin and drag it to the site; don't roll it. If your plant is large, or if you have several, it pays to rent a special plant-moving hand cart from a nursery or equipment rental shop.

7  Lower the rootball into the hole, covering and all. Remove any synthetic wrappings or fastenings. Leave natural burlap and twine in place (they'll rot quickly), but cut away any burlap around the trunk; if it sticks out above ground it will wick moisture away from the roots.

8  Fill the hole about halfway with soil and tamp it lightly with your foot to remove large air pockets. Make sure the tree or shrub is standing straight up, then water slowly to saturate the soil and remove any remaining air pockets.

### ✱ Tips

Unless you're planting a small shrub or a street or patio tree in a small, confined space, avoid amending the soil in the planting hole. The "good" soil will encourage the roots to confine themselves within that small area rather than spread out as they need to.

Deep, thorough watering is the key to healthy shrubs and trees. Give new trees at least an inch of water a week all around the root zone. (The roots of a woody plant extend about the same distance as its branches.)

### ⚠ Warning

Even small B-and-B shrubs are heavy. Unless you're dealing with tiny specimens, don't risk your back or the plant's roots and limbs—get help at planting time.

### Things You'll Need

❏ shovel

❏ flat stake

❏ tarpaulin

❏ mulch

9  Finish filling the hole with soil. Use any extra to build a temporary berm at the drip line (the place on the ground directly below the outer edges of the foliage) and water again.

10  Keep the soil moist for the first year after planting. Mulch to retain moisture, but keep at least 6 inches bare around the trunk. Check frequently; if you see yellow leaves or the soil feels dry, water immediately.

## 335 | Plant a Tree or Shrub From a Container

Many common nursery plants are sold in containers of various sizes and materials. Unlike bare-root and B-and-B, container-grown plants can be planted even while growing vigorously.

### ⊙ Steps

1  Plant a container-grown tree or shrub in spring or autumn for best results, especially if it's an evergreen. If that timing doesn't fit your schedule, though, any time except midsummer will work, as long as the soil is not bone-dry, saturated or frozen.

2  Dig a hole that's at least 6 inches wider than the container on all sides and about the same depth. Then roughen up the sides of the hole with your shovel.

3  Remove the plant from its container even if the label says you don't need to; the roots will spread out more quickly. With a small tree or shrub, it's easy to do this job before you lower the plant into its hole; with a larger plant, it's easier to handle if you set it into the hole first and then cut away the container.

4  Knock a plant out of a rigid plastic container. Simply tilt the pot onto its side, tap it lightly, and gently slide out the rootball. If the container is made of metal or a soft material such as peat, cut the pot away using a knife, clippers or tin snips.

5  Gently tease out any roots that are encircling the rootball with your fingers so that they are free, taking care not to break up the ball of soil. Then clip off any damaged roots.

6  Place a stake in the hole if you're planting a tree that will need support.

7  Set the plant into the hole at the same depth it was growing in the pot, and begin filling the hole, checking as you go to make sure the plant is standing straight up. Add about 4 inches of soil and gently firm it with your foot or a hoe to remove any air pockets. Repeat the process until the hole is filled.

8  Water slowly to saturate the soil and remove any remaining air pockets.

9  Use any extra soil to build a temporary berm at the drip line (the place on the ground directly below the outer edges of the foliage) and water again.

10  Keep the soil moist for the first year after planting. Mulch to retain moisture, but keep at least 6 inches bare around the trunk. Check frequently; if you see yellow leaves or the soil feels dry, water immediately.

### ✱ Tips

Unless you're planting a small shrub or a street or patio tree in a small, confined space, avoid amending (improving) the soil in the planting hole. The "good" soil will encourage the roots to confine themselves within that small area rather than spread out as they need to.

Deep, thorough watering is the key to healthy shrubs and trees. Give new trees at least an inch of water a week all around the root zone. (The roots of a woody plant extend about the same distance as its branches.)

When purchasing a tree or shrub in a container, make sure no roots are growing through the holes at the bottom of the container. The appearance of roots indicates that the plant is root-bound and may be under stress.

### Things You'll Need

❑ shovel

❑ mulch

❑ knife, clippers or tin snips

❑ stake (optional)

# Sow Seeds Indoors

Starting plants from seed indoors is a great way to get a jump-start on spring. Although it takes a bit of a knack, it's not hard—especially when you know a few tricks of the trade.

## ⊙ Steps

1 Consider your timing. Some plants need to be planted as much as 12 weeks before your region's last average frost date, while others do best when started just two weeks before.

2 Choose your seed-starting container. Nearly any container with drainage will do, but good candidates include milk carton bottoms, egg cartons, plastic produce boxes, peat pots and special seed-starting flats. (Punch drain holes into containers that need them.)

3 Plant seeds in sterile seed starting mix. It has no soil to cause disease problems and is lightweight—perfect for baby plants to get off to a good start. Sprinkle vermiculite over seeds that require covering. Its lighter color helps you see just what you've covered.

4 Follow seed package directions about the depth of planting. As a rough rule, the larger the seed, the deeper it's planted. Some very small seeds are just scattered directly on the soil and not covered up at all.

5 Water gently. Either set the container in 1 to 2 inches of warm water and allow the water to wick up to the soil surface, water gently from above with a special bulb-type hand sprinkler, or dribble water from your hand.

6 Slip the container into a clear plastic bag to minimize drafts and conserve moisture. Twist the end shut.

7 Put the seeds in a spot with the correct temperature. (Check the seed packet.) Keep the seeds out of direct sunlight or risk fatally overheating them. Seeds usually need either cool temperatures of 50 to 65 degrees F or warm temperatures of 70 to 85 degrees F. Find an especially warm or cool spot by checking with a thermometer in different locations in your house.

8 Check the seeds daily. If water drops form inside the bag, open the end to vent it. Once the seeds germinate, remove the plastic and put the seedlings in the brightest indoor spot possible.

9 Put the new seedlings in a sunny, unobstructed south-facing window. Or set them a few inches below a shop light equipped with one warm and one cool fluorescent light. Use an inexpensive light timer to automatically keep the lights on 14 to 16 hours a day.

## ✱ Tip

If you've planted the seedlings more than a couple of weeks before the last frost date, it's a good idea to pick them out and transplant them into individual pots so they have plenty of room to grow. To do this, lift the seedlings out gently with a pencil or table knife and plant them in regular potting soil.

## ⚠ Warning

When you're planting seeds, it's critical that the soil be neither soggy nor too dry. Soggy conditions contribute to fatal diseases, while too little water is just as fatal.

## Things You'll Need

❑ seeds

❑ containers

❑ seed-starting mix

❑ vermiculite

❑ clear plastic bag

## 337 | Sow Seeds Outdoors

Whether you're planting flowers, vegetables or herbs, sowing seeds outdoors is a snap. All it takes is good garden soil and a little follow-up care to get loads of great plants.

### ⊙ Steps

1   Read seed-packet directions carefully. Many annuals and perennials can be sown directly in the ground, but some should be started in containers, then transplanted.

2   Consider your timing. Some plants like to be planted outdoors in early spring, while temperatures are cold. Others must wait until after your area's average last frost date. Again, consult the packet.

3   Prepare the soil. Most seeds demand optimum conditions. Work in plenty of compost with a spade or spading fork to a depth of at least 1 foot. The soil should be loose and crumbly and moist before planting. Rake smooth.

4   Sow the seed. Follow package directions on sowing depth. As a rough rule, the larger the seed, the deeper it must be planted. Some very small seeds are just scattered directly on the soil and not covered up at all.

5   Water gently. It's easy for seeds to be washed away by heavy watering. Use the mist attachment on a watering wand or a watering can that has a gentle sprinkle. Be sure to keep soil moist until seedlings are up.

6   Thin out seedlings by gently pulling them out, if the seed packet directs, once they are an inch or so high. This will ensure that those you want to survive have adequate room to grow big and healthy.

7   Pinch back most seedlings when they've made three sets of true leaves. Just snip the top part of the tiny plant off with your fingernails to encourage bushy growth and more roots. Check the package to determine whether pinching is recommended.

8   Baby your seedlings. Make sure they continue to have all the sun they need. Also keep the seedlings watered and weeded. Add an inch or two of organic mulch as soon as seedlings are up and growing.

### ✽ Tips

Some plants are easier than others to start from seed: marigolds, zinnias, squash and corn are good easy-to-start examples.

It's better to trim crowded seedlings off at soil level than to disturb the ones you want to keep by pulling the crowding ones out by the roots.

### Things You'll Need

❑ seeds

❑ spade or spading fork

❑ rake

❑ watering wand or can

❑ mulch

## 338 | Transplant Seedlings

Whether you grow your fledgling plants from seed or buy them at the nursery, extra care at planting time will get them off to a good start in your garden.

### ⊙ Steps

1   Double-check the planting date on the seed packet, in a comprehensive garden book or on the plastic tag stuck into the soil (for plants you bought at a nursery). You must hold off planting most flowers and vegetables until all danger of frost has passed. Some cold-tolerant varieties such as cauliflower can go into the ground a bit earlier; heat lovers such as tomatoes should wait until the ground has thoroughly warmed up.

### ✽ Tip

If the plant has been growing in a peat pot, break away a few pieces from the bottom or sides so the roots won't be confined, and loosen the soil a little with your fingers.

2  Prepare the planting bed. Use a spade or spading fork to work the soil to a depth of 10 to 12 inches; incorporate organic matter as needed.

3  "Harden off" your seedlings by leaving them outdoors for longer and longer periods. Start by sheltering the young plants under a porch or bench by day, then bringing them back in by night or during inclement weather. After two or three days, you can safely keep them in the sun for half a day. By the end of a week, they'll be tough enough to soak up the rays all day.

4  If you can, transplant the seedlings to the garden on an overcast day to ease the shock of transition from pot to ground. If a light mist is falling, so much the better. Water both the outside ground and the plants before you move them into the garden.

5  Remove each plant from its pot by turning it upside down and tapping lightly on the bottom; it will slide out easily. Gently run your fingers through the roots to loosen them a little.

6  Use a trowel to dig a hole about twice the size of the rootball and set the plant into the hole so the rootball will be covered by about ¼ inch of soil. Press the soil firmly around the roots to ensure good soil-to-root contact.

7  Space the plants according to the directions.

8  Water well immediately after transplanting and again every day until the plants are well established and growing—usually within a week. If some plants show signs of wilting, shield them with a lath screen or a piece of lattice until they perk up, which shouldn't take more than a few days.

## ⚠ Warning

If you live where late frosts can hit unexpectedly, be prepared to protect your tender seedlings. When the weather forecast predicts low temperatures, cover them with Styrofoam cups, plastic milk jugs with the tops cut off or one of several commercial products made for the purpose. Or invest in some cloches. These beautiful, bell-shaped glass covers have been used for centuries to shield tender plants from sudden cold snaps, or simply to prolong the growing season.

## Things You'll Need

- ❑ seedlings
- ❑ spade or spading fork
- ❑ organic matter
- ❑ garden trowel
- ❑ watering can or garden hose

---

## Design and Prepare a Flower Bed                          339

A well-prepared flower bed not only looks good but promotes good drainage, has plenty of nutrients, makes watering and weeding a snap, and discourages disease and pests.

### ⊙ Steps

1  Choose a spot for the bed and walk around it. Visualize plants of different shapes and sizes. Consider their needs for sun and shade. Make rough sketches.

2  Sketch a plan of the bed you want to plant. Tall plants should go at the back of a bed that's adjacent to a wall or fence and in the middle of a bed that will be viewed from all sides. Plants that need frequent attention, such as pruning, grooming or spraying, should go where they can be reached without your crushing other plants.

3  Sprinkle household flour to trace the outline of your prospective flower bed. If you don't like the way it looks, brush the flour away and start over.

4  Use a trowel or small shovel and cut along the flour lines you've just made.

5  Have your soil tested, or test it yourself with a home kit, and amend as necessary. A local nursery can recommend the best amendments to use.

6  Control severe weed problems by mowing and then spraying the area with a nonselective herbicide, following directions carefully, especially regarding how long to wait until planting. Or, as a nonchemical alterna-

### ✱ Tips

There's no need to limit your bed to a rectangular shape. Flower beds can be any size or shape you wish.

Unless you've got a budget big enough to buy full-grown perennials, the plants you put in the ground now will look very different in a year or two. Leave room for them to grow. You can fill in bare spots with annuals.

### ⚠ Warning

This method for creating a new flower bed works only if the soil is reasonably good. In areas with very sandy or very clay-laden soil, raised beds are your best bet. Or if you don't mind the work, dig out and dispose of the

tive, mow the area and then dig it up or till it. Then let it set for at least two to three days to allow annual weeds seeds to germinate. Hoe or till it a second time.

7   Spread 3 to 4 inches of compost and any other soil amendments over the top of the area you intend for the bed, grass and all.

8   Till or dig up the soil to a depth of at least 8 to 10 inches, up to 24 inches if you're planting perennials.

9   Toss out any chunks of sod or tufts of grass that appear on the surface.

10  Rake smooth with a ground rake, and you are ready to plant.

11  Install edging, if desired. Edging isn't a must but does help keep out grass and some other weeds while creating a neat appearance.

problem soil, and replace with a mixture of compost and high-quality topsoil.

## Things You'll Need

❑ all-purpose flour

❑ trowel

❑ compost

❑ tiller or spade

❑ rake

---

## 340 | Plant a Garden Bed

After you've prepared the soil and raked it smooth, the next step is to add the plants. Here's what to do.

### ⊙ Steps

1   Remove seedlings from their containers, and loosen the roots gently if they're root-bound. Place the unpotted plants back into the nursery flat, lying on their sides with the foliage all facing the same direction. Work quickly so the roots don't dry out.

2   Begin planting at the back of the garden bed. This way you won't be stepping all over the plants you've just put into the ground. Keep the flat of plants where you can easily reach it.

3   Use a trowel to make a hole for each plant. Stab the trowel into the soil, trying to gauge the depth so that the hole is only as deep as the rootball. The crown (the area where the foliage meets the rootball) of the plant should be at the surface of the soil.

4   Pick up the rootball of a plant with your free hand.

5   Lower the plant into the prepared hole.

6   Adjust the depth if necessary. With your trowel, shovel in a little soil to fill the hole around the plant, or scoop out a little more soil to make room for the plant. You want the top of the rootball to be at the surface of the soil.

7   Push the soil into place around the roots with your trowel.

8   Continue working backward, planting as you work toward the front of the bed.

9   Cover your footsteps by fluffing up the soil with your trowel. Tender young roots push through soft, uncompacted soil much faster than through compacted soil.

10  Water the newly planted garden immediately after you've finished planting the entire bed. Use a hose at low volume or a watering can. Try not to get water on the foliage; apply it near the roots to settle the soil.

### ✱ Tips

Plant in the early morning or late afternoon hours to prevent roots from drying out.

Avoid using fertilizer until you begin to see new growth.

Stand up and stretch your back every 15 minutes while planting.

## Things You'll Need

❑ seedlings

❑ garden trowel

❑ garden hose or watering can

## Mulch Flowers 341

A mulch is a layer of material applied to the soil's surface. It cuts down on weeds and conserves moisture so you water less.

### ⊙ Steps

1  Choose your mulching materials. Grass clippings, wood chips, shredded bark, pine needles, cocoa bean hulls and many other materials all make excellent mulch materials, but vary in cost and have subtle advantages and disadvantages. Check with your local agricultural extension or garden center for advice on the best mulch to use in your area.

2  Apply the mulch to your flower bed in late spring after your region's last frost date. Otherwise, you'll prevent the soil from warming up—and you need adequately warmed soil for good plant growth.

3  Spread the mulch 1 to 3 inches thick, depending on the size and sturdiness of the flowers. Large, mature perennials can handle 3 inches of mulch, while small, newly planted annuals might get lost.

4  Spread mulch right up to the plant but don't push mulch against the base.

5  Plan on replacing mulch annually; it breaks down into the soil.

### ✱ Tip

It's easy to confuse mulching that you do in the spring and mulching you do in the fall (to protect plants over the winter). Mulch applied in the fall often covers part or all of a plant and is usually very airy and lightweight (straw, pine boughs, shredded autumn leaves) so the plant doesn't suffocate.

### Things You'll Need

☐ mulch

☐ shovel

## Grow Annuals 342

Plunk annuals (plants that live one season only) in the ground at the right time of year and they'll provide long-lasting color that few perennials can match.

### ⊙ Steps

#### Choosing Annuals

1  Determine if you want to start your annuals from seed or from established plants. Established plants are fastest and easiest but cost much more and are available in a limited variety. Starting from seed takes a bit of skill and more time, but you can have hundreds of flowers for what you'd spend on just one flat of established annuals.

2  Browse the catalogs or display racks carefully when buying seeds. Beginners should choose annuals that are touted as being especially easy or that perform especially well. Also look for fast germination times. A plant that germinates in 4 or 5 days is easier to grow than a plant that germinates in 20.

3  Look for short, stocky (not leggy) established plants that don't have flowers on them and don't have roots coming out of the drainage holes at the bottom of the pot. Blooms indicate that the plant is putting too much energy into flowering when you want it first to put energy into root development at planting time; roots coming out of the bottom of the pot are a sign that the plant has been in the pot too long.

4  Read the label or packet carefully and note the plants' needs for sun, soil, water and other conditions. Make sure you're able to provide those conditions.

### ✱ Tips

Annuals are usually divided into two groups, cool-season annuals and warm-season annuals. Cool-season annuals do best when temperatures regularly stay below 80 degrees F. Warm-season annuals like warm conditions best. If planted too early in spring, they'll languish in cold soil or will be nipped by frost.

Never let annuals wilt. Instead, feel the soil to see if it's dry or water whenever the glossy leaves lose their sheen.

### ⚠ Warning

Never buy a plant that is showing signs of disease or wilting. It's likely to go downhill once you take it home and may spread disease to other plants in your garden.

## Planting Annuals

1 Prepare the planting area well, as described in 339 "Design and Prepare a Flower Bed." Also work a little slow-release granular fertilizer into the planting area if desired. Fertilizer can help fast-growing annuals reach their maximum height and bloom. Follow the package directions exactly.

2 Pinch off any flowers on the plant. (There will be some in most cases.) This will help the plant get established and produce more flowers in the long run.

3 Plant annuals about 25 percent closer than what the label recommends. Those distances are recommended for maximum plant health, not for the best visual effect. Plant in groups. Most annuals look far better when grouped in plantings of 12 or more.

## Caring for Annuals

1 Mulch most annuals (see 341 "Mulch Flowers"). Use a mulch such as grass clippings, wood chips or pine needles. Mulch suppresses weeds, conserves moisture and prevents some soil-borne diseases. Apply a layer 1 to 3 inches thick.

2 Keep annuals appropriately watered (see 345 "Water Flowers"). Most annuals are fairly thirsty—they'll need about 1 inch of water per week, either as rainfall or watering. It's better to water them deeply and occasionally rather than giving them just a little water here and there.

3 Deadhead most annuals regularly (see 351 "Deadhead Flowers"). This means trimming or pinching off spent blooms every few days. This not only keeps the plant tidy-looking, but it encourages more flowers.

4 Fertilize regularly during the growing season, using food formulated for flower production; follow label directions.

5 Tear out annuals when they're spent. For cool-season annuals, this usually means that hot or very cold weather has hit. For warm-season annuals, this usually means a heavy frost has blackened their leaves. Dispose of healthy annuals in a compost heap. If disease has been a problem, put them in a separate area or in the garbage.

### Things You'll Need

- ❏ annuals seeds or seedlings
- ❏ spade or spading fork
- ❏ rake
- ❏ compost
- ❏ fertilizer
- ❏ mulch
- ❏ garden shears

---

## 343 | Grow Perennials

Perennials come back to flower for more than one season of bloom. Most die back partially or fully at the end of the season, but many stay evergreen in mild climates.

### ☉ Steps

#### Choosing Perennials

1 Look for perennials at nurseries from spring through fall, or year-round in mild climates.

2 Choose perennials that grow well in your climate.

3 Buy perennials in 4-inch to 1-gallon containers.

4 Choose healthy-looking plants that have signs of new growth in leaf and flower bud in spring and summer.

**✳ Tip**
Check individual plant requirements, because not all perennials need the same treatment.

**How to Do (Just About) Everything**

## Planting Perennials

1  Choose a spot for perennials that is well-suited to their needs—"sun" means 6 hours of sunshine a day; "light shade" or "dappled shade" comes from tall trees; "dark shade" comes from something solid like a house; and "part shade" means 3 hours of sunshine a day.

2  Prepare the planting area as described in 339 "Design and Prepare a Flower Bed."

3  Add a light application of organic fertilizer to the planting hole.

4  Place the plants no deeper than they were growing in the containers.

5  Set the plants an appropriate distance apart, depending on how wide they grow.

6  Mulch the plants—place 1 to 3 inches of organic compost around but not on top of the plants—to help retain water and keep down weeds while the plants are getting established.

7  Water new plants well, until soil is completely moist. Do this weekly during their first summer.

## Caring for Perennials

1  Cut back old stems and flowers in late fall (for spring-flowering perennials) or early spring (for perennials that bloom summer through fall).

2  Apply an organic fertilizer to the soil in early spring—except for perennials that do not need yearly fertilizing.

3  Mulch around but not on top of the plants with 3 inches of organic compost in early spring (see 341 "Mulch Flowers").

4  Cut old flower stems off spring-blooming plants to a place on the stem just above where you see new leaves growing. This will encourage the plant to bloom again.

5  Water most perennials well until soil is completely moist; do this weekly in summers with no rainfall.

### Things You'll Need

- ❏ perennial plants in containers
- ❏ spade or spading fork
- ❏ rake
- ❏ garden trowel
- ❏ organic fertilizer
- ❏ mulch
- ❏ garden shears

---

# Care for Roses                                    344

Roses have an undeserved reputation for being fussy, hard-to-care-for plants. Some roses do require more maintenance than others, but growing roses is something even a beginner can do.

## ⊙ Steps

1  Prune roses in winter or early spring once the rose starts to show signs of new growth, usually in the form of tiny red buds swelling. These buds will become new branches.

2  Cut out any obviously dead or damaged branches first. Then cut out all but four or five healthy main stems.

3  Cut the stems back by a third to a half, depending on how tall you want the bush to be. Make these cuts right above an outward-facing bud—that is, a red bud that's on the outside of the rosebush. This directs the

### ✱ Tips

Use sharp hand shears for most pruning. To cut branches more than ½ inch thick, use long-handled loppers.

Many "landscape" or shrub roses do not require the typical pruning described in the steps. Instead, simply shear them back by a third.

bud to grow up and out, leaving the center of the rose bush open for a prettier shape and better air circulation.

4 Start fertilizing roses regularly at the start of the growing season. Roses are hungry plants, demanding lots of nutrients for best growth and flowering. Fertilize roses with a liquid fertilizer every three to four weeks during the growing season or according to package directions.

5 Water diligently. Roses need a steady source of water during the growing season, about 1 inch a week from rain or watering. In arid regions of the country, consider installing a drip irrigation system.

6 Mulch. Roses need less weeding and watering and have fewer diseases if you lay down 1 to 2 inches of organic mulch, such as wood chips, pine needles, grass clippings or other biodegradable material.

7 Deadhead. This simply means trimming off spent roses to encourage the bush to produce more. While some roses bloom only in one big flush in June, others are bred to keep producing off and on all season long.

8 Spray. If your rose bush becomes diseased or has an insect infestation, you may want to deal with it by spraying. (Try simply trimming off the affected portion of the plant and giving the buggy plant a good strong blast from a hose.) Identify the problem by trimming off the affected part and taking it to a reliable garden center, where the staff can prescribe the correct treatment.

9 Stop fertilizing roses in early autumn, at least one month before your region's first annual frost date. Fertilizing too long into autumn encourages roses to produce tender new growth that will get nipped by cold.

10 Protect roses as needed in late autumn, after your region's first hard freeze. In regions where temperatures don't fall below 20 degrees F, no additional winter protection is needed. In cooler regions where temperatures don't fall below 10 degrees F below zero, a simple mounding of several inches of soil over the base of the rose should suffice. In cold-winter regions where temperatures get colder than 10 degrees F below zero, mound to about a foot about a month after your region's last average frost date; additionally, two weeks later, the entire plant should be wrapped in burlap to protect the upper parts.

If your rose is a climbing or rambling rose, prune with caution. Some will bloom only on old wood from the previous year.

Each rose grower has his or her own favorite feeding method. One of the easiest is to buy a slow-release granular rose food and work it into the soil so it can feed the plant all season long.

## ⚠ Warnings

Read pesticide and fungicide lables carefully. Even organic products can be hazardous if used incorrectly, so follow package directions to the letter.

It's best to avoid those white plastic cones for winter rose protection. Not only do they look unattractive, but they also can trap heat during a late-winter thaw, harming the rose.

## Things You'll Need

❑ garden shears

❑ lopping shears

❑ fertilizer

❑ mulch

❑ burlap

---

## 345 | Water Flowers

Water your annual and perennial flowers badly and you'll waste time—and have sickly plants. Water them well and you'll save yourself time and be rewarded with healthy, beautiful blooms.

## ⊙ Steps

1 Water early in the day. Watering in the cool of morning (even before dawn) minimizes evaporation if you're using a sprinkler. It also allows foliage to dry off quickly, preventing fungal diseases.

2 Avoid wetting the blooms. Some blooms close up if wet or fall off in a hard spray.

3 Water occasionally and deeply rather than often and lightly. You want water to soak in as deeply as possible, encouraging the plant to send

## ✱ Tips

In optimum (loamy) soil conditions, most plants need 1 to 2 inches of water per week.

As you design and plant your garden, try to cluster plants according to watering needs.

down deep roots. The soil should be moist to the bottom of the plant's roots when you insert your finger into the soil.

4   Learn to look for signs of dryness before flowers wilt, including a loss of sheen on leaves and hard soil surrounding the plant. Never let flowers wilt. This weakens them and makes them more prone to a host of diseases.

5   Check flowers in containers once or even twice a day, since they can need watering that often in hot, sunny or windy weather.

6   Let technology help you. If you have difficulty keeping up with watering needs, check out your local garden center's supplies of soaker hoses, drip emitters (including some for containers), and timers to connect to your outdoor faucet. Or try adding water-absorbing polymer crystals to your containers—the crystals can cut watering needs significantly.

7   Mulch (see 341 "Mulch Flowers"). Not only does this suppress weeds, but it keeps the soil around your flowers cool and moist, minimizing the need for water.

## ⚠ Warning

Avoid planting flowers whose watering needs will be difficult to keep up with. If you live in New Mexico, for example, it's silly to fight nature by planting water-guzzling plants.

---

# Water Vegetables

## 346

Most vegetables need about an inch of water (about 62 gallons per 100 square feet) per week to survive. In most years, in most places, rain alone won't supply enough.

### ⊙ Steps

1   Pull back any mulch, dig down 4 or 5 inches, scoop up a handful of soil and squeeze it. If the soil holds together, it's moist enough; if it crumbles in your hand, you need to water. Very sandy soil never forms a ball. If it feels gritty and sticks to your fingers, it's moist; if the particles flow through your fingers, the soil is too dry.

2   Cultivate before you water to loosen the soil; otherwise, the water will cause a crust to form on the soil's surface, preventing both water and air from reaching the roots.

3   Water in the morning. Avoid watering during the heat of the day, when a lot of water will be lost to evaporation, or in the late afternoon or evening; water that remains on stems or foliage overnight encourages fungus disease.

4   Apply water slowly and uniformly to a depth of 5 to 6 inches; you'll encourage deep roots that can seek out water at different levels in the soil. Adapt your technique to the particular needs of vegetables—flood the furrows if you grow in rows; sink a reservoir made of a perforated pipe or coffee can next to melons and squash; and locate sprinklers close to the ground for less evaporation around large leaves.

5   Install a drip irrigation system for maximum watering efficiency and ease. This will deliver water to individual plants, not to your driveway or the weeds growing in the garden path. A large nursery can supply and install the system for you. It's not cheap, but it can cut your water costs in half.

6   Accomplish similar results at a lower cost with a drip soaker: either a hose with holes punched in it or a porous hose that oozes water along its length. You simply lay the hose in place so that it reaches the base of each plant.

### ✳ Tips

Amend your soil with organic matter to improve the way it handles water.

Use mulch to conserve moisture.

### ⚠ Warnings

Some vegetables need more water than others. Heavy drinkers include celery, artichokes and asparagus. Beets, tomatoes and peppers are modest imbibers. Many herbs, including marjoram, oregano, thyme and garlic, need very little liquid sustenance. In fact, they'll taste best if you hold off watering until they look ready to wilt.

Too much water will cause as much damage as too little: it will drown plant roots and wash away nutrients.

#  347 Grow Popular Vegetables

Home-grown produce almost always tastes better. Look for seeds and seedlings in nurseries and catalogs and on Web sites, and choose with an awareness of what will grow best in your region and climate.

chart

| | SOIL AND SUN | PLANTING | SPECIAL CARE | WATERING | HARVESTING |
|---|---|---|---|---|---|
| Beans, snap | Choose a site in full sun (partial afternoon shade in very hot climates) with well-drained soil. Add organic matter. Install supports for pole beans. | Sow after threat of frost has passed and the soil temperature is at least 60 degrees F. Seeds should be an inch deep and 2 to 3 inches apart in rows 3 to 4 feet apart. | Thin so that bush varieties are 5 to 6 inches apart, pole beans 6 to 8 inches. In humid climates, increase this distance. Mulch with compost when plants show second set of leaves. | Give about 1 inch of water a week, a little more when pods are developing. Don't over-water. Water the ground, not the plants. | Pick beans when they're young and tender, before you notice the seeds swelling. |
| Carrots | Choose a site with full sun. Dig at least 12 inches deep, and remove all rocks and debris. Add plenty of organic matter. | Sow directly in the ground about two to three weeks before the last expected frost in cool regions; in warm climates, plant in fall, winter or spring. | Thin seedlings before tops entwine. Mulch with compost. | Water young plants at least 1 inch a week; cut back as they near maturity. | Begin harvesting when roots have turned bright orange. |
| Corn | Choose a site with full sun. Corn needs soil that's rich, moisture-retentive and well-draining. Dig in plenty of compost and well-cured manure. | Buy plants if growing season is short. If not, plant seeds outdoors at least a week after the last frost, when soil is 55 degrees F (65 for supersweet varieties). Sow 1 to 2 inches deep, 4 to 6 inches apart. | Thin to a foot apart when 3 to 4 inches tall. Mulch when the ground has warmed. Fertilize when plants reach 10 inches and then 18 inches, and when tassels appear. | Make sure plants get at least an inch of water a week. Never water from above. | Harvest when husks are bright green, silks are dry and brown but still supple, and full-size kernels reach to the top of the ear—for most varieties, about 20 days after silks appear. |
| Lettuce | Plant in full sun in cool weather, partial sun in summer. Till soil thoroughly, breaking up clumps and removing stones and debris. Dig in plenty of compost and well-cured manure. | Sow seeds outdoors as soon as soil can be worked in spring. Set plants 8 to 16 inches apart. | Mulch to conserve moisture and keep the soil cool. Feed every three weeks with liquid fertilizer. | Keep the soil moist, but avoid watering in the evening; foliage that stays wet overnight is prone to disease. | Begin cutting leaf lettuces as soon as they're big enough to use. Harvest heading types when heads are firm and fully formed. |
| Peas | Choose a site with full sun and well-draining soil. Dig in plenty of compost. Avoid any high-nitrogen soil additives. | Sow directly outdoors as soon as soil can be worked. Plant an inch deep, 3 to 4 inches apart, in rows 3 feet apart. Install supports. | Help ensure heavy yields by using liquid fertilizer twice during growing season. Guide vines upward as soon as they're long enough to climb. | Give young plants about ½ inch of water a week (1 inch in very sandy soil). When plants begin to flower, give them 1 inch per week. | Expect peas to be ready for picking about three weeks after the plants begin to flower. |
| Tomatoes | Tomatoes need full sun and plenty of warmth. Amend the soil with compost. | Move seedlings to the garden when nighttime temperatures remain above 50 degrees F. Dig a hole the size of a basketball for each plant. Mix in a shovelful of compost. Set plants 12 to 18 inches apart. | Mulch soil and install any supports the plants will need as they grow. Feed with low-nitrogen fertilizer: two weeks after transplanting, after the first flowers appear, when fruits are as big as golf balls, and when you spot the first ripe tomato. | Give plants between 1 and 2 inches of water every week. | Pick tomatoes when their color is glossy and even, and their texture is midway between soft and firm. |

## Prevent Weeds 348

Fighting weeds is a constant battle during the growing season. The key is to get them under control and then prevent them from returning.

### ⊙ Steps

1 Dig, chop, hoe or remove any weeds that have invaded your garden. You need to start with a clean slate in the war against weeds.

2 Place a thick layer of mulch over the clean soil. Mulch can be anything that covers the surface of the soil, including ground bark, newspaper, leaves, rocks or even old carpet. It prevents weeds from germinating by shading the soil and keeping it cool. A 3- to 4-inch-thick layer will prevent all but the most noxious weeds from growing.

3 Encourage shrubs to grow to full size by fertilizing during the growing season. Shrubs will shade the surface of the soil and choke weeds before they become established.

4 Use fast-growing ground covers such as vinca or hypericum to choke weeds out of existence. Once the surface of the soil is covered with foliage, the weeds won't have anywhere to grow.

5 Pull stray weeds as they appear, and never allow them to go to seed in your garden.

### ✳ Tip

Use a thick layer of mulch around new plantings until shrubs and ground covers become well-established.

### ⚠ Warnings

Always start out with the least toxic method of weed control.

There are chemicals, called pre-emergents, that control weeds before they grow. Use pre-emergent herbicides only after the soil is cleared of weeds.

If you do use chemicals for weed control, wear protective clothing, including a long-sleeved shirt and pants, neoprene gloves, a respirator and goggles.

## Trap Garden Gophers 349

Gophers are territorial rodents that bulldoze their way around your property, eating nearly every kind of plant. Trapping is considered the most effective form of eradication.

### ⊙ Steps

1 Purchase two gopher traps at a local gardening supply store.

2 Set up the traps according to the directions that come with them.

3 Use a metal pole to find the gopher's main tunnel. Unused runs will be full of debris and not easy to penetrate.

4 Use a shovel to excavate dirt until you find the main tunnel and open it.

5 Place two traps in the main tunnel; the traps should be placed into the exposed tunnel and faced away from each other so that the gopher will be trapped no matter which way it is moving in the tunnel.

6 Bait each trap with vegetables or dry cat food if you wish.

7 Wedge the traps into the tunnel tightly. Cover the excavation with a board and fill in the ends with soil.

8 Check and reset the traps as necessary, moving them to another spot if you haven't caught the gopher within a few days.

9 Remove the dead gopher from the trap and dispose of it; wrap it tightly in paper and plastic before putting it into the garbage.

### ✳ Tips

Keep human scent off traps by wearing gloves when you set them up.

Using fumigants or flooding the holes with water usually brings only limited success.

If you prefer not to kill gophers, try various frightening devices and wire baskets around roots. Cats and dogs can also discourage gophers.

### ⚠ Warning

Poison pellets and other toxins aren't recommended, since they can be pushed to the surface by the gopher and eaten by birds and pets. Or a pet might eat a poisoned gopher, with lethal results.

## 350 | Protect Your Garden From Deer

They're cute, they're furry and they're graceful, and they'll wreak havoc on your garden. Don't shoot! Here are some ways to keep deer from eating your plants.

### ⊙ Steps

1 Landscape with plants that deer don't like to eat. Contact a local nursery to discover which local plants are less appealing to deer.

2 Surround your property with fencing that is at least 8 feet high—higher on a slope so the deer won't be able to leap over.

3 Create a barrier by erecting parallel 4-foot-high fences, 5 feet apart. Deer won't attempt to jump the shorter fences if they see another obstacle.

4 Use only wire mesh or solid fencing. While those types of fences may be less attractive, deer can miraculously squeeze through just about any spaces between slats or gaps in wood fencing. (Mesh now comes in a variety of colors and can blend in better with your surroundings.)

5 Install electric fencing around the perimeter of your garden. This will definitely do the trick, but it will also zap unintended animals and children, so use it as a last resort and away from trails and houses.

6 Fence in or enclose specific trees or beds with mesh or screen. The barriers should be tall enough (up to 6 feet high) for the deer not to eat over and at least 2 feet from the foliage so the deer cannot graze through fences.

7 Spray your garden with deer repellents. Unfortunately, the ingredients that work best are ground chicken feathers and sewage, and the smell may keep more than just the deer away.

8 Hang bars of deodorant soap from trees throughout the garden. Add enough of the pungent bars so no tempting leaves are more than 3 feet from a bar. Deer are skittish about any unfamiliar smell, so change the bars to new brands regularly.

9 Get a dog. Deer are cautious animals and won't enter a yard with a lurking canine.

### ✳ Tip

Deer are creatures of habit and often return regularly to easy targets. These steps make your yard less attractive to them and will send the deer off to more available food sources.

### ⚠ Warning

Late in the summer when wild vegetation becomes scarce and dried out, or in winter when food is less available, the deer get hungry and it becomes more difficult to keep them away.

## 351 | Deadhead Flowers

A flowering plant's goal is to set seed. If you repeatedly dead-head—trim off the spent flowers—the plant goes into overdrive, putting out more and more flowers in an effort to reproduce.

### ⊙ Steps

1 Deadhead when a flower starts to brown, wither, shatter or otherwise go downhill.

2 Deadhead tall flowers that sit atop long, slender stems by cutting the stem at the base of the plant.

3 Trim bushy plants with many small flowers with handheld grass shears or small hedge clippers. Trim the whole plant at once—even if there are

### ✳ Tip

Plants respond differently to deadheading, depending on climate, variety, rainfall and other variables. Experiment. Take comfort in the fact that in most cases, the worst you can do is give them a bad haircut. It's almost impossible to kill a plant by deadheading.

**How to Do (Just About) Everything**

still some nice flowers—rather than trying to tediously trim one flower at a time.

4   Deadhead other plants by simply snapping or pinching off the flowers with your hand or cut them off with garden shears, a knife or scissors.

5   Treat annuals and perennials that have dying or ragged foliage by cutting back (shortening) the foliage by one-third to two-thirds. Do this either when the plant has stopped blooming or when it starts to get that overall "ratty" look. They'll usually send out a new flush of healthy, fresh foliage with flowers.

**Things You'll Need**

❑ garden shears, grass shears or small hedge clippers

---

## Train a Vine                                                                          352

Climbing vines are quick-change artists that can hide garden eyesores. There are four basic types of vines, each growing in a different way.

### ⊙ Steps

1   Plant climbing vines such as English ivy or climbing hydrangea at the base of any wall or fence you want to cover. Stand back and watch them scramble upward. They will send out rootlets that will cling to any support they encounter.

2   Plant tendril vines such as grapes and sweet peas where they can hang on to their supports. Their tendrils grow out from their stems and can wrap themselves around thin supports such as string, wire or the stems of other plants. Match the support to the size and weight of the mature plant; a grapevine needs a sturdy arbor with strong wires, while sweet peas need only a simple wire or nylon mesh trellis.

3   Plant twining vines such as clematis, morning glory and kiwi near any trellis, arbor or openwork fence. As the plants grow, they'll twine themselves around both vertical and horizontal supports. Guide the first shoots up the fence and fasten them loosely; once they start weaving their way through the openings, they will need no more help.

4   Fasten procumbent vines (they crawl along the ground and have no means of self-support) such as jasmine directly to a fence or trellis. Secure the shoots loosely using plastic-coated wire or nylon twine. To cloak a wall or solid fence, drive in galvanized nails at 18-inch to 2-foot intervals, and as the shoots grow, tie them to the nails.

**✳ Tips**

Look to the future if you plant a perennial vine. Wisteria, for instance, will live 50 years or more, and a mature plant is heavy. It needs a sturdy, well-designed structure that will both show off its beauty and bear its weight.

Arrange the shoots of tendril vines in the direction you want them to grow, and fasten them loosely with twine or coated twist ties for a day or so until the tendrils begin to grip.

**Things You'll Need**

❑ twine or other vine ties

❑ trellis

❑ galvanized nails

## 353 Shape and Revive a Plant

Many plants benefit from occasional barbering, whether the purpose is to promote more bloom or simply to produce a more pleasing shape. The method to use depends on the plant.

**Things You'll Need**

- ❑ garden shears

### ⊙ Steps

1 Deadhead (trim or pinch off regularly) the spent flowers of all annuals and the many perennials that bloom over a period of time instead of all at once (see 351 "Deadhead Flowers"). There are dozens of long-blooming perennials, including balloon flower, yarrow, sage and peony.

2 Pinch back annual flowers, vegetables, herbs and late-blooming perennials such as chrysanthemums and asters. You'll help the plants produce more flowers and make them fuller and denser.

3 Shape perennials that bloom in a single flush, such as lavender and false indigo, to produce a form that blends well with other plants in your garden. Use sharp shears to cut foliage back by about a third, creating a shape that blends in with later-maturing plants in your garden.

4 Cut plants prone to legginess all the way back to the ground after they bloom. Hardy geraniums, Japanese anemone and black-eyed Susan all lend themselves well to this treatment.

## 354 Trim Hedges

Plant a hedge to mark boundaries, form a barrier, create a background or define a planting bed. All hedges will look best if kept trimmed and in good health.

### ❋ Tip

The ideal hedge plant has scaffolding branches that start at the ground. Boxwood, holly, juniper and privet are all excellent choices for hedging.

### ⚠ Warning

Evergreen hedges such as juniper and cypress should never be trimmed below the foliage or they won't grow back. Clip only a few inches from the previous year's growth.

### ⊙ Steps

1 Begin trimming hedges when they're first planted. Young plants respond well to shaping and training.

2 Cut a few inches off the top of a hedge plant as soon as it has been planted. This will help form bushy plants.

3 Use a string guide to keep your hedges even. Place a bamboo stake at either end of the hedgerow. String a line between the two stakes at the desired height of the finished hedge. Use hedge trimmers and follow the string line.

4 Shape the hedge so that it's wider at the bottom. Sunlight will reach all the leaves if the hedge is pruned this way. Taper the plants in as you near the top.

5 Trim during the active growing season. You may have to trim more than once, but you'll avoid making mistakes that can't be rectified.

6 Trim lightly at the end of the growing season to keep hedges looking good throughout the winter months.

**Things You'll Need**

- ❑ hedge shears
- ❑ string
- ❑ bamboo stakes

# Divide Perennials

**355**

Are your perennials blooming less prolifically or getting too crowded? Then it's time to divide them. The method depends on your plants' growth habit.

## ⊙ Steps

### Dividing Clump-Forming Perennials

1 Dig up the entire root system using a spade or spading fork—including all the soil from about 6 to 8 inches around the roots.

2 Separate the root clumps with your hands by shaking off excess soil and pulling the roots apart into divisions.

3 Separate tightly growing clumps with two forks. Stick them between clumps with their back sides together, then push the handles apart.

4 Replant the new divisions in the ground, or plant them in containers filled with soil mix.

5 Water new plantings well until soil is completely moist.

6 Discard the oldest section at the center of the clump if it looks woody and has little new growth.

### Dividing Single-Stem Perennials

1 Use the following method for perennials that have runners (underground stems) and those that spread by growing roots through the soil and sending up more stems above ground.

2 Plunge a shovel or spade straight down into the soil between groups of upright, stems that are above ground. This separates the whole plant into sections.

3 Dig up a clump of soil that has roots and three or four stems growing out; dig about 4 or 5 inches down. These are your new plants.

4 Replant or pot the extra divisions.

5 Refill the original hole with compost.

6 Water the remaining plant and the new divisions well, until the soil is completely moist.

### ✱ Tips

Most perennials can be divided in late fall or early spring.

Dividing perennials means you get more and more plants every year—plants you can use in your own garden or share with friends.

### Things You'll Need

❑ spade

❑ two spading forks

❑ compost

---

# Winterize Your Garden

**356**

Readying your garden for winter is essential in cold-winter regions, where freezing, drying conditions can tax even hardy plants. Even in warmer climates there's plenty to do.

## ⊙ Steps

1 Plant spring-blooming bulbs such as tulips and daffodils. Plant them any time from September in colder regions through December in warmer climates—as long as the ground can be easily worked.

2 Rake leaves and dispose of them, preferably in a compost heap. Failing to rake leaves can result in a dying or diseased lawn.

### ✱ Tip

Save your favorite plants before frost hits. Small annuals and herbs are wonderful for digging up and planting in pots to spend the winter in a sunny window inside.

3 Pull up any annual flowers or vegetables felled by frost. Dispose of these in the compost heap; if you suspect disease, throw them in the garbage.

4 Cut back almost to the ground any perennials whose foliage has become unsightly. The seedheads and dried foliage of some perennials add interest during the winter months, while others just look messy.

5 Weed. Fall action prevents weeds from getting a head start next spring, saving you work in the long run.

6 Dig up tender bulbs. Cannas, tuberous begonias, gladiolus, dahlias and most other summer-blooming bulbs don't survive the winter in USDA Zone 9 and colder. Store bulbs in vermiculite in a paper bag in a cool (65 degrees F or cooler), dry spot.

7 Protect roses as needed (see 344 "Care for Roses").

8 Apply a winter mulch to perennials where winter temperatures generally fall below minus 10 degrees F. Simply lay a lightweight organic mulch, such as shredded autumn leaves, pine needles or straw, over beds to protect plants from winter's extremes. Avoid more compact mulches and whole leaves (which can mat), since they can suffocate plants.

9 Protect broad-leaved evergreens, such as rhododendrons and holly, with an antidesiccant spray. This prevents water loss from drying winter winds.

10 Water evergreens and small trees and shrubs if the fall weather is especially dry. Their foliage and stems need to be nice and plump to prevent damage from drying winds now through early spring.

## ⚠ Warning

Don't fertilize or prune plants at the end of their seasons. Either could promote tender new growth that will get nipped by cold. The exception is trimming out dead or damaged branches or foliage.

## Things You'll Need

❑ leaf rake

❑ garden shears

❑ mulch

❑ antidesiccant spray

---

## 357 | Water Houseplants

**More houseplants die from too much water than from not enough. Here's how to determine when your plants need water.**

### ◎ Steps

1 Poke your finger right into the dirt, about an inch below the surface or up to your first knuckle. If the soil feels dry to the touch below the surface, it's time to water. If it feels damp, wait a day or two and test again.

2 Use an inexpensive moisture meter to check the moisture level in the soil as an alternative to the fingertip test.

3 Provide extra water to plants that require moist soil, such as ferns and philodendrons. The soil should feel like a wrung-out sponge.

4 Use self-watering pots if you don't have the time to check your plants daily. These handy pots allow the plants to help themselves to a drink. You will need to check the pots' water reservoirs every two weeks.

5 Use tepid or warm water to water tropical plants. Allow the water to sit in the watering can overnight so that chlorine and chemicals can evaporate. This is called "seasoning" the water.

6 Use water from a freshwater aquarium. It contains nutrients, is the proper temperature and has no chemicals or chlorine.

7 Mist plants frequently. They do take in moisture through their leaves, and the humidity mimics their tropical environment.

### ✳ Tips

Plants in bright light will use more water than those in low-light areas.

Make a humidity tray by placing gravel in the saucer. When you water, moisture will evaporate from the gravel up through the foliage.

### ⚠ Warning

Never allow plants to sit in standing water. Drain saucers a half-hour after watering.

## Fertilize Houseplants                 358

You need to fertilize houseplants during their growing season, which is spring and summer.

### ☉ Steps

1. Select a liquid fertilizer formulated for houseplants, and use it as directed during the growing season (spring and summer).

2. Add the concentrated fertilizer directly to the watering can.

3. Remove a plant from its saucer and place it in an area where water can run freely through the soil, such as in a sink or bathtub.

4. Pour the fertilizer solution onto the surface of the soil. Make sure it flows from the pot's drainage hole.

5. Allow the water to drain through the pot thoroughly before replacing the plant on its saucer.

6. Consider another method: Use a slow-release fertilizer in the form of granules or spikes. Apply the product according to label directions.

### ⚠ Warnings

Don't fertilize more than is recommended, or you may burn your plants or get a salt buildup on the clay pot.

Try not to get any fertilizer on the foliage; it may burn the leaves and cause spots.

### Things You'll Need

- ❏ liquid fertilizer
- ❏ watering can
- ❏ slow-release fertilizer

## Propagate Houseplants From Cuttings          359

Propagating from stem cuttings is an economical way to add to your houseplant collection.

### ☉ Steps

1. Cut the tips (including the end leaf and the second and third leaves in from the end) off vining or branching houseplants such as monstera, wandering Jew or *Ficus benjamina*.

2. Remove the bottom two leaves. Roots will form at the nodes where the leaves were removed, not from the leaves themselves. If left on the cutting, the leaves may rot and foul the water.

3. Dip the cut end of the cutting into a rooting hormone product. Rooting hormones encourage new root growth.

4. Place the prepared cutting into a small pot filled with damp quarry or river sand. You may also use damp perlite or vermiculite.

5. Set the cuttings in a bright, warm location, away from direct sunlight. To increase humidity while roots are forming, place the cuttings (in their containers) in a clear plastic bag. To prevent the bag from collapsing onto the young plants, place two or three chopsticks into the sand to support the bag. Tie the plastic bag loosely at the top with twist ties or rubber bands.

6. After roots form, transplant the cutting into a small pot filled with damp potting soil. Tug gently on the plant to check for root development. If the plant pulls out of the sand easily, it's not ready. If there's some resistance, roots have formed and the cutting is ready to transplant.

7. Treat your new plant as you would any other houseplant. Be extra careful about proper moisture and light until the plant has fully established itself.

### ✳ Tips

Cuttings from foliage plants should not be longer than 3 to 4 inches, unless the plant is very large. Take several cuttings to ensure success in propagation.

African violets can be grown from a single leaf. Remove the leaf from the plant, dip the cut end into rooting hormone, place the cutting in damp sand, then transplant when roots form.

### Things You'll Need

- ❏ garden shears
- ❏ rooting hormone
- ❏ small pots
- ❏ quarry or river sand
- ❏ clear plastic bag
- ❏ chopsticks
- ❏ twist ties
- ❏ potting soil

## 360 | Select a Basic Set of Kitchen Equipment

You'll be able to prepare most recipes with just a few basic pots and pans.

### ◉ Steps

1  Assess your needs. Basic cookware is adequate for those who mostly cook for themselves and don't go gourmet too often.

2  Look for basic cookware at larger markets and kitchen stores. Quality yet affordable cookware is available at larger kitchen and housewares stores. Supermarket cookware will work but often is of lesser quality.

3  Choose a 9- or 10-inch skillet or sauté pan, a 4- or 5-quart pot and a baking or roasting pan to start. You can cook most recipes with these three items.

4  Add to your basic set with an extra sauté pan, a 1- or 2-quart saucepan, and an 8- or 10-quart stockpot.

5  Avoid plastic handles if possible—they can't withstand high oven temperatures—and choose cookware with riveted or welded handles. (There's nothing worse than a handle's coming off in your hands as you attempt to remove a pot from the stove.)

6  Choose stainless steel or thick aluminum cookware if possible.

7  Start out with a spatula, tongs, a vegetable peeler and a few wooden spoons as your basic cooking utensils.

8  Be sure to get at least one high-quality, sharp knife; a good choice is the all-purpose, medium-size kind often labeled "chef's knife."

### ✳ Tip

Nonstick surfaces such as Teflon or Silverstone work well but are usually necessary only in sauté pans. Use only wooden or coated utensils when cooking with non-stick surfaces.

### Things You'll Need

❑ 9- or 10-inch skillet

❑ 4- or 5-quart pot

❑ baking or roasting pan

❑ 1- or 2-quart saucepan

❑ 8- or 10-quart stockpot

❑ spatula

❑ tongs

❑ vegetable peeler

❑ wooden spoons

❑ chef's knife

## 361 | Season a Cast-Iron Skillet

Seasoning a cast-iron skillet with oil gives it a protective coating that keeps food from sticking and the pan from rusting. Do this when the pan is new or food is starting to stick to it.

### ◉ Steps

1  Scrub a new skillet with steel wool or a plastic scrub pad and mild, soapy water to get it very clean. (If reseasoning an old skillet, just scrub with hot water and a brush.) Rinse well and dry thoroughly.

2  Use a paper towel to coat the skillet lightly with solid vegetable shortening (don't use butter).

3  Heat the skillet, uncovered, in an oven for 1 hour at 350 degrees F.

4  Let it cool before use and store uncovered.

### ✳ Tips

Once you've seasoned a skillet, avoid washing it with soap. Clean instead by wiping with a damp cloth after each use—use a little salt as a mild abrasive to remove bits of stuck food, then coat with solid vegetable shortening.

If you must wash it, clean with mild soap, rinse and wipe dry. Then grease lightly with solid vegetable shortening.

## Sharpen Kitchen Knives

A sharpening steel, a whetstone and a commercial knife sharpener all can help keep an edge on your good chef's knives. Here are the basics on all three.

### ⊙ Steps

#### Sharpening Steel

1 To maintain the edge, use a sharpening steel—a metal rod with a handle and a crosspiece to keep the knife from hitting your hand—every time you use the knife.

2 Hold the steel handle in one hand and the knife handle in the other. Place the heel of the knife blade near the tip of the steel.

3 Move the knife blade down the steel in the direction of the cutting edge and along the edge from heel to knife tip, at about a 10- to 20-degree angle. Repeat on the blade's other side.

#### Whetstone

1 Use a whetstone to give a knife back its edge. Choose wet or dry— experts differ on which is best. Choose one with a coarse side and a smooth side.

2 Place the whetstone on a stable surface, coarse side up. Position the knife blade at about a 20-degree angle to the stone.

3 Draw the knife across the stone several times in the direction of the cutting edge and along the edge from heel to knife tip. Repeat the process on the other side of the blade, about 10 times per side.

4 Repeat the same process a few more times on the fine side of the stone.

#### Commercial Sharpener

1 Use a commercial sharpener to sharpen and maintain blades. First, find out about the variety available: electric and manual, with a variety of sharpening surfaces, including ceramic and diamond. The best automatically position the knife blade at the correct angle.

2 Search online for "knife sharpeners" to find suppliers, knife-sharpening tutorials and discussion forums about the different products. Expect to pay anywhere from $25 to $150 for a sharpener.

### ✱ Tips

Make sure yours is a good knife that can be sharpened. Most high-quality chef's knives today are made of high-carbon steel.

Store good knives in a knife block or on a magnetic rack—not tossed randomly into a drawer— and cut only on cutting boards.

A professional sharpening service can do a great job on your knives if you're willing to be without them for a little while. Check online directories or the yellow pages for ones near you. Cutlery and cookware shops, as well as full-service butcher shops, also sometimes offer this service.

### ⚠ Warning

Using a whetstone correctly takes practice and can be frustrating—consider having a cooking teacher or chef show you how to do it.

## Chop an Onion

Chopping an onion may very well be the most common kitchen task other than washing dishes. Still, it can be daunting.

### ⊙ Steps

1 Make sure you have a firm, clean cutting board and a sharp knife.

2 Use a knife that's at least twice as long as the onion. You'll need the length to slice through the vegetable.

### ✱ Tips

To avoid tears, make sure your kitchen is well-ventilated so the sulphuric compounds released from the cut onion are quickly dispersed.

3   Place the onion on the board so you can see both the root and the stem.

4   Hold the onion carefully and position the knife's blade along the onion so that it will cut it in half vertically, through both the root and stem ends.

5   Start the cut and then stop to make sure the blade is lined up properly.

6   Take your hand off the onion and place it on top of the knife, so that if the knife slips it won't cut you.

7   Finish cutting the onion in half.

8   Place each half on the cutting board, cut side down.

9   Cut off about ½ inch from the root and stem ends, and either discard them or save them for stock. Remove the peel from the two halves.

10  Hold one half of the onion against the cutting board with the fingers of one hand at the very top, the fingertips curled under to keep them away from the knife blade.

11  Hold the knife in the other hand with the flat of the blade parallel to the cutting board. Cut the onion into a stack of horizontal slices, still connected at the root end—that is, don't cut all the way through it.

12  Turn the knife so the tip is pointing toward the root end and the blade is perpendicular to the board. Cut the horizontal slices into sticks, still not cutting through the root end.

13  Point the knife tip away from yourself and cut the sticks crosswise to make dice. Repeat with the other half of the onion.

A truly sharp knife makes this process a breeze.

All onions, including shallots, are basically the same and can be cut the same way. If using leeks, discard the dark green part and wash the remaining white part well between each layer. Leeks don't need to be peeled.

Do not cut onions in half horizontally, so the stem is on one half and the root end on the other. Onions are difficult to work with and to keep together when cut this way.

Chop the onion more finely (if desired) using the "hinge" method: Hold the knife with one hand and place the fingers of your other hand on top of the knife, down by the tip, to keep the tip lightly pressed to the cutting board. Use a rocking motion, with the tip of the knife acting as a hinge, to chop the onion into smaller pieces.

---

## 364 | Chop Fresh Herbs

Fresh herbs are an important part of many recipes, and chopping them to the right size helps blend in their flavors.

### ⊙ Steps

1   Rinse your herbs in cold water and carefully dry them with paper towels.

2   If using herbs with a woody or thick stem, like rosemary, basil or older thyme, strip the leaves off the stems with your fingers.

3   Remove the lower, leafless stems from herbs like parsley or cilantro.

4   Pile the herbs on a clean cutting board.

5   Chop the herb pile roughly first, drawing the herbs back into a pile as you rechop them.

6   Finely chop the herbs using the "hinge" method: Hold the knife with one hand, and place the fingers of your other hand on top of the knife down by the tip, to keep the tip lightly pressed to the cutting board. Raise the knife handle up and down rapidly, using a rocking motion, with the tip of the knife acting as a hinge.

7   Use the knife to draw the herbs back into a neat pile after every few strokes to make sure they are chopped evenly.

8   Use the herbs in your recipe as soon as you've finished chopping them.

### ✳ Tip

The best knife for chopping herbs is a sharp one with a wide blade, such as a chef's knife or a Chinese cleaver, that lets you chop without hitting your fingers on the cutting board. Don't use a serrated-edge knife because it won't cut cleanly.

## ✓ 365 Choose Produce

Follow the pointers in this chart to select the best tasting, ripest fruits and vegetables. If you have any doubts or questions, ask the produce-department manager. Note that imported produce may be available in seasons other than those listed.

| | WHAT TO LOOK FOR | PEAK SEASON |
|---|---|---|
| Apples | Bright color, firm texture; no bruising or wrinkling | September through November (but available year-round) |
| Asparagus | Straight stalks with closed (not open or mushy) tips | February through June (hothouse asparagus available year-round in some regions) |
| Avocados | Heavy weight for size; no bruises or cuts; ready to use if they give to gentle pressure; ripen further if still firm | Hass avocados—summer; Fuerte—fall and winter |
| Bananas | Bright yellow with green tips need further ripening; perfectly ripe when speckled with brown spots | Available year-round |
| Broccoli | Florets closed, dark green or purplish; not soft and mushy; fresh smell | October through April (but available year-round) |
| Cherries | Attached stems; firm but not hard; not soft or bruised | May through August |
| Citrus fruit | Heavy for their size; faint, sweet fragrance appropriate to variety | Available year-round (lemons peak in the summer) |
| Corn | Golden-brown silk; bright green, snug husk; rows of tightly packed, plump kernels extending to the tip | May through September |
| Grapes | Silver-white bloom on skin; no brown spots; firmly attached to moist, flexible stems | Domestic grapes—June to November (but may be available longer if stored under controlled conditions) |
| Mangoes | Red blush over yellow skin when ripe; choose larger rather than smaller ones | May through September |
| Melons | Slightly sweet fragrance; slight softness at blossom end for muskmelons; dull, not shiny, rind for watermelons; sound hollow when thumped; avoid bruised melons | Muskmelons (such as cantaloupe and honeydew)—late summer to early fall; watermelons—May to September, but peak from mid-June to late August |
| Mushrooms, button | Light color; closed caps; pleasant, earthy smell; dry-looking, not slimy | Available year-round, but peak in fall and winter |
| Papayas | Rich color; give slightly to gentle pressure; if still a bit green, will ripen at room temperature | Summer, but can be found as early as January |
| Peaches and nectarines | Intense fragrance; yellow, pink or white (not green) background color; give slightly to pressure | Peaches—May to October; nectarines—May to late September, with a peak during July and August |
| Pears | Firm texture (avoid pears with soft spots); blemish-free skin; fresh fragrance | Mid to late summer through early November (and later if pears are from storage) |
| Persimmons | Deep red-orange, glossy, smooth skin; Hachiya very soft, juicy; Fuyu firm, almost like an apple | Fall |
| Pineapples | Fresh-looking, leafy green crown; no visible bruises; sweet pineapple smell at stem end | Available year-round, but peak from March to July |
| Potatoes | Red, white, brown or purple skin free of discoloration; no decay, blemishes, green or sunken spots | Year-round (one variety or another) |
| Strawberries | Bright color, plump and glossy with green caps still attached; avoid moldy, soft berries | April to midsummer |
| Squash | Blemish-free skin with no mushy spots; summer squash firm, heavy and smooth-skinned; winter squash firm, hard and heavy | Summer squash—early through late summer; winter squash—early fall through the winter |
| Tomatoes | Heavy for size; firm and well-shaped; give slightly to pressure; rich color characteristic of variety | Available year-round, but peak from June through September |

chart

## 366 | Dice Vegetables

A diced vegetable is cut into small cubes. It's easy to dice quickly and evenly—just think "slices, sticks and cubes."

### ⊙ Steps

1   Clean your cutting board and knife.

2   Peel the skin from the vegetable, if necessary, and discard it.

3   For round vegetables like carrots and potatoes, cut in half lengthwise and place them cut side down on the board. This will keep the vegetable from rolling.

4   Cut the vegetable lengthwise into even slices, then stack the slices and cut them into long sticks. (Long, relatively thin vegetables like celery and leeks need only be sliced into sticks.)

5   Gather the sticks and cut them crosswise into cubes. Make sure to cut the cubes as evenly as you can.

### Dicing Tomatoes

1   To dice a tomato, cut it in quarters vertically, through the stem. It is not necessary to cut out the stem just yet.

2   Cut away the inner pulpy part of each tomato quarter, removing the stem with it.

3   Slice the remaining outer flesh into thin strips, then cut the strips crosswise into dice.

### Dicing Cucumbers

1   To dice a cucumber, peel the skin with a vegetable peeler and cut the cucumber in half lengthwise.

2   Using a teaspoon, scrape the seeds and pulpy interior from each half.

3   Slice the cucumber into thin strips and then cut crosswise to dice.

### ✻ Tips

A small dice is generally considered to be a ¼-inch cube, a medium dice is about ½ inch, and a large dice is between ¾ and 1 inch.

This technique will vary for specific vegetables, but you will almost always be aiming to get the vegetable into strips, which you can then easily cut into cubes. Vegetables made up of flowers, such as broccoli and cauliflower, are not typically diced, but broken into "flowerets" or "florets."

To julienne vegetables (a type of cut that makes long, thin strips), follow steps 1 through 4 to slice the vegetables into even strips ¼ inch thick and about 2 inches long.

## 367 | Peel and Mince Garlic

Garlic is one of the most common ingredients in cooking. Using fresh garlic that you peel yourself gives the best results.

### ⊙ Steps

1   Select a whole bulb of fresh garlic whose cloves are held tightly together and are not discolored.

2   Separate the cloves by placing the garlic bulb, root side down, on a cutting board and pressing down on it firmly with the heel of your hand.

3   To peel the cloves, arrange them on the cutting board and whack or press them firmly with a heavy object, like the flat side of a chef's knife, a kitchen mallet or a small pan.

### ✻ Tips

Wetting your fingers with water from time to time will prevent them from getting sticky from the garlic.

If salt is called for in your recipe, try adding a little to the garlic as you're mincing it. The salt will make the garlic less slippery and make mincing easier.

*How to Do (Just About) Everything*

4   Cut away the end of the garlic clove where it was attached to the bulb.

5   Discard the skins and clean the cutting board before mincing.

6   First chop the garlic coarsely. Use the same technique as with an onion:
    Make a series of horizontal cuts on the clove (separating it into thin
    slices), then a series of vertical cuts (separating it into thin sticks). Then
    cut the sticks crosswise to make tiny dice.

7   Mince the diced garlic by chopping it with a rocking motion: Keep the tip
    of the knife on the cutting board and move the handle up and down.

8   Stop every few strokes and use the knife blade to draw the garlic pieces
    back into a neat pile before continuing. Scrape off the garlic that has
    stuck to the side of the blade.

## Peel and Seed Tomatoes                                              368

So often, recipes call for peeling and seeding tomatoes. But
how do you do it? Here you go.

### ◎ Steps

1   Place a saucepan three-quarters full of water over high heat and bring
    to a boil.

2   Immerse tomatoes in the boiling water for 1 minute.

3   Remove tomatoes with tongs or a slotted spoon and set aside to cool
    enough so that you can handle them.

4   Barely pierce a tomato's skin with the tip of a sharp knife. Loosen the
    skin with the knife and peel away.

5   Cut the peeled tomatoes in half horizontally—that is, not cutting through
    the stem end.

6   Hold a tomato half in your hand over a small bowl.

7   Gently squeeze the tomato half so that the seeds and the clear pulp
    surrounding them drip into the bowl. Discard.

8   Use tomatoes as the recipe requires.

### ✳ Tips

Some people cut a small X in the
base of the tomato before dipping it in the boiling water. The
skin splits slightly around the X;
peel back the corners of the X to
remove the skin.

If the tomatoes don't peel well,
dip them in the boiling water for
another 30 seconds.

## Bone a Fish                                                         369

You can bone fish either before or after cooking. The bones
separate quite easily after cooking, but it's often more pleasant
to eat fish when the bones have been removed beforehand.

### ◎ Steps

1   Place the gutted and rinsed fish on a cutting surface. The following
    steps give you fillets.

2   Hold the fish by the head (if the head is still attached) and slice into the
    fish behind the gill until you feel the knife touch the backbone.

### ✳ Tips

The sharper the knife, the better.
Fish flesh is usually very delicate,
especially trout and smaller fish,
and requires a very sharp knife to
cut cleanly. Serrated knives and
electric knives are not recommended—they will make a mess.

3   Turn the knife so it's flat against the backbone, touching the ribs. The cutting edge should face the tail.

4   Cut along the backbone from head to tail, under the fillet.

5   Turn the fish over and repeat this cut. At this point two sets of bones will remain in the fillet.

6   Cut away the rib cage bones, which will be visible, by sliding the edge of the knife between the rib bones and the meat of the fillet.

7   Pull out the smaller set of bones, called pin bones, that run through the center of the fillet. Use your finger to feel for the pin-bone tips sticking out of the fillet. Use tweezers or needle-nose pliers to grab the tips and pull them out.

Raw fish should be gutted and rinsed in clean water.

## 370 Take the Skin Off Chicken

**Chicken skin contains most of the bird's fat, and by removing skin you can lower the amount of fat in your diet. Many recipes call for skinless chicken meat.**

### ◉ Steps

1   Place a whole raw chicken on a clean cutting board with the breast facing down.

2   Slice through the skin along the backbone.

3   Cut off the wings at the first joint.

4   Cut around the end of each drumstick to loosen the skin from the legs.

5   Carefully peel the skin away from the chicken, starting with the cut you made at the backbone.

6   Cut or pull the skin from the breastbone.

7   Skin a single piece of raw chicken by grasping one end of the skin firmly and pulling it.

8   To skin a whole cooked chicken or a cooked chicken piece, wait until it is cool enough to handle, then pull the skin away.

**✳ Tip**

Leave the skin on during cooking and peel it away afterward—meat won't absorb a significant amount of fat from the skin during cooking. Skin will also protect the meat from drying out during cooking and will add a little extra flavor.

## 371 Bone a Chicken Breast

**The more work done to prepare chicken before sale, the more it costs per pound: Skinless, boneless breasts are much more expensive than the bone-in variety.**

### ◉ Steps

1   If the recipe allows, cook the chicken breast with bones intact. They protect the meat as it cooks, which helps keep it juicy, and they help the breast retain its shape.

**✳ Tips**

When you're finished cutting raw chicken, be sure to thoroughly clean everything the chicken touched.

2   If you want to cook with a boneless breast, place the raw chicken breast, skin side down, on a clean cutting board. The bones will face up.

3   Look for the rib bones. Breasts sold with the bones attached still retain the ribs and part of the breastbone.

4   Hold the breast by the rib bones, and use the tip of the knife to make a thin incision between the ribs and the breast meat.

5   Use the knife tip to make small cuts across the rib cage, between the ribs and the meat, so you gradually separate the meat along the entire length of the rib cage.

6   Follow the contours of the rib cage with the tip of the knife, holding the breast by the ribs.

7   Continue making small cuts until the meat has completely separated from the bone.

8   The meat is now ready for your recipes.

9   Save the bones for stock or discard them.

A sharp boning knife is best for cutting chicken. Boning knives have thin, flexible blades about 6 inches long that can maneuver around the bird's small bones.

# Shuck Oysters                                                     372

Shucking oysters requires practice to do just right and preserve most of the oysters' liquid. It's a good idea to use a specialized sturdy oyster knife to make the job easier and safer.

## ⊙ Steps

1   Make sure the oysters are still alive by checking that their shells are tightly closed.

2   Scrub the oysters with a stiff brush under running water.

3   Hold an oyster in the palm of your hand with a towel so that you don't cut yourself. Or wear leather oyster gloves to protect your hands.

4   Work over a bowl so that you can catch the oysters' juices.

5   Position the oyster in your hand with the cup side down—so that its curved shell faces down and its flatter side faces up.

6   Insert a strong paring or oyster knife between the shells, near the hinge.

7   Twist the knife so that the oyster's muscles are detached.

8   Remove the top shell.

9   Scrape the meat from the top shell into the bottom shell.

10  Use the knife to cut the oyster free from the bottom shell.

## ✳ Tip

Always try to determine that shellfish originated in a body of water untainted by pollution or other hazards. The best way to do this is to become the regular customer of a reputable fishmonger. Try calling a restaurant chef or your local newspaper food section for recommendations.

## Things You'll Need

❏ stiff brush

❏ leather gloves

❏ oyster knife

## 373 | Devein Unshelled Shrimp

The "vein" is actually the shrimp's digestive tract. You don't have to take it out, but many people prefer to remove it for appearance's sake.

### ◎ Steps

1   Cut down the back of the shell with a knife or kitchen scissors to make it easier to access the vein.

2   Use your fingers and a "shrimp pick" (a small pick), a skewer or the tip of a small, sharp knife to remove as much of the vein as you can. Keep pulling out pieces until all of the vein has been removed.

3   Rinse in cold water.

### ✴ Tip

You can devein the shrimp and leave the shell on; the shell adds flavor to the dish and can protect the meat if you're grilling the shrimp.

## 374 | Clean and Crack Cooked Hard-Shell Crab

With its pincers and hard shell, a live crab can be intimidating to handle—and a cooked one only a little less so. But the reward of sweet crabmeat is worth it.

### ◎ Steps

1   Place a cooked crab on a work surface, belly side up.

2   Pull off the triangular-shaped belly flap, or "apron."

3   Turn the crab over and remove the top shell by inserting your thumb between the body and shell at the rear end of the crab and pulling up on the shell.

4   Pull off the spongy gills and small paddles at the front of the crab's body and discard them.

5   Use a spoon to scoop out crab meat and roe ("crab butter") from inside the body. Keep the roe if you like.

6   Twist off the claws and legs. (Note: Some people like to leave the smaller blue's legs on as handles to hold while they pick out the meat.)

7   Use a knife to cut the crab's body in half lengthwise and then into quarters, if desired, or simply snap the body in half. Pick out meat.

8   Use a nutcracker or small hammer to crack open the leg shells. Tap the shells sharply to break them into pieces that you can then remove.

9   Pick out meat from the legs and body of the crab with a lobster pick, fork or tip of a crab claw.

### ⚠ Warning

Watch out for live crabs' pincers. They are strong enough to cause injury.

## Boil an Egg   `375`

Just in case your mother never explained this to you, here are the simple steps involved in boiling an egg.

### ⊙ Steps

1 Place the egg in a saucepan.

2 Run cold water into the saucepan until the water is 1 inch above the top of the egg.

3 Place the saucepan on a stove and turn the heat to medium.

4 When the water begins to boil, reduce the heat to low.

5 Continue simmering for 2 to 3 minutes for soft-boiled eggs or 10 to 15 minutes for hard-boiled eggs.

6 Remove the egg with a spoon or ladle and let it cool slowly, or run cold water over it to cool it more quickly.

### ✳ Tip

Cooking times given are for room-temperature eggs (70 degrees F). Allow a couple of minutes more for eggs right out of the refrigerator.

## Separate Egg Whites From Yolks `376`

Working slowly is the secret, as is getting a good first crack.

### ⊙ Steps

1 Lightly crack an egg on the edge of a bowl.

2 Turn the egg upright and carefully open the shell into two halves, keeping the egg in the lower half.

3 Over the bowl, pour the egg from one half of the broken shell into the other, letting the egg white fall into the bowl but keeping the yolk intact in the shell halves as you pour.

4 Repeat until all of the white has fallen into the bowl and only the yolk remains in the shell.

### ✳ Tip

If you plan to whip the egg whites, take care not to get any yolk in them, separating each egg over a small bowl before transferring the yolk and white to separate larger bowls. Whites that have yolk or any fat at all in them will not whip properly. It's usually not a problem to have a little white left in the yolk.

## Shell a Hard-Boiled Egg  `377`

Don't crack the egg too sharply or you'll sacrifice some of the egg along with the shell.

### ⊙ Steps

1 Hold a boiled egg in one hand and a spoon in the other.

2 Lightly strike the egg midway on its side with the edge of the spoon.

3 Rotate the egg 90 degrees and repeat.

4 Continue until the egg is cracked all the way around.

5 Hit the side of the egg above the crack.

6 Slightly squeeze the egg in the middle.

### ✳ Tips

Squeeze the egg just a little or you will crush it.

The fresher an egg, the harder it is to peel when cooked. If you can't get the shell off, put the egg in the freezer for a few minutes and try again.

7   With a slight twisting motion, lift off the shell's top.

8   Hit the side of the egg below the crack.

9   With the same twisting motion, lift off the shell's bottom.

## 378 Stew Anything

Stewing is a good way to prepare foods that don't do too well with other cooking methods. A great use of leftovers, stews are easy to make, freeze and reheat.

### ◉ Steps

1   Start the stew by cutting the ingredients into pieces roughly the same size so that they cook evenly. Stews are usually made up of smaller pieces of meat and vegetables so that they can be bite size and their flavors can mingle.

2   Heat a large saucepan or stockpot over medium-high heat and add a few tablespoons of oil—enough so that the ingredients won't stick.

3   Season the meat with salt and pepper and add it to the pan. The pan should be hot enough for the meat to sizzle. Brown the meat thoroughly, but don't cook it all the way through.

4   Remove the meat when it is browned and add sturdy vegetables (but not potatoes just yet). Most stews use a mixture of onions, celery and carrots. Cook these for a few minutes, stirring them around, and then add a generous sprinkle of flour. This will thicken the stew as it cooks. (Add about 1 tbsp. flour for each pint of cooking liquid you will use in step 7.)

5   Stir the flour into the vegetables and cook for a few minutes before returning the meat to the pot.

6   Add herbs, such as bay leaf or thyme, if desired.

7   Cover the stew with liquid. Most stewing liquid is water, stock, wine or a combination. Homemade stock is best, of course, but low-sodium canned stock will do. Any dry wine will work; different wines will give your stew different tastes—just don't use a sweet wine.

8   Bring the mixture to a boil, lower the heat to simmer, and cook until the meat is done (see Tips for approximate cooking times). Add any potatoes, cut in quarters or large cubes, about 40 minutes before the end of the cooking time. Check for doneness by removing a piece of meat and tasting it; it should be tender but not mushy.

9   Sprinkle on freshly chopped parsley or another herb and serve.

### ✳ Tips

Stew made with vegetables only takes 20 to 35 minutes to cook. Check such a stew constantly because, unlike meat stew, vegetable stew is easy to overcook.

Poultry stews take about an hour to cook, lamb and veal stews about 90 minutes, and beef stews up to 3 hours.

Tougher cuts make the best stew meat, because the slow cooking tenderizes the meat, while long stewing will actually make tender cuts tougher. Look for "stew meat" In the store. It's usually the least expensive. If using beef, cubed chuck makes the best stew.

Potatoes are indispensable in many stews. The trick is to add them after the stew has simmered for a while so that they don't overcook and disintegrate.

## Marinate Meat 379

Marinating meat is one of the best ways to give it more flavor and tenderize it at the same time. It's foolproof if you follow a few simple guidelines.

### ◎ Steps

1 Trim the meat so that it's ready for cooking. You shouldn't have to cut or trim the meat after it's been marinated.

2 Mix the marinade according to its recipe (see 380 "Make a Basic Marinade" or 381 "Make a Red Wine Marinade").

3 Notice whether the marinade contains any of these three key ingredients: an acidic ingredient (such as wine, lemon juice or vinegar), salt and alcohol. Each one reduces the amount of time the meat should marinate.

4 Combine the meat and marinade in a nonreactive, sealed container. Make especially sure not to use aluminum or cast iron, and try to avoid metal altogether, if possible.

5 Marinate in a sealable plastic bag if you can. You can turn these over often, ensuring that all surfaces get coated.

6 Immediately place the container in the refrigerator. Never marinate meat at room temperature.

7 See Tips for marinating times.

8 When the marinated meat is ready to cook, be sure to treat it with the same care you would treat any raw meat.

9 Discard the marinade after use.

### ✳ Tips

Any marinade that contains acidic ingredients, alcohol or salt should not be used for very long, because it will chemically "cook" or denature the food in it. In general, marinate food for less than 4 hours; however, marinades that contain no salt, acidic ingredients or alcohol can be used to marinate overnight or, in some cases, longer. Marinades that contain citrus juices, especially lemon or lime juice, should be used for 2 hours or less.

Although marinades thwart bacterial growth, remember that the food in them is still raw and must be treated as such.

### ⚠ Warning

Do not reuse a marinade or baste with it less than 5 minutes before food is done cooking.

## Make a Basic Marinade 380

This easy marinade will add great flavor to chicken, fish and shrimp. You can use many different combinations of fresh herbs. This makes enough for 1 to 2 pounds of food.

### ◎ Steps

1 Mince the garlic and place it in a mixing bowl.

2 Rinse the herbs in cold water and dry them carefully with clean paper towels. Parsley, thyme, oregano and marjoram are good in this marinade, in virtually any combination. Cilantro and basil lose their flavor quickly and are best avoided for marinades. Use them fresh, instead, on the finished dish.

3 Chop the herbs into small pieces and place them in the bowl with the remaining ingredients. If using rosemary, remove the leaves for use and discard the woody stems before chopping.

4 Mix the ingredients well.

5 Carefully place the food to be marinated in a sealable plastic bag or a clean container.

### ⚠ Warning

Once raw food has been stored in this marinade, discard the marinade immediately after use and do not use it again.

### Ingredients

❑ 6 to 8 cloves garlic

❑ ½ c. chopped fresh herbs (parsley, thyme, oregano or marjoram)

❑ 1 c. olive oil

❑ 1 tbsp. freshly cracked black pepper

❑ 1 tsp. red pepper flakes

6   Pour the marinade over the food and mix everything together well.

7   Marinate food in the refrigerator for several hours or up to two days. Because this marinade contains no salt or acid, food can be left in it for longer periods of time.

8   Use the marinade on fish, shellfish (such as shrimp) and poultry, especially white meat from chicken and turkey.

9   Take the food out of the marinade and cook it on an outdoor grill for the best flavor. You can also roast or sauté marinated foods.

10  Make this marinade in advance for more convenience. Store it in a covered container in the refrigerator for several weeks.

---

## 381 | Make a Red Wine Marinade

Here is the quintessential marinade for beef, especially tougher cuts such as pot roasts and ribs. This recipe makes about 3 cups, enough for one pot roast or 2 to 3 pounds of short ribs.

### ⊙ Steps

1   Place all ingredients in a nonreactive saucepan and bring to a boil over high heat. Boil briskly for 5 to 6 minutes.

2   Remove the saucepan from the heat and allow the marinade to cool.

3   Use the marinade as a cooking liquid in a stewed or braised dish. Once it cooks for a while with beef, it makes a fantastic sauce.

### Ingredients

☐ 1 (750ml) bottle red wine

☐ 1 carrot, chopped

☐ 1 medium onion, chopped

☐ 5 or 6 sprigs fresh thyme

☐ 5 or 6 sprigs fresh parsley

☐ 1 bay leaf

☐ 1 tsp. black peppercorns

---

## 382 | Sauté Anything

Sautéing is the same as pan-frying—cooking quickly in a little fat. It comes from the French word meaning "to jump," because the food in the pan is sometimes quickly stirred or tossed.

### ⊙ Steps

1   Sautéing is a quick cooking method, so have everything ready to go and near the stove before you begin.

2   Set a burner to medium heat or higher.

3   Place the skillet on the burner and allow it to heat. This is an important step; the skillet should never be cold when you add the cooking oil or the food. Cookware with a nonstick coating shouldn't be heated dry for more than 30 seconds. Add the cooking fat before this, because the nonstick coating will degrade if heated dry for too long.

4   When the skillet is hot, add enough oil or other cooking fat to thinly coat the bottom. Sautéing properly depends on the cooking fat's forming a

### ✱ Tips

The high heat is necessary to brown the outside and cook foods quickly enough so that the inside doesn't dry out. This is especially true of meat, in which the fibers contract as they cook, squeezing out moisture as they do so.

Almost anything can be sautéed, as long as it's reasonably thin and isn't too wet. Use paper towels to dry damp items, because sautéing depends on enough heat to vaporize the water in the layer between the food and the pan, so make sure you use enough. Too little oil will cause food to cook unevenly and probably stick. Yet if you use enough and heat the pan properly, the food won't absorb a lot of fat.

5   Don't overheat the oil; it should never start smoking. One common test to see whether the pan is hot enough is to drop a minute pinch of flour into it; if the flour bubbles and sizzles rapidly, the pan is hot.

6   When the oil is hot, add the food you're going to sauté. Place it in the pan carefully, because the pan should be hot enough now for it to sizzle rapidly. The sound should tell you whether the pan is hot enough. No sizzle means it's too cold, and if it splatters and pops, the pan is too hot.

7   Foods that have been cut up, perhaps for a stir-fry, will need to be stirred regularly so that each piece has the same amount of contact with the bottom of the pan. Larger pieces, such as chicken breasts and fish fillets, are best left undisturbed and flipped only once, so that each side gets the same amount of contact with the pan.

outer layer of foods, which leads to browning. Too much water will cause the food to steam instead.

Canola, safflower, or olive oil will work in virtually all recipes, but if you use the latter, make sure your dish will benefit from its taste—also be aware that extra-virgin olive oil has a low smoking point. Butter can't be heated as much (the dairy solids in it burn), so it's best used for eggs, vegetables and other foods that cook fast and at lower temperatures. Animal fats such as lard and bacon fat work especially well, but add distinctive flavor.

## Stir-Fry Anything                                                    `383`

Stir-frying is an Asian technique for cooking meat and vegetables quickly. It typically involves a quick sauté over high heat, occasionally followed by brief steaming in a flavored sauce.

### ◉ Steps

1   Invest in a nonstick or carbon-steel wok. While you can stir-fry in any old skillet, the wok's depth and sloping sides (it's cooler there, so you can move ingredients up and away from the hot bottom) are ideal.

2   Cut all your vegetables and meats and prepare your sauce before you begin to stir-fry. Stir-frying is fast; you won't have time to chop the broccoli while the onion is cooking.

3   Make sure that your vegetables and meats are all cut approximately the same size—bite size, as a matter of fact. Stir-frying uses high heat, so pieces must be small enough to cook through without burning.

4   Learn the different cooking times of meats and vegetables, so that you can add ingredients according to how long they take to cook. (For example, you'd add onions first and stir-fry for about 2 minutes, then add broccoli florets and stir-fry for 3 to 4 minutes, then add red bell pepper and stir-fry for 2 more minutes.) If you've got a wok-full, stir-fry the meat completely first and remove it, then add it back in at the end.

5   Follow this order when stir-frying: Heat the pan first, then add oil. When the oil is hot, add aromatics, such as ginger and garlic, and stir-fry for a few seconds, or until you smell them. Then start adding your other ingredients, according to their approximate cooking times. When the food is about two-thirds done, add your sauce. If the food will take more than a few additional minutes to cook, cover and steam until done. If it will take a short time, continue to stir-fry.

6   Practice the basic technique of lifting the food in the wok with a spatula or other flat utensil and moving it to the side.

**✳ Tip**

For a basic stir-fry sauce, combine 2 tbsp. soy sauce, 2 tbsp. water or broth, 1 tbsp. plain or rice vinegar, 1 tbsp. Chinese rice cooking wine or dry sherry, a pinch of sugar, and 1 to 2 tsp. of Asian chili garlic sauce (or a few dashes of hot pepper sauce). Whisk 1 tsp. cornstarch into the cold mixture as a thickener.

## 384 | Keep Food From Sticking to Pans

From stovetop pots to baking pans, follow these tips to keep food from sticking.

### ◉ Steps

#### Pots and Frying Pans

1  Buy high-quality, heavy pots and pans. Thin pots and pans can develop "hot spots," which cause food to burn and stick. Heavy nonstick pans are great for cutting down on sticking, but some cooks believe that food doesn't brown as well in them, and even the highest quality nonstick coating degrades over time.

2  Make sure your pots and pans are completely clean before you use them. Old food buildup can burn and make food stick. Black spots indicate food buildup. Scrub it off with a nonabrasive cleanser.

3  Try to have your food at room temperature before adding it to the pan.

4  Heat the pan, then add a small amount of cooking oil or other fat. When the oil is also hot, add the food. (Nonstick pans are an exception: Heating them without oil for more than 30 seconds will damage the coating.)

5  If food does burn, wait for the pan to cool, then soak it in hot water.

#### Baking Pans

1  Buy well-made pans, and keep them free of food buildup.

2  Follow your recipe carefully. Most recipes will indicate if a pan should be greased, greased and floured, or left ungreased.

3  If in doubt, grease. Use nonstick cooking spray or wipe on butter or shortening with a paper towel. Coat thinly and evenly.

4  To grease and flour a pan (usually for baking a cake), coat the pan with cooking spray, then add a tablespoon of flour to the pan. Knock the pan from side to side to coat until the pan is dusted evenly with flour. Dump out the excess.

### ✳ Tips

If you overcook food, it is more likely to stick to the pan.

If you use nonstick pans, don't use metal utensils, as these can scratch the coating.

Season cast-iron pans and carbon-steel woks before you use them, to prevent sticking (see 361 "Season a Cast-Iron Skillet").

Nonstick cooking sprays can leave a gummy buildup on pans, causing food to stick later. If you do use a nonstick spray, apply it to a cold pan, then put the pan on the heat. If your pan feels sticky or gummy after you've washed it, remove the buildup with a nonabrasive cleanser.

Avoid using metal scrubbers to clean pots, as these can leave tiny scratches in the finish where food can build up and stick.

## 385 | Braise Anything

Braising is a cooking method usually used for tougher cuts of meat, and sometimes for vegetables. The food cooks in liquid, similar to stewing, and the result is meltingly tender.

### ◉ Steps

1  Make sure that all your ingredients are roughly the same size so they will cook evenly.

2  Heat the pan, then add a little oil and heat that, too.

3  Season the meat or vegetables on both sides with salt and pepper, or whatever seasonings your recipe requires.

### ✳ Tips

Pot roasts, chuck roasts, ribs and shanks, and poultry legs and thighs are best for braising.

If you want to use the braising liquid as a sauce, leave the pan uncovered so that moisture can evaporate, thus concentrating

4   When the pan is hot, add the meat or vegetables and sauté at high heat to quickly brown the outside. This adds color and flavor.

5   When they're nicely browned, add enough liquid to the pan to come about halfway up the sides of the meat or vegetables. Liquid used for braising is usually water, stock, wine or a combination.

6   Lower the heat and simmer the ingredients slowly until everything is tender, or place the whole dish (provided the pan is ovenproof) in the oven and bake it. What's important is that the meat or vegetables cook slowly in the liquid and that the liquid never evaporates. (See Tips to decide whether to cover the dish.)

7   Check for doneness according to what you're cooking. Be aware that braising is a slow-cooking method. Most braised dishes take from 30 minutes (or less, for vegetables) to 6 hours (for tough shanks and ribs).

the flavors. Only do this with cuts that take less than 90 minutes or so to cook. Add other ingredients, such as vegetables or herbs and spices, to flavor the liquid. Make sure the liquid level doesn't get too low, or you'll be baking and not braising.

Vegetables that braise well include onions, fennel, carrots and beets; you can even braise fruit such as pineapples and apples. In each case, it's easiest to cut the vegetable or fruit in half and brown it on the flat cut side.

## Steam Vegetables                                386

Steaming is one of the best ways to cook vegetables. It leaves more of the vegetable's natural taste, texture and color intact than any other method, and it requires no added fat.

### ⦿ Steps

1   Bring an inch or two of water to a boil over high heat in a large pot. Always use high heat to steam vegetables. Since steam is hotter than boiling water, vegetables will cook faster and will absorb less water.

2   If you're using a steaming rack or a bamboo steamer (works great!), make sure it's clean and have it ready.

3   Trim and cut your vegetables when the water is boiling. It's best to do this as close to cooking as possible so they won't dehydrate or oxidize. Cut all the vegetables the same size so they'll cook evenly.

4   Place the vegetables in the steamer or steamer rack and cover.

5   Steam them only until they're done; most cut vegetables only need to steam for a minute or two. Thicker pieces might steam for 2 to 3 minutes. Potatoes take 15 to 30 minutes.

6   Serve immediately, because the longer the vegetables sit, the mushier they'll get.

**✸ Tips**

A bamboo steamer is preferred to all other utensils because the wood inhibits water condensation. Choose bamboo steamers that are 100 percent bamboo. Some contain metal linings or metal racks, and these will allow condensation, which can lead to soggy veggies. Bamboo steamers are best used in a wok.

The most important tip is not to overcook steamed vegetables.

## Blanch Vegetables                                387

By boiling vegetables briefly, chilling them in ice water, then reheating them slowly, you can preserve texture, color and flavor. The boiling and chilling technique is known as blanching.

### ⦿ Steps

1   Bring a large pot of water to a rapid boil over high heat. Add enough salt so that the water tastes faintly salty.

**✸ Tips**

Blanching is best for vegetables like asparagus, broccoli, cauliflower, green beans and spinach. If you were to serve these

2   While the water heats, fill a medium bowl about three-quarters full with ice, then add enough cold water to come just to the top of the ice.

3   When the water is boiling and the ice bath is ready, trim the vegetables to the size you need. It's best to trim them just prior to cooking so they won't oxidize or dehydrate.

4   Add the vegetables to the boiling water in batches small enough to ensure that the water doesn't lose its boil.

5   Boil the vegetables only until they're barely cooked through but still tender. To test, remove one piece with a slotted spoon, dip it into the ice bath to cool, and eat it.

6   As soon as the vegetables are done, remove them as fast as you can and submerge them in the ice bath.

7   Remove them from the ice bath as soon as they are no longer warm.

8   To reheat the vegetables, you can use any cooking method you wish, such as sautéing, grilling or boiling; just make sure to barely heat them up and not to cook them again.

vegetables right out of the boiling water, they would continue to cook and might become too mushy. These vegetables, blanched, are also great for crudités (vegetable platters). Serve with aioli (garlic mayonnaise) or another dip.

You can also boil and chill pasta this way, for cold pasta dishes or for pasta you plan to reheat later.

---

## 388 | Make Mashed Potatoes

In some families, making mashed potatoes is an art form. Here's a recipe that will be a hit. Makes six servings.

### ⊙ Steps

1   Peel, cut into large chunks and boil four to six medium-size potatoes for 20 to 25 minutes or until tender when pierced with the tip of a knife.

2   Drain the potatoes, return them to the pot they were boiled in and shake over medium heat until the potato pieces are dry and mealy.

3   Purée the potatoes by passing them through a food mill or potato ricer, by whipping them with an electric mixer, or by mashing them with a potato masher or heavy fork. Work out lumps as best as you can.

4   Whisk in 2 to 4 tbsp. melted butter, a pinch of salt, pepper to taste and 1/3 to 1/2 c. warmed milk. Whisk potatoes to desired smoothness.

5   Serve immediately.

### ✱ Tip

Never use a food processor to make mashed potatoes. They will become gooey and gluey.

### Ingredients

❑ 4 to 6 potatoes

❑ 2 to 4 tbsp. butter

❑ salt and pepper to taste

❑ 1/3 to 1/2 c. milk, warmed

---

## 389 | Toast Nuts

There are two ways to toast nuts—in the oven or in a skillet. Both use high heat and short cooking times to bring out the nuts' best flavor.

### ⊙ Steps

1   Make sure the nuts are shelled and of uniform size.

2   For toasting in the oven, spread nuts in a single layer in a baking pan (one with walls is best). Cook at 400 degrees F for 7 to 10 minutes or until the nuts start to turn golden. Shake the pan halfway through toasting.

### ✱ Tips

Toasted nuts have a deeper, more concentrated flavor than raw nuts.

Nuts have high concentrations of natural oil, so it is not necessary to add oil when toasting them.

3    For toasting in a skillet, place nuts in a single layer. With the skillet over medium-high heat, stir or shake the nuts continuously.

4    Cook the nuts only until they start to turn golden and parts of them still appear raw, about 5 to 7 minutes; they should smell toasty, though. Don't let them get any darker than light brown or they won't taste good. Remove them from the cooking pan as soon as they're done. Let cool before using.

## Choose a Steak                                                          390

To pick the best steak for your money (and it can be a lot of money), pay attention to the type of cut and the grade—as well as to a few things that are not so obvious.

### ☉ Steps

1    Get to know the cuts, which are sold under many different names. Tenderloin, also known as filet, is boneless and is the most expensive; strip, also known as New York, is boneless and has real beef flavor; T-bone and porterhouse, which are similar, have a large bone; rib steak (with a bone) and rib eye (boneless) are fattier, with rich flavor; and top sirloin is leaner and less expensive.

2    Determine how tender you like your steak. The most tender cuts come from the part of the animal that gets the least exercise. From most to least tender: tenderloin, strip, porterhouse and T-bone, ribeye, top sirloin.

3    Use the U.S. Department of Agriculture's grades as a basic guide to quality. Prime beef has the most marbling, or fat within the meat, but is found mainly in restaurants, rarely in grocery stores. Choice, with good levels of marbling, is juicy and tender, and the most widely available. Select tends to be leaner and less flavorful, and dries out more easily.

4    Check with your butcher to find out if the meat has been aged, which tenderizes and mellows the flavor.

5    Allow at least 4 oz. of steak per serving—double or triple that for hungry eaters, or if the steak contains a bone.

**✳ Tips**

The more marbling, or streaks or flecks of fat, the more flavorful the steak. Be sure that the marbling is evenly distributed.

Look for meat with a smooth, tight grain.

A general rule of toughness: The closer the meat is to a hoof or horn, the tougher it will be.

The porterhouse is also known as the sweetheart steak because it is actually two steaks, providing two servings in one.

## Broil Meat                                                             391

Broiled meat is cooked very close to the heating element. Because it takes such high, direct heat, broiled food gains a pleasantly brown exterior, and it usually cooks quickly.

### ☉ Steps

1    Choose tender steaks and chops that can be cooked quickly—or sliced ham, bacon, fish or baby beef liver. Preheat the broiler at least 5 to 7 minutes. It needs to be very hot.

2    Season the meat and place it on a broiler pan, or on a rack in a shallow baking pan.

**✳ Tip**

Broiling works best on quick-cooking cuts—less than 1 inch thick. Thicker cuts can be browned in the broiler and finished in a 325-degree F oven.

3   Put the pan in the oven about 5 inches from the heat source. Place thicker foods farther from the heat, thinner foods closer. Cuts that are too thick must be cooked another way.

4   Broil until the side closest to the heat turns a pleasant, deep golden brown. Take care that the meat doesn't burn. Depending on the cut, start checking after about 5 minutes.

5   Turn the food over and cook the other side to desired doneness. Test for doneness with an instant-read cooking thermometer (the most accurate way), or cut steaks or chops in the thickest portion to determine doneness. Most red meat is rare at an internal temperature of about 130 degrees F, medium rare at 145 degrees and medium at 150 degrees. Pork and poultry should be completely cooked through—at least 160 degrees for pork, 170 for poultry breast meat and 180 for poultry thigh meat. Fish should flake easily.

6   Learn to test for doneness by pressing with a finger; meat firms as it cooks. Be careful not to burn yourself.

## △ Warning

If something catches fire, do not pour water on it, because this can splash flaming grease. Shut the oven door and immediately turn off the broiler. Most broiler fires will suffocate themselves. If the fire persists, use a fire extinguisher.

---

## 392 | Roast Meat

**Roasting is used for large, tender cuts. Beef rib cuts, pork loins, legs of lamb and whole poultry all roast well.**

### ⊙ Steps

1   Preheat the oven to 450 degrees F.

2   Assess the size of the roast. If it's small enough for you to quickly brown the outside in a very hot pan or a barbecue grill, season the roast with salt and pepper, oil it lightly and brown it.

3   Put the meat in a roasting pan, fat side up.

4   If the meat is already browned, lower the heat to 325 degrees F and cook it until done.

5   If the meat is too large to brown before roasting, cook it at 450 degrees F for about 20 minutes, then lower the heat to 325 degrees F and cook it until done.

6   Test for doneness with an instant-read kitchen thermometer. Beef, lamb and veal are generally rare at about 130 degrees F, medium-rare at about 145 degrees F, and medium at 150 degrees F. Pork and poultry should be completely cooked through—at least 160 degrees for pork, 170 for poultry breast meat and 180 for poultry thigh meat.

7   Place foil over the meat and wait 10 to 20 minutes to carve it. (Waiting helps to ensure that juices settle back into the meat, rather than spilling all over the cutting board.)

### ✳ Tips

If you don't have a meat thermometer, refer to a meat chart in an all-purpose cookbook to determine cooking time per pound.

In general, don't cover a roast; you don't want it to steam in its own juices. If, however, you're cooking a large roast or turkey and it browns too quickly, cover only the browned parts with foil.

## Use a Meat Thermometer 393

The best way to tell if meat is done is to use a meat thermometer. These directions are for the type of thermometer you leave in during cooking.

### ⊙ Steps

1  Push the thermometer into the thickest section of the meat you are cooking before you place the meat in the oven.

2  Make sure the thermometer is not touching bone but is embedded deeply in the meat itself.

3  Put the meat in the oven at the recommended temperature.

4  Leave the thermometer in the meat throughout the cooking process.

5  Check the thermometer close to when the recommended cooking time for the cut of meat you are preparing is almost finished. The reading on the thermometer—check the levels for the kind of meat you are cooking—will indicate when the meat is cooked throughout.

### ✳ Tips

Meat thermometers come in a variety of styles, including instant-read, dial types, probes and stand-up types. Some probe thermometers allow you to connect the thermometer to a countertop unit that gives you the temperature reading without having to open the oven.

Instant-read thermometers are not left in the meat while it cooks. They register temperatures within a few seconds of insertion.

## Make Beef Stock 394

Beef stock, or beef broth, is readily available in cans. But you'll feel like a real pro making your own—and it does taste better. Makes about 2 quarts.

### ⊙ Steps

1  Preheat the oven to 450 degrees F.

2  Put the soup bones in a large, shallow roasting pan.

3  Bake the bones for about 30 minutes, or until they're well browned, turning at the 15-minute point.

4  Put the soup bones in a large pot. Pour 1/2 c. water into the roasting pan and stir with a wooden spoon to scrape up and dissolve any crusty browned bits. Add the water mixture to the pot.

5  Add carrots, onions, celery, parsley, peppercorns, basil, bay leaves, garlic and salt to the pot.

6  Add 10 c. water to the pot and bring to a boil. Reduce heat, cover and simmer 3 1/2 hours. Remove the soup bones.

7  Line a colander with two layers of cheesecloth. Set it over a heatproof bowl and pour the broth into the colander to strain.

8  Discard the vegetables and seasoning.

9  Chill the broth, then lift off the solidified fat.

10  Store the broth in a covered container in the refrigerator for up to three days, or freeze for up to three months.

### Ingredients

- ❑ 4 lbs. meaty soup bones (short ribs or beef-shank crosscuts)
- ❑ 10 1/2 c. water
- ❑ 3 carrots, chopped
- ❑ 2 medium onions, chopped
- ❑ 2 celery stalks with leaves, chopped
- ❑ 8 sprigs fresh parsley
- ❑ 10 black peppercorns
- ❑ 1 tbsp. dried, crushed basil
- ❑ 4 bay leaves
- ❑ 2 halved garlic cloves
- ❑ 1 1/2 tsp. salt

## 395 | Make Chicken Stock

Homemade stock is the best! It's so easy, and it also fills your kitchen with great aromas. Makes about 2 quarts.

### ⊙ Steps

1 Warm the vegetable oil in a stockpot or large saucepan over high heat.

2 Brown the vegetables for a few minutes, until they are golden in places.

3 Add the wine, water, chicken, salt, peppercorns, bay leaves, parsley and dill and bring to a simmer. Skim any foam from the surface.

4 Reduce the heat to low, cover partially and simmer for 2 hours.

5 Remove the chicken.

6 Strain the stock into a bowl, reserve the meat for later use and discard the remaining solids. Taste the stock. If it seems too bland, bring it to a boil and reduce it (let it boil and evaporate) until it tastes rich enough.

7 Chill the broth, then lift off the fat.

8 Store the broth in a covered container in the refrigerator for up to three days or freeze for up to three months.

### Ingredients

❏ 1 tbsp. vegetable oil

❏ 2 large yellow onions, chopped

❏ 3 celery stalks with leaves, coarsely chopped

❏ 3 carrots, coarsely chopped

❏ 1 c. dry white wine

❏ 2½ qts. water

❏ 1 (3½ to 4 lb.) chicken, cut into quarters to fit in stockpot

❏ 1½ tsp. salt

❏ 6 peppercorns

❏ 2 bay leaves

❏ 10 sprigs fresh parsley

❏ 5 sprigs fresh dill

## 396 | Make Vegetable Stock

A savory vegetable stock is a staple of vegetarian cooking. It doesn't get better than this. Makes 3½ to 4 quarts.

### ⊙ Steps

1 Preheat the oven to 450 degrees F.

2 In a roasting pan, roast the carrots, leeks, celery, yellow and red onions, and garlic, uncovered, for 1 hour (cut vegetables to fit in the pan).

3 Transfer the vegetables to a large stockpot.

4 Add the thyme, bay leaf, peppercorns and water. Turn the heat to high.

5 Bring to a boil, reduce heat and simmer, covered, for 1 hour.

6 Remove from heat. Strain through a fine-mesh sieve.

7 Chill the stock. Store in a covered container in the refrigerator for up to three days or freeze for up to three months.

### Ingredients

❏ 5 carrots

❏ 3 leeks

❏ 3 celery stalks

❏ 2 yellow onions

❏ 1 red onion

❏ 1 head garlic

❏ 2 thyme sprigs

❏ 1 bay leaf

❏ 5 peppercorns

❏ 4 qts. water

## Make and Use a Roux 397

A roux is a cooked mixture of flour and a cooking fat, such as vegetable oil, that is used to thicken sauces and gravies.

### ⊙ Steps

1 Pour about ¹⁄₄ c. oil in a small, sturdy pan and place the pan over medium-low heat.

2 When the oil is warm but not too hot, start stirring in flour with a wooden spoon until the mixture is thick—about the texture of wet concrete or plaster of Paris. Add more oil or flour until the consistency is right. Roux is usually equal parts by weight of flour and fat, but most chefs make it by simply adding flour to hot oil and looking for the proper thick texture.

3 Stir continuously with the wooden spoon over the heat so the roux cooks. The flour will gradually begin to brown. The roux can be used when the flour is light golden in color. The darker you cook the roux, the more flavor it will add to the sauce. Don't cook it past a mahogany color, though.

4 Transfer the roux to another container to cool.

5 Store the roux in the refrigerator for a week, or freeze in tablespoon-size wafers for later use.

6 To thicken a sauce with roux, let it cool so it won't splatter and whisk it into your boiling sauce base, such as broth or pan drippings. One tbsp. of roux will thicken 1 to 1¹⁄₂ c. of liquid.

7 Lower the heat to a simmer and continue to whisk until all the roux has been absorbed.

8 Simmer the sauce for at least 20 minutes until it has thickened and the texture is smooth.

### ✳ Tips

Any cooking fat can be used to make a roux, including bacon fat or chicken fat.

Butter should be used only for very light-colored roux. The milk solids in the butter will burn easily if it's cooked too long.

For best results, reserve some roux and some liquid when making your sauce so you can adjust the thickness later.

Roux-thickened sauces will thicken further as they cool.

### Ingredients

❑ about ¹⁄₄ c. vegetable oil

❑ about ¹⁄₄ c. all-purpose flour

## Thicken a Sauce 398

There are hundreds of ways to thicken sauces, but only a handful are commonly used, and here are four of them. In each case, you'll need to start with some sort of base liquid.

### ⊙ Steps

1 Thicken most broths for gravies with roux, a cooked mixture of flour and a cooking fat such as vegetable oil (see 397 "Make and Use a Roux"). Roux needs to be cooked first, but gravies made with it are virtually lump-free. Many cream soups are also thickened this way.

2 Use a cornstarch slurry to thicken fruit and vegetable juices. To make a slurry, dissolve 1 tbsp. cornstarch or flour in 2 tbsp. ice water, then whisk the slurry into 1 c. of boiling liquid. Simmer the sauce at least 15 minutes to allow the starch to work. Cornstarch is commonly also used to thicken stir-fries and many other Asian dishes.

3 Use a cooked-vegetable purée to make a rustic sauce. For example, sautéed onions braised with a pot roast can be strained out, puréed

### ✳ Tips

Most sauces benefit from some simmering before you thicken them. This allows them to reduce, which means that excess moisture will evaporate and what's left will be more concentrated.

Reducing sauces can be tricky, because the amount of salt and other seasonings will also concentrate, so make sure to underseason everything and correct it only at the end.

and whisked back into the liquid to create a flavorful sauce with no added fat.

4   Use butter to thicken powerfully flavored liquids such as wine and concentrated pan juices. Butter softens the flavors and smooths the texture. Whisk in partially softened cubes of butter over very low heat, tasting as you go, and serve these sauces in tiny amounts. Don't heat them, or they'll separate.

**Ingredients**

☐ vegetable oil

☐ all-purpose flour

☐ cornstarch

☐ butter

---

## 399 | Make Hollandaise Sauce

**Essential to many dishes, including eggs Benedict, hollandaise sauce is about as rich and luxurious as a sauce gets. It's excellent with fish. Makes about 2 cups.**

### ◉ Steps

1   Place the white wine, white wine vinegar, shallots, peppercorns and red pepper flakes in a saucepan and bring to a simmer.

2   Simmer until the liquid has reduced to 1/2 c., and then strain the liquid into another container. Discard the seasonings.

3   Bring about 2 inches of water to a simmer in the bottom of a double boiler.

4   Melt the butter completely in a small saucepan over low heat.

5   Skim off and discard the white foam that rises to the top. Ladle off and reserve the clear yellow liquid in the middle (this is clarified butter) and discard the milky liquid at the bottom.

6   Place the egg yolks in a medium metal bowl or in the top of a double boiler and whisk them together.

7   While whisking the egg yolks continuously, place the bowl over but not touching the simmering water for about 20 or 30 seconds, and then remove it and whisk for a few more seconds. Repeat.

8   Heat the yolks slowly so that they don't form scrambled curds. If they scramble, you'll need to start over.

9   Keep whisking until the yolks thicken. Look for the ribbon stage, when they're firm enough that when you lift the whisk out of the yolks and drizzle some back onto the surface, it forms a ribbonlike pattern that lasts for a few moments before sinking back into the yolks.

10  Slowly drizzle some of the melted clarified butter over the beaten yolks, whisking constantly. When a ladle or two of butter has been blended in, begin alternating between the melted butter and the vinegar mixture.

11  Notice when the mixture has thickened and begins resembling a sauce, then season with salt and begin tasting. If it's too tart, whisk in more melted butter—if it's not tart enough, squeeze in some lemon juice.

12  Keep the sauce in a warm place until you're ready to use it. It will thicken as it sits.

### ✱ Tips

An overly thick sauce can be thinned by whisking in a little hot water. The same remedy will help a sauce that begins to separate.

This sauce can't be reheated and will separate if you try to do so.

### Ingredients

☐ 1 c. white wine

☐ 1 c. white wine vinegar

☐ 2 shallots, chopped

☐ 1 tsp. black peppercorns

☐ 1/2 tsp. red pepper flakes

☐ 1 lb. unsalted butter

☐ 3 egg yolks

☐ juice of 1 lemon

☐ salt

## Make Turkey Pan Gravy     `400`

This recipe assumes that you have just roasted a turkey and are set to make pan gravy from its drippings. Makes 4 cups.

### ⊙ Steps

1   Set the turkey aside after it is done cooking. Pour all the drippings from the turkey's roasting pan into a glass measuring cup that can accommodate 1 quart of liquid. Leave any browned bits on the bottom of the pan. (These are actually quite tasty and help give the gravy its flavor.)

2   Let the drippings stand until the fat rises to the top of the measuring cup. Spoon off the fat and reserve.

3   Add stock so that there are 4 c. of liquid in the measuring cup.

4   Set the roasting pan over medium-low heat. (You may need to use two burners at once.)

5   Spoon out 6 tbsp. of the reserved fat and put it back in the roasting pan. Discard the remaining fat.

6   Sprinkle the flour over the fat and whisk. Whisk the flour and fat for 1 to 2 minutes until the flour turns golden brown.

7   Pour the drippings and stock mixture into the pan and, with a wooden spoon, scrape off the encrusted bits on the bottom of the pan.

8   Simmer the mixture for 2 to 3 minutes, whisking every so often.

9   Adjust the thickness of the gravy. If it is too thin, simmer it, whisking often until the gravy is as thick as you want it. If it is too thick, whisk in a little more stock.

10  Season the gravy with salt and pepper to taste.

11  Strain the gravy if you want to get rid of any remaining bits you loosened earlier. Pour the gravy into a gravy boat and serve.

### ✳ Tip

You can substitute canned chicken stock for the turkey or chicken stock.

### Ingredients

❑ turkey drippings

❑ 6 tbsp. all-purpose flour

❑ turkey or chicken stock

## Store Leftovers     `401`

Handling your leftover lunch or dinner safely helps prevent foodborne illness (otherwise known as food poisoning).

### ⊙ Steps

1   Wash your hands well with soap and warm water before and after handling leftovers, each time.

2   Refrigerate leftovers within 2 hours of the time they were prepared.

3   Cool food in the refrigerator instead of on the counter. Small portions of leftovers cool down faster. Stir or turn larger quantities frequently so they cool evenly and completely. Don't put piping-hot foods in the refrigerator, though, for they can raise the temperature of chilled foods inside.

4   If you have large amounts of leftovers, divide them among several clean, shallow storage containers.

### ✳ Tips

Use a refrigerator thermometer to make sure your fridge stays between 35 and 40 degrees F.

Bacteria grows most easily between 40 and 140 degrees F, so keep hot food hot and cold food cold.

Remember to get restaurant doggie bags in the fridge within 2 hours of preparation, too.

5   Make sure that storage-container lids seal tightly, or cover them with aluminum foil or plastic wrap.

6   Place storage containers at least 2 inches apart in the refrigerator—this allows cold air to circulate.

7   Use leftovers containing meat within three days; use other foods within five days.

## 402 | Make a Basic Vinaigrette

A vinaigrette is a basic sauce, usually used as a salad dressing, that can be made from a few simple ingredients in about 3 minutes. Makes 1 to 1¼ cups.

### ◎ Steps

1   Whisk the mustard and vinegar together in a medium bowl.

2   Season lightly with salt and pepper.

3   Continue whisking the mustard/vinegar mixture and drizzle in the oil in a thin, steady stream.

4   Start tasting the mixture when about half of the oil has been incorporated. You may need to add some more salt and pepper. The basic ratio for vinaigrette is one part vinegar to three or four parts oil. Use whatever ratio tastes right to you, though; some people like significantly more vinegar, some less.

5   Keep whisking in the oil until the vinaigrette tastes smooth and slightly tart. If it's too sour, keep whisking in oil.

### ✱ Tips

You can substitute any acidic liquid for the balsamic vinegar, such as lemon or other citrus juice, other vinegars, or Champagne.

Add fresh herbs, such as basil, parsley, thyme or marjoram.

### Ingredients

❑ 1 tbsp. Dijon mustard

❑ ¼ c. balsamic vinegar

❑ salt and pepper

❑ ¾ to 1 c. olive oil

## 403 | Fry Chicken

Here is a simple but classic method for making that Southern delight, fried chicken. This recipe uses a flour coating rather than batter. Makes four servings.

### ◎ Steps

1   Put flour, salt, pepper, paprika and cayenne pepper in a plastic bag. Shake to mix.

2   Add chicken pieces, with or without bones, to the bag. (Smaller pieces cook more quickly, so consider cutting each breast half in two.) Shake to coat the chicken with the seasoned flour.

3   Heat ¾ inch oil in a heavy frying pan (preferably cast-iron) over medium-high heat, until it reaches 350 degrees F. Use a 2-inch-deep pan if possible to reduce spatters.

4   When the oil is hot, shake any excess flour off the chicken and add the pieces to the pan a few at a time. Don't allow the pieces to touch in the pan. Fry the chicken in batches if your pan won't hold them all with space to spare.

### ✱ Tip

Frying chicken is messy business. Spread newspapers on the floor in front of the stove to keep the floor clean. Consider moving anything on the stovetop out of the way so it won't acquire a coating of grease.

### ⚠ Warning

Be very careful when working with hot oil. It can splatter and cause bad burns. Add chicken carefully to the pan, handling it with long metal tongs if possible.

5  Cook the chicken pieces for about 10 minutes per side. Regulate the heat as the chicken cooks, keeping the oil temperature below 375 degrees—use a deep-frying thermometer to check the temperature.

6  Check the chicken for doneness. The meat should no longer be pink, and the juices should run clear when the meat is pierced.

7  Drain the chicken on paper towels.

### Ingredients

- 1 c. all-purpose flour
- 1 tbsp. salt
- 1 tsp. pepper
- 1/2 tsp. paprika
- 1/2 tsp. cayenne pepper
- 1 (3- to 4-lb.) frying chicken, cut into at least six pieces
- 4 c. canola oil

## Bake Chicken                                                    404

Chicken can be baked whole or in pieces. Leave the skin on during cooking, even if you discard it later, to protect the meat from drying out. Makes four to six servings.

### ⊙ Steps

1  Preheat the oven to 350 degrees F.

2  Season the chicken with salt and pepper.

3  Coat the chicken with a marinade, glaze or bread crumbs if desired.

4  Place a whole chicken in a roasting pan or large ovenproof skillet, or place pieces skin up on a lightly greased baking pan.

5  Cook a whole chicken for 1 to 1 1/2 hours, uncovered. Cook pieces for 35 to 40 minutes.

6  Use a meat thermometer to check the chicken during cooking. When the internal temperature reaches 170 degrees for breast meat, 180 for thighs (measured in the thickest part not touching the bone), the chicken is done.

7  Test for doneness without a thermometer by cutting into the thickest part of the thigh. If the meat is no longer pink and juices run clear, it's done.

### ✳ Tips

Try rubbing the raw chicken with different dry seasonings.

Squeeze a lemon over the chicken (and inside the cavity of a whole chicken) before you cook it.

To avoid contamination, be sure to carefully clean everything the raw chicken touched.

### Ingredients

- 1 (2 1/2 to 5 lb.) chicken
- salt and pepper
- marinade, glaze or bread crumbs (optional)

## Roast a Chicken                                                 405

Roasting a chicken is far easier than the browned and succulent result would make it seem. Your guests don't need to know. Makes four to six servings.

### ⊙ Steps

1  Preheat the oven to 400 degrees F.

2  Remove the chicken from its plastic bag, if it is in one.

### ✳ Tips

Try rubbing the bird with 1 tbsp. Dijon mustard mixed with 1 tbsp. olive oil. Put fresh herbs in the cavity of the bird, or squeeze a lemon inside it and leave the lemon halves inside.

3   Remove the bag of giblets from the cavity of the bird.

4   Remove any large deposits of fat from the cavity.

5   Trim any loose skin with a sharp knife.

6   Remove the tail, if you want, or leave it on. Rinse the chicken inside and out with cold water. Pat dry with a paper towel.

7   Place a roasting rack in a baking pan with sides at least 1 inch high.

8   Place the bird on the rack with its breast side up.

9   Grind fresh pepper onto the bird, and sprinkle with a little salt. Salt and pepper the cavity as well. Rub the bird all over with olive oil and stuff it with fresh herbs and a quartered lemon if desired.

10  Place the baking pan on an oven rack in the oven's lower-middle part.

11  Roast 45 to 70 minutes or until the juices run clear when a sharp knife is inserted into the joint between the body and the thigh, or until a meat thermometer registers 170 degrees for breast meat, 180 for thighs.

12  Remove the chicken from the oven, cover it loosely with foil and let it rest for 10 minutes before carving.

If the chicken seems to be browning too much, cover it loosely with foil.

Make sure your kitchen is well ventilated. In small spaces, the roasting process has been known to set off smoke alarms.

## Ingredients

❏ 1 (2½- to 5-lb.) chicken

❏ black pepper

❏ salt

❏ olive oil

❏ fresh herbs (optional)

❏ lemon (optional)

❏ Dijon mustard (optional)

## 406 | Roast a Turkey

The turkey in this recipe is not stuffed, so you might want to prepare a stuffing on the side. Makes six servings. For a turkey this size, allow ¾ to 1 lb. per serving.

### ◎ Steps

1   Preheat the oven to 325 degrees F.

2   Remove the turkey from its wrapping and remove the neck and giblets from inside the cavity. Set them aside to make gravy later.

3   Rinse the turkey inside and out with cold water. Dry with paper towels.

4   Put the oven rack on the lowest level.

5   Place the turkey on a roasting rack, breast side up, in a roasting pan.

6   Rub the outside of the turkey with olive oil.

7   Salt and pepper the turkey's body and cavity.

8   Roast the turkey about 3 hours for a 12- to 14-pound bird, or until a meat thermometer inserted in the thickest part of the thigh registers 175 to 180 degrees F.

### ✱ Tips

A turkey should be roasted 10 to 12 minutes per pound if it is not stuffed and 12 to 15 minutes per pound if it is stuffed.

In general, you shouldn't cover a roasting turkey; you want the skin to get a deep brown all over, and you don't want it to steam. However, you can loosely cover parts that are browning too quickly with aluminum foil.

### Ingredients

❏ 1 (12- to 14-lb.) turkey

❏ olive oil

❏ salt and pepper

## Carve a Turkey 407

After hours of preparation and anticipation, make sure to carve the turkey in a way that preserves its flavor and texture.

### ◉ Steps

1 Choose a sharp, thin-bladed knife. Running your knife along the bottom of the turkey, find the places where the thighbones meet the body.

2 Slip your knife into the joint to separate thigh from body on each side.

3 Separate the drumstick from the thigh using the same technique (cut through the joint, not the bone, wiggling the drumstick to locate the joint).

4 Running your knife along the bone, separate the meat from the thigh and drumstick—try to get as much as possible in one piece.

5 Cut thigh and leg meat into thin slices.

6 Use your knife to find where the wings and body connect.

7 Slip your knife into the joint to separate wings from body on each side.

8 Carve thin slices off one side of the breast, cutting parallel to the breast.

9 Repeat with the other side of the breast.

### ✳ Tips

If you are carving soon after roasting, cover the turkey with foil and let it stand for 15 minutes first.

Cut dark meat before light meat, as it will stay moist longer.

## Make Glazed Holiday Ham 408

Hams are easy to prepare because most are precooked and require only warming up. This ham is glazed with an orange marmalade sauce. Makes six to eight servings.

### ◉ Steps

1 Heat the oven to 325 degrees F.

2 Trim the ham of most visible skin and fat and place it in a roasting pan.

3 Place the marmalade and sugar in a saucepan. Warm over low heat to dissolve the sugar, stirring continuously to prevent burning.

4 Remove the mixture from the heat when the sugar has dissolved, and stir in the mustard and cloves.

5 Stir in just enough cider vinegar to thin the glaze to the consistency of a thick sauce. You won't need much.

6 When the ham is halfway through its cooking time, start brushing the glaze on it. Add glaze every half-hour throughout the cooking time.

7 Cook the ham for about 3 hours, or until its internal temperature reaches 140 degrees. You can check the temperature by inserting a meat thermometer into the ham away from the bone. Remember, the ham is already fully cooked.

8 Transfer to a carving board and carve. Use excess glaze as a sauce.

### ✳ Tips

Use only a precooked, bone-in ham for this recipe.

Ham leftovers make delicious sand-wiches.

### Ingredients

❑ 1 (8- to 10-lb.) bone-in cooked ham

❑ 1 c. orange marmalade

❑ ½ c. brown sugar

❑ 1 c. Dijon mustard

❑ pinch ground cloves, or to taste

❑ 2 to 4 tbsp. cider vinegar

## 409 | Grill Hamburgers and Hot Dogs

Grilled hot dogs and hamburgers are a hit with kids of all ages.

### ⊙ Steps

1  Season the ground beef as desired by adding seasoning salt, chopped onions, dry onion-soup mix, Worcestershire sauce, salt and pepper.

2  Form ground beef into patties using hands or a mold: Grab a tennis ball–size piece of beef and flatten it into a patty. Be sure the patty is the same thickness on the edges as it is in the middle. Each patty should be about 3/4 inch thick.

3  Stack ground-beef patties on a plate, separating them with pieces of waxed paper. Refrigerate the patties until time to cook.

4  Prepare a fire in a charcoal grill or turn a gas grill to high.

5  Place hamburgers and hot dogs on the grill.

6  Hot dogs should be turned often until slightly blistered on all sides, 5 to 6 minutes.

7  Cook hamburgers on one side until brown (approximately 10 minutes).

8  Using a spatula, flip hamburgers over and cook the other side.

9  When hamburger juices are no longer pink, use a small knife to cut into one hamburger and check for doneness. If one is done, the rest will be also. If making cheeseburgers, let cheese melt on top of burgers for about 1 minute before removing burgers from the grill.

10  Place grilled hamburgers and hot dogs on a clean plate.

11  Serve as desired—plain or on buns—with such accompaniments as cheese, lettuce, tomatoes and onions.

### Ingredients

- ❑ ground beef (about 6 oz. per serving)
- ❑ seasoning salt
- ❑ chopped onions
- ❑ dry onion-soup mix
- ❑ Worcestershire sauce
- ❑ salt and pepper
- ❑ hot dogs
- ❑ buns
- ❑ mustard and ketchup
- ❑ cheese, lettuce, tomatoes and onions

## 410 | Grill Vegetables

Grilled vegetables can be an easy accompaniment to other grilled foods or the centerpiece of a vegetarian meal.

### ⊙ Steps

1  Choose vegetables that take well to grilling, such as peppers, eggplant, tomatoes, corn on the cob, mushrooms and summer squash.

2  Clean and trim the vegetables. Cut large ones into smaller pieces.

3  Boost flavor by marinating vegetables for 15 minutes before grilling (see Tips). Or just brush them lightly with oil so they don't stick to the grill—unless you will use a foil pouch or vegetable basket.

4  Prepare a medium-hot fire in a charcoal or gas grill.

5  Put the vegetables directly on the grill grid, on skewers or inside a foil pouch or vegetable basket. Start vegetables first that take the longest to cook. The time for cooking vegetables varies greatly. Tomatoes may take 3 minutes per side, while whole peppers can take up to 20 minutes total.

### ✳ Tips

Marinades can be made the day before and stored, covered, in the refrigerator.

Try this basic marinade: Combine 2 parts olive oil and 1 part lemon juice with 1 peeled and crushed garlic clove.

### Ingredients

- ❑ vegetables
- ❑ marinade, oil or butter

**How to Do *(Just About)* Everything**

6  Turn the vegetables often, brushing on more marinade as needed.

7  Remove the vegetables when they can be easily pierced with a fork.

## Grill Fish     `411`

Grilling on your barbecue is a superb way to cook fish. Most fish take well to quick cooking over direct heat. Use fish fillets no more than an inch or so thick.

### ⊙ Steps

1  Light your grill and set it at its highest heat setting. Let it heat up for at least 20 minutes or so.

2  Season the fish well with salt and pepper or your desired dry seasoning.

3  Make sure that you have all your tools next to the grill, along with a clean plate or dish to hold the cooked fish.

4  Oil the grill grate lightly, then repeat. This coat of oil will prevent the fish from sticking and will promote the formation of grill marks.

5  Lay the fish in the center of the grill directly above the heat source. It should sizzle audibly. Avoid cooler sections and indirect heat.

6  Wait about 2 minutes, then slide the prongs of a broiler fork between the bars of the grill grate and slide them under the fish. Gently lift up a section of fish to check the cooking and look for grill marks.

7  When grill marks have formed, use the broiler fork to lift up a corner of the fillet, and slide a spatula under the fish.

8  Turn the fish over and cook the other side.

9  Use the broiler fork to flake open a section of one fillet to check for doneness. If the interior is no longer translucent, the fish is cooked.

10  Remove the fillets as soon as they're done.

### ❋ Tips

Almost every species of commercially available fish can be grilled. Salmon and halibut grill especially well, whereas more delicate fish, such as smaller flatfish and trout, will require extra care.

High heat is important to sear the fish instantly and keep it firm. Lower temperatures and slower cooking will dry out the fish and make handling it more difficult.

The ideal size for a piece of grilled fish is the size of your spatula, for easy flipping.

### Ingredients

❑ 1 (6- to 8- oz.) fish fillet per serving

❑ salt and pepper

❑ vegetable oil

## Steam Clams     `412`

A brine soak helps clams rid themselves of sand and grit before they're cooked. Many clam fans believe the best dipping sauce is the cooking juices, some melted butter and fresh lemon.

### ⊙ Steps

1  Soak the clams for 15 minutes in a brine solution of ⅓ c. salt and 1 gallon cold water. Repeat with fresh brine for another 15 minutes. Discard any clams with gaping shells.

2  Scrub the clams under cold running water, using a stiff brush.

3  Place 1 inch water in a kettle or pot with a cover. Place the clams on a rack over the water (not in it). Bring the water to a boil.

### ❋ Tip

Serve steamed clams with small bowls of melted butter for dipping. Or make garlic butter with 1 to 3 cloves fresh garlic, minced, per ¼ pound of butter.

4   Steam the clams in the covered pot for 5 to 10 minutes, until their shells open.

5   Discard any clams that do not open after steaming for 5 to 10 minutes. Remove clams as their shells open and serve as soon as all are open. Serve with melted butter and lemons.

### Ingredients

- ❑ 6 to 9 clams per person
- ❑ salt
- ❑ melted butter
- ❑ fresh lemons
- ❑ fresh garlic (optional)

## 413 | Boil Lobster

Boiling is an easy way of preparing lobster. You can eat the lobster by itself—it's simple and elegant with some melted butter—or use the meat in recipes such as crêpes, salads or risotto.

### ◎ Steps

1   Fill a large stockpot with enough water to cover the lobsters, and bring to a boil over high heat.

2   Salt the water (2 tbsp. salt per quart of water) and add lemon juice.

3   Put live lobsters headfirst into the boiling water. If you choose to kill them quickly before boiling, do this now (see Tips).

4   Allow the water to boil again, and then turn the heat down to medium.

5   Cover the pot and cook 5 minutes for the first pound of a lobster's weight and an additional 3 minutes for each additional pound. Like all shellfish, lobsters overcook almost instantly, so remove them from the water as soon as they're done.

6   Remove the lobsters from the water and drain them on paper towels.

7   To prepare the lobsters for the table, twist off each large claw, leaving the claw joints intact (there's a lot of meat in the joints). Crack the claw shell with a nutcracker or mallet.

8   Hold the body of a cooked lobster with a clean kitchen towel (the lobster should still be hot) and twist off the tail with your hands. Remove the tail meat by separating and removing the tail shell with your fingers.

### ✱ Tips

To kill the lobsters quickly just before boiling them, place the tip of a sharp knife on top of a lobster's head where the lines in the shell form a T. Push the knife down with a quick cutting motion.

At the fishmonger, select the liveliest lobster. Make sure the tail curls under, the shell is not damaged and the claws are secured with bands.

### Ingredients

- ❑ lobsters
- ❑ salt
- ❑ fresh lemon juice

## 414 | Eat Lobster

The shell is a small obstacle to that rich, tender lobster meat. Here's how to get at your dinner.

### ◎ Steps

1   Allow the lobster to cool after cooking.

2   Remove the large claws from the body by twisting them off at the joints.

3   Crack the claws. A nutcracker works well for this.

### ✱ Tip

You can mash the tomalley, add a little stock or cream, and use it as a sauce.

4  Bend the body back from the tail—it will crack, and then you can remove the tail. Break off the small flippers on the tail.

5  Push the tail meat out of the tail. It should come out in one piece. Remove the black vein in the tail and discard it.

6  Dip the lobster meat in melted butter and enjoy. Repeat as you unshell more of the meat.

7  Find the tomalley (the liver; it's green) and eat or discard it.

8  Note that the coral-colored roe in a female lobster is also edible.

9  Crack the body apart to find the meat in the four cavities where the small legs join the body.

10 Look for meat in the small walking legs, too, if you have a lobster weighing more than 2 lbs. Push a skewer into the legs to get the meat out.

## ⚠ Warning

Pregnant women and nursing mothers are advised not to eat the tomalley in Maine lobster due to high dioxin levels. Others are advised to limit consumption to one meal per month.

# Boil Pasta                                   415

Boil some pasta, make a quick sauce or open a jar, and you have the quintessential quick, easy meal.

## ◉ Steps

1  Fill a large pot three-quarters full with cold water.

2  Place the pot on the stove and turn the burner to high.

3  When the water begins to boil, add 1 to 2 tsp. salt, depending on how much pasta you're making.

4  Add the desired amount of pasta and stir.

5  Return the water to a boil.

6  Cook for as long as the package instructs. Stir occasionally so the pasta doesn't stick to itself.

7  To test when the pasta is done, taste it at the earliest time indicated on the package. It should be tender but still firm to the bite ("al dente," which means "to the tooth" in Italian). If you can still see a little uncooked core in the pasta, it needs another minute or so. But keep in mind that it will continue to cook a little after you remove it from the stove.

8  When the pasta is done, remove the pot from the burner immediately and carefully pour the contents into a colander in the sink.

9  Shake out any excess water over the sink.

10 If you want, use a couple of drops of olive oil to prevent the pasta from sticking; but if you're saucing the pasta, you really don't need to.

11 Serve immediately.

### Ingredients

❑ salt

❑ pasta

❑ olive oil

## 416 | Make 10-Minute Tomato Sauce

This recipe uses canned whole tomatoes and tastes fresher than any bottled sauce. It can be used on its own or as the base for other sauces. Makes enough for a pound of pasta.

### ⊙ Steps

1 Heat the oil in a saucepan and sauté the garlic for 30 seconds.

2 Open the can of tomatoes and add it to the pan.

3 Bring the liquid to a fast simmer and cook for about 5 minutes.

4 Blend or chop the tomato. You can use a hand blender to coarsely purée the tomatoes or use a large spoon to mash them right in the pot; or transfer the mixture to a blender or food processor.

5 Season to taste with salt and pepper and continue mashing or puréeing until the sauce is evenly coarse.

6 Add the basil and serve.

### ✳ Tip

Don't worry too much about precise measurements. Season to taste.

### Ingredients

❑ 1 tbsp. olive oil

❑ 2 tsp. minced or chopped garlic

❑ 1 (28-oz.) can whole tomatoes

❑ salt and pepper

❑ about ¼ c. fresh chopped basil

## 417 | Make Lasagna

Here is a recipe for lasagna at its simplest. Modify it to your own taste by adding any extra ingredients you like to the sauce. Makes six to eight servings.

### ⊙ Steps

1 Break or tear the basil leaves with your fingers. Set aside.

2 Warm the olive oil in a saucepan over medium-low heat, and add the garlic. Allow the garlic to sizzle for 3 to 4 minutes without letting it get too brown. Remove the garlic.

3 Add the tomato sauce to the hot oil and stir. Add the basil.

4 Turn the heat to very low, cover the pan and allow the sauce to simmer for 30 minutes, stirring occasionally.

5 As the sauce simmers, fill a large pasta pot with 4 to 5 qts. of water and a large pinch of salt. Bring to a boil.

6 Carefully place the lasagna noodles in the boiling water and stir occasionally to ensure that the noodles do not stick together. Cook until al dente, or tender but still chewy.

7 Drain the noodles but don't rinse them.

8 Generously oil the bottom of a baking dish.

9 Cover the bottom of the dish with a layer of lasagna noodles.

10 Spread the sauce over the noodles with a spoon and top the layer with a little of each cheese.

11 Repeat until the pan is full, saving most of the cheese for the top.

### ✳ Tip

Lasagna is a flexible dish: Try adding a pound of cooked veal, chicken or ground beef to the sauce. Or chop leftover vegetables and add them to the sauce.

### Ingredients

❑ 1 large sprig of fresh basil

❑ ⅓ to ½ c. extra-virgin olive oil

❑ 1 garlic clove, cut in half

❑ 1 (12 to 16 oz.) can tomato sauce

❑ salt

❑ 1 (16-oz.) box lasagna noodles

❑ 8 oz. grated Parmesan cheese

❑ 8 to 12 oz. ricotta cheese

❑ 8 oz. shredded mozzarella cheese

12  Top with remaining sauce and cheese.

13  Cover and bake at 350 degrees F for 20 minutes. (You may need to cover the lasagna for the first 10 minutes to melt the cheese, then uncover it for the last 10 minutes to brown it.)

14  Let the lasagna stand for 10 minutes before serving.

## Make Basic Cheese Enchiladas                                            418

**The zesty sauce in this recipe can be used for most types of enchiladas. Makes four to six servings.**

### ⊙ Steps

#### Making the Sauce

1  Bring the chiles and water to a boil in a gallon-size pot. Remove from the heat and let cool.

2  Remove the chiles from the water. Save the water for puréeing.

3  Purée the chiles and garlic in a food processor. Add enough water to the food processor to give the purée a gravylike consistency.

4  Heat 2 tbsp. of lard or canola oil in a saucepan over medium-high heat and add the flour while constantly stirring. Add the chile purée, garlic powder and salt.

5  Simmer 15 minutes, stirring occasionally. If the sauce gets too thick, stir in a little more chile water.

#### Making the Enchiladas

1  Preheat the oven to 350 degrees F.

2  Heat the remaining lard or canola oil in a small sauté pan over medium-high heat. Using tongs, dip a tortilla quickly in the oil and place it in a baking dish that will hold 12 rolled enchiladas in a single layer.

3  Sprinkle an ounce or so of the jack cheese in a line across the middle of the tortilla. Starting at an edge of the tortilla that is directly across from the line of cheese, roll the tortilla until it just folds over itself.

4  Place the rolled enchilada in the baking dish, flap side down. Repeat this process until all tortillas and cheese are used.

5  Pour enough chile sauce over the tortillas to just moisten the entire surface. Bake for 20 minutes uncovered.

6  Remove the enchiladas from the oven and sprinkle with the queso cotija.

7  If desired, garnish the enchiladas with shredded iceberg lettuce, chopped plum tomatoes and chopped green onions.

### ✳ Tip

For a quicker version, canned red enchilada sauce makes a good substitute.

### Ingredients

❑ 12 stemmed and seeded dried Anaheim chiles

❑ 1 qt. water

❑ 1 garlic clove, peeled

❑ 6 tbsp. lard or canola oil

❑ 2 tbsp. flour

❑ ³/₄ tsp. garlic powder

❑ ½ tsp. salt

❑ 12 corn tortillas

❑ 1 lb. shredded Monterey jack cheese

❑ ¼ lb. queso cotija (aged Mexican cheese) or Romano or Parmesan cheese

❑ shredded iceberg lettuce (optional)

❑ chopped plum tomatoes (optional)

❑ chopped green onions (optional)

## 419 | Make Refried Pinto Beans

If you've never had the real thing before, the tastiness of this homemade version will surprise you. Makes eight servings.

### ⊙ Steps

1 Inspect the pinto beans carefully by placing ½ c. of beans at a time on a plate and discarding any stones or bad beans.

2 Place the beans in a strainer and rinse under cold water.

3 Put the beans and 8 c. of water in a large pot and bring to a boil. Skim off any gray foam that rises to the surface as the beans boil.

4 Lower the heat to medium, add the onion and let the beans simmer rapidly for 30 minutes.

5 Add the salt and oregano and continue to simmer for another 1½ hours, or until the beans are very soft.

6 In a large cast-iron skillet or heavy-bottomed pan, heat ¼ c. vegetable shortening over medium-high heat. When the oil is hot, add a cup of the beans and their juice.

7 Using a potato masher, mash the beans in the pan while they fry. The beans should have a fairly smooth consistency, with whole beans here and there.

8 Place the beans in a large, heavy bowl and add a pinch of salt and some of the cheese. Repeat with the remaining beans and cheese.

### Ingredients

- ❑ 2 c. dried pinto beans
- ❑ 8 c. water
- ❑ 1 medium onion, peeled and coarsely chopped
- ❑ 1 tsp. salt, plus more for frying
- ❑ ¼ tsp. dried oregano, crumbled between fingers
- ❑ ¼ c. vegetable shortening (or canola oil )
- ❑ ¼ lb. shredded Monterey jack cheese

## 420 | Make Fried Rice

Fried rice is an easy and filling dish—you just have to remember to have cooked rice on hand. Makes two or three servings.

### ⊙ Steps

1 Heat a wok or large skillet over high heat.

2 Add a little oil and wait a few moments for it to heat up. You only need a tablespoon or so to keep the rice from sticking.

3 Break the eggs into the wok and stir quickly to scramble.

4 When the egg is well set, remove it and chop it into bite-sized pieces.

5 Wipe out the wok and add a little more oil. Wait for it to heat.

6 If the rice is clumpy, break it up with your hands to separate the grains.

7 Add the cold rice to the wok. Move the rice quickly around the hot pan by sliding your spoon or spatula under the rice and turning it over. (This is the basic stir-frying technique.)

8 After a minute or so, add the carrot and stir-fry it with the rice.

9 After 3 minutes, add the peas and stir-fry.

10 After 2 minutes, add the scallions, egg and meat, if using.

### ⚠ Warning

Don't use hot rice; you'll have a gloppy mess. Cooling the rice makes the grains separate.

### Ingredients

- ❑ oil
- ❑ 2 eggs
- ❑ 4 c. cooked rice, cold
- ❑ 1 carrot, finely diced
- ❑ ½ c. frozen peas
- ❑ 4 minced scallions
- ❑ ½ c. leftover meats, chopped (optional)
- ❑ salt or soy sauce

11  Once the ingredients are well mixed, season the rice with salt or soy sauce. Cook another minute or until everything is heated through.

12  Remove from heat and serve.

## Make Chow Mein 421

This recipe calls for chicken, but you can substitute beef, pork, seafood or vegetables. Makes four to six servings.

### ⊙ Steps

1  Look for fresh Chinese egg noodles in the supermarket refrigerator section. These are best to use. Pick them apart (they will be stuck together in a clump) before you cook them.

2  Toast sesame seeds by tossing them in a dry, hot pan for a minute or until golden.

3  Cook the noodles according to package directions and drain. Toss with a small amount of the peanut oil to prevent sticking.

4  Heat a wok or skillet over medium-high heat. Add the remaining oil and garlic and cook, stirring, until the garlic is golden but not brown.

5  Add the chicken and stir continuously until it is no longer pink. Add the bamboo shoots, mushrooms and celery, and cook for 3 minutes.

6  Add 2 c. of the broth to the pan and bring to a boil. Cover, reduce the heat to medium and cook for 7 minutes.

7  Add the onion and cook for another 2 minutes. Add the bean sprouts and stir until most of the liquid has evaporated.

8  Mix the cornstarch with the remaining broth and soy sauce; stir into the pan. Stir until the sauce thickens, then add the noodles.

9  Toss to heat through and taste. Add more soy sauce if preferred.

10  Serve in a large bowl, garnished with the sesame seeds and cilantro.

### Ingredients

- ❑ 1 lb. Chinese egg noodles
- ❑ 2 tbsp. white sesame seeds
- ❑ 3 tbsp. peanut oil
- ❑ 3 garlic cloves, peeled and minced
- ❑ 1½ lbs. chicken breast or thigh meat, cut into thin slices
- ❑ 2 small cans bamboo shoots, drained
- ❑ ¾ lb. button mushrooms, stemmed and thinly sliced
- ❑ 2 celery stalks, rinsed and sliced thinly crosswise
- ❑ 2½ c. chicken broth
- ❑ 3 small onions, peeled and sliced thinly
- ❑ ¾ lb. bean sprouts
- ❑ 3 tbsp. each cornstarch and soy sauce
- ❑ 2 tbsp. freshly chopped cilantro

## Use Chopsticks 422

Practice makes perfect when it comes to using chopsticks. The key is that the bottom chopstick remains still while the upper chopstick moves to grasp the food.

### ⊙ Steps

1  Position one chopstick so that it lies at the base of your thumb (on the joint) and at the lower joint of the middle finger. This chopstick shouldn't touch your forefinger.

2  Place the other chopstick between your thumb and forefinger so you can move it up and down.

### ✹ Tip

If you have trouble maneuvering the chopsticks, try supporting the second chopstick against your ring finger as well.

3 Keeping the tips of the chopsticks parallel and the first chopstick stationary, practice moving the second chopstick toward the first.

4 Use this technique to position the chopsticks around a piece of food.

5 Hold the food firmly as you lift it toward your mouth.

⚠ **Warning**

Though you may be tempted to spear food with your chopsticks as an act of desperation, it is considered impolite.

---

## 423 | Make Basic Biscuits

Biscuits are fast and easy to make, and homemade biscuits are a whole lot better than store-bought. Makes about 10 biscuits.

### ◎ Steps

1 Preheat the oven to 450 degrees F.

2 Use a dry fork to stir together flour, baking powder and salt in a medium-size mixing bowl.

3 Cut in shortening, using a pastry blender, two knives or your fingertips, until the mixture looks like coarse crumbs.

4 Make a well in the center of the mixture and add the milk. Stir with a fork until the mixture is moist.

5 Place the dough on a lightly floured surface. Knead gently, turning the dough, until it's soft and smooth. Don't overknead the dough or the biscuits will be tough. Just knead until it all comes together nicely.

6 Roll out the dough to a 1/2-inch thickness. Cut biscuit shapes out of the dough using a biscuit or cookie cutter.

7 Place biscuit rounds on an ungreased cookie sheet, brush with melted butter, and bake 10 minutes or until golden on the bottom.

### Ingredients

- ❑ 2 c. all-purpose flour
- ❑ 1 tbsp. baking powder
- ❑ 1/4 tsp. salt
- ❑ 1/3 c. shortening
- ❑ 3/4 c. milk
- ❑ melted butter

---

## 424 | Make Oatmeal

Oatmeal is easy to make. Try this cinnamon-raisin version for variety. The same procedure works for plain oatmeal. Makes four servings.

### ◎ Steps

1 Combine oats, raisins (or other dried fruit of your choice), nuts (if desired), brown sugar, cinnamon, salt and nutmeg. Set aside.

2 Bring the water, or water and milk, to a boil in a medium-size saucepan. Slowly add the oat mixture to the boiling water, stirring constantly. (For a creamier texture, put the oatmeal in the cold liquid, then bring to a boil.)

3 Cook for 1 minute, stirring.

4 Cover, remove the pan from the heat, and let it stand 1 to 3 minutes, or until the oatmeal is of desired consistency.

5 To make ahead, cook to this step and store, covered tightly, at room temperature for a half-hour or so.

6 Serve with milk, or simply plain.

### Ingredients

- ❑ 1 1/2 c. quick-cooking rolled oats
- ❑ 1 c. raisins
- ❑ 1/4 c. chopped nuts (optional)
- ❑ 1/4 c. packed brown sugar
- ❑ 1/2 tsp. cinnamon
- ❑ 1/4 tsp. salt
- ❑ 1/4 tsp. ground nutmeg
- ❑ 3 c. cold water (or 1 1/2 c. water, 1 1/2 c. milk)
- ❑ milk (optional)

## Make Buttermilk Pancakes | 425

Forget that mix. Pancakes are easy to make from scratch.
Makes four servings (about 16 pancakes).

### ⊙ Steps

1 Preheat the griddle to about 375 degrees F.

2 Sift all dry ingredients into a large mixing bowl.

3 Melt the butter and combine it with the buttermilk and eggs.

4 Pour the buttermilk mixture into the dry mixture and stir just until all dry ingredients are moist.

5 Add a teaspoon or two of butter or oil to the griddle and swirl to coat.

6 Pour the batter on the hot griddle using a ¼-c. measuring cup, or make larger pancakes by pouring batter from a pitcher.

7 Let the pancakes cook on one side until bubbles hold their shape on the uncooked side of the pancake and the edges appear slightly golden.

8 Flip the pancakes and cook on the other side—the second side always takes about half as much time.

9 Serve with butter and syrup.

### ✳ Tip

It's normal for the batter to be lumpy after you stir it.

### Ingredients

❑ 1 tsp. salt

❑ 1 to 2 tbsp. sugar

❑ 2 c. sifted all-purpose flour

❑ 1 tsp. baking soda

❑ 2 tbsp. butter, plus more for cooking and topping

❑ 2 c. buttermilk

❑ 2 lightly beaten eggs

❑ maple syrup

## Make Waffles | 426

Waffles are a tasty treat, whether served for breakfast, brunch or dinner. Dress them up with fruit, syrups or powdered sugar.
Makes two or three servings.

### ⊙ Steps

1 Close the lid to the waffle iron and plug it in. Follow the manufacturer's instructions for the correct setting.

2 Separate the eggs (see 376 "Separate Egg Whites From Yolks") and beat the yolks well in a medium mixing bowl. Add the vanilla.

3 Stir in the buttermilk.

4 Combine the flour, baking powder, baking soda, salt and sugar. Add to the egg-buttermilk mixture.

5 Add melted butter; stir until combined.

6 Beat the egg whites until stiff; fold them into the batter.

7 Check the waffle iron to be sure it's hot. If the waffle iron has a thermostat indicator or light, this will show that it is ready.

8 Open the lid of the waffle iron. If it isn't a nonstick waffle iron, grease it following the manufacturer's instructions.

9 Using a measuring cup, pour about 1 c. batter into the bottom of the waffle iron. (Check the manufacturer's instructions if you are not sure how much batter to add to your waffle iron.)

### Ingredients

❑ 3 eggs

❑ 2 tsp. vanilla extract

❑ 1½ c. buttermilk

❑ 1¾ c. all-purpose flour

❑ 2 tsp. baking powder

❑ 1 tsp. baking soda

❑ ½ tsp. salt

❑ 2 tbsp. sugar

❑ 1 stick butter, melted (½ c.)

❑ maple syrup

www.ehow.com

10  Close the lid.

11  Let the waffle cook until steam no longer comes out of the waffle iron or until the waffle is light brown and slightly crisp.

12  Carefully remove the cooked waffle with a fork. Top with maple syrup.

---

## 427 | Scramble Eggs

Scrambled eggs are easy, but to make your eggs creamy, you need to cook them slowly over low heat. Makes one serving.

### ◉ Steps

1  Crack one to three eggs into a bowl.

2  Add a splash of milk.

3  Add a dash of salt and pepper.

4  Beat with a fork or whisk until well-combined.

5  Heat a skillet over medium-low heat.

6  Melt the butter in the skillet.

7  Pour the beaten eggs into the skillet.

8  Let the eggs cook undisturbed until they begin to set, then push them gently from the bottom of the pan.

9  Continue cooking until the eggs are the consistency you like.

10  Stir cheese or any other additions into the eggs 1 or 2 minutes before you're going to serve them.

### ✻ Tip

Eggs cooked for a shorter period of time are "scrambled soft." If cooked longer, they are "scrambled hard." The "ideal" scrambled eggs are soft and creamy.

### Ingredients

❑ 1 to 3 large eggs

❑ milk

❑ salt and pepper

❑ 1½ tsp. butter

---

## 428 | Make Hash Browns

Homemade hash browns don't take long to prepare, and they're always a hit. Makes four servings.

### ◉ Steps

1  Peel the potatoes and coarsely shred them. You should wind up with about 3 c.

2  Rinse the shredded potatoes. Pat dry well with paper towels; or use a salad spinner if you don't want to pick damp potato shreds off towels.

3  Combine the potatoes, onion, salt and pepper.

4  Melt the butter in a large skillet over medium heat.

5  Using a spatula, pat the potato mixture into the skillet. Reduce heat to medium-low and cook about 10 minutes or until the bottom is crisp.

6  Cut the hash browns into four wedges and turn (if you are using a non-stick skillet, use a plastic utensil for this). Cook another 8 to 10 minutes or until golden and the potatoes are cooked through.

### Ingredients

❑ 3 medium potatoes (1 lb.) such as russet

❑ ¼ c. finely chopped onion

❑ ¼ tsp. salt

❑ ⅛ tsp. black pepper

❑ 3 tbsp. butter

---

## Make Sugar Cookies 429

These sugar cookies are perfect for rolling out, cutting into various shapes and decorating. Makes about three dozen cookies.

### ◉ Steps

1 Mix together the flour, salt and baking powder. Set aside.

2 Beat the butter until creamy, then add the sugar, vanilla and lemon extract, and beat for 1 minute.

3 Beat the egg and egg yolk into the butter mixture.

4 Stir in the flour mixture only until incorporated. Stop stirring the instant the dough is uniform.

5 Form into a log, wrap in plastic wrap and chill for at least 2 hours.

6 Heat the oven to 350 degrees F.

7 Divide the dough and roll it out between two sheets of wax paper; make your cutouts. Work with just a little dough at a time. Keep the rest in the refrigerator to stay chilled.

8 Place the cookies on a nonstick baking sheet and decorate with colored sugar, sprinkles, candies or other foods that won't melt in the oven.

9 Cook for 12 to 15 minutes, or until the cookies just start to turn golden around the edges. If the cookies turn golden before 10 minutes have passed, lower the oven temperature.

### ✱ Tip

Be sure not to skip the chilling step. This dough needs to be cold, cold, cold.

### Ingredients

- ❑ 1½ c. all-purpose flour
- ❑ ⅓ tsp. salt
- ❑ 1½ tsp. baking powder
- ❑ ⅔ c. softened unsalted butter
- ❑ ⅔ c. sugar
- ❑ 2 tsp. vanilla extract
- ❑ ¼ tsp. lemon extract
- ❑ 1 egg
- ❑ 1 egg yolk

## Make Chocolate Chip Cookies 430

We eat more chocolate chip cookies than any other type, and for good reason. They're the most familiar and most satisfying. Makes about two dozen cookies.

### ◉ Steps

1 Stir together the flour, baking soda and salt. Do not sift.

2 Beat the butter until creamy, then add the sugars and vanilla and stir them in until combined.

3 Add the egg and yolk one at a time, mixing well after each addition.

4 Stir in the flour mixture. Stop the instant it's all been incorporated.

5 Stir in the chocolate chips until they are distributed evenly.

6 Form the dough into a log, wrap it and chill for at least 30 minutes. Chilling the dough is an important step. It allows the flour to relax, the sugars to partially dissolve and the flavors to begin to come together.

7 Heat the oven to 350 degrees F and grease some cookie sheets.

8 Cut the dough into thin rounds, place on baking sheets and bake for 10 minutes or until the edges begin to turn golden.

### Ingredients

- ❑ 2½ c. all-purpose flour
- ❑ 1 tsp. baking soda
- ❑ ½ tsp. salt
- ❑ 1 c. softened unsalted butter
- ❑ ¾ c. brown sugar
- ❑ ¾ c. sugar
- ❑ 1 tbsp. vanilla extract
- ❑ 1 egg
- ❑ 1 egg yolk
- ❑ 2½ c. semisweet chocolate chips

## 431 | Make Peanut Butter Cookies

These all-time favorites taste great and are easy to make. Try using "natural" peanut butter (the kind that separates—stir it together first) or crunchy. Makes about two dozen cookies.

### ⊙ Steps

1 Use a wooden spoon or electric mixer to beat the butter and peanut butter until combined, about 30 seconds.

2 Add the sugars, and the baking soda and baking powder, and beat until combined.

3 Add the vanilla and the egg, and beat until combined.

4 Stir in the flour until it's incorporated. The dough will become thick and difficult to work at this point; you may want to chill it for an hour or so until it's easier to work with.

5 Heat the oven to 325 degrees F.

6 Roll the dough into 1-inch balls and place them a few inches apart in rows on cookie sheets.

7 Butter the tines of a large fork and use it to press the cookies flat. Make a design of perpendicular lines with the fork. Re-butter the fork as necessary. You can also dip the buttered fork into granulated sugar before pressing; some of the sugar will then stick to the cookies.

8 Bake for 15 to 18 minutes or until the cookies start to brown around the edges.

9 Remove the cookies from the cookie sheet to cool.

### Ingredients

- ❑ ½ c. unsalted butter
- ❑ ½ c. peanut butter
- ❑ ½ c. sugar
- ❑ ½ c. dark brown sugar
- ❑ ½ tsp. baking soda
- ❑ ½ tsp. baking powder
- ❑ 1 tsp. vanilla extract
- ❑ 1 egg
- ❑ 1½ c. all-purpose flour

## 432 | Make Brownies

For pure decadence, try frosting these brownies when cool with a chocolate fudge frosting. Makes 24 small brownies.

### ⊙ Steps

1 Preheat the oven to 350 degrees F.

2 Grease the baking pan with cooking spray. Set aside.

3 Melt the butter and chocolate, either in a double boiler or in a medium-size saucepan over low heat (if you do it this way, take care not to burn the chocolate). Remove from heat.

4 Stir in the eggs, sugar and vanilla with a wooden spoon. Beat lightly until just combined.

5 Stir in the flour and nuts.

6 Spread the batter in the baking pan. Bake 30 minutes. Don't overbake.

7 Cool the brownies in the pan on a wire rack. Cut into bars.

### Ingredients

- ❑ ½ c. unsalted butter
- ❑ 2 oz. unsweetened chocolate
- ❑ 2 eggs
- ❑ 1 c. sugar
- ❑ 1 tsp. vanilla extract
- ❑ ¾ c. all-purpose flour
- ❑ ½ c. chopped nuts (optional)

## Make Yellow Cake    433

Don't buy it in a box—make it yourself! It's easy enough. Chocolate frosting is the classic accompaniment to yellow cake. Makes 10 to 12 servings.

### ⊙ Steps

1  Have all the ingredients at room temperature. Preheat the oven to 350 degrees F.

2  Grease and lightly flour the two cake pans and set aside.

3  Combine the flour, baking powder and salt in a small mixing bowl and set it aside.

4  Beat the butter or margarine with a hand mixer at medium speed for 30 seconds in a large mixing bowl.

5  Add the sugar and beat well.

6  Add the eggs, one at a time, beating well after each. Add the vanilla.

7  Add the dry flour mixture and milk alternately, beating on low speed after each addition until just combined.

8  Pour the batter into the prepared cake pans.

9  Bake until a toothpick inserted in the center of the cake comes out clean, 30 to 35 minutes.

10  Cool the cakes in pans on a wire rack for 10 minutes.

11  Invert the pans to remove the cakes. Cool thoroughly on racks.

12  Fill with frosting, or with your favorite pudding or mousse recipe. Frost or just dust the top with powdered sugar.

### Ingredients

- ❑ 2 1/2 c. all-purpose flour
- ❑ 2 1/2 tsp. baking powder
- ❑ 1/2 tsp. salt
- ❑ 3/4 c. butter or margarine
- ❑ 1 1/2 c. sugar
- ❑ 2 eggs
- ❑ 1 1/2 tsp. vanilla extract
- ❑ 1 1/4 c. milk

## Make White Cake    434

Have fun dressing up this basic cake with your favorite frosting. Makes 10 to 12 servings.

### ⊙ Steps

1  Have all the ingredients at room temperature. Preheat the oven to 350 degrees F.

2  Grease and lightly flour the cake pans. Set aside.

3  Combine the flour, baking powder, baking soda and salt in a small mixing bowl. Set aside.

4  Beat the butter or margarine in a large mixing bowl with a hand mixer at medium speed for 30 seconds.

5  Add the sugar. Beat well.

6  Add the egg whites one at a time, beating well after each. Add the vanilla.

7  Add the dry flour mixture and buttermilk alternately to the batter, beating on low speed after each addition, until just combined.

### ✱ Tip

Real butter will give the best flavor in a simple cake like this.

### Ingredients

- ❑ 2 c. all-purpose flour
- ❑ 1 tsp. baking powder
- ❑ 1/2 tsp. baking soda
- ❑ 1/8 tsp. salt
- ❑ 1/2 c. butter or margarine
- ❑ 1 3/4 c. sugar ➤

8  Pour the batter into the prepared pans and bake until a toothpick inserted in the center of the cake comes out clean, 30 to 35 minutes.

9  Cool the cakes in the pans on wire racks for 10 minutes.

10  Invert the pans to remove the cakes. Cool thoroughly on racks.

11  Fill with frosting, or with your favorite pudding or mousse recipe. Frost or just dust the top with powdered sugar.

❑ 4 egg whites

❑ 1 tsp. vanilla extract

❑ 1 1/3 c. buttermilk

---

## 435 Frost a Cake

Frosting helps seal the moisture in a cake—not to mention adding extra flavor. Make sure the layers are cool and free of crumbs before you apply the frosting.

### ◉ Steps

1  Cool the cake layers in pans on the wire rack for 5 minutes.

2  Cover another rack with a towel; place the rack, towel side down, on top of the layer and invert as a unit. Remove the pan.

3  Place the original rack on the bottom of the layer; turn over both racks (as a unit) so the layer is right side up. Remove the top rack and towel.

4  Repeat with the other layer. Allow the layers to cool completely.

5  Before frosting the cake, brush loose crumbs from the sides and edges of the cooled layers. Support the cake firmly with one hand and brush crumbs with the other.

6  Place one layer, rounded side down, on the cake plate and spread about 1/2 c. of frosting to within 1/4 inch of the edge.

7  Place the second layer, rounded side up, on the frosted layer. Coat the side with a very thin layer of frosting to seal in crumbs.

8  Swirl more frosting on the side, forming a 1/4-inch ridge above the top of the cake.

9  Spread the remaining frosting over the top, just meeting the built-up ridge around the side. Make swirls or leave the top smooth for decorations.

### ✳ Tips

If you don't let the cake cool, the frosting will melt on it and run all over.

If your cake is bumpy or has a hump in the middle of it, slice off the bumps to make the layer level. If the cake falls apart or part of it sticks to the pan, try "gluing" it together with the frosting.

Scatter candy sprinkles in spirals or strips, or around the edge for a border.

Decorate with candles, crushed candy, coconut or chopped nuts.

Dip the spatula in hot water as you frost to give the frosting a smooth look.

---

## 436 Make Basic Piecrust

The secret to tender, flaky pie dough is not to overwork it. The moisture in the cold bits of shortening creates steam, separating the layers into flakes. Makes two 10-inch piecrusts.

### ◉ Steps

### Making the Dough

1  Sift the flour and salt together into a bowl; cut in the chilled solid shortening with a fork, two knives or a pastry blender until the mixture resembles coarse meal.

### ✳ Tips

You can also use a combination of cold butter and shortening.

If your recipe calls for prebaking the bottom crust, put a piece of aluminum foil on the dough and

2 Add the egg, white vinegar and cold water to the flour-shortening mixture. Use a fork to mix until just combined.

3 Gather the dough into two balls and chill for at least 20 minutes.

## Rolling the Crust

1 Flour a board lightly. Also flour the rolling pin.

2 Roll the dough into an 11- to 12-inch circle, about 1/8 inch thick, using fairly firm pressure. Roll from the middle of the dough out to the edges, not back and forth. Press the dough together to mend any cracks.

3 To transfer the dough to the pan, loosely roll it around the rolling pin, and then unroll it in the pie dish. You can also try folding the dough into quarters, and then unfolding it in the dish.

4 Trim the crust edges so that there's a 1-inch overhang around the rim.

5 Unless your recipe calls for the shell to be prebaked, add the filling.

6 For a one-crust pie, make a decorative edge by pressing the tines of a fork into the dough, or pinching it into scallops.

7 For two-crust pies, place the top crust on the filling, using either the rolling pin or folding method.

8 Trim the dough to a 1-inch overhang.

9 Fold the top crust under the bottom crust and pinch the edges together, and then crimp as for a one-crust pie.

10 For a two-crust pie, score the top with a knife to let steam escape.

weigh the crust down with dry beans or pie weights to prevent bubbles.

Don't stretch the dough into the pie dish. It will shrink when baked.

Flakiness is enhanced by handling the dough as little as possible. Make every attempt not to reroll the dough.

Brush beaten egg white over piecrust before baking to yield a beautiful glossy finish.

### Ingredients

☐ 3 c. all-purpose flour

☐ 1 tsp. salt

☐ 1 1/4 c. solid shortening, chilled

☐ 1 egg, slightly beaten

☐ 2 tsp. white vinegar

☐ 5 tbsp. cold water

---

## Make Apple Pie                                           437

Use tart apples for your pies—Granny Smiths and pippins are good choices. Makes one 9-inch pie.

### ⊙ Steps

1 Make piecrust (see 436 "Make Basic Piecrust" for instructions) or use frozen piecrust.

2 Preheat the oven to 400 degrees F.

3 Peel and core the apples, then cut them into 1/2-inch-thick slices.

4 Toss the apples lightly with the flour, sugar, lemon juice, spices and salt.

5 Roll out dough for the bottom crust and place it in the pie pan. Trim the edge to a 1-inch overhang.

6 Drain the apples and add to the pan. Top with the pieces of butter.

7 Roll out dough for the top crust. Place it over the pie and trim the edge, leaving a 1-inch overhang.

8 Fold the top edge of the upper crust over the lower crust and squeeze them together.

9 Crimp the edges by pinching small sections of dough with your fingers.

### Ingredients

☐ 5 c. sliced tart cooking apples

☐ 2 tbsp. all-purpose flour

☐ 3/4 to 1 c. sugar

☐ 1 1/2 tbsp. fresh lemon juice

☐ 1/2 tsp. ground cinnamon

☐ 1/4 tsp. ground ginger

☐ 1/2 tsp. ground allspice

☐ 1/4 tsp. grated nutmeg

☐ 1/4 tsp. salt

☐ 1 1/2 tbsp. butter, cut into pieces

☐ basic piecrust

10  Use a sharp knife to cut five 1-inch steam vents in the top.

11  Sprinkle the upper crust with sugar for sparkle.

12  Bake for 40 to 50 minutes, until the crust is golden.

## 438 | Make Pumpkin Pie

Pumpkin pie is the quintessential autumn treat. For a firmer pie, use just two eggs. For a creamier custard, use three eggs. Makes one 9-inch pie, about eight servings.

### ◉ Steps

1  Have all the ingredients at room temperature. Put an oven rack in the center of the oven and preheat to 375 degrees F.

2  Put the eggs in a large mixing bowl and whisk well.

3  Add the pumpkin, evaporated milk, sugar, brown sugar, cinnamon, ginger, nutmeg, cloves and salt, and whisk well. Set aside.

4  Warm the piecrust in the oven until it is hot to the touch, approximately 5 minutes.

5  Pour the filling into the warmed piecrust and bake 35 to 40 minutes, or until the filling is set but still a bit quivery, like gelatin, when nudged.

6  Cool the pie on a rack and then refrigerate. Serve either cold, at room temperature or slightly warmed.

### Ingredients

- ❑ 2 or 3 eggs
- ❑ 2 c. pumpkin purée
- ❑ 1½ c. evaporated milk
- ❑ ½ c. sugar
- ❑ ⅓ c. firmly packed brown sugar
- ❑ 1 tsp. ground cinnamon
- ❑ 1 tsp. ground ginger
- ❑ ¼ tsp. nutmeg
- ❑ ¼ tsp. ground cloves
- ❑ ½ tsp. salt
- ❑ unbaked 9-inch, deep-dish piecrust

## 439 | Make Cheesecake

The traditional choice for the purist, this recipe is the basic New York cheesecake with a simple graham cracker crust. Makes one 9- or 10-inch cheesecake, about 12 servings.

### ✳ Tip

Use any fruit or sour cream topping you wish.

### ◉ Steps

1  Heat the oven to 350 degrees F. Have all ingredients, especially the cream cheese, at room temperature.

2  Stir together the graham cracker crumbs, cinnamon and melted butter until well combined.

3  Pack the crust mixture into the bottom and up the sides of a springform pan. Use the flat bottom of a glass to press the crust flat.

4  Place the cream cheese, zests and vanilla in a mixing bowl and beat by hand or with an electric mixer until just smooth.

5  Add the sugar and flour gradually and beat just until incorporated. Scrape down the sides of the mixing bowl.

### Ingredients

- ❑ 1¾ c. graham cracker crumbs
- ❑ ½ tsp. cinnamon
- ❑ ½ c. melted butter
- ❑ 1¼ lb. cream cheese
- ❑ 1½ tsp. finely grated lemon zest

6  Add the eggs and cream. Mix thoroughly.

7  Pour the filling over the crust. Place the filled springform pan in a water bath—a shallow pan filled with enough water to come halfway up the sides of the springform pan.

8  Bake for approximately 1 hour, turning the cake about 15 minutes before the baking time is up.

9  Check the cake for doneness. The center should jiggle slightly when the pan is nudged. Avoid using a knife or toothpick to check for doneness.

10  Leave the cake in the oven, with the door partly open, for an hour after cooking; then let cool completely at room temperature.

- ❏ 1 tsp. finely grated orange zest
- ❏ 1 tsp. vanilla extract
- ❏ ¾ c. sugar
- ❏ 1 tbsp. all-purpose flour
- ❏ 4 eggs
- ❏ 2 tbsp. heavy cream

## Make Hot Chocolate                                                           440

Chocolate was actually first enjoyed as a drink, by the Aztecs. You can use low-fat milk, but whole milk gives the best consistency. Makes about 10 servings.

### ◉ Steps

1  Chop the chocolate into small pieces and place in a mixing bowl.

2  Heat the milk in a saucepan over medium-low heat until it steams and is very hot.

3  Add the sugar and vanilla and stir the mixture until the sugar has dissolved. Remove from the heat.

4  Ladle out about 1 c. of the milk and pour it over the chocolate.

5  Let the chocolate melt slowly. Stir it with a whisk to blend all the chocolate into the milk.

6  Continue adding the remaining milk and stir until all the milk has been incorporated. Serve hot.

### ✳ Tip
Six oz. of bittersweet chocolate equals about 1 c. of chopped chocolate.

### Ingredients
- ❏ 6 oz. high-quality bittersweet chocolate
- ❏ 8 c. whole milk
- ❏ 1 c. sugar
- ❏ 1 tsp. vanilla extract

## Brew a Pot of Coffee                                                         441

Drip, or filtered, coffee can be made in an electric drip coffeepot or simply by placing a filter holder over a pot or cup.

### ◉ Steps

#### Using an Electric Drip Coffeepot

1  Fill the coffeemaker's carafe with fresh, cold water.

2  Place a filter in the coffeemaker's filter basket.

3  Add 2 tbsp. coffee to the basket for every 6 oz. of water. (Sometimes the cups marked on the carafe are more than 6 oz., so check the coffeemaker's instructions.)

4  Pour the water into the coffeemaker's reservoir and replace the carafe.

5  Turn on the coffeemaker.

### ✳ Tips
Use finely ground coffee—about the consistency of granulated sugar—with a cone filter. Use a slightly coarser grind with a flat-bottomed filter.

## Using a Filter Holder (Manual Method)

1 Boil water, then let it rest briefly to achieve the optimum brewing temperature (195 to 205 degrees F).

2 Place a filter holder over a coffeepot or cup.

3 Place a filter in the holder.

4 Add 2 level tbsp. ground coffee to the filter holder per 6 oz. of water, or 2 oz. coffee per each qt. of water.

5 Pour about 3 tbsp. of water over the grounds to wet them.

6 Wait a few seconds for the grounds to expand.

7 Pour the rest of the water over the grounds. Let it drip through the grounds, but be sure to remove the grounds before the last of the water has drained into the pot or cup. Coffee grounds can overextract and get a bitter taste.

Keep coffee warm on a burner or hot plate for no more than 20 minutes. After 20 minutes, coffee takes on a "stewed," bitter taste. Reheating coffee increases its bitterness and is not recommended.

---

## 442 | Brew a Pot of Tea

If you don't like tea, perhaps it's because you've only been treated to lukewarm water and the stuff in a bag. But a proper pot of tea is quite reviving—especially when you feel parched.

### ⊙ Steps

1 Fill a kettle with fresh, cold water, adding enough to make the desired amount of tea, plus some extra to allow for evaporation and to prewarm the teapot.

2 Wait until the water is near boiling, then pour a little into the teapot and swirl it around. This warms the pot so that it is at an optimum temperature for holding the tea. Empty the pot.

3 For each cup of tea, place 1 rounded teaspoon of leaves into the warmed pot. (If your pot has a strainer basket, use that.)

4 Allow the water in the kettle to reach a brisk, rolling boil.

5 Pour the water from the teakettle over the leaves in the teapot.

6 Let the tea steep for 3 to 5 minutes, depending on the size of the leaves. Allow a longer steeping time for larger leaves.

7 Stir just before serving, then strain the tea into cups. Depending on the tea, you might add sugar, milk, honey or lemon. (Or a combination, but don't use lemon and milk together.)

8 Keep the pot covered with a cozy to keep the tea warm, and enjoy.

### ✳ Tips

If you do not want to use a strainer, place the tea leaves in a tea infuser, filter or mesh tea ball instead. You can also purchase teapots with removable infusion baskets. You can use tea bags in a teapot, but the quality of tea in bags is never as good as that of loose tea.

Transfer steeped tea into another heated teapot to avoid the bitter taste that can result from its sitting on the leaves for a long period of time.

## Make Sun Tea 443

**Capture summer in a jar by brewing tea in the warm sun.**

### ⊙ Steps

1 Choose a clear glass jar that can hold the amount of tea you want to make and has a working lid.

2 Fill the jar with fresh, cold water.

3 Select your tea, either bags or loose tea. Four tea bags or 4 rounded tsp. tea will make 4 c. iced tea.

4 For loose tea, either use a tea ball, tie up the tea in a little cheesecloth, or don't use anything (which means you'll have to strain the tea).

5 Put the tea bags or loose tea in the water. Close the lid.

6 Set the jar in the sun.

7 In an hour, check for strength and color. If you used loose tea without a container, strain the tea when it has finished brewing.

8 Pour the tea over ice and serve.

### ✱ Tips

Don't leave the tea in the water too long or the tea will be bitter.

If you use teabags, tie the strings together and hang the tags outside the jar.

### Ingredients

❑ clear glass jar with lid

❑ cold water

❑ 1 teabag (or 1 tsp. loose tea) per cup of water

---

## Make Lemonade 444

**Lemonade, that classic summer quencher, is easily made from scratch. The best version combines a simple sugar syrup and freshly squeezed lemon juice. Makes two servings.**

### ⊙ Steps

1 Make sugar syrup: Combine the sugar and 1 c. water in a saucepan and heat to boiling. Remove from heat, stir to dissolve sugar completely and allow to cool. (You'll only use a couple of tablespoons per serving—but this is a good item to make ahead and store in the refrigerator, covered. It keeps for weeks.)

2 For each serving, combine the juice of half a lemon, 2 tbsp. of the sugar syrup and 8 to 10 oz. cold water in a tall glass.

3 Add ice and sprigs of mint. Serve immediately.

### Ingredients

❑ 1 c. sugar

❑ 1 c. water

❑ 1 large lemon

❑ 16 to 20 oz. cold water

❑ mint sprigs

---

## Make a Dry Martini 445

**The classic, elegant martini has undergone quite a resurgence lately. Makes one martini.**

### ⊙ Steps

1 Pour gin and vermouth over ice in a cocktail shaker.

2 Shake or stir well.

### Ingredients

❑ 1¼ oz. gin

❑ dash of extra-dry vermouth ➤

3    Strain into a chilled martini glass.

4    Serve straight up with an olive. (To make this drink a Gibson, serve with a pickled onion.)

❑ 3 or 4 ice cubes

❑ cocktail olive

## 446 | Make a Cosmopolitan

A Cosmopolitan is a fruity, refreshing drink of fairly recent origin that has become a classic. Makes one serving.

### ◉ Steps

1    Wet the rim of a chilled martini glass with cranberry juice in a saucer and dip in sugar in another saucer.

2    Put ice in a cocktail shaker.

3    Add the vodka, 1 oz. cranberry juice, lime juice and Cointreau to the ice.

4    Shake twice.

5    Strain into the cocktail glass.

6    Garnish with a lemon twist.

### Ingredients

❑ 1 oz. cranberry juice plus extra for dipping glasses

❑ granulated sugar

❑ 3 or 4 ice cubes

❑ 2 oz. vodka

❑ 1 oz. lime juice

❑ dash of Cointreau

❑ lemon twist

## 447 | Mix a Frozen Margarita

Break out the chips and salsa: You're making frozen margaritas! Call 'em "blended" if you prefer. Just serve them as soon as they're made, for best results. Makes one serving.

### ◉ Steps

1    Rub a cut lime around the rim of a margarita glass and then dip the glass into a plate of coarse salt if desired.

2    Put the tequila, fresh lime juice and triple sec or Cointreau in a blender with the crushed ice.

3    Blend at medium speed for 5 to 10 seconds and pour immediately.

4    Garnish with a lime wedge.

### Ingredients

❑ cut lime

❑ coarse salt

❑ 2 oz. tequila

❑ ¾ oz. fresh lime juice

❑ 1 oz. triple sec or Cointreau

❑ 1 c. crushed ice

❑ lime wedge

## Choose a Cabernet 448

Some of the world's best red wines are made from cabernet sauvignon grapes. Follow these general rules to ease the difficulty of choosing the right cabernet.

### ⊙ Steps

1 Base your cabernet purchase on quality and price.

2 Learn about cabernet styles. Where a wine comes from is probably the most important factor in what it will be like, so look for the country of origin on the bottle.

3 Understand that the two largest regions producing cabernet today are California and France. Cabernets from France tend to express fewer of the fruity characteristics of the grape but seek a balance between the nonfruit and fruit aspects. California cabernets tend to emphasize the fruit first.

4 Realize that weather is a big reason for stylistic differences. Grapes have a difficult time ripening during any season in Bordeaux, which is France's major cabernet-producing region. On the other hand, California rarely sees a season when grapes don't fully ripen. Fully ripe grapes yield more fruity characteristics than do less ripe grapes.

5 Learn to look for subregions and producers as well as general regions. For example, "California" on a wine label is the lowest designation a wine can have. There are many good cabernets in this category, but very few great ones. Remember that the smaller and more specific the regional designation on the label, the higher the quality and price usually are.

### ✱ Tips

Australia, Italy and Chile are all making wonderful cabernets, but not at the volume of California and France.

If a wine lists a subregion, such as "North Coast" or "Central Coast," the quality should be slightly higher, with a truer cabernet profile. If a wine lists a specific region, such as "Napa County," "Oakville" or "Rutherford Bench" on the front label, the quality should be higher still. If a wine lists a specific vineyard or circumstance, such as "Morisoli Vineyard" or "Microclimate 3," on the front label, the wine should be of the highest quality and probably will have a correspondingly high price.

## Choose a Chardonnay 449

White wines made from chardonnay grapes are as popular as they are esteemed. This general outline makes it easy to choose a good one.

### ⊙ Steps

1 Take some time to learn about styles of chardonnay. The country or state where the wine is produced makes a difference, influencing everything from growing conditions to style of winemaking.

2 Compare chardonnays from different regions. You'll notice that chardonnays from France tend to express fewer of the fruity characteristics of the grape but seek a balance between the nonfruit and fruit aspects, while California chardonnays tend to emphasize the fruit and rely on much more oak influence.

3 Find out about the effects of weather on different styles of wine. Grapes have a difficult time ripening during any season in Burgundy, which is France's major chardonnay-producing region. But California rarely sees a season when grapes don't fully ripen. Riper grapes yield more fruity characteristics.

### ✱ Tip

Some outstanding Australian chardonnays can now compete with the best examples from France and California.

4    Explore subregions. A wine with a designated subregion is usually of a higher quality than one with just a general regional designation. Notice when a label says "Carneros" or "Santa Maria Valley," for instance, instead of just "California" or "North Coast."

5    Notice that some wines are labeled even more specifically, and see if you detect a higher-quality wine to go with the predictably higher price.

6    Remember the vintage, winery and any other label characteristics of the chardonnays you like, so you can find them again.

---

## 450 | Open a Wine Bottle

**It's actually pretty simple to open a bottle of wine. These steps are for a double-action, or wing, corkscrew, which has two arms (or wings) that help lever the cork out of the bottle.**

### ◎ Steps

1    Remove the top of the lead or foil capsule by cutting around the rim of the bottle with the sharp point of the corkscrew. The arms of the cork-screw will have to be raised for this step. You can also make a slit in the foil and remove the whole capsule before beginning.

2    Stand the bottle on a flat, hard surface at mid-chest level or lower. Lower the arms of the corkscrew. Holding the corkscrew as vertically and straight as possible, place the sharp end directly into the middle of the cork.

3    Securely grasp the top of the bottle and the lower end of the corkscrew with one hand.

4    With the other hand, begin turning the handle of the corkscrew clock-wise, applying an even, constant downward pressure into the cork. As the corkscrew goes into the cork, its arms will begin to rise.

5    Apply more pressure if the corkscrew will not penetrate the cork.

6    Keep turning the handle until the arms of the corkscrew are completely raised and the screw is well into the cork.

7    With one hand on each arm of the corkscrew, press the arms down. This will lift the cork out of the bottle.

8    Wrap your hand around the base of the corkscrew and lift straight up.

9    Remove the foil, if necessary.

10    Twist the cork off the corkscrew.

11    Wipe the rim of the bottle with a clean, damp towel before serving, to remove any stray pieces of cork and, more important, any lead left by the foil.

### ✳ Tips

Avoid corkscrews that penetrate the cork with a solid, ridged metal screw, which won't grip a draw cork well and can tear it apart. Instead, use a corkscrew with a metal spiral resembling a cartoon pig's tail.

If for some reason you just can't get the cork out on the first try, twist the corkscrew into a differ-ent part of the cork until the arms are raised, and repeat the process. But if you keep turning the corkscrew handle until the arms are completely raised, you shouldn't need to do this.

### Things You'll Need

❑ double-action (wing) corkscrew

##  ✓ 451 Pair Wine and Food

Choosing the right wine for a meal can strike fear into the heart of a host. But experts say that the first rule is to serve the wine that you personally feel will go best with the dish. If you're still unsure, check below for some guidelines.

### Seafood

- For grilled fish, try a full-flavored, smoky French or California Central Coast viognier or a full-bodied California chardonnay.

- For rich seafood such as salmon, consider French Chablis, a full-bodied California chardonnay or an elegant pinot noir.

- Pair delicate, subtly sauced seafood with more delicate wines: a muscadet or vouvray from France, or a California sauvignon blanc.

- For shellfish such as oysters, crisp muscadet, Chablis and sparkling wine are classic. For richer shellfish, such as lobster, try a California Central Coast chardonnay or a Chablis.

- For spicy seafood dishes, try a spicy wine such as a gewürztraminer or a German riesling or dry California sparkler.

### Poultry

- Pair delicately flavored chicken dishes with crisp, delicate white wines: a savennières from the Loire Valley of France or a pinot gris from Oregon.

- For any grilled poultry, try a medium-bodied red Burgundy or California pinot noir, or a fruity California zinfandel.

- For heavily spiced chicken or turkey, try a spicy wine, such as an off-dry pinot blanc from Alsace or a fruity gewürztraminer from California.

- For rich duck dishes, consider a rich, gamey red from Burgundy, Hermitage or Châteauneuf-du-Pape, or a high-acid wine: Italian sangiovese or a white burgundy.

- Pair game birds with earthy reds: French red burgundy or Châteauneuf-du-Pape—or a mature cabernet-based wine.

### Meat

- For grilled meats, choose intense, smoky reds: Italian Barolo or Barbaresco, French Côte-Rôtie, a big Napa Valley cabernet sauvignon or an Australian shiraz.

- Pair full-flavored dishes such as pepper steak with spicy reds such as grenache from California, Australia or Gigondas in France. Also good: Châteauneuf-du-Pape (a Rhône blend) or a peppery California zinfandel.

- For hearty, spicy stews, pick spicy syrah-based Rhône wines from Hermitage and Côte-Rôtie or California's Central Coast. California zinfandel is another option.

- Lighter meats can sometimes go well with big or off-dry whites. Try an oaky chardonnay with veal, for example, or a riesling or gewürztraminer with baked ham.

### Vegetarian

- Pair strongly flavored dishes, such as those made with garlic, with robust reds: syrah or cabernet sauvignon. Try a sangiovese for tomato-based dishes.

- For more subtle dishes, try a crisp white: a sauvignon blanc from California, New Zealand or Sancerre in France.

- For strong, mushroomy dishes, select pinot noir for its delicate, earthy aromas.

- For Mexican or Southwestern dishes with corn or green chiles, try a crisp Chablis from France or a slightly grassy California or New Zealand sauvignon blanc—as long as the dish isn't too spicy.

- For spicy dishes, such as curry, try a slightly sweet German riesling, gewürztraminer or a French rosé.

reference

## 452 | Choose Champagne

Sparkling wine—called Champagne if it comes from the Champagne region of France—is made from chardonnay, pinot noir, muscat and other grape varieties.

### ⊙ Steps

1 Learn to look for the words "methode champenoise" on the label. True Champagnes and the best sparkling wines from other regions are made by this process of double-fermentation—once in barrels or vats and a second time in bottles.

2 Learn the different types of sparkling wines, from extra-brut (the driest) to extra-dry (extra-sec), sec, demi-sec and doux (sweet). The great vintage Champagnes are found in the brut category.

3 Taste various types of sparkling wine and Champagne to get an idea of what kinds appeal most to you. One way to do this is to check the wine merchants' events calendars and attend Champagne tastings.

4 Ask friends whose taste you respect for advice and recommendations, and talk to wine merchants, too.

5 Learn the histories and winemaking styles of various sparkling wine houses in France, California and elsewhere. Remember that Germany, Spain and Italy also make sparkling wines.

### ✱ Tips

Sparkling wine terms can be confusing. "Brut," for example, is drier than "extra dry."

Only sparkling wines from the Champagne region of France are correctly called Champagnes— but the term is still casually used for all sparkling wines, especially in the United States. Some California sparkling wines will even say "Champagne" on the label.

Less expensive sparkling wines are usually made by the charmat bulk process, in which all the fermentation takes place in vats.

## 453 | Open a Champagne Bottle

It takes some skill to open a bottle of Champagne so that the bubbly ends up in the flutes and not all over your guests.

### ⊙ Steps

1 Remove the foil from the cork.

2 Angle the bottle away from everyone so that if the cork pops out, it won't injure anyone.

3 Untwist the wire restraint securing the cork.

4 Wrap the bottle's neck and cork in a dish towel.

5 Take hold of the cork with the towel and gently untwist.

6 Continue untwisting, or hold the cork in place and twist the bottle itself.

7 Slowly ease the cork out of the bottle's neck. Wait for a soft pop. Pour.

### ✱ Tips

Keep glasses nearby and ready to catch the foam.

To preserve and best appreciate the effervescence of any sparkling wine, use the tall, narrow glasses known as flutes. Old-fashioned wide Champagne glasses cause bubbles to dissipate quickly.

# Make Mulled Cider                                          454

This warm, comforting drink, spiked or unspiked, is easy to prepare and is a great finale for a holiday meal. Makes 1 quart—three or four servings.

## ◉ Steps

1  Pour the cider into a nonreactive saucepan and turn the heat to low.

2  Cut the zest from the orange with a sharp paring knife or a vegetable peeler. Try to get only the orange part. If any of the bitter white pith comes with the zest, cut this off and discard it.

3  Lightly pound the orange zest to release the aromatic oils, and place it in the cider.

4  Place all remaining ingredients in the cider and simmer over low heat, stirring occasionally.

5  When the cider is very hot and has begun to steam, it's ready to serve. Taste it at this point to make sure that it's sweet enough and there is enough seasoning. Add more if necessary.

6  Shut off the heat and ladle the cider into mugs.

## ✳ Tips

Apple juice can be substituted for apple cider.

Always use only a stainless steel, heatproof glass, ceramic or non-stick pot to make the mulled cider.

## Ingredients

- ❑ 1 qt. apple cider
- ❑ 1 orange
- ❑ ½ c. dried cranberries
- ❑ ⅔ c. honey
- ❑ 6 to 8 whole cloves
- ❑ ½ tsp. vanilla extract
- ❑ 1 cinnamon stick
- ❑ ½ c. brandy (optional)

# Make Eggnog                                                455

"Nog" derives from an old English term for strong ale or liquor. However, this version can be made plain or spiked. Makes eight small servings.

## ◉ Steps

1  Heat the milk, cloves and peppercorns over low heat in a nonreactive saucepan until the mixture steams and is very hot.

2  Meanwhile, place the egg yolks, nutmeg, sugar and vanilla in a bowl and beat thoroughly.

3  When the milk mixture is hot, shut off the heat and strain out the cloves and peppercorns.

4  Start whisking the egg yolk mixture vigorously, and slowly ladle about ¼ c. milk into it.

5  Switch the whisk to the saucepan and whisk the hot milk while slowly pouring the egg/milk mixture into the saucepan.

6  Return the saucepan to low heat and stir continuously with a wooden spoon or heatproof flexible spatula. Make sure to stir the mixture off the bottom so the portion in contact with the pan doesn't overcook. The mixture will thicken as it cooks.

## ✳ Tips

If rum extract is not available, substitute ½ tsp. orange extract.

To spike this eggnog recipe, add a jigger (1 to 2 oz.) of rum, brandy or whiskey per serving.

## Ingredients

- ❑ 2 c. whole milk
- ❑ 5 or 6 cloves
- ❑ 10 white peppercorns
- ❑ 6 egg yolks
- ❑ ½ tsp. nutmeg
- ❑ ¾ c. sugar
- ❑ 1 tsp. vanilla extract ➤

7   Test for doneness by dipping the spoon or spatula in the mixture and dragging your finger across the back of it; the eggnog is done when your finger leaves a path through the thickened milk and the milk doesn't run. (This might take as long as 20 minutes. Keep the heat low and don't rush it, or you might curdle the eggs.)

8   Pour the mixture into a mixing bowl. Stir in the remaining extracts and the half-and-half.

9   Chill thoroughly before serving.

☐ .1 tsp. rum extract

☐ ½ tsp. almond extract

☐ 1 c. half-and-half

## 456 | Set the Table

Whether your dinner is very formal or not so formal, there are a few basic guidelines to setting a table.

### ⊙ Steps

1   Figure out how many guests will be attending. If several children will be in attendance, consider having a children's table. If you would like to include the children at the main table, consider booster chairs if the children are small.

2   Determine where everyone should sit. For convenience, the cook may want to sit near the kitchen door. Parents should sit next to their children. If there is a male guest, he is traditionally seated on the hostess's right. A female guest is traditionally seated on the host's right. For large parties, determine who would interact best with each other. Some hosts like to alternate men and women, but this isn't necessary. You may want to use place cards to avoid everyone's rushing for a seat at the last minute.

3   Decide if you will use a tablecloth. If the tablecloth is damask, you will need a pad under it to prevent it from slipping. Also, the middle crease should be arranged so that it runs in a straight and unwavering line down the center of the table from head to foot. The tablecloth should hang down about a foot and a half for a seated dinner. For a buffet table, it should hang down to the floor.

4   Once you've put the tablecloth, if you're using one, on the table, you can set it. Begin by folding napkins and placing them in the center of each diner's place.

5   Place the large dinner fork to the left of the napkin and the smaller salad fork to the left of the dinner fork.

6   Place a salad plate to the left of the forks. The dinner plate should not be on the table when guests sit down.

7   Place a knife to the right of the napkin. For poultry or meat, you might want to use steak knives.

8   If serving soup or dessert, you will need one spoon for each. A small dessert spoon (or fork) may be placed horizontally across the top of the setting. Place the soup spoon to the right of the knife. (You can also wait and bring the dessert spoons or forks out just before dessert.)

### Things You'll Need

☐ tablecloth

☐ napkins

☐ silverware

☐ china

☐ water goblets

☐ wineglasses

☐ coffee cups and saucers

9  Place a bread plate with a butter knife (if you have them) about 2 inches above the forks, with the knife across the top of the plate.

10  Place a water goblet about 2 inches above the knife. Place wineglasses to the right of the goblet and slightly closer to the dinner guest.

11  If you will serve coffee, the cup and saucer should go to the right of the glasses, with a coffee spoon on the right side of the saucer.

## Eat at a Formal Dinner     **457**

The silverware is placed on the table in the order in which it will be used, starting with the outside pieces. Let this be your guide as you work your way through a meal.

### ◉ Steps

1  Put your napkin on your lap. Unfold it, but don't spread it.

2  Use the outside fork for the first course, unless soup is served—then use the outside spoon.

3  When you are finished with the course, place your fork at the right end of your plate, on a slight diagonal. This signifies that you are finished. For a soup course or another course that uses a wide bowl, place the spoon on the plate below the bowl. If a shallow bowl is used, place the spoon on the bowl in the same manner as a fork on a plate.

4  Continue by using the new outside fork. If the course requires a knife, use the knife farthest to the right.

5  Use the fork closest to your plate to eat your entrée. The spoon or fork at your plate's head is for dessert.

6  Drink water from the largest glass at your setting.

7  Drink red wine from the big-bowled glass; drink white wine from the narrower-bowled glass.

8  If a little bowl of water is on the table at your place, or appears with the dessert, it is a fingerbowl. Wash the tips of your fingers in it. Dry them with your napkin.

9  Place your napkin on your chair if you leave the table temporarily. Place it next to your plate (don't fold it) when you leave the table.

### ✻ Tips

It is proper etiquette for the guests to wait for the host or hostess to unfold the napkin and begin eating before they do the same.

If you're uncertain about how or when to use a certain utensil, watch others and do what the majority of them do.

When eating bread, tear off pieces with your fingers—don't cut it or take bites from larger pieces. Also, butter the piece you've just torn right before you eat it; don't butter the whole piece first.

To eat soup, dip the spoon into the soup, then remove it in a motion away from your body, not toward it. Quietly sip the soup off the side of the spoon, rather than placing the whole spoon in your mouth.

## 458 | Whistle

If singing is not your biggest strength, try whistling your favorite tunes. Follow these steps and practice until you can whistle with comfort and ease.

### ☉ Steps

1 Purse your lips into a tiny O shape, leaving a small opening for air.

2 Place the tip of your tongue behind your bottom teeth or against your inside bottom gums.

3 Gently expel air through your mouth.

4 Adjust your tongue position and the small O opening formed by your lips until you hear a note.

5 Once you can sound one note, experiment with your tongue position and the strength of your breath to produce different notes.

6 Practice!

### ✳ Tips

Try not to blow too hard at first; it's much easier to whistle with a small amount of air.

You may find it easier to produce a strong, pure note if you wet your lips first.

## 459 | Waltz

The waltz, which evolved from a German folk dance, is danced to a triple beat. It's popular throughout Europe and the United States, especially at formal social events.

### ☉ Steps

1 Get into position by facing your partner. If you are the leader, place your right hand on your partner's waist slightly around the back and extend your left hand to your side with your elbow bent and your palm raised, facing her. With that hand, grasp your partner's right hand in a loose grip, and make sure your partner has her left hand on your right shoulder, with her elbow bent. She should mirror your movements.

2 On the first beat, step forward gracefully with your left foot. Your partner should follow your lead by doing the opposite of what you do on each beat—in this case, stepping back with her right foot.

3 On the second beat, step forward and to the right with your right foot. Trace an upside-down letter L in the air with your foot as you do this.

4 Shift your weight to your right foot. Keep your left foot stationary.

5 On the third beat, slide your left foot over to your right and stand with your feet together.

6 On the fourth beat, step back with your right foot.

7 On the fifth beat, step back and to the left with your left foot, this time tracing a backward L. Shift your weight to your left foot.

8 On the final beat, slide your right foot toward your left until your feet are together; now you're ready to start over with your left foot.

9 Repeat steps 2 through 8 turning your and your partner's orientation slowly to the left by slightly varying the placement of your feet.

### ✳ Tips

It helps to count as you go—"one, two, three; one, two, three"—placing the emphasis on the "one" as you count.

Practice to a slow waltz until you become comfortable with the moves.

# Tango **460**

Born in the brothels of Argentina, the tango is synonymous with passion. Although the dance is relatively free-form, you can do a lot with two basic moves: the walking step and the rock step.

## ⊙ Steps

1 Face your partner and stand closer together than you would in most other ballroom dances—close enough that your torsos are touching.

2 If you're the leader, place your right hand on the middle of your partner's lower back. Extend your left hand out to your side with your arm bent and grasp your partner's right hand in a loose grip. Your partner should place her left hand on your right shoulder and place her right hand lightly in your palm with her right elbow bent.

3 On the first beat, walk forward slowly with your left foot, placing down your heel first and then your toes. Your partner will mirror each of your movements on every beat throughout the dance—in this case, moving her right foot backward, landing her toes and then her heel.

4 On the second beat, step forward slowly with your right foot so that it moves past your left. You should feel like you are slinking forward.

5 On the third beat, step forward quickly with your left foot, then immediately slide your right foot quickly to the right side and shift your weight to that foot.

6 On the fourth beat, bring your left foot slowly to your right, leaving your left leg slightly bent as your feet come together. Your weight should still be on your right foot.

7 Now, shift your weight to your left foot and do a right forward rock step: While making a half-turn clockwise, step forward quickly on your right foot, and then quickly shift your weight back to your left foot. With your right foot, slowly step forward to complete the half turn.

8 Bring your feet together, bring your left foot up next to your right and repeat steps 3 through 7.

**✳ Tips**

Keep in mind that your feet barely leave the floor as you dance.

This isn't a subtle way to meet people.

# Salsa **461**

Listen to the rhythm of the music as you learn this popular Latin dance. You can learn the basic salsa steps in less than an hour, and sashay all over the dance floor before you know it.

## ⊙ Steps

1 Get in position by facing your partner. If you are the leader, place your right hand on your partner's waist, slightly around the back. Extend your left arm diagonally to chest height with your elbow bent at a right angle and your palm raised. Grasp your partner's right hand in a loose grip; your partner's left hand should be on your right shoulder.

2 On the first beat, step forward with your left foot. Your partner will mirror each of your movements throughout the dance; for example, on the first beat she will step backward with her right foot.

**✳ Tips**

You can add more complicated moves once you've got the basic salsa step down.

Act sassy while dancing, but don't use exaggerated hip movement. That sexy swing will come naturally as you let yourself feel the rhythm.

3  Step in place with your right foot on the second beat.

4  Step back with your left foot on the third beat so that you are back in the starting position, and hold in place for the fourth beat.

5  Step back with your right foot on the fifth beat.

6  Step in place with your left foot on the sixth beat.

7  Step forward with your right foot on the seventh beat so that you are back in the starting position, and hold for the eighth beat.

8  Repeat, starting at step 2.

Some salsa clubs offer free or inexpensive introductory classes or specials on certain nights of the week.

## 462 | Swing Dance

There are several different styles of swing, including East Coast, West Coast, Savoy swing and the lindy. This six-count basic step is East Coast swing style.

### ⊙ Steps

1  Get in position by facing your partner. If you are the leader, turn very slightly to your left and place your right hand in the middle of your part-ner's back. Extend your left hand at hip level with your palm up, grasp-ing your partner's right hand in a loose grip. Your partner should place her left hand on your right shoulder and mirror your movements through-out the dance.

2  Do a triple step on counts one and two: Quickly make a small step on your left foot, then your right, and then back to your left. (Your partner will do the reverse.) You may want to move slightly to the left during this step, but it's more a shifting of weight back and forth than actual steps. Say "triple step" to get the rhythm.

3  Do another triple step on counts three and four, starting with your right foot, this time moving slightly to the right if you like.

4  Place your left foot behind your right on the fifth count, rocking back on the ball of your left foot. This should open up a space between you and your partner as she mirrors your movements, rocking back on the ball of her right foot.

5  On the sixth count, bring your weight back to your right foot into the original starting position while simultaneously launching back into the triple step as described in steps 2 through 4.

### ✱ Tips

Start out to slower music while you're learning the steps, and count the beats as follows: "one-and-two, three-and-four, five, six."

Yell out, "Yeah, yeah, go Daddy-O!" occasionally.

Some swing clubs offer free or inexpensive introductory classes or specials on certain nights of the week.

## Write a Sonnet

The sonnet, a 14-line poem, has two main types: English (or Shakespearean) and Italian (or Petrarchan). Here, we present the format for writing a Shakespearean sonnet.

### ◎ Steps

1   Select the subject matter for your sonnet. Themes have often focused on love or philosophy, but modern sonnets can cover almost any topic.

2   Divide the theme of your sonnet into two sections. In the first section you will present the situation or thought to the reader; in the second section you can present some sort of conclusion or climax.

3   Compose your first section as three quatrains—that is, three stanzas of four lines each. Write the three quatrains with an *a-b-a-b, c-d-c-d, e-f-e-f* rhyme scheme, where each letter stands for a line of the sonnet and the last words of all lines with the same letter rhyme with each other. Most sonnets employ the meter of iambic pentameter (see Tips), as seen in these three quatrains from Shakespeare's "Sonnet 30":

*When to the sessions of sweet silent thought* **(a)**
*I summon up remembrance of things past,* **(b)**
*I sigh the lack of many a thing I sought,* **(a)**
*And with old woes new wail my dear time's waste:* **(b)**
*Then can I drown an eye, unused to flow,* **(c)**
*For precious friends hid in death's dateless night,* **(d)**
*And weep afresh love's long since canceled woe,* **(c)**
*And moan the expense of many a vanished sight:* **(d)**
*Then can I grieve at grievances foregone,* **(e)**
*And heavily from woe to woe tell o'er* **(f)**
*The sad account of fore-bemoanéd moan,* **(e)**
*Which I new pay as if not paid before.* **(f)**

4   Compose the last section as a couplet—two rhyming lines of poetry. This time, use a *g-g* rhyme scheme, where the last words of the two lines rhyme with each other. We refer once more to "Sonnet 30":

*But if the while I think on thee, dear friend,* **(g)**
*All losses are restored and sorrows end.* **(g)**

### ✱ Tips

An iamb is a type of metrical "foot" used in a poem. It is composed of two syllables, with the accent on the second syllable. Examples: "to-*day*" or "en-*rage*." Pentameter means that there are five metrical feet per line. Iambic pentameter means that each line of the poem consists of five iambic feet, or 10 total syllables. An example from Shakespeare: "Good pilgrim you do wrong your hand too much."

In the Italian sonnet, use an *a-b-b-a-a-b-b-a* rhyme scheme for the first section (called the "octave"), and a rhyme scheme of *c-d-e-c-d-e* or *c-d-c-d-c-d* in the second section (called the "sestet").

## Write a Short Story

The model described here is the pyramid plot: The upward slope establishes setting and characters and builds tension; the tip is the climax; and the downward slope is the resolution.

### ◎ Steps

1   Choose a narrative point of view. You can write your story as if you were one of the characters (first person), as a detached narrator who presents just one character's thoughts and observations (third-person limited), or

### ✱ Tips

There are many possible variations of this model, all of which allow for perfectly good short stories.

as a detached narrator who presents the thoughts and observations of several characters (third-person omniscient). A first-person point of view will refer to the central character as "I" instead of "he" or "she."

2   Create a protagonist, or main character. This should be the most developed and usually the most sympathetic character in your story.

3   Create a problem, or conflict, for your protagonist. The conflict of your story should take one of five basic forms: person vs. person, person vs. himself or herself, person vs. nature, person vs. society, or person vs. God or fate. If you choose a person vs. person conflict, create an antagonist to serve as the person your protagonist must contend with.

4   Establish believable characters and settings, with vivid descriptions and dialogue, to create a story that your readers will care about.

5   Build the story's tension by having the protagonist make several failed attempts to solve or overcome the problem. (You may want to skip this step for shorter stories.)

6   Create a crisis that serves as the last chance for the protagonist to solve his or her problem.

7   Resolve the tension by having the protagonist succeed through his or her own intelligence, creativity, courage or other positive attributes. This is usually referred to as the story's climax.

8   Extend this resolution phase, if you like, by reflecting on the action of the story and its significance to the characters or society.

Keep your language concise, specific and active. For example, write "Steve ate the apple" instead of "The fruit was eaten by someone."

---

## 465  Write a Limerick

There once was a fellow named Larry,
Who sought to write limericks for Mary.
Perplexed, our dear poet
With eHow's help wrote it—
And Mary he later did marry.

### ◉ Steps

1   Prepare to write five lines of verse. If you're stumped, try starting off your limerick with the traditional "There once was a ..."

2   Create the following stress pattern in lines one, two and five: da-*da* da-da-*da* da-da-*da*-da. For example, "There *once* was a *fel*-low named *Jer*-ry...." You can omit the last, unstressed syllable if you prefer.

3   Create the following stress pattern in lines three and four: da-*da* da-da-*da*-da. For example, "Per-*plexed*, our dear *po*-et." As before, you have the option of omitting the last syllable.

4   Make sure your limerick's rhyme scheme is *a-a-b-b-a*. In other words, the first, second and fifth lines all rhyme with one another; the third and fourth lines rhyme with each other.

5   Exploit puns and wordplay.

### ✳ Tips

The racier, the better. Limericks are notoriously bawdy and obnoxious.

The last line should deliver a punch, be it surprising, funny or naughty.

## Paint a Landscape With Watercolors 466

Painting outdoors is a peaceful way to enjoy a beautiful day. Keep a backpack full of painting supplies and you can be ready to go whenever the inspiration strikes.

### ⊙ Steps

1 Tape a piece of watercolor paper to a heavy piece of cardboard using masking tape. Run the tape along the entire edges of all four sides of the paper.

2 Use a soft lead pencil to begin your painting with a simple sketch.

3 Locate and draw the horizon line, which is the line formed where the sky and the land meet.

4 Sketch in the background objects: hills, mountains, distant trees. Background objects are typically smaller and have less detail than objects in the foreground.

5 Sketch the objects in the foreground. These objects will be larger and more detailed.

6 Use clear water and a flat brush to dampen the sky area of your picture.

7 If you're painting on a sunny day, use a medium round brush to paint a blue sky over the sky area while the paper is damp. This is applying what is called a "wash."

8 Create clouds by blotting the sky with a crumpled tissue while the paint is still wet.

9 Use the same wash technique to paint in large areas of background color such as hills, mountains, water and grass.

10 Wait until the watercolor paper is dry or almost dry to paint details; your paintbrush should also be nearly dry. This technique, which gives you more control over the paint flow, is called "dry brush."

11 Paint in details using a small round brush. Mix paint with more water to create softer, lighter hues. Use less water to create darker, more vivid colors and harder edges.

12 Allow your finished painting to dry completely, then carefully peel away the masking tape from the edges of the paper. This will leave a nice white border around the edge of your painting.

### ✳ Tips

Consider buying a watercolor block, which is a pad of watercolor paper that is glued on all four sides. A watercolor block is rigid, which makes it easy to take anywhere so you can do without a drawing board.

Postcard-size watercolor pads are available in many stores, and they're fun to take on trips. Friends will appreciate receiving a hand-painted landscape postcard from you.

### Things You'll Need

❑ cardboard

❑ masking tape

❑ watercolor paper

❑ pencils and erasers

❑ watercolor paints

❑ water and container

❑ watercolor brushes

❑ facial tissue

## Finger Paint 467

Finger painting is an easy way to show off your artistic talents, it's great for both the beginner and the advanced artist, and it has always been very popular with kids.

### ⊙ Steps

1 Gather your supplies together: finger painting paper, butcher paper or thick construction paper, and tempera paint, which is most commonly used. However, almost any nontoxic water-based paint will work.

### ✳ Tips

To reduce the paint's chipping or cracking, avoid leaving thick concentrations of paint on your paper.

2   Select your work area. A large, smooth, flat surface that is easy to clean is best. Cover it with newspaper or plastic, and wear old clothes or an apron that you don't mind getting dirty.

3   Lay out your paper. Using a brush, sponge or even your hand, dampen the surface of your paper with water. This smooths out the paper and makes it easier to spread paint.

4   Pour the paint into baking tins or bowls.

5   Use your fingers, a spoon or a brush to scoop a generous amount of paint onto the paper.

6   Smear the globs of paint around with your fingers to create your painting. Don't be timid when finger painting; lots of bright colors and bold strokes are the keys to great results. Use your fingers, hands and even feet for effect.

7   If your paint begins to dry before you're finished, add water to keep the paint fluid and easy to work with.

8   Sign your masterpiece when you're finished and let it dry on a flat surface. It's better not to hang your picture for drying, as the paint may run.

9   Clean up with soap and water.

You can also use oil paint with your fingers, though it's more difficult to clean up and not good for beginners or kids. Wear latex gloves when finger painting with oil paint, since it is toxic.

Sprinkle glitter on your painting before it dries.

### ⚠ Warning

Use nontoxic paints when painting with children.

### Things You'll Need

❑ finger painting paper

❑ butcher or construction paper

❑ tempera or other water-based paint

---

## 468 | Start a Collection

An informed collector is a happy collector. Know what you're buying and the best price before you purchase the item.

### ⊙ Steps

1   Figure out what kind of items or genre of items you are interested in collecting, or determine if you already have three or more of a certain object. You may have begun a collection without knowing it.

2   Subscribe to collecting magazines or newsletters that are devoted to your object(s) of interest.

3   Purchase books and do the research required to become an expert in your subject of interest. It will save you money in the long run because you'll recognize bargains and rip-offs when you see them.

4   Allocate a space in which to store the collection. It's best if this space is easily viewed so that you can enjoy the fruits of your obsession. Purchase display cases or shelves if necessary.

5   Set a budget so you don't spend too much money on the collection.

6   Use the Internet or newsletters to form a loose network with other collectors and sellers.

7   Thoroughly research each item before you purchase it.

8   Keep a ledger listing your contacts, the items in your collection and the date and cost of purchase.

### ✳ Tips

Monitor online auction sites, such as eBay, to find out general price ranges and typical rates.

Let family and friends know that you are starting a collection. It will help them come up with gift ideas for you.

Many collections can be assembled or started without making special purchases with items such as matchbooks, bottle caps, seashells or pinecones.

## Find the Books You Loved as a Child 469

New books get published every year, but the ones you loved as a child are like comfort food. It's natural to want the kids you love to have the books that were your childhood favorites.

### ◎ Steps

1 Remember as much about the books as you can. Titles and authors' names are, of course, exceedingly useful, but any tidbit, including the setting (Maine? San Francisco?), the main character's name (Betsy? Harriet? Tom?) or the theme (a magic garden? a swan that can play the trumpet?) can come in handy. Make notes as you mull it over.

2 Ask the librarian at your child's school or at the children's desk in your public library for help, especially with books you don't remember well. Most children's librarians have not only a deep passion for children's literature, but also an encyclopedic memory for plots and characters.

3 Frequent garage sales, especially in turnover neighborhoods (those suburban blocks that were once chock-full of children). People are having fewer kids and having them later, and would-be grandparents who are moving to Florida may decide it's more important that the books be read than that they be saved for a particular child.

4 Find out if there's someone in your local used bookstore who specializes in children's books. It's a common passion, and these people tend to be knowledgeable. Some will even keep wish lists and notify you when they find the book you're seeking.

5 Keep an eye out for library book sales. Many collectors look askance at "ex libris" books (books that were once in a library) because they're less than pristine. Still, they're often in surprisingly good condition—well loved, but not destroyed.

6 Check out online services. Most of the larger online stores offer book-search services, while sites that specialize in used and out-of-print books (such as Bibliofind.com and Alibris.com) link networks of small book dealers all over the United States and even abroad.

### ✱ Tips

Memory can play tricks on you, and even reference books can contain typographical errors. Whether you're searching in reference books or online, check a few different spellings if you can't find what you're looking for.

Make this a family project. Ask your family and your same-aged friends to help you jog your memory.

## Make Decorative Paper 470

Give scrap paper a new life by blending it with water to make decorative paper. You will need a fine screen and a tub larger than the screen to do this project.

### ◎ Steps

1 Gather a pile of scrap paper and tear it into small bits.

2 Boil water, remove it from heat, and soak the paper bits in the hot water for 2 to 3 minutes. The ratio should be two parts water to one part paper.

3 Blend the water and paper bits in a blender. Run the blender for a few seconds at a time until the mixture is a very fine pulp.

4 Pour the mixture into a large plastic tub (a baby bathtub works well) or a large baking pan.

### ✱ Tips

If the mixture is too thick, add more water to thin it out. If your mixture is too thin, add more paper bits. Then blend again.

In place of glitter you can add sequins, slivers of aluminum foil, flower petals or waterproof ink to the pulp. Add these items to the pulp mixture in the tub before you dip in the screen.

5   Use a large spoon or your hands to stir the mixture until the pulp is evenly distributed in the tub or pan.

6   Repeat with more scrap paper until the mixture in the tub is deep enough to dip the screen into.

7   Add some glitter to the tub and stir again until the glitter is evenly distributed throughout the mixture.

8   Submerge the screen in the mixture, dipping it below the mixture at a shallow angle and then holding it in a horizontal position.

9   Use your hands to distribute the pulp on the screen evenly and then slowly lift the screen up and out of the tub, keeping it horizontal.

10  Hold the screen over the tub until water stops dripping from the bottom (this should take less than a minute). Gently turn it from side to side to make sure all excess water drains out.

11  Quickly flip the screen over and lay it pulp side down on a short stack of lint-free towels.

12  Gently lift the screen off the layer of pulp so that the pulp remains on the towels in one piece.

13  Place another stack of towels on top of the pulp layer to blot the pulp.

14  Press firmly on the stack with your hands or use a rolling pin to squeeze out the water.

15  Carefully transfer the pulp to a new, dry stack of towels if the original stack becomes soaked. Continue blotting until hardly any water comes out when the stack is pressed.

16  Gently remove the sheet of paper and place it on a flat, dry surface to air-dry overnight.

17  Once the paper is dried, use scissors to trim the edges as desired. Some people prefer to leave the edges naturally rough.

You can use stacks of newspapers to blot the paper instead of stacks of towels; however, the ink in the newspapers may run into the pulp.

### Things You'll Need

❏ fine window screen

❏ plastic tub or baking pan

❏ scrap paper

❏ blender

❏ glitter

❏ lint-free towels

❏ rolling pin

❏ scissors

---

## 471 Dry Flowers

Dried flowers are wonderful for year-round floral arrangements. You can dry flowers by hanging them or by placing them in a box of desiccant, which better preserves the blossoms.

### ⊙ Steps

#### Air-Dry Method

1   Pick flowers when their blossoms are half-open, and leave the flowers on their stems.

2   Strip the lower leaves from the stems; don't remove the leaves closest to the flower on the stem.

3   Gather 8 to 10 stems together, and tie them with string or secure them with rubber bands.

4   Hang the bundle upside down in a well-ventilated area. After 10 days (in warm weather), the flowers should be dry. When drying multiple bundles of flowers, leave space between them to ensure thorough drying.

### ✳ Tips

Make floral arrangements out of dried flowers or use them in crafts projects.

Rapid drying in a warm, dry and brightly lit place (near a sunny window, for example) will provide bright blossoms; slower drying in a more humid spot (for instance, near a water heater) will produce more muted colors.

You can find borax in the laundry section of the grocery store.

## Box Method

1  Line a box with fine, dry sand, borax or silica gel.

2  Place the whole heads of the flowers face down in the box. Dahlias, roses and zinnias dry well using this method.

3  Sift more sand or borax onto the flower heads until they are covered.

4  Place the box in a warm, dry area for two weeks.

### Things You'll Need

❑ flowers

❑ string or rubber bands

❑ box

❑ dry sand or borax

---

# Play Charades                                                           472

Charades, believed to have originated in 18th-century France, is a classic party game that's fun for all ages. You'll need at least six people to play.

## ◉ Steps

### The Game

1  Divide the group into two teams of at least three people each. Decide on a time limit—between 3 and 5 minutes—for each round.

2  Have each team write titles of books, TV shows or movies, or other phrases (see Tips), on individual scraps of paper, then fold them to hide the writing. Each team then places its scraps in a separate bowl.

3  When it's your turn, close your eyes and pick a piece of paper from the other team's bowl. Read its contents to yourself.

4  Without speaking, help your team try to guess the title by giving signals using appropriate gestures (see the following section).

5  Stop when your team guesses the title or time runs out.

6  Sit down and watch the other team draw a title and act it out.

7  When it's your team's turn again, watch as one of your teammates draws a new title out of the bowl; now it's your turn to try to guess what your teammate is acting out.

8  Record how many clues it takes each team to guess correct titles (or add up the number of correct guesses per team) to determine the winner.

### The Clues

1  To indicate a book title, put your hands together as if you are praying, then unfold them flat.

2  To indicate a film title, form an O with one hand to pantomime a lens while cranking the other hand as if you are operating an old-fashioned movie camera.

3  Indicate a television show by making a box with your fingers.

4  Make quotation marks in the air with your fingers to indicate a quote.

5  Pose like Napoleon (with a hand on your chest and the tips of your fingers tucked partway into your shirt) to indicate a famous person.

### ✳ Tips

In addition to book, movie and TV titles, popular charades topics include well-known quotations, song titles and names of famous people, rock bands and places.

Arrange other signals with your partners before the game, if you wish, but remember that it's against the rules to arrange an "alphabet code" to act out the spelling of a word.

It is improper to point to people or objects in the room for hints.

6  Pull on your ear to indicate that the word being guessed sounds like another word.

7  Hold up fingers to indicate the number of words in the title, quotation or name; hold up a number of fingers again to indicate which word you want your teammates to guess.

8  Hold fingers against your arm to indicate the number of syllables in a particular word.

9  Pinch your thumb and forefinger or open them up to indicate a short or long word.

10  Confirm that your partners have guessed a word correctly by tapping your index finger on your nose and pointing to the person or persons who made the correct guess.

11  Wipe your hand across your forehead to let your teammates know that they are getting hot.

12  Cross your arms and shiver to let them know that they are getting cold.

## 473 | Play 20 Questions

This is a terrific way to occupy children on a rainy day or during a long car ride. One player thinks of an object and the other players ask questions to determine what that object is.

### ◎ Steps

1  Choose one person to start. This person must think of an object. To make the game easier, he or she can classify the object as animal, vegetable or mineral.

2  Have another player ask a question about the object that can be answered yes or no.

3  The person who has the object in mind should answer the question with a simple yes or no.

4  After hearing the answer, the questioner is allowed to guess the object. The players are allowed to ask a total of 20 questions.

5  If the guess is correct, the winning questioner now thinks of a new object. If the answer is incorrect, another player is allowed to ask a yes or no question.

### ✱ Tips

If the players use up their 20 questions without guessing the object, the player with the object in mind reveals it and thinks of a new one.

This game works best with four or fewer players.

## 474 | Play Checkers

Checkers has been around for centuries, but that doesn't mean it's just for nice old guys hanging out in the park. Check it out.

### ◎ Steps

1  Flip a coin to decide who will play red and who will play black. Whoever wins the toss chooses. The red player will make the opening move.

### ✱ Tips

If one of your checkers is in a position to jump, you must jump; the alternative is to forfeit the

2 On the red player's side, place one red checker on each black square in the first three rows of squares.

3 On the black player's side, place one black checker on each black square in the first three rows of squares.

4 Make sure there are 12 staggered checkers on each side of the board with two empty rows in the middle.

5 The red player begins by moving one red checker forward diagonally onto an adjacent free black square.

6 Take turns moving one checker, one square forward diagonally, at a time.

7 "Jump" your opponent's checker if it is in a square directly diagonal and adjacent to your own checker and there is a free square on the other side. To do this, move your checker over your opponent's checker and place it on the opposite square. Take possession of your opponent's jumped checker by removing it from the board.

8 If you jump a checker and land in a position to jump another of the other player's checkers, jump that checker as well during the same turn.

9 "King" one of your checkers when it reaches the farthest row from your starting side (your opponent's back row). Signify a kinged checker by having your opponent stack one of your jumped checkers on top of the kinged checker. Kinged checkers can move both forward and backward, but still can only move diagonally to adjacent black squares, one square at a time. Only a kinged checker can move backward and forward.

10 The first player to remove all of the opponent's checkers from the board by jumping them wins the game.

game. If more than one of your checkers is in a jumping position, you may choose which one will jump.

Red and black are the most common colors for checkers. Other popular color pairs are black and white (white goes first) and white and red (red goes first).

These rules are for standard American checkers. Other variations exist.

---

## Do a Crossword Puzzle 475

Crossword puzzles provide hours of wordplay enjoyment, and they also increase your vocabulary. With some practice and a few hints, you'll be scribbling down the answers with ease.

### ⊙ Steps

1 Use a pencil so that you can erase mistakes easily.

2 Fill in obvious answers, both across and down.

3 Look at across questions and down questions again to see if anything new pops up—an easy answer you didn't notice before, or one that has now become clear because of the letters that are filled in.

4 Look for multiples in clues, such as "friends." Put an *S* in the last position, which may help you figure out adjacent words.

5 Pay attention to clues in the past tense. Try putting *ED* in the last two positions. (This doesn't always work, however.)

6 Familiarize yourself with frequently used—and often obscure—little words that crossword assemblers need to fill in niches here and there.

7 If you're completely stumped, put the puzzle down for a while and try again later. Or look at the clue another way—for example, maybe "Getting to first base" refers to romance rather than baseball.

### ✱ Tips

If the clue contains an abbreviation, then the answer is also an abbreviation.

A question mark at the end of a clue means the answer is somehow sneaky or a pun. For example, one *New York Times* puzzle creator, Manny Nosowsky, gave "Where a person uses an ID to get mail?" as a clue to the answer "Idaho."

The highly esteemed *New York Times* puzzles are easiest on Monday and get progressively harder throughout the week, with a larger puzzle on Sunday.

Helpful aids include a crossword dictionary, an atlas and an almanac.

## 476 | Play Darts

If you're competitive, think about mastering this game in the family room den before braving the scene at the local watering hole. Here's how to get started.

### ⊙ Steps

1 Hang the dartboard so that the center is 5 feet 8 inches from the floor.

2 Mark the throwing line, called the "oche" (rhymes with "hockey"), with nonskid tape. The line should be 7 feet, 9¼ inches from the face of the dartboard (not the wall), according to the World Darts Federation.

3 Make sure the tape mark lies so that the front edge is the actual line. In other words, a player may step on the tape, but not past it.

4 Give each player or team three darts, and determine who throws first by having each player or team representative throw one dart. The player or team whose dart is closest to the center, or bull's-eye, gets to go first.

5 Warm up, as competitive dart players do, by alternating throws until each person has thrown nine darts.

6 Once the game begins, take your turn by throwing your three darts.

7 Add up the score. Each part of the board has a number, and that is the dart's score.

8 Count a dart that misses the board completely as a throw. The score for that dart is zero.

9 Remove your darts and allow the other player to throw.

10 Alternate until the game is over. There are numerous dart games, including the simple one in which players throw five sets, and whoever has the highest score wins.

### ✳ Tip

Another popular game is to have each team begin with a set number of points (such as 301 or 501) and then try to reduce its score to exactly zero. Whatever number you hit with the dart is subtracted from the total. The team that hits zero first wins.

## 477 | Play Jacks

True classics never die, and this childhood game doesn't require much to keep it thriving: a little bouncy ball, at least 10 jacks, and a hard, level playing surface.

### ⊙ Steps

1 Sit on the ground (blacktop, sidewalk or floor) unless you're playing on a table, in which case standing is usually better than sitting on a chair.

2 Toss the 10 jacks gently out onto the playing surface.

3 Toss the ball into the air with your throwing hand.

4 While the ball is in the air, pick up 1 jack using only your throwing hand.

5 Catch the ball in your throwing hand before the ball hits the ground.

6 Repeat steps 3, 4 and 5 until you've picked up all 10 jacks.

7 Toss the 10 jacks out onto the playing surface again.

### ✳ Tips

Another way to play is to bounce the ball on the playing surface rather than throw it in the air, and try to pick up as many jacks as you can before the ball bounces again.

There are ways to make the game more difficult, such as not touching jacks you don't pick up and placing the jacks you do pick up in your other hand before catching the ball.

8  Toss the ball into the air, and now pick up 2 jacks each time and catch the ball before it hits the ground.

9  Continue tossing the ball, picking up jacks and catching the ball—increasing the number of jacks you pick up when the ball is in the air until you pick up all 10 at one time.

10  It's the other player's turn when you don't pick up the correct number of jacks or you miss the ball.

11  Begin where you left off when it's your turn again. If you were picking up 3 jacks at a time, toss the 10 jacks onto the playing surface and pick up 3 each time.

12  Declare a winner if you want to when you or your friend succeeds at "onesies" through "tensies" (1 jack through 10 jacks).

**⚠ Warning**

Keep the jacks and ball away from small children and pets—the small pieces could cause choking.

## Play Marbles 478

Although most of us think of marbles as an old-fashioned pastime, the game is still fun for kids of all ages and is played around the globe.

### ⊙ Steps

1  Draw a circle 2 to 3 feet wide. Use chalk on asphalt or concrete, a stick in dirt, or a string on carpet or tile.

2  Select your shooter and place any marbles you wish to play with as targets inside the circle; the other players do the same. Shooters are designated marbles used to knock targets out of the ring. Your shooter should be larger than the other marbles so it's powerful enough to do its job. It should also look different from other marbles so you can distinguish it from them easily.

3  Take your turn when the time comes by shooting your marble from outside the ring at any marble or marbles inside the ring. Shoot by kneeling on the ground and flicking your marble out of your fist with your thumb.

4  Gather any marbles you've knocked out of the ring.

5  Shoot again if you knocked any marbles out of the ring. Let the next player shoot if you haven't knocked any marbles out and/or your shooter remains in the ring.

6  Continue shooting in turn until the ring is empty.

7  Count your marbles at the end of the game. The winner is the player with the most marbles.

8  Return the marbles to their original owners unless you're playing "keepsies." In that case, each player keeps the marbles he or she won during the game.

**✱ Tips**

These are the rules for a version of "ring taw" marbles, an older, more common variant. There are many other ways to play.

One way to decide playing order is called "lagging." The players line up opposite a line 10 feet away (the "lag line") and shoot their marbles at it. The player whose marble ends up closest to the line goes first, the next closest goes second, and so on.

**479 Choose Gifts for Kids of All Ages**

Are birthdays or holidays approaching? Use this chart to help you find the right gift for everyone on your list—but don't follow it too rigidly. Children develop at different rates, and any of the gifts may interest either gender, so check both columns and adjacent ages. Be careful to buy age-appropriate toys for children under 3, as they tend to put everything into their mouths.

| AGE | FEMALE | MALE |
|-----|--------|------|
| One | Board books or cloth books, clothes, blocks, push toys, toy phone, stuffed animals | Music, shape sorters, clothes, blocks, noise makers, ride-on fire truck |
| Two | Sponges and toys for the bath, a pail and shovel for the beach, toy stroller, plastic tea set, doll, hammer-the-pegs toy | Red wagon, play cooking set, board books, wooden cars, sand box, wood puzzles, tricycle |
| Three | Simple memory games, doctor's kit, books, clothes for dress-up, tricycle | Train set, toy earth mover for a sand box, toy car to ride in, video of trucks, clothes with animals on them |
| Four | Software, board game, tricycle, stuffed animals, an outing to the park or zoo, picture book, puppets, backyard slide | Glow-in-the-dark stars; action figures; pajamas with a favorite animal; alphabet puzzles, blocks or magnets; trucks, trains |
| Five | Watercolor set, dollhouse, gift certificate for clothes, lunch box, marbles, insect-collecting kit, sticker set, puzzles, books | Software, books, music, sports equipment, simple board games, activity kits, school supplies, puzzles, paints |
| Six | Childproof camera, small basketball, concentration game, golf or gymnastics lessons, tea party set, beginning reader book, board games | Kite, soccer or swimming lessons, electric railroad, school supplies, book about losing teeth, crafts set |
| Seven | Adventure book, backyard basketball hoop, makeup kit, computer game, trip to a movie or theme park | Rocket or car model kit, board game, outing to a sporting event or water park, book about planets, card game |
| Eight | Kids' magnetic poetry kit, electronic memory game, board game, watch, personal radio, posters for room, mystery novels | Remote-controlled airplane, computer adventure program, sporting equipment, adventure and suspense books |
| Nine | Three-dimensional puzzle, bath gel, make-your-own-jewelry kit, book on horses, inflatable furniture, kite, CDs, clothes | Construction kit, radio-controlled helicopter, mini-planetarium, book about astronomy, adult-level puzzles |
| Ten | Diary, chess set, manicure set, "young adult" book, trendy clothes, tape recorder, teen music, school supplies, software | Word game, kids' cookbook, aquarium, whale- or bird-watching trip, ship-model kit, radio-controlled plane, clothes, school supplies, software |
| Fifteen | Magazine subscription; day-planner; address book; software; camera; portable CD player; gift certificate for CDs; tickets to a theme park, movie theater or sporting event; perfume; sunglasses; watch; hair accessories; cosmetics; earrings; cash | Magazine subscription; day-planner; address book; software; camera; portable CD player; gift certificate for CDs; tickets to a theme park, movie theater or sporting event; baseball; battery-operated games; cologne; pocket knife; tools; cash |
| Twenty-five | Clothes; gift certificate for CDs; gym membership; luggage; gift certificate for a massage, facial, manicure or pedicure; golf or tennis lessons; TV; VCR; aromatherapy candles; perfume; cosmetics; jewelry; bottle of wine | MP3 player, gift certificate for CDs or dinner at a favorite restaurant, concert tickets, tickets for a sporting event, clothes, TV, VCR, beer-of-the-month club membership, something for his car or computer, gym membership |
| Sixty-five | Gift certificate for hair styling, manicure or pedicure; gift basket of "splurge" foods; jewelry; magazine subscription; family portrait; homemade gifts from her grandchildren; membership in a local museum or another attraction she enjoys | Gift certificate to a local restaurant or movie theater, round of golf or a fishing trip, year's pass to a national or state park, magazine subscription, book, prepaid tickets to the local car wash, family portrait, point-and-shoot camera |

chart

# Juggle 480

Juggling is a matter of learning to catch and throw at the same time. Work up from one ball to two balls to three balls.

## ⊙ Steps

1 Hold a ball in your right hand.

2 Be aware that as you juggle, you'll be moving your hands in two independent circles—your right hand clockwise and your left hand counter-clockwise. The left hand lags about half a rotation.

3 Throw the ball with your right hand so that the apex—the highest point—of its path is about head-high.

4 Catch the ball as it drops into your left hand, then throw it up again, catching it with your right hand. Practice this maneuver until you go blind with boredom.

5 Proceed with a ball in each hand and continue as you did with one ball, throwing the second ball just as the first reaches its apex, and catching each ball with the other hand.

6 Practice with two balls until you feel confident. Try starting with the left hand once you've mastered starting with the right.

7 Add a third ball by starting with two balls in your right hand and one ball in your left hand.

8 Begin as you did with two balls, by throwing one of the balls from your right hand and then throwing the ball from your left hand when the first ball reaches its apex.

9 Catch the first ball with your left hand.

10 Throw the third ball (from your right hand) when the second ball reaches its apex.

11 Catch the second ball in your right hand.

12 Throw the first ball from your left hand as the third ball reaches its apex.

13 Catch the third ball in your left hand.

14 Keep throwing each ball just as the ball thrown from the opposite hand reaches its apex. You will always have at least one ball in the air, and you will never have more than one ball in either hand.

## ✱ Tips

Juggle facing a wall to keep the balls from running away from you. Also, try juggling things that don't bounce—like bean bags—so you don't have to chase after them.

Stand over your bed or sofa while juggling so you don't have to bend down as far to retrieve dropped balls.

If you're having trouble reacting quickly enough, try throwing the balls higher to give yourself more time to catch them, or try using handkerchiefs, which fall more slowly. You'll have to flick your wrists to toss them high enough.

# Walk on Stilts 481

Stilt-walking is an ancient art that only requires a pair of stilts, optional protective padding and lots of practice. Soon you'll be able to view the world from a whole new perspective.

## ⊙ Steps

1 Begin with a low pair of stilts that place your feet about 1 foot off the ground. If you're concerned about injuring yourself in a fall, you might also want to wear a helmet and protective padding on your knees, elbows and wrists.

## ✱ Tips

Learn how to fall correctly. You want to curve yourself inward a little and try to land on a wide part of your body, such as your shoulders, which can better absorb the impact.

2   Select a firm, even surface on which to walk—the stilts could sink into softer ground, making them difficult to maneuver. Also, try to position yourself next to a wall that you can use as support, or between two low surfaces that you can use to prop yourself up, the way a gymnast uses parallel bars.

3   Make sure you have someone to "spot" (or catch) who can handle your entire weight. Alternatively, string a rope tightly across your training area at the level where your hands will be when you're on stilts. Use this for support and balance.

4   Grasp one stilt in each hand, set one foot on the little ledge sticking out from one stilt, and straighten your leg. Have your spotter prop you up if need be.

5   Once the first stilt feels secure, raise your other foot onto the second stilt and straighten this leg.

6   Practice stepping in place to get a feel for lifting your legs with the stilts properly. Begin walking only after you feel comfortable taking steps.

7   Take your first step forward and then keep moving—it's easier to keep your balance that way.

8   Pretend you're marching—picking up each stilt high as you walk—so you don't trip on bumps in the road.

9   Practice until you feel comfortable.

10  Progress to taller stilts as you feel ready.

Take slow, small steps in the beginning to avoid "the splits." It's pretty easy to figure out what this means.

---

## 482 | View a Lunar Eclipse

A lunar eclipse occurs when the sun, earth and moon are aligned such that the earth partially or totally blocks the sun's rays from reaching the moon, casting it in shadow.

### ⊙ Steps

1   Consult an astronomy field guide, hot line or Web site, or check with local weather forecasts for the date and time of an upcoming lunar eclipse. On average, lunar eclipses occur at least twice a year, but the majority are not total eclipses, nor are they visible everywhere.

2   Drive to the darkest place possible on the appointed night, as far away from streetlights and city lights as possible. Although the moon is widely visible, you'll enhance your view by eliminating any extra light.

3   Place a blanket on the ground.

4   Lie on your back and look up at the moon; binoculars will magnify your view but are not necessary.

5   Observe the umbra, or darker part of the earth's shadow, as it slowly starts to cover an edge of the moon.

6   Watch the shadow gradually cover more and more of the moon.

7   Expect the disk of the moon to be dark and reddish when the eclipse is complete. For the next hour or two, gradually less and less of the moon will be in shadow.

### ✸ Tips

An entire lunar eclipse usually takes at least a few hours. Most people are content to watch just the beginning of the eclipse plus the moment of totality if it's a total eclipse.

Remember to bundle up or even take a sleeping bag if the weather is going to be chilly. You'll lose body heat very quickly lying quietly on the ground.

### Things You'll Need

❏ blanket or sleeping bag

❏ binoculars

## View a Partial Solar Eclipse483

In a solar eclipse, the moon moves between the sun and the earth. Here's how to view solar eclipses with an indirect viewing system—never look directly at the sun.

### ⊙ Steps

1 Pick a viewing area that's not too crowded and has a good view of the sky. Visit the site beforehand to make sure no trees or buildings will block your view of the eclipse.

2 Punch a small hole into the center of a white piece of cardboard with a sharp pencil or a pin. The hole should be about the size of a pencil point. Thick paper will also work if cardboard is unavailable, but make sure it is opaque.

3 Turn your back to the sun during the eclipse, and hold the punched cardboard about 1½ feet above a second sheet of cardboard. The sun should be shining through the hole in the cardboard.

4 Adjust the distance between the sheets to get a clear, sharp image of the eclipse. Moving the sheets closer to each other will give you a smaller, sharper image.

5 View the eclipse as it occurs by looking at the image projected onto the second piece of cardboard. As the moon moves across the sun, a similarly shaped shadow will move across the bright disc of the sun's image on the cardboard.

### ✳ Tip

Most solar eclipses are partial, occurring when the moon crosses the sun only part way. Total solar eclipses occur when the moon passes directly in front of the sun; they last only a few minutes. In annular solar eclipses, the moon passes in front of the sun but is too far from Earth to cover the sun's disc. This creates a dark circle in the middle of the sun, surrounded by a bright ring.

### ⚠ Warning

Never look directly at the sun during a solar eclipse.

### Things You'll Need

❑ 2 pieces of white cardboard

❑ sharp pencil or pin

## Bird-Watch484

Birding is one of the fastest-growing hobbies in the United States. If you're looking for a new pastime, join the eager amateur ornithologists.

### ⊙ Steps

1 Choose a beginning field guide that covers the birds of your region.

2 Study the book and learn the characteristics of different bird families.

3 Use the book's range maps and identify the birds of your region.

4 Invest in a pair of binoculars to help you see birds more closely.

5 Begin to identify the larger birds you see in your yard with the naked eye.

6 Try to identify smaller birds, such as warblers and hummingbirds.

7 Start a journal listing the birds you have seen and positively identified. List the bird type, location and date.

8 Expand your birding explorations from your yard to local wildlife refuges, creeks, wetlands and other habitats. Continue to keep notes and lists about birding activities.

9 Join a bird club to further expand your horizons.

10 Plan birding trips to other states or countries.

### ✳ Tips

Keeping a list of all the birds you have seen in your life is a common practice among birders. This is called a "life list." Other lists you may want to keep include a state list, county list, yard list, North American list or world list.

Call local colleges, museums or nature preserves to ask about birding classes or special docent-led birding excursions.

### Things You'll Need

❑ birding guide

❑ binoculars

❑ birding journal and pen

## 485 | Make a Simple Bird Feeder

You don't need to spend a lot of money on a fancy bird feeder to attract feathered visitors to your yard. Try this easy make-it-yourself model.

### ⊙ Steps

1 Wash an empty 1-gallon plastic milk jug thoroughly, removing any milk residue from it.

2 Put the cap on.

3 Stand the milk jug right side up on your work surface.

4 Cut large holes—about 3 to 4 inches in diameter—in two adjacent sides of the jug opposite the handle. Cut the holes in the middle of the side and high enough that the seed won't spill out of the jug when you put it in.

5 Use a large nail to punch a smaller hole below each of the large holes, and insert a dowel, which the birds will use for perching, through diagonally. The perch should be long enough to stick out about 2 inches on both sides to provide perching spots for your birds.

6 With the large nail, punch two holes in the neck of the milk jug, about 1 inch below the cap.

7 Run a 2-foot-long piece of wire through these two holes, twisting the wire tightly above the cap with several turns.

8 Fill the feeder with birdseed and use the wire ends to hang it from a strong branch or other support. Use black oil sunflower seeds, which will attract the largest variety of birds.

### ✻ Tip

Clean your bird feeder every time you change the seed or whenever the seed gets wet.

### ⚠ Warnings

Adults should supervise children using scissors, nails and wire.

Make sure that the feeder is located in an area safe from neighborhood cats.

### Things You'll Need

❑ 1-gallon plastic milk jug

❑ scissors

❑ large nail

❑ dowel or smooth stick

❑ 2 feet of thin but sturdy wire

❑ birdseed

## 486 | Make a Snowman

Building a snowman provides an entertaining, creative way to get some fresh air on a lazy winter day. You'll need a few inches of snow on the ground; wear gloves or mittens.

### ⊙ Steps

1 Test to see if you have "packing snow," which clumps together easily and isn't too wet. The snow must pack to make a snowman.

2 Shape a handful of snow into a ball. Continue adding more snow and packing the ball until it's too large to hold.

3 Place the ball on the snow in front of you and slowly roll it away from you. As more snow accumulates on the outside of your ball, pack the snow by pressing on it with your gloved hands.

4 Roll and pack the ball over and over until it is the size you want for the bottom of the snowman's body.

5 Repeat for the midsection and head. The bottom should be the biggest ball, and the top should be the smallest.

### ✻ Tips

If you're having a hard time rolling and packing the snow into sections, try using buckets. Find three that are of descending size and pack them with snow, then upend them, dumping the snow from one bucket on top of the other.

You can spray your snowman with colored water to add rosy cheeks.

Your snowman's days are numbered, so take plenty of pictures.

6   Pack some extra snow between the layers to make them stick together. Place sticks down the center where the sections meet if your snowman is having trouble standing erect.

7   Give the snowman a face. Use coal, rocks, buttons or anything dark and round for the eyes. A horizontal stick or twig will make a good mouth, and a carrot is fine for the pointy nose. If you don't have a carrot, a banana or a candy cane will do the job.

8   Cover the top of his head with an old plant for hair, or give him a knit hat to wear. Top hats will blow away unless secured.

9   Add arms, legs and other accessories. Push sticks into the sides of the middle section and hang old mittens on the ends, then place boots at the bottom for legs. Also consider adding items such as a shirt, a scarf or sunglasses.

**Things You'll Need**

❏ gloves or mittens

❏ coal, rocks or buttons

❏ stick or twig

❏ carrot

❏ hat

❏ other accessories

# Build a Sand Castle
### 487

Why spend money on clay when you can use beach sand for free? Indulge your artistic side and create medieval fantasies by building your very own sand castle.

## ◉ Steps

1   Draw a rough sketch of the castle you'd like to build.

2   Choose a square site near the water, but not so close that waves will destroy your castle as the tide comes up. Make sure the square is large enough for your castle plans.

3   Dig a hole down to the water table, where the sand is dark and moist, or bring up large buckets of water from the ocean or lake.

4   Scoop wet sand onto the center of the area in which you'll be working. Work fast so the sand stays wet.

5   Build towers by forming and stacking sand patties about the size and shape of thick pancakes. Place larger patties on the bottom, and gently shake the patties from side to side as you pile them so that the sand settles. Seal your towers by gently pouring water over them.

6   Build walls to connect the towers of your castle by jiggling—gently shaking from side to side—wet sand into brick shapes and laying them on top of each other.

7   Carve the towers and the walls into shapes using tools such as a small trowel, a putty knife or plastic utensils.

8   Dig a moat around the castle to protect it from invaders, such as breaking waves and dogs.

## ✳ Tips

Extremely wet sand is easiest to work with. Use a spray bottle to wet down the sand if your castle begins to dry and crumble during construction.

Be sure to jiggle the sand while building, as pounding, beating or pushing the sand might destroy your castle. Another popular method is the drip method, where you squeeze a fistful of extremely wet sand and let it drip out of your hand into piles.

## Things You'll Need

❏ paper and pencil

❏ shovel or trowel

❏ buckets

❏ putty knife or plastic utensils

❏ spray bottle

## 488 | Skip Rocks

Nothing accompanies deep thought better than skipping rocks across a body of water.

### ⊙ Steps

1 Select a rock that's round, flat and smooth.

2 Stand at the edge of a large, placid body of water.

3 Hold the rock horizontally—flat side down—with your index finger curling around one edge.

4 Aim the rock. Envision a convex arc a few inches above the water.

5 Throw the rock low and parallel to the water's surface. Throw sidearm so that your hand travels past your waist and the rock travels horizontally across the water.

6 Release the rock with a snap of the wrist to give it a horizontal spin. Your elbow will be next to your hip as the rock leaves your hand.

7 Count the number of times the rock skips.

### ✽ Tips

The harder you throw the rock, the higher it may ricochet after the first skip. Three or more skips is very good. Eight is extraordinary. More than 12 is mythical.

You want the flat part of the rock to skip along the water's smooth surface.

## 489 | Pan for Gold

Put yourself in the shoes of the tens of thousands of forty-niners who traveled west in search of gold during the wild 1849 California gold rush.

### ⊙ Steps

1 Buy a gold pan from a mining supply store. In California's gold country, hardware stores often carry them. Look for one that has riffles—bars or slats—and a catch hole in the bottom, since these help the gold to separate from other particles more easily. Plastic pans are generally preferred over metal pans because they are lighter, have shallower angles (which reduces the risk of gold's being tossed out of the pan), and because gold is easier to spot against plastic than against shiny metal.

2 Before you begin, familiarize yourself with the recreational prospecting regulations of the area in which you wish to pan for gold.

3 Choose a location along a river or creek to pan. Places where the water slows down noticeably, such as behind sandbars or large rocks, are usually good spots for panning. You can also ask park officials or local prospecting organizations for recommendations about the best places to pan.

4 Fill the pan almost to the top with sand from the edge of the creek or river. Try sand from various depths. Use a shovel to dig deeper.

5 Dip the pan's edge into the stream and fill it with water.

6 Hold the pan with one hand and swirl it to mix the sand. Any gold will start settling toward the bottom of the pan.

7 Swirl the pan faster. You will lose some of the water, along with lighter particles of sand, as you go.

### ✽ Tips

Try running the sand through a sieve or screen to get rid of larger particles before placing it in your gold pan.

Pyrite, or fool's gold, looks like the real thing but has no value. There's lots of it out there, and it's fun to find even though it won't make you rich.

To make sure you've found gold and not fool's gold, rub the stone against something white, like porcelain. If it leaves a black streak, it's fool's gold. If it leaves a yellow streak, it's gold. Gold is also much softer than fool's gold.

Gold can be found farther downstream from its usual source after heavy rains, since the rush of water dislodges it and carries it away.

8 Begin scraping the top sand out of the pan with your free hand.

9 Continue until much of the pan is empty, leaving only small bits of gold—if you're lucky—in a little water.

10 Use tweezers or a pipette to retrieve tiny gold particles and pick out larger samples with your fingers.

11 Keep all gold samples in plastic vials or sample bottles.

**Things You'll Need**

❑ plastic or metal pan

❑ shovel

❑ tweezers or a pipette

❑ vials or bottles

## Make Papier-Mâché Paste                                                490

Making a piñata, dinosaur or bowl is fun, easy and economical with papier-mâché. The first step is mixing up the paste, which helps to hold all the newspaper strips together.

⊙ **Steps**

1 Gather all your materials and spread a plastic cover over your work area, including the floor.

2 Pour equal parts flour and water into a plastic bucket or bowl and blend with a mixing spoon. The amount you make depends on the size of the project. Two cups each of flour and water is good for a smaller project; you can always make more if you run out.

3 Add flour to thicken the mixture or water to thin it until you reach the desired consistency—a smooth liquid with no lumps. The paste should stick smoothly to paper strips without dripping off.

4 Add salt to the paste to keep it from getting moldy; add white glue for extra stickiness.

**Things You'll Need**

❑ all-purpose flour

❑ water

❑ mixing spoon

❑ plastic bucket or bowl

❑ salt

❑ white glue

## Make a Papier-Mâché Bowl                                               491

Use a bowl of almost any shape or size as a mold for this papier-mâché creation, as long as it's completely concave.

⊙ **Steps**

1 Choose a bowl for your mold, and spread a thin, even coat of petroleum jelly on the inside of it. This will prevent the paper from adhering to the inside of the bowl.

2 Tear newspaper into strips 2 to 3 inches wide. Each strip should be long enough to cover the interior of the bowl from rim to rim and extend about 2 inches past the rim at each end.

3 Make papier-mâché paste (see 490 "Make Papier-Mâché Paste").

4 Coat one newspaper strip at a time with the paste: Dip it into the bowl of paste and then run the strip through your fingers to ensure an even coating and get rid of excess paste.

5 Cover the interior of the bowl with the strips, placing each strip in the bowl as soon as it's dipped. Start at the center of the bowl and work

**✳ Tips**

Have a rag handy to keep your hands clean while you work. It will be difficult to run the strips through your fingers if you allow paste to build up on them.

You can use a variety of concave or cylindrical household containers to create other papier-mâché vessels.

outward, placing the strips all the way across the bowl; each strip should overlap the previous strip by about 1 inch.

6  Repeat the previous step six or seven times, making crisscrossed layers: After you lay down one layer, turn the bowl 90 degrees and lay down another layer. The number of layers you need depends on how large a bowl you're making: A larger bowl requires more layers. Allow the paper to dry at room temperature for 36 to 48 hours.

7  Remove the paper bowl from the mold; use a butter knife to gently loosen it from the mold, if necessary. Place it upside down to continue drying on a baking rack, and let it dry at room temperature for another 12 hours or so.

8  Use scissors to trim the bowl's rim evenly to the desired width.

9  Lightly sand the interior and exterior of the bowl.

10  Paint the bowl with two coats of a solid-color tempera or other water-based paint—white makes a good primer. When that's dry, paint your designs on the bowl and lightly apply a protective varnish, if desired.

### Things You'll Need

❏ concave bowl

❏ petroleum jelly

❏ newspapers

❏ papier-mâché paste

❏ scissors

❏ sandpaper

❏ tempera or other water-based paint

❏ varnish (optional)

---

## 492 | Make Beanbags

Small, easy-to-make beanbags can help kids learn how to play catch. Plus, they put your scrap fabric to good use. Follow these steps to make 10 beanbags that are 4 inches square.

### ◉ Steps

1  Start with your own fabric scraps, or search through the remnant bins at fabric stores to find suitable material. Any sort of closely woven fabric will do. To make 10 beanbags 4 inches square, you'll need approximately 1/2 yard of 45-inch-wide fabric.

2  Purchase enough filling material for the desired number of bags. Use fiberfill or plastic pellets sold especially for beanbags. These items can be found at most fabric and craft stores.

3  Use a yardstick or ruler to draw a 4 1/2-inch square on heavy paper or cardboard (the extra 1/4 inch on each side is for stitching together the edges of the fabric). Cut out this square to use as your template.

4  Iron your fabric, if necessary, and lay it down on a flat surface, wrong side up.

5  Place your template on the fabric and use a fabric-marking pen or chalk to trace 20 squares. Use scissors to cut out the squares.

6  Pin two pieces of fabric together to make one beanbag, right sides together (inside out).

7  Use a sewing machine to stitch a 1/4-inch seam (i.e., 1/4 inch from the edge) around the edges of the fabric square, starting 1 inch from any corner. When you reach a corner, keep the needle inserted in the fabric, lift the presser foot of your sewing machine and swivel the fabric 90 degrees. Then release the presser foot and sew the next side. Stop sewing 2 inches short of where you began, to allow an opening that will let you turn the bag right side out.

### ✱ Tips

Make your bags from a variety of fabrics. The total yardage needed does not have to come from just one piece of fabric.

Make your beanbags any size you desire. Just be sure to make your template 1/4 inch larger all around—for the seam allowance.

Avoid using beans, rice or birdseed for bag filling. These items can work very well as filling but they have a tendency to attract insects.

### Things You'll Need

❏ fabric

❏ fiberfill or plastic pellets

❏ heavy paper or cardboard

❏ fabric-marking pens or chalk

❏ scissors

❏ dressmaker's pins

❏ sewing machine or needle and thread

8 Turn your bag right side out at the 2-inch seam opening, and fill your bag with the fiberfill or pellets.

9 Use a needle and thread or a sewing machine to stitch up the opening.

10 Repeat step 6 through 9 to make the remaining beanbags.

## Make a Beaded Necklace 493

You only need a few items to complete this necklace. Once you're done, you'll have the basic skills necessary to tackle more complex beading and jewelry projects.

### Steps

1 Choose a length for your necklace and purchase that much beading thread, plus a few extra inches.

2 Make sure you have enough beads, including spacer beads (the small beads that go between the larger beads). You will also need a clasp and two bead tips, which are used to secure the ends of your necklace so that the clasp can be attached.

3 Lay your beads out on a flat surface, on top of a towel to keep them from rolling away. Determine the design of your necklace and in what order the beads will be strung.

4 Knot a thread end and use scissors to trim off the excess thread. The knot should be at the very end of the thread, but not so close that it runs the risk of unknotting.

5 Push the unknotted end of your thread through one open end of the bead tip and thread it through the hole. Pull the thread all the way through so that the knot you made rests firmly against the hole.

6 Place a small amount of craft glue on the knot to keep it from coming undone, and allow it to dry.

7 String your beads and then thread on the other bead tip so that the open end of the tip faces away from the strung beads.

8 Tie a loose knot in the thread end and use a long, straight pin to push the knot down into the open end of the bead tip. The knot should rest securely against the hole. Trim the excess thread and use pliers to close the bead tip.

9 Affix one clasp piece onto one bead tip hook so that the loops at the end of each are joined. Use the pliers to close one ring over the other. Repeat with the remaining clasp piece at the other end of the necklace.

### ✱ Tips

Look for bead tips under the name "clam shells" or "oyster shells," so named because of their shape.

Use a double strand of beading thread for extra strength.

Place glue along 1 to 2 inches at the end of your thread before stringing the beads and allow it to dry. This will stiffen the thread end and make the beads a lot easier to string.

### Things You'll Need

❑ beading thread

❑ beads

❑ jewelry clasp

❑ 2 bead tips

❑ towel

❑ scissors

❑ craft glue

❑ straight pin

❑ flat-nose pliers

## 494 | Make Bubble Mix

Reuse bubble jars and blowers again and again by making your own bubble mix. For just pennies, you can make enough mix to fill an entire afternoon with bubbly fun.

### ⊙ Steps

1 Combine ½ c. liquid dishwashing soap, 2 tsp. sugar and 1¼ c. water in a mixing bowl.

2 Mix gently. This recipe yields 1¾ cups of bubble mix.

3 Use immediately or store in a plastic container.

 **Tips**

This mixture is very sticky—it's best used outside.

Use baby shampoo in place of soap, if desired.

## 495 | Make a Giant Bubble Wand

A giant bubble wand is a big hit with kids and works on the same principle as the smaller, store-bought versions. This wand is simple and quick to make.

### ⊙ Steps

1 Bend a wire clothes hanger into a circle; for large bubbles, the more perfect the circle, the better it works.

2 Twist the hook opposite the circle to form a handle.

3 Wrap the handle with electrical tape, taking special care to cover the wire's two sharp ends with tape.

4 Wrap the circle with cotton twine to absorb more soap mixture so you can make bigger bubbles.

**Tip**

Use floral wire to make smaller wands with interesting shapes.

**Things You'll Need**

❑ wire clothes hanger

❑ electrical tape

❑ cotton twine

## 496 | Make a Paper Airplane

You don't need to be a pilot to get an old-fashioned introduction to aviation. Grab a piece of paper and start flying jets in your own backyard.

### ⊙ Steps

1 Find a piece of paper shaped like a rectangle. A sheet of computer printing paper or school notebook paper is a good size and weight.

2 Lay the paper on a table with one of the long edges closest to you.

3 Fold the paper in half lengthwise. When the two edges match up, use your thumbs to make a sharp crease along the fold.

4 Take the upper left corner of the top layer of paper and fold it diagonally down toward the first crease you made. When the edges match up, use your thumbs to make a sharp crease along the new fold, which should create a small triangular flap.

 **Tips**

Experiment with the size and weight of the paper.

Experiment with the location of the tab.

Make sharp creases to ensure a good flight.

5 Turn the paper over.

6 Take the upper right corner of the top layer of paper and fold it diagonally toward you, until the edge lines up with the first crease you made. When the edges match, make a sharp crease along the new fold. (This is a mirror of what you did in step 4.)

7 Take the newly formed diagonal edge on the right side of the paper, and fold it straight down toward the first crease you made. When the edges match, make another sharp crease.

8 Turn the paper over, and again fold the diagonal edge down toward the first crease you made; make another sharp crease. The paper should now look like a triangle with a 90-degree angle.

9 Form the wings by flipping the airplane over and repeating steps 7 and 8.

10 Hold the paper in one hand along the first crease you made. Let the wings of the plane flare out.

11 At a point 4 or 5 inches from the nose of the plane, make a 1/2-inch rip in the bottom part of the plane; make another rip 1/2 inch behind it. Fold this tab up.

12 Hold the airplane near the tab and toss the plane with an overhand, horizontal forward motion.

## Fly a Kite                                                     497

A windy day in the park might keep you from flying a paper airplane outdoors, but it could be the perfect day to practice launching a kite.

### ☉ Steps

1 Check your local weather report to determine if conditions are favorable for kite flying. Look for light to moderate winds if you're a beginning kite flier, or gustier winds if you are more experienced. A wind speed of 5 to 15 mph is best for kite flying.

2 Find a large and windy open area free of trees and power lines—two things that are notoriously dangerous for kites and their owners.

3 Hold the kite in both hands and toss it lightly into the wind until the wind catches it. This works well when the wind is moderately strong.

4 Alternatively, let out a small length of kite string and, holding the string in your hand, run with the kite behind you until the wind lifts it.

5 Begin letting out string until the kite reaches a height with which you are comfortable. Good heights generally range from 50 to 100 feet.

6 Keep an eye on your kite, as it may come crashing down because of sudden changes in wind. If it dips, run or pull in the string a bit to give it some lift.

7 Bring the kite down by slowly winding the kite string around a kite spool.

8 Reach out and grab the kite before it hits the ground to avoid damaging it.

### ✱ Tips

Tighten the string around a spool and secure the spool to the ground if you want to tend to other activities.

Tie additional ribbon or strips of cloth to the tail to increase the stability of diamond kites in gusty winds.

### ⚠ Warning

Stay away from electrical lines! If a kite becomes entangled, leave it there. And never fly your kite during a thunderstorm.

## 498  Make Food Green for St. Patrick's Day

All you need is some imagination and a bottle of green food coloring to get your family into the spirit of St. Patrick's Day.

### ⊙ Steps

1  Start off the morning by serving your kids a glass of green milk with their breakfast (a bowl of Lucky Charms, perhaps?).

2  Put a few drops of green food coloring in a clear citrus-based soda to make a fun, fizzy, green beverage. To improve the taste, you can also add lime-flavored syrup to the soda.

3  Impress your friends and family by making pasta and serving it with green Alfredo sauce or pesto sauce. Or serve chicken with green gravy and green mashed potatoes (with green vegetables, of course).

4  Bake a loaf of fresh green bread by adding a few drops of food coloring to your bread mix.

5  Make a traditional dessert more festive by preparing some green whipped cream as a topping. If you like, add a touch of mint extract to match the color with a mint flavor.

6  Whip up a batch of sugar cookies, adding a couple of drops of green food coloring to the dough, or add green food coloring to a white cake mix.

### ✳ Tips

For most foods (especially liquids), a drop or two of food coloring goes a long way.

The lighter-colored the food, the easier to make it green, and the better it will look. Dark foods require more food coloring and tend to look moldy when colored.

### ⚠ Warning

Think about hiding the food coloring from your kids after you're done with it. They might decide that everything should be green.

## 499  Hollow Out an Egg

Lots of egg-decorating projects call for hollow eggshells. After you empty the egg, save the white and yolk to make scrambled eggs, quiche or an omelette.

### ⊙ Steps

1  Wash and dry a raw egg.

2  Insert a long needle into the large end of the egg to make a small hole. Twist the needle as you push it into the eggshell as far as you can while still grasping it.

3  Use the needle to make a slightly larger hole in the small end.

4  Push the needle into the center of the egg and move it around to break the yolk.

5  Hold the egg over a bowl with the small end down.

6  Place your lips over the hole at the large end of the egg and blow firmly until all the egg comes out the hole at the small end.

7  Rinse out the egg by running a thin stream of water into the larger hole.

8  Blow out the water the same way that you blew out the egg.

9  To dry the eggshell, prop it up in a dish drainer with the large end facing down.

### ✳ Tip

Save empty egg cartons for storing the hollow eggs before and after you decorate them.

### ⚠ Warning

Do not ingest any of the raw egg. Raw eggs can carry the salmonella bacteria, which can cause serious illness.

## Dye Polka Dot Eggs

500

Save your used birthday candles to make these eye-catching polka dot eggs.

### ◉ Steps

1 Hard-boil or hollow out several white eggs to decorate (see 499 "Hollow Out an Egg").

2 Lay out newspaper on your work area to protect it from dripping wax.

3 Choose your dye colors—you'll want a lighter base color for the polka dots and a darker color for the rest of the egg surface. Prepare the dye according to the directions on the package.

4 Dye the egg your base color. It should be a light color, such as yellow or pale pink.

5 Place the egg on a paper egg holder (see Tips) and let it dry thoroughly.

6 Light a candle. For this project, you will need the small candles that are sold as birthday candles.

7 Hold an egg in one hand and the lighted candle in the other.

8 Allow the melted candle wax to drip onto the egg, forming small circles of wax on the shell. Take care not to burn your fingers.

9 Turn the egg slowly so that the wax cools as you go and drips of wax cover the top half of the egg evenly, spacing the circles evenly apart to create a polka dot effect. It's difficult to control exactly where the drops of melted wax will fall on the egg. However, the spontaneity of the drops adds to the beauty of the finished egg.

10 Set the egg on a paper egg holder to allow the wax to cool and harden. You won't be able to wax the whole egg without burning your fingers, so do one end, let it dry, then repeat steps 7 through 9 to do the other.

11 Dye the egg with the darker color to tint the surface that does not have wax on it.

12 Allow the egg to dry.

13 Remove the wax by scraping it off with your fingernail if the egg is hard-boiled. Or, if you're using a hollowed-out egg, wrap the egg in foil and place it in the oven at 200 degrees F for 5 minutes, or until the wax softens. Then wipe off the wax with a paper towel.

### ✳ Tips

You can make a simple egg holder by rolling up a strip of thick paper into a small cylinder about 2 to 3 inches high and about 1 inch in diameter and then securing it with tape. A section of a toilet paper roll could also work.

You can dye the egg more than two colors. Follow steps 1 through 12. Then scrape off some of the wax dots and dye the egg in the darkest color before scraping away the remaining wax dots. A good dye sequence would be yellow, orange, red, or yellow, green, blue.

### ⚠ Warnings

Handle burning candles with extreme caution. Both the flame and the hot wax can cause serious burns.

Never allow children to handle burning candles or matches.

### Things You'll Need

❑ eggs

❑ egg-dye kit

❑ birthday candles

❑ matches

## Carve a Pumpkin

501

Jolly jack-o'-lanterns are a traditional welcome for trick-or-treaters, an invitation to stop by for a Halloween surprise. Just remember that carving a pumpkin takes more tenacity than skill.

### ◉ Steps

1 Select a fresh pumpkin in a shape that pleases you. Some folks prefer their pumpkins low and round, while others like them tall and oval-shaped.

### ✳ Tips

Coat the cut edges with cooking oil to keep your jack-o'-lantern fresh longer.

2  Draw a circle or hexagon on top of the pumpkin in preparation for making an opening large enough for your hand to reach through.

3  Cut through the stem end of the pumpkin along your outline with a sharp knife. Use a back-and-forth slicing motion to cut through the thick, tough skin.

4  Remove the stem end, which will act as a cap, making sure you scrape off any seeds or pulp.

5  Use a large spoon to scoop out the seeds and pulp from inside the pumpkin. Hold the spoon by its bowl to get extra leverage while scooping.

6  Draw a pattern for the face on the clean pumpkin with a felt-tip pen, or scribe the lines into the skin using a pencil. Be sure to make the eyes, nose and mouth large enough; you'll have a hard time cutting out tiny features when you're using a big knife blade to saw through tough skin.

7  Follow your pattern as you cut all the way through the pumpkin.

8  Push the cut-out features gently from the inside of the pumpkin and discard the pieces.

9  Place a votive candle inside the pumpkin to create an eerie glow.

During the Halloween season, many craft stores and some supermarkets sell sturdy, serrated plastic pumpkin-carving tools.

### ⚠ Warnings

Candles should be used with care, especially around children.

Always cut away from your body.

### Things You'll Need

- ❑ pumpkin
- ❑ sturdy, sharp knife
- ❑ large spoon
- ❑ felt-tip pen or pencil
- ❑ votive candle

---

## 502 | Carve a Fancy Pumpkin

With this technique, you remove the tough orange skin from some areas, and carve out other sections completely to let the light from a candle or small flashlight shine through.

### ◎ Steps

1  Select a pumpkin with a smooth surface.

2  Draw a pattern on a separate piece of paper. Some suggestions are bats, skulls, spiders and ghosts.

3  Cut away the top section of the pumpkin surrounding the stem, and remove any seeds and pulp from inside.

4  Follow the pattern and draw the design on the pumpkin, thinking about which areas you'll cut out completely, and where you'll remove just the orange skin. Areas where the orange skin is left in place will appear darker than those where the skin is removed. In the case of a ghost, for example, you would completely carve out the eye holes and perhaps a mouth, but remove only the pumpkin's skin in the area of the ghost body.

5  Cut an outline around your design using a sharp knife.

6  Remove the areas that are to be completely cut.

7  Cut around any raised areas, such as folds of fabric or spider legs.

8  Slowly and carefully remove the orange skin from the desired areas with a vegetable peeler, an X-Acto knife or a dedicated pumpkin-carving tool. Take your time, as this is the hard part. Variations in depth will create a more interesting design.

9  Place a votive candle or battery-powered light inside the pumpkin to create an eerie glow.

### ✳ Tips

A slip of the knife can sometimes be mended by pinning the skin back in place with a toothpick.

Try cutting off the bottom of the pumpkin and removing the insides from this end, especially if the pumpkin is lopsided or the stem is very small.

### ⚠ Warnings

Be extremely careful. Carving tools are sharp.

Be especially careful with candles near small children.

### Things You'll Need

- ❑ pumpkin
- ❑ sturdy, sharp knife
- ❑ vegetable peeler, X-Acto knife or special pumpkin-carving tool
- ❑ votive candle or small battery-powered light

## Make a Haunted House 503

Create the spookiest entertainment on the block, and terrify children and adults alike on Halloween night.

### ⊙ Steps

1   Find a safe place large enough to accommodate all the things you plan to do. You can use your house, basement or yard—or if you really want to be extravagant, you can rent a large, vacant building.

2   Draw up a plan. Using a diagram of the space available, figure out what you want to have in your haunted house and where it might go. Plan an entrance and an exit.

3   Do the hard stuff first. Order or construct props, including such items as fake headstones, guillotines and coffins.

4   Put the haunted house together. Make it dark using black plastic trash bags or blankets over windows, then add eerie lighting. Include lots of unexpected scary sounds and sensory experiences to startle visitors. Keep in mind the need for adequate ventilation.

5   Use peeled grapes as eyeballs, placing them where people will touch them in the dark. Use Styrofoam heads from a beauty supply house and turn them into monsters.

6   Spritz visitors' faces with cold water in the dark, or have visitors walk through spider webs made of stretched cotton or wet string.

7   Create a bubbling-cauldron effect with the aid of dry ice. Fill a rubber glove with water colored with food coloring and freeze it, then remove the glove and float the "frozen hand" in the cauldron.

8   Invite several adults to participate with you. They can dress in costume and be part of the haunted house, but can also keep an eye on things and help supervise participants.

9   Advertise. Whether the haunted house is simply for trick-or-treaters in your neighborhood or a community affair, put up a sign telling kids where to find some haunted fun on Halloween.

### ✳ Tips

Start planning early in the year and gather or make the necessary items in time for Halloween.

Check out your local costume or specialty shop, or browse online to find items for your haunted house. If your library has an audio section, you may find some scary music there.

Mix citrus soda and blue punch for a bright green beverage.

### ⚠ Warnings

Small children may be terrified of the goings-on in a haunted house. Set an age limit, or post a sign warning children of the level of scariness within.

Do not allow dry ice to touch anyone's skin.

Keep anything wet safely clear of electrical effects or outlets. Do not use any candles or other live flames.

Always remember: Safety first.

## Create a Unique Costume 504

Forget the passé ghosts and goblins this year. Instead, crank up your imagination and create a costume that will be the talk of the town.

### ⊙ Steps

1   Toss out any clichés immediately. Forget anything related to traditional Halloween costumes, such as witches, werewolves and monsters.

2   Play off common words, titles or phrases in unexpected ways. For example, a doctor's outfit with chili peppers pinned to it is "Dr. Pepper." A surfer costume covered with fake spider webbing is a "Web surfer."

3   Make a list of themes that are unique to you. Play off your name, a nickname, a personal legend or an unusual physical attribute.

### ✳ Tips

Consider dyeing old clothes or accessories to fit your costume. You'll save money and cut down on shopping time.

Surf the Web, watch cartoons or check out your local bookstore for ideas to help spark creativity.

4   Shop at thrift stores. These treasure troves are home to some of the most unusual and utilitarian clothes and accessories.

5   Use common household items to transform your look. Burn a piece of cork and rub it on your face for a 5 o'clock shadow, or use eyelash glue to attach fake fur to your face for a beard.

## 505 | Make Scary Spiders

Spiders are a snap to make using cardboard egg cartons. This project is easy for young children, although they'll need supervision when cutting or painting. One carton makes 12 spiders.

### ◎ Steps

1   Spread several layers of newspaper on your work surface.

2   Cut or tear the top off an empty cardboard egg carton.

3   Paint the entire bottom of the egg carton, inside and out, using black tempera paint.

4   Let the paint dry for a few minutes, then cut the egg carton cells apart. Touch up the edges with black paint.

5   Turn the cells so the open side is down, and insert eight black pipe cleaners into each cell, four on each side. Bend the pipe cleaners to look like legs.

6   Glue on googly eyes from a craft store, or make eyes for the spiders out of construction paper.

7   Hang each spider using a needle and piece of thread. Thread the needle and tie a knot at one end; then pierce it through the egg carton cell from the bottom. Use a light-colored thread to make it less noticeable.

### ✱ Tip

Make several spiders and hang them together for a spooky effect, especially in low light.

### Things You'll Need

❑ cardboard egg carton

❑ black tempera or other water-based paint

❑ paintbrush

❑ black pipe cleaners

❑ glue

❑ googly eyes

❑ needle

❑ thread

## 506 | Make a Cornucopia

A cornucopia, also known as a horn of plenty, is a cone-shaped ornament or receptacle overflowing with abundance, signifying the wealth of the harvest at Thanksgiving.

### ◎ Steps

1   Purchase an actual ready-to-fill cornucopia, available at most crafts stores year-round and at many drugstores and supermarkets during the holidays. You can also buy a cone-shaped basket, but then you'll have to shape the narrow end by steaming it and bending it slightly to resemble the horn of a goat.

2   Place a large tray or flat basket on a table.

3   Gather colorful autumn leaves and place them on the tray, or use decorative paper autumn leaves, sold in craft and kitchen-supply stores.

### ✱ Tips

When you build the cornucopia on a tray, it becomes portable.

Select colorful vegetables with waxy skin; these last the longest without refrigeration. You can expect your harvest display to last for one to two weeks.

4   Fill the cornucopia with straw, excelsior or raffia to act as a filler and to support the vegetables. This way, you don't have to use so many fruits and vegetables to fill the horn.

5   Set the cornucopia on top of the tray covered with leaves.

6   Begin placing the largest vegetables and fruits inside the cornucopia to serve as the foundation of those to come.

7   Continue filling the cornucopia with fall-harvested fruits and vegetables such as gourds, pomegranates, small apples, miniature pumpkins, peppers, artichokes and dried ears of Indian corn.

8   Allow the fruits and vegetables to spill out of the cornucopia over the fall leaves on the tray.

9   Spill a variety of nuts and berries over the arrangement. (Make sure to choose hardy berries, such as cranberries.) Allow them to drop into the cracks and spaces.

10  Finish by tucking more colorful leaves among the vegetables and fruit.

### Things You'll Need

❑ cornucopia or horn-shaped basket

❑ tray

❑ autumn leaves

❑ straw, excelsior or raffia

❑ autumn fruits and vegetables

❑ nuts and berries

---

# Make an Evergreen Wreath                                507

After the Christmas tree, wreaths are the traditional Christmas decoration. Wreaths are easy to make from common greens found right outside your home.

## ◎ Steps

1   Gather a large shopping bag full of 6-inch garden trimmings. Some suggested trimmings are cedar, pine, fir, redwood, magnolia and oak. Remember to include holly or other red berries in your collection. The tip ends of the branches work best.

2   Use a wire wreath frame or make your own from a wire coat hanger. (Simply unbend it from the familiar shape into a circle; you can use the hook to hang your finished wreath.)

3   Attach #24 floral wire—sometimes called paddle wire—anywhere along the wire wreath frame. Tie it to the frame at that point and keep unspooling it and wrapping as you go around the frame with the bundles of greens.

4   Select several of the garden trimmings and place them together in a bunch with the stems at one end.

5   Place this bundle on top of the frame where the floral wire is connected.

6   Hold the bundle in place and wrap the floral wire around the bundle and frame. You will need two hands for this: one to hold the bundle in place against the frame and one to wrap the wire.

7   Wrap the floral wire around the bundle a second time and then pull it tight. Make sure to leave the wire attached to the frame—you still have a long way to go.

8   Gather another bundle of foliage and place it so that the leaves overlap the first bunch and cover the stems. Make sure that the stems on both bunches face the same direction.

## ✳ Tips

Thick bundles make fat wreaths. The more plant material you add, the fuller your wreath will appear.

Make a bright red bow and attach it with wire to the top of your wreath.

Wreaths make wonderful hostess gifts during the holiday party season.

## ⚠ Warning

Once your family and friends see your wreath, they will all want one. Buy or make plenty of wreath frames to supply the overwhelming demand.

## Things You'll Need

❑ scissors or pruning shears

❑ garden trimmings

❑ wire wreath frame or wire coat hanger

❑ #24 floral or paddle wire

❑ pinecones

9  Continue overlapping the bunches of foliage and wiring them to the frame until you complete the circle.

10  Add pinecones by twisting a new piece of paddle wire around the base of the cone, leaving a tail of 8 to 10 inches. Tie the wired cone's tail to the wreath.

11  Lift the first bundle that you wired onto the frame and tuck the last bundle under it.

12  Twist the wire tightly around the last bundle. Knot the wire onto the frame, leaving 1 inch of wire with which to hang the finished wreath.

13  Trim the wire with scissors or pruning shears when you're finished.

---

## 508 | Make an Evergreen Garland

Garlands are traditional decorations for doorways or banisters during the holiday season. You can easily make one yourself from evergreen trimmings collected from your own garden.

### ⊙ Steps

1  Gather a wheelbarrow full of evergreen trimmings. Some suggestions are cedar, pine, fir, juniper, redwood, oak, bay laurel and asparagus fern.

2  Cut the trimmings to a length of 6 inches.

3  Lay a 10-foot length of string or twine on a large, flat surface. Tie a loop in one end of the string.

4  Attach #24 floral wire—also called paddle wire—to the loop end of the string. Keep the wire attached to the spool and unravel it as needed.

5  Select several foliage pieces and place them together in a bunch, with the stems at one end. You can mix different kinds in one bundle.

6  Place the bundle of foliage at the loop end of the string with the stems pointing toward the long end of the string.

7  Wrap the floral wire around the stems and string to secure them in place.

8  Wrap the floral wire around the bundle twice and then pull it tight. Make sure to leave the wire attached to the string.

9  Gather another bundle of foliage and lay it so that the stems overlap the first bunch and cover the stems. Make sure that all the stems are facing the same direction.

10  Continue the process of overlapping the bunches of foliage and wiring them to the string until you run out of string.

11  When you get to the end of the string, twist the wire tightly around the last bundle's stems, and knot the wire and the string together. Leave 12 inches of wire (to attach the garland where you want it) and cut the wire with scissors or pruning shears.

### ✱ Tips

It's best to use the tips of the branches when gathering evergreen trimmings.

If you need the finished garland to be longer than your spool of string, you can wire two completed garlands together.

Wire small pinecones to the finished garland by twisting a length of floral wire around the bottom half of a cone.

Hang the garland from evenly spaced tacks, nails or picture hooks so it droops uniformly between the hooks.

### ⚠ Warning

This is a dirty job! Work over newspaper, and have plenty of soap and water ready to clean your hands when you're done.

### Things You'll Need

❏ scissors or pruning shears

❏ garden trimmings

❏ string or twine

❏ #24 floral or paddle wire

## Paint Holiday Windows 509

You don't have to go shopping to enjoy festive seasonal windows—here's how to create your own at home.

### ⊙ Steps

1 Measure the window you will be painting, and note its dimensions and shape. Be sure the window has some protection from rain and snow, such as an awning. Window paint will wash off if it gets wet.

2 Consult coloring books and greeting cards for ideas, then decide what designs or images you want to paint. Or create your own original design.

3 Draw your design, actual size, on a piece of butcher paper.

4 Tape the butcher paper to the inside of the window with the design facing out. This will be your guide for applying paint.

5 Don't bother washing the windows right before painting; a light coat of dust will help the paint adhere to the window.

6 Prepare the work area by placing newspaper on the ground.

7 Plan the colors you'll use for each area of your design. Tempera paints are most commonly used.

8 Pour paint from the bottles into small plastic cups.

9 Paint large areas of the design first, using a wide brush. Use smaller brushes to paint smaller areas and add details.

10 Outline your design and add finishing touches and highlights using a fine-tipped brush with black or white paint.

### ⚠ Warning

Use caution when working on a ladder. Make sure the ladder is stable before climbing on.

### Things You'll Need

❑ tape measure

❑ coloring books and greeting cards

❑ butcher paper and pencil

❑ masking tape

❑ tempera paint

❑ plastic cups

❑ paintbrushes

## Make a Snowman Pop-Up Card 510

Let your kids send their own 3-D holiday greetings with this easy pop-up card.

### ⊙ Steps

1 Use a blank greeting card or a piece of card stock that has been cut to the desired size and folded in half. A folded card measuring 6 by 8 inches works well for this project.

2 Draw or trace a snowman shape onto a separate piece of heavy white paper. Card stock or cardboard is best. The snowman should be one-half to three-quarters of the length of your greeting card (4 to 6 inches) and three-quarters of the width of the open greeting card (4½ inches).

3 Outline the snowman shape with a black felt-tip pen or permanent marker. Use crayons, acrylic paint or markers to decorate the snowman.

4 Use a ruler and pencil to draw one vertical line along each side of the snowman. Place each line 2 inches from the snowman's widest point.

### ✱ Tips

Use a snowman-shaped cookie cutter as a template for your snowman. You can also make other shapes, such as a star, angel or heart to create pop-up cards.

Make sure that the tabs are the same color as the interior of the greeting card. You may have to draw your snowman on a white piece of paper and then glue it onto paper that matches the greeting card.

5 Use scissors to cut along the outside of the snowman outline so that the black marks made in step 3 remain. Leave uncut the 2-inch-long tab of paper on the center of each side of the snowman. Make sure both tabs are centered and even with each other. (Note: if your card is smaller than 6 by 8 inches, make the tabs 1 inch instead of 2 inches.)

6 Fold the snowman in half vertically, blank sides together. Make a sharp crease and unfold. Fold the tabs on the sides of the snowman under by 1/2 inch. Make a sharp crease.

7 Position the snowman over the open greeting card so that the snow-man's centerfold lines up with the center of the card; keep in mind that the snowman fold should oppose the card fold. Determine where to place the tabs depending on how far you want the snowman to pop up. Mark the two spots for the tabs with a pencil, making sure that they are equidistant from the edges.

8 Glue the 1/2-inch, folded-back portion of the tabs to the surface of the greeting card so that the pop-up shape remains in the position deter-mined in step 7. Allow the glue to dry.

### Things You'll Need

❏ card stock paper

❏ black felt-tip pen or permanent marker

❏ crayons, acrylic paints or markers

❏ ruler

❏ pencil

❏ scissors

❏ glue

---

## 511 | Make Pomanders

Pomanders—fruits studded with cloves—have been used for centuries for their fragrance. They will add a wonderful holiday scent to your home.

### ◉ Steps

1 Choose a variety of fruits for your pomanders. Apples, lemons, tanger-ines and oranges work best.

2 Use a toothpick or a wooden or metal skewer to pierce the skin of the fruit. Insert cloves into the fruit so that cloves form close, vertical rows. Make patterns with the cloves, if you desire. The goal is to cover the fruit with cloves as completely as possible.

3 Combine the powdered orrisroot, ground cinnamon, ground allspice and ground nutmeg in a large zipper-lock bag. (This mixture will cover approximately two pieces of fruit.)

4 Place the fruit in the bag, and roll the fruit around in the spice mixture. Cover the entire fruit with spices.

5 Remove the fruit from the bag and shake off excess spice powder.

6 Wrap the fruit in tissue paper and store in a cool, dry place for three to four weeks.

7 Unwrap the pomander and display as desired.

### ✱ Tips

Hang pomanders in doorways, on mantles or even on a Christmas tree.

Display four or five pomanders in a bowl filled with potpourri.

### Things You'll Need

❏ apples, lemons, tangerines or oranges

❏ toothpick or skewer

❏ cloves

❏ 1 tbsp. powdered orrisroot

❏ 1 tbsp. ground cinnamon

❏ 1 tbsp. ground allspice

❏ 1 1/2 tsp. ground nutmeg

❏ large zipper-lock bag

❏ tissue paper

## Wrap a Gift 512

These instructions are for a rectangular gift box, but they can be applied to any size or shape of box.

### ☉ Steps

1 Gather your materials and lay them out on a flat work surface. Remember to remove the price tag from the gift before wrapping it.

2 Place the box along the length of wrapping paper and unroll enough paper to wrap it around the box, leaving at least a 2-inch overlap. Make sure there is enough wrapping paper at each end of the box to cover the ends completely when folded over them.

3 Use a pencil to mark where this overlap ends and cut the wrapping paper in a straight line at this point. Fold the paper or use a yardstick to guide you in cutting a straight line.

4 Eyeball the wrapping paper at the ends of the box. Trim away any extra paper so that the remaining flaps are long enough to cover the box but short enough to fold over smoothly into flaps.

5 Open the paper you've just cut and lay the box in the center of the unprinted side, top down.

6 Bring one lengthwise edge of the wrapping paper to the center of the box and secure it with tape. Turn the opposite edge of the paper under approximately 1 inch and bring this to the center of the box as well so that it overlaps the first edge, and tape it down.

7 Position the box so that one short end is facing you. Grasp the left and right edges of the wrapping paper and push the sides in so that top and bottom flaps are formed. Make sure the edges are pushed in as far as they will go without ripping the paper. Tape the edges to the box.

8 Bring the upper flap down against the side of the box, making sure the flap is sharply creased at its folds. Tape the flap to the box.

9 Bring the lower flap up against the side of the box. Crease and secure it as you did the upper flap.

10 Repeat for the opposite end of the box.

11 Position the package so the seamless side is facing down.

12 Wrap a long piece of ribbon around the box lengthwise, then twist the ribbon at the lengthwise seam to wrap it around the box widthwise.

13 Turn the box over so that the seamless side is facing up and tie the ribbon into a bow on top of the present where the ribbons cross.

14 If you have a card, slide it under the ribbon and secure it with tape on the underside. If you have a gift tag, use the loose ends of the ribbon to secure the gift tag (if it has a hole in it), or adhere it directly to the gift (if it has adhesive on it.)

### ✱ Tips

If your gift is not rectangular, find a box you can put it in to make it easier to wrap.

Check the label on any package of gift-wrapping paper to make sure there is enough paper to wrap your gift box.

Choose gift-wrapping paper that comes on a tube instead of precut sheets of paper that come folded into squares. The latter have deep creases, which can give your package a crumpled, untidy appearance.

Transparent cellophane tape, especially the nonglossy kind, will give your package a tidier appearance than can be achieved with other types of tape.

### Things You'll Need

❑ wrapping paper

❑ pencil

❑ scissors

❑ transparent cellophane tape

❑ ribbon

❑ card or gift tag

## 513 | Be Happy

Happiness has different meanings for everyone; we each have to define and seek it for ourselves.

### ⊙ Steps

1   Figure out what is important to you in life. For example: Do you value a certain kind of job; material things; a relationship; time alone or with others; time to relax or to be creative; time to read, listen to music or have fun? These are just a few of the possibilities.

2   Think about times when you have felt happy, good or content. Where were you? Whom were you with? What were you doing, thinking or feeling that made you feel happy?

3   Decide to make more time in your life to do more of what is important to you and makes you feel happier. To be happy, you have to make happiness a priority in your life.

4   Start with little things and work up to bigger ones. Little things might include reading an engrossing book for 15 minutes; taking a walk; calling a friend; or buying great-smelling soap, shampoo, candles or tea that you will enjoy every time you use it.

5   Focus on what is positive about yourself, others and life in general instead of dwelling on the negative. In a journal, write down as many positive things as you can think of. Keep it handy to read over, and continue adding to it.

6   Appreciate what is working in your life right now. In the major areas of your life, such as your health, job, love life, friends, family, money and living situation, what is going well?

### ✱ Tips

Ask other people, "What makes you happy?" or "What is something that makes you feel good?"

It's OK to ask for professional help. Talk to someone such as a psychotherapist, career counselor or spiritual adviser (minister or teacher) to help you sort out what would make you happy.

Read books on the subject of happiness. Wise people have been writing about it for hundreds of years. In the bookstore, look under psychology, spirituality or philosophy.

## 514 | Overcome Shyness

Everyone feels shy sometimes, but being too shy can hamper many aspects of your life.

### ⊙ Steps

1   Determine why you're shy in the first place. For example, are you afraid of what someone might say about your physical appearance? Remember, there's an underlying reason for how you react in situations.

2   Act as if you're not shy. In private, behave as if you're oozing confidence. Hold your chin up, stand up straight and tall, stride confidently and speak firmly. It may seem ridiculous, but you will see results when you're out in public.

3   Practice making eye contact and smiling when you have interactions with others. Strike up casual conversations with strangers about the weather or current events.

4   Look your best. One way to reduce self-consciousness is to always look good and limit opportunities for being self-critical.

### ✱ Tip

See 842 "Overcome a Phobia" for progressive relaxation techniques. These same steps can be applied to situations that bring out shyness.

5   Decrease your fear of rejection by imagining the worst possible out-
    come. If you approach someone, he or she may say no to your overture
    or may just walk away. Everybody has been rejected at some point, but
    no one has to dwell on it.

6   Look and learn. Watching friends or even strangers who aren't shy is a
    good way to learn some tips firsthand.

7   Develop a positive feeling about yourself, don't get frustrated, and have
    fun. Keep in mind that the real goal is to meet people who will like you
    for who you are.

## Find the Best Places to Meet People                                515

**Still looking for the date of your dreams? If you're wasting hours
on end hanging out at the corner bar or the local gym, you
might want to change your strategy.**

### ⊙ Steps

1   Choose a place that interests you. This increases your chances of meet-
    ing people who are interested in similar things.

2   Be creative about where you go. Parties and other social gatherings are
    the most obvious places to make new acquaintances, but don't leave
    out other options, such as club meetings and classes.

3   Go academic: College and university campuses are great places to meet
    people if you still attend school.

4   Mingle: Parties, dances and movie lines are fun places to meet people
    who make an effort to go out.

5   Don't overlook opportunities in public places: Grocery stores,
    Laundromats, bookstores, coffeehouses and restaurants are all casual
    spots to meet new people.

6   Ask around—friends and relatives are good sources for helping you get
    exposed to other people.

7   Look in your neighborhood. Proximity plays a big part in friendships as
    well as romantic relationships, and you may find that the special some
    one you seek is right around the corner.

8   Look in your community. Familiar places like your church, temple or
    mosque are good venues for seeing who's out there.

9   Use the newspaper. Place a personal ad or respond to one.

10  Try meeting people online. There are numerous Web sites that feature
    chat rooms, personal ads and individual photos.

### ⚠ Warnings

If you meet a potential romantic
partner at work, think carefully
before proceeding—is it worth
the possible complications?

Try not to look desperate—
people may find this unattractive.

## 516 | Flirt

**Not a natural flirt? Don't worry—anyone can learn the basic social skills that will attract others.**

### ⊙ Steps

1 Be confident—it's the magical charm that makes others want to get to know you.

2 Smile, smile, smile.

3 Think playful thoughts when gearing up to flirt. Flirts are fun and engaging, and they love to play with others.

4 Compliment a stranger or acquaintance on his or her clothes, eyes, smile or sense of humor, for starters.

5 Keep your body language open and inviting: Make eye contact, lightly touch the person's hand or arm when telling a story, toss your head back when you laugh.

6 Initiate stimulating conversation. At a loss for words? Ask open-ended questions about the flirtee's job, hometown, family, recent movies seen, or thoughts about a painting on the wall.

7 Open up about yourself, giving someone even more reason to like you. But don't go on and on—the goal is to engage and intrigue, not bore.

8 Gauge the person's interest carefully. If you sense a flashing red light— or worse, smug ridicule—make your exit graciously and immediately. You've got nicer people to meet.

9 Progress in your flirtation, paying attention to cues from the object of your interest. If you perceive a sensual or sexual connection, make a bold move—ask for a date.

### ✳ Tips

Avoid negative body language such as crossing your arms, scowling, appearing overly stressed, looking downward or walking in a hurry when you don't really need to.

Give yourself time to learn what types of conversation starters work for you. Practice flirting wherever you can—at the grocery store or Laundromat, or with your friends.

### ⚠ Warning

Sexually suggestive remarks or touching is inappropriate among co-workers. Keep any office flirting G-rated at all times.

## 517 | Survive the Bar Scene

**You agreed to go out with your friends to a bar or club. Instead of dwelling on how you allowed such a thing to happen, have fun by following these simple tips.**

### ⊙ Steps

1 Enjoy yourself, first and foremost. Would you rather be home alone washing dishes? If the answer is yes, keep thinking of mundane chores until you find the one you would not want to be doing at the moment.

2 You see someone you think you'd like to know better. He or she blows you off? So? Pat yourself on the back for knowing that your soul mate is not necessarily hanging out in a meat market. Let it go and find someone else with better manners.

3 Be someone you're not—try on a new hat. Play the part of the spoiled rich girl, the alpha-wolf guy, the dumb blonde.

### ✳ Tips

Be sure you know how you're getting home before you go out.

Interestingly enough, 71 percent of men report success when they use the pickup line "Hi."

### ⚠ Warning

Don't put yourself into a dangerous situation, such as being alone in a dark alley with a strange man—or woman.

4   Be careful not to drink too much, in case you are approached by some-one with a bad pickup line. "May I end this sentence with a proposi-tion?" might work on you if you have tipped a few too many.

5   Remember, though, that as lame as pickup lines might be, the person is making an effort to show interest in you. If you are even remotely inter-ested, laugh, say hello and begin a normal conversation.

6   Be polite if someone wants to talk to you and you aren't interested. If the person won't leave you alone, say that you have a boyfriend or girlfriend.

7   Save your flirting for when you really want to use it.

## Make Small Talk                                                   518

Small talk can be a big challenge, but preparation and confidence are all you really need.

### ◉ Steps

1   Practice. Converse with everyone you encounter: cashiers, waiters, peo-ple you're in line with, neighbors, co-workers and kids. Chat with folks unlike yourself, from seniors to teens to tourists.

2   Read everything: cookbooks, newspapers, magazines, reviews, product inserts, maps, signs and catalogs. Everything is a source of information that can be turned into interesting conversations.

3   Force yourself to get into small-talk situations, such as doctors' waiting rooms, cocktail parties and meetings at the office. Accept invitations, or host your own gathering.

4   Immerse yourself in culture, both high and low. Television, music, sports, fashion, art and poetry are great sources of chat. If you can't stand Shakespeare, your dislike of the bard is also a good topic for discussion.

5   Keep a journal. Write down funny stories you hear, beautiful things you see, quotes, observations, shopping lists and calls you made. That story about the time when the long-distance operator misunderstood you could become an opening line.

6   Talk to yourself in the mirror. Make a random list of topics and see what you have to say on the subjects. Baseball, Russia, butter, hip-hop, shoes ... the more varied your list, the better.

7   Expand your horizons. Go home a new way. Try sushi. Play pinball. Go online. Paint a watercolor. Bake a pie. Try something new every day.

8   Be a better listener. Did your boss just say that she suffers from migraines? Did your doctor just have twins? These are opportunities for making small talk.

9   Work on building your confidence, overcoming shyness and banishing any feelings of stage fright. Remember, the more you know, the more you know you can talk about.

### ✳ Tips

Be yourself. Confidence and uniqueness are superb substi-tutes for comedic genius.

Keep a few exit lines in mind. For example, "Thanks for the won-derful conversation, but now I have to make believe I'm inter-ested in everybody else."

### ⚠ Warning

Keep your fellow chatterers in mind; naughty stories and loose language will be frowned upon in many circles. Similarly, your French quips and scientific dis-courses will be wasted on some.

## 519 | Know if Someone Is Lying

There are often cues and signs that a person may be lying. But there may also be understandable reasons for the lie.

### ⊙ Steps

1 Look for body language that might indicate someone is lying, such as not looking you in the eye when speaking to you, being fidgety, or acting nervous or uncomfortable.

2 Listen for inconsistencies in what the person tells you, such as different stories on different days, different time frames, mistakes in remembering details or mixing up details.

3 Notice if the person steadfastly resists answering any of your questions. Extreme defensiveness could mean that he or she is hiding something.

4 Notice if the person accuses you of lying or being deceitful when you haven't been. This could reflect the accuser's own underlying behavior, which he or she is projecting onto you rather than owning up to.

5 Listen to your gut and intuition. You may just know someone is lying. If you are not sure, don't jump to conclusions. Try to get some evidence to back up your hunch.

6 Consider asking directly if the person has lied to you. Many people feel bad getting caught lying and find it a relief to finally be honest.

7 Try to be understanding and listen to the person's reasons for lying. Was he trying not to hurt you? Was she afraid you would be angry or upset?

8 Look at your possible role in the situation. Are you someone who gets so upset hearing the truth that others feel they can't be honest with you?

### ⚠ Warning

Try not to assume that someone is lying unless your evidence is solid. Body language and intuition can provide clues but not proof.

## 520 | Compliment a Man Who Catches Your Eye

A cute guy has just entered the café. What do you do? A straightforward compliment can lead to a beautiful friendship — or at least brighten his day.

### ⊙ Steps

1 Be sincere and friendly; compliment him in the same way you would want to be complimented.

2 Smile at him as he walks by. Giving special attention and obvious appreciation might be all you need to do.

3 Mention that he has a nice smile — but don't be lecherous. Simply say, "You've got a nice smile."

4 Note an attractive part of his outfit: "Great frames!" "Cool sweater!"

5 Don't gawk.

6 Keep your appreciation of his Adonis-like features or body to yourself — anything you say about his physique will probably sound cheesy.

### ✱ Tip

Try not to be too extravagant, like saying you love something of his. Simple, straightforward compliments are best and leave little room for misinterpretation.

### ⚠ Warning

Use compliments sparingly lest you come off as insincere.

7   Give him credit for his spunk and originality if he sports a magenta, green or blue hairdo.

8   Compliment him in the context of the situation at hand. For example, tell him you admire his taste in reading material.

## Compliment a Woman Who Catches Your Eye　521

You spot an intriguing woman and must establish contact or live with regret for the rest of the day. How do you compliment her without appearing too aggressive? Or, worse, tasteless?

### ⊙ Steps

1   Think about commenting on actions over looks: "Great moves!" for the groover on the dance floor, or "Healthy diet!" for the cutie buying greens at the supermarket.

2   Commend a woman for her wit or intelligence ("Funny joke!" "Great idea!") rather than her beautiful breasts.

3   Compliment a woman's appearance—hair, clothes, jewelry—only if you can do so with a sincere smile, or she'll think you're tossing her a line and will tune you out.

4   Consider compliments that may lead to conversation: "Love your bike— where do you like to ride?"

5   Consider asking her first if she likes receiving compliments. If she smiles encouragingly, tell her she's got a great smile; if she gives you a dirty look, pretend you're on Maui and look the other way.

6   Get creative. If a woman has unbelievable violet eyes or an extraordinary and exotic name, she's probably used to getting compliments about these unusual features. Compliment her on something less obvious— she'll appreciate that you noticed what others don't.

### ✳ Tip

Watch out for half-compliments that could do more damage than good: "You're going to look so beautiful when you finally get your braces taken off."

### ⚠ Warning

Avoid sarcasm and smirking when you give compliments, especially if those behavioral no-nos tend to occur when you're nervous.

## Know if Someone Likes You Romantically　522

Sometimes the direct approach is best—just ask. But if that seems too bold, look for some of these telling signs.

### ⊙ Steps

#### Behavior

1   Pay attention to your conversations with the person in question. Does this person show a special interest in talking with you and, once it's started, make an effort to keep that conversation going?

2   Does this person "accidentally" run into you in places where he knows you will be, such as at your desk? At the Laundromat on Tuesdays? At your brother's birthday party?

3   Notice whether this person mentions future plans to spend time with you: "That band is coming to town soon. We should really get tickets."

### ✳ Tips

Trust in your intuition and listen to your feelings.

Feel flattered if a friend or co-worker likes you romantically, but don't view it as a personal crisis if you can't return the affections. Your admirer will probably move on once you make it clear that you don't feel the same way.

4   Notice if the person is making an effort to spend time alone together. Canceling other plans in order to be with you longer, or finding excuses not to leave, could be a sign of romantic interest.

5   Has the person been calling for seemingly random reasons, such as, "I was wondering if you knew what that pizza place down the street is called," followed by, "Are you hungry?"

6   Has the person taken a sudden interest in your life and hobbies? This is a sure sign that she is interested in something—and it's probably not your stamp collection.

7   Observe how the person acts around your friends—he might be extra friendly to your closest pals for a reason.

## Body Language

1   Sometimes seeing someone you have a crush on results in telltale physiological signs. Does the person in question blush when you look at her? Her sympathetic nervous system is probably going into overdrive. Does she jumble her words when talking to you?

2   See if the person mirrors your motions: When you lean back, he leans back; when you put your elbows on the table, he does the same.

3   Note whether this person sits or stands in the open position—that is, facing you with arms uncrossed, or crossing her legs in your direction if the person is a woman.

4   Does he move closer to you and/or touch you subtly, such as patting your hand or touching your cheek?

5   Look for other elements of body language such as frequent eye contact, holding your gaze and looking down before looking away, energetic speech coupled with open hands, or flashing palms.

6   Does the person you're wondering about just plain smile at you a lot?

---

## 523  Ask for a Phone Number

Say you're at the grocery store and out of nowhere comes your dream mate. Don't just stand there speechless in aisle 9—ask for a phone number!

### ⊙ Steps

1   Approach the person. Remember that eye contact and a gentle smile are crucial in appearing friendly.

2   Enter the conversation with a compliment, then introduce yourself. Try not to be too cute with your delivery; sincerity goes over better than an elaborate pickup line.

3   Talk. You'll get a strong sense of whether the person would be willing to give you a phone number. If no eye contact or smile is coming your way, and you're making a solid effort, then maybe you should give up.

4   Ask for the number if you're getting positive signals. Try not to be pushy, and show respect for the person's private information. Avoid "How about

### ✱ Tips

Opt for a person's work number if he or she appears uncomfortable with giving you a home number.

If you get a phone number, wait two days before calling so as not to appear desperate. Avoid waiting too long, though; he or she may forget about you.

giving me your number?" and go with "It would be great to get to know you better. Is there a number where I can reach you?"

5   Offer your own phone number after getting the other person's, if you feel comfortable doing so. Some women are not comfortable giving out their number, so if a woman declines to give you hers, you may still want to offer your own.

# Ask Someone on a Date                                              524

You'll never know whether the other person is interested unless you ask. So gather up all your courage and follow these steps.

## ⊙ Steps

1   Introduce yourself to that person you've been admiring from afar.

2   Ask for the person's telephone number, or tell a common friend that you would like the number.

3   Call at a time that's not intrusive. Make the call when you're comfortable, regardless of what your friends might say about romantic protocol.

4   Reintroduce yourself once you're on the phone by saying something like, "Hey, it's Shirley. We met at the drag strip."

5   Using as little pretense as possible (ideally none), ask the person if he or she would like to meet for a cup of coffee or do something similarly informal. If you are politely refused, take the hint and get off the phone.

6   Arrange to get together casually for a brief time—half an hour or so. If that goes well, suggest a more formal date, such as lunch.

### ✱ Tips

Some of the best ideas for a date are the things you love to do the most, such as going to an art museum or getting muddy on a mountain bike ride.

If your invitation is rejected, congratulate yourself for trying and move on.

### ⚠ Warning

Going to see a movie may not be ideal for a first date; it shows a lack of creativity and does not allow the two of you to spend much time talking.

# Plan a Date on a Budget                                            525

You don't need to blow your bank account or rack up debt on your credit card to plan a fantastic date. All you need is a little imagination and the following pointers.

## ⊙ Steps

1   Determine how much you can spend and the types of things you and your date might enjoy doing together.

2   Opt for the less expensive meet-at-a-café date or the drink-after-work date for a blind date, or if you don't yet know your mutual interests.

3   Consider an afternoon bike ride, swimming in a local lake, sitting on docks watching sailboats go by, or ice skating in the park if the weather is nice and your date likes the outdoors.

4   Plan an evening picnic in the park, weather permitting. Coordinate with a free outdoor musical, play or opera, and pack a bottle of wine, along with cheese and bread.

### ✱ Tip

Ask the person to lunch and a matinee on the weekend— the inexpensive version of a Saturday-night dinner-and-a-movie date.

### ⚠ Warning

Avoid pretending you have money when you don't. But don't draw attention to the fact that you have little to spend—financial distress is never a turn-on.

5 Consider inviting your date to a party; make any necessary introductions to your friends, have fun, then leave together after a short time and grab a drink.

6 Try cooking dinner and renting a movie. (This may or may not be an appropriate first date.)

## 526 Refuse a Date to Ensure No More Requests

**Unless you want to be asked out again by this person, be direct and leave no room for misinterpretation.**

### ⊙ Steps

1 Be clear, consistent and gracious in your refusal. Be politely neutral rather than emphatic.

2 Don't hesitate, procrastinate or ask to think about it.

3 Express regret, if you'd like, but never say anything you don't mean, such as, "Maybe another time."

4 Devise an impersonal, generic explanation if you prefer, such as, "I never date co-workers" or "I'm involved with someone else." Otherwise, simply refuse the invitation with a polite "Thank you for thinking of me. I'm sorry I'll have to say no."

### ✻ Tip

If a person persists in asking you out, just persist in being firm and clear. Sooner or later, you'll get the message across.

## 527 Refuse a Date to Ensure Another Request

**Sometimes circumstances are beyond your control. Here's how to refuse a date when you truly wish you could accept.**

### ⊙ Steps

1 Smile and make eye contact if the invitation is made in person.

2 Communicate your complete attention if the request is made by phone. Consider saying something like "Excuse me while I close the door" or "I was hoping you'd call."

3 Express your thanks in whatever style is genuine and comfortable for you—a joke, a simple thanks, a great big "Wow!"

4 Communicate your regret at having to refuse, and explain why you need to decline the invitation.

5 Suggest another specific day, or express your general wish to find another time that works for both of you. A straightforward "I can't this time because I have to go to Chicago, but I would love to make it another time. How's next Friday?" has candor to recommend it.

### ✻ Tips

People look for acceptance, so be open and enthusiastic.

If you simply say that you can't make it, the person may interpret that as a brush-off. Always provide an explanation.

Be clear, candid and gracious.

### ⚠ Warning

Asking someone out can be difficult, so make it as easy as possible for the other person.

## Cancel a Date at the Last Minute

You've changed your mind about your date—or life has simply gotten in the way. How do you cancel at the last minute?

### ◉ Steps

#### If You Want to Be Asked Out Again

1 Call as soon as possible. It's not likely you'll be forgiven easily if you let your date show up and wait for you, just to have you cancel.

2 Blame it on outside circumstances: an unexpected meeting, deadline or assignment. You really, really want to go, but ...

3 Tell the truth: You're tired, you don't feel well, you've had a rotten day. You'd rather stay in and rest than go out and not be very much fun.

4 Create an excuse: You forgot that you were meeting your friends for dinner, you need to go to your grandmother's to move furniture, you lost your keys and can't leave until you find them.

5 Leave the conversation open for another invitation.

6 Suggest an alternative date.

7 Offer to make it up to him or her—and then do it. Send a card or a bouquet of flowers.

8 If your date calls later to check up on you, be where you said you'd be and thank him or her for being thoughtful.

#### If You Don't Want to Be Asked Out Again

1 Call as soon as you realize you want to cancel. Keep in mind how much easier canceling is on the phone than in person.

2 Blame it on outside circumstances. Believable: You are really busy at work and don't have time for dating. Unbelievable: Your power has been shut off so you haven't had a shower in four days.

3 Tell the truth: You're not interested; you've had a revelation that he or she is not The One.

4 Tell a white lie: You're seeing someone else, or you've decided that you don't want to date anyone just now.

5 Stay on the phone only long enough to deliver your message; be careful not to give the impression that you are interested.

### ✱ Tip

If you don't want another date, keep the conversation short. Don't apologize for not wanting to go out with this person. Ever.

## 529 | Create a Romantic Atmosphere

When planning an intimate dinner or other event, use your imagination and ingenuity to arouse the senses with beautiful sights, sounds, flavors and aromas.

### ⊙ Steps

#### Indoors

1 Set the mood by playing some soft, romantic music. Classical music is usually a safe bet, as are jazz and soul.

2 Fill the room with a dramatic array of flowers to add visual interest as well as inexpensive elegance.

3 Light the room with either bright, slow-burning candles or, if possible, the glow from a fireplace to add a warm, intimate tone to the evening.

4 Plan and prepare a simple yet elegant meal. Try to find out beforehand which foods your date particularly enjoys and serve them.

5 Include classic romantic fare, such as Champagne and strawberries.

6 Use your best china and flatware, and select table linens and napkins in soft and sumptuous fabrics. If chosen well, these items can be purchased for little money but appear stylish and sophisticated, giving your date the impression that you've gone all out for the occasion.

#### Outdoors

1 Coordinate your plans with seasonal or natural events such as a sunset, a full moon or the turning of the leaves during the fall.

2 Plan and prepare a simple yet elegant meal. If possible, include your date's favorite foods. Don't forget the wine or Champagne.

3 Pack the meal and the necessary utensils in a picnic basket. Again, use the best china and flatware you have.

4 Bring along a picnic blanket as well as a big, soft blanket for warmth, should the night turn cold.

5 Build a fire if your location allows, or bring along some candles or torches to provide light and warmth. Citronella candles are especially handy for warding off insects.

### ✳ Tips

Flowers are a staple of romance—use them liberally.

When planning an outdoor event, be sure to check the weather forecast and have an alternate plan in mind, just in case.

### Things You'll Need

❑ music

❑ flowers

❑ candles

❑ romantic food and drink

❑ china and flatware

❑ table linen and napkins

## 530 | Keep a Dozen Red Roses Fresh

To make that special and romantic gift last as long as possible, follow these guidelines.

### ⊙ Steps

1 Store the roses in a cool place—ideally a refrigerator—if you can't get them into water immediately. A cool environment will help to slow the deterioration process.

### ✳ Tips

There are many other factors that go into the duration of a cut rose, including rose type, gardening

2  Fill a vase with warm or tepid water. Make sure it's no cooler than room temperature. Warm water will be absorbed more quickly.

3  Add floral preservatives to the water if you have some available. Follow the package instructions.

4  Cut off any foliage that will lie below the waterline (it will rot), as well as any torn leaves.

5  Cut off about 1 inch of the stems, either straight across or at a slant, using a knife rather than scissors. Do this while the stem is submerged in a basin of warm or tepid water.

6  Place the roses in water immediately after cutting them.

7  Change the water and recut the stems daily, taking extra care to remove any leaves that may have wilted or dipped into the water. This will help prevent bacteria buildup. If you're using preservatives, add more solution every other day.

8  Keep the flowers in a cool, dry place, away from direct sunlight, heaters, air conditioners and drafts. At night, move your roses to the coolest part of the house. This will help them last longer.

methods and climate; however, following these steps will allow you to keep your roses fresh for as long as possible.

You can make your own floral preservative using a citrus-based soft drink. Add one part soft drink for every three parts water.

## Make a Great First Impression on a Date          531

Want to make sure your date will be eager to go out with you a second time? No problem.

### ⊙ Steps

1  Dress attractively but comfortably. Don't wear clothes that make you feel stiff or self-conscious.

2  Be aware of your posture—it speaks volumes about you. You want to appear alert and confident by sitting up straight.

3  Compliment your date. Don't just say "I like your shirt." Be sincere and notice something that he or she took time with.

4  Learn to flirt (see 516 "Flirt") and try it out. Don't overdo it, though.

5  Realize that you don't have to tell people how great you are. It's better to show them instead.

6  Be interested and interesting. Listen actively to what your date says. Ask questions and don't interrupt.

7  Enjoy yourself, no matter what. If you're easygoing and fun to be around, and if you can roll with whatever comes your way, you can't help but make a great impression.

8  Thank the other person for the date—always, without exception. Good manners will get you far.

### ✳ Tips

Don't talk about anything negative or complain on a first date.

Be cautious about drinking—it will give you a false sense of confidence and your inhibitions will be lowered. You may say or do things you'll regret later.

## 532 | Read Your Date's Body Language

Your date claims to be having fun, yet you catch him or her yawning uncontrollably. Body language says a lot about what your date is really thinking.

⊙ **Steps**

**Positive Body Language**

1 Notice if your date's posture is good yet relaxed. A slouched date probably isn't having a good time. A date who's sitting up is paying attention.

2 Observe whether your date makes good eye contact. If he keeps looking into your eyes, you've got it made.

3 Is your date leaning forward? Then you aren't a stranger anymore.

4 Be aware of any physical contact. Holding hands is a great sign.

5 Notice if your date has her palms up, which indicates a friendly warmth.

6 Know that your date is listening to you if he nods at appropriate times during conversation; this indicates that your words are being heard.

7 Pay attention to whether your date is in sync with you and constantly reflecting your behavior. Does she shift in her seat when you do? Does he pick up your speed and tone when he's speaking? This occurs unconsciously and indicates a good rhythm between you—it's not just a copycat game.

**Negative Body Language**

1 Take note if your date's arms are crossed. This suggests there's a wall between the two of you.

2 Beware if your date is yawning. This is a bad sign—unless it's because she was up all night thinking about you.

3 See if your date is nodding at inappropriate times or seems to be nodding constantly during your conversation. Your date may be thinking about something else.

4 Is your date looking at everything but you? Be worried.

5 Notice if your date is keeping some distance between you. Personal space is one thing, but if your date is not standing next to you when you're waiting in a movie line together, that's a bad sign.

**✱ Tip**

Interpreting body language isn't cut-and-dried; allow for the fact that your interpretation may be wrong.

**⚠ Warning**

Avoid pointing out your date's body language to him or her—this may put your date on the defensive.

## 533 | Kiss on a Date

The date's gone well, and now it's almost over. Here are some tips on the how and when of kissing.

⊙ **Steps**

1 Look for positive body language, such as eye contact, uncrossed arms and head tilted toward you.

2 Do it. Waiting just makes the moment awkward.

**✱ Tip**

Keep the kissing simple for now. Use a soft touch that will calm your date, especially if this kiss is the first one.

3   Maintain eye contact as you close in. Try not to close your eyes until after making lip contact.

4   Tilt your head slightly to one side to avoid bumping noses.

5   Press your lips gently against your date's. Try not to suck his or her breath away just yet.

6   Release. Look into your date's eyes. If he or she isn't looking back at you the same way, then you probably shouldn't continue.

7   Kiss your date again. There's more flexibility to this kiss.

8   Explore—softly kiss your date's neck, ears and eyelashes. By this time, you'll have a better feel for how and where to kiss your date.

## Decide Whether to Go on a Third Date                          534

You made it past the first and second dates. Now it's time to decide: Is this worth pursuing?

### ⊙ Steps

1   Assess the relationship. Who is making the plans? Is it both of you or just one of you? Are the decisions truly mutual?

2   How interested are you? You probably don't know each other very well yet, but are you beginning to feel comfortable with this person? Can you talk about some of your thoughts and feelings?

3   Does he or she seem interested in you?

4   Think about your shared interests. Do you have any of the same hobbies? Do you enjoy the same kinds of weekend activities?

5   Take note of your differences. Some can be a problem, while others may add interest. Do you have fun listening to his fishing stories, even though you'd never go yourself? That's a good sign. Are you put off by her vocal political opinions? Better forgo the third date.

6   Do your conversations keep getting more interesting? Or are you already running out of things to talk about?

7   Do you talk on the phone apart from setting up dates?

8   Have you seen any signs of psychological gamesmanship? If so, don't continue this unless you really enjoy the abuse.

9   Were you thanked on the first two dates? Regardless of who paid, it's nice to know that someone appreciated spending time with you.

10  How comfortable would you be meeting his or her parents? That may tell you a lot about how well you're clicking.

### ✳ Tips

If you decide to go on a third date, make sure to take it slow. Even though all the signs are looking positive, you need time to get to know each other better before getting serious.

If you decide against a third date, be firm and respectful in letting the other person know. Treat him or her the way you would like to be treated in this situation.

## 535 | Know When It's Over

**Is it time to call it quits?**

### ⊙ Steps

1 Be realistic. If you're being abused, hurt, cheated on or lied to, it's time to cut your losses and get out.

2 Think about the future you're creating. If your partner is jealous, obsessive, possessive or overly emotional, consider the extra burden you are carrying in dealing with those behaviors.

3 Is he a shameless flirt? Is she bossy? demanding? insecure? These are more signs of a rocky road ahead.

4 Do you truly enjoy each other's company, or do you find yourself relieved whenever you part company? If the latter, it doesn't bode well.

5 Evaluate your role in maintaining the relationship. If you feel as if you're doing all the work, it's time to talk or walk.

6 Does he promise to call and then forget? Is she terminally late? Be honest with yourself. Is this what you want?

7 Do you feel accepted and appreciated? If not, move on.

### ✳ Tip

Make sure you want to end the relationship because the person is wrong for you and not because you fear commitment. You don't want to send Prince Charming packing just because you have commitment jitters.

## 536 | Break Up Peacefully

**If you're ready to end a relationship, consider how you can break up without conflict.**

### ⊙ Steps

1 Acknowledge that the relationship is really over. Come to terms with your own feelings and make a firm decision to end the relationship.

2 Don't delay the inevitable. Once you decide to break up with your partner, immediately think about how, when and where you will take action.

3 Make sure you're the one who personally delivers the news. Don't give a third party the opportunity to tell your partner that you want to break up before you have the chance to discuss the matter alone.

4 Select a private place to meet with your partner to end the relationship.

5 Find or schedule an appropriate time. Approach the topic when both of you are calm and rational. Don't announce your intention to break up during a heated argument or a moment of anger.

6 Show your resolve by being firm, decisive and honest. Help your partner understand why you want to end the relationship. Be tactful, not brutal.

7 Remind your partner that you'll never forget the positive qualities in your relationship, but emphasize that you're ready to move on with your life.

8 Give your partner the closure that he or she needs to accept the breakup; answer questions and talk it over instead of leaving loose ends.

9 Stay positive as you both make plans to go your separate ways.

### ✳ Tip

Let go of old grievances during a breakup. The end of a relationship isn't the appropriate time to bring up old grudges.

### ⚠ Warning

If your partner does not agree to the breakup, don't allow him or her to manipulate you into staying in the relationship.

**How to Do** *(Just About)* **Everything**

## Handle a Breakup 537

Whether you're the one doing the dumping or the one getting dumped, breaking up is always hard to do. Although you might feel as if you'll never get over this, you will.

### ☉ Steps

1 Call all of your friends—even the ones you may have ignored during your recent relationship—and make plans immediately. Now is not a good time to be alone.

2 Vent when the need arises. Good friends will let you take out the photo album (again) and cry (again) and rant (again)—and they'll still love you.

3 Allow yourself time to grieve. If you don't let yourself wallow in self-pity for a while and mourn the good times lost, your heart may harden to future relationships and love.

4 Realize that this sadness will pass.

5 Distract yourself with fun once you're tired of mourning. Movies, group sports, classes or a favorite CD can help get your mind off your loss.

6 Indulge yourself when you're feeling lonely. Try a massage, a weekend trip away with a best friend, a great new outfit—whatever helps you feel good about yourself.

7 Begin dating again when you're ready. Have friends set you up, and go to all those parties you might otherwise skip.

8 Analyze what went wrong in the relationship only after you have rebuilt your self-esteem. If you attempt to do this too soon, you're headed for another downward spiral.

9 Remember the good aspects of the relationship (there must have been some), and then get excited about the new direction your life is suddenly taking. Change can be awesome!

### ✸ Tip

Keep in mind that clean breaks are generally better than those minibreaks or sort-of breakups that are a bit easier to deal with at the time. Upon breaking up, attempt to resolve lingering issues, then take some time away from each other, even if you intend to remain friends.

### ⚠ Warnings

Never sleep with an ex unless you like to torture yourself.

While you're upset, don't do anything you'll regret later. The transition back into single life is a highly vulnerable time. Get support from your friends.

## Know if You're in Love 538

Determining if you're in love involves serious soul-searching.

### ☉ Steps

1 Clarify what love is for you. Write down all your thoughts and feelings about what a loving relationship would be like for you. Ask other people how they define love or know if they love someone.

2 Distinguish between love (as you've defined it) and lust or infatuation. Lust is an intense sexual desire. Infatuation refers to the initial stage of a relationship, when you are "crazy" about your new love interest; this feeling usually fades over time.

3 Write down how you do feel about the person. For example: You enjoy his or her company, have similar interests, feel safe, trust the person, think he or she is attractive, and so on.

### ✸ Tips

Infatuation, when you may think you are in love and have found the perfect person, lasts about six months. But it often takes more time to tell if you are truly compatible and if you can love the whole person.

4   Think about how well the two of you relate to each other. For example, how well do you communicate with each other? How do you deal with conflict? Do you bring out good or bad parts of each other? Can you show different sides of yourself?

5   Ask yourself if you see and accept your love interest as a whole person. True love isn't just about loving the parts of someone that are easy to appreciate, but choosing to love that person overall.

Read books on the subject of love. Wise people have been writing about it for hundreds of years.

## 539  Say "I Love You"

Ready to take the plunge and introduce that most romantic phrase into your relationship's dialogue?

### ⊙ Steps

1   Decide if you do, indeed, love your mate. Most partners can see through a halfhearted "love ya"—which won't do your relationship any good.

2   Consider the possibility that your partner might not respond with the hoped-for "I love you, too." If you can handle that and still want to express your love, go for it. If you can't, then consider holding off until either you're certain your partner will respond as hoped or you're OK with it if he or she doesn't.

3   Think about how you'd like to let your partner know the way you feel, keeping in mind that uttering those words may give birth to a lifelong memory. If spontaneity works for you, wait for the perfect moment. If you're more methodical, consider writing a love letter first, then telling your mate in person the next time you get together.

4   If you decide in advance when to reveal your love, plan a special evening around it. Such relationship milestones warrant celebration.

5   When you tell your partner you love him or her, do so while making total eye contact, and while you are holding each other. This gives the moment the intimacy it deserves.

### ✱ Tip

Avoid saying the "L" word for the first time in the heat of passion—your partner may doubt the sincerity of your proclamation.

## 540  Write a Love Letter

Here is how to profess everlasting love for your one and only in a proper love letter.

### ⊙ Steps

1   Select stationery appropriate to your personality and sentiment. Decide whether you prefer torn-out notebook paper, perfumed sheets covered with flowers, or elegant note cards.

2   Determine the letter's purpose. Are you writing to tell your longtime love that you miss him or her, or initiating contact with someone you don't know very well?

3   Date your letter for posterity's sake.

### ✱ Tips

Handwrite the letter. Laser printing isn't very romantic.

Write a draft, set it aside briefly, then read it again. Tone the letter down if necessary.

4  Begin with Dear, Dearest, Beloved, My Precious, or whatever endearment or salutation feels appropriate for the depth of your relationship.

5  Be sure to thank your lover if you're responding to a letter, and mention the number of times you've reread it. Flatter your lover by repeating a couple of choice phrases he or she used.

6  Describe how your loved one makes you feel. Try to be original, but put sincerity ahead of creativity. The purpose of the letter is to express your feelings, not to stun your partner with a brilliant metaphor.

7  Mention his or her adorable traits. Bring up specific qualities or idiosyncrasies you appreciate. Be sparing with references to eyes and smiles, which can seem forced or clichéd, and try not to get melodramatic.

8  Recall your past times together and describe your hopes for the future.

9  Close with an exhortation to write back quickly, a mention of the next time you expect to see each other, or another appropriate comment.

10  Affix a proper valediction—such as "Sincerely," "Love" or "Feverishly Awaiting Your Letter"—depending on how you feel.

11  Read your letter aloud to check for awkward or stilted phrasing.

12  Finish your letter or envelope with a wax seal. Consider affixing a flower to it or enclosing a poem.

Consider other creative means of expressing your devotion: Scrawl confessions on a mirror, fan or piece of cloth. Fire off a quick succession of postcards.

## Make a Long-Distance Relationship Last  541

**Whoever first said that absence makes the heart grow fonder never contended with the weekend airport rush. Here are some ways to hold on to your long-distance lover—and your sanity.**

### ◉ Steps

1  Keep in touch daily. If large phone bills are a concern, send e-mail, letters, cards and even faxes.

2  Plan reunions to keep both of you pleased about the relationship. If your partner needs closeness, set up plans to meet often. Having a date to look forward to can help you through the rough times.

3  Reaffirm your love and commitment to one another. Try not to assume that the relationship is thriving. Listen to your partner's concerns and communicate your own before they become bigger problems.

4  Keep your partner informed about your life. You may live separately, but sharing information about your activities and friends is still important.

5  Trust in one another. Suspicion will only break the relationship down.

6  Keep the relationship a high priority. Avoid canceling reunions or putting off a phone call.

7  Focus on the future. Make plans to live in the same city eventually.

### ✳ Tips

Plan a reunion in a city other than the ones you live in. Having a weekend getaway or vacation together can help recharge the relationship and reinforce your commitment.

Find ways to reduce the costs of travel and phone calls so you can meet and talk more often.

Surprise your loved one with an unexpected visit or a bouquet of flowers to keep the passion alive.

Be patient—it may take time for long-term plans to work out.

## 542 Ask for Forgiveness

Saying you're sorry can seem awfully tough, but it gets easier with practice and delivers bountiful rewards.

### ◉ Steps

1 Think about what happened and what it is you are sorry for doing.

2 Write down your apology; this will help you organize your thoughts and calm your nerves.

3 Practice what you plan to say until you feel comfortable with it.

4 State clearly what it is you are sorry for doing.

5 Acknowledge your actions without making excuses.

6 Share your feelings about what happened—avoid blaming, exaggerating or saying empty words.

7 Listen to the other person's response without getting defensive.

8 Offer to make amends if appropriate.

9 Move on. Once you've apologized, let it go.

### ✱ Tips

Think of an apology as a commitment to the relationship rather than an act of weakness.

Be honest. Only apologize for things you truly feel responsible for; don't apologize just to make an unpleasant situation go away.

Say it in writing if a personal confrontation is just way too scary.

Give the other person some time to sort out his or her feelings—don't be discouraged if you aren't completely forgiven the moment you apologize.

## 543 Forgive

Forgive and forget, let go and lighten your load. A grudge can be a heavy weight to bear.

### ◉ Steps

1 Think about what happened.

2 Acknowledge all of your feelings. There is often anger lurking behind any hurt or sadness you might feel.

3 Express your feelings—write them out, talk to a friend or simply allow yourself to feel what you feel.

4 Accept responsibility for your own emotions. Although you were wronged and your emotions may be justified, it is still up to you to decide when you're ready to stop feeling angry or upset.

5 Talk to the other person about the behavior that upset you and how it made you feel. The odds are that you won't feel truly ready to forgive until you know this person has heard and understood your perspective.

6 Try to understand the other person's perspective, even if you don't really agree with it.

7 Rebuild trust in the relationship. Make agreements about acceptable future behavior whenever appropriate.

8 Make the decision to forgive, and communicate your forgiveness to the other person. Once you've done this, make every effort to move on and let it go completely.

### ✱ Tips

You can forgive someone without condoning his or her behavior; forgiveness isn't the same thing as approval.

Avoid a defensive reaction by first venting your emotions outside the presence of the wrongdoer—this will help the interaction to be more productive.

Wait until you are truly ready to forgive. Respect your feelings and take all the time you need.

## Know if You Will Marry Your Significant Other 544

Is the object of your affections the right one for you? Keep your eyes open for signs that this is the person you want to marry.

### ◉ Steps

1 Examine your conversations. Does your partner include you in her plans when she talks about the future?

2 Consider the compatibility of your activities and values. Are you interested in your loved one's work and hobbies? Does your partner seem to be interested in your job and pastimes, even if she doesn't share your passion for them?

3 Consider whether you're both traveling along the same pathway in life. Do you want the same things, such as kids, stability, money, career?

4 Evaluate how your partner treats you in private and in public. Does he brag about you? Does he seem proud to be with you, or does he avoid being seen with you in public? Does he stick around when you're having a bad day, or does he disappear when you need him the most?

5 Evaluate how your significant other treats your friends and family. Is she willing to be nice to them, even if she doesn't like them?

6 Assess your partner's honesty and trustworthiness. Does he do what he says he's going to do? Do you feel you can trust him?

7 Think about all the reasons why you really like this person. Remember that infatuation fades, but genuine compatibility endures.

8 Communicate with your partner and discuss these issues to figure out if you're meant for each other.

###  Tip

If the person seems secretive or ashamed to be seen with you in public, reevaluate your relationship. He or she may be trying to hide something or someone from you.

## Get Him to Propose 545

You've found the man of your dreams, and you know you're meant for each other, but he needs a little nudge. Here's how to point him in the right direction.

### ◉ Steps

1 Make him aware of your interest in a lifetime commitment. Drop subtle hints from time to time, such as, "We'd make a great team" or "I can't imagine my future without you," rather than incessantly bombarding him with demands about marriage.

2 Point out your shared interests, values and common goals. Open his eyes so he'll realize that you're the one for him.

3 Remember that actions speak louder than words. Show him what a great lifetime partner you could be through thoughtful actions, sincerity, kindness and other appealing traits.

4 Create opportunities for him to pop the question. Plan a candlelight dinner, arrange a romantic evening out or have a weekend away together.

### ✴ Tip

Make sure not to fixate on this issue, as it may have a detrimental effect on the relationship. Give him the time he needs to sort things out.

5   Remind him of several happily married couples who are mutual friends of yours, pointing out how much you have in common with them and how successful their marriages are.

6   Express your happiness, love and devotion to him. Show him by your actions and words that you've found the man of your dreams—and you're ready to marry him!

## 546 | Propose Marriage to a Man

You're not the type of girl to wait around for Prince Charming. You know what you want, so why not ask for it? Here are some thoughts on how to propose to the man in your life.

### ◎ Steps

1   Know your beloved well and anticipate his response. Will he be swept away by this romantic gesture? Or could he feel threatened by a woman's proposing marriage? (If so, you may want to reconsider.)

2   Set the stage. Pick his favorite place—whether you consider it romantic or not—to pop the question. This might be a secluded camping site, a fancy restaurant, a golf course at sunset ... or even a sports bar. Let your love's taste be your guide.

3   Keep your plans flexible. You may have an evening of French cuisine and fine wine in mind; he may be in the mood for burgers and beer. Unless your plans involve other people or events, go with the flow.

4   Make a splash if your beloved appreciates the theatrical. Put your question up in lights at a ballgame, or bring in a soloist to croon over pasta.

5   Keep the occasion subtle if your honey tends to like things more subdued. Pop the question over dessert, or during a private game of pool.

6   Bring or plan an engagement gift. Sure, you could get him a ring, but a puppy with a note tied around its neck might be a better choice. Or a motorcycle. Something that will last for a long time.

7   Give him some time to be surprised and tongue-tied. Remember, even though he loves you for the unconventional woman you are, he probably won't see this one coming.

### ⚠ Warning

If you've already been dropping hints and he hasn't been receptive, don't use a proposal to force the issue. Your attempt at romance may backfire.

## 547 | Propose Marriage to a Woman

This is a moment that will be recounted over and over to friends, family and even your children. Make it memorable.

### ◎ Steps

1   Try to keep your plans to yourself.

2   Consult your intended's father before asking, if you are a traditional kind of guy.

### ✱ Tip

It may be best to pop the question first and buy the ring together later, especially if you're not sure of her taste.

3 Make sure the proposal reflects your personal style. Get on one knee and propose at the top of a mountain, during a romantic weekend or while you're on a tropical vacation.

4 Have Champagne and flowers waiting.

5 If your partner says yes, call the people that matter to let them know.

6 Be prepared to start talking about wedding plans immediately.

7 Don't be offended if your new fiancée is not taken with the ring you selected. She can choose another setting later if she desires.

## Buy an Engagement Ring     548

Bucking tradition might be necessary when it comes to selecting an engagement ring that she'll wear for the rest of her life. It's always best to get input from the bride.

### ◉ Steps

1 Discuss styles, stones and budget with your bride-to-be if you're going to be shopping together.

2 Expect to pay about $2,500 to $3,500 per half carat for a quality diamond. This is a rough estimate that will depend on several factors, including the diamond's size—larger diamonds are rarer, and therefore more valuable (see 704 "Buy a Diamond").

3 Go shopping with your intended after your proposal, or shop alone so that you can surprise her.

4 If you shop alone and aren't sure what style she wants, buy just the stone, make an appointment with a jeweler to return later for a setting, and pop the question using a fun dime-store ring. After she's accepted, go back and pick out a setting together.

5 Have the ring made or buy one ready-made, once you've discussed styles with your sweetheart.

### ✳ Tips

Despite the old adage that the ring should be worth two months' salary, if you can't spend that much money, go for a simple design that can be dressed up with the wedding band.

Use the stone from a family heirloom to make a unique and less expensive ring she'll treasure.

If you buy the ring without the bride's input, don't fret if she doesn't like your choice. Get a basic setting with an understanding from the jeweler that you can come back and trade up.

## Plan a Wedding     549

Now that you've recovered from the delightful shock of your engagement, take a deep breath, grab a notebook and your address book, and then let the countdown to the Big Day begin!

### ◉ Steps

1 Envision your wedding from beginning to end. Where and when have you dreamed the wedding would take place? How formal would you like the event to be? What will the wedding party wear? What kind of food would you like to serve?

2 Pick a date.

3 Set a budget—one that is functional and provides for some flexibility. Here is where you must combine fantasy with practicality.

### ✳ Tips

Ask your parents early on in the planning stage for their input.

Be kind to yourself and your betrothed—this can be an extremely stressful time.

4 Ask friends and family to recommend a reputable jeweler. Order your engagement and/or wedding rings.

5 Book the wedding and reception sites.

6 Meet with the officiant of your wedding. Now is the time to be clear about rules and restrictions regarding the ceremony and ceremony site.

7 Select your wedding attendants—your wedding party can be as big or small as you like.

8 Choose a dress and wedding attire for the rest of the wedding party.

9 Make a guest list. You may have to compromise on the number of guests if your budget is limited.

10 Plan your pre-wedding parties, ceremony, reception and honeymoon—consider menus, decorations, favors and music.

11 Interview and hire vendors: wedding coordinator, photographer, video professional, caterer, florist and entertainment.

12 Check state requirements for obtaining a marriage license, and find out how long the license will remain valid.

13 Take care of the rest of the paperwork, from ordering invitations to signing up with gift registries.

Keep a notebook to fill with things like swatches of fabric, notes and vendor contracts.

Be sure to take time away with your partner and give attention to your relationship.

## 550 | Register for Marriage

There are just a few things you absolutely have to do before the big day. One of them is to register with the state in which you plan to be wed. Here's how to go about it.

### ⊙ Steps

1 Contact the government office that handles registrations in the city, county or state where your wedding will take place. The specific office may be called Public Records or Registrar. Call the main administrative number if you're unsure.

2 Check with this office a minimum of three months before your wedding date, although the mandatory registering date is often a mere three days before your wedding.

3 Make a list of any documents the office tells you to bring with you when applying for a marriage license.

4 Be prepared to provide the bride's and groom's legal names, addresses, ages and previous marital histories, if any. If either of you has been married before, you will have to show records of annulment or divorce, or the previous spouse's death certificate.

5 Ask about fees. Cash and credit cards are usually accepted.

6 Be prepared for a waiting period, although this varies across the country.

7 Keep in mind that special rules may apply if your prospective spouse is not a U.S. citizen. Be sure to ask about this.

8 Remember to ask what you must do once the ceremony is completed, in case there are any follow-up forms that need to be filled out.

### ✳ Tips

It's usually best if you have all the paperwork out of the way before the big day.

Marriage requirements vary by state. For example, some states require blood tests. In addition, you may need a birth certificate or a positive identification such as a driver's license or passport.

## Register for Wedding Gifts                551

Make it easy for yourself and your guests—be organized and offer them a wide selection in both price and types of gifts.

### ⊙ Steps

1  Discuss what you truly want as a couple, and draw up a wish list.

2  Explore your options. You can go the traditional route—home accessories, formal place settings, silverware and fancy linens—or you can break the mold and sign up for tools, contributions toward a trip or a special purchase such as a home, or donations to a selected charity.

3  Scout around—visit a number of stores until you find one that suits your personal taste and satisfies your needs.

4  Consider registering at two or three stores, a good option if you and your betrothed want to cover more ground or you simply can't agree on a single registry theme.

5  Set up a registry soon after your engagement, but not more than nine months prior to the wedding day.

6  Give as much detail as possible when filling out the registry form—make the experience easier on guests by providing information about brand, pattern or model, size and color.

7  Find out whether the store or chain has a computer database for tracking; whether it takes phone, fax or online orders; whether it offers direct shipping; and what kind of refund and exchange policy it has.

8  Ask the store for a complete list of what you've registered for, so you can verify that your list and your mailing address have been entered accurately in the store's database.

9  Jot down the name of a contact person at the store so you'll know whom to contact should complications arise.

### ✱ Tips

Keep the registry active for at least a year after the wedding—guests have a year to buy their gift and remain within the bounds of etiquette.

Avoid including registry information in your wedding invitations or other wedding mail that comes directly from you. Your guests can learn where you've registered by asking your parents or your wedding party.

Keep track of who sent what as soon as gifts arrive. This will help you later on when you are writing thank-you notes.

### ⚠ Warning

Double-check the stores' return deadlines and policies.

---

## Write a Wedding Invitation                552

Send out invitations at least six weeks before the ceremony to give your guests plenty of time to make travel arrangements.

### ⊙ Steps

1  Decide who is announcing the wedding—the couple's parents or the bride and groom themselves.

2  Determine if your invitation will be formal or informal. You can say "Mr. and Mrs. Marcus Melendy request the honor of your presence" or use a more casual phrase like "please join us."

3  In general, use the term "the honor of your presence" if the ceremony will be held in a place of worship. Otherwise use "the pleasure of your company" or another less formal phrase.

4  For a traditional invitation, list the bride's name—usually first and middle—after her parents' names. For example, "Mr. and Mrs. Marcus Melendy

### ✱ Tips

Invitations to a small or informal wedding are usually handwritten, not engraved. In designing them, feel free to use your imagination.

Include all the guests' names on the envelope. Avoid impersonal terms such as "and family."

request the honor of your presence at the marriage of their daughter, Wendy Sue."

5   Follow the bride's name with the full name of the groom: "to John Jacob Williams." You may choose to name the groom's parents: "son of Mr. and Mrs. Robert Williams."

6   Write out the date: "Friday, the ninth of June, two thousand one."

7   Mention the time of the ceremony: "at ten o'clock."

8   List the location and full address.

9   Enclose a separate map and a stamped, self-addressed reply card.

If you want to depart from the traditional wording, consult your stationer for ideas—or look at wedding invitations you've received, and decide which ones you like best.

---

## 553 | Handle Family Tension at Your Wedding

Tensions between relatives can dampen the joy of your wedding day, but with the right attitude and a positive approach, you can practically eliminate family friction.

⊙ **Steps**

1   Present a united front with your spouse-to-be. Talk about your apprehensions and decide how you'll face them as a couple.

2   Open a checking account expressly for wedding expenses, and have all contributors (parents, in-laws) each submit a predetermined amount. This will prevent unnecessary comparisons and the "I paid for this" superiority complex.

3   Sit down with everyone involved (individually, if the situation is awkward) and air your concerns. Explain that your wedding day should be one of your happiest and that family members can help by putting aside their differences for one day.

4   Split up wedding duties—if you want to ask the bride's biological father to give her away, consider granting her stepfather the first dance with her at the reception.

5   Separate hostile parties. At the ceremony, seat your mother and her spouse in the front row and your father and his spouse in the third row; at the reception, avoid forcing them to sit at the same table.

6   Talk to your officiant if things seem too hard to handle. This person can talk you through your concerns and can be a positive source of support.

✱ **Tip**

Show affection and respect when communicating with family members—let them know you value their opinions and beliefs.

---

## 554 | Be a Best Man

Being chosen as best man is an honor and a responsibility. Here's how to fill the role.

⊙ **Steps**

1   Arrive on time or early to every event connected with the wedding.

2   Plan a bachelor party that suits the groom's personality.

✱ **Tips**

Save your roasts for the bachelor party and make a more formal toast at the wedding.

---

3 Oversee the ushers' tuxedo rentals and fittings—make sure the tuxedos are picked up and ready the day before the event, as well as returned on time after the wedding.

4 Hold the bride's ring until it is needed, unless a ring bearer is present.

5 Be sure the groom has the marriage license. You are an official witness and may sign it.

6 Remind the groom to be ready with his suitcases for the honeymoon, tickets and anything else he may forget.

7 Help the groom get dressed before the wedding.

8 Get the groom to the wedding with plenty of time to spare.

9 Make the first toast to the bride and groom at both the rehearsal dinner and the wedding reception.

10 Read any congratulatory Mailgrams at the reception.

11 Dance with the bride and attendants during the reception.

12 Unless the couple plan to drive away on their own, arrange for a ride, or drive them from the ceremony to their hotel or the airport.

13 Order Champagne for the newlyweds' hotel room.

Remember that the other ushers as well as the groom will be affected by your attitude, so be enthusiastic and have fun.

## Be a Groomsman                555

It's a rare groom who can carry the wedding load single-handedly. That's where groomsmen come in: to help him cope with formalities and jitters and to make sure he gets to the altar.

### ⊙ Steps

1 Let the groom know that you are honored to be one of his groomsmen, and assure him that you will fulfill your role with dignity—without sacrificing the fun.

2 Attend as many prenuptial events as you can—and give the groom one less thing to worry about by being punctual.

3 Help the best man throw a bachelor party for the groom.

4 Rent your own tuxedo and shoes, per instructions from the groom.

5 Arrive 45 minutes early at the wedding site to go over the seating plan and to help the groom take care of any last-minute preparations.

6 Serve as an usher by escorting guests from their cars and leading them to their seats as specified by the seating plan. (For every group of guests that arrives, seat the oldest woman first.) You may also have to direct guests to parking facilities and restrooms and give directions to the reception site.

7 Perform ceremonial duties such as escorting the bridesmaids down the aisle and, most important, standing at the altar with the groom.

8 Dance with the bridesmaids during the first dance (after the newlyweds and their parents)—you may be the ones to jump-start the party.

### ✳ Tips

Stay flexible and on your toes. You may be called upon to handle unexpected circumstances.

Respect the groom's wishes if you throw a bachelor party. Be inventive, but stay within the boundaries of reason. He may have made some promises to his bride-to-be regarding his "last night of freedom."

Perform your duties with dignity during the ceremony.

Make the experience fun—humor is a good tonic for nerves—but be sure to keep the antics to a minimum, especially on the wedding day. What seems hilarious when you are plotting with fellow groomsmen can turn into a fiasco and result in hurt feelings.

9   Toast the couple at the reception after the best man does so.

10  Bedeck the bride and groom's getaway vehicle with flowers, signs, streamers and balloons.

## 556 | Be a Maid of Honor

As one of the bride's closest friends or relatives, you'll have a major part in the wedding festivities.

### ⊙ Steps

1   Ask the mother of the bride if you can help in any way aside from performing your ceremonial duties.

2   Consider offering housing to out-of-town guests if you live near the place where the wedding is being held.

3   Offer your support as the bride plans (and perhaps obsesses over) every wedding detail—from floral arrangements to dinner menus.

4   Orchestrate a shower and/or bachelorette party. Help the bride keep track of gifts she receives at these gatherings.

5   Help the bride get dressed before the wedding.

6   Tend to the flower girl and ring bearer if there is no one else available to direct them.

7   Serve as one of the official witnesses to the wedding, if asked.

8   Hold the bride's bouquet and the groom's ring during the ceremony. Help the bride with her veil or train if necessary.

9   Act as a liaison between the bride and the bridesmaids during the reception.

10  Give a toast at both the rehearsal dinner and the reception—usually after the best man.

11  Dance with the best man and possibly other groomsmen.

12  Help the bride prepare for her departure after the reception. Alert the bride's and groom's parents when the newlywed couple is ready to leave the reception.

### ✱ Tips

Keep any negative opinions of the bridesmaids' dresses or any other wedding details to yourself.

Save a roast for the bachelorette party and give a more formal toast at the wedding.

## 557 | Be a Bridesmaid

Whether the bride is an old schoolmate, a favorite new friend, a trusted sister or your brother's fiancée, be honored that she has asked you to share in this joyous—and hectic—time in her life.

### ⊙ Steps

1   Let the bride know you feel privileged to be chosen as a bridesmaid. She will appreciate your enthusiasm.

### ✱ Tips

Be sensitive to the bride's wishes, if and when you throw a bachelorette party. Remember, it is your friend's wedding and you'll want to respect her desires.

2 Offer to help the bride and maid of honor with any tasks they'll be facing prior to the big day. This could include housing out-of-town guests.

3 Coordinate a shower—or assist the maid of honor in doing so—to be held for the couple or the bride.

4 Keep in mind that your bridesmaid dress is part of the big picture—if you are not crazy about the material or design, keep it to yourself. It is your responsibility to pay for the dress, shoes and lingerie.

5 Attend as many prenuptial events as you can—and give the bride one less thing to worry about by being punctual.

6 Contribute to the bridesmaids' gift to the bride, in addition to your own.

7 Pack an emergency kit for the bride for the wedding day: bobby pins, safety pins, hair spray, hair dryer—anything she may forget to bring and can't live without.

8 Be ready to fill in doing odd jobs, such as serving as an impromptu seamstress if the need should arise.

9 Jump-start the party—dance with the groomsmen and bring other guests onto the floor.

10 Mingle and help everyone feel comfortable.

11 Toast the newlyweds at the reception, alone or with another bridesmaid.

Budget your expenses for the months to come. The costs for parties, meals and clothes may add up to more than you expect.

## Change Your Name After Marriage 558

**Whether the wife takes the husband's name as tradition dictates, he takes hers, or both make the decision to hyphenate, follow the necessary steps to make it official.**

### ⊙ Steps

1 Order extra certified copies of your marriage certificate for agencies that require originals before allowing you to change your name on documents, such as the department of motor vehicles.

2 If you're a man changing your name at marriage, check your marriage certificate to see if there is a space to indicate a name change. If not, you will need court papers to legally change your name. Contact a local attorney to find out the procedure for name changing in your state. (This is not necessary for women.)

3 Request a new Social Security card or cards reflecting the name change. Call the Social Security Administration at (800) 772-1213 to obtain forms and instructions.

4 Make an appointment to visit the department of motor vehicles for a new driver's license. Ask in advance which documents you'll need to bring in order to certify the validity of your name change.

5 Obtain and complete a Passport Amendment/Validation Application. Send this along with appropriate fees, your current passport(s), and a certified documentation of your name change (such as a certified copy of a marriage certificate or court papers) to the nearest passport agency.

 **Tip**

Because a woman traditionally takes her husband's name when she is married, a certified copy of your marriage certificate is sufficient documentation for a woman's name change, even if it doesn't contain a space for your new name. A man may need court papers, not just a marriage certificate, to get new documents after marriage If he wants to change his name.

6   Order replacements for checks, business cards, credit cards and other documents that contain your old name.

7   Call employers and schools (if you are a student) to let them know your new name, and ask them to change it in their records.

8   Change your name on your car registration, with your insurance and mortgage companies, and with your frequent-flier program.

9   Contact the post office, utility companies and registrar of voters.

10  Make the announcement to friends and family (ideally to your in-laws first), using stationery or thank-you cards with your new name printed on them, or order name-change cards designed for such an occasion.

## 559 | Write a Wedding Thank-You Note

Send personalized thank-you notes to all of your gift-bearing wedding guests. This is your chance to let them know how much you appreciate their thoughtful presents.

### ⊙ Steps

1   Consider ordering formal note cards with your married name or monogram on them. These cost about $150 and up for 50 cards, depending on the quality of paper and number of details you include. Order these notes at the same time that you order your invitations.

2   You can also opt for preprinted thank-you notes from a card or stationery store. These are much less expensive, and there are lots of styles to choose from. Expect to pay $5 to $10 for eight cards.

3   Be sure to purchase plenty of extra cards. You may receive more gifts than you expected.

4   Handwrite each note.

5   Mention each gift and tell the giver how you will use the item, if possible.

6   Refer to any special effort the person went to for you, such as traveling a long distance to attend the wedding or giving a special toast.

7   Consider adding a line telling invited guests who were unable to attend the wedding how sorry you were that they couldn't be there with you.

8   Send separate notes for shower and wedding gifts. Even if you received two gifts from the same person within a short period of time, each one deserves its own acknowledgment.

9   Be timely. According to etiquette guru Amy Vanderbilt, a thank-you note should be written within two to three weeks of receiving a gift—six to eight weeks at the very most.

### ✳ Tips

Use collectors' stamps from the post office for creative flair.

If possible, include a photograph of you taken with the person who gave the gift, at your wedding. People will enjoy this gesture.

Send thank-you notes to all of your wedding vendors to show how much you appreciated their efforts. Also send notes to your wedding party to thank them for taking part in your big day.

### ⚠ Warning

Even if you thanked guests in person, you are still expected to send out a formal note.

## ✓ 560 Select a Wedding Anniversary Gift

Whether you're celebrating your own anniversary or buying a present for another couple, these traditional and modern themes can give you some ideas. Feel free to interpret these suggestions either literally or creatively—for example, a diamond anniversary could mean diamond jewelry, or it might mean a family outing to your favorite baseball diamond.

| | TRADITIONAL | MODERN |
|---|---|---|
| 1st | Paper (stationery, book, scrapbook) | Clock (watch, grandfather clock) |
| 2nd | Cotton (clothing, linens, towels) | China (teacups, garden art) |
| 3rd | Leather (luggage, jacket, armchair) | Glass or crystal (champagne flutes, vase, lamp) |
| 4th | Fruit, flowers, linens (gift basket, bouquet, flowering plant) | Electrical appliance (cappuccino maker, ice cream maker, blender) |
| 5th | Wood (picture frame, firewood, cello) | Silverware (cake server, silver chopsticks) |
| 6th | Sweets, iron (candy dish, cast-iron pot) | Wood (jewelry box, salad bowl, tree) |
| 7th | Copper, wool (pots and pans, sweaters) | Desk set |
| 8th | Bronze, rubber (sculpture, rubber stamps) | Linens, lace (napkins, lacy curtains) |
| 9th | Pottery, willow (vase with willow vines) | Leather (boots, gloves, book, journal) |
| 10th | Tin and aluminum (antique tin toy, aluminum lamp or picture frame) | Diamond jewelry (tiny studs for her, diamond cufflinks or tie tack for him) |
| 15th | Crystal (glassware, chandelier) | Watch or clock (stopwatch, kitchen timer) |
| 20th | China (cake plate, gravy boat, figurine) | Platinum (watch, cake server, figurine, pin) |
| 25th | Silver (earrings, cufflinks, vase) | Silver (desk accessories, picture frame) |
| 30th | Pearl (tux studs, strand of pearls) | Diamond jewelry (earrings, cufflinks) |
| 35th | Coral (earrings, necklace, ring) | Jade (jewelry, sculpture, paperweight) |
| 40th | Ruby (necklace, ring, earrings) | Ruby (decorative box, picture frame) |
| 45th | Sapphire (earrings, bracelet, tie tack) | Sapphire (blue glass, sapphire-cut steel) |
| 50th | Gold (ring, bracelet, cufflinks) | Gold (hair accessories, picture frame) |
| 55th | Emerald (necklace, tie tack, ring) | Emerald (stick pin, vase) |
| 60th and 75th | Diamond (necklace, cufflinks, bracelet, earrings, ring) | Diamond (watch, photo in diamond-shaped frame, baseball tickets) |

chart

## 561 | Create a Successful Marriage

As with most good things, a long and satisfying marriage takes time and effort—on the part of both spouses. Your reward is happiness of the highest order.

### ⊙ Steps

1 Cherish compatibility. Seek out the things that interest, please and delight both of you.

2 Respect and treasure your differences. Learn from one another. Appreciate and understand your spouse's distinctive style, approach and personality—especially when it diverges from yours. Differences can often turn into delight.

3 Cultivate patience. Give your spouse enough time to reach a comfortable middle ground in his or her own way.

4 Learn how to be understanding, and develop the ability to see through your spouse's eyes.

5 Share your feelings in regular talk sessions. A nice atmosphere in a good restaurant helps open the doors to intimacy and sharing. Really listen to your partner. Be sure to look directly into the eyes of your loved one.

6 Strive for a high ratio of positive to negative in comments and actions.

7 Allow time to pass when you're surprised by a disappointment. Solutions will become evident when there is patience. A good night's sleep will help additional insights to surface.

8 Resolve the inevitable differences in a way that strengthens and deepens your love. Strive to communicate your feelings without being aggressive or defensive. Listen to each other with an open mind and seek resolutions that you both can be happy with.

9 Learn to express thankfulness for the smallest things. This gratitude can be brief and must be genuine.

**✳ Tip**

Especially after kids arrive, schedule time to be alone together, and make it fun. Enjoy each other's company and laugh together.

## 562 | Impress Your In-Laws

In-law jokes have been part of world cultures for centuries. It can sometimes be tricky to forge a positive relationship with your spouse's parents, but it's a good idea to try.

### ⊙ Steps

1 Treat your spouse well. Nothing pleases parents more than knowing that their son or daughter is being well-loved and cared for.

2 Present a united front. Never squabble with your spouse in front of his or her parents. If you think hot issues may come up, discuss how you will deal with them ahead of time.

3 Contact them without waiting for them to contact you, and invite them over before they invite themselves. This allows you to get your home ready and to prepare yourself emotionally for a visit on your own terms.

**✳ Tip**

Begin making your own cherished family holiday traditions at home, especially if family holidays become a tug-of-war about whose family to visit and it isn't possible to visit both. Or go out of town and enjoy the holidays in an entirely different way.

4 Ask their advice, regardless of whether or not you plan to take it. Your spouse's parents will be glad to feel that they still have some influence on their child's life.

5 Be creative. If it bothers you that your mother-in-law always tries to do your dishes after dinner, offer her another task, such as serving coffee or playing with the baby.

6 If you and your in-laws are completely incompatible, just handle it as gracefully as possible, avoid contact whenever you can, and remember that even if you will never love your in-laws, they did something wonderful when they created your spouse.

### ⚠ Warnings

Avoid confrontations with your in-laws. Try to let criticism or differences of opinion wash over you.

Try to get along well with your in-laws, but don't let them take over. This can be especially important when grandchildren arrive. Set reasonable ground rules for everyone in the family.

---

## Resolve Conflict in a Marriage    563

Of course, there will be disagreements in any marriage. The key is how you resolve them. Do it right and your marriage will grow stronger and deeper by the day.

### ◉ Steps

1 Separate complaints, which can be destructive, from constructive criticism, which you can learn from and build upon.

2 Understand your spouse's emotional needs. Listen to what your spouse is saying, but also try to understand why he or she is saying it.

3 Learn to communicate nondefensively and nonaggressively. Presenting facts or feelings in a neutral manner helps avoid escalation.

4 Stay calm and be direct. Be truthful with your spouse and with yourself. What are you really feeling?

5 Keep studying those first four steps. Practice makes perfect. And perfecting your marriage is worth all the practice you can put into it.

### ✱ Tip

Practice conflict resolution with small matters, such as picking out silverware, before moving up to complex, possibly disharmonious decisions such as choosing pets and naming children.

---

## Be a Better Listener    564

As you've probably heard, good communication is the most important part of a successful marriage. And careful listening may be the most important part of good communication.

### ◉ Steps

1 Position yourself so that you can be engaged with your spouse and the conversation: Face your spouse and make eye contact. If you are doing something else (for example, typing or reading the paper), stop.

2 Close the door to minimize interruptions and let your partner know you're willing to listen.

3 Pay attention to your spouse's words. Stop daydreaming and letting your mind wander elsewhere.

4 Pay attention to nonverbal cues: Notice pitch, tone and inflection. Observe facial expressions and posture. Is your partner slouched, turned

### ✱ Tips

Your questions and comments reflect how closely you have been listening. Good listeners might incorporate bits of what the speaker has said, sometimes much earlier in the discussion, into their questions.

Keep an open mind and avoid jumping to conclusions.

away from you, or sitting with his arms crossed? These postures may indicate that he is upset—try to find out why.

5 Be conscious of your spouse's personality—and your history together—when you're evaluating his words.

6 Try to determine what your spouse wants from you, even if it's not explicitly stated. Sympathy? Advice?

7 Try to rid yourself of biases or preconceptions that can distort what you hear or your understanding of it.

8 Avoid interrupting the speaker before he is done talking. You might be thought rude, but more important, you might misinterpret what your partner is saying if you don't let him finish.

9 Respond appropriately. Encourage your partner with an understanding nod or say "I see" or "That makes sense."

10 Ask questions to clarify what you don't understand and to demonstrate your interest. Open-ended questions (such as "How did that make you feel?") promote further discussion.

## ⚠ Warnings

Avoid turning the focus of the conversation onto you. For example, if your spouse is trying to confide a personal problem, avoid saying "That's just like the time I ..." and digressing into unhelpful stories about yourself or your own problems.

Avoid trying to plan your next comment while the other person is talking—this can detract from listening and hearing.

Don't let your emotions cloud what the other person is saying.

## 565 | Get a Divorce

It has been estimated that about half of all marriages end in divorce. The process boils down to controlling what you can— and normally, what you won't be able to control is your spouse.

## ◉ Steps

1 Make every effort toward keeping your relations amicable. The angrier your spouse is, the uglier your divorce will be.

2 Consult an attorney—most will meet for an initial consultation just to explain the process and your immediate options—or research the divorce process in your area. Divorce laws differ among states, and each county may have its own rules.

3 Take a trip to your local family law courthouse or the family law department within the local courthouse.

4 Gather your financial documents, including tax returns for the last five years, all retirement accounts and all financial accounts.

5 Close or freeze joint accounts. You and your spouse may want to divide equally all funds accumulated during your marriage.

6 Keep track of all debts incurred or paid (credit cards, repairs to the family home and so forth) once you separate from your spouse.

7 Determine whether alimony or child support is warranted. If you are the spouse in need of support, make sure to initiate court proceedings as soon as possible, because you won't receive support until you file. Consult an attorney or other resource.

8 Keep track of any money you give your spouse as alimony or child support, and write checks rather than giving cash.

9 Realize that most states have a waiting period between the time when you file for divorce and the time when your divorce is final.

 **Tip**

It's best to consult with an attorney who specializes in family law, even if you plan to represent yourself throughout the process.

## ⚠ Warnings

Expect the divorce process to be long and potentially costly.

Remove your emotions from the legal process by seeking therapy to deal with them. Don't use your lawyer or the system to retaliate against your spouse; it will just cost you more money.

10  Research your spouse's pension plans, retirement accounts and other savings accounts. You may not be aware of all the plans to which your spouse contributes, or to which an employer contributes on behalf of your spouse.

11  Negotiate a custody plan if children are involved; you will have to. Most courts offer free assistance.

---

## Date as a Single Parent                                               566

**As a single parent, you may feel reluctant to date again. Take it slowly, listen to your instincts and try to have fun.**

### ⊙ Steps

1  Date when you feel you're ready, not when others tell you that you should (see 524 "Ask Someone on a Date").

2  Ignore guilt. You're a human being and you need adult companionship. You deserve an occasional night out.

3  Take it slowly. Don't fill your calendar with dates all at once. It will take time for you and your children to adjust to the idea of your dating.

4  Make sure your children are cared for by someone you trust while you're on a date.

5  Talk to your children. Explain that you're going to spend some time with a person you like. Do not talk about remarriage or new daddies or mommies, but be honest about its being a date. Answer any questions your children have, but keep personal details to yourself.

6  Decide whether you want the person you're dating to meet your children. On a first date it is probably not advisable. When you do introduce them, keep it light, easy and quick. Don't plan any "family" outings yet.

7  Try not to talk about your kids too much during dates, but don't feel you need to hide their existence, either.

8  Introduce the new person to your children gradually if you feel that your relationship is becoming more serious.

9  Avoid letting your children see you in bed with anyone.

10  Consider how much affection you're comfortable expressing in front of your children. Follow your instincts. You can always kiss after the kids are in bed.

11  Be prepared for your children to be angry, resentful, hostile, sad, shy or nervous about the situation. Help them through it as best you can.

12  Be patient. It may take time to become comfortable on dates after being out of practice for so long.

13  Keep your ex-spouse out of it. He or she is bound to find out about your dating and may try to discuss it with you or become involved. Remember that you are divorced and it is your life to live as you please, so long as your children are not harmed.

### ✱ Tip

If you or any of your children are having a very difficult time coping with the situation, consult a counselor or therapist.

## 567 | Prepare Siblings for a New Baby

Whether baby makes four, five or six, the change in your family will undoubtedly both excite and confuse your children.

### ⊙ Steps

1 Wait until Mom is showing before breaking the news; this will make the wait seem shorter for siblings-to-be.

2 Involve your children by letting them listen to Mom's belly and feel for hiccups and kicks.

3 Allow young ones to ask questions about the baby's impact on their lives.

4 Give your children a doll to introduce them to the concept of a new baby. Teach them how to change diapers and bathe the doll.

5 Show your children the ultrasound photo of the new baby, then bring out their own ultrasound photos and discuss similarities and differences.

6 Read books together about children who have brothers and sisters.

7 Bring a present to the hospital for each of the siblings so they can receive it as soon as their new brother or sister is born. Explain that the present is from the baby.

8 Give the baby a small present from each brother and sister, and let the siblings find a good place for the gifts in the baby's room.

### ✳ Tip

Children may have serious concerns about where the baby will sleep, whether the baby will play with their toys, and how much he or she will divert Mom and Dad's attention from them. Respond to all questions thoughtfully and with reassurances.

### ⚠ Warning

Although your goal is to encourage a bond between siblings and new babies, caution your older children specifically about any actions that could harm the baby—for example, accidentally smothering the baby with a blanket, hitting the baby or trying to feed the baby solid food.

## 568 | Host a Baby Shower

When celebrating an event as joyous as a baby's imminent arrival, you can be as silly—or as traditional or creative—as you want to be.

### ⊙ Steps

1 Give yourself plenty of time to plan. Showers usually take place in the seventh or eighth month of pregnancy.

2 Decide whether the shower is for women only. Traditionally, you throw a baby shower for the mother-to-be, with only female friends and relatives as guests. But today, showers that include men—with both expectant parents as guests of honor—have become increasingly popular.

3 Determine the time of day and location—making sure above all that it's convenient for the guest(s) of honor—and approximately how many guests you'd like to invite.

4 Decide whether to make the shower a surprise. Keep your honorees' personalities in mind—remember that not everyone likes surprises.

5 Think about possible shower themes, such as teddy bears, bottles or balloons. Or pick a gift theme like "Around the House," assigning each guest to bring a baby gift for use in a different room—the kitchen, the bedroom, the bathroom and so forth. (It's OK to ask for more than one gift per room.)

### ✳ Tip

Consider coordinating the gifts if you know the guests well, so Mom and Dad don't end up with 13 diaper bags. Or several guests can go in together on a big gift such as a crib, stroller or gift certificate.

### Things You'll Need

- ☐ invitations
- ☐ decorations
- ☐ centerpiece
- ☐ small gifts
- ☐ food and drinks
- ☐ cups, plates, napkins, utensils

6   Create a guest list. If the shower is not a surprise, consult the guests of honor about whom they'd like to invite; if it is a surprise, consult a close friend or relative to make sure you don't leave anyone out.

7   Send out invitations at least three weeks in advance. Include directions, surprise-party instructions if applicable, and the theme, if you've chosen one. If possible, mention the color scheme and theme of the baby's room as well.

8   Find out if the parents-to-be are registered for gifts at a particular store. Have this information ready in case any of the guests ask.

9   Make a table centerpiece composed of flowers, a basket and candles, bouquets of baby socks or a baby doll—or buy a centerpiece at a party store. Coordinate the centerpiece and decorations with your theme, if you've chosen one.

10  Decide if you want guests to play any games. If so, buy small gifts for the winners—some possible prizes could be plants, blank books, candles and bookmarks.

11  Make food, buy takeout or hire a caterer. Don't forget supplies—cups, plates, napkins and utensils.

12  At the shower, keep track of presents as the guests of honor open them—this will help them when they're writing thank-you notes.

# Ask for Maternity Leave                                            569

**Gearing up for maternity leave can be a tough business, especially if it's your first baby.**

## ◎ Steps

1   Pay attention to how other women at your company handle maternity leave; ask people you trust for strategic advice.

2   Read your company's personnel handbook for official company policies. Talk to the human resources representative, if your company has one.

3   Learn about state and federal disability and maternity leave policies.

4   Think through your ideal: How long will your leave be? Do you want to come back part-time at first? Work from home? Modify your job responsibilities or hours?

5   Sick, vacation and personal days, disability and paid and unpaid time can be part of your leave; develop a clear and thorough proposal.

6   Wait to talk to your boss until your pregnancy is well-established—but tell before you're obviously showing.

7   Consider your boss's possible reaction and think through how to respond to any questions and concerns. Have suggested solutions ready for any problems or challenges your absence might cause.

8   Negotiate for the length and type of leave you want.

9   Give your boss and co-workers time to adjust to the idea of your absence.

## ✻ Tips

If your company has more than 15 employees, you can't be fired for being pregnant.

The Family Medical Leave Act, a federal law passed in 1993, guarantees both men and women 12 weeks of unpaid leave (with the same or a similar job waiting for them when they return) to care for a new baby. This law applies to public agencies as well as private-sector commerce-related employers of 50 people or more.

**570 Choose a Traditional Name for Your Child**

If you want your child to grow up honoring his or her heritage, a name may be a good way to start. If family names don't suit you, you can try the chart below. It lists some traditional names, along with their meanings, from a variety of ethnic groups and languages.

| | BOY | GIRL |
|---|---|---|
| **Arabic** | Adil, righteous; Akbar, greatest; Alam, universe; Cemal, attractive; Fadil, generous; Haidar, lion; Nailah, success; Nazeer, friend; Nizam, leader; Roni, joy is mine | Aisha, life; Najma and Najmah, star; Nureen, light; Rashieka, descended from royalty; Sadiya, lucky; Shula, bright; Razi, my secret |
| **Chinese** | Ho, good; Hu, tiger; Lei, thunder; Li, strong; Liang, excellent; Lok, happy; Kong, sky; Yong, courageous; Yu and Yue, universe | Lian, graceful willow; Ling, delicate; Mei, pretty; Meiying, beautiful flower; Xiaoli, small and beautiful; Xiu Mei, beautiful plum; Yang, sun; Yen, yearning |
| **French** | Antoine, praiseworthy; Bernard, brave as a bear; Guillaume, determined guardian; Henri, leader; Jean, Marc, Luc and Jacques, love | Aimée and Cheri, love; Annette, gracious; Chantal, song; Charlotte, little and womanly; Juliette, youthful; Nicole and Nicolette, victorious people |
| **German** | Baldric, brave ruler; Bardolf, bright wolf; Dieter, army of the people; Len, brave as a lion; Medwin, faithful friend; Ottokar, happy warrior; Otto, rich | Annchen, gracious; Delana, noble protector; Gretchen, Greta and Gretel, pearl; Hedy, delightful and sweet; Katrina, pure; Mina, love; Raina, mighty |
| **Greek** | Alexander, defender of humankind; Constantinos, firm or constant; Nicos and Nicholas, victorious people; Platon, broad-shouldered | Alexandra, defender of humankind; Athena, wise; Callista, most beautiful; Helena, bright one; Kay, rejoicer; Katina, pure; Philana, love |
| **Hebrew** | Ethan, strong and firm; Gibor, powerful; Levi, joined in harmony; Joel, God is willing; Joshua, God is my salvation; Josiah, fire of the Lord; Jonah, dove | Ahava and Haviva, beloved; Aliza, joyful; Evelyn, life or life-giving; Ariel, lioness of God; Danielle, God is my judge; Dara, compassion; Liora and Meira, light |
| **Irish** | Aron, strength; Conn, Conan and Quinn, intelligence; Eoin and Owen, gift from God; Jack, John and Sean, grace; Kacey, brave; Kevin and Keeley, beautiful | Aingeal, angel; Caronwyn, Eavan and Keeley, beautiful; Dara and Ida, intelligence; Grace, Hannah and Jane, grace; Shauna and Siobhan, gift from God |
| **Italian** | Angelo and Angelino, angel or messenger; Davide and Amadeo, love; Giovanni, has favor with God; Nicolo and Nicolas, victorious people | Angela and Angelina, angel or messenger; Beatrice, blessed; Isabella, dedicated to God; Lucia, light; Natalia, Christmas; Pia, devout; Sofia, wisdom |
| **Japanese** | Juro, long life; Hideaki, intelligence; Hisoka, reserved; Kioshi, quiet; Tomi, rich; Kaori and Takeshi, strength; Dai and Montaro, big boy | Akiko, bright light; Keiko and Kioko, happy child; Kishi, Kameko and Sen, longevity; Mai, brightness; Mio, strength; Tomo, intelligence; Tori, bird |
| **Native American** | Alo (Hopi), spiritual guide; Honi (Arapaho), wolf; Hurritt (Algonquin), beauty; Misu (Miwok), rippling water; Onacoma (Cherokee), white owl; Tyee (Bannock), chief; Wohali (Cherokee), eagle | Ahawi (Cherokee), deer; Nita (Choctaw), bear; Nova (Hopi), chases butterfly; Talisa (Creek), beautiful water; Winema (Moquelumnan), woman chief |
| **Polish** | Andrzej, manly; Czeslaw, rocky fortress; Dawid, beloved; Eryk, peaceful ruler; Jan, God is gracious; Krzysztof, Christbearer; Leon, lion; Pawel, small | Agnieszka, pure; Ala, truthful; Elka, Elzbieta and Izabella, consecrated to God; Filomena, loved one; Janina, God is gracious |
| **Russian** | Aleksandr, Aleksey and Sasha, defender of humankind; Danila, God is my judge; Leonid, brave as a lion; Misha, like God; Nikolai and Koyla, victorious people; Vitya, conqueror; | Anya, gracious; Dodya, love; Katya and Ekaterina, pure; Nika, belonging to God; Nikita, victorious people; Sonya, wisdom; Tania, fairy queen |
| **Spanish** | Alfonso, noble and eager; Alejandro, defender of humankind; Carlos, strong and manly; Fernando, daring and adventurous; Jose, God will increase; Pablo, small; Pedro, small rock | Alicia, truthful; Carmencita, song; Clarita, bright and clear; Juana, God is gracious; Monica, adviser; Paloma, dove; Rosa, rose; Susana, lily; Teresita, reaper |
| **Swedish** | Anders, strong and manly; Bjorn, brave as a bear; Erik and Frederik, peaceful ruler; Ernst, sincere; Hans, God is gracious; Per, small rock | Astrid, divine strength; Britta, strong; Carina and Karin, pure; Elsa, noble; Erika, peaceful ruler; Inga, beautiful daughter; Kerstin, Christian |

chart

# Name a Baby 571

Whether you decide to go with a traditional name or with a more unusual one, make sure the name will fit your baby throughout life.

## ⊙ Steps

1 Decide whether you lean toward unusual names or more traditional ones (see 570 "Choose a Traditional Name for Your Child").

2 Collect names from both partners' family trees. Look for names of people who have played a meaningful role in either of your lives or who have names you both like.

3 Write down your favorite artists and writers; favorite characters from novels, movies or plays; and figures from history or mythology.

4 Think about cities and countries significant to you and your partner— geographically inspired names have become popular in recent years.

5 Think about your heritage. Do you want to recognize a particular nationality or ethnic background in your baby's name? Could you use other elements in your family's history, such as place names?

6 Buy a book of baby names and highlight the ones you both like.

7 When you've compiled a list, think about how your favorites sound with the baby's last name. You'll probably want to avoid rhymes, long first names combined with long last names, or combinations that add up to a celebrity's name or a pun, or that have any unflattering nicknames.

8 Using all of the above information, narrow your list down to two girls' names and/or two boys' names (depending on whether you know the sex of the baby).

9 After the baby is born, either bestow a name immediately or, if you prefer, observe your baby for a day or two and decide which of your choices seems most appropriate.

## ✳ Tip

Try not to divulge your top choice. It's a fun surprise when the day finally comes. Plus, you don't want someone else who's also expecting to poach your favorite name.

# Write a Birth Announcement 572

As a new parent, you're probably eager to share all the details about your new baby with your family and friends.

## ⊙ Steps

1 Write down all the information you want to include. Remember to list the baby's full name, date and time of birth, and length and weight. Include both parents' names, and mention the grandparents' names if you like.

2 Select the type of birth-announcement card you will use. Check with card or stationery stores to see the wide range of choices.

3 Consider purchasing packs of ready-made announcements. Prices begin at about $50 to $75 for 50 cards and envelopes; the price goes up for more expensive paper stock and added embellishments such as stickers or bows.

## ✳ Tips

Consider asking a photography shop to make birth-announcement cards out of a baby photo.

Ask a family member or friend to help you address the envelopes, since you are doubtless busy taking care of the new baby.

4   Splurge for custom-printed announcements if you prefer. These can cost about $200 to $250 for 50 cards and envelopes. You can purchase these through copy and print shops and some specialty card stores.

5   Consider shopping online to save time. You can e-mail your information to an online stationer and have the cards printed and shipped to your home. Do a keyword search for "birth announcements" on your favorite search engine to find Internet vendors.

6   Consider having the envelopes shipped to you before the baby is born. This way you can have them preaddressed and ready to go as soon as you provide the information on the cards.

7   Include a photo of the baby with the announcement.

8   Type up the announcement information and send it to your local newspaper office.

9   Find out if the newspaper will run a photo with the announcement. If you provide one, write the baby's name and address on the back so it doesn't get confused with the photo for another baby's announcement.

Save a copy of the birth announcement in the baby book, or frame it and hang it on your child's wall.

## 573 | Be a Good Parent

A big part of good parenting is establishing respect between parents and children. Your child needs to know what you expect of her, and you in turn must learn to listen and wait.

### ◎ Steps

1   Slow down. Babies and children live in a different time frame from adults'—usually a much slower one. Keep this in mind as you talk to your child, care for her and go about your day together.

2   Observe your child. You'll be amazed at how well you'll get to know your child by sitting back and watching. This focused awareness will help you better understand moods, abilities and temperament. Listening is important, too.

3   Stay optimistic. Optimism is contagious; so is negativity. Show your child through your behavior how to overcome minor setbacks. Children emulate their parents' attitudes and habits, so it will help if you have a positive outlook.

4   Accept and acknowledge your child's feelings and desires. Let her know it's OK if she feels sad, scared or angry. You can say, "It looks like you're sad because your friend went home" or "It seems that you're mad because I put the ball away."

5   Tell your child your expectations. Children won't always comply right away, but they need to understand clearly what a parent expects: "I want you to put on your sweater. We're going outside," or "I want your feet to stay off the couch."

6   Set appropriate limits. Even when you acknowledge a feeling or desire, you must make a child aware of appropriate behavior and rules: "I can see you're mad at your friend because he took the toy from you, but I won't let you hit him. Hitting is not something we do in our family. What else can you do?"

### ✱ Tips

Build more time into your schedule so you can slow down with your child and enjoy your time together. Continuous hurried behavior creates stress for both you and your child.

Start a baby-sitting cooperative with neighborhood parents so you can have a few hours to yourself or a date with your partner. Ask friends, Grandpa or a responsible teenage niece to baby-sit. Get out of the house and have some adult fun.

### ⚠ Warning

Monitor your child if she's having a dispute with a friend. Feelings can quickly escalate, and a parent may need to intervene. Safety should always be your No.1 consideration.

7   Wait. Let your child do as much as she can on her own—learn to walk, put on her socks, resolve conflicts with her friends. Anxiety or the desire to help often tempts parents to rush in and solve the problem for the child. A better response would be to wait and see what your child can manage on her own. She might surprise you.

8   Behave genuinely. Just as you accept your child's moods, though not always his behavior, it's OK to have a sad or angry thought yourself and express it appropriately: "I'm really tired right now but I'm listening to you." A parent's genuineness prepares a child for life.

9   Nurture yourself and your marriage. Make arrangements to have some guilt-free time to take care of your own needs. Plan a date with your partner and forget the kids for a while. You'll be a happier person and a better parent.

## Breast-Feed Your Baby Successfully                                574

Breast-feeding is nature's way to feed an infant—but that doesn't mean it comes naturally. Here's how to get started.

### ⊙ Steps

1   Make sure your hands are clean.

2   Choose a breast-feeding position: on your lap (cradle hold), baby at your side (football hold) or lying on your side (reclining position). Use pillows to support your back and arms as necessary.

3   Hold your baby very close, with his head, shoulders and hips facing you. While his mouth is close to your breast, tickle his mouth with your nipple. When he opens his mouth (the "rooting" reflex), bring him in the rest of the way. If he is latched on correctly, his lips will be flared out and he will take a good portion of your areola into his mouth.

4   Expect to feel a pulling of the nipple, or even some pain initially. If pain lasts beyond a few seconds, the baby is probably sucking on just the tip of the nipple; remove him from the breast and try latching him on again.

5   Let your baby nurse on the first breast as long as he wants, to ensure that he gets enough to eat and that your milk supply will keep pace with his needs.

6   To remove your baby from the breast, insert a clean finger into his mouth to release the suction, and then pull him off.

7   Burp your baby after he finishes the first side, then offer the other breast. If he doesn't take the other breast, offer that breast at the next feeding.

8   Nurse at least 10 to 12 times a day, or whenever your baby seems hungry. Signs of hunger include increased alertness or activity, mouthing and rooting. Crying is a late indicator of hunger.

### ✳ Tips

Eat a balanced diet and drink plenty of fluid. You may want to have water or juice nearby as you nurse.

Delay bottle feedings for at least three to four weeks to avoid nipple confusion. If a delay is not possible, ask a lactation specialist about alternative feeding methods.

You will know that breast-feeding is going well if your baby gains weight on schedule. He will lose some weight in the first week, but should be up to his birth weight by two weeks and start to gain steadily after that.

### ⚠ Warning

If breast-feeding isn't going well, get support. Some hospitals employ lactation specialists. La Leche League is an excellent support group for nursing mothers; visit www.lalecheleague.org or call (847) 519-7730.

## 575 | Store Breast Milk

Whether you are pumping breast milk daily so you can return to work or you're just doing it before a night out, storing it properly is essential.

### ⊙ Steps

1   Express your breast milk using a breast pump.

2   Pour the milk into either clean, opaque plastic bottles or plastic bottle-liner bags.

3   Store the breast milk in 2- to 4-oz. portions. These cool down more quickly than larger portions.

4   Cap the bottles tightly. Tape the bags shut or use ones with built-in twist ties.

5   Label each bottle or bag with the date.

6   Refrigerate or freeze breast milk as soon as possible after collecting it.

7   Store breast milk in the refrigerator for up to 72 hours; if you need to store it longer, use the freezer. The freezer inside an older, single-door refrigerator can keep breast milk safely frozen for up to two weeks; the frozen-food compartment of a double-door refrigerator can store milk for three months.

### ✳ Tip

Wash bottles well with hot, soapy water and a brush. Rinse and dry them before adding milk.

### ⚠ Warnings

Throw out any breast milk that has been at room temperature for more than 6 hours.

Some studies have indicated that chemicals may leach from plastic bottles made out of polycarbonate, which is normally used in clear plastic bottles. If you have any clear plastic bottles, replace them with opaque ones made of polyethylene, which is safe.

## 576 | Choose the Right Baby Formula

The first step in selecting the right baby formula is to discuss your baby's nutritional needs with your pediatrician. Then consider two other factors: cost and convenience.

### ⊙ Steps

1   Be aware that breast milk is the ideal baby food. If you can't breast-feed, or if you choose not to, commercial iron-fortified infant formula is your next-best option.

2   Select a formula with a composition of proteins, sodium, fats and sugars simulating that of breast milk. (Most commercial formulas do.) Read labels carefully.

3   If your baby has diarrhea or gas or seems fussy, he or she may be having trouble digesting cow's milk, on which most formulas are based. Check out lactose-free formulas, but consult your doctor first.

4   Decide what formula type will work best for your lifestyle and budget: powdered, concentrated or ready-to-use.

5   Know that powdered formulas are the cheapest and can be bought in bulk; on the other hand, they're more time-consuming to prepare, since you must mix them with water before feedings.

6   Understand that concentrated liquid (ready-to-pour) formulas come in cans, and you must dilute them with water before using. Discard leftovers within a day.

### ✳ Tip

Ask your pediatrician for formula samples so you can experiment with them before buying in bulk.

### ⚠ Warnings

Test the formula's temperature on your inner wrist before giving it to your baby: It should be no more than tepid. Hot formula will burn your baby's mouth.

If your baby spits up too much, he or she might have gastro-esophageal reflux and may benefit from a formula with added rice starch; check with your doctor.

If your baby projectile-vomits after consuming formula, call your doctor immediately.

7   Note that ready-to-use formulas packaged in individual bottles are the most convenient choice; all you need to do is attach a sterilized nipple. However, this is also the most expensive option.

8   Read and follow the directions carefully when mixing formula.

9   Talk to your doctor if you think your baby has a problem with a chosen formula. Avoid switching formulas without consultation.

Check the expiration date before using any formula. Throw away outdated formula, and don't reuse leftover formula, which can harbor harmful bacteria.

## Heat a Baby's Bottle 577

Whether they take breast milk or formula, some babies prefer having their bottles warmed up. It takes off the chill and generally helps infants accept the bottle.

### ⊙ Steps

1   Dispose of any clear plastic bottles and replace them with opaque ones, since some studies have indicated that chemicals may leach from plastic bottles made out of polycarbonate.

2   Defrost breast milk if necessary, either by thawing it in the refrigerator overnight or putting it in a bowl of warm water for half an hour.

3   Warm a bottle of either formula or defrosted breast milk by submerging it in a bowl or pan of warm (not boiling) water, by running the bottle under warm tap water, or by using a commercial bottle warmer, available at baby stores.

4   Test the temperature of the milk or formula in the bottle by shaking a few drops onto your inner wrist. It should feel tepid, not hot.

5   Continue warming the milk or formula until it's the desired temperature.

6   Some babies also like to have the nipple of the bottle warmed; run it under warm tap water or submerge it in a pan of warm water for just a few seconds. Test it on your inner arm to make sure it's just warm, not hot.

### ✱ Tip

To make life more convenient when you are out and about, you may want to start introducing a bottle closer to room temperature—so your baby does not grow accustomed to always having a nice, toasty bottle.

### ⚠ Warnings

Avoid microwaving formula or breast milk; it distributes heat unevenly in the bottle.

For your baby's safety, never reuse formula or breast milk once you've heated it. Bacteria may have formed in the liquid.

## Get Dad Involved With Baby Care 578

It's important for new fathers to help care for their babies—it promotes family bonding, gives new mothers much-needed support, and is emotionally rewarding for dads and babies alike.

### ⊙ Steps

1   Make sure Dad is there at his baby's birth. For many fathers, the bonding experience begins when they help cut the baby's umbilical cord. If you have to deal with any birth complications or a cesarean section, he can spend time with the baby while you're recovering.

2   Give Dad a special, unique task of his own. In many families, fathers take care of bath time, diapering or burping.

### ✱ Tips

If you're looking for a sling that Dad can wear, too, get one with adjustable straps. Some slings even come in larger sizes to accommodate tall men.

Take photographs and videos of Dad and baby together. It will give you a record of the special

3 Trust him to work things out for himself (as long as everyone stays safe). He may not perform all baby-care tasks exactly as you do, but the difference may not matter. So what if the baby's outfit isn't color-coordinated?

4 Let him share in the nighttime parenting. Dancing, cuddling and rocking are wonderful ways for a father to nurture his baby. Even a middle-of-the-night diaper change can offer a tranquil moment of bonding between father and child.

5 Encourage him to play with his baby. Even very tiny infants benefit from Daddy time.

6 Let him carry his baby in a sling or other infant carrier. When the baby gets older, Dad can carry his tyke in a backpack.

7 Give Dad reading material, such as the many books on fatherhood that can help him deal with his new role.

moments they share and encourage Dad to stay involved as your baby grows.

## ⚠ Warning

If you're breast-feeding exclusively, resist the urge to let Dad give an occasional bottle, at least in the early stages; using artificial nipples in the first three to four weeks of life can cause nipple confusion and may lead to breast-feeding difficulties.

---

## 579 | Reduce the Risk of Sudden Infant Death Syndrome

Most parents worry about sudden infant death syndrome (SIDS), but the chances of an average baby dying from SIDS are less than 2 in 1,000. These steps can help further reduce the risk.

### ◉ Steps

1 Place your baby on her back to sleep, not on her tummy.

2 Give your baby a firm mattress.

3 Keep your baby away from secondhand smoke.

4 Never put your baby to sleep on a water bed or beanbag chair.

5 Don't use plastic top sheets or allow plastic bags or film near the crib.

6 Make sure your baby doesn't get overheated—avoid multiple layers of clothing and hot blankets.

7 Keep stuffed toys, pillows and heavy comforters out of the crib along with anything else that might smother the baby.

8 If your baby suffers from sleep apnea (cessation of breathing), which can be life-threatening, consider purchasing a monitor that signals you if your baby suddenly stops breathing.

### ✱ Tips

Babies who have survived a life-threatening incident in which they turned blue, stopped breathing and required significant intervention or resuscitation are at a higher risk for SIDS. Premature and low–birth weight babies may also be more susceptible.

Most deaths occur between the second and fourth months, at home, in the crib, in cold weather and between midnight and 8 a.m. Consult your pediatrician for more information about SIDS.

---

## 580 | Change a Baby's Diaper

Not much has really changed since the days of diaper pins—whether you choose to go the route of cloth or disposable diapers, you'll follow more or less the same procedure.

### ◉ Steps

1 Lay a fresh diaper on a changing table, or on a towel or mat on the floor.

### ✱ Tip

Wash your hands before and after all diaper changes, and remember that frequent changes help prevent diaper rash.

2   Place your baby, tummy side up, on top of the clean diaper.

3   Unfasten the diaper tabs on the soiled diaper.

4   Hold your baby's feet together and very gently lift them up, raising the baby's bottom. Use the clean part of the diaper to wipe away any excess stools, then fold over the soiled section of the diaper and set the old diaper aside.

5   Wipe your baby's buttocks and genitals gently from front to back with baby wipes. Don't forget the lower back and the skin folds of the thighs. (A baby girl might get stools around her labia and vagina, so clean that area gently with baby wipes.)

6   Lower your baby's bottom onto the clean diaper.

7   Pat the area dry with a towel; cornstarch powder is optional.

8   Apply diaper-rash cream to the area if necessary.

9   Make sure to pull up the back of the clean diaper high enough to prevent leaks. Position the front of the diaper just under the baby's abdomen.

10  Bring the tabs around from the back of the diaper and fasten them to the front.

11  Turn diapering into a game of peek-a-boo to distract your baby.

## ⚠ Warnings

Never leave your baby unattended on a changing table.

Talcum powder or baby powder that contains talc can cause upper respiratory problems in babies. Instead, use cornstarch powder, and apply it carefully to prevent inhalation.

## Things You'll Need

❑ changing table

❑ diapers

❑ baby wipes (or wet washcloth or cotton balls)

❑ towel

❑ cornstarch powder (optional)

❑ diaper-rash cream

---

# Burp a Baby                                                    581

Burping a baby can reduce spitting up and relieve bloating caused by swallowed air. Here are some tried-and-true methods.

## ◉ Steps

1   Put a clean towel, cloth diaper or receiving blanket over your shoulder or wherever your baby's head will rest.

2   Position the baby over one shoulder with his stomach against your chest and with his head resting on your shoulder.

3   Gently pat your baby on the back and rub it in a circular motion until he burps.

4   Try the "bulldoggy burp." Place one hand across the baby's chest, supporting his chin with your thumb and index finger. Lean your baby across that support hand and gently pat or rub his back with your free hand.

5   Opt for a "lap burp." Position yourself so that you can comfortably place the baby's head on one thigh and his stomach on the other. Using an upward and circular motion, gently pat the baby's back until he burps.

6   Try getting exercise while you walk and burp your baby. Stand up and place your arm under the baby's rib cage, with the baby's back to your chest. Walk around slowly, leaning the baby over your arm until he burps. And be patient: Sometimes burping takes several minutes.

## ✳ Tips

Never try to burp a baby while he is spitting up.

Don't worry if your baby spits up occasionally—what looks like a lot of liquid is probably no more than a teaspoon. Very frequent spitting up or projectile vomiting could signal a problem; contact your doctor.

Breast-fed babies tend to swallow less air than bottle-fed babies, so don't worry if your breast-fed baby rarely burps, as long as he seems comfortable.

If breast-feeding, burp the baby when you switch sides or finish feeding. If bottle-feeding, burp after every few ounces or whenever he seems uncomfortable.

## 582 Get a Baby to Sleep

You just put her down for a nap, and now she's awake and crying again. You could let her cry it out, or try these ideas to get her back to sleep.

### ◉ Steps

1 Rock your baby. Most babies enjoy rocking and cuddling as part of their bedtime routine.

2 Nurse your baby. Babies love to fall asleep while breast-feeding; in fact, sometimes it's hard to keep them awake long enough to finish a meal. But don't let this become such a habit that your baby will never sleep without nursing first.

3 Swing your baby. Mechanical swings or rocking cradles can calm fussy babies and help them drift off to sleep.

4 Swaddle your infant. Many newborns enjoy the feeling of being snugly wrapped—though others don't enjoy being swaddled.

5 Dance with your baby. A good lullaby or smooth jazz CD, a dark room and a slow dance often send a baby to sleep.

6 Bathe your baby. A warm bath about an hour before going to bed is a great way to relax your baby and help her sleep.

7 Go for a drive or walk. Many babies who resist falling asleep in a crib or bed will happily drift off in a car seat in a moving vehicle, in a sling or frontpack, or in a stroller or carriage.

8 Read, talk and sing to your baby. Even if she's too young to understand the words, the gentle rhythms of your voice may help her get to sleep.

9 Turn on a fan or other source of white noise. The steady buzz of a fan, or even the static from a baby monitor with the transmitter turned off, can help a baby tune out other sounds.

10 Do laundry. The gentle vibration and white noise of a laundry room often help a baby get to sleep. Some desperate parents even put the baby in her car seat on top of the dryer.

11 Develop a routine. Mealtime, bath time, cuddle time and story time will naturally lead to bedtime once your baby gets used to the pattern.

### ✱ Tips

Some babies are night owls by nature. If your baby is like this, don't worry about enforcing a 6 p.m. bedtime. If she falls asleep at 9 or 10 p.m., she may sleep later in the mornings, giving you time to yourself at the start of the day.

Get opaque blinds for the room where your baby will sleep. This will help keep the room dark for naps and ensure that your baby doesn't always get up with the sun.

### ⚠ Warning

Avoid leaving your baby in a swing for too long; extended periods of sitting upright can hinder spinal development in young babies.

## 583 Calm a Colicky Baby

About one in five babies has colic—a set of symptoms that include inconsolable screaming, clenched fists, increased bowel activity and gas. The cause is unknown.

### ◉ Steps

1 Rock your baby in your arms, a carriage, a swing or a cradle (but not until your baby is at least six weeks old). Experiment with a variety of rocking positions, since all babies are different.

### ✱ Tips

Always consult your pediatrician about colic. A pediatrician can make a proper diagnosis, eliminating possible causes such as an intestinal problem or an allergy

2  Sing a lullaby to your baby.

3  Walk around with your baby in a sling or backpack.

4  Wrap your newborn snugly in a soft blanket, as some infants are soothed by being swaddled.

5  Gently massage your baby's back, tummy and thighs.

6  Give your baby a warm bath if he likes it.

7  Place your baby across your lap, tummy down, and stroke his back.

8  Walk around to relieve pressure, placing your forearm under your baby's rib cage with the baby facing outward.

9  Soothe your baby with sound: Some babies enjoy rhythmic noises, such as music, a vacuum cleaner or a dishwasher. They may also find riding in a car very soothing.

to formula. She may recommend a medication for gas relief, or a different baby formula.

Most babies outgrow colic by the end of their fourth month.

⚠ **Warning**

Never rock or shake your baby vigorously.

# Wash an Infant                                                    584

As soon as the umbilical cord and circumcision have healed, your baby is ready for a bath. Bathing your baby is not only easy, it can be fun for you both.

⊙ **Steps**

1  Place an infant bathtub in the kitchen sink.

2  Fill it with lukewarm water. Test the water on the sensitive skin inside your wrist or elbow to make sure it's lukewarm, not hot.

3  Add a few squirts of baby wash.

4  Carefully place your baby in the tub, being careful to support his head and neck.

5  Wash the infant with a baby washcloth, patting and rubbing gently.

6  Gently dab your baby's face with the washcloth.

7  Pour warm water onto your baby's hair from a small plastic cup, shielding his eyes.

8  Apply a dime-size dollop of baby shampoo and wash the baby's head and scalp.

9  Shield the baby's eyes and rinse his head with lukewarm water, again using the cup and being careful to avoid the eyes.

10  Lift your baby out of the bath.

11  Wrap him in a soft, warm towel.

⚠ **Warning**

Never leave a baby unattended in the bath, even for a few seconds. Infants and toddlers can drown in very shallow water.

**Things You'll Need**

❑ infant bathtub

❑ baby wash

❑ baby washcloth

❑ small plastic cup

❑ towel

## 585 | Clean a Baby's Eyes, Nose and Ears

A daily sponging is all that's really required to keep your baby's eyes, nose and ears fresh and clean.

### ⊙ Steps

1 Dip a clean, soft baby washcloth or cotton ball into warm water and squeeze it to remove any excess water. (Since baby skin is very sensitive, avoid using soap on the face.)

2 Sing or talk softly to your baby to distract her as you clean.

3 Use the cloth or cotton ball to clean the corners of your baby's eyes, wiping gently from the inside corner to the outside edge of each eye.

4 Use a soft, damp washcloth or baby wipe to remove mucus around your baby's nose, wiping gently around each nostril.

5 Use a washcloth to wipe the outer part of your baby's ears, but not inside. Check behind each ear, and wipe away any dirt or debris.

### ✱ Tip

Earwax keeps ears clean and naturally moves outward. But if wax buildup seems excessive or doesn't move outward, talk to your pediatrician.

### ⚠ Warning

Never put anything inside your baby's eyes, nose or ears. Cotton swabs or fingers could rupture the eardrums or make the walls of your baby's ears bleed.

## 586 | Wean Your Baby Off the Bottle

When you decide to wean your baby from a bottle to a cup, a variety of techniques can make the transition easier on you both.

### ⊙ Steps

1 Offer your baby a cup instead of a bottle, and follow his cues. He may seem interested and may drink from it properly; if he has trouble or just refuses, try again in a few days.

2 Make a family policy that your baby can't walk around with his drink or play with his bottle. This will make it clear that he needs to eat at regular meal and snack times, rather than always holding on to the bottle. Follow similar rules yourself so you don't send mixed messages.

3 Substitute other things that will comfort your baby if he seems to be using his bottle as a pacifier. These should include extra attention and affection, as well as special games, toys and books.

4 If your baby gets thirsty at night, keep a spillproof cup of water nearby and offer it to him in lieu of a bottle when he wakes. The nighttime bottle is often the most difficult to lose, but doing so is important. Using formula, milk or juice at night harms your baby's dental health, as the liquid will pool in the mouth, coat the teeth and lead to severe decay. Bottles also pose a choking hazard.

### ✱ Tips

If your baby does not seem fond of cow's milk, don't despair. There are many other excellent sources of calcium and protein, such as tofu and yogurt.

Remember that your baby still needs good nutrition; a 1-year-old should drink about 4 cups of milk daily, depending on how much solid food he takes in.

Many babies become addicted to juice during weaning; try to make it an occasional treat rather than a regular part of your baby's diet.

Try using a cup that features your child's favorite book, TV or movie characters; this may help him get excited about using it.

## Wean Your Baby Off the Breast **587**

Weaning can be a difficult time for both mother and baby, but doing it gradually with lots of love can ease the transition.

### ⊙ Steps

1 Proceed slowly. Your baby may find abrupt weaning traumatic, and it can lead to uncomfortable engorgement and mastitis in your breasts. Mastitis is an infection that can cause fever and flulike symptoms, as well as pain, hardness, redness, or heat in your breast—usually just one breast, not both.

2 Eliminate one daily feeding session at a time over a period of weeks or even months, starting with the nursing session that seems the least important to your baby emotionally.

3 Offer your baby a substitute for the breast. If she is less than 1 year old, you may need to substitute formula in a bottle to make sure she gets the nutrition she needs. If she is past her first birthday, eating a variety of foods and drinking from a cup, you may be able to offer her food or distract her with a fun game or activity.

4 Give extra affection. Weaning can make babies feel vulnerable for a while, and your baby may need added reassurance that you still love her.

5 Keep your baby occupied by going to the park, taking a walk or playing in the garden.

6 If your baby clearly wants to nurse, and if your attempts to distract her with other snacks or activities aren't working, it's OK to nurse. This way, you can avoid a battle of wills.

7 Continue to nurse for comfort if necessary. Often, a more or less weaned baby will want to nurse after a fright or a fall. This is OK. It will take her a while to get used to the other forms of comfort you offer.

8 Contact your doctor, a lactation professional or your local La Leche League if you experience pain or engorgement while waiting for your milk to dry up. They can offer some solutions for a safe and pain-free transition.

9 If you wean your baby from breast to bottle, avoid putting her to bed with a bottle. It poses a choking hazard and promotes tooth decay. If she gets thirsty at night, keep a spillproof cup of water nearby and offer it to her when she wakes.

### ❋ Tips

The American Academy of Pediatrics recommends breast-feeding for at least the first four to six months of your baby's life. After the first year, weaning often becomes easier, as you can offer your baby a wider variety of foods.

Avoid feeling that you have to wean your child; many mothers nurse beyond the first year, and some nurse their babies well into toddlerhood. Eventually, all children lose interest in nursing, so follow your heart and do what feels right.

When substituting other liquids for breast milk, avoid offering your baby large quantities of juice or sugary drinks; they will fill your baby up without providing adequate nutritional value, and can cause tooth decay.

## Take a Baby or Toddler to a Restaurant **588**

Don't let your family outing turn into a food fight or the quickest meal on record. These strategies can make eating out together fun for everyone.

### ⊙ Steps

1 Plan to go to a restaurant during your child's normal mealtime.

### ❋ Tips

Ask other families about restaurants geared to kids. Some restaurants have generous children's menus, pass out balloons

2   Make a reservation if you have a large party. Often restaurants take reservations for parties of more than six people. If not, ask about the wait. Hungry tummies and long waits do not mix.

3   Inquire about the availability of high chairs and boosters. Take a hint if the restaurant doesn't have high chairs or boosters on hand: This may not be the best place for young kids.

4   Keep a portable booster in your car in case the restaurant has already given out all its high chairs.

5   Change your baby's diaper before entering a restaurant.

6   Try to sit near other families. Other parents tolerate squeals and tantrums much better. Plus, with other kids around, any noise and commotion that occurs at your table may just blend in rather than drawing unwanted attention.

7   Consider sitting outside or near a window to provide distractions for your child, and to keep any noise away from the central dining area.

8   Assess the table arrangement. Move out of reach all sharp utensils, breakable plates, glassware and any other objects not safe for young children to handle or hurl.

9   Bring food or a bottle for your child or baby and offer it early in the meal. If ordering food for your child, flag down the waiter soon after sitting down to get food to the table as soon as possible.

10  Provide age-appropriate books and toys for your child to play with while you are eating.

11  Investigate how to place your infant carrier safely on a chair. Some carriers can sit atop a high chair or on a regular chair. Booths work well.

12  Tip big—give some respect to staff who must clean up after your family leaves, including any mess under your baby's seat.

or crayons, or sing silly songs for birthdays.

Save four-star restaurants for nights out with your partner.

## ⚠ Warning

Avoid placing the infant seat on the ground when your baby is sleeping, in case of spilled beverages.

---

## 589 | Deal With Stranger Anxiety in Babies

Stranger anxiety, which starts as early as three months, is a normal, self-protective process. The anxiety should lessen after the first birthday as your child learns to handle new faces.

### ◎ Steps

1   Greet a friend or relative who's new to your baby with a handshake, a kiss or whatever seems appropriate. This will give your baby a hint that Mom or Dad accepts this stranger.

2   Stay in view of your baby when you're at the market, the doctor's office or any place where strangers are present. Hold or comfort your baby if she's anxious.

3   Don't force a child to be held or kissed by anyone who seems to cause anxiety, even if that person is a friend or relative. Babies go through phases when even Grandma or a neighbor can provoke anxiety.

4   Ask grandparents, friends or anyone to whom your baby has become sensitive to approach her slowly so that she has time to warm up to them.

### ✳ Tips

Talk to your baby. You can say, "This is Aunt Carol. We went to her house last week. Remember?"

Avoid telling your baby there's nothing to be scared of. The fear that babies and children experience is real to them.

**How to Do** *(Just About)* **Everything**

# ✓ 590 Keep a Child's Immunizations Up-to-Date

Vaccinations will prevent your child from contracting potentially deadly diseases. Keeping up-to-date on immunizations is also important because day care centers and schools require it. The following recommendations come from the U.S. Centers for Disease Control and Prevention. Consult a pediatrician for the most up-to-date information.

### 2 months

- Hepatitis B*
- Diphtheria, tetanus and pertussis (DPT)
- Haemophilus influenza type B (Hib)
- Polio (IPV)
- Pneumococcal vaccine

### 4 months

- Hepatitis B*
- Diphtheria, tetanus and pertussis (DPT)
- Haemophilus influenza type B (Hib)
- Pneumococcal vaccine

### 6 months

- Diphtheria, tetanus and pertussis (DPT)
- Haemophilus influenza type B (Hib)
- Polio (IPV)
- Pneumococcal vaccine

### 12–18 months

- Hepatitis B*
- Measles, mumps and rubella
- Chicken pox (varicella)
- Diphtheria, tetanus and pertussis (DPT)
- Polio (IPV)
- Haemophilus influenza type B (Hib)
- Pneumococcal vaccine

### 4–6 years

- Polio (IPV)
- Measles, mumps and rubella
- Diphtheria, tetanus and pertussis (DPT)

### 11–12 years

- Tetanus and diphtheria booster (Td)
- Hepatitis B if not vaccinated earlier in life
- Measles, mumps and rubella if not vaccinated twice earlier in life
- Chicken pox (varicella) if not vaccinated earlier in life (and if he or she has never had the disease)

calendar

* If you test positive for hepatitis B virus, get your child an injection of immune globulin within a week, or even within 12 hours if possible.

## 591 | Feed a Finicky Toddler

Some toddlers are so reluctant to eat that they seem to live on air. Even a finicky child can still get adequate nutrition fairly easily, though.

### ⊙ Steps

1 Don't worry if your child's weight gain slows or even stops. Many children stop gaining weight for a short period around the time they hit toddler-hood; that's because their intense activity level causes them to burn off lots of extra calories.

2 Maintain a positive and matter-of-fact attitude about food. Don't turn it into an emotional issue. Often, a child may resist eating even more if he figures out that he has pushed one of your hot buttons.

3 Don't take food too seriously. Playing with food is a natural part of a tod-dler's development and is not likely to become a behavior problem.

4 Make sure you are offering your child foods from all the necessary food groups every day; this will help him maintain a balance of nutrients as he grows.

5 Offer your child choices, but don't overwhelm him with them. Two or three options are easier to deal with than five or six.

6 Try to reduce or remove distractions at mealtimes. This will teach your child that mealtimes are for focusing on food and family, not on TV, toys or other activities.

7 Consider presenting food in imaginative ways. For example, you could use cookie cutters to turn toast, a sandwich or French toast into fun shapes. This may encourage your toddler to eat more.

8 Follow your child's cues as much as possible while still providing a bal-anced mix of healthy foods. If he shows a preference for mashed foods, for example, you may get him to eat more than just bananas and pota-toes by mashing other foods you offer him.

9 Offer small servings—about 1 tablespoon of each food for each year of your child's age.

10 Keep track of your child's weekly nutritional intake rather than worrying about it every day. Some kids may eat a lot on some days, then next to nothing on others. This almost always balances out over the course of a few days. As long as you are offering a range of healthy food choices, you will probably find that your toddler is eating fairly well overall.

### ✱ Tips

Many children prefer to eat small, frequent meals and snacks, rather than three large meals each day.

To get a rough idea of how many calories he should take in each day, multiply your child's height in inches by 40 (this works for kids between the ages of 1 and 3). For example, a 30-inch-tall child should consume about 1,200 calories a day. Or multiply your child's weight in pounds by 50 for another rough estimate. Keep in mind that these are just approximations; a pediatrician or dietitian can give you a better idea of your child's needs.

### ⚠ Warning

If your child begins to lose weight rapidly, refuses to eat altogether for more than a few hours, or shows any other signs of malnu-trition (including bleeding gums, brittle hair and nails, or loose, wrinkled skin), contact your doc-tor immediately.

# Discourage Temper Tantrums 592

A tantrum is a natural way for a young child to experiment with feelings. But you can take some steps to help her work through frustration and bring emotions like anger under control.

## ⊙ Steps

1 Set a good example. If you act aggressively when you are frustrated or angry, it is only natural for your child to react the same way when faced with the same emotions. Try to remain calm and neutral in voice and posture when dealing with tantrums or other frustrating situations.

2 Talk openly about your emotions. Say things like, "Mommy gets angry when you throw your food on the floor. I get frustrated when you throw your toys around the room. It looks messy and is more work for me. I feel sad and angry when you yell at me and call me names." Teach your child how to express feelings verbally by expressing yours.

3 Observe your child. If you see a tantrum coming on, go and sit near your child. Ask whether something is bothering her and whether you can help in some way. Helping your child learn to work through a problem is a valuable lesson.

4 Once a tantrum gets started, try to ignore it. If your child is not a threat to herself or others, let her work through the anger or frustration. By ignoring the tantrum, you are telling your child that you are not interested in the behavior.

5 Resist the urge to reason with your child. Your child is very preoccupied with emotions and can't listen to or comprehend reason.

6 Remind your child, in a friendly, uncritical voice, of the appropriate response. Say things like, "I know you are angry. Let's try again. Why don't you take your toy to your room to be alone? You can be angry and cry, but you cannot hit."

7 Try not to give in. If your child is throwing a tantrum because you took something or said no, giving in to your child's demands will encourage more tantrums in the future.

8 Remove your child from the room if necessary. Especially if you are in a public place, sometimes your child needs a quiet or empty room to work through frustration or anger.

9 If ignoring the tantrum isn't working or isn't an option, try distracting your child with another toy or activity. Because young children have naturally short attention spans, redirection is an effective way to draw attention away from a frustrating activity and channel energy into a more constructive activity.

## ✽ Tips

Praise your child often for good behavior.

Keep behavior charts for older children. Teach your child to monitor and control behavior by marking charts and setting behavior goals.

Keep track of your child's tantrums, and try to eliminate or reduce the occurrence of situations that bring on a tantrum.

## ⚠ Warning

It is natural at times for a parent to feel frustrated or angry when a child has a tantrum. If you experience extreme frustration or anger when trying to discipline your child, however, consult your family doctor or another health care professional.

## 593 | Toilet Train Your Toddler

There are many ways to toilet train your child, and various experts consider many of them controversial. Remember that your child will give you signs to indicate readiness for the big step.

### ⊙ Steps

1   Assess your toddler's readiness for toilet training. Ask yourself these questions: Does your toddler follow simple instructions? Dislike having a soiled diaper? Know words for stool and urine? Sit for 5 minutes or more attending to a project? Understand the physical signals indicating the presence of urine or stool? Have dry periods for 2 hours or longer? Wake up dry from naps? These are all good indications that you can start introducing your toddler to the potty.

2   Buy a potty or toilet seat. Choose one that will suit the needs and preferences of both you and your toddler. Do you want one you can take with you anywhere? Do you want one that will rest safely on public toilets? Do you want one that makes music? Don't be surprised if your child doesn't agree with the one you think is right.

3   If you feel comfortable, have your child sit on his potty with clothes on while you, your spouse, or another person of the same sex as your child goes to the bathroom. Don't try to restrain your child or force him or her to sit down. If your toddler shows extreme fear or disdain for the potty, put it away and try again, or let your child explore the toilet seat independently.

4   Sit your child on the toilet seat without a diaper when he or she shows no signs of fear. Explain to your child what is supposed to happen on the potty. Don't be surprised if nothing happens for a long time. After two-plus years of passing urine and stool in a diaper, change will come slowly.

5   Create a toilet routine. Following a routine will set up your child for success. Place your toddler on the toilet at specific times of day—first thing in the morning, right before or after a nap, and right before bed.

6   Be patient. Some children become urine-trained before becoming stool-trained. Other children wet the bed up to age 7 or 8. All children develop and accept change differently.

### ✳ Tips

Reward your child for making it to the potty.

If your child has an accident on the floor or in training pants, use gentle, encouraging words. Let your child know that he or she is learning something new and that accidents are OK.

Read toilet-training books for kids together to show your toddler that other children learn this skill, too.

## 594 | Throw a Children's Birthday Party

With a little planning and imagination, you can help your child have the best birthday celebration ever.

### ⊙ Steps

1   Decide on the number of guests to invite. Some schools with small classes have a rule that if you invite more than half a class, you should invite the remainder of the class to avoid making anyone feel left out. Even if it's not an official rule, you may want to follow this guideline to avoid hurt feelings.

### ✳ Tips

For younger guests, plan the party for around midafternoon, after their naps. Plan on the party lasting no more than 2 hours, and allot time accordingly for eating and playing games.

2   Get your child's input. Let him or her decide on a theme, such as a cartoon character, a movie, or a favorite sport or other activity.

3   Select party favors, room and table decorations, snacks and games to illustrate this theme.

4   Pick a locale for the party, whether it's at home, in a park, or at a family fun center or restaurant. Make sure the environment is appropriate for the kids' age and energy level.

5   Choose entertainment for the guests, such as arts and crafts or old-fashioned games like musical chairs and pin the tail on the donkey. If your child is older, consider throwing a pool or slumber party.

6   Keep foods simple—pizza, ice cream, chips, cookies, fruit and juice are perennial favorites.

7   Decide, based on the age of the guests, whether you want to include a time for opening presents or wait to open them later. Keep in mind that younger guests may get confused as to whom the presents are for.

8   Mail invitations directly to the guests, or send them in care of their parents or guardians, and ask for an RSVP. When the guardians call to confirm, you can discuss party logistics, such as food and dress.

9   Request that an adult accompany children under 5. Provide for the needs of the adults at the party as well. For older kids who are being dropped off, be sure to let the parents know when they can expect to pick their children up.

When entertaining guests under 6 years of age, avoid choosing competitive games, which may upset them.

If you're giving out goody bags (a popular practice at kids' birthday parties), keep in mind that a modest, well-thought-out bag can be just as much fun as a more expensive one. Try linking the goody bags to the party's theme.

## Things You'll Need

❏ invitations

❏ party favors and decorations

❏ snacks and drinks

❏ games

# Discourage Thumb Sucking                                    595

Children who suck their thumbs after around age 6 may become the target of teasing and criticism; they may also end up with dental and speech problems.

## ◉ Steps

1   Wait for the problem to go away. Most children, but not all, outgrow the habit by the time their permanent teeth come in (about age 6). After this age, thumb sucking can cause dental and speech problems, but before then, many children still have a fairly strong impulse and need to suck.

2   Start to work on kicking the habit a little while before you expect your child's permanent teeth to come in. That way you can deal with it before it becomes a real problem.

3   Try to keep your child talking, which will make it hard for her to keep her thumb in her mouth.

4   Offer her activities to keep her hands busy: crayons or pencils and paper, squishy balls or toys to fiddle with, or models and puzzles to work on.

5   Consider working out a reward or praise system, using stickers and a chart or calendar.

6   Encourage your child with positive reminders that she is a big kid, and that big kids don't need to suck their thumbs.

## ✳ Tips

Encourage your child to wash her hands frequently to avoid constant transfer of germs from her hands to her mouth.

Take a look at your child's thumb. If it is callused or sore from sucking, she is almost certainly sucking it too much.

Look for hidden stress in your child's life if she suddenly develops a thumb-sucking habit. Dealing with the source of the stress may eliminate the problem.

7   Explain to your child in simple terms why it is important for this habit to go away, and ask her to suggest a few possible solutions. Many children will come up with some creative possibilities.

8   Try putting a brightly colored adhesive bandage on your child's thumb as a reminder not to suck.

9   If your child sucks her thumb at night, consider having her wear a glove or sock on her hand while she sleeps.

10  Talk to your dentist, who may have helpful suggestions and who can also explain the dental consequences and options for treatment if thumb-sucking continues when the permanent teeth come in. Ask your dentist to have a talk with your child, if you think it will help.

11  Be patient with your child. Although thumb sucking is an unattractive habit, many children can't help themselves. Take the time your child needs to eliminate the habit gently and gradually, rather than criticizing or punishing.

## 596  Teach Your Child Manners

It's never too early—or too late—to teach your child about proper etiquette.

### ⊙ Steps

1   Set a good example. It's unfair to expect politeness of a child if his parents are not polite themselves.

2   Teach your child manners in stages, as his comprehension and skills develop. It probably won't do any good to ask a 2-year-old to stop chewing with his mouth open; he probably lacks the understanding and physical coordination to comply. But by 4 or 5 years of age, your child should have the ability to grasp the reasoning behind such a rule.

3   Start using words and phrases like "please," "thank you," "excuse me," "I'm sorry," and "may I?" as early as possible around your child. Encourage your child to do the same.

4   Take care what language you use around children; they mimic the way adults speak.

5   Ask your child to address adults with a certain degree of formality—that is, Ms. Lee, Mrs. Doe, Mr. Smith—unless the adult tells them to do otherwise.

6   Review the other basics of etiquette with your child whenever necessary. He should learn how to shake hands, show respect for older people, behave quietly in public places, and avoid interrupting other people in conversation. He should also learn not to play with other people's belongings unless given permission to do so.

7   Avoid ignoring bad behavior or waiting to talk about it. Address a rule as soon as your child breaks it.

8   Bring up the behavior again in private so you can discuss it more thoroughly and make sure your child understands how to behave in the future.

9   Praise your child for good behavior.

**✱ Tip**
When teaching or correcting manners, try never to embarrass your child in public.

## Encourage Young Siblings to Share                  597

Refereeing in the never-ending game of which toy belongs to whom can lead to premature gray hair. These steps can help you spend more time playing and less time blowing the whistle.

### ⊙ Steps

1  Set aside a specific time when you will interact and play with your children. Young children learn and remember best when a parent works with them directly for consistent periods of time.

2  Suggest some toys to play with, and help your children get them out. Bring the toys to an open area so you all have room to play.

3  Establish a positive and constructive play activity while letting your children remain in control of their play. If you want your children to play with blocks instead of climbing on the furniture, start building a tower.

4  Monitor your children and their play. Watch for an older sibling teasing a younger one. Keep mental notes of how long a turn one child takes with a toy other siblings want to play with.

5  If one child takes a toy from another, give the upset child a toy the other child likes. If she also tries to take away that toy, tell her she must give one of the two toys to the upset child. Explain that sharing is fair.

6  If a child refuses to share toys, place her in a time-out area—a predesignated spot, separate from the play area, where she can be alone, calm down, and get ready to return in a more cooperative mood. She must give the upset child a toy and apologize before returning to play.

7  Praise your child for sharing or helping independently. Say things like, "What a good sharer you are. Nice manners!"

8  Follow these steps during playtime and use them during the course of the day to reinforce the skill of sharing.

### ✽ Tips

Maintain a calm, neutral tone when explaining how sharing works: "It is nice manners to share. Look how Tommy gets upset when you take away a toy. Please be nice and share with your brother."

Try to use positive terms by telling your children what you want them to do instead of telling them what you *don't* want them to do. For example, say "Please give Tommy a truck to play with" instead of "Don't take that away!"

## Teach Your Child Financial Responsibility         598

From piggy banks to credit cards, there's plenty you can teach your child about money matters at any age.

### ⊙ Steps

1  Start talking about money with your child as early as age 3. Take her to the market and explain that you earn money so that you can buy things you need.

2  Give your child a small amount of money and let her buy something on her own.

3  Begin giving your child a small weekly allowance when she is 6 or 7 years old, and set guidelines about how she can use the money.

4  Pick a date, such as a birthday, on which to give your child an annual raise. Increase her responsibilities as you increase her allowance.

5  Avoid withholding allowance if your child doesn't fulfill a responsibility; choose another form of discipline instead. It's hard for a child to learn

### ✽ Tips

When deciding on an allowance amount, consider the child's age, her needs and your family's financial situation. Talk to other parents if you'd like to get an idea of typical allowances in your area, or do an online search to find various national polls on the topic.

Encourage your older child to work and save by offering to match each deposit she makes to a savings account.

budgeting skills if she doesn't know how much money will be coming in each week.

6 Start talking about long-term goals, such as saving for college or a car, when your child is between 11 and 14. Encourage her to earn extra money by mowing the neighbor's lawn or shoveling snow off driveways.

7 Consider opening a bank account in your child's name as an aid to saving and spending her earnings.

8 Consider encouraging your child to find a part-time job when she is 16 to 18 years old.

9 Consider giving her a credit card when she enters college, and discuss how to use it responsibly. Determine together what expenses you will pay for and what she must pay for. If the card is to be used only in emergencies, make that clear.

10 Teach your child about social responsibility as you teach her about money—for example, you could both donate money to a charity or volunteer your time at a shelter.

## ⚠ Warning

Keep your college-age child's credit card use under careful supervision, providing guidelines as well as clearly stating the consequences of misuse.

---

## 599 | Talk to Your Daughter About Menstruation

A young girl may find the onset of menstruation both an exciting and an anxiety-provoking time, and it's important that she enter this phase of her life with the information she needs.

### ◉ Steps

1 Make sure to talk to your daughter early so she won't be surprised when she gets her first period. Some girls can begin menstruating as early as age 9 or 10, so age 8 can be a good time to discuss it. If your daughter is beginning to develop breasts and pubic hair, menstruation is probably coming soon.

2 Approach the subject tactfully. Girls just entering puberty are often sensitive and easily embarrassed.

3 Make sure she knows you are proud of her. Make it clear to your daughter that entering womanhood is a wonderful event, and that there is no reason to feel uncomfortable or ashamed of the changes in her body.

4 Be realistic. While menarche is an important rite of passage, menstruation is also a physical event your daughter will go through every month throughout her childbearing years. Let her know what to expect physically and emotionally. Tell her in as straightforward a way as possible, without either overstating or sugarcoating the facts.

5 Discuss her options. Present the pros and cons of pads and tampons, and discuss how to deal with any premenstrual symptoms or cramps. See if she wants to chart her cycle on a calendar or in a journal.

6 Reassure her. On a practical level, menstruation won't change her life all that much. Women of earlier generations may have avoided certain activities during menstruation, but it is now common knowledge that women can swim, exercise and go on with life as normal during their periods.

### ✳ Tip

Prepare yourself in advance with any books and materials you may need to help you explain the more technical aspects of menstruation to your daughter.

**How to Do** *(Just About)* **Everything**

7 Talk about the implications. Once your daughter begins menstruating, she has the ability to bear children. Hopefully, you have already discussed sexuality, reproduction and contraception with her, but if not, now is the time.

## Talk to Your Child About Sex 600

More than 25 percent of 15-year-olds have had sexual intercourse—many start as early as age 12 or 13—so it's wise to broach the subject of sexual responsibility early.

### ◎ Steps

1 Prepare for this important conversation beforehand by thinking through what questions your child may have, and gathering any information you may need to answer them clearly.

2 Ask what your child knows about sex so you'll have a starting point. Depending on your child's age and knowledge level, you might begin by explaining the physical aspects of sex, or answering questions about this—even older kids may be unclear on some points. Be direct and use the exact words for sex organs so there's no room for misinterpretation.

3 If your child is mature enough, discuss the emotional side of sexual intimacy. Acknowledge that sex can be pleasurable, but point out that emotions surrounding it can at times be complicated, confusing or even wrenching, and that these issues may be more difficult to deal with if a teen becomes sexually active early. Remind your child that it's up to him or her to decide when he or she is ready for sex, and to stick to that resolution, even if it means resisting peer pressure or pressure from a girlfriend or boyfriend.

4 Remind your teen that there is never any excuse for pressuring or coercing someone into sex. Make it clear that if your teen is coerced into sex, he or she is not to blame—and should not continue in that relationship.

5 Address the topic of pregnancy. Adolescents are often incapable of thinking far into the future. Familiarize your child with the possible consequences of living for the moment. Discuss contraceptive options, and remind your adolescent that none of these are foolproof.

6 Explain the risks of contracting a sexually transmitted disease. Teens account for about one-quarter of the 20 million new cases of sexually transmitted diseases annually. Stress that abstinence is a viable option and that contraceptives are always available. Even if you emphasize abstinence, make sure your teen understands how to protect himself or herself when he or she does decide to become sexually active.

7 Anticipate questions your child might have, whether those involve facts or advice about decision making, and be prepared to provide concrete answers and support. If you don't have answers to every question, consult your family doctor, a therapist, or a medical book or Web site that specializes in this area.

8 Strive to maintain open lines of communication with your teen. Make sure he or she knows that you are always available for advice or assistance, whether that means sorting out relationship issues or finding a reliable form of contraception.

### ✻ Tips

Your primary goal as a responsible parent should be to provide your teen with enough information to make intelligent choices.

Clarifying your own thoughts and values beforehand will help you decide on the exact message to convey. This, in turn, will help you avoid delivering an ambiguous message that could be challenged or, worse, ignored.

### ⚠ Warning

Avoiding this topic could have strong negative effects, such as your child becoming pregnant or contracting a sexually transmitted disease.

## 601 | Plan a Teen Sleepover

Some planning—and some rules—will help everyone sleep a little easier.

### ⊙ Steps

1  Sit down with your teen and decide how many kids to invite. Consider the size of your living room (or whichever room the teens will sleep in), how light a sleeper you are, and any other specifics of your house that affect how many teens can fit in your house.

2  Send out invitations a week ahead of time, or pass the word by phone. Ask guests to RSVP. Make it clear that the party will be supervised, with an adult present for all of the activities.

3  Ask everyone to bring a sleeping bag and pillow.

4  Have at least three or four age-appropriate videos for the kids to watch, and make the sleepover spot convenient to the TV and VCR if possible.

5  Be prepared in case the kids want to bake cookies, go swimming or play games.

6  Stock up on snacks and beverages. If you have concerns about spills on your carpet or furniture, limit eating to the kitchen.

7  Don't forget to lay in supplies for breakfast. Bagels and orange juice are fine, or you can get more elaborate.

8  When the kids arrive, spell out the rules from the start. Discuss what rooms the kids can use and when they can make noise, and set limits on phone and kitchen use. If you don't want them to leave the house for any reason, tell them up front. If you're not sure your teen will be comfortable laying out the ground rules, take the responsibility yourself.

### ✸ Tip

If you don't want the teens going off on their own in the middle of the night, or if you don't want any members of the opposite sex showing up during the night, make those rules very clear at the beginning.

### Things You'll Need

☐ invitations

☐ videos

☐ games

☐ snacks and drinks

## 602 | Teach a Teen to Drive

Patience and calm are your best friends when teaching a teenager to drive. If you can't handle it, have your spouse, a trusted friend or relative, or a driver-training teacher take on the job.

### ⊙ Steps

1  Make sure your teen has a learner's permit, license or any other requirement necessary before beginning driver training.

2  Review the rules of the road the teenager learned during the required classroom hours.

3  Drive to an empty parking lot or driving course.

4  Explain the basic workings of the entire car, inside and out, before letting your teen start the engine. Go over each part and process in detail, including everything under the hood, the dashboard controls, the gas tank, the tires and the emergency equipment. Repeat until you're sure your teenager understands.

### ✸ Tip

For your teen's safety as well as your peace of mind, teach him or her how to change a flat tire before driving alone (see 945 "Change a Flat Tire").

### ⚠ Warning

Discuss the dangers of and laws against drinking and driving or using drugs and driving. Also discuss the hazards of driving when tired or when distracted by rowdy passengers, blaring music or difficult weather conditions.

5   Demonstrate how everything works: the lights, seat belts, windshield wipers, blinkers, horn, emergency lights, transmission, seat adjustment, steering wheel, mirrors and defroster.

6   Sit in the passenger seat and have your teen start the engine.

7   Point out how acceleration, braking and smooth transmission shifts feel.

8   Give corrections, warnings and tips as you make your way around the course, and discuss overall points when you've finished.

9   Sprinkle your lesson with what-if scenarios. Cover such possibilities as a child running across the road, traffic signals going out, emergency vehicles pulling up behind, a tire going flat, and so forth.

10  Remind your teen that it's important to always have the car's registration and insurance information accessible in the car, and to carry a driver's license or permit.

11  Note skill improvements and make the course progressively more diffi-cult, finally going out into traffic when you think your teen is ready.

12  Practice again and again.

# Set Rules for Using the Car — 603

Make the rules clear and fair so you won't have to renegotiate every time your teen wants to use the car.

## ⊙ Steps

1   Decide who will pay for the teen's insurance coverage, which can be a big expense, especially for young male drivers. You can add your teen to your existing policy, which will drive up the rate, or obtain a new one. Either way, you can pay for it yourself, require your teen to pay for it, or split the cost in any way you think is appropriate.

2   Discuss gas usage and who will pay to fill the tank.

3   Write out a schedule of times when the teen can have access to the car.

4   Clarify permissible destinations, such as within a 25-mile radius of the house, to school, to work or to the beach.

5   Set down any other conditions for use of the car. For example, you could say that the teen can use the car after completing homework, cleaning up the bedroom, or earning all Bs or above on a report card.

6   Make rules concerning who is allowed in the car when the teen is driv-ing. Letting a carload of friends accompany a new driver is not a good idea. (In fact, it may not even be legal; check with your state's depart-ment of motor vehicles for specific rules.)

7   Explain your policy regarding lending the car to friends or letting friends drive it.

8   Tell your teen what you expect when he or she is using the car. Issues may include removal of litter, adjusting radio stations, locking the car in the driveway after use, or washing the car.

## ✱ Tips

Even if a teen has his or her own car, parents remain financially responsible until the driver reach-es age 18.

Make certain your teen driver understands what to do in case of an accident.

Many states have license condi-tions for new drivers. Contact your state's department of motor vehicles for specifics.

## 604 | Encourage Responsible Teen Dating

This parenting hurdle takes particular patience and understanding. You'll find a sense of humor a valuable asset.

### ◉ Steps

1   Broach the subject of dating early on, perhaps during your child's junior high school years, or even sooner.

2   Set down some basic rules, including what you consider a proper dating age for both your teen and the teen's dates. Also discuss expectations about group or single dating, curfews, and appropriate destinations. For example, you might feel that only group dating is appropriate until age 16, or that teens should not leave your town or city on their dates.

3   Put all of your rules and expectations in an informal written document that you share with your teen. As your teen matures, bring it out and make changes if appropriate.

4   Talk with your teen about issues of sex and morality. In addition to discussing your moral views, talk about AIDS, sexually transmitted diseases, pregnancy and emotional issues related to sex—critical issues for teens. If you have trouble communicating about these issues with your teen, or if you feel that your child is experiencing problems that are too large for you to handle, get help from a counselor, clergy member or medical professional.

5   Explain that if your teen winds up in a difficult situation, you are willing and available to pick him or her up—whenever or wherever that might be, no questions asked.

6   Tell your teen where in the house to find some extra cash in case he or she is going out and doesn't have money available. Your teen should always carry enough cash to take a cab home in case of emergency.

7   Insist that your teen's date come into the house upon arrival for an introduction. Small talk and friendly questions are fine—this is not the best time for interviews, warnings or giving the third degree.

8   Make yourself available after the date to talk if your child wants to. Show your interest, but avoid prying. If you decide not to wait up that night, be sure to let your child know beforehand that you'll be available to chat in the morning.

9   Keep your ears, eyes and mind as open as possible. A parent's intuition will often spot the first signs of trouble, whether that means alcohol, drugs, an abusive relationship, a significant age difference, or anything else that worries you.

### ✳ Tip

If your teen doesn't have a cellular phone, give him or her change for a pay phone in case of emergency. Make sure the teen has a phone number for reaching you or a trusted friend.

### ⚠ Warning

Consider counseling if you feel a dating situation has gotten out of hand and you can't effectively communicate with your teen about it.

**How to Do *(Just About)* Everything**

## Help a Teen Find a Job                    605

Networking, answering ads and creative thinking are the keys to a successful teen job search.

### ⊙ Steps

1   Sit down together and assess skills, expectations and requirements, just as you would do for yourself.

2   Discuss options, taking into account your teen's time availability and transportation needs.

3   Think creatively: If your daughter wants to be a tennis star, maybe she can work at the local tennis club. Or your wannabe reporter can call local newspapers and radio stations for a go-fer or intern position.

4   Help your teen create a résumé, even if this is her first working experience. A teen résumé can include academic and extracurricular information and can mention awards, honors and relevant skills and interests.

5   Role-play with your teen. Listen to her ask for the job and describe her strengths, and coach her on what she should say in response to questions the interviewer may pose.

6   Make a list of possible contacts, including both yours and your child's. Get phone numbers and encourage the teen to call for job possibilities.

7   Check local newspapers for lawn-care, baby-sitting, hauling or painting jobs around town.

8   Once your teen has applied for a job, encourage her to make a follow-up call if the management doesn't respond within a week.

### ✱ Tips

Usually, a child must be 16 to legally get a traditional job, although there are exceptions.

Make sure your teen knows about good grooming and the importance of articulate, respectful and punctual behavior.

## Plan a Family Reunion                    606

Organize a memorable family reunion to renew lost contacts, introduce new ones and celebrate your heritage.

### ⊙ Steps

1   Make a list of family members, including spouses, partners and children. Get contact information for all the people on your list.

2   Choose a date when most people can attend. Summer months are often ideal, since children are off from school.

3   Decide how long you want the reunion to last and where to have it. Hold it near most family members, if you're clustered in one area; or if you're scattered, pick a central location.

4   Develop a budget and decide how much each family will need to contribute. Avoid making costs prohibitively high.

5   Visit reunion sites—such as hotels, inns and country clubs—and reserve one early.

6   Determine the menu—perhaps one that celebrates your family's heritage. Find a caterer or restaurant that can supply food for the event.

### ✱ Tips

If your reunion is large, consider organizing a reunion committee, with a secretary for mailings, a treasurer and a social-events planner.

Have attendees send checks several weeks before the reunion so you can shop for food, prizes or whatever else you'll need.

Try making family reunions a consistent event—every one, two or five years—at the same time of year.

7   Appoint a family historian to take photographs or videos during the event.

8   Plan social activities for the reunion—icebreaker games, sports, contests and talent shows. Include activities that will appeal to all ages. Buy prizes for your games or for distinctions such as oldest family member or longest distance traveled to attend.

9   Send an initial mailing to gauge interest and preferences, and to ask for help with planning. Send invitations later, with relevant information, directions and a map. Ask for a check from each family for its part of the reunion expenses.

## 607 | Make a Family Time Capsule

A time capsule can be a great family project to commemorate a special occasion. Fill it with photographs and mementos, and put it away for as long as you like.

### ⊙ Steps

1   Determine how long you want to put your time capsule away. Is it something you want to look at in 5 years? 10? 20? Will you take it out for a special occasion, such as an anniversary or a 21st birthday? Or do you want to hide it away for the next generation to find?

2   Decide where to put it. Keep in mind that you may move before the appointed time, so think about putting it where you can easily find it.

3   Decide what container to use. You can buy containers designed for time capsules, or use any waterproof, airtight and preferably fireproof vessel.

4   Ask everyone in the family to contribute an item—clippings, photographs, letters, arts and crafts, toys or just about anything else that fits into the capsule.

5   Protect the contents from decay. Put them into individual, airtight plastic bags and store them in a cool, dry location. For extra protection, consider copying them onto acid-free paper first.

6   Store photographs correctly—ask at a photography or crafts store if you aren't sure how to treat your photos.

7   Leave out any substance that could decay and damage the other contents of the box. This includes rubber, wool, wood, PVC, and any perishable or edible item. If you must include any of these, put them in an airtight plastic bag.

8   Mark everything clearly so you or others will know where each item came from and who included it when the time comes to open the capsule. Don't assume you will remember all the details. You may also want to include a detailed inventory of all the items.

9   Fill the capsule and seal it, then put it out of sight and out of mind. Make sure you store your capsule in a place where your kids won't get impatient having to look at it every day.

10  Leave yourself a reminder about the time capsule in a place where you are likely to find it if you move or if your home suffers any damage.

### ✱ Tips

Black-and-white photos last longer than color photos and will not fade as much—use them whenever possible.

Have each family member include a letter to the older version of himself or herself, or to future generations, if the capsule will be stored that long. Mention favorite foods, music, books, movies and hobbies.

If you plan to seal the time capsule away for more than a generation, include instructions for using any equipment or recordings you include. Your compact discs and videocassettes may very well be obsolete 100 years from now.

### Things You'll Need

☐ container

☐ memorabilia

☐ plastic bags

☐ acid-free paper

# Plan a Funeral

Planning a funeral is a difficult task, in which you must consider the wishes of the deceased as well as the survivors.

## ⊙ Steps

1   Meet with the other principal mourners to discuss their wishes and preferences. Find out if the deceased left any instructions regarding the funeral. Discuss religious preferences and how much money the family is willing to spend.

2   Consult with a religious leader or a funeral home if you would like help with any of the details, including location of a burial site or disposition of ashes, casket or cremation container selection, transportation, legal issues, flowers and music.

3   Choose the site where the funeral will take place. This is most often a church or temple, but it could also be a funeral home or at the graveside. (You may also decide on a more informal memorial service.)

4   Select someone to conduct the service. This could be a religious leader, funeral home personnel or a friend of the family.

5   Appoint pallbearers if you are having a formal funeral. Pallbearers can include special friends or business associates of the deceased, though the funeral home can usually provide them if there are no preferences.

6   Assign someone to give the eulogy. Typically, the family will choose a family member, religious leader or close friend. Contact the person who will give the eulogy as soon as possible to give him or her time to talk with the family and organize notes for the service.

7   Consider including music in the service. Choose a piece with special meaning for the family, perhaps having a family friend be a vocalist or instrumentalist.

8   Choose flowers for the service. What is appropriate depends on the family's wishes and the amount of money it wishes to spend.

9   Place an obituary in the local newspaper announcing the date, time and place of the funeral.

10  Consult the funeral home about having printed programs for the funeral service. Get input from the family regarding their design.

11  Buy a guest book for guests to sign as they arrive, if one is not provided.

12  Coordinate all of the above with the funeral home, which will arrange to transport the coffin to the funeral, remove the coffin to the burial site, or take care of other details as requested.

## ✳ Tip

You are not obliged to purchase any goods or services from the funeral home, and doing some things yourself can save a great deal of money. Ask the funeral home for a general list of all the services it offers—with prices—and choose only what you want to pay for or can't do yourself.

## 609 | Give a Eulogy

A eulogy is a speech in praise of a person who has died. One of the most important elements of a funeral, it can be given by a family member, friend of the departed or religious leader.

### ◉ Steps

1  Talk to the family of the deceased. Write down details of the person's life, major awards or recognition he or she received, names of family members, and special memories that family members share. Ask if the family would like you to say anything specific during the eulogy.

2  Take your notes home. Try to find a theme or ethic that defined the person's life and build the eulogy around it. For example, was family most important to the deceased? Did he or she have a great sense of humor?

3  Begin at the beginning. Most eulogies begin with the departed person's birth and give a brief outline of his or her life. Include anecdotes, memories and details that capture the person's spirit.

4  Try to quote a memorable statement made by the person or relay specific incidents that bring him or her to life for family and friends. Anything that paints a portrait of the individual is perfect.

5  Use your personal memories of the individual, if you have any. For example, if you knew the deceased in your youth, recall those times.

6  Infuse your eulogy with a little humor, especially if the deceased was a jokester or had a good sense of humor. Keep all humorous references appropriate to the occasion.

7  Be as brief as you can while still doing justice to the life of the deceased. Brevity is the key to a well-received eulogy.

### ✳ Tips

Try to avoid high-flown, moralistic speeches, and don't portray the deceased as a saint unless he or she truly was.

If you're not sure how much time you should take to deliver the eulogy, ask the person conducting the funeral or the family what they expect.

You may want to rehearse the eulogy a few times so you'll feel more comfortable delivering it. You don't need to memorize it, though; using typed sheets or note cards is perfectly acceptable.

If you find yourself becoming too emotional to continue, stop for a moment and try to collect yourself. If you feel you are unable to resume, you can ask the clergy member who has been officiating to read the eulogy for you.

## 610 | Comfort a Grieving Person

Comforting a grieving person entails offering support and allowing the person to go through whatever he or she is feeling.

### ◉ Steps

1  Allow the person to talk about his grief and express his feelings. Listen without offering advice or interrupting.

2  Be patient with the grieving person's changeable moods. It's normal for someone who is grieving to alternate between anger, sadness, numbness and acceptance.

3  Give the person as much time as he needs to grieve. Telling him to "get over it" or "let it go" won't help him grieve any faster.

4  Ask the bereaved what you can do to help. Try not to get frustrated if he doesn't know what he needs.

5  Offer suggestions of what you could do to help. For example, does the grieving person need more space? Does he want you to be around more? Are there tasks or errands he needs done?

### ✳ Tips

There is no "correct" amount of time to mourn a loss. The grieving period varies with the individual.

Be sensitive to significant dates such as birthdays, holidays and the anniversary of the death or loss; the grieving person may find these especially difficult times.

6   Show affection such as hugs or hand-holding if the bereaved seems receptive. If he seems uninterested in affection, try not to get irritated—this will pass with time.

7   Encourage the grieving person to join a grief support group. He can call his doctor for a referral or look in the community service section of the yellow pages for grief support services.

8   Urge the grieving person to get professional help if he's so depressed that he's unable to function day to day. Assist him in setting up an appointment with a doctor to discuss counseling or possible medication.

# Find Vital Records     611

**You can find official birth, death, marriage and divorce certificates in state, city or county records offices. Follow these directions when writing for a copy.**

## ⊙ Steps

1   Find out the address of your state or local vital-records office by referring to the National Center for Health Statistics (NCHS) Web site at www.cdc.gov/nchs, or call the NCHS at (301) 458-4636. The NCHS will also tell you the fee for the record you're requesting in your state.

2   Include the following when requesting a birth or death record: full name of the person whose record you are requesting; sex; parents' names, including mother's maiden name; place of birth or death and name of hospital (city, county and state); reason for requesting the certificate; and your relationship to the person whose record you are requesting, even if it is your own.

3   Provide the following information when asking for a marriage record: full name of bride and groom; month, day and year of marriage; place of marriage (city, county and state); reason for requesting the certificate; and your relationship to the people whose record you are requesting.

4   Give the following when requesting a divorce record: full names of bride and groom; date of divorce or annulment; place of divorce or annulment (city, county and state); type of final decree; your reason for requesting the certificate; and your relationship to the people whose divorce record you are requesting.

5   Write a check or money order payable to the office that holds your certificate, making sure it is the correct amount for the number of copies you are requesting.

 **Tip**

The federal government does not hold files on official certificates of birth, death, marriage or divorce.

## 612 | Deliver Puppies

Your dog's whelping (delivering) puppies can be an exciting and educational experience for your family. Most likely you will only have to observe and be available in case of emergencies.

### ◎ Steps

1 Contact your veterinarian to schedule a pre-whelping exam and consultation. Your veterinarian can offer last-minute advice and will be familiar with your dog should she need assistance during delivery.

2 Provide a whelping box of sturdy material that the puppies can't chew through and that's big enough for the mother dog to lie in and stretch out with her puppies. The sides of the box should be at least 6 inches high—high enough to prevent 4- to 6-week-old pups from escaping, but low enough to allow the mother to get in and out easily.

3 Present the whelping box to your dog one to two weeks before delivery and place it in semiprivate, familiar surroundings. Put soft, clean towels in the box.

4 Check the temperature of the mother-to-be daily after day 50 of pregnancy. When her temperature drops to 99 degrees F, labor will begin in 10 to 24 hours.

5 Look for signs that the dog is ready to give birth, such as her licking the genital area, or the appearance of an amber fluid or a bulge (the amniotic sac) protruding from the birth canal. This indicates that a puppy should be delivered within a few minutes.

6 During labor, avoid upsetting the dog. Remain calm when she is restless, nervous, anorectic (not eating), vomiting, pacing, shivering or panting. These can be normal behaviors for dogs in labor.

7 If the mother has not removed the amniotic membrane from her pup within 1 minute after delivery, intervene. Gently grasp the puppy in a clean towel and pull away the slimy material. Make sure that the nose and mouth are free from fluid and tissue.

8 Don't panic if the mother delivers a puppy without expelling the placenta. Sometimes the placenta of the previous birth will be expelled with the following birth.

9 Cut the umbilical cord about 2 inches from the puppy's body, using sharp, sterilized scissors. (Use isopropyl alcohol to sterilize scissors.)

10 Consult a veterinarian if your dog is in active labor for more than 30 minutes but has not yet delivered a puppy. If you notice that a puppy seems to be stuck, gently grasp it and pull it from the birth canal, twisting slightly if necessary.

11 Make sure all puppies are safe and warm and are not getting stepped on as the mother is delivering the other puppies. Multiple births followed by resting is common, but a delay of more than 1 hour between births warrants a call to the veterinarian.

12 Make sure each puppy nurses soon after delivery. It's essential that puppies nurse within the first 24 hours to acquire vital antibodies supplied by their mother's milk.

### ✳ Tips

Labor lasts 6 to 12 hours. Stage one of labor begins with uterine contractions and ends with the full dilation of the cervix. This is not externally visible. Stage two of labor begins with full dilation of the cervix and ends with full delivery of the first puppy. Stage three begins after delivery of the first puppy and ends with the expulsion of the placenta. The length of the second and third stages is variable—anywhere from 10 to 30 minutes.

If you suspect a puppy is not breathing, rub it with a towel along the shoulders and back to stimulate breathing. A healthy cry or whimper indicates an unobstructed airway.

### ⚠ Warning

Prepare yourself and your children for the possibility of a stillbirth. Should this happen, bury the puppy yourself or take it to the veterinarian.

### Things You'll Need

☐ cardboard box

☐ clean towels

☐ sterilized scissors

☐ commercially prepared milk replacer for puppies

13 Be prepared to give the puppies commercially prepared milk replacer in case the mother doesn't have enough milk or some other emergency arises. This is available wherever pet supplies are sold.

14 Take the mother and her puppies—in the whelping box, with a blanket for warmth—to the veterinarian for an exam. Do this within 24 hours after the last puppy is born.

---

## Deliver Kittens                                                           613

Mother Nature can usually guide the birth, but if you do get involved, follow these steps to ensure your cat's safe and comfortable delivery of her kittens.

### ⊙ Steps

1 Contact your veterinarian if you think your cat is pregnant to ensure that you will have professional help if needed.

2 Choose a quiet, warm location to place a basket or box lined with clean towels large enough for the mother cat to lie in and stretch out with her kittens. The sides should be at least 4 to 6 inches high—high enough to keep 4- to 6-week-old kittens from escaping, but low enough so that the mother can get in and out easily.

3 Avoid disturbing the mother during delivery, but observe her closely every few minutes to see how she is doing. Delivery should begin within 20 minutes of the first strong contraction; birth of the first kitten may take up to 60 minutes, but you should call your veterinarian if a kitten has not been delivered within 30 minutes since it may take a while to track down some help. Signs of labor include licking of the genital area, and straining in general.

4 Watch for amber fluid or a bulge (the amniotic sac) protruding from the mother's birth canal—this indicates that a kitten should be delivered within a few minutes.

5 If the mother has not removed the amniotic membrane within 1 minute after delivery, intervene and gently grasp the kitten in a clean towel and pull away the slimy material. Be certain the nose and mouth are free from fluid and tissue.

6 Rub the kitten with a towel along the shoulders and back to stimulate breathing. A healthy meow indicates an unobstructed airway.

7 If the mother has not chewed through the umbilical cord, sever it about 2 inches from the kitten's body, using sharp, sterilized scissors (sterilize with isopropyl alcohol). Gently pull the afterbirth from the birth canal.

8 Expect kittens to be delivered 15 to 45 minutes apart, but call your veterinarian if strong labor continues for 30 minutes without producing a kitten. Average litters contain three to six kittens.

9 Make sure that nursing begins in a few minutes. It is essential for the kittens to nurse from the mother to provide protection against disease. Supplement with commercially prepared milk replacer, available wherever pet supplies are sold, following your veterinarian's advice.

### ✳ Tip

Make sure the basket or box is readily accessible so you can closely observe the mother during her delivery.

### ⚠ Warnings

Watch closely when the mother is cleaning the newborn kitten. She may attempt to eat the afterbirth (placenta), and may inadvertently injure a kitten if it is wrapped tightly in the tissue.

Once in a while a kitten will be born dead—prepare yourself and your children ahead of time. Should this happen, bury the body or take it to the veterinarian.

### Things You'll Need

☐ basket or box

☐ clean towels

☐ sterilized scissors

☐ commercially prepared milk replacer for kittens

10 Take the mother and her kittens to the veterinarian for an exam in a covered container or box. Do this within 24 hours after the last kitten is delivered.

## 614 | Have Your Pet Spayed or Neutered

Having your pet spayed (an ovario-hysterectomy, for females) or neutered (castration, for males) will help stop pet overpopulation and contribute to your pet's well-being.

### ⊙ Steps

1 Contact your veterinarian about recommendations concerning age, vaccination requirements and other health-care issues as soon as you adopt your pet.

2 Understand that spaying or neutering information will vary depending on the type, age and sex of the pet you have chosen. Surgery at an early age—6 to 12 weeks—is now widely accepted for dogs and cats.

3 Ask the local animal shelter or your veterinarian about special programs available to have your pet spayed or neutered at a reduced cost. Programs exist everywhere for single or multiple animals and can save you money.

4 Ask the staff what is involved in the surgery and about pre- and post-operative care. This helps you make an educated choice about where to have the procedure done and how much you should pay.

5 Realize that postoperative pain management is a standard part of any acceptable surgical protocol; the veterinarian of your choice should recommend pain medication.

6 Schedule an appointment for surgery, and follow the veterinary hospital or clinic staff's instructions about presurgical care.

7 Take your pet to the veterinary hospital or spay/neuter clinic.

8 Pick up your pet as soon as allowed after the surgery, and administer postsurgical care as directed. Some veterinarians will discharge your pet the day of surgery, while others prefer to keep pets hospitalized overnight for observation.

9 Watch for signs of swelling, discharge or complications such as not eating or vomiting. You should have an after-hours contact number to call if you suspect anything is wrong.

10 Call the clinic the day after surgery, and let the staff know how your pet is doing. They should be interested in your pet's recovery.

11 Make sure to keep your pet from licking at the incision or chewing out any sutures—your vet may provide a special collar to help prevent this.

12 Schedule an appointment for a follow-up exam and suture removal.

### ✳ Tip

Contact the humane society or animal-control agency in your area to ask about reduced costs for licensing spayed or neutered animals.

### ⚠ Warnings

Spaying or neutering your pet is a major surgical procedure that should be performed by a qualified veterinary surgeon, under a general anesthetic, in a sterile surgical environment. Exercise care and good judgment when selecting someone to do this once-in-a-lifetime procedure on your pet.

General anesthesia and surgery do involve risk, but the benefits to pet and pet owner greatly exceed the risk involved.

## License Your Dog     **615**

All dogs are required to be licensed. Licensing helps the recovery of lost or stray animals and helps protect the public from rabies, since licensed dogs must have proof of vaccination.

### ◉ Steps

1 Have your dog vaccinated for rabies. Your veterinarian will let you know when your puppy is ready for this inoculation.

2 Contact your local animal-control agency for licensing information.

3 Take proof of vaccination to the appropriate animal-control agency— typically, the local humane society if you live within city limits.

4 Prepare to pay a fee. Fees are less for spayed and neutered dogs and are considerably less for dogs owned by senior citizens.

5 Affix the license tag to your dog's collar and place the dog license with your other legal documents.

6 Renew the license as required. The animal-control agency should notify you when it's time for renewal.

## Choose the Right Dog for Your Family     **616**

By evaluating the dog's breed and background as well as your home and lifestyle, you can assure your family of a fun and loving companion.

### ◉ Steps

1 Consult a veterinarian, who can provide useful advice on a breed's behavior and temperament as well as potential medical problems. A vet's opinion is apt to be less biased than that of a breeder, who is trying to sell a particular breed.

2 Consider your daily routine. Are you or someone else home often enough to care for a dog? If not, consider adopting a more independent pet, such as a cat.

3 Think about your family. Do you have young kids in the house? If so, be sure to choose a breed that generally gets along well with children.

4 Evaluate your living environment. Is it rural or urban, an apartment or a house? A Chihuahua or Yorkshire terrier may love your one-bedroom apartment, but larger breeds need more room to roam.

5 Supplement the information you receive from a veterinarian with further study about different breeds. For an overview of breed characteristics, see 618 "Select a Dog Breed" or check the pet section of your local library. Talking to dog owners can provide additional advice.

6 Decide whether you want a purebred or a mixed-breed dog. If you plan to show or breed your dog, then choose a purebred. If not, keep in mind that mixed-breed dogs can be just as loyal and lovable.

### ✱ Tips

Be aware that the average life span of a dog is 12 to 15 years, depending on the breed.

Adopting an adult can save you from the surprise of not knowing what the size, appearance and disposition of the dog will be as it gets older.

### ⚠ Warning

It's not fair to the animal to adopt it and then "return" it if you decide things aren't working out. Do your research and soul-searching beforehand, and once you've made a decision, try your best to honor the commitment.

7   Decide whether you want a puppy or an adult dog. Many wonderful pup-
    pies and adult dogs have been abandoned or given up to animal shel-
    ters or breed rescue groups, and adopting a pet from one of these
    sources may mean saving a life.

8   Ask the seller to tell you about particular habits or personality traits the
    dog exhibits.

9   Ask the seller about the parents of the puppies when visiting a purebred
    litter. Be sure that each parent belongs to an entirely different family and
    has been screened for common genetic or inheritable diseases.

---

## 617 | Introduce Your New Dog to Your Home

**Prepare yourself and your home so that your new dog can
quickly become comfortable in his new abode.**

### ⊙ Steps

1   Collect supplies for your new puppy or dog: a comfortable bed or crate,
    dog food and treats, food and water dishes, toys, a collar, a leash and
    an identification tag.

2   Dog-proof your home. Check and repair any damaged fencing, gates,
    doors, windows or screens. Place poisons out of reach, remembering to
    check behind the fridge for small objects or forgotten rat or mouse poi-
    son (see 653 "Protect Dogs and Cats From Household Dangers").

3   Pick up your puppy or dog at a time when you or someone else will be
    around the house for a couple of days.

4   Introduce the newcomer to other pets and family members, and then let
    him explore the house.

5   Supply a nice, plush bed or a cozy crate. Consider placing the bed or
    crate in an area where your new pet can keep an eye on you when he
    beds down.

6   Take your puppy outside to relieve himself after meals, after playtime,
    upon waking and, if necessary, every 15 minutes. Adult dogs can wait
    2 hours or longer.

7   Listen for your puppy's cues that he needs to relieve himself in the mid-
    dle of the night. It may take a while before he can sleep through the
    night without a potty break. Remember, it was your choice to get this
    puppy (see 641 "House-Train Your Puppy").

8   Play with your pet on and off throughout the day.

9   Take your pet to a veterinarian for a checkup and vaccinations as soon
    as possible.

10  Obtain a license from the proper agency (see 615 "License Your Dog").

### ⚠ Warning

Dogs will eat or drink anything—
that's how they explore and
learn—so be thorough in removing items that pose a risk to your
dog.

## ✓ 618 Select a Dog Breed

No matter where you live or what your lifestyle, there's likely to be a dog breed that will suit you. Here are brief descriptions of popular breeds recognized by the American Kennel Club (AKC); for details visit the AKC Web site at www.akc.org.

| BREED | APPEARANCE | CHARACTERISTICS | CARE |
|---|---|---|---|
| Airedale terrier | Large; tan and black | Gentle, protective | Exercise twice daily |
| Akita | Large; erect ears | Intelligent; loyal; good watchdog | Sheds heavily; prone to bloating |
| Alaskan malamute | Large; muscular; thick coat | Affectionate, obedient | Sensitive to heat and humidity |
| Australian shepherd | Medium-sized; medium-length coat | Energetic; good watchdog | Exercise daily |
| Basset hound | Medium-sized; large ears | Friendly, loyal, calm | Exercise to keep weight down |
| Beagle | Small; short, dense coat | Friendly with people and pets | Exercise daily |
| Boston terrier | Small; brindle, seal or black and white | Friendly, intelligent | Good indoor dog |
| Boxer | Large, muscular | Friendly, protective | Needs a yard |
| Bulldog | Medium-sized, stubby | Friendly; loyal; gentle with children | Clean face to avoid skin problems |
| Chihuahua | Small; large eyes and ears | Attentive; suspicious of visitors | Sensitive to cold |
| Chinese shar-pei | Medium-sized; wrinkled head | Loyal; excellent watchdog | Sensitive to heat |
| Cocker spaniel | Medium-sized; silky coat | Obedient; gets along well with people and animals | Coat needs regular trimming and grooming |
| Collie | Large; long or short hair | Loves people, good with children | Sensitive to heat |
| Dachshund | Small; low body | Bold, curious, adventurous | Walk or exercise daily |
| Dalmatian | Large; white with spots | Energetic, playful | Daily jog or walk; prone to deafness |
| Doberman pinscher | Large, powerful, regal | Loyal; intelligent; good watchdog | Likes warmth; not an outdoor dog |
| German shepherd | Large; strong; agile | Intelligent; loyal; excellent watchdog | Sheds heavily |
| Golden retriever | Large, powerful; golden coat | Playful; energetic; friendly; reliable | Sheds heavily; lots of exercise |
| Great Dane | Large, powerful; glossy coat | Gentle; friendly; eager to please | Twice as much food as other dogs |
| Jack Russell terrier | Small; smooth coat | Energetic; affectionate; athletic | Space and exercise; loves to dig |
| Labrador retriever | Medium-sized and strong; short, dense coat | Gentle; outgoing; eager to please | Very active, lots of exercise |
| Miniature schnauzer | Small; hard, wiry coat | Playful; spirited; obedient | Groom once or twice a week |
| Pekingese | Miniature; long, full coat | Dignified; stubborn | Groom weekly; sensitive to heat |
| Pug | Small; stocky; smooth coat | Even-tempered; playful; charming | Excessive shedding; indoor dog |
| Rottweiler | Medium-large and robust; black with rust markings | Headstrong; confident; excellent watchdog | Lots of exercise, training, companionship |
| Saint Bernard | Large, powerful, imposing | Loyal; friendly; calm | Lots of exercise and food; drools; sensitive to heat |
| Scottish terrier | Small; wiry coat | Bold; stubborn, feisty | Groom two or three times a week |
| Shih tzu | Miniature; long, full coat | Outgoing; happy, affectionate | Groom and exercise daily |
| Siberian husky | Medium-sized; well-furred | Energetic; independent; impish | Fenced-in yard; may try to escape |
| Standard poodle | Large and elegant | Intelligent; obedient | Groom a few times a week |
| Weimaraner | Medium-sized; sleek; gray | Active; headstrong; friendly | Exercise; fenced-in yard, training |
| Yorkshire terrier | Miniature; long steel-blue and tan coat | Spirited; independent | Groom daily; must live indoors |

reference

## 619 | Tame a Feral Cat or Kitten

With a little patience and time, most feral (wild) cats can be tamed into loving pets.

### ◎ Steps

1   Enclose the cat or kitten in a small space at first—a bathroom or bedroom works best.

2   Turn out the light if the cat is terrified; this often has a calming effect.

3   Put a bed, a litter box, food and water in the room. If the cat is very young (6 to 12 weeks), put her in a large carrier with a grated door and small windows.

4   Spend at least 2 to 3 hours a day with the animal. Just sitting quietly in the same room will allow the cat to learn that you are not a threat.

5   Gently compel the cat to let you touch her. Carefully wrap a blanket around her if you have to, hold her on your lap and pet her. Stroke her coat and touch her ears, face and neck as you talk to her in soothing tones. Even if the animal doesn't seem to be enjoying the attention, she is. Hold the cat by the scruff of the neck if she attempts to leave. (The mother cat will do this to carry or train a kitten—it doesn't hurt, and it actually relaxes the animal.)

6   Present special treats such as chicken or tuna, and leave them if the cat will not eat from your hand.

7   Gradually allow the cat to roam about in more rooms.

8   If the cat tries to run away from you repeatedly, enclose her in a smaller space and start again.

### ✷ Tips

Don't get discouraged early on; young feral cats can become very affectionate pets.

Younger cats are more apt to adjust quickly: 6- to 8-week-old kittens typically take two to three weeks to adjust to a domestic environment. An older cat that has been wild for a long time is difficult and sometimes impossible to tame, and may be better left outside. If you catch one, have the animal spayed or neutered and vaccinated, and then turn the cat loose where caught, or contact a professional.

### ⚠ Warning

Handle feral cats with extreme caution. Use gloves and protective clothing as required. Cat bites and scratches can result in serious health problems.

## 620 | Move to a New Home With Your Cat or Dog

Don't let your four-legged friend get lost in the shuffle of a move. Relocating your pet to a new home can be a smooth transition for everyone involved if you follow these simple steps.

### ◎ Steps

1   Obtain a copy of your pet's medical records to give to a veterinarian in the new area. Make sure all vaccinations are current.

2   Get a health certificate and proof of rabies vaccination if you're moving out of state, and ask your veterinarian about any other requirements to move animals out of state.

3   Call the animal-control agency or humane society in the new locale. Ask about licensing requirements.

4   Arrange for your pet to travel with you in a car or by air; buy a crate if he'll be traveling by air. Pets normally aren't allowed on trains or buses.

5   Feed your pet 5 to 6 hours before traveling. Give him water 2 hours before traveling. Give your pet medication to calm him, with your veterinarian's advice, if he becomes overexcited or anxious while traveling.

### ✷ Tips

Get your pet used to the crate a few weeks before the move so he will feel comfortable and secure while riding in it.

As soon as you know your new address and phone number, order a pet-ID tag with this information in case your pet gets lost in the new neighborhood.

If your cat is missing, check open vents and crawl spaces. Cats have been known to crawl between walls and other small spaces in an effort to hide and feel secure in a new place.

6   Bring food and water along. If you're traveling by car, make frequent stops to let your pet stretch, relieve himself and drink water.

7   Keep your pet confined when you get to the new home. He can easily escape during the moving process. Release him once all doors and windows are closed, and allow him to become familiar with the house.

8   Use familiar bowls, bedding and toys. Put them in locations similar to where they were in the old house.

9   Accompany your pet outside until he's familiar with the area. It's best to keep cats indoors for about two weeks after the move until they are accustomed to their new home. Disoriented cats sometimes run away in an attempt to get back to their old homes.

10  Try to stick to a regular schedule in the first days after the move.

11  Locate a veterinarian in your area. Make an appointment for your pet, and take your pet's records along.

⚠ **Warning**

Check your new home closely for dangers such as discarded poisons or chemicals inadvertently left by others.

---

## Introduce Dogs and Cats                                       621

The best time to introduce dogs and cats is when they are young. If possible, start when puppies are less than 12 weeks old and kittens are less than 7 weeks old.

### ⊙ Steps

1   Realize that kittens usually attach themselves to adult dogs, who in general aren't threatened by kittens.

2   Understand that dogs instinctively chase animals that run or move suddenly, even if they're used to being around other cats.

3   Introduce the kitten while the dog is either closely monitored by someone else or is on a leash. Do this several times over a period of several weeks, to allow time for each animal to grow comfortable.

4   Make introductions a positive experience for the dog, and reward her with plenty of praise and treats when she shows appropriate behavior.

5   Give an immediate and sharp "No!" if the dog is unfriendly toward the kitten, but avoid shouting if the dog behaves inappropriately.

6   Realize that an adult cat may perceive the dog as a threat to his status and may protest by marking his territory. This is normal behavior for a cat under stress.

7   Avoid allowing a puppy or dog to roam the house freely during the first few weeks of her introduction to an adult cat.

8   Provide a special area for the cat that's inaccessible to the dog. Be sure to place food, water and a litter box in the area.

9   Be aware that both the dog and the cat need space and special attention; bathing and grooming should take place in private.

10  Place the cat on a table and pet him for reassurance, while having the dog sit on the floor nearby.

✱ **Tips**

Don't fret if your dog and adult cat never bond. Most adult cats don't do well with change and are independent and solitary by nature.

Trim your cat's nails prior to introductions (see 640 "Trim Your Cat's Nails").

If after two weeks there are no improvements in relations, you may have to relocate one of the pets. Contact a pet behaviorist.

⚠ **Warning**

A dog can injure or kill a cat with a single bite, so proceed with caution. Avoid leaving the two together for even a brief period without supervision.

11 Alternatively, place the puppy or dog in a cage, and let the cat approach.

12 Allow the cat to swat at the dog (within reason) when they finally meet nose to nose. This is a cat's way of establishing space boundaries.

## 622 | Introduce Your New Baby to Your Dog

Introducing your new baby to your dog is almost like bringing a baby home to a sibling—if handled incorrectly, it can cause rivalry and hurt feelings. Take a few simple precautions.

### ◉ Steps

1 If you need to change house rules, change them before the baby arrives. Otherwise, your dog may associate the baby's arrival with her sudden banishment from the couch.

2 Consider a series of obedience classes before the baby arrives, especially if your dog doesn't know the basic commands: sit, come, stay.

3 Have your dog thoroughly checked out by a veterinarian before your baby comes home. This will give you time to deal with parasites or other problems that could pose a family health risk.

4 Let your dog get used to the sights, smells and sounds of a baby in advance. Let her sniff baby blankets and lotions, and get her used to the sounds of rattles and other baby toys.

5 Before bringing your baby home from the hospital, send home a blanket or gown that the baby has been wrapped in. This will get your dog used to the baby's scent.

6 Let Dad or someone else carry the baby inside at the first homecoming, so that Mom is free to greet the dog with open arms. That way the dog will be less jealous of her attentions to the baby.

7 Praise your dog when you're near the baby so she will think of the child as a positive influence on her life—she gets praised more when the baby is around.

8 Reassure your dog, each time your baby cries, that this is a normal sound, and train her not to bark when she hears it. Use positive reinforcement as much as possible—a treat or a hug for doing the right thing.

9 Spend one-on-one time with your dog while the baby is napping, or during walk time (your baby can ride along in a sling or front-pack).

10 Be patient—it may take some time before your dog is really comfortable around your baby.

### ✱ Tips

Teach your dog to heed a "Quiet!" or "Hush!" command if she tends to bark when someone comes to the door. This will mean she can still do her job of guarding the house, but you can quiet her quickly if your baby is sleeping.

Keep your dog's nails trimmed (see 639 "Trim Your Dog's Nails"). Train her not to jump on people if this has been a problem.

### ⚠ Warning

Never leave your dog alone with your baby, no matter how well-trained and friendly the dog may be. Even the best-behaved dog can become frustrated with a baby's cries, and will act instinctively rather than rationally in some situations.

## ✓ 623 Select a Cat Breed

When you're buying a pedigreed cat, you have the choice of a "pet-quality," "breeder-quality" or "show-quality" animal, each showing greater conformance with breed standards at a correspondingly higher price. When you're selecting any kitten, inspect her to make sure she's healthy. Get a written health guarantee from the breeder, and bring your kitten to a veterinarian for a checkup as soon as possible. For more information about breeds, visit the Web site of one of the many ailurophile organizations, such as the Cat Fanciers' Association (www.cfainc.org).

| BREED | APPEARANCE | CHARACTERISTICS | HEALTH AND CARE |
|---|---|---|---|
| Abyssinian | Solid brown, fawn, blue or red, with large ears and almond-shaped eyes | Active, playful, affectionate | Susceptible to kidney disease. Brush teeth weekly to help prevent gingivitis. |
| American curl | Unusual curled ears, a genetic mutation | Loving; adapts well to other animals | Don't force the ears to uncurl, or you could break the cartilage |
| British shorthair | Stocky and sturdy; dense and firm, short hair | Reserved yet affectionate; loves children | Prone to hemophilia B (hereditary bleeding disorder) |
| Burmese | Sleek and silky, with round gold eyes. Sable is the most popular color; other colors are blue, champagne and platinum. | Playful, affectionate, intelligent; a great lap cat | Hardy and long-lived if kept indoors |
| Korat | Silver-blue fur, luminous green or amber eyes | Extremely loyal, with a gentle disposition; highly acute hearing | Prone to corneal dermoids, treatable surgically |
| Manx | Tail length varies from nonexistent to normal | Mellow and affectionate, but may attack intruders; likes high places | Prone to severe spinal defects |
| Maine coon | Shaggy tail, tufts on paws and ears, longer fur on belly | Gets along well with other cats, even dogs; can be trained to walk on a leash | Tends to inherit hip dysplasia and hypertrophic cardiomyopathy |
| Persian | "Smooshed-in" face and long, flowing fur | Serene, quiet, dignified | Sometimes has respiratory problems such as wheezing and eye drainage |
| Siamese | Blue eyes and either triangular or apple-shaped face; darker shadings on feet, ears and tail | Affectionate, good with children; vocal and demanding | Sometimes cross-eyed; occasionally has a kinked tail. May inherit heart defects. |
| Somali | Available in blue, fawn, red (sorrel) and ruddy colors—or in Europe, more commonly silver tones | Personable and active; likes to snooze on laps, but also needs to run and play | Needs a special "PCV" blood test. May be prone to autoimmune hemolytic anemia (AIHA) and renal amyloidosis. |
| Sphynx | Appears to be hairless, but color and pattern are visible in a downy coat and on underlying skin | Gregarious, active, affectionate; gets along well with other animals | Needs a warm indoor environment to maintain its hairlessness. Prone to sunburn, even through a sunny window. Must be bathed often to combat oily skin; ears are prone to wax buildup. |

reference

## 624 | Introduce Your New Baby to Your Cat

When you bring your new baby home, your cat may not be favorably impressed—but there's a lot you can do to help the two of them become good friends.

### ⊙ Steps

1   If you need to change house rules, change them before the baby arrives. Otherwise, your cat may associate the baby's arrival with his sudden banishment from the foot of your bed.

2   Set up a crib or bassinet for your baby ahead of time and train your cat not to sleep in it. Cats and infants should not sleep together, because it poses a risk of suffocation or allergic reaction for the baby.

3   Have your cat thoroughly checked out by a veterinarian before your baby comes home. This will give you time to deal with parasites or other problems that could pose a family health risk.

4   Before bringing your baby home from the hospital, send home a blanket or gown that the baby has been wrapped in. This will get your cat used to the baby's scent.

5   Let Dad or someone else carry the baby inside at the first homecoming, so that Mom is free to greet the cat with open arms.

6   When introducing your baby to your cat, don't hold or restrain the cat; let him approach and explore the baby at his own pace.

7   Spend time with the cat while your baby is sleeping. Cuddle him, brush him and play with him as much as possible to reassure him that you still love him.

### ✴ Tips

As your baby grows and becomes mobile, teach her as early as possible how to pet your cat gently, and make sure she doesn't grab at your cat's tail or ears. This will help your child and your pet to become friends rather than adversaries.

Be sure to keep your cat's nails trimmed (see 640 "Trim Your Cat's Nails"). Don't declaw him, though—especially if he spends any time outdoors. Just train him to be gentle around your baby.

### ⚠ Warning

If your baby will be sleeping in a nursery, consider making it a cat-free zone. Your cat probably won't hurt your baby deliberately, but it is dangerous to leave them together unsupervised.

## 625 | Find a Pet Sitter

Use a pet sitter as an alternative to a kennel when you travel. Here's how to find a loving pet nanny.

### ⊙ Steps

1   Ask your veterinarian or pet groomer for references, or check the yellow pages for a pet sitter.

2   Call Pet Sitters International, at (800) 268-SITS, or the National Association of Professional Pet Sitters, at (800) 296-PETS.

3   Have the potential sitter come to your home for an interview. Introduce your pet, to gauge both parties' reactions. If your pet is a dog, have them go for a walk to see how the sitter handles your dog on a leash.

4   Determine how the potential sitter would handle problems such as a medical emergency or the escape of your pet.

5   Expect the potential sitter to ask you if your pet's vaccinations are up-to-date, how your pet behaves when he is out among other animals and people, and what to do if the sitter must suddenly leave the job before you have returned home.

### ✴ Tip

Pet sitters should be bonded or insured for their protection and yours.

6 Once you've selected a sitter, provide him or her with the names, phone numbers and addresses of your pet's regular veterinarian, the closest emergency veterinary hospital, a nearby friend, and the place where you can be reached.

7 Go over what and when to feed your pet, any medications to be given, and the duration and preferred location of outings.

## Find Doggy Day Care 626

If you worry about leaving your dog home alone during the day, you may want to consider enrolling him in doggy day care, where he can socialize with four-legged friends.

### ⊙ Steps

1 Do a search online or in the yellow pages to find a program that's near your home.

2 Ask other dog owners you meet at the park to recommend a program they have used, or check with a local pet store, veterinarian or grooming parlor for references.

3 Call the humane society in your area to see if it runs a day-care program for dogs or can direct you to one.

4 Browse the Sunday classifieds section of your local newspaper to find ads for local programs.

5 Visit the day-care center you are considering before enrolling your dog. Find out what types of activities are planned for the dogs during the day.

6 Make sure your dog is old enough to attend the program you choose. Five or six months is usually the minimum age.

7 Have your dog spayed or neutered in advance to avoid pregnancy.

8 Take your dog to your veterinarian to be sure your dog is current on vaccinations, is parasite-free and is in good health before his first day of attendance at the program.

9 Expect to pay $15 to $25 or more for a full day of care.

**✱ Tips**

Doggy day-care centers should be clean and odor free, and the dogs should be well-supervised. Check to make sure that there are enough caregivers to provide proper supervision.

Even if you don't enroll your pet full-time, you may want your dog to attend day care if you have any maintenance people coming to your house during the day. This is also a good option to ease your mind during a particularly stressful week at work or when planning a special event at your home.

## Feed Your Dog a Balanced Diet 627

No single dietary plan can be considered ideal for every dog. Here are some general guidelines to follow that can keep your dog healthy and her appetite satisfied.

### ⊙ Steps

1 Be sure to choose a reputable brand of dog food. Check with your veterinarian for recommendations.

**✱ Tips**

When switching dog foods, do it gradually over a week by increasing the ratio of new food to old food. This will help avoid digestive upsets.

2　Select a high-quality dog food that's appropriate for your dog's age, weight, activity level or size. Make sure to feed your dog dry food as well as moist canned food to help keep his teeth clean.

3　Be sure that protein ratios are appropriate for your dog's breed and age. Typically, dog food with 20 to 30 percent protein content provides a healthy balance.

4　Avoid overfeeding, since obesity can lead to a variety of medical problems, including musculoskeletal problems, and can aggravate hip dysplasia (abnormal growth or development of the hip joint).

5　Avoid feeding your dog table scraps—it encourages begging and may not be good for her digestive system. If you must give her "people food," put the scraps in her dog bowl after the family has finished the meal. Be careful to avoid giving her onions or chocolate.

6　Feed your dog a measured amount twice daily, but keep in mind that some dogs prefer to eat one meal a day.

Consult a veterinarian before adding vitamin and mineral supplements to your dog's diet.

Dry food is better than canned food at preventing dental tartar.

## ⚠ Warnings

Avoid oversupplementing your dog's diet with vitamins and minerals. Excess dietary supplements cause nutritional imbalance and medical disorders. Some vitamins and minerals are toxic in high dosages.

Never feed your dog chocolate. Chocolate is toxic for dogs.

---

## 628 | Feed Your Cat a Balanced Diet

**No single dietary plan can be considered ideal for every cat. Here are some general guidelines to help keep your cat healthy and her appetite satisfied.**

### ⊙ Steps

1　Be sure to choose a reputable brand of cat food. Check with your veterinarian for recommendations.

2　Feed your cat dry food as well as wet, canned food. Dry food helps keep her teeth cleaner. Read the label to be sure the nutrient level is appropriate to your cat's stage of life. Usually, cat food containing 34 to 38 percent protein and 19 to 22 percent fat provides a healthy balance.

3　Remember that most cats are snackers or nibblers and like to eat small amounts of dry food throughout the day.

4　Know that cats with digestive problems may require higher fiber content in their diet. Check with your veterinarian.

5　Remember that cats begin to show their age at 8 to 10 years, with diminished abilities to smell, taste, chew and digest. Make sure an older cat has food that is highly digestible and palatable.

6　Feed your cat a small, measured amount of canned food twice a day. Leave the dry food out so that he can snack throughout the day.

### ✱ Tip

Cats with kidney or heart disease might need reduced protein, phosphorus and sodium in their diets. Purchase these foods from your veterinarian.

### ⚠ Warnings

Never feed a cat dog food. Cats require more protein and fat in their foods.

Make sure not to overfeed your cat. Obesity in cats contributes to disease and can lead to premature aging and early death.

## Determine if Your Cat or Dog Is Overweight     629

Obesity in a pet can lead to health problems—and can itself be a sign of a serious medical condition. Monitor the weight of your cat or dog with this simple test.

### ⊙ Steps

1 Check that your pet's ribs are easily felt but not visibly sticking out. This indicates that your cat or dog is at a desirable weight.

2 Look at your pet from above. Some indentation between the rib cage and the hips, depicting an hourglass shape, indicates that your pet is at a desirable weight.

3 Check your pet's belly. If the belly of a cat protrudes, the cat may be overweight. (A protruding belly on a cat is called an apron.) A dog should also have a trim abdomen.

4 Feel your pet's hips. Anything more than light fleshiness indicates that your pet is above normal weight.

5 Always consult a veterinarian before putting a pet on a diet. Your veterinarian can recommend a special diet appropriate to your pet, and can examine your pet to rule out the possibility that a serious medical condition is causing the obesity.

### ✳ Tips

Regular exercise helps your pet lose weight.

A dog or cat's weight at 1 year of age often reflects the animal's optimal body weight, although this is not true of pets that are already obese at 1 year. A veterinarian can provide weight guidelines.

### ⚠ Warning

Visible ribs or excessive thinness could be a sign of hyperthyroidism (overactive thyroid) in cats, especially in those over 12 years of age. Consult a veterinarian if your pet is chronically underweight.

---

## Walk Your Dog     630

Dogs that are confined to the house for long periods need relief from boredom, an outlet for their energy and a chance to explore the world.

### ⊙ Steps

1 Make sure your dog is trained for basic obedience commands, such as "Heel," so that you can keep him under control at all times.

2 Resist the urge to let your dog run wild and free on public property—keep him safe by putting him on a leash. If you're concerned about restricting him too much and your dog is well-trained, consider purchasing a retractable leash.

3 Take your dog on a 1-hour walk or two 30-minute walks each day, even if you're home for part of the day and spend lots of time with him.

4 Adjust the walking distance and pace to the age and health of your dog.

5 Allow your dog time to stop and smell the ground. Dogs gather information this way—they can determine what animals have passed and what changes have occurred since the last walk.

6 Let your dog greet people and other dogs appropriately while on the walk. This will help develop him social skills.

7 Carry a pooper-scooper or small plastic bags to clean up after your dog as you go.

### ✳ Tip

Walking your dog regularly helps alleviate inappropriate behaviors at home such as barking, chewing or digging.

### ⚠ Warning

Reduce the time and distance of the walk in extremely hot or cold weather, especially if your dog is old or in poor health.

## 631 | Run With Your Dog

Dogs are great companions for runners, and they offer visible security. Vigorous exercise can also help keep your dog fit.

### ◉ Steps

1 Check with your veterinarian before starting your dog on an exercise program. Make sure running is the right kind of exercise for your dog.

2 Warm up your dog. Put the animal through a few sprints to loosen up her muscles and get her heart pumping. Dogs may show signs of stiffness after the initial run, just like humans.

3 Build up slowly, and watch for signs of fatigue. If your dog lies down during a workout, end the session.

4 Keep water on hand before, during and after a workout.

5 Watch the running surface. If your dog is not accustomed to running on pavement, build up gradually.

6 Keep your dog on a leash and by your side when running.

### ⚠ Warnings

Avoid running with your dog in very hot weather. Dogs do not sweat and can easily become overheated.

Running on hot pavement can cause blisters on your dog's pads—check the pavement with your own bare hands or feet before taking the dog out in hot weather.

Take care not to overdo it. Animals don't always know when to quit, so don't let your dog run until she drops.

## 632 | Wash Your Dog

Your pooch is dirty, and he stinks. Instead of making him suffer under a cold hose, give him a bath indoors.

### ◉ Steps

1 Place a medium-sized bucket, three large towels and a hair dryer in a warm bathroom.

2 Make certain a shower mat is securely in place to keep the dog from slipping in the tub.

3 Isolate the dog in the bathroom before running the water.

4 Make certain the water is comfortably warm, and fill the tub with about 3 inches of water. Put the dog in the tub.

5 Protect your dog's eyes from the shampoo by using a lubricating eye ointment, which your veterinarian can provide. A drop of olive or baby oil will also do.

6 Use the bucket to wet the dog from the head down toward the tail, including the undersides, being careful not to get water in his eyes.

7 Apply a small amount of dog shampoo—available at pet stores—to the top of the head. (Do not use dish soap, as it can dry and irritate a dog's skin.) Be extremely careful to keep it away from the eyes. Lather down to the tail, including the neck and underside fur. If using a flea shampoo, leave the lather on for the recommended time.

8 Keep a hand on your dog, because he will want to shake the lather off. Be ready to turn your head away.

9 Pull the tub drain and run the water again; adjust the temperature.

### ⚠ Warnings

Trembling is not uncommon during a bath—for the dog, that is.

Your dog may snap at the hair dryer if you hold it too close to his face.

### Things You'll Need

☐ medium-sized bucket

☐ 3 large towels

☐ hair dryer

☐ shower mat

☐ eye ointment

☐ dog shampoo

10  Use the bucket to carefully and completely rinse the head first, avoiding the eyes and inner ears. Work the water toward the dog's back and undersides. Use your hands to work the water through the suds.

11  Turn off the water. While your dog is still in the tub, let him shake excess water off his fur.

12  Drain the water from the tub and dry the dog with towels from head to toe. Concentrate on the areas of thickest fur and between his toes.

13  Remove your dog from the tub. Turn on the hair dryer to a medium setting, testing the heat with your fingers. Aim first for the thickest hair, running your fingers or a comb through it until it is just slightly damp. Keep the hair dryer approximately 6 inches from the skin to prevent burning and overdrying.

## Wash Your Cat                                                633

If your cat is infested with fleas, you'll probably want to give her a bath. Otherwise, wash your cat as you deem necessary—since cats wash themselves, they do not often need bathing.

### ◉ Steps

1  Adopt a calm, positive attitude before and during the bath—it will help ease your cat's anxiety.

2  Consider trimming your cat's claws beforehand to reduce your risk of getting scratched (see 640 "Trim Your Cat's Nails").

3  Bring your cat into the bathroom. Close the door and keep it closed until you are finished.

4  Fill the bathtub with enough lukewarm water to cover your cat's paws.

5  Gently set your cat in the tub.

6  Give your cat free rein in the bathtub using minimal restraint, but gently hold on to the back of her neck if she tries to escape.

7  Apply lubricating eye ointment (available from your veterinarian) or a drop of baby or olive oil to your cat's eyes to prevent irritation from the shampoo.

8  Scoop water in a plastic cup, and pour it over the cat until her fur is wet, making sure to avoid her eyes.

9  Apply a regular shampoo made for cats, or a flea shampoo if needed, and rub it into the cat's fur. Use caution around the eyes.

10  Hold your cat under the faucet or scoop clean water over her to rinse.

11  Quickly pat or rub your cat dry with a towel.

12  Comb through your cat's fur to spend quality time together as she dries, then give her a special treat such as catnip or kibble for a job well done.

### ✳ Tip

If your cat's fur is matted or soiled from contact with hard-to-clean substances such as oil, gum or paint, it is best to have the cat bathed by a professional groomer.

### ⚠ Warning

Be sure to remove all soap when rinsing, since cats will groom themselves and ingest anything left on their fur.

### Things You'll Need

- ❑ plastic cup
- ❑ eye ointment
- ❑ cat shampoo
- ❑ towel
- ❑ pet comb
- ❑ cat treats

## 634 | Get Skunk Smell Out of Your Pet's Fur

Did your cat or dog get sprayed during your weekend away at the cabin? Keep your pet outdoors until you get rid of the obnoxious skunk odor with the following solution.

### ⊙ Steps

1 Mix 4 c. hydrogen peroxide with 4 tbsp. baking soda and 1 tsp. dish-washing soap.

2 Put cotton balls in your pet's ears to protect the inner-ear tissue from the cleaning mixture, which could easily drip in.

3 Don rubber gloves to protect your hands during this process.

4 Start with your pet's head, taking care not to get the solution into his eyes, ears or mouth. Apply a drop of olive or baby oil to his eyes to prevent irritation.

5 Rub the mixture evenly into your pet's coat. It will probably be more pleasant to do this outdoors.

6 Rinse the coat with clean water.

7 Repeat if the smell persists.

### ✱ Tips

Tomato juice also neutralizes the effects of skunk odor. Rub it into your pet's fur, let it soak for approximately 15 minutes, then wash it off with water.

Skunk-odor remover or douches that remove skunk scent from fur are sold in pet stores. Ask your veterinarian for advice on which product works best.

### ⚠ Warning

Skunks can carry rabies, so make sure your pet's vaccinations are current before you visit areas frequented by skunks.

## 635 | Clean Your Dog's Ears

If your dog's ears are smelly or look dirty, or if he's scratching them a lot, it may be time for a cleaning.

### ⊙ Steps

1 Use an ear wash formulated for cleaning animals' ears, as recommended by your veterinarian.

2 Soak a cotton ball thoroughly in the ear wash. Squeeze out the excess.

3 Place the cotton ball in your pet's outer ear and gently rub up and down.

4 Allow your pet to shake off excess moisture. This is important for preventing ear infections.

5 Soak the tip of a cotton swab in the ear wash and run it along the nooks and crannies of the outer ears, being careful never to push into the ear canal. Clean only the flaps and visible parts of the ear. Dogs' ear canals are deep and don't drain like human ears.

6 Leave cleaning down inside the ear canal to the veterinary medical staff.

### ✱ Tip

Some dog breeds, such as poodles, need hair removed from their ear canals to prevent infections. Consult your veterinarian.

### ⚠ Warning

If your pet has chronic ear infections (symptoms include excessive itching, discharge, pain around the ears, redness or swelling of the ear canal, unusual tilting of the head, or bad odor), consult a veterinarian.

## Brush Your Cat's or Dog's Teeth

Brushing your cat's or dog's teeth is simple after you've had a few practice sessions. Try to do this every day to promote healthy teeth and gums.

### ⊙ Steps

1 Have a veterinarian check your pet's teeth before you start a tooth-brushing program. If your pet has gum disease or damaged teeth, the process will be painful and he will associate pain with tooth brushing. He may even bite you. Get your cat or dog used to your looking into his mouth. After each time you do so, reward him with a treat or praise.

2 Buy a pet dental kit, including toothpaste (made for dogs and cats) and a toothbrush, at a pet store or from your vet. Follow the kit's instructions for use.

3 Place your cat or dog on a comfortable surface while brushing his teeth.

4 In general, try to use minimal restraint on your pet while brushing—especially if it's a cat. However, it may be easier to handle an especially reluctant cat by wrapping him in a towel to keep him from scratching or trying to escape.

5 Brush your cat's or dog's teeth with a gentle, massaging motion.

6 Reward your cat or dog with a tartar-control treat after the procedure.

### ❋ Tips

Starting at age 3, bring your dog or cat to the veterinarian for an annual teeth cleaning.

Try to brush as part of daily quality time with your pet. He will come to associate tooth brushing with affection and praise.

Research alternatives, such as a finger toothbrush, if your pet refuses to let you brush his teeth with a toothbrush. Ask your veterinarian for suggestions.

### Things You'll Need

❑ pet dental kit

❑ tartar-control treats

---

## Prevent Bad Breath in Your Cat or Dog

Bad breath may be a sign that your cat or dog has a buildup of bacterial growth in the form of plaque, or possibly a more serious condition, such as gingivitis.

### ⊙ Steps

1 Understand that brushing your cat's or dog's teeth is the best method for preventing bad breath and other dental problems (see 636 "Brush Your Cat's or Dog's Teeth").

2 Look for abscessed teeth and other dental problems while you're brushing, and have a veterinarian properly treat any such problems.

3 Consider offering your cat or dog mouthwash; some mouthwashes made for pets claim that they can deter dental tartar buildup.

4 Consider your pet's diet. Some soft canned foods are particular offenders when it comes to bad breath. Make sure your cat or dog eats dry food in addition to soft food, unless he is elderly and needs to eat soft food exclusively.

5 Be sure that your veterinarian includes a dental examination and cleaning as part of your pet's regular examinations.

6 Consider other possible causes of bad breath—such as gastrointestinal disease—if it persists in spite of clean teeth and proper food. Bring your pet to the veterinarian for a checkup.

### ❋ Tip

Some pet foods are designed to help prevent tartar buildup and gum disease. Certain chew toys also can help prevent and remove tartar buildup.

## 638 | Care for Your Cat's or Dog's Paws

Keep your pet's paws in good shape by inspecting them on a regular basis.

### ⊙ Steps

1 Trim nails as needed (see 639 "Trim Your Dog's Nails" or 640 "Trim Your Cat's Nails").

2 Check regularly between toes for foxtails, stickers and other foreign bodies. They can sometimes be deeply embedded between toes.

3 Pull out any irritants you can locate, using tweezers.

4 Check for cuts on paw pads. If cuts are small, wash them gently with antibacterial soap. If they are large or bleeding excessively, contact your veterinarian for care.

### ⚠ Warnings

Running on pavement can wear out your dog's pads—check them regularly if you run with your dog. Also, avoid running with your dog on hot pavement, since it can burn his pads.

Take your pet to the veterinarian to be checked and treated if he's limping and excessively licking a paw.

## 639 | Trim Your Dog's Nails

Your dog's nails should just touch the ground when she walks. If her nails are clicking on the floor or getting snagged in the carpet, it's time for a pedicure.

### ⊙ Steps

1 Use trimmers designed for pets. Ask your veterinarian or a groomer for advice about what types of nail trimmers are best for your dog and how to use them properly.

2 Make sure the trimmers are sharp.

3 Start at the tip of the nail and snip a little at a time. When you can see a little bit of moisture, stop clipping.

4 Avoid cutting into the quick, which contains nerves and blood vessels. It is painful and will bleed easily. On white nails, the quick is the pink section. Be extra careful when cutting dark nails, because the quick is difficult to see.

5 If the tip of the nail begins to bleed, apply pressure using styptic powder or a substitute such as baby powder or cotton. Avoid wiping the blood clot off the tip of the nail once the bleeding has stopped.

6 Remember to trim the dewclaw nail, on the inside of the leg. Since it doesn't touch the ground, it wears down less rapidly than the others.

7 Give your dog a treat after trimming her nails.

8 Trim your dog's nails once or twice a month. The quick will lengthen if you don't trim the nail regularly, and long nails can cause problems with traction or become ingrown.

### ✱ Tip

If you have not cut your dog's nails since she was a puppy or you're uncomfortable with the task, ask your veterinarian or groomer to demonstrate proper nail trimming or to do it for you.

### ⚠ Warning

Never attempt to trim your dog's nails with clippers designed for use on humans.

### Things You'll Need

☐ pet nail clippers

☐ styptic powder

☐ dog treats

## Trim Your Cat's Nails                                   640

If your cat has the not-so-charming habit of using his nails inappropriately on you or the furniture, a regular trimming can help.

### ⊙ Steps

1   Get your cat accustomed to having his feet and nails handled; whenever you're snuggling, take a moment to massage each paw.

2   Turn on a strong light. Trimming your cat's nails in good light will help you see the quick—the part of the nail containing nerves and blood vessels. Cutting into the quick is painful and will cause bleeding.

3   Have everything ready before you start. Cats don't like restraint, especially for long periods.

4   Place your cat in your lap, and gently hold one of his paws.

5   Unsheath your cat's retractable nails by placing your index finger underneath one toe and your thumb over the top of the same toe. Squeeze your fingers together gently. As you do this, you'll see the toenail protrude; it will remain extended until you release your hold.

6   Trim each nail just beyond the point where it starts to curve downward, using trimmers specifically designed for cats.

7   Start gradually, clipping a few nails in one sitting, using positive reinforcement such as petting or treats as you clip.

8   If bleeding occurs, apply pressure to the tip of the nail using styptic powder or a substitute such as baby powder or cotton balls.

9   Work up to trimming the nails on all four paws in one sitting.

### ✱ Tips

Cats usually have five nails on each front foot and four on the rear, although they can be born with extra toes. The nails on extra toes tend to become ingrown and should be trimmed more frequently.

This is often a job for two people—one to hold the cat and one to trim the nails.

Avoid punishment or negative reinforcement if your cat protests the pedicure—cats generally don't respond well to this approach. Try again when you sense that your cat might be more cooperative.

### Things You'll Need

- ☐ pet nail clippers
- ☐ styptic powder

## House-Train Your Puppy                                 641

A puppy isn't born knowing that your carpet is not an acceptable place to relieve himself. Here's a relatively easy way to train him that doesn't require punishment.

### ⊙ Steps

1   Watch your puppy's behavior while relieving himself outdoors so you can detect the warning signs and intercept him when indoors.

2   Stay outside as often as possible during nice weather so your puppy can develop a preference for eliminating outdoors. Help him develop a liking for surfaces like dirt and gravel by taking him outdoors to eliminate after eating, playing and sleeping—or, ideally, every 15 minutes.

3   When it's time, go straight to a predesignated area and don't leave until the puppy urinates.

4   Tuck your puppy into a cozy crate in your bedroom at night. Dogs are den animals and don't like to soil the area where they sleep.

5   Carry the puppy outdoors when he becomes restless in the middle of the night, and wait until he's finished relieving himself.

### ✱ Tip

Corrections and punishments for indoor accidents will only teach your puppy not to eliminate around you (even when outdoors), but won't stop him from eliminating indoors when you're not around. If you catch the puppy in the act, say "No!" sharply and carry the puppy outside.

### ⚠ Warning

Avoid giving your dog the message that relieving himself is wrong. Don't rub his nose in the mess, and don't hit him with a newspaper.

6  Supply a litter box (filled with sand or kitty litter) during the night, unless you plan on getting up every couple of hours to take him outside. If you do want to take him outside, set your alarm if you sleep too deeply to notice that your puppy has started fidgeting, and carry him outside at those times.

7  Carry the puppy outside first thing in the morning so he won't soil the floors as he walks outside.

8  Be consistent with training. Consult a pet behaviorist if you have problems.

9  Reward your dog with puppy treats and praise every time he successfully eliminates outdoors.

## 642 Train Your Dog

**The key to proper training is positive reinforcement—treats and unlimited praise. Be patient and avoid harsh punishment, and you and your dog will both benefit.**

### ⊙ Steps

1  Enroll your dog in a basic obedience class to learn the "Heel," "Sit" and "Stay" commands.

2  When your dog is learning a command, say "Good" the instant she exhibits proper behavior, and then follow up quickly with a reward of treats and more praise.

3  Begin increasing your expectations very slowly. For example, lengthen by a few seconds the time your dog must sit before you shower praise.

4  Reward even the slightest sign of effort your dog is making to meet your increasing expectations.

5  Move on to other commands once your dog is comfortable with "Heel," "Sit" and "Stay," and with training in general.

6  Train throughout the day, when you have free time, in a quiet area free from distractions. Limit each session to 5 to 10 minutes.

7  Train in a busier environment only after your dog understands the command entirely, but realize that you may need to start from scratch—dogs are situational learners.

8  Reduce food rewards gradually, but always give an abundance of praise.

### ✱ Tips

Check with your local humane society or community college to find out about obedience classes.

Be consistent in training—always use the same words, body language and tone of voice for the same command. You will confuse your dog otherwise.

Be patient. Your dog needs time to understand what you want from her. If she isn't responding, reconsider your approach. Most of the time it's the trainer's fault that a dog doesn't understand what's wanted.

Teach your dog a release command, such as "OK" or "Free," early on, so she will know when the task is over and it's OK to relax.

## 643 Train Your Cat to Come When You Call

**Follow these steps, and even your aloof, independent cat will come to you when he hears you say a special word.**

### ⊙ Steps

1  Talk to your cat—a lot. Encourage him verbally to come to you, and regularly pet him and brush him.

### ✱ Tips

Choose a dry, crunchy snack that is nutritious and also good for the teeth.

2 Choose a special dry snack that he has shown he likes—and use it only when you call him. It cannot be his regular dry food.

3 Pick a special word for his snack— such as "snack" or "dessert"—and plan to always say it in the same tone of voice.

4 Use your special word during his next snack time. In his presence, place one piece of the food in his empty dish and say the special word.

5 Say the word again after he eats the first piece. Place another piece of the food in his dish and say the special word again.

6 Walk away. If he is giving you "I am really starving" cries, say your word again and give him one more piece. Then walk out of the room.

7 Repeat the procedure in 5 minutes. Cats learn very quickly when they are motivated.

8 Follow this procedure for the next several days.

Use the special word daily, not only when it's time for a trip to the veterinarian or when it's bath time. On those occasions, give him the snack and try to allow a few minutes before following through on your hidden motive.

⚠ **Warning**

Use your special word only when you will follow through with the snack, or you may confuse your cat.

---

## Teach Your Dog Not to Beg at the Table  644

**Teach your dog from the very beginning that begging isn't allowed. It's much easier to prevent the habit from starting than to end it.**

◎ **Steps**

1 Avoid feeding your dog at the table at all times.

2 Ignore your dog completely while you eat, to discourage begging behavior. That means no eye contact, no talking and no reprimanding throughout the training phase.

3 Train your dog to perform a "Down, stay" and sustain it (see 642 "Train Your Dog").

4 Give your dog a Buster cube—a rolling toy filled with food that drops out as the dog plays—while you eat. Mini Buster cubes are available for smaller dogs.

5 Reward your dog with plenty of praise and affection and a treat (away from the table) after you've finished your meal.

6 Be consistent in your training. Giving in now and then will only confuse your dog.

✱ **Tip**

If you can't resist giving your dog table scraps, keep him in the other room while you eat and give him the scraps later in his food bowl.

---

## Stop Your Dog's Excessive Barking  645

**Barking is a perfectly natural behavior in dogs, but that's not a good enough explanation for angry neighbors in the middle of the night. Here are a few hints for turning down the volume.**

◎ **Steps**

1 Try to determine why your dog barks—eliminating the cause will increase your chances of success.

✱ **Tips**

Some breeds tend to bark more than others. Check with other owners to find out if your dog's barking habits are normal.

2   Have your dog's favorite treat within reach.

3   Praise the dog for barking once he starts by saying "Good job" and then "What's the matter?"

4   Tell the dog, "Be quiet."

5   Wave the treat in front of your dog's nose. Most dogs will instantly quiet down, because they will be concentrating on smelling and attempting to lick the treat, rather than barking.

6   Keep praising the dog. Tell the dog that he is a good dog for being quiet.

7   Let the dog have the treat after 3 seconds of quiet time.

8   Wave another treat in front of your dog if he starts to bark again. This time, try not to let your dog have the treat until 5 seconds of quiet time have elapsed. Your dog should learn that after each successful quiet-time interval, he will be rewarded.

9   Scold your dog every time he makes a mistake. If the dog barks, even for just an instant, as you're waving the treat in front of his nose, say "Be quiet," in a louder voice. Then reward the dog immediately after he stops barking.

10  Increase the quiet-time intervals by 3 seconds each time: from 3 seconds to 6 seconds to 9 seconds and so on. It is possible to continue to a couple of minutes of quiet time during the first session, which would mean significant progress in curbing your dog's barking habit.

It takes time to get your dog to break the habit of excessive barking. Remain calm and patient, and eventually he will bark only when it's appropriate.

If you have trouble getting your dog to stop barking, consult a veterinarian trained in behavioral problems.

## 646 | Prevent Your Dog From Chewing on Furniture

It's common for dogs under 2 years old to chew on everything from your best shoes to your windowsill. Here's how to show your growing dog that there are better things to chew on.

### ◎ Steps

1   Determine whether the chewing stems from teething, curiosity, boredom or a behavioral disorder. Discuss these options with your veterinarian or an animal-behavior specialist.

2   Give a teething puppy a teething ring or a frozen washcloth to chew on.

3   Watch your puppy constantly. Use a baby gate to keep him in the same room as you, or crate-train your puppy and put him in the crate with toys for short periods when you're unable to supervise.

4   Divert your puppy's attention to something appropriate, such as a dog toy, when you catch him chewing. Have toys of soft and hard textures available, and rotate them to preempt boredom.

5   Set aside specific times for your puppy to interact with you: practicing obedience training exercises, learning tricks, exercising and going on outdoor adventures.

6   Exercise your puppy, and play with him using toys. If he's tired, he won't have the energy to chew.

### ✱ Tips

Use chew toys designed for dogs. They are inexpensive and safe and will teach your dog what is OK to chew on.

Some household items that are safe for your dog to play with, under your supervision, are cardboard boxes and paper bags.

### ⚠ Warning

Obedience training by itself won't change behavioral disorders. You may need to correct the underlying problem with the help of an animal-behavior specialist.

7  Establish a routine with an adult dog, which should include feeding schedules, elimination times and exercise periods he can count on. Adult dogs usually chew out of boredom or frustration.

8  Avoid punishing your dog for chewing, as chewing is a natural behavior in dogs. It will just make him feel conflicted and anxious.

9  Consult a veterinarian who specializes in animal behavior if you suspect a behavioral disorder. Common motivations for chewing include separation anxiety, phobia, or a desire to escape or seek attention.

**Things You'll Need**

- ☐ teething ring or frozen washcloth
- ☐ baby gate
- ☐ dog crate
- ☐ chew toys

## Stop Your Cat From Scratching Furniture     647

**Cats scratch to mark their territory, sharpen their claws and stretch their muscles. Here's how to help your cat curb the urge (or at least redirect it away from the sofa).**

### ◉ Steps

1  Provide scratching posts and place them in locations where your cat likes to linger—by a sunny window, for instance.

2  Keep in mind that individual cats like different textures (cardboard, wood or rugs) and post orientations (horizontal or vertical). Experiment with different types of posts to find the best ones for your cat.

3  Encourage kittens to use posts, and reward them with food and praise.

4  Consider giving your cat extra attention when he stirs from a nap, and then placing him near the scratching post, since many cats scratch when waking up.

5  Avoid punishing your cat if he scratches an inappropriate area. Punishment teaches the cat not to scratch in your presence, but it won't deter a cat from scratching when you're not around.

6  Avoid letting your cat scratch an old couch, even if you plan to get rid of it soon—this will only encourage him to scratch the new couch as well.

**✳ Tip**

Using unpleasant-tasting substances doesn't help, since scratching does not involve the taste buds.

**⚠ Warnings**

Scratching is a natural behavior, so blocking the cat's access to one area will simply encourage him to scratch elsewhere.

Consult your veterinarian about alternative treatment options before you give up. Destructive behavior is a leading reason why people surrender their cats to animal shelters.

## Stop Your Dog From Digging Up the Lawn     648

**Digging can be either a characteristic of your dog's breed or evidence of separation anxiety or a desire to escape.**

### ◉ Steps

1  Avoid punishing your dog for digging—this only teaches her not to dig in your presence. She may resume digging when you're not around.

2  Take her on walks. Dogs often dig to expend energy, and walking is a less destructive way to accomplish this.

3  Put up a fence to keep your dog out of areas—like your well-manicured lawn—where you don't want her to dig.

4  Confine your dog in a dog run with toys, shade and water.

**✳ Tips**

Digging is often a result of boredom, so keep your dog occupied with other activities.

5   Keep your dog's sleeping area shaded in hot weather, and supply a wading pool if it's hot outside. Dogs often dig in search of a cool place to lie down.

6   Turn on the sprinklers or spray your dog with a hose each time she starts digging—this may discourage her from digging if she doesn't like water sprayed on her.

Give your dog her own place to dig—a sandbox or dirt area—and encourage digging in only that spot by hiding treats for her to find. This allows your dog to enjoy the natural behavior of digging without ruining your yard.

---

## 649 | Approach an Unfamiliar Dog

Attacks by dogs in the United States result in an average of 12 deaths a year. Teach your child to be careful when approaching an unfamiliar dog, and take the same precautions yourself.

### ⊙ Steps

1   Never approach a dog that is chained, tied, enclosed in a pen, behind a fence, or in a car or the bed of a pickup truck. Also don't touch or disturb a dog that appears to be sleeping or is unaware of your presence.

2   Recognize signs of aggressiveness such as barking, growling, snarling with teeth bared, holding the ears erect or tight against the head, holding the tail up stiffly, keeping the legs rigid, or bristling the hair. Keep your distance from a dog exhibiting any of these signs, even if the dog is wagging his tail. If the dog advances, move away slowly, in a sideways direction; do not turn and run. Say "No" or "Stay" in a firm voice.

3   To be on the safe side, only approach a dog that is with his owner and on a leash. Make sure the owner approves and invites you to approach and pet the dog.

4   Squat or crouch in front of the dog and allow him to approach you before attempting to pet him. Avoid staring directly into the dog's eyes, as this may be seen as a challenge.

5   Avoid reaching out to touch the dog, even if he appears to be friendly, as the dog may interpret this as a threat.

6   Do not tease or make any sudden movements or loud noises as you approach the dog. This may excite him and cause him to attack.

7   Let the dog keep any items that are in his possession—food, toys, chew bones and so on.

8   Offer a treat to the dog once contact is made, provided the owner says it's OK to do so.

### ⚠ Warnings

Remember that children comprise more than 60 percent of dog-bite victims, so always take extra precautions when children are present around puppies or dogs.

Never approach stray dogs or dogs who are not within sight of their owners.

## Break Up a Dog or Cat Fight | 650

Breaking up a fight between two dogs or two cats can be dangerous and challenging. Depending on your size and abilities, you have a few options to choose from.

### ⊙ Steps

1  Avoid hitting the dogs or cats or getting your hands anywhere near their mouths. Hitting could make the situation worse and could cause the attack to be redirected toward you.

2  Enlist another person and separate two dogs by grabbing their hind legs and walking them backward like wheelbarrows. Secure the dogs away from each other before releasing them. This is not for cats.

3  Spray the aggressor with a water hose. If this doesn't make a difference, aim for the nostrils.

4  Hold a broom between the dogs or cats to separate them.

5  Use a noisemaking device such as an air horn to drive the animals apart, and be prepared to move away quickly or defend yourself.

**✱ Tip**

Consider keeping your cat inside. Abscesses resulting from cat fights can pose serious health risks and are expensive to treat.

**⚠ Warning**

Most cases of feline immunodeficiency virus (FIV) are spread through bites—such as in a cat fight.

## Help Your Pet Cope With Loud Noises | 651

Fear of loud noises is a common behavioral disorder in pets. The symptoms range from mild (trembling) to extreme (panic attacks, destructive behavior, running away).

### ⊙ Steps

1  Be aware that controlling reactions to loud noises may require the help of a veterinarian or trainer using medication or behavioral modification.

2  Desensitize or countercondition your pet through repeated exposure to sounds. Start with a greatly reduced volume, and gradually intensify the sounds over time. This may result in controlling the problem.

3  Invest in nature recordings with sounds of thunder or pounding rain to help your pet get used to these sounds.

4  Keep your pet company if there is potential for exposure to loud noises.

5  Bring your pet inside if loud noises are likely. Do not leave a pet in a run or cage or tied with a rope, chain or cable.

6  When loud noises occur, confine the pet in familiar surroundings that are insulated from sound, are dimly lit and present no opportunity for escape. A basement or a room without windows is ideal.

7  Play soft music or videos, or leave the television on during a loud storm or noisy event. This may calm or distract your pet.

8  Find a suitable boarding facility at especially high-risk times, such as Independence Day.

9  Avoid punishing a pet to suppress a fearful response to loud noises.

**✱ Tips**

Pets can sense your anxiety, so stay calm. Try not to overreact; your reaction could cause the condition to worsen.

Tranquilization may be required. Use only drugs developed especially for animals—not people—as prescribed by a veterinarian.

## 652 | Treat Your Dog's Separation Anxiety

Barking, whining, escaping, destructive behavior or, in severe cases, self-mutilation can be your dog's way of expressing anxiety over your absence.

### ⊙ Steps

1 Consult your veterinarian to get a correct diagnosis of separation anxiety. Your veterinarian will help you with treatment or refer you to an animal behaviorist who can prescribe effective drug therapies to alleviate your dog's anxieties.

2 Practice leaving your dog alone for short periods of time. Pick up your keys and leave for 1 minute.

3 Gradually increase the amount of time you stay away. This will accustom your dog to your absence.

4 Avoid overly emotional good-byes and greetings. Instead, pat your dog on the head and offer a quick good-bye or hello.

5 Keep your dog confined in a safe area while you are away. Be sure to leave a bowl of water and plenty of chew toys.

6 Exercise your dog for an hour each day in places other than your yard or home. This helps your dog feel comfortable in other locations and lets her blow off steam.

7 Praise your dog often to build self-confidence, rather than punishing her for exhibiting frightened behaviors. Punishment only increases anxiety and makes the situation worse.

### ⚠ Warning

The first time you administer medication to control separation anxiety, stay with and watch your dog carefully in case she has an adverse reaction. Take her to the veterinarian if you witness odd behavior, as the dosage may need adjustment.

## 653 | Protect Dogs and Cats From Household Dangers

Accidents such as falling, being dropped or crushed, or ingesting a foreign body are the leading causes of injury for dogs and cats in the home. Here are some simple precautions.

### ⊙ Steps

1 Keep your cat or dog away from toxic plants. Toxic plants commonly found around the house include mistletoe, schefflera, philodendron, dumbcane (dieffenbachia) and caladium. Talk to your local nursery about which toxic outdoor plants are common in your area.

2 Keep objects that are small enough to be swallowed away from your cat or dog. A small ball or loose string is easy to swallow and may cause bowel obstruction.

3 Store toxic chemicals, as well as dangerously sharp objects and utensils (knives, razors and scissors), in closed containers inside cupboards and cabinets.

4 Avoid confining your cat or dog in areas where cleaning products and other chemicals are stored.

### ✳ Tip

Animal behaviorists compare cats and dogs to children when it comes to understanding and avoiding hazards. Be vigilant in protecting your pet.

5  Clean up any spilled chemicals thoroughly—especially antifreeze—before letting your pet into the area where a spill has occurred (see 662 "Detect Antifreeze Poisoning in Your Pet").

6  Keep chocolate in areas where your dog cannot reach it. Chocolate is toxic to dogs.

7  Secure electrical cords behind appliances, hidden from your pet's view, and tape them to the wall if necessary. Discourage your pet from chewing on them by spraying the cords with bitter apple spray or other unpleasant flavors (see 654 "Prevent Your Pet From Chewing on Electrical Cords").

8  Check and repair any damaged fencing, gates, doors, windows or screens where your cat or dog might escape.

9  Be cautious—watch for your cat or dog as you drive in and out of your garage to make sure you don't run over her or get her caught in the garage door.

10 Keep medications and vitamins out of your pet's reach, and never give her medication labeled for people unless directed by your veterinarian. For example, acetaminophen is toxic for cats, and ibuprofen can cause kidney failure in dogs.

## Prevent Your Pet From Chewing on Electrical Cords          654

Chewing on electrical cords can burn or shock your pet, causing respiratory problems, cardiac arrest and even death. His sharp teeth and inquisitive nature can put him at high risk.

### ⊙ Steps

1  Tape cords to the wall with electrical tape to help prevent your pet from gaining access to them.

2  Stow excess lengths of cord behind furniture or appliances, hidden from your pet's view. Cats are attracted to dangling cords and may think they are toys.

3  Block access to visible cords by wrapping flexible safety cable (available at hardware stores) around them.

4  Place contact paper, sticky side up, in the general area of electrical cords to discourage your pet from approaching them.

5  Apply unpleasant-tasting substances to exposed cords. These could include bitter apple spray, hot-pepper sauce, menthol, toothpaste, mouthwash or lemon juice. Experiment with different flavors, since pets' taste aversions vary.

6  Have favorite toys available to distract your pet from the cords, and rotate toys every few days to prevent boredom.

7  Keep your pet out of any room with exposed electrical cords until your furry friend loses interest in chewing on them.

### ⚠ Warning

Electrical-cord injuries are most common in puppies and kittens, especially when they are first adopted, so be extra vigilant with the young ones when you bring them home for the first time.

### Things You'll Need

☐ electrical tape

☐ flexible safety cable

☐ contact paper

☐ bitter apple, hot-pepper sauce, menthol, toothpaste, mouthwash or lemon juice

☐ pet toys

# ✓ 655 Give Veterinary Medicine

If you've never administered medication to your pet, ask your veterinarian for a hands-on demonstration; also ask about any danger in handling the medication if you are pregnant. When you give a pet medicine, keep other pets or unfamiliar people out of the room, and stroke and praise your pet before and after the procedure. Before administering medicine to an animal with a dropper, practice using lukewarm water.

## To a bird by dropper

1 Close all doors and windows and remove any other pets before you open the cage.

2 Fill the dropper with the prescribed dose of medication and place it within easy reach.

3 Try giving the medicine with a dropper while the bird is on a perch.

4 If this doesn't work, capture the bird and hold him gently in your hand or wrapped in a towel, head exposed and tilted upward.

5 Gently but firmly restrain his wings and legs in your grasp to prevent injury or escape.

6 Place the dropper at the corner of his beak and slowly dispense by squeezing the bulb.

7 Allow the medication to trickle down between the upper and lower beak.

8 Release the bird if he struggles intensely.

## To a cat by dropper

1 Place your cat on a flat surface such as a table, facing the same way as you are.

2 Fill the dropper with the prescribed dose.

3 Stand along the cat's left side (your right).

4 Grasp his head with your left hand, holding the mouth closed by placing your thumb on the bridge of the nose and your fingers under the lower jaw.

5 Tilt the head upward at a 30-degree angle.

6 Pick up the dropper with your right hand and insert it between the lips and teeth at the corner of the mouth on the right side.

7 Slide the dropper to the back of the cheek pouch and deposit the medication there.

8 Loosen your grasp on the head, but do not let go. Tilt the cat's nose down at an angle of about 30 degrees to make him swallow.

## To a dog by dropper

1 Place your dog in a sitting position—or if she's small, in your lap.

2 Fill the dropper with the prescribed dose.

3 Grasp the muzzle gently with your left hand, fingers under the lower jaw, thumb on the bridge of the nose.

4 Tilt the nose upward at a 30-degree angle.

5 Pick up the dropper in your right hand and insert it into the corner of the mouth, between the lips and teeth, on the right side of the dog's muzzle.

6 Gently slide the dropper between the lips and teeth.

7 Squeeze the bulb to deposit the medication at the back of the cheek pouch.

8 Release the muzzle to let the dog swallow.

## To a cat, dog, or horse by pill

1 Give your pet a treat without medication to whet her appetite. Offer cats a lump of butter. For dogs, consider a bite size portion of hot dog, cheese or peanut butter. Give horses grain with molasses.

2 For cats or dogs or dogs, break the pill into small pieces if necessary, and enclose it completely within the hot dog, cheese, peanut butter or lump of butter.

3 For horses, grind up the pill and add it to the grain with plenty of molasses to hold the mix together.

4 Be sure the treat is large enough to cover the pill or pieces of the pill, but not so large that your pet will chew, discover the medicine and spit it out.

## Pack a First Aid Kit for Your Pet     656

Keep a first aid kit for your pet accessible at home or in your car when traveling. Gathering the necessary items ahead of time could help save your pet's life in an emergency.

### ◎ Steps

1 Get a durable, waterproof (or at least water-resistant) container that opens and closes easily yet securely. It should be large enough to hold the items mentioned below.

2 Start off with bandage material, such as gauze pads or cotton gauze, and adhesive tape or masking tape.

3 Add hydrogen peroxide and antibacterial ointment or cream.

4 Include diarrhea medication, but seek your veterinarian's approval before using it. Check expiration dates and replace as needed.

5 Add a pair of scissors, plus tweezers or forceps.

6 Include a few eyedroppers for dispensing liquid medication (see 655 "Give Veterinary Medicine") or for cleaning superficial wounds.

7 Be sure to include syrup of ipecac to induce vomiting in the event your pet is poisoned. Consult your veterinarian before inducing vomiting.

8 Find activated charcoal at any health food store. This remedy is good for poisoning or diarrhea and controls flatulence resulting from any stomach or intestinal upset.

9 Store blankets in the kit to keep your pet warm in extreme conditions.

10 When traveling, call ahead to your destination to see if there are any particular dangers, such as snakes, poisonous plants or extreme heat, that you will need to consider when packing your first aid kit.

11 Include the phone numbers of your pet's regular veterinarian and of a nearby emergency veterinary hospital.

### ⚠ Warnings

Muzzle an injured dog if possible, since overly stressed dogs are more likely to bite.

Never give your cat aspirin or acetaminophen (the active ingredient in Tylenol). It is extremely toxic to cats. Avoid giving ibuprofen to dogs, as it can cause kidney failure.

### Things You'll Need

☐ waterproof container

☐ bandages

☐ hydrogen peroxide and antibacterials

☐ diarrhea medication

☐ scissors and tweezers

☐ eyedroppers

☐ syrup of ipecac

☐ activated charcoal

☐ blankets

---

## Get Rid of Fleas     657

Fleas can transmit disease and tapeworm. Keeping your pet and his environment clean is the single most important part of a successful flea-control program.

### ◎ Steps

1 Understand the life of the flea. An adult female can lay one egg per hour for every hour of her life (usually three months). Fleas thrive in heat and humidity and are most active in summer and fall.

2 Help prevent fleas indoors by vacuuming your home thoroughly and frequently, paying close attention to corners, cracks and crevices. Dispose of vacuum cleaner bags conscientiously, as adult fleas can escape.

3 Remove fleas from your pet using a fine-toothed comb, and drop the fleas into soapy water to drown them.

### ✱ Tips

Be diligent in your exterminating efforts. A flea pupa while in the cocoon is impervious to treatment and can live for eight months without feeding.

Veterinarians are skeptical of homemade flea remedies such as garlic, vinegar, vitamin C and kelp.

4   Wash pet bedding in hot, soapy water weekly; this is the most likely site for flea eggs and larvae.

5   Prune foliage and keep grass trimmed short to increase sunlight, as flea larvae cannot survive in hot, dry areas. Remove piles of debris in areas close to your home.

6   Bathe pets weekly if possible. If bathing is not an option, speak to your veterinarian about appropriate alternatives.

7   Watch your pet for signs of flea trouble: excessive scratching and biting, especially around the tail and lower back; "flea debris" (black, granular dried blood) and fleas themselves on the skin; and possibly raw patches where the animal has been biting and scratching himself.

8   Talk to your veterinarian about various treatments for your flea-plagued pet: a flea adulticide applied monthly to the skin; a monthly pill that prevents fleas from reproducing but doesn't kill adult fleas; and multipurpose products that prevent flea reproduction and control heartworms, hookworms, whipworms and roundworms. Also consider flea collars and flea powders.

9   Look into chemical flea-treatment products to apply by hand around the environment in spray or powder form. Ask your veterinarian for a recommendation on the best product and how to use it.

Call on a professional exterminator for severe indoor and outdoor infestations.

## ⚠ Warnings

Be very careful with all insecticides to be used on pets or around your home. Read directions carefully.

Never apply a flea product to a cat or kitten unless it is labeled as safe for cats. Cats are very sensitive to insecticides.

Ingesting fleas could give your pet tapeworm (see 659 "Prevent Worms in Cats and Dogs").

---

## 658 | Remove Ticks From Pets

Ticks thrive in woody, grassy and brushy areas and carry diseases such as Rocky Mountain spotted fever and Lyme disease. That's why it's essential to keep them off your pet.

### ◎ Steps

1   Check your pet for ticks daily if he spends a lot of time outdoors, especially if you live in an area known for ticks.

2   Put on latex gloves to avoid direct contact with the tick and contaminated skin, as diseases can be transmitted from tick to pet to human.

3   Feel your pet all over, especially around the neck, head and ears. If you encounter a lump like a small pea, move the fur on your pet to see if you have found a tick.

4   Look to see if a tick is protruding from the skin. Ticks are tiny black, brown, reddish or tan disklike arachnids (having eight legs), about the size of the head of a pin. If they have attached themselves to their host (your pet), then they can swell up to the size of a grape in some cases.

5   Put your pet in a comfortable position. Ask a friend or family member for help in distracting your pet.

6   Grasp the tick with tweezers as close to your pet's skin as possible; make sure not to pinch your pet's skin.

7   Pull the tick out using a straight, steady pulling motion. Be gentle; pulling too hard on the tick can cause its head to remain lodged in your pet's skin, which can lead to inflammation and secondary infection.

### ✳ Tips

Consider using a flea and tick shampoo if you find several ticks in your search.

Obtain a tick collar from your veterinarian. Also ask about anti-tick products that you can apply to your pet's skin.

### ⚠ Warning

Contact your veterinarian if you suspect that your pet has been infected with Lyme disease. The most common symptoms are a rash (visible if you part the hair), followed by recurring joint pain (which the pet may manifest by limping).

8 Dispose of the tick by throwing it into a fire, or by squishing it in a tissue using the tweezers and then flushing it down the toilet. Do not smash it with your foot or your bare hands.

9 Apply antiseptic ointment to the bite.

10 Remove and wash the gloves, and wash your hands thoroughly.

11 Clean the tweezers with hot water or isopropyl alcohol or by holding them over a flame.

**Things You'll Need**

☐ latex gloves

☐ tweezers

☐ antiseptic ointment

☐ isopropyl alcohol

## Prevent Worms in Cats and Dogs | 659

Roundworms, hookworms and tapeworms are some of the common parasites that can infest your pet. They can cause diarrhea, weight loss or vomiting.

### ⊙ Steps

1 Get puppies and kittens tested as early as three weeks after birth. They will often already be infested with worms and will need to be treated.

2 Take your pet in for an annual exam. Ask your veterinarian to recommend broad-spectrum preventive products. The newest products protect against roundworms, heartworms, ticks and fleas.

3 Control fleas (see 657 "Get Rid of Fleas"). Fleas can transmit tapeworm if your pet ingests them.

4 Avoid exposing your pet to stray animals or wildlife, as they are often carriers for fleas and other parasites. Dog parks that are not well maintained are a common source of parasites.

5 Prevent your pet from eating animal carcasses, such as those of birds, rabbits and rodents. Carcasses can carry immature worms that can then mature after your pet has ingested them.

6 Prevent your dog from eating feces—his own or that of other dogs and other animals. Contact with fecal material from another animal is the most common way for a dog to get intestinal parasites.

7 Take precautions when traveling with your pet. Before you go, check with your travel agent or veterinarian about risks at your destination.

8 Inspect your pet's anus and feces to spot signs of tapeworms. Tapeworm segments are small, white and flat, resembling grains of rice.

9 Have a stool specimen checked by your veterinarian to be certain that your pet remains parasite-free.

### ✱ Tips

Parasite types vary, depending on locale and whether the animal is an indoor or outdoor pet.

Infestations can be asymptomatic until triggered by stress.

### ⚠ Warnings

Avoid over-the-counter and home remedies. These are generally less effective and can also be dangerous.

Contact your veterinarian immediately if your pet shows any signs of illness (vomiting, diarrhea, tremors or poor coordination) after administration of worm medication.

## 660 | Care for a Dog Who Has Allergies

Canine allergies are a lot like human allergies—dogs can react to allergens in the air, in food or on their skin. Learn to recognize canine allergy symptoms, then provide relief.

### ◉ Steps

1   Look for allergy symptoms in your dog. The most common signs of an allergy to inhalants or fleas are frequent itching, chewing and biting, especially on the tail, the stomach and the insides of the hind legs, as well as licking and chewing the paws. Inhaled allergens can also result in sneezing, coughing and watery eyes. Vomiting, itching and diarrhea can be symptoms of food allergies. Hives and rashes can be symptoms of various types of allergies.

2   Consider the season: Allergies to airborne mold and pollen erupt in the spring and fall. Flea allergies are most prominent during the flea season, which is summer in most areas but can range from early spring to late fall.

3   Take your dog to a veterinarian if you observe any of the above symptoms, especially vomiting or diarrhea, as they could be caused by a more serious underlying medical condition.

4   If you suspect an allergy to food, realize that typical canine food allergens include corn, beef, dairy products, wheat and soybeans—ingredients in most pet foods.

5   Talk to your veterinarian about putting your dog on a special restricted diet to determine which food she is reacting to. Follow the veterinarian's guidelines to gradually introduce other foods into the diet until the allergen is found. Your veterinarian may also recommend food-allergy tests to find the allergen.

6   If you suspect an allergy to inhalants, vacuum and dust frequently. Culprits include dust, mold spores and pollen grains.

7   Treat your dog to a cool bath, and shampoo or rinse with aloe vera or oatmeal to help soothe itchy skin. Your veterinarian may also recommend medicated shampoos, antihistamines or other drugs to keep the itching at bay while the skin heals and contact with the allergen is diminished.

8   Check your dog for fleas, as your dog could be suffering from fleabite dermatitis (an allergy to a flea's saliva). Careful grooming and frequent examinations for fleas and flea droppings can help alleviate this allergy. Ask your vet about flea products such as sprays, shampoos, topical ointments and pills. Again, an oatmeal or aloe vera bath can help soothe the itching.

9   Consider the possibility of contact allergies, realizing that the symptoms will be limited to areas of contact. Some dogs are allergic to bedding (cedar wood chips and wool are two possible offenders), grass or plastic food bowls. If your dog has acne on his chin and uses a plastic feeding bowl, try switching to a steel, glass or ceramic feeding bowl.

10  Talk to your veterinarian about a referral to a board-certified veterinary dermatologist if your dog is not responding to recommended treatments.

### ✳ Tips

Frequent baths (once or twice a week) can help eliminate many skin problems suffered by dogs (see 632 "Wash Your Dog").

It only takes one or two flea bites to set off a dog's allergies to fleas.

Certain dog breeds, such as golden retrievers, are more prone to allergies than others. If buying a purebred dog, ask the owner whether the parents have allergies, since allergies can be inherited.

### ⚠ Warnings

Bring your dog to the veterinarian when the itching first manifests itself, to avoid the possibility of skin infections caused by excess chewing and scratching.

Novor apply flea products to irritated or broken skin; the chemicals could further irritate and injure the skin.

## Detect Skin Cancer in Your Pet 661

Early detection of skin cancer in your pet is the key to successful treatment. Here is how to spot the disease in the initial stages of development.

### ⊙ Steps

1 Examine your pet monthly, at a minimum. Check for tumors; areas of color change; or scaly, crusty lesions.

2 Use your fingers to separate the hair, and look closely at the skin.

3 Take note of any new growths, as well as any changes in the color or size of existing growths. If you find changes, continue to observe the growths and call your veterinarian for advice.

4 Be concerned if you find tumors that bleed easily or any areas that refuse to heal.

5 Pay attention if your pet is licking at one area continually. Examine that area closely.

6 Call your veterinarian at once if you notice a swelling in your pet's breast tissue or discharge from a nipple. Check under his tail for any suspicious lumps or areas of discoloration.

7 Look closely at your cat's eyelids and lips and inside his mouth for irregular areas or color changes. If your cat's nose or ears are white, check them closely for scaly, bumpy or reddened areas.

8 Check your pet's mouth. Look for masses or tissue that seems different from surrounding areas.

9 Bathe, groom and massage your pet frequently; this will help you to detect any small changes as you feel for unusual masses or other suspicious areas. Fingers can often find things that are camouflaged by fur.

10 Report all things that are not normal to your veterinarian right away.

### ✳ Tips

Dogs frequently develop soft masses under the skin, called "lipomas." Your veterinarian should quickly be able to tell this from skin cancer.

Orange tabby cats often develop smooth dark spots on their lips and eyelids as they age; these are not cancerous.

Chronic infections from cat-fight wounds that will not heal may resemble skin cancer.

### ⚠ Warnings

Delay in treatment of skin cancer can result in serious harm to your pet's health.

A long, thick coat may obscure tumors that would otherwise be seen easily.

## Detect Antifreeze Poisoning in Your Pet 662

The taste and smell of antifreeze are attractive to animals, and ingesting it can be deadly. Here's how to spot possible ingestion so you can seek help immediately.

### ⊙ Steps

1 Prevent antifreeze poisoning by keeping antifreeze away from animals, including antifreeze puddles that sometimes form under cars.

2 Take your pet to the veterinarian immediately if you catch him tasting antifreeze or think he has done so.

3 Visit the veterinarian immediately as well if you notice signs of ingestion such as stupor, swaggering, weaving, listlessness, frequent urination, excess thirst or vomiting.

### ⚠ Warnings

An animal must be taken to the veterinarian within 12 hours of ingesting antifreeze. After 12 to 24 hours, kidney failure will occur, followed eventually by death.

In freezing weather, the only water that's not frozen may contain antifreeze. so don't allow your pet to drink from puddles.

4 Understand that in the second stage of poisoning, the liver will metabolize ethylene glycol into more toxic substances.

5 Consider using new, safer propylene glycol antifreeze, which is less hazardous to animals.

## 663 | Take Your Pet's Temperature

Take your pet's temperature when she is healthy so that you'll recognize when her temperature is above normal in the future.

### ⊙ Steps

1 Use a rectal thermometer specific to your animal's size. These are available at many pet stores. Human thermometers also work.

2 Sterilize the thermometer by dipping it in rubbing alcohol.

3 Allow it to dry, then apply petroleum jelly or a similar lubricant to the tip.

4 Allow your pet to stand, or lay her on her side, and gently hold her down.

5 Shake the thermometer until it reads below 100 degrees F.

6 Insert the thermometer three-quarters of the way into the rectum and wait 1 to 3 minutes. Your pet may respond to this uncomfortable procedure by scratching or snapping. As you proceed, gently stroke her and talk in a gentle, soothing tone. If this doesn't work, try again later—most pets eventually allow their temperature to be taken.

7 Take the thermometer out and read it.

8 Wipe or rinse the thermometer after use, and then sterilize it by dipping it in rubbing alcohol.

9 Reward your pet with a treat.

### ✱ Tips

Digital thermometers designed for humans work well on pets. They can be used orally or anally and deliver a reading in a matter of seconds.

The average temperature for a dog or cat is 100.5 to 102.5 degrees F.

### ⚠ Warning

Do not try to take a bird's temperature using these instructions.

### Things You'll Need

❑ pet thermometer

❑ petroleum jelly

❑ pet treat

## 664 | Determine if Your Dog Needs Medical Care

Since your dog can't talk, you'll need to watch carefully for signs of illness. Spotting the symptoms early can dramatically affect the outcome—and expense—of treatment.

### ⊙ Steps

1 Learn your dog's daily routine. Observe her activities—such as her eating and drinking habits and her patterns of urination and defecation—closely, so you can quickly detect variations from her normal behavior.

2 Learn to do simple things like monitoring her heart and respiratory rates and taking her temperature (see 663 "Take Your Pet's Temperature"). Normal temperature for a dog is 100.5 to 102.5 degrees F.

3 Watch for symptoms such as persistent vomiting, retching or gagging; diarrhea; or straining to defecate or urinate. These can signify serious medical problems. Call your veterinarian immediately.

### ✱ Tips

Listlessness and refusal to eat or drink are usually the first symptoms of illness. Hot weather causes dogs to become inactive and eat less, but they will also drink more.

Ask any children in your household if they think the dog is sick. They often see things that busy adults overlook.

4   Notice lethargy or weakness, a reluctance to eat or drink, or persistent coughing or sneezing, coupled with a change of behavior. These are sure signs that your dog needs medical attention.

5   Be aware that excessive drooling and shaking or generalized tremors, convulsions, seizures or labored respiration can indicate poisoning. Call your veterinarian immediately.

6   Try not to confuse normal behavioral changes and mood swings, which can be caused by alterations in your daily routine or variations in household activities, with true signs of illness.

⚠ **Warning**

Take action as soon as you notice a problem. Delays in calling your veterinarian will often result in prolonged treatment, increased stress on you and your dog, increased expense and possibly the loss of your pet.

## Determine if Your Cat Needs Medical Care          665

Disguising symptoms of illness is one of your cat's specialties, so he may have been sick for days before you notice. Here's how to tell if something's wrong.

### ◉ Steps

1   Watch your cat closely. Become familiar with his normal habits and patterns of activity, such as eating, sleeping and defecating. The slightest variation may indicate the beginning of illness or disease.

2   Prepare yourself to do simple things like monitor his heart and respiratory rate and take his temperature. Normal is 100.5 to 102.5 degrees F.

3   Groom him daily, checking for masses, swellings and sensitive areas.

4   Understand that lethargy, refusal of food or water, and reluctance to play are often the first symptoms of illness. Sick cats dehydrate quickly, so prompt response is essential.

5   Be aware that even the slightest elevation in temperature will account for his listlessness.

6   Notice any symptoms, such as sneezing, runny eyes or nose, or labored breathing, that may indicate respiratory illness, and call the veterinarian for advice.

7   Remember that coughing or hacking could simply mean that your cat has a hairball. But If these symptoms persist, call his doctor.

8   Know that straining to urinate, especially in male cats, is considered a sign of urinary-tract obstruction. Get medical help immediately, as this can be life-threatening.

9   Be aware that violent retching, attempting to vomit or unusual panting are symptoms of serious illness or pain in cats, so call your veterinarian right away.

10  Call your veterinarian as soon as you think your cat is sick. Delaying the call often leads to greater risk for the cat, prolonged recovery and increased expense.

✱ **Tips**

Cats are finicky eaters, so refusal to eat a new food may not indicate that your cat is sick.

Ask any children in your household if they think the cat is sick. They often see things that busy adults overlook.

⚠ **Warning**

Use caution when handling a sick cat. He may react suddenly and bite or scratch when he would not normally do so.

## 666 Calm a Pet's Fear of Visiting the Veterinarian

A fearful or aggressive pet is difficult for veterinary staff to examine. If your pet has an extreme aversion to visiting the veterinarian, help her get acquainted with that environment.

### ◎ Steps

1 Visit the veterinary hospital or office with your pet once a week until your pet is habituated.

2 Take treats and have the staff give them to your pet. Make it a fun experience, and then take your pet and leave.

3 Use a gradual approach if your pet is already fearful and won't accept treats. For example, play with her on the front lawn of your vet's office and make her feel comfortable. Over a period of a few weeks, gradually bring her to the front door and progress to standing in the front lobby and visiting with the staff.

4 Give treats for calm behavior.

5 Attempt to get your pet acquainted with a single staff member so she has a friend—pets, like people, get along with some individuals better than others.

### ✱ Tips

Ask your veterinarian if a previsit tranquilizer might be the best solution.

If your pet is fearful and an exam is essential, give her to the staff and leave. Sometimes pets do much better when alone with the veterinarian. Animals sense your anxiety.

## 667 Find Your Lost Pet

If your pet is missing, don't give up hope. Take the following measures to recover your furry or feathered friend and bring him back home.

### ◎ Steps

1 Organize a search party. Travel on bikes, by foot and by car and search the area.

2 Walk slowly and call your pet's name. Listen for any response—a meow, bark or chirp. He may be hiding, afraid to come out in the open.

3 Make familiar sounds likely to attract your pet: Shake a box of his favorite dry food, whistle or open a can of wet food.

4 File a lost-pet report with all animal-control agencies, newspaper lost-and-found departments, and animal shelters in the surrounding area.

5 Call your local veterinary and emergency clinics to see if someone has presented your pet for treatment.

6 Search your neighborhood thoroughly late at night. Look closely under cars and around garbage cans.

7 Make fliers that include the date of loss, the pet's name, a description, any unique markings, a picture and your phone number.

8 Put the fliers up around your neighborhood and at shopping centers, veterinary clinics, pet shops and anywhere else you can think of—including your old neighborhood if you've recently moved.

### ✱ Tips

To help prevent your pet from becoming lost in the first place, equip him with tags and a microchip. A microchip is a tiny identification chip injected under the skin. It is read with a special scanner that humane societies, veterinarians and agencies have, and it contains information that can help these organizations find you.

If your pet is small, check open vents and crawl spaces and listen for noises. Sometimes pets venture into small spaces and get stuck between walls or in vents.

9   Check the "found" section of your local newspaper daily, and be sure to pay a visit to your local animal shelter and humane society—don't rely on a phone call.

10  Place familiar-smelling items such as T-shirts you've worn and not washed in a cardboard box, and then place the box in your yard, as far away from the house as possible. Regularly check it late at night and early in the morning.

## Slow the Aging of Your Dog                          668

Dogs age more quickly than people, so start working to keep your dog young when you adopt her. Paying close attention to a few details may add years to her active life.

### ⊙ Steps

1   Get your dog annual physical exams, and follow the veterinarian's advice on preventive health-care measures. Preventing disease while maintaining optimal health is the first step toward a long, healthy life.

2   Spay or neuter your dog as soon as possible. Having puppies, especially repeated litters, is stressful and will contribute to premature aging.

3   Feed high-quality food designed for the life stage of your dog. Your dog's nutritional requirements will change throughout her life.

4   Talk to your veterinarian about adding vitamin and mineral supplements, including antioxidants, and extra fiber to your dog's diet.

5   Exercise your dog daily. Playing, running or swimming will help prevent obesity and keep her active well into old age.

6   Groom and bathe your dog regularly, paying particular attention to her ears and skin. Chronic infections and inflammation are stressful and speed the aging process.

7   Have your dog's teeth cleaned professionally. Good dental health is a key component of longevity.

8   Provide adequate shelter and bedding, especially during inclement weather. Sleeping on cold, hard surfaces such as concrete will promote joint disease, stiffness and aging.

9   Avoid subjecting your dog to environmental stresses such as second-hand smoke, harassment by other animals, noise or crowding.

10  Shower your dog with love and attention. Keeping her feeling young at heart will promote a strong desire to stay active so she can join you in all activities.

11  Look for signs of arthritis—stiffened joints and limping—early on to get proper pain medication to help your dog avoid unnecessary suffering.

### ✳ Tips

Find a veterinarian with a special interest in aging who keeps abreast of advancements in this rapidly developing area of pet care.

Research this subject on your own. Experts' understanding of the aging process is changing rapidly, and knowledge gained about humans is often applicable to animals.

Mental fitness is important in delaying aging in dogs, just as in people, so challenge your dog with commands and have her do tricks even as she ages.

### ⚠ Warnings

Consult your veterinarian, and use caution and common sense, when tempted to try supplements or "miracle cure" products that promise unrealistic results.

Also consult your vet before offering your elderly dog pain medications. Some products that people consume safely—such as ibuprofen—are poisonous to dogs.

## 669 | Slow the Aging of Your Cat

Cats may not have nine lives, but they can live longer than many people think—18 to 20 years is common. Here's how to keep your cat purring into advanced old age.

### ⊙ Steps

1 Take your cat to the veterinarian at least once a year for a complete physical exam, and follow your veterinarian's advice regarding preventive health-care measures. Preventing disease and maintaining optimum health are the first steps toward a long, healthy life.

2 Spay or neuter your cat as soon as possible. Having kittens, especially repeated litters, is stressful and will contribute to premature aging.

3 Keep your cat inside at all times to reduce the risk of accidents, injuries from fights or disease.

4 Feed your cat high-quality food designed to meet the specific nutritional requirements during all stages of his life.

5 Prevent obesity at all costs by controlling your cat's diet and engaging him in play activities.

6 Talk to your veterinarian about adding vitamin and mineral supplements, antioxidants and extra fiber to your cat's diet.

7 Have your cat's teeth cleaned professionally. Good dental health will add years to his life.

8 Groom your cat daily, checking for abnormalities, and seek medical help promptly when you discover anything suspicious (see 661 "Detect Skin Cancer in Your Pet").

9 Make sure no harmful chemicals such as pesticides or household cleaners find their way onto your cat's fur, since cats groom themselves with their tongues constantly. Even small amounts of harmful chemicals on their bodies can have adverse effects if consumed over many years.

10 Protect your cat from environmental dangers such as household cleaners and secondhand smoke.

11 Help your cat avoid the stress of harassment from other animals by providing a quiet place for undisturbed catnaps.

12 Provide your older cat with a heat source such as a heating pad set on low, since cats more than 12 years old require extra heat. You'll notice a difference in his attitude and activity level.

13 Give your cat daily full-body massages and lots of love. Despite their aloof demeanor, cats thrive on affection.

### ✳ Tips

Find a veterinarian with a special interest in aging who keeps abreast of advancements in this rapidly developing area of pet care.

Research this subject on your own. Experts' understanding of the aging process is changing rapidly, and knowledge gained about humans is often applicable to animals.

### ⚠ Warning

Call your veterinarian before giving your cat any product not specifically approved for cats. Some products, such as acetaminophen, commonly consumed safely by people or dogs, are poisonous to cats.

## Teach Your Parrot to Talk {#670}

670

As satisfied bird owners can attest, teaching a parrot to talk takes patience but is well worth the effort.

### ⊙ Steps

1 Begin teaching your parrot to talk when she is 4 to 6 months old at the latest. Try a simple "Good morning" to your bird at the start of each day. Keep in mind that some parrots will pick up words sooner than others.

2 Hold the bird in front of your mouth when you teach her, so that you have her attention.

3 Repeat words or phrases, such as family members' names and common expressions. Be sure to show lots of excitement in your voice. Your parrot will gradually begin to repeat after you.

4 Repeat certain words or phrases every time you do something, such as "Up" when you lift your bird up, to teach her to associate a certain movement with certain words.

5 Reward with treats when your parrot mimics you.

6 Consider playing recordings of words you want her to learn for up to 15 minutes at a time—longer than that can cause boredom.

### ✱ Tips

Don't let your bird hear sounds or words you don't want her to mimic. Discourage unwanted utterances by simply ignoring them.

Some experts believe that parrot owners should teach their birds to talk before teaching them to whistle, as whistling can interfere with learning words.

Mynah birds and certain types of parakeets can also learn to repeat words.

## Trim Your Bird's Wings {#671}

671

Trimming a bird's wings allows him to flutter to the ground safely—but not fly out the window.

### ⊙ Steps

1 Have a veterinarian show you how much to trim the first time, and take notes so you'll know how to trim the feathers on your own. The amount to trim depends on the strength and body weight of the bird.

2 Have someone assist you in restraining the bird.

3 Examine all feathers of the wing.

4 Look for emerging feathers, which have blood in the shafts (see Tips). These feathers should never be cut.

5 Locate the primary feathers on each wing. These feathers start at the leading edge of the wing and are followed by secondary and tertiary groups of feathers.

6 Use scissors to cut the primary feathers on each wing, just behind the protective coverts (small feathers) overlying the flight feathers. You may want to cut just one or two feathers a day until you see a sufficient reduction in flying ability.

7 If you cut or damage a blood feather, pluck it out at the base with tweezers or needle-nose pliers to stop the blood loss.

8 Be sure to clip both wings evenly, as clipping only one may leave the bird unbalanced.

### ✱ Tips

Newly emerging feathers, called "blood feathers," have soft, dark shafts that contain a nourishing blood supply. When the feather is completely grown in, the blood supply is closed off and the shaft turns hard and whitish. These are the feathers you can trim.

Having wings clipped is painless for the bird, much like having your hair or fingernails cut.

### ⚠ Warning

Cutting secondary feathers may cause the bird to fall straight down rather than flutter to the floor.

## 672 | Care for Your Rabbit

Rabbits need affection from their owners and can become wonderful pets if properly socialized. You can even house-train them like cats. Follow these guidelines for a happy, healthy bunny.

### ⦿ Steps

1. Have your rabbit examined by a veterinarian when you first get him, and continue with regular checkups as recommended.

2. Keep your rabbit in an indoor cage with walls and ceiling composed of stainless steel bars. At least part of the floor should be a flat surface rather than wire mesh to prevent foot injury. The cage should have one square foot for every pound of rabbit. Line the cage with newspapers and wood chips.

3. Make sure to keep the cage in a cool environment, as rabbits are very sensitive to hot temperatures. If you live in a hot climate and keep your rabbit in a hutch outdoors (instead of in an indoor cage), provide shade and ice packs to help prevent heatstroke—frozen 2-liter bottles make good ice packs.

4. Provide fresh water daily in a water bottle that attaches to the cage, and clean the water bottle once a week.

5. Give your rabbit 4 to 6 oz. of rabbit feed (depending on his size and age) once a day, and keep a salt spool in the cage.

6. Provide chew toys designed specifically for rabbits to keep his teeth worn down. Rabbits' front teeth (incisors) grow continuously.

7. Have your rabbit spayed or neutered, even if he lives alone. This will promote well-being, reduce aggressiveness and prevent some common health problems.

8. Note that you can house-train a rabbit and allow him to roam indoors. Begin by placing a cat litter box in the cage where your rabbit usually relieves himself. Once he learns to use it, you can leave the cage open and place an additional, larger litter box elsewhere in the house. The cage can serve as the rabbit's nest, where he sleeps and eats, as well as his primary spot for relieving himself.

9. Place a few handfuls of timothy hay in your rabbit's litter box. Rabbits like to munch on the hay and use the litter box at the same time. This will encourage your rabbit to use his litter box more often.

10. Trim your rabbit's nails regularly, just as you would trim a cat's nails (see 640 "Trim Your Cat's Nails").

11. Clean your rabbit's cage at least once a week and replace the lining.

### ✳ Tips

Pick up your rabbit by placing one hand under his chest and the other under his hind legs. Then, gently hold your rabbit at your chest with one hand under his belly and the other under his neck. If your rabbit starts squirming, drop to one knee so he won't fall very far if you lose your grip.

Rabbits are available in regular and dwarf sizes, and with erect or lop ears.

### ⚠ Warning

Rabbits love to chew on just about anything. Keep them away from electrical wires and both indoor and outdoor plants (see 654 "Prevent Your Pet From Chewing on Electrical Cords").

### Things You'll Need

- ☐ cage
- ☐ water bottle
- ☐ rabbit pellets
- ☐ salt spool
- ☐ chew toys
- ☐ timothy hay

# Care for Your Hamster                                      673

Hamsters are perfect first pets for youngsters and can live for two to five years. They fit in the palm of your hand, they're lovable and cuddly, and caring for them is easy and inexpensive.

## ⊙ Steps

1 Buy a hamster that is between 4 and 7 weeks old. They're easier to tame when they're young.

2 Keep the cage away from drafts and direct sunlight.

3 Cover the cage floor with a thick layer of bedding. Wood shavings are best, because they are absorbent and nontoxic. Keep the bedding warm and dry—moisture can cause fatal infections.

4 Keep a filled, clean water bottle attached to the side of the cage.

5 Provide plenty of chew toys. Hamsters love the cardboard tubes found inside rolls of toilet paper and paper towels. Attach hamster wood chews to the side of the cage.

6 Make a small box for your hamster to sleep in. Cut a 2-inch doorway into a closed box. Place the box in a far corner of the cage. The hamster will fill the box with bedding and chewed-up pieces of cardboard from the toilet paper tubes and will use the box as a bedroom. He will not urinate in the box, so you can use it for many months before replacing it.

7 Feed your hamster a commercially prepared hamster-food mix once or twice a day. Supply a small amount of fresh fruits and vegetables year-round. When you introduce new foods, initially feed small portions so his system can get used to them.

8 Exercise your hamster by putting an exercise wheel in his cage. Let him exercise outside his cage inside a specially designed plastic hamster ball, available at pet stores. Close the doors to your bedroom, take him out of his cage, and let him run around in the hamster ball.

9 Wash your hamster's cage at least once a week. Remove the hamster and dip the cage in water that has a few drops of household disinfectant added to it.

10 Remove any uneaten fruits and vegetables after a few days. Fresh foods that turn moldy can make your hamster sick.

11 Don't bathe your hamster. Hamsters clean themselves. If you think your hamster smells bad, the odor is probably coming from dirty bedding. Clean the hamster cage more often.

12 Always be careful when handling hamsters. Although normally they bite only when they are frightened, they do have very sharp front teeth.

13 Take your hamster with you or find someone to take care of him if you are going on vacation for more than three days.

## ✱ Tips

If you put your hamster in a plastic exercise ball, be sure to keep the ball away from steps. Falling down a flight of stairs can result in serious injury.

Hamsters are active at night. The best time to clean the cage or exercise the hamster is in the evening or morning, rather than at midday when the hamster prefers to rest undisturbed.

Care and housing requirements for rodents vary. If you plan to acquire a gerbil or guinea pig, a veterinarian who specializes in "pocket pets" can provide more detailed information.

## ⚠ Warnings

Consult a veterinarian promptly if your hamster needs medical care, since hamsters die quickly.

Hamsters can catch the human cold virus, so avoid contact if you are sick.

## Things You'll Need

☐ hamster cage
☐ wood shavings
☐ water bottle
☐ chew toys
☐ small box
☐ commercially prepared hamster-food mix
☐ exercise wheel
☐ plastic hamster ball
☐ household disinfectant

## 674 | Care for Your Chinchilla

These fur-bearing relatives of the guinea pig and porcupine make excellent pets, though they're shy and easily frightened. Most live 8 to 10 years; some can live to 18.

### ⊙ Steps

1   Have your new chinchilla examined by a veterinarian who specializes in small or exotic animals, and continue to bring her in for regular check-ups as recommended.

2   Feed your chinchilla commercially prepared rabbit pellets mixed with alfalfa and grass hay.

3   Give dried fruits as treats, but in moderation. These supplements should make up only 10 percent of the entire food intake.

4   Supply a water bottle, and change the water daily.

5   Provide a wire mesh cage, with or without a solid floor, of at least 3 by 3 by 3 feet—more than adequate for one chinchilla during playtime.

6   Be sure the cage is located in a cool, dry, and draft-free area, preferably in a temperature range of 60 to 70 degrees F. Keep your chinchilla's cage indoors to provide better temperature control.

7   Allow your chinchilla supervised evening romps outside her cage. Use a leash designed for small animals like rabbits and chinchillas if you take her outside.

8   Provide your pet with a dust bath twice a week by mixing nine parts silver sand with one part fuller's earth, or buy a specially prepared chinchilla dust-bath mixture.

9   When holding a chinchilla, grasp her at the base of the tail with one hand and support the body with your other forearm. Hold her gently, close to your body. Rough handling can cause hair loss. Note that chinchillas may urinate when annoyed or nervous.

10  Provide chew toys for her such as wooden blocks and other items designed for chinchillas.

### ✱ Tips

Care for your chinchilla conscientiously. Poor nutrition, boredom and hot temperatures can lead to serious medical problems.

Some chinchillas can develop health problems due to an overgrowth of molars. Regular veterinary checkups are essential.

### Things You'll Need

❏ rabbit pellets mixed with alfalfa and grass hay

❏ dried fruits

❏ water bottle

❏ wire-mesh cage

❏ leash designed for small animals

❏ chinchilla dust-bath mixture

❏ chew toys

## 675 | Care for Your Ferret

Ferrets are ultradian animals—they have short bursts of activity separated by hours of rest. They can adapt their schedules to yours so they'll be awake and ready to play when you are.

### ⊙ Steps

1   Feed your ferret a high-quality ferret or kitten food that's high in protein (34 to 38 percent) and fat (19 to 22 percent) but low in fiber. Make this readily available throughout the day, as ferrets digest food quickly and eat 7 to 10 meals a day. Avoid giving your ferret any moist, canned cat food, which can contribute to dental-tartar formation.

### ✱ Tip

Some states don't allow ferrets to be kept as pets. Contact your local wildlife or fish and game department or the humane society to find out if ferrets are legal in your area and whether you'll need a license to own one.

**How to Do *(Just About)* Everything**

2   Offer treats such as meats, starches, vegetables and fruits. Give no more than 1 tsp. a day, and mash or chop food into small pieces to make it easier for him to consume. Examples are bits of mashed banana, pieces of seedless melon, green peas and chopped cucumber.

3   Provide a cage that's equipped with a water bottle and lined with news-paper on top of linoleum. Make sure the cage is large enough for exercise. For one or two ferrets, the cage should measure 18 by 30 by 36 inches and contain at least two levels. Keep your ferret in his cage unless supervised.

4   Place a litter box inside the cage filled with kitty litter. A ferret will learn to use the litter box to relieve himself, much like a cat. If he does not figure it out himself, encourage him to use the litter box by placing him there when you suspect he needs to go.

5   Give your ferret 2 hours of playtime and exercise outside the cage each day. Be sure to ferret-proof your home by removing hazardous products before allowing him to roam the house. If you take your ferret outside, always keep him on a leash made for small animals.

6   Protect your ferret from extreme weather and temperatures, especially direct sunlight and heat (anything over 80 degrees F can be harmful).

7   Have a ferret-savvy veterinarian vaccinate your ferret for rabies and canine distemper. Also, remember that ferrets can get fleas, heartworm and intestinal parasites. Consult a veterinarian for preventative measures and treatment (see 657 "Get Rid of Fleas" and 659 "Prevent Worms in Cats and Dogs").

8   Spay or neuter your pet ferret. This is especially critical for females, as female ferrets are induced ovulators (they ovulate when bred). If she is not bred when in heat, she can die from anemia.

9   Give your ferret toys such as tennis balls, cardboard boxes and cat toys. Make sure none of your ferret toys have small, removable parts, as your ferret can ingest these and develop an obstruction in the digestive tract.

10  Pick up your ferret from behind. Use one hand to support his chest and the other to support his hips.

## ⚠ Warning

Ferrets can catch colds from people, so stay away from your ferret if you are feeling sick.

## Things You'll Need

❑ ferret or kitten food

❑ treats

❑ cage

❑ water bottle

❑ litter box

❑ small-animal leash

❑ toys

---

## Care for Your Vietnamese Potbellied Pig   676

These good-natured miniature pigs—raised for food in Southeast Asia—are intelligent and headstrong. Caring for them requires space and a mellow attitude.

### ◉ Steps

1   You can keep your pig either indoors or outdoors. They're generally clean animals, and they prefer to relieve themselves outside. When your pig's tail stops wagging and becomes horizontal, it's a sign that she needs to relieve herself.

2   Feed your pig twice a day with commercially prepared potbellied-pig food that's formulated to meet your pig's nutritional needs. Have a

## ✳ Tips

Potbellied pigs are considered livestock, so check with your city officials before moving one into your neighborhood.

Livestock veterinarians usually treat these pets.

veterinarian advise you on the proper amount to feed, since food requirements vary with the pig and depend on age and weight. Be sure to watch your pig's weight closely.

3  Train your pig to use a litter box if she must be kept indoors for long periods of time. Keep the box far away from her food and bedding area.

4  Avoid lining the litter box with items your pig may like to eat. Instead, use a large plastic cement-mixing tub (available at home-improvement stores), lined with newspapers and pine chips.

5  Take an indoor pig out daily so she can act like a pig and get exercise. Provide a rooting box, such as a child's swimming pool filled with sand, dirt and toys.

6  Provide a warm, dry, draft-free environment such as a large doghouse, with plenty of blankets and straw, if your pig is kept outdoors. The more blankets, the happier the pig.

7  Monitor your pig carefully when temperatures drop below freezing or rise above 80 degrees F, since pigs are sensitive to extreme temperatures and cannot sweat. Make sure the pig has access to a shaded area.

8  Provide your pig with a child's swimming pool filled with water for cooling down when it's hot. Apply sunscreen (the type used on humans) if your pig often gets sunburned—pig hair doesn't offer much protection.

9  Spay or neuter your pig at 8 to 10 weeks. Neutering helps to reduce aggressive behavior in males.

10  Have your pig vaccinated once a year, and get her hooves trimmed when necessary.

11  Give a good foot stomp and a strong "No!" to stop your pig from engaging in unwanted behavior. Spoiled pigs can become unruly, destructive and demanding.

12  Be prepared for your pig to reach a shoulder height of 18 inches and a weight of 60 to 110 pounds. Keep in mind that potbellied pigs have an average life span of 20 to 25 years.

Potbellied pigs are very smart and can easily be trained to do tricks, just like dogs.

## Things You'll Need

- ☐ commercially prepared potbellied-pig food
- ☐ litter box
- ☐ pine chips
- ☐ child's swimming pool
- ☐ sand
- ☐ blankets
- ☐ straw
- ☐ toys
- ☐ sunscreen

---

## 677 | Care for Your Turtle

**Proper temperature, water quality and feeding are important aspects of maintaining the health of semiaquatic turtles and aquatic turtles (which are called terrapins).**

### ⊙ Steps

1  Set up two-thirds of your turtle's aquarium for swimming and one-third for basking, using a full-spectrum ultraviolet light source. Basking is critical for drying and preventing shell problems. And since turtles can't store vitamin $D_3$, they must be exposed to UVB light for absorption.

2  Keep the temperature at 77 to 95 degrees F for aquatic and semiaquatic species. Use an aquarium heater when needed; turtles and terrapins become sluggish and stop eating in low temperatures.

3  Keep the water clean to prevent health problems. Use an aquarium filtration system to maintain optimal water quality.

### ⚠ Warning

Common medical conditions are improper mineral balance, vitamin deficiency and excessive protein levels. The biggest problem for turtles and terrapins is a metabolic bone disease caused by improper feeding and lighting and lack of exercise.

4  Prevent your turtle's environment from becoming soiled by either netting or siphoning off all fecal matter as soon as possible. Fecal buildup can cause health problems.

5  Clean the entire aquarium (including the filtration system) at least once a month. Clean ponds or large enclosures where the animal spends time at least every three to six months.

6  Offer a complete commercial diet made specifically for turtles and terrapins. Check with experts for exact dietary requirements and amounts for your species.

7  Supplement the diet with appropriate snacks: Earthworms, crustaceans, small fish, mouse pups, algae, leafy green vegetation and fruit are examples of suitable foods for terrapins. Semiaquatic species tend to be herbivorous—they tend to eat plants only.

8  Feed your pet two to three times a week in a small holding tank that is separate from its normal enclosure; uneaten food can attract disease-causing microorganisms.

9  Rinse off your turtle after a feeding with slightly warm water before returning him to his enclosure.

10  Find a veterinarian who specializes in reptiles, amphibians and other exotic pets to provide care for your turtle.

### Things You'll Need

- ☐ aquarium
- ☐ full-spectrum ultraviolet light source
- ☐ aquarium heater
- ☐ aquarium filtration system
- ☐ commercially prepared turtle or terrapin food

---

## Care for Your Fish                                                      678

Fish need an optimal environment. These general guidelines apply to most freshwater fish in pet stores but not to saltwater or tropical fish, which have different requirements.

### ◉ Steps

1  Start off with healthy fish. View every fish in that tank before you purchase one. They should move about the tank with purpose and not display any signs of sickness, such as cloudy eyes or slimy-looking bodies.

2  Keep new fish in a quarantine tank with the same water quality as the main tank. They should stay there for at least two weeks (preferably three) before you introduce them to the new tank. When you start getting impatient, think about how much trouble it would be to treat the entire population for infection instead of just one fish.

3  Place the tank against an inside wall—away from windows, doors and heating systems—to prevent drafts and sudden temperature changes.

4  Maintain the water quality. Test the ammonia, nitrite and pH levels regularly with a special kit. Chemical imbalances are a leading cause of sickness in fish. Once the water quality is acceptable, use a special filtered siphon to change 20 percent of the water every 10 days. A pet store that sells fish should also sell test kits and siphons.

5  Provide your fish with a diet of commercially prepared fish food. Store it in a cool, dry place for no more than a few months.

6  Remove waste and uneaten food with a net every other day. Rinse the net thoroughly before and after use to avoid the potential spread of infection.

### ✱ Tip

Make sure your tank is large enough—about 30 square inches of surface area per inch of fish. Increase the size of the tank by 50 to 100 percent before adding more fish.

### ⚠ Warnings

Mixing faster and stronger fish with slower, weaker ones is a bad idea. The slower fish will not get enough to eat, and the others will be overfed.

Discuss what types of fish are compatible in a tank and which to keep separate—some species can be very territorial and will kill other fish.

### Things You'll Need

- ☐ two fish tanks (one for quarantine) ➤

7 Keep a canopy or hood over the tank at all times. Some fish are jumpers.

8 Don't let your fish get stressed by poor water conditions, drastic lighting changes or constant activity outside the tank. These things will lower their resistance to disease.

☐ fish food

☐ fish net

## 679 | Wash Your Goldfish's Bowl

Because goldfish are a cold-water species, they don't need a heated tank. If you're one of those people who love the classic look of a fishbowl, read on.

### ◎ Steps

1 Plan on cleaning out your fishbowl every two weeks, if not weekly.

2 Catch your fish with a small net and place it in a smaller secondary bowl full of room-temperature water from the original bowl.

3 Empty the primary fishbowl into the sink. Catch any rocks or other objects in a strainer as you pour the water out.

4 Rinse the bowl thoroughly with hot water, scrubbing the sides with a paper towel, if needed.

5 Pour out the dirty water, and repeat with more hot water. This will help kill germs and bacteria.

6 Clean your bowl using a chemical cleaner designed specifically for goldfish bowls. Never use soap or detergent when washing a fishbowl.

7 Rinse the bowl out thoroughly with cold water.

8 Run cold water over the objects in the strainer (gravel, plastic plants) until they are clean. Return them to the bowl.

9 Refill the bowl and let the new water sit for 24 hours to allow the chlorine in the tap water to evaporate and to bring the water to room temperature.

10 Return your fish to the primary bowl.

**✻ Tip**

Transfer the fish quickly from one bowl to another. A fish out of water can suffocate and die within minutes.

**⚠ Warning**

Ask at the fish store about special chemical cleaners designed to safely clean your bowl in the event that your fish has died and bowl sterilization is necessary.

## 680 | Feed Your Goldfish

Keeping goldfish properly fed is easy when you do it right.

### ◎ Steps

1 Purchase the right kind of food for your fish. Goldfish need protein and a wide range of vitamins and carbohydrates, so choose a nutrient-rich food specifically for goldfish. Use either flake-form or floating pellets. Ask at the aquarium store for food recommendations for the specific type of goldfish you own.

2 Consider occasionally offering snacks, such as leafy vegetables (lettuce and spinach) or live food (brine shrimp and mosquito larvae), for variety.

**✻ Tip**

Buy a vacation food block if you are going to be away from the tank for more than a weekend.

**⚠ Warning**

Overfeeding pollutes the tank, endangering the fishes' lives.

3 Feed your fish once a day by adding one small pinch of food to the tank at a time. In general, provide as much food as the fish will consume in 2 minutes. (Vary this accordingly for larger fish.) Remember to offer just a tiny amount in each pinch.

4 Remove excess food with a net after the feeding session, to avoid polluting the water.

5 Consider using a feeding ring, which attaches to the side of the tank and allows better control, thus reducing the risk of overfeeding your fish.

**Things You'll Need**

☐ goldfish food

☐ fishnet

☐ feeding ring

## Help Your Child Cope With the Death of a Pet     681

The loss of a family pet can be a child's first experience with death. Helping children cope with grief will help them understand a very painful aspect of life and begin the healing process.

### ◎ Steps

1 Talk about the pet's health and any decisions to be made prior to the animal's death, if possible.

2 Respond to your children honestly and age-appropriately. While young children will not understand the concept of death, they will feel a tremendous loss. Older children may want to discuss the decline of the pet's health, plans for the body and the concept of death itself.

3 Avoid the commonly used phrase "putting to sleep." This phrase can confuse young children, and even scare them as they prepare to go to bed at night.

4 Try to explain the concept of "dog years" or whatever is applicable to the species of your family pet. But make it clear that Mom and Dad live in "people years" and are not going anywhere.

5 Ask your veterinarian to answer any medical questions for your children. Older children may have questions about euthanasia—how it is done, what the pet will feel, what equipment is used and what happens to the animal's body.

6 Say good-bye to the pet in a ceremony to make it official. Bury it in a special place (a pet cemetery is an option) so your children can remember the pet whenever they visit this spot.

7 Memorialize your pet in a way that is unique to your family. Plant a tree in your pet's favorite spot in the garden, write down thoughts about fun times spent with the pet, draw pictures, or hang a favorite photo of the pet in your home for all of the family to share.

8 Show your own grief. Children will grow to understand their own feelings better if they see that their sadness is shared by other family members.

9 Encourage children to talk about their feelings, memories of the pet and favorite times spent together.

10 Share the loss with your children's teachers or counselors to explain any changes in behavior and to add further support.

### ✳ Tips

Many books are available for different ages about dealing with the death of a family pet. Reading such a book with your child may help him talk about feelings of loss.

When the family is ready, think about adopting another pet. After a period of mourning, this addition to the family will bring a new set of experiences and will not take anything away from your child's memories of his previous loving companion.

Seek advice from professional grief counselors who specialize in pet loss.

## 682 | Write an Invitation

Your invitation sets the tone for your party—take time to think about what you want it to communicate.

### ◎ Steps

1 Decide on the tone, voice and level of formality you're going to use, based on the event itself. This will dictate whether you handwrite the cards or have them printed, and whether you choose a preprinted or personalized invitation.

2 Consider making a theme invitation—using such items as travel postcards, photographs and envelopes studded with confetti—for a casual, festive occasion.

3 Choose the type of card you want, and order or buy a few more than you think you'll need. This will permit you to add some guests to your list at the last minute, if necessary.

4 Determine the wording based on the level of formality. For example, a formal invitation might say, "Dr. and Mrs. Stanley request the pleasure of your company," whereas a more casual note might say, "Please join us."

5 Include the names of the host and/or hostess, as well as the place, time, date and purpose of the party, even if it's a simple get-together. Make sure to add RSVP information.

6 Include a respond-by date in a formal invitation so you can get an accurate head count in time to adjust the amount of food, number of place settings and room size. For a wedding, charity function or other formal event, consider including a response card and a stamped, self-addressed envelope inside the big envelope.

7 Mail invitations three weeks before most events, four weeks before a formal affair. For events held during the December holidays, send invitations around Thanksgiving.

### ✳ Tips

Use precisely the kind of RSVP method that best serves the occasion: a response card for a head count, a telephone number for expediency, or an e-mail address if you know that the invitees have computers.

Large dinner parties, debuts, receptions and weddings call for written invitations.

Count out those who don't respond, but be prepared for a few nonresponders to show up.

Printing invitations costs much more but is worthwhile if you are planning a formal or large event.

For less formal occasions, consider using social-planning Web sites, such as www.evite.com, to e-mail your invitations.

## 683 | Respond to a Written Invitation

Responding to an invitation properly demonstrates your good manners, and it is also a mark of respect and consideration for your host.

### ◎ Steps

1 Read the invitation carefully. Often it gives a hint as to a preferred mode of response.

2 If a response card with envelope is provided, fill it out and send it off in a timely manner. If the invitation gives a phone number, call as soon as you know whether you will attend.

3 Use your personal stationery or a blank card to respond to a formal invitation that doesn't come with a response card. Write some variation of the following: "Joseph Mackenzie and guest, Rachel Helfond, accept with pleasure the invitation to dine with the Stellmans on 15 June 2001."

### ✳ Tip

RSVP is an abbreviation for the French phrase *répondez s'il vous plaît,* which means "please reply."

### ⚠ Warning

If you don't respond—unless specifically instructed not to—your host's horrified face shouldn't surprise you when you make an appearance anyway.

Or if you cannot attend, send your regrets: "I regret that I will not be attending the dinner party, as I must be out of town."

4   Mail the response in time to assure at least one week's notice.

5   Keep in mind that "Regrets only" means you should respond only if you do not plan on attending the event.

## Buy a Wedding Gift                                                   684

Wish the lucky pair well with a heartfelt and useful gift.

### ⊙ Steps

1   Find out where the couple has registered by calling a member of the wedding party. You can also call, visit or go online to specific stores to determine where they've registered.

2   Search the wedding registry, making sure you have the full names of both bride and groom, as well as the wedding date, to make the search easier. The registry should give an updated list of gifts the couple hasn't yet received.

3   Select a gift from the registry that's within your price range, even if that means you can only buy one cup and saucer.

4   Have it gift-wrapped, and include an enclosure card with your address to simplify the couple's thank-you writing.

5   Address the gifts to the bride before the wedding, and to both the bride and groom afterward.

6   Send your gift instead of bringing it to the wedding; this is much easier for the wedding party. Most stores will mail it for you, especially if you order it online or by telephone.

7   If you prefer to give money instead of a gift, present it on the day of the ceremony. Make a check payable to both the bride and groom.

### ✱ Tips

As a rule of thumb, select a gift from the registry since the couple has expressly requested these items. Refrain from buying a print by your favorite artist or an antique cake platter you love unless you are absolutely positive the couple will also love it.

Consider purchasing a large gift with a group of friends.

Shop early when buying a gift off the registry. You'll have wider choice in your price range.

### ⚠ Warning

Avoid monogramming your gift. The couple can't return or exchange a monogrammed gift, and you may not know what names the couple will choose.

## Be a Proper Wedding Guest                                            685

Keep in mind these quick pointers for being a perfect wedding guest, and you'll help the wedding day go smoothly for the bride and groom.

### ⊙ Steps

1   Make your hotel and plane reservations early, especially if you receive a "save the date" notice.

2   Purchase gifts early, and use the registry. It is designed to make your life—and the lives of the bride and groom—easier.

3   Respond, or RSVP, as soon as possible after you get the invitation. Only bring a guest if you receive an invitation addressed to you and a guest.

### ✱ Tips

If you have questions about attire, whether to bring children to the ceremony, or other logistics, call the best man or maid of honor, who is often much more accessible than the bride or groom.

Keep in mind that the bride and groom want to see and talk to

4   Dress appropriately. If the invitation says black tie, men should wear tuxedos and women should wear formal dresses. If you are unsure of the dress code, you're safer erring on the side of dressing up too much.

5   Bring children only if the invitation expressly mentions them. Weddings are formal events and typically not appropriate for little ones.

6   Arrive 15 minutes before the ceremony begins. Tradition dictates that friends and family of the bride sit on the left and friends and family of the groom sit on the right. Typically, an usher will lead you to your seat.

7   Wait in the receiving line, if there is one, to congratulate the newlywed couple and their parents after the ceremony. Keep your greeting upbeat and brief.

8   Remain quiet and attentive during toasts at the reception, and while the couple cuts the wedding cake.

9   Wait for the bride and groom to have their first dance before you hit the dance floor. Then get up, dance and enjoy the party; the couple will be pleased to see all the guests having a good time.

10  Avoid engaging the bride or groom in conversation for too long—they have many guests to greet, and a honeymoon suite awaits them.

every guest, so don't feel disappointed if you don't get to chat with them for long.

Mail your gift ahead of time to make it easier on the bride and groom. If you do bring the gift, take it to the reception and place it on the gift table.

---

## 686 Be a Proper Guest at a Party

A great guest responds promptly to the invitation, arrives fashionably late, acts cheerful and friendly, and isn't the last one to go home.

### ◉ Steps

1   Respond to the invitation in a timely manner. Use the method indicated: phone, mail or e-mail.

2   Bring a friend only if you receive an invitation for you and a guest. Your hosts may have a food, budget or space limitation.

3   Go with the spirit of the party. If there's an occasion, such as a house-warming, bring a gift. If it's dressy, wear your fancy duds. Costume required? Dig into your closet and get creative.

4   Prepare. Read up on current events; think of a few good stories; recall a few movies, books or plays. Try hard not to be shy or cranky—for your host's sake, if not your own.

5   Arrive reasonably close to the starting time. The starting time for a cocktail party tends to be looser than it is for a dinner party, which requires punctuality. Fashionably late means no more than 30 minutes past the indicated time.

6   Seek out your host or hostess and say hello as soon as you arrive.

7   Make an effort to mix and mingle cheerfully. Don't just hide out in a corner chatting with a clique.

8   Know your alcohol limits and don't exceed them. Take into consideration your energy level, food intake and drink size. Nothing's ruder than ruining a party with inappropriate behavior.

### ✳ Tips

If you know your hosts, you might call and ask about the dress code, if the invitation doesn't make it clear. Or ask another guest who's attending.

Decide whether a gift is appropriate. Flowers or a bottle of wine is a nice thought for a dinner party; a six-pack of beer or soda is a good idea for a barbecue.

### ⚠ Warning

Never arrive early; your hosts may not be ready to receive guests.

9   Treat your host's home as you would your own—no wet glasses on the furniture, no cigarettes ground out in the plants, no hors d'oeuvre toothpicks on the floor.

10  Leave at a reasonable hour. Some hosts close the bar half an hour before they want the party to end. Take a hint when others start slipping on their coats.

11  Find your hosts to say thank-you and good night personally. It's also thoughtful to call the next day and let your host know how much you enjoyed the event.

## Introduce People                                                    687

Want to meet new people and improve your social graces? Here's how to make proper introductions at parties, dinners and other social situations.

### ⊙ Steps

1   Introduce individuals to each other using both first and last names.

2   If you're introducing someone who has a title—a doctor, for example—include the title as well as the first and last names in the introduction.

3   Introduce the younger or less prominent person to the older or more prominent person, regardless of the sex of the individuals. (However, if a considerable age difference lies between the two, it is far more courteous to make introductions in deference to age, regardless of social rank.) For example: "Arthur Prefect, I'd like you to meet Dr. Gertrude Smith."

4   If the person you are introducing has a specific relationship to you, make the relationship clear by adding a phrase such as "my boss," "my wife" or "my uncle." In the case of unmarried couples who are living together, "companion" and "partner" are good choices.

5   Use your spouse's first and last name if he or she has a different last name than you. Include the phrase "my wife" or "my husband."

6   Introduce an individual to the group first, then the group to the individual. For example: "Dr. Brown, I'd like you to meet my friends Kym Hsu, Shawn Kampbell and Michael Via. Everyone, this is Dr. Kurt Brown."

### ✱ Tips

If you've forgotten a name, you'll seem impolite if you try to ignore the need for the introduction. It's less awkward (and better manners) to apologize and acknowledge that the name has escaped you.

If your host neglects to introduce you to other guests, feel free to introduce yourself, but make your relationship to the host clear in your introduction.

### ⚠ Warning

Formal etiquette censures repeating names and adding phrases such as "charmed" and "a pleasure," as it may appear insincere or detract from the introduction. Instead, offer a friendly "Hello," or "Gertrude has told me so much about you."

## Shake Hands                                                         688

Historically used to show that both people were unarmed, the handshake today is a critical gauge of confidence, trust, sophistication and mood.

### ⊙ Steps

1   Extend your right hand to meet the other person's right hand.

2   Point your thumb upward toward the other person's arm and extend your arm at a slight downward angle.

### ✱ Tip

A two-handed handshake is not for first meetings. It is a sign of real affection, and you should reserve it for friends and intimates.

3   Wrap your hand around the other person's hand when your thumb joints come together.

4   Grasp the hand firmly and squeeze gently once. Remember that limp handshakes are a big turnoff, as are bone-crushing grasps.

5   Hold the handshake for 2 to 3 seconds.

6   Pump your hand up and down a few times to convey sincerity. (This gesture is optional.)

⚠ **Warning**

Handshakes are not appropriate in all cultures. Investigate local customs if you will be visiting a foreign country.

---

## 689 | Remember Names

The ability to remember the names of people you meet will always serve you well in social situations.

### ◉ Steps

1   Pay attention when you are introduced to someone. A few minutes after you meet the person, say his or her name to yourself again. If you have forgotten it, talk to the person again and ask for the name.

2   Write down the new name three times while picturing the person's face; do this as soon as possible after meeting someone.

3   Ask how to spell a difficult name, or glance at the spelling on the person's business card, if it's offered. If you know the spelling of a word and can picture it in your mind, you'll remember it better.

4   Connect a name to a common word you will remember. For example, the name Salazar could sound like "salamander," "bazaar" or "sell a jar."

5   Make a connection to the person's hobby or employment. "Bill the pill" might help you remember the name of your pharmacist, for example.

**✱ Tip**

Writing down new names is generally a very successful memorizing technique that doesn't require a lot of work.

---

## 690 | Propose a Toast

A few carefully selected words can add a personal touch to any social gathering. People make toasts over festive beverages such as champagne, sparkling cider or wine.

### ◉ Steps

1   Let the host or hostess make the first salute at a dinner party. If she or he does not do so, initiate a toast after the dishes from the main course are cleared.

2   Make certain that everyone, no matter what he or she is drinking, has a full glass to raise.

3   Stand up and tap your glass to get everyone's attention.

4   For a formal occasion, have everyone (except for the person you are toasting) stand up. If it is less formal, guests may remain seated.

5   Direct your toast toward the host or hostess or the guest of honor. Speak loudly and slowly so that all can hear you.

**✱ Tips**

If you know ahead of time that you will be giving a toast, write down some thoughts on note cards and practice delivering the toast before the big event.

Remember that the toast puts the spotlight on the honoree, not on you.

If you are the recipient of a toast, remain seated and refrain from drinking when everyone drinks to you.

6    Keep it brief, sincere and to the point; choose simple but substantial words to convey your feelings. Some of the best toasts are just a single sentence or two.

7    If you are feeling more creative, you can begin with an appropriate quotation, a poem or an amusing anecdote.

8    Consider mentioning an unusually brave, heroic, romantic or awesome act performed by the honoree.

9    Weave humor into your toast, but don't embarrass the honoree. If the assembled group is close-knit, it's all right to refer to shared experiences, but don't make the toast a private joke between you and a few of the people present.

10   When you have finished your toast, lift your glass to the recipient and lead the group in drinking to that person.

## ⚠ Warning

Make sure your toast is appropriate for everyone at the event. For example, a best man's speech at a wedding ceremony shouldn't refer to bachelor-party escapades.

---

# Leave a Party Graciously                              691

**Arriving at the party is the easy part. When you are ready to leave, exercise tact and always thank the host or hostess before you depart.**

### ◎ Steps

1    Wait until the host is not in conversation or caught in the middle of cooking or serving duties.

2    Express your gratitude for the invitation, and compliment the host on one particular aspect of the party.

3    Make a tentative reference to the next time you will see each other. For example, saying "We should get together for drinks soon" takes the emphasis off your departure.

4    Acknowledge everyone in the room, if possible. If the party is too large to permit this, express a parting gesture to those guests with whom you spent time talking.

5    Make your parting words short and sweet in an attempt to let everyone else get back to the festivities.

## ✱ Tips

Avoid long and effusive apologies. Others will look upon your departure negatively if you insist on apologizing for it.

If the party invitation included an ending time, don't stay too long after the time indicated.

---

# Write a Thank-You Note                                692

**You can fill even short thank-you notes with appreciation and meaning. And remember, "better late than never" applies—the recipient will always enjoy your thanks.**

### ◎ Steps

1    Mention the gift, favor or party you attended.

2    Talk about the appropriateness of the gift or favor: "Your baby-sitting for my children has truly been a lifesaver in these difficult times." (You can describe a gift that didn't quite suit your taste as "a conversation piece" or "unique.")

## ✱ Tips

Many people consider it unnecessary to write thank-you notes for gifts given in person, with the exception of wedding gifts, as long as you thank the giver verbally. But when in doubt, a written note is always a good idea.

3   Tie the appropriateness of the gift to the person who gave it to you: "You've always understood my taste in clothes."

4   Talk about how you plan to use the gift (or substitute this step for step 2): "I have a picture of my parents that would look perfect in your frame." If you received a gift of money, mention how you will spend it.

5   Add a small personal note to update the giver about your life: "I have completely recovered from my cold and plan to hit the slopes again as soon as I can."

6   Consider sending a token of appreciation along with your note if you're thanking someone for a good deed. Possibilities include flowers, chocolate or an invitation to lunch (your treat).

A newly married couple should write individual, handwritten notes to all gift givers, and mail these out within three months of the wedding (at the very latest).

Send a thank-you note for birthday and holiday gifts within three days of when you receive them.

## 693 | Tie a Tie

**Once you've mastered the technique, you won't need a mirror to look dapper in your favorite tie. These instructions will teach you to tie a four-in-hand knot.**

### ◎ Steps

1   Lift up the collar of your shirt and put the tie around the back of your neck. The wide end should hang down about twice as low as the thin end; it can hang closer to your right or left hand, depending on what's most comfortable for you.

2   Wrap the wide end around the thin end twice, a few inches below your neck. The wide end should go over the thin end at first.

3   After wrapping the wide end around the second time, push it through the back of the V shape made by the partially formed knot.

4   Tuck the wide end through the front loop of the knot.

5   Gently pull down on both the thin and wide ends below the knot until it is tight.

6   Hold the thin end and slide the knot up to your neck.

7   If the thin end hangs below the wide end, untie the tie and begin again, with the wide end hanging lower than it did the first time.

8   If the wide end hangs too low, untie the tie and begin again, with the wide end hanging higher than it did the first time.

9   Flip your collar back down once you and your tie look dapper.

### ✱ Tip

When untying a tie, follow the directions in reverse rather than just pulling the narrow end through the knot. Otherwise, you may distort the shape of the tie.

# ✓ 694 Dress to Flatter Your Figure

Not all of us are able—or willing—to spend hours in the gym in quest of a perfect body, so it's good to know that there are much less painful ways to hide flaws and enhance attributes. Here's how to meet a few common fashion challenges.

## Minimize a large bottom

- Wear wide-leg pants. Steer clear of back pockets or any detailing around the buttocks. Opt for styles that hang full from the middle of the bottom. Front pleats and pockets will help balance your silhouette.

- Choose full or A-line skirts that hang loosely.

- Pair a short jacket with a long skirt and a long jacket with a shorter skirt.

- Select jackets that are slightly fitted and taper gently.

- Wear "empire" dresses for evening. Avoid clingy bias-cut styles.

- Attract admirers' eyes to your upper body. Wear brightly colored or patterned tops and consider neckline accessories.

- Wear slimming dark colors such as navy, dark brown, charcoal and black.

## Minimize a large stomach

- Direct attention toward your upper body. Accessorize your neckline or choose tops with detailing above the breasts.

- Choose pants with a narrow or tapered leg. Leggings and stirrup pants are great if they are not too tight.

- Select skirts that do not gather at the waist. Straight skirts will narrow your silhouette.

- Wear tunic-style tops and sweaters, and square jackets that cover the stomach.

- Look for sheath dresses that create a column from your shoulders to your lower leg.

- Avoid belted or drawstring looks, which draw attention to your waist.

- Choose pants with details around the cuffs to draw attention down your leg and away from your stomach.

## Make breasts appear larger

- Stand up straight.

- Buy a padded push-up bra.

- Insert foam pads into your bra. Place them in special pockets built into the bra, or place them In the cup under the breast.

- Apply blush, a shade darker than your skin tone, between the breasts to suggest shadows and cleavage.

- Remember that too much padding or blush can be obvious. Try to go for a subtle, subliminal effect.

- Wear a tight Lycra top over your bra and under your shirt to add an extra layer.

- Choose clothing material that hugs and draws attention to the bustline.

## Appear more slender

- Choose clothing all in one color to give yourself a long, lean look.

- Wear black, which looks slimming.

- Avoid shapeless clothing. Loose clothes often make you appear wider or heavier.

- Choose softly tailored—not tight—pieces, which define but don't constrain.

- Steer clear of horizontal stripes, which make you appear wider.

- Consider vertical stripes, which make you look longer and leaner.

- Wear blocks of color that draw the eye away from less-than-perfect areas.

- Wear shoulder pads and wide necklines.

- Choose pants with narrow or tapered legs.

reference

## 695 | Buy a Perfect Little Black Dress

Every woman needs a little black dress. It's the one garment you can always slip on when you aren't sure what to wear for the evening, but you need to look fabulous.

### ◉ Steps

1 Think about your body type. If you need to wear a bra when you go out for the evening, you may not be comfortable in halters, backless numbers and sheer shoulders. But remember that there are plenty of other ways to look sexy.

2 Identify your key assets. Is your back worth showing off? Want to expose a little shoulder? Is the low-cut look for you? Do your legs deserve the spotlight?

3 Find a dress that's comfortable. Eliminate any dress that makes it hard to walk, sit or dance.

4 Choose a well-constructed dress of a good fabric—a light wool or silk crepe is best—with a lining. The lining will smooth your figure so the shell hangs neatly.

5 Follow the 3-1 ratio—three parts conservative to one part racy. Choose a little black dress that's plain except for that one saucy feature: crisscross straps in back; a daring neckline; a deep slit in the side, back or front.

6 Accessorize for understated drama: fishnet stockings, a bold bracelet, a choker, or leopard pumps with a matching bag.

### ✳ Tip

Surprisingly, some well-made spaghetti-strap dresses work well even if you're on the busty side—they offer a good way to show a little skin without feeling too exposed.

## 696 | Buy a Man's Business Suit

Everyday business attire may have become more casual, but the suit is still the anchor of any man's formal wardrobe. Start with a classic navy suit and move on to gray, khaki or camel.

### ◉ Steps

1 Choose a jacket style. The two-button, single-breasted jacket is a popular style, but three- or four-button jackets are also available. Keep in mind that fashions change for men's clothing, just as they do for women's. Only thin men should wear formal double-breasted jackets, which add bulk to the figure. These should be kept buttoned at all times, as the jacket hangs awkwardly otherwise.

2 Select a fabric color and pattern. If you opt for a patterned fabric, check to see that patterns line up at shoulder and lapel seams.

3 Choose a suit fabric. High-quality worsted wool is the most seasonally versatile. Cotton and linen are good for summer wear. Avoid blends that are made with too much polyester, as they don't breathe well and may look cheap.

4 Crumple the fabric to make sure it bounces back instead of wrinkling, unless you've chosen a fabric that's meant to wrinkle, such as linen.

### ✳ Tips

Tall men should emphasize horizontal lines and avoid pinstripes. Double-breasted suits often flatter tall, thin men. Short men should consider single-breasted, shorter jackets in pinstripes or dark solids. Heavier men should also opt for pinstripes and avoid double-breasted suits.

When you buy a suit off the rack, you may have to take whichever pants come with the jacket. If this is the case, the jacket style, which is more noticeable, should take precedence over the pants style. Keep in mind that cuffs can be added to or removed from most pairs of pants.

5 Select a pants style. Pleats make pants dressy and provide room for movement, while flat-front pants are slimming. Cuffed legs are formal, add weight to the suit and can make the leg seem shorter; uncuffed pants elongate the leg and are more informal.

6 Test the jacket for fit. Make sure the collar lies flat against the back of your neck and shows a ¼-inch rim of shirt collar. Shoulders should be lightly padded and neither too boxy nor too sloped. Sleeves should reveal ¼ to ½ inch of shirt cuff and fall 5 inches above the tip of your thumb.

7 Button the jacket and sit down to verify that it is comfortable and doesn't bunch up.

8 Make sure the pants sit on the waist, not hips, and drape over and break slightly at the tops of your shoes. Check that your socks aren't visible when you walk.

Buying a jacket and pants separately will give you more style choices, and is a good approach if you need a special fit (if you have a large chest and a small waist, for example). It may be difficult to match the garments, though.

# Rent a Tuxedo 697

A tuxedo is customary for a trip down the aisle, opening night at the opera and other formal occasions. When renting a tux, plan ahead to ensure the proper fit and best selection.

## ⊙ Steps

1 Check the phone book for tuxedo-rental shops in your area. When renting for wedding attendants, look for stores with multiple locations or stores that will fit a tux based on measurements—this helps ensure a consistent look.

2 Visit your chosen store four to eight weeks prior to the event to have your measurements taken. Good sales associates measure around your chest (both including and excluding the width of your arms); your naked waist at belt height; your hip girth, including your seat; your neck circumference; and your sleeve length from the center of your back.

3 Consider cuts that complement your build and accommodate the formality of the occasion. In contrast to the rule for business suits, double-breasted tux jackets and those with wider lapels look great on a broad-chested, heavier-set man. A cropped jacket will elongate the height of a shorter man.

4 Prepare to pay between $100 and $150, excluding tax, for a rental that includes pants, jacket, shirt, tie, cummerbund, shirt buttons, cufflinks, socks and shoes. Prices vary depending on the cut and make of the tux, and on whether you want a vest, a special necktie, or fancier cufflinks and buttons. You usually leave a deposit when you have your measurements taken, and pay the balance before leaving with tux in hand.

5 Schedule a final fitting one week before the event. The rental price includes alterations—you may need a lift in the sleeve or a tuck in the waist to be dancing through the wee hours comfortably and in style.

6 Pay attention when the sales associate explains how to get dressed in a tux. You may find you're all thumbs with the special buttons, cufflinks, cummerbund and tie if you do not understand how to put them together.

## ✱ Tips

Rent from establishments that offer in-store inventory. Should you have any last-minute changes or additional needs, they can offer you an alternative.

A white bowtie and cummerbund paired with a coat and tails is the most formal choice, but a black bow tie and cummerbund are acceptable at any formal event.

## ⚠ Warnings

If you're coordinating tuxedo rentals as the best man, don't expect your groomsmen to remember all the dates and details about their rentals. It's a good Idea to confirm that they've hit all the deadlines for measurement submission and have made appointments for fittings.

If the store you're using doesn't have multiple locations, encourage out-of-town members of your wedding party to have measurements taken professionally at a tuxedo-rental store or tailor shop near them, then send the figures on to the store providing all the tuxes. Self-measurements can be very inaccurate.

7   Plan to return your tuxedo the day after your event, although some stores may give you a few additional days. You are seldom required to dry-clean the rental, but damages and excessively late returns will add to your final bill.

## 698 | Dress for a Cocktail Party—Men

Cocktail parties give you a chance to mingle among friends, acquaintances, and current and potential business associates. Look sharp and dress appropriately for the occasion.

### ⊙ Steps

1   Consider the type of invitation. If it came by phone or e-mail, chances are the party is casual. If you received a formal invitation, and especially if the event benefits a charity or association, consider it a dressier affair.

2   Think about the season. Wear lighter-weight fabrics and brighter colors for spring and summer get-togethers. Stick to dark, muted tones in heavier fabrics for fall and winter gatherings.

3   Dress up casual business attire for a more formal after-work cocktail party. Add a blazer to khaki pants and a button-down shirt, or pair a sport coat with black jeans and a black mock turtleneck. Switch sandals or athletic shoes for dark leather loafers or lace-up shoes.

4   Treat cocktail parties on weekend afternoons less formally than those scheduled in the evening. Go dressy business casual for a more formal late-afternoon gathering; opt for a suit in the evening. For a less formal event, wear a nice casual outfit in the afternoon and dressier business casual clothes in the evening.

### ✳ Tips

Athletic socks and shoes are inappropriate for a cocktail party. Shorts are also not advisable even on summer afternoons. Opt for lightweight pants in cotton or linen instead.

Check a formal invitation for terms like "semiformal" or "black-tie optional." If you see these indications, a suit and tie is your best option.

Coordinate your outfit with your date's.

## 699 | Dress for a Cocktail Party—Women

Cocktail parties are the perfect occasion for the famous little black dress (see 695 "Buy a Perfect Little Black Dress"). Whatever your attire, keep it dressy and elegant, but not too formal.

### ⊙ Steps

1   Think about your invitation. If it came by phone or e-mail, chances are it's a more casual affair. If you received a formal invitation, and especially if the event benefits a charity or association, consider it a dressier affair.

2   Choose dress and skirt lengths from mini to just above the ankles. Save anything resembling a full-length sequined gown for a different occasion.

3   Choose fabric according to the season. Wool and wool blends are perfect for fall and winter; satin, silk, rayon and fine-gauge knits are great for the spring and summer months. These materials can be dressed up or down with jewelry, handbags, shoes, wraps and hairstyles.

### ✳ Tips

Colors such as gray, crimson, black, dark brown and dark blue flatter for evening, fall and winter events. During the summer and spring, consider florals and seasonal shades like light pink, sky blue, pale green, pale yellow and other pastels.

Choose a dress that flatters your figure—don't squeeze into a dress that's too tight or low-cut.

4   Attend a more formal after-work party in a business suit, or if you wear more casual clothes to work, bring an outfit to change into. A black wool dress with stockings and pumps is a simple solution for fall or winter. Pair a strapless or spaghetti-strap dress with an embroidered cardigan and slingback pumps or strappy sandals for a spring or summer event.

5   Head to a more casual after-work gathering in a dressy-casual outfit. Pair a wool skirt with a fitted turtleneck and leather flats for winter parties. Consider a fine-knit twinset, slim satin pants and low-heeled mules in the summer.

6   Wear a printed A-line sundress to a cocktail party on a weekend afternoon. A party scheduled for a weekend evening warrants a more flirty or elegant ensemble. Pair a colorful satin or silk empire-waist dress with a velvet or silk shoulder wrap.

7   Accessorize. Show off your gold charm bracelet or favorite pair of dangling earrings. Match hair adornments and a handbag to the motif, material or colors in your outfit.

## Dress Business Casual—Men     `700`

Many businesses allow somewhat casual attire at least once a week, but dress codes vary. Here are some guidelines for dressing business casual, which is a notch below business formal.

### ⊙ Steps

1   Ask your human resources department for official guidelines. Business casual means different things at different companies. At a large corporation, it may mean a sport coat with a tie; at a smaller company, it may mean khakis and a polo shirt.

2   Before you go casual, check your daily planner to make sure you don't have any meetings that require formal business attire.

3   Select clean, pressed and wrinkle-free clothes. Your outfit should communicate professionalism.

4   Wear a collared shirt with an undershirt. You can break up the oxford shirt monotony by wearing a linen or flannel shirt or one with a band collar. Knitted shirts and polo shirts are also generally acceptable. A casual sport coat is appropriate.

5   Wear khakis, chinos, corduroys or other nondenim slacks. Check your company's policy before you decide to wear jeans to work.

6   Be sure to wear a belt, and have it match the color of your shoes.

7   Wear socks that match the color of your pants—leave white socks or tube socks in your gym bag.

8   Choose oxfords, loafers, or rubber-soled leather shoes or boots for casual day. Wingtips are often too formal. Worn-out shoes, sandals or athletic shoes don't make the grade.

### ✱ Tips

Observe what others are wearing to get an idea of what is acceptable, if your company has no written guidelines.

Your casual-day outfit should be formal enough that you can throw on a sport coat and meet a client.

### ⚠ Warning

Casual days generally do not include the option of not shaving.

## 701 | Dress Business Casual—Women

Women can often get away with a wider range of attire than men. Let comfort and professionalism guide you when you're dressing for business casual occasions.

### ⊙ Steps

1 Ask your human resources department for official guidelines. Business casual means different things at different companies. At a large corporation, it may mean slacks or a business skirt; at a smaller company, it may mean a cotton sweater and a floral skirt.

2 Before you go casual, check your daily planner to make sure you don't have any meetings that require formal business attire.

3 Select clean, wrinkle-free clothes.

4 Wear a good-quality blouse or knit shirt. Include a casual blazer or cardigan if appropriate.

5 Don pressed khakis or other slacks, or a dress or skirt. If a dress is sleeveless, wear a blazer or cardigan over it. Check your company's policy before you decide to wear jeans to work.

6 Wear shoes that are comfortable and appropriate for your outfit. Funky platform athletic shoes or strappy sandals might be formal enough for some companies; however, it's more typical to wear closed-toed leather shoes. Avoid worn-out shoes.

7 Keep the makeup light. Let your natural beauty shine through.

8 Accessorize with a silk scarf or classic bracelet to give your casual outfit a polished look.

### ✳ Tips

A basic pair of black slacks is a must for any work wardrobe.

Business casual attire is more formal than weekend wear. Faded T-shirts, shorts, torn clothing and risqué attire are not appropriate.

## 702 | Choose a High-Quality Garment

Check the quality of clothes before you spend your hard-earned money. The following is a quick rundown on the particulars of good craftsmanship.

### ⊙ Steps

#### Fabric and Stitching

1 Inspect fabrics to make sure patterns line up at the seams—especially at the shoulders, collar and sewn-on (patch) pockets.

2 Hold fabric up to the light and make sure the weave is tight, even and uniform, with no loose or undone threads. If the fabric has beads or sequins, make sure they're securely attached.

3 Check the grain of the fabric. The vertical grain should run straight up and down the garment, and the horizontal grain should run at a 90-degree angle to this line.

4 Crumple heavier fabric, such as wool, to see if it bounces back, either immediately or in several minutes, indicating resistance to wrinkling.

### ⚠ Warning

Take note of stains on a garment, particularly lipstick and other makeup marks around the neck area. If you notice a stain and still want to buy the item, find out if the store will dry clean it, or ask for a discount. Alternatively, find out if you can get a refund if you can't remove the stain at home.

5  Verify that all stitches are secure and straight. You should see about 8 to 12 stitches per inch.

6  Examine hems, which should be nearly invisible. Hemmed bottoms should hang straight and not curl or pucker.

## Other Details

1  Compare fabric lengths: Fold pants, shirts, skirts and other garments in half lengthwise to ensure that the right and left sides are symmetrical. Check that the right and left sides of the collar are equal in shape, size and positioning.

2  Confirm that patch pockets lie perfectly flat against the cloth, with no space between the pocket and the front of the garment. While holding the garment upright, make sure that the pocket doesn't hang away from the front.

3  Hold up clothing to ensure that the lining follows the cut of the garment, falls smoothly and does not extend below the hemline. In general, women's slacks are fully lined, while men's slacks are lined only in front to just below the knees.

4  Verify that buttons and buttonholes are sewn tightly, with no unraveled thread. In general, the more buttons a shirt has, the higher quality it is; spare buttons are an added plus.

5  Try on a shirt before buying it. Button it fully, making sure that buttons are placed well so that the shirt doesn't gape open across the chest.

6  Pull zippers up and down a few times to make sure that they run smoothly and don't snag.

---

## Choose High-Quality Shoes                                                   703

You don't have to spend a fortune to buy well-made shoes that fit comfortably—you just need to know what to look for.

### ⊙ Steps

#### Ensuring Fit

1  Ask a salesperson to measure both your feet, as right and left foot sizes often differ slightly.

2  Try on shoes with socks of appropriate thickness—bring nylons, dress socks or athletic socks, depending on the type of shoe you're thinking of buying.

3  Press on the shoe to locate your longest toe. You should feel at most a thumb's width between your longest toe and the end of the shoe.

4  Walk several paces with the shoes on and feel how they fit around your heels, insteps, balls and toes.

5  Make sure the shoe doesn't scrape against your anklebone.

6  Keep in mind that shoes should feel comfortable from the start; don't rely too much on "breaking them in" over time, despite what the salesperson may say.

### ✱ Tips

When deciding on shoe size, consider the shoe material's ability to stretch. For example, calfskin stretches more than do manufactured materials.

Shop for shoes in the late afternoon rather than the morning. Your feet may swell slightly over the course of the day.

Determining where the shoe is made can help you assess quality: Italian materials, design and assembly, for example, often indicate a shoe of high quality.

## Ensuring Quality

1   Examine the sole to make sure it is firmly attached to the shoe. Keep in mind that some soles are cemented to the upper shoe and others are stitched. Either type is acceptable, and some shoes (mainly men's shoes and athletic shoes) will be both cemented and stitched.

2   Check the heel. High-quality dress shoes have leather heels, sometimes with a layer of rubber or nylon on the back edge of the heel. Heels on high-heeled shoes for women are usually made of plastic and covered with leather. The higher the price, the higher quality the plastic.

3   Inspect the shoe's interior. Leather interiors absorb foot moisture best. Good-quality shoes are fully lined from front to back.

4   Consider the shoe material. Shoes with an oiled, natural finish are durable, while patent- and polished-leather shoes resist dirt. Suede shoes stain easily and need to be sprayed with a protectant.

5   Examine buckles and any adornments on the shoe. They should be securely attached and reinforced with even, smooth double stitching.

### ⚠ Warning

You should not find bits of glue anywhere on the shoe. This is especially true for athletic shoes.

---

## 704 | Buy a Diamond

Choosing a diamond involves more than a casual trip to the jewelry store. Armed with the proper knowledge, you can make an informed decision and a wise investment.

### ⊙ Steps

1   Decide how much you can spend. If you are buying an engagement ring, the general rule is two months' salary, but the sky's the limit if you're in pursuit of the perfect stone.

2   Choose the shape of diamond you prefer. Although the round, or brilliant, cut is most popular, diamonds come in many cuts, including oval, square or even heart-shaped.

3   Inspect the diamond's clarity (the degree of transparency). A "flawless" diamond, free from all inclusions or blemishes, is very rare. Other diamonds are rated on a clarity scale that grades diamonds from "flawless" to "obvious inclusions"—the higher the diamond's rating on this scale, the greater its value.

4   Examine the diamond's color. Although you may not generally think of diamonds as having color, some have a yellow, gray or brown cast. Pure, colorless diamonds are at the top of the color scale. Diamonds are also available in "fancy" colors such as red, blue or purple. These diamonds are rare and more expensive than the normal clear to yellow variety.

5   Examine the diamond's cut, which is crucial to the brilliance of the stone and a major factor in its value. A well-cut diamond reflects and disperses light in beautiful ways, thanks to qualities such as symmetry and depth (the bottom of the diamond shouldn't be too shallow or too deep). Diamonds are graded according to the cut quality, and this grade should carry a great deal of weight in your decision.

6   Determine the weight, which is measured in carats. The greater the carat weight, the more valuable the diamond. Keep in mind that since larger

### ✳ Tips

Inquire about a certificate from the Gemological Institute of America (GIA). The GIA, the largest impartial diamond-grading authority in the world, issues a grading report and details the diamond's specifications after examining it. Many stores keep the certificate on hand.

A nicked and scratched stone is almost certainly fake, but only a jeweler can detect some fakes. Have a questionable stone professionally appraised.

Buy from a jeweler who will guide you through the process. A good jeweler will help you assess how much you can spend, show you a wide selection of diamonds, and explain the four C's.

Buying a loose diamond gives you the option of designing a setting around the stone.

If you buy a ring band, opt for platinum or white gold: Metals other than yellow or rose gold enhance the brilliance of the diamond due to their color.

stones are more rare, two $\frac{1}{2}$-carat diamonds are less expensive than a single 1-carat diamond.

7   Compare several diamonds side by side and get a good idea of what you can find in your price range. No two diamonds are alike, so examine all of them carefully for their unique qualities.

8   Make your final decision based on which diamond offers the best combination of the four C's: clarity, color, cut and carat. Ignore any of these attributes, and you jeopardize your chances of getting the best diamond for your money.

### ⚠ Warning

Don't try to get the largest possible diamond for your money. This can mean overlooking quality in favor of size and ending up with an inferior stone. Balancing all factors is the best approach to choosing a quality diamond.

## Buy Pearls                                                                705

Versatile and classic, pearls are a worthwhile investment that can soften a business suit or add more elegance to a dress. Here's what to look for.

### ◉ Steps

### General Considerations

1   Decide whether you want natural, cultured or imitation pearls. Keep in mind that imitation pearls are costume jewelry and are of very little value; natural pearls are almost impossible to find in stores and often aren't as high in quality as cultured pearls.

2   Choose a pearl shape: round, symmetrical or baroque and/or irregular. Spherelike round pearls are the most expensive and highly prized. Symmetrical pearls, such as those shaped like teardrops, should be evenly shaped.

3   Consider pearl size, the most important factor in price. The larger the pearl, the costlier it will be.

4   Decide if you want a double-strand necklace of smaller pearls (cheaper) or a single strand of larger pearls (more expensive).

5   Place pearls directly under a light on a flat, white surface in order to inspect them.

6   Inspect each pearl for luster. Lustrous pearls have a shiny surface, good contrast between light and dark areas, and strong, crisp reflections. Avoid pearls that resemble dull, cloudy white beads.

7   Look at the pearl's "orient," a play of iridescent rainbow colors—characteristic of high-quality pearls.

8   Examine pearl color, which can be white, yellow, black, gray or various other colors. Ask whether the color is natural or dyed; the latter is less expensive. More exotic natural colors are more expensive.

9   Inspect the pearl's "overtone," a tint secondary to the main body color. Pinkish overtones can increase pearl price, while green or blue tints may lower the price.

10  Verify the pearl's cleanliness by checking that it has minimal surface blemishes such as nicks, cracks, pits or discoloration.

### ✱ Tips

Natural pearls, which are rare and valuable, form when oysters reflexively coat a foreign particle with nacre. Cultured pearls start off with an artificially implanted bead nucleus that triggers the same response in the oyster. Imitation pearls are composed of glass or plastic.

The only certain way to distinguish between a natural and a cultured pearl is to have the pearl X-rayed.

If you're buying a pearl necklace, it should have a knot between each pearl to hold the necklace together in case the string breaks.

Compare a pearl with others in the same strand. Verify that pearls within a strand match in color, tint and size. Comparing one strand of pearls with another might help you assess luster and color more accurately.

### ⚠ Warning

Pearls offered at unbelievably low prices are probably fake.

11  Turn the pearl in your hands to examine it from all angles. Color, shape, smoothness and luster all may vary within a single pearl. Roll a strand of pearls on a flat surface to test them for roundness—round pearls roll more smoothly and evenly.

## Distinguishing Real Pearls From Imitations

1  Run the pearl lightly along the biting edge of your front teeth. A real pearl will feel slightly gritty or sandy, whereas a fake pearl will feel smooth. This is a standard test for authenticity that most sellers will allow, as long as you ask first.

2  Look at and feel the pearl. Absolutely flawless-looking pearls, as well as those that feel unusually light when you bounce them in your hands, are probably fake.

3  Examine the pearl under a 10× magnifier (a loupe). Imitation pearls appear grainy.

---

## 706 | Clean Jewelry

Before cleaning your jewelry, examine it carefully to make sure that all settings, clasps and prongs are secure. Once you've done that, you're ready to proceed.

### ◎ Steps

#### Gold, Platinum and Gemstones

1  Use a nonabrasive jewelry cleaner, which you can purchase at a local jewelry store. Or use a cleaning solution of mild dish soap and water.

2  Dip the jewelry in the cleaner or cleaning solution.

3  Rinse in warm running water.

4  Buff dry with a soft, lint-free cloth until it's shiny.

#### Silver

1  Clean the silver with a nonabrasive silver polish.

2  Apply the polish with a soft cloth, gently working it into stains.

3  Wipe away excess polish and buff the jewelry with a soft, lint-free cloth until it's shiny.

4  Keep in mind that frequently wearing silver jewelry can keep it from becoming tarnished.

### ✳ Tips

Store jewelry carefully to avoid damage. Sturdy cases with partitioned, soft interiors protect and organize items.

Jewelers recommend having jewelry professionally cleaned at least once a year.

### ⚠ Warnings

Do not use jewelry cleaner on pearls and porous stones, such as emeralds, rubies, lapis lazuli, coral and turquoise. Wipe them clean with a soft, damp cloth or have them cleaned professionally. Consult a jeweler when in doubt about a particular stone.

Exposure to perfume, cosmetics or perspiration can stain gemstones.

# ✓ 707 Buy a Gemstone

When you're shopping for jewelry set with precious or semiprecious stones, it pays to buy from a reputable and trusted jeweler. Here are a few guidelines for judging quality; also see 704 "Buy a Diamond" and 705 "Buy Pearls."

| | CUT OR SHAPE | COLOR | CLARITY | ADDITIONAL NOTES |
|---|---|---|---|---|
| **Amethyst** | Comes in a variety of cuts. | Deeper purple stones are more valuable. | Look for perfect clarity with no visible flaws. | The regal purple color is purported to ward off drunkenness and is prized in the crowns of royalty. |
| **Aquamarine** | Comes in a variety of cuts. | Dark blue stones are more valuable; those with green less so. | Make sure the gem is free of flaws or inclusions. | Said to be a favorite of mermaids and a protection against evil, fear and marital discord. |
| **Emerald** | The rectangular step-cut—or "emerald cut"—is most popular. | Color should be a deep, vivid green. | Although perfect clarity makes an emerald exceptionally valuable, some inclusions may be acceptable as long as they are not so deep as to weaken the stone. | The emerald is a symbol of love, rebirth and youth. |
| **Garnet** | Many garnets are quite small, but larger ones can be cut in a variety of shapes, including hearts. | The rarest and most valuable are of the green demantoid variety. Pink and red rhodolite garnets are among the most popular. | The light should reflect evenly off the surface. Check for obvious flaws and inclusions. | Most garnets are reasonably priced. They are said to protect travelers from harm and sleepers from nightmares. |
| **Ruby** | Rubies are usually cut in an oval shape; other shapes are available. | The best stones are pure red with a fiery intensity. The center of the stone should not appear dark. | You will see no inclusions in a perfect, transparent ruby. The star-shaped highlights of star rubies result from tiny inclusions. | Because large rubies are so scarce, you may not be able to find a stone larger than five carats. |
| **Sapphire** | Oval shapes are popular, but sapphires come in a variety of cuts. | The most valuable sapphires are deep, pure royal blue, although sapphires come in a range of colors. Valuable "color-change" stones have different hues in natural and artificial light. | Hold the stone face up and be sure the light reflects evenly. There should be no scratches, and the center of the stone should not appear dark. | Sapphires can be heated to give them a better color and clarity. It is estimated that more than 90 percent of those on the market have undergone this process, which does not affect value. |
| **Topaz** | Topaz can be cut into a variety of shapes. | The rarest topaz is light pink or red. Other colors include yellow, brown, green, blue and peach. | Be sure the stone has no visible flaws or inclusions. It should reflect light evenly when held face up and should not show any scratches. | Clear topaz can also be irradiated to become blue. Topaz treated this way is more affordable than the rare blue topaz found in nature. |
| **Turquoise** | Turquoise can be cut into a variety of shapes. | The most valuable turquoise is pure blue without any greenish cast. The presence of veins is a matter of personal taste. | Check the condition of the stone. It should have no chips or fractures. | Turquoise is fairly soft, so it often is coated with acrylic resin to make it more resilient. |

chart

## 708 | Sew On a Button

Don't let that shirt or sweater that has lost a button gather dust in the fix-it pile; a few minutes of handiwork with a needle and thread can put it back in your regular rotation.

### ⊙ Steps

1 Select a button if you don't have the original. Look inside the seam or lining for the extra button that manufacturers sometimes include, or buy one that closely matches the size and color of the other buttons.

2 Choose thread that matches either the thread color used on the other buttons, the color of the button or the color of the material.

3 Cut a piece of thread about 1/2 yard long (approximately finger to elbow).

4 Thread the needle, feeding the thread through the eyehole. Moisten the thread with your tongue first to stiffen it and make this easier.

5 Move the needle to the middle of the thread and fold the thread in half. Tie a knot at the end of the thread, where both ends meet. Tie another knot so that you've double-secured the end. You're ready to sew.

6 Place the button on top of the material where you intend to sew it into place. You can put a match or toothpick between the button and the material to give the thread the necessary slack.

7 Push the needle up from under the material through one of the holes on the button. Pull the thread all the way through until you've anchored the knot against the material.

8 Push the needle down through the next hole on the button and through the material.

9 Repeat steps 7 and 8 three times, going up through the material and then down through the button and material, so that you've secured each hole with multiple strands.

10 End with the needle on the material side. Stitch through the material only and up again, forming a knot against the material with the needle and thread. Do this twice, forming two knots against the material to ensure that your button will stay secure. Snip off the remaining thread.

### ✱ Tip

Your button may have two or four buttonholes, or it may be the kind of button you attach from underneath via a shank—you follow approximately the same steps in either case. For four-hole buttons, you can crisscross the thread to form an X on the top of the button, or you can go straight across the top of the button to form two lines. Use whichever pattern matches the thread on the other buttons.

### Things You'll Need

❏ button

❏ thread

❏ scissors

❏ needle

## 709 | Darn a Sock

You can use the darning technique to repair small holes in socks and other clothing. With a darning needle and yarn, you'll form a network of stitches across the gap.

### ⊙ Steps

1 Find thread or yarn that matches the sock in color and texture; you can use embroidery floss (a type of thread) to repair a crew sock, while wool yarn is appropriate for a wool sock. Choose a darning needle as well.

2 Place a lightbulb in the sock and position the hole over the lightbulb. Your needle will glide smoothly over the bulb's surface, making your stitching go faster.

### ✱ Tips

Use a darning needle for your repairs. The eye of this needle is large enough to accommodate a thicker yarn.

Sew a running stitch by bringing the needle up through the fabric, then down again, then up again. Space stitches evenly.

3   Thread the darning needle with the yarn or thread and leave the end unknotted. The darning process should create a tight weave that makes knots unnecessary.

4   Start your work on either side of the hole. Take several small vertical running stitches in the intact fabric of the sock, about 1/2 inch to the left or right of the hole. Turn the sock upside down and make another row of stitches next to the first.

5   Increase the number of running stitches you make as you come closer to the hole. When you reach the point at which the hole begins, your stitching line should extend from 1/2 inch above the hole to 1/2 inch below it.

6   Continue making vertical running stitches. When your stitching reaches the hole, take your thread or yarn over the hole and into the fabric on the other side, forming what resembles a vertical bridge over the hole. Stitching should extend 1/2 inch beyond the hole at both the top and bottom edges.

7   Cut the thread end once you have covered the hole with vertical threads and extended the stitching 1/2 inch past it so that both sides of the hole look identical.

8   Thread your darning needle and begin your work 1/2 inch from either side of the hole at either the top or bottom. Take the threaded needle and weave it under and over the vertical threads that cover the hole (as well as the vertical threads that lie within 1/2 inch of the hole).

9   Turn the sock upside down once you reach the opposite end of the hole, and weave another yarn strand next to the first. Continue stitching back and forth until you've completely filled the hole. Trim excess thread.

Lay both your running-stitch lines and crosswise threads as close together as possible to create a tight weave.

You can replace the lightbulb with another round, smooth object of similar dimensions, such as a hard plastic ball.

## Things You'll Need

❑ thread, yarn or embroidery floss

❑ lightbulb

❑ darning needle

❑ scissors

---

## Hem Pants     `710`

Whether you're tailoring new clothes or adapting hand-me-downs, you'll want to get the hem right.

### ◉ Steps

1   Select thread that matches the color and thickness of the thread used in the original hem.

2   Use small scissors or a seam ripper to undo the existing hem carefully.

3   Try on the pants and fold each pant leg inward to the length that looks correct for the new hem. Pin it in place.

4   Take off the pants, turn them inside out, and use a tape measure or ruler to determine the length of the fabric folded inward to form the new hem length. Use this measurement as your gauge for folding the pant legs all the way around.

5   Measure and pin the new hem length into place on both legs according to the measurement you just made.

6   Iron the edge of the new hem on both legs to create a good crease. (If you want to hide the unfinished edge of the fabric to prevent fraying, fold it approximately 1/4 inch toward the inside of the pant leg and iron it in place.)

### ✱ Tips

Try on pants with the appropriate shoes and hem accordingly.

With lined pants, the lining is typically hemmed slightly shorter than the pants.

### Things You'll Need

❑ thread

❑ pins

❑ tape measure or ruler

❑ small scissors or a seam ripper

❑ needle

❑ iron and ironing board

7  Try on your pants after you have pinned and ironed the new hem, to ensure that both legs match in length. If the original pant length was excessive, you may need to trim some fabric before securing the hem.

8  Sew the hem into place by hand, lightly catching a few threads on the inside of the garment to avoid having the stitches show on the outside, and forming one line equidistant from the edge of the leg.

## 711 | Iron Pants

**Almost all pants, aside from jeans, require ironing.**

### ⊙ Steps

1  Turn the pants inside out. Look for the tag that gives ironing and fabric information for the garment.

2  Choose the heat setting on your iron appropriate for that fabric. Linen and 100 percent cotton take a high setting; wools and cotton blends call for medium heat; polyester, rayon, nylon, silk, acetate and acrylic all require a low heat setting.

3  Fill the iron with distilled water if you will be using the steam setting on cottons or linens.

4  Test the iron on a small area to make sure you don't have the setting too high—this can damage or discolor the fabric.

5  With the pants still inside out, iron the waistband, pockets (on both sides), fly area, seams and hems, in that order.

6  Turn the pants right side out and pull the waistband over the pointed end of the board. Iron the waistband area and any pleats along the front of the pants below the waistband.

7  Lay the pants lengthwise along the ironing board with both legs together and carefully line up any preexisting creases.

8  Take the hem of the top pant leg and bring it toward the waistband, folding the top leg away from the bottom leg. Iron the inside (hem to crotch) of the lower leg. Turn the pants over and repeat for the other leg.

9  Smooth out both legs carefully and iron the outside of the top leg. Give extra attention to cuffs, if the pants have them.

10  Turn the pants over and iron the outside of the other leg.

11  Hang warm pants immediately to avoid wrinkling. Fold them through a suit hanger to avoid crushing them in a pant hanger.

### ✱ Tips

The material in many suits can become shiny with too much ironing. You can avoid this by placing a clean cotton cloth over the area before ironing it.

Avoid spot-cleaning pants just before ironing. Any wet spots may become permanent stains if ironed.

### ⚠ Warning

Irons are very hot and heavy; avoid ironing when small children are near, and never leave a hot iron unattended.

## Iron a Shirt                                                        712

Even so-called no-iron shirts often require ironing—but if you learn to do it yourself, you'll save enough on laundry bills to buy several more.

### ⊙ Steps

1   Locate the tag on your shirt that indicates the materials that were used in the garment.

2   Plug in the iron and set the dial to the recommended setting for that fabric. Linen and 100 percent cotton take a high setting; wools and cotton blends call for medium heat; polyester, rayon, nylon, silk, acetate and acrylic all require a low heat setting.

3   Fill the iron with distilled water if you will be using the steam setting on cottons or linens.

4   Test the iron on a small area to make sure you don't have the setting too high—this can damage or discolor the fabric.

5   Iron the back of the collar first, then the front, taking care to iron in from the edges a little at a time to avoid creases.

6   Open the cuffs fully. Iron inside first, then outside.

7   Iron the sleeves after smoothing them flat to avoid creases. Do the sleeve backs first, the fronts second.

8   Hang the shirt over the board so that you can extend one front panel of the shirt flat (with the collar at the narrower end of the board). Iron from shoulder to shirttail.

9   Rotate the shirt over the board so that you iron the back next, and the other front panel last.

### ✱ Tips

Hang your warm shirt on a hanger immediately to avoid rewrinkling it.

If you'll be wearing a buttoned jacket all day and are short of time, you need only iron the collar, sleeves and top of the front. If you'll be wearing a sweater all day, iron only the collar.

### ⚠ Warning

Irons are very hot and heavy; avoid ironing when small children are near, and never leave a hot iron unattended.

## Prepare Your Clothes for Dry Cleaning              713

Distressed about the stain you found on your favorite silk blouse? You can take several steps to ensure that your dry cleaner gets the best results possible.

### ⊙ Steps

1   Keep care tags or labels on garments.

2   Do not wash, dry or iron in stains if you know you are going to take the item to the cleaners anyway.

3   Avoid pretreating stains, especially those on delicate fabrics and on clothes that are dry-clean only. You'll get best results when you leave these stains untouched and bring the item in immediately.

4   Include a note that explains the source of the stain and how long it's been there. Better yet, explain this to the cleaner personally.

5   Empty pockets of makeup, change and other items at home.

### ✱ Tips

Dry cleaners are professionals, but some stains lie beyond even their cleaning capabilities.

Fabrics that generally require dry cleaning include silk, wool, linen and rayon.

6    Notify dry cleaners ahead of time of any preexisting tears or damage. Otherwise, they might not clean your garment for fear you'll think they caused the damage.

## 714 | Do Laundry

Has a parent, spouse or someone else determined that it's time you did your own laundry? You'll soon discover it's a snap to clean your own clothes.

### ◉ Steps

1    Sort your clothes, making separate piles for whites, bright colors and darks. If you mix whites with colors in the wash, the colors may bleed onto and ruin your whites. Also separate clothes that tend to produce lint (towels, sweatshirts, chenille and flannel) from clothes that tend to attract lint (corduroy, velvets and permanent-press clothes).

2    As you sort, close zippers to prevent snagging, and empty pockets (you don't want soggy shreds of facial tissue all over your clothes!).

3    Pretreat heavy stains with laundry detergent or stain remover, heeding instructions on the product label.

4    Use the measuring cap of the detergent bottle or the cup found in detergent boxes to measure according to the manufacturer's instructions.

5    Pour the soap into your washer or its detergent dispenser. Add liquid fabric softener, if desired, according to the product instructions.

6    Choose the water temperature for the wash cycle—hot, warm or cold; save on energy and opt for a cold rinse cycle for any load. Consult the labels on your clothes, your washing machine's instruction manual or the detergent container for recommendations. In general, use cold water to protect colors and darks from bleeding or fading, and to avoid shrinkage. Use warm or hot water for durable fabrics like cotton (make sure they're preshrunk), and to ensure that your whites stay white.

7    Start the washer before adding clothes, if you have time, to allow the detergent to dissolve in the water. The regular cycle suffices for most clothes, but use the gentle cycle for sheer or delicate fabrics. Adjust the water level to the size of your load.

8    If you need to add bleach, allow the machine to run for a few minutes to mix the detergent and water, then add about a cup of bleach to the washer or the bleach dispenser.

9    Add your clothes, close the lid and let the machine do its dirty work.

10   Put the clothes (and an anti-static sheet, if desired) in the dryer after the wash is complete. Hang delicates (such as bras and certain sweaters) to air dry. Check tags if in doubt.

11   Remove lint from the dryer's lint tray and then turn on the dryer.

12   Once the clothes are completely dry, remove them from the dryer or drying rack and fold them.

### ✳ Tips

If you stuff too many clothes into the washer, it won't clean them very well.

Handle bleach carefully. Avoid splashing it directly onto clothes or yourself.

### ⚠ Warning

Remember that you should typically dry-clean some fabrics—silk, wool, linen and rayon, for example. You should hand-wash lingerie in the sink to preserve delicate lace and other elements.

### Things You'll Need

☐ stain remover

☐ laundry detergent

☐ fabric softener

☐ bleach

☐ anti-static sheets

# ✓ 715 Remove Stains From Clothing

The first step in removing a stain is to know what caused it. There are several basic categories of stains, each requiring a different treatment. Use the reference below to guide you in identifying and treating the stain. Once you've run the stain through the wash, make sure it's completely gone before throwing the garment in the dryer; otherwise the heat could set it permanently. If you are at all in doubt about how to treat a stain, take the stained article to a dry cleaner for professional advice.

## Protein stains

Caused by protein foods such as meats, milk and eggs, as well as by blood, urine, feces, grass and perspiration.

- If a urine stain is still wet, cover it with salt until all the liquid is absorbed. Rinse. If the stain remains, use white vinegar or hydrogen peroxide.

- Soak the garment before washing, using an enzyme presoak product according to instructions on the product label.

- Wash in cold water if you are dealing with blood stains.

- Do not use chlorine bleach to treat protein stains.

## Grease stains

Caused by cooking oil, butter, margarine, mayonnaise, motor oil and cosmetics.

- Use a prewash stain remover as soon as possible after the stain occurs.

- If you're using a spray or liquid pretreatment product, launder the garment as usual immediately after treating it.

- If you're using a stick or gel product, let the garment sit for as long as a week before laundering.

- If the stain remains, pretreat and launder again.

## Tannin stains

Caused by coffee, tea, ketchup, juice, wine, chocolate and soft drinks.

- If you can treat a red wine stain immediately after a spill, cover the spot with salt to absorb the liquid. Then soak it in cold water.

- If you have a chocolate stain, use an enzyme treatment before washing.

- Use chlorine bleach if that's safe for the fabric. If it's not, soak in oxygen bleach and launder in the hottest water safe for the fabric.

- Check that the stain is gone; if not, repeat the treatment.

## Miscellaneous stains

- To remove mustard, treat with a prewash stain remover, then use chlorine bleach. If that's not safe for the fabric, use oxygen bleach, which is milder.

- If you're removing chewing gum, rub it with ice to harden it. Then scrape off as much as possible with a dull knife. Treat with stain remover and wash.

- For ink stains, apply denatured alcohol to the stain using a clean cotton swab. Wash the fabric as usual.

- To remove nail polish, use nail polish remover; rinse, then launder. If the fabric is acetate or triacetate, treat with glycerin, then take to a dry cleaner.

reference

## 716 | Wash a Cashmere Sweater

Instead of sending your cashmere sweater to the dry cleaner, wash it! Many people don't realize that cashmere can be hand-washed, and that such care will prolong the life of the garment.

### ⊙ Steps

1   Buy a detergent specifically intended for fine garments.

2   Fill your sink or basin with lukewarm or cool water, depending on the garment's washing instructions. Add the recommended amount of fine-garment detergent to the basin.

3   Briskly run your hand through the water to distribute the detergent and generate suds.

4   Submerge the sweater and gently squeeze the suds through it.

5   Let it soak for 20 minutes.

6   Drain the sink and rinse your sweater with lukewarm water until the water rinses clear.

7   Gently press water out of the sweater and place it lengthwise on a clean, dry bath towel.

8   Roll up the towel. Press with your palms to squeeze out excess water.

9   Remove the sweater from the towel and smooth it out so it is back in its original shape.

10  Lay the sweater flat on a dry towel and let it air dry, or use a drying rack if you have one.

### ✻ Tip

Dry-cleaning cashmere is also a viable option. However, as cashmere is a delicate fiber, excess chemical treatments may shorten your sweater's life.

### ⚠ Warnings

Wringing out your sweater may pull it out of shape.

Sunlight can fade your sweater, and other heat sources may wear fibers prematurely. It's better to let your sweater dry naturally indoors, away from sunny windows and heat vents.

### Things You'll Need

☐ fine-garment detergent

☐ towel

## 717 | Shine Shoes

Want to keep your shoes looking as good as new? Learn how to shine them like a pro.

### ⊙ Steps

1   Clean dust and dirt from the surface of your shoes or boots with a shoeshine brush or damp cloth.

2   Select a wax or cream shoe polish that matches the leather's color.

3   Use a shoe-polish brush (a small, soft brush that's distinct from the large, bristly shoeshine brush) to apply a conservative amount of polish to the surface of the leather. Brush in circular motions until the leather has a dull coating. Get into tight spots using an old soft-bristled toothbrush.

4   Wait up to 15 minutes, or until the polish completely or nearly dries, depending on the instructions for the polish.

5   Brush the shoes or boots with a shoeshine brush.

6   Buff them to a gleaming shine with a clean cotton cloth, such as an old sock or T-shirt.

### ✻ Tips

Don't polish suede or patent leather.

"Instant" or "EZ" shoe polishes generally do not last and can harm shoe leather.

Don't attempt to change the color of leather with polish. Have a shoemaker dye the shoes.

## Clean Athletic Shoes  `718`

Being busy is no excuse for having dirty, smelly sneakers. These instructions work for athletic shoes of various materials.

### ⊙ Steps

1 Prepare a solution of water and a neutral cleaner (such as liquid dishwashing detergent or another mild product).

2 Remove laces and inserts and rinse the shoes with water inside and out.

3 Use a soft brush and the cleaning solution to scrub every part of both shoes, including liners and insoles.

4 Remove scuff marks with a white nylon-backed scrub pad.

5 Rinse the shoes thoroughly with water.

6 Stuff the shoes with paper (not newspaper—the ink will run and make a mess) to absorb excess water and to help the shoes keep their shape. Allow them to drip-dry.

7 Wash the laces in a load of laundry. Allow the inserts to air out, and apply baking soda to them if they're smelly.

8 Replace the inserts and laces after the shoes dry completely.

9 Apply white cream shoe polish to white leather parts and black polish to black leather parts.

### ✻ Tips

Many athletic-shoe retailers sell special shoe-cleaning kits for use with specific brands and models.

If your athletic shoes will hold up through the cycle, run them through your washing machine to get them clean.

### Things You'll Need

❑ liquid dishwashing detergent or other mild cleaner

❑ soft brush

❑ white nylon-backed scrub pads

❑ paper

❑ white or black cream shoe polish

---

## Prevent Shoe Odor  `719`

Bacteria, which thrive in moist, dark areas, cause foot odor. It is essential to keep your feet and shoes clean and aired out to prevent shoe odor from occurring.

### ⊙ Steps

1 Wash your feet thoroughly with antibacterial soap, and scrub between your toes. Dry your feet completely after washing.

2 Apply antiperspirants to your feet to control moisture if your feet sweat excessively. Use antiperspirants specifically designed for feet rather than underarm products. You can also apply antibacterial gels to your feet to control bacterial growth, or antifungal powder to prevent athlete's foot.

3 Wear absorbent socks, such as cotton, and avoid nylon socks, which don't absorb sweat very well. Change socks once or twice a day if your feet sweat a lot.

4 Wear shoes that breathe, such as sandals or shoes made from mesh and canvas. Allowing your feet to air out reduces bacterial growth.

5 Avoid wearing shoes two days in a row—let them air out for 24 hours between uses.

6 Remove the insoles and allow them to air out for 24 hours after an excessively sweaty day, or if your shoes get wet.

### ✻ Tips

If fashion dictates that you wear your shoes without socks, shake in a bit of talcum powder to absorb sweat.

If your shoes ever get drenched on a rainy day, let them dry completely before wearing them again.

### Things You'll Need

❑ antibacterial soap

❑ foot antiperspirant

❑ antibacterial gel

❑ antifungal powder

❑ absorbent socks

7    Wash your shoes, if appropriate, making sure to dry them thoroughly. If your shoes are not washable, replace the insoles every few months or even more frequently, and put baking powder in them to absorb odors. You can also try special odor-reducing sprays and inserts.

8    If you have a severe problem with foot odor, consult a doctor to get prescription medicine that controls bacterial growth and perspiration.

---

## 720 | Control Perspiration

Perspiration, or sweating, is your body's way of regulating its temperature and responding to stress. But it can also lead to foul odors and damp clothing.

### ⊙ Steps

1    Use a product that contains both deodorant and antiperspirant. The deodorant only helps control odors, whereas the antiperspirant helps block sweat.

2    Sprinkle cornstarch or talcum powder in problem areas to absorb moisture.

3    Dress in layers so you can control your temperature, thereby reducing your body's need to sweat. Wear a white or light-colored hat to reflect sunlight on hot days, since your head is an important temperature-control point on the body.

4    Wear natural fabrics such as wool, silk and cotton that allow air to circulate around your body easily.

5    Drink plenty of fluids and stay fit. Fluids and a fit body help regulate your temperature and reduce sweating.

6    Relax as much as possible using regulated breathing, yoga or meditation. This can reduce stress, a perspiration trigger.

**✳ Tip**

Cotton socks and foot antiperspirants can minimize foot sweat. (see 719 "Prevent Shoe Odor"). Cotton panties help to prevent sweating, too.

**⚠ Warning**

If you perspire even when you're relaxed and the temperature is cool, see your doctor—it could be a sign of an underlying health problem.

---

## 721 | Find the Perfect Fit in a Bra

Whether you choose a bra to enhance, minimize, support or show off your bust, fit is crucial—it's the key to keeping you comfortable and supporting your breasts properly.

### ⊙ Steps

1    Use a measuring tape to measure around your bare rib cage, just beneath your naked breasts. Add either 4 or 5 inches to this number to bring it up to an even-numbered measurement. This number indicates the band size most appropriate for your figure.

2    Measure the widest part of your bust, sliding the tape around the middle of your back. Hold the tape as level as possible to ensure accuracy.

3    Note the difference between the two measurements. Use the following as a guide, and try on a range of sizes above and below your measurement: If your bust measurement is up to 1/2 inch larger than your band

**✳ Tips**

Remember that all bras are not made equal. Experiment to find the brand or style that best suits your figure.

Wash bras by hand, or in the delicate cycle of a washing machine in a mesh bag. Avoid shrinkage and prolong life by hanging bras to air-dry instead of machine-drying them.

size, then your cup size is an AA. A measurement of ½ inch to 1 inch more than the band size indicates an A cup, 1 to 2 inches indicates a B cup, 2 to 3 inches indicates a C cup, 3 to 4 inches indicates a D cup, and 4 to 5 inches indicates a DD or E cup.

4   Select a range of bras according to your band and cup size.

5   Try on a bra. Place your hands through the straps and bend over to allow your breasts to fall into the cups. The cups should contain your breasts—unless you're trying a demibra or an enhancing bra—and should center your nipple in the fullest part.

6   Close the bra using the middle hook. Look for a band that fits snugly but doesn't cut into your rib cage. If it's too tight, try adjusting the hook closure before proceeding to a larger size.

7   Adjust the straps so the band fits comfortably under the breasts and around the rib cage. If the bra seems to slip forward, if you find yourself pulling up on the straps, or if it feels as if your breasts are falling out of the bottom of the cups, the band size is too big.

8   Check the fabric or bridge between your breasts. This should lie flat on the breastbone. If it sticks up or stabs your breastbone uncomfortably, try a larger cup size. If it puckers, try a smaller size.

9   Move up a cup size if your breasts bulge from the bra. Move down a size if you notice wrinkles in the cup material.

## Choose a Flattering Swimsuit 722

A flattering swimsuit makes the most of the proportions of a woman's figure. It's all about a careful mixing of color, print, and the right lines and silhouette.

### ◎ Steps

1   Use blocks of color to divert attention from wide hips or a belly bulge. Wear one-piece suits with a dark-colored, solid lower half and a lighter-colored or printed bodice.

2   Choose suits with at least 15 percent spandex to minimize flabby areas. If you have wide hips, opt for styles that cut across the hips rather than hanging below them.

3   Enhance a small chest with a lightly padded halter top or a demi cut with an underwire; the demi cut resembles a bra, but it's not a full cup. Also look for suits that offer texture, like ruffles or smocking, and material with a small print—these are guaranteed to deflect attention from your bust.

4   Minimize a full chest with a dark, monochromatic bodice that has a high or square-cut neck. Make sure the suit offers your bust ample support to resist drooping or sagging, and choose a wider-cut bottom to balance your overall look.

5   Elongate a petite frame with a one-piece suit that has thin vertical stripes. Lend short legs length with a suit cut high on the hip.

6   Give a square or boyish figure the appearance of a waist with a one-piece or tankini (a bikini with a top shaped like a tank top) that has a

### ✳ Tips

Nowadays, you can essentially create your own two-piece suit. Look for companies that offer a variety of mix-and-match, coordinated tops and bottoms.

Wear your swimsuit with a long sleeveless blouse, print sarong or wraparound skirt if the thought of walking around in your swimsuit makes you uncomfortable.

### ⚠ Warning

You generally can't return bathing suits. Check restrictions prior to purchase.

darker color from the crotch to the middle ribs and a lighter color over the chest. Consider a skort—a combination short and skirt—to conceal and divert attention away from a too-round bottom.

7   If you have toned legs and sexy shoulders, flaunt them in a string bikini or cutout one-piece swimsuit.

## 723 Choose Sunglasses

Sunglasses not only look fashionable, but they also help protect your eyes from the harmful rays of the sun.

### ⊙ Steps

1   Check labels to make sure the sunglasses provide 100 percent UVA and UVB protection.

2   Look for sunglasses that filter out at least some blue light, which can damage the retina and lead to macular degeneration (vision loss from degeneration in parts of the eye). To make sure, try wearing them outside; a blue sky should appear gray with these on. Also ask about polarization, a type of filtering that helps reduce glare.

3   Choose a lens color based on your preferences and comfort level. Gray doesn't affect color perception; orange-brown lenses are a good choice for those with macular degeneration, since they filter out UV and blue light rays for maximum retinal protection; green lenses distort color less than other shades, such as red or yellow.

4   Opt for lightweight, plastic, shatterproof sunglasses if you're going to be wearing them when playing sports.

5   Purchase sun goggles for total protection of your eyes. These cover a large area and include side shields. As an added bonus, they also fit over prescription glasses.

### ✱ Tips

A darker lens does not necessarily indicate better protection, and lighter-tinted lenses offer better visibility. Check labels to find sunglasses that provide the best protection possible.

To ensure against mislabeling, you may want to purchase a UV card, a credit card–size device for testing sunglasses. Contact an optometrist, or look for the product online.

For added eye protection, wear a hat with at least a 3-inch brim.

## 724 Choose Flattering Eyeglass Frames

Glasses these days have a dual purpose: They improve your vision, and they serve as a fashion accessory that can enhance, rather than detract from, your looks.

### ⊙ Steps

1   Pull your hair back in a ponytail (if necessary) and inspect your face shape in front of the mirror.

2   Keep in mind that oval faces are egg-shaped and balanced on top and bottom, and can support any type of frame.

3   Make a long, thin face seem wider and shorter with larger frames in round or triangular shapes. Or try a wide, rectangular shape. Frames that have color, width or embellishment near the sides will also broaden your face.

### ✱ Tips

Make sure that your eyes are positioned in the middle of the lens. If your eyes are close-set, avoid large frames.

Your eyebrows should align with the top bar of your glasses.

Avoid wearing frames that have shapes similar to your face, as a general rule. In other words, don't wear round frames if you

**How to Do** *(Just About)* **Everything**

4   Try round frames made of thin metal to soften the angular look of a square face, which has a wide forehead and cheeks, and an angular chin.

5   Remember that round faces are fuller, with a gentle chin, wide cheeks and small cheekbones. Avoid round frames, which make the face look larger; wear boxy or rectangular ones instead. Dark frames can weigh down your face, making it appear heavier.

6   Balance a heart-shaped face, which has a wide forehead that angles down to a small chin, with frames that are wider at the bottom than at the top.

7   Flatter a diamond-shaped face, which has a narrow forehead, wide temples and an angular chin, by wearing small frames in geometric or oval shapes to minimize the horizontal distance between your temples.

8   Choose smaller frames if you have facial hair such as a beard. Large frames will further mask your features.

9   Stick with small frames if you have a small head. Make sure your glasses aren't any wider than the widest part of your face.

10  Select large frames that fit comfortably if you have a large head. Avoid glasses that appear to squeeze your face or temples.

have a round face. Rather, choose frames in a different cut from your face shape.

## Choose a Hairstylist                                    **725**

**Finding a good hairstylist may take some searching, but it's worth the time investment to locate the right one for your look and hair.**

### ◉ Steps

1   Ask your friends and acquaintances about their stylists. If you see someone on the street who has a haircut you admire, don't hesitate to ask for the stylist's name—most will be flattered and only too happy to tell you.

2   Pick a salon with a good reputation and ask for a stylist who specializes in your type of hair, or choose one based on what you've heard.

3   Schedule a consultation, for which the salon shouldn't charge you.

4   Make sure the salon looks clean and orderly.

5   Find out as much as you can about that particular stylist—how long he or she has been in business and what products he or she prefers.

6   Inquire about the beauty school the stylist attended if you wish, but keep in mind that the work is more important than where he or she studied.

7   Evaluate the stylist's own hair to see if it's chic and healthy-looking.

8   Note whether the stylist asks appropriate questions about your hair history and how much time you're willing to spend styling your hair.

9   Consider asking for a new haircut, if you're a risk-taker, and letting the stylist do his or her best work.

### ✱ Tips

Plan ahead—a skilled stylist may book several weeks in advance.

If you're looking for a stylist to do your wedding, he or she will most likely charge for a consultation because your hair requires complete styling at that time so you can see how it will look on your wedding day. This amount is like a down payment that the stylist will subtract from the bill for the big day.

## 726 | Choose a Flattering Hairstyle

If you are a woman who knows what she wants, you will make the job of the hairstylist easier. Use these guidelines to help the stylist create the look that's best for you.

### ⊙ Steps

1   Tie your hair back, if necessary, and examine your face shape in front of a mirror. Decide if your face is oval, long, square, round or heart-shaped.

2   Show off an oval face—egg-shaped and balanced on top and bottom, and widely considered ideal. Since any type of hairstyle flatters this face, explore a variety of looks.

3   Make a long face look shorter with hair that sits above the shoulders. Long layers work well, as do bangs. Since midline parts elongate the face, use a side part instead.

4   Choose curvy hairstyles to soften your face if it's square, with a wide forehead, wide cheeks and an angular chin. Wearing layers around your jawline frames your face and can mask a strong, angled chin. Avoid sharp, straight lines.

5   Elongate a round face—full, with a small chin, wide cheeks and small cheekbones—with longer hair that extends below your chin. Layers on top add volume and height; layers around the cheeks narrow your face. Avoid bangs and chin-length styles.

6   A heart-shaped face has a wide forehead that angles down to a small chin. Try shoulder-length hair, adding layers from the chin down. Curl or flip out these layers to create a fuller bottom that balances your small chin. A chin-length bob also works well. Avoid any look that adds fullness to the top and tapers down to wisps on the bottom.

### ✱ Tips

In addition to face shape, consider your hair texture when deciding on a hairstyle. A long hairstyle can render fine hair flat and difficult to manage. A shorter cut adds more body. Wavy hair looks nice in chunky layers, and thick hair is suited to soft, textured layers.

Although most hairstylists learn the above guidelines, some do not choose hairstyles this way. Ask during the consultation if your hairstylist will help you choose a style based on your face shape.

## 727 | Blow-Dry Hair Straight

Want to calm the frizzies or straighten your curls for a day? All you need is a round brush, a blow dryer, some hair products and about 30 minutes.

### ⊙ Steps

1   Towel-dry your just-washed hair.

2   Apply a heat protectant to your hair, paying special attention to the ends.

3   Place a quarter-size dollop of straightening balm in your palm. Rub your palms together to distribute the product in your hands, then massage it evenly throughout your hair.

4   Comb through your hair with your fingers while gently drying it on a low setting. This removes excess water.

5   Pull your hair into three sections, two at the sides and one at the back. Clip the two sides up.

6   Select a small portion of the hair from the unclipped section.

### ✱ Tips

Always point the dryer down as you are blow-drying the hair; blowing hair upward can cause frizzies.

Tame flyaway hair with an antifrizz serum or pomade. Place a few drops in your hand, rub gently to distribute it, then apply it your hair according to the product instructions.

7   Using a thick, round brush and beginning at the roots, gently pull the brush through the hair to the ends while you blow-dry it. Pull the hair away from your head, stretching and straightening it as you go.

8   First pull the brush through the underside of your hair so that you expose it directly to the heat of the dryer. Once that area is mostly dry, switch to the top of the hair.

9   Keep the tension consistent and evenly distribute heat over the section of hair you're working on. This ensures uniform hair texture and prevents overdrying of certain areas.

10  Continue with the other sections of damp hair.

### Things You'll Need

❏ towel

❏ heat protectant

❏ straightening balm

❏ hair dryer

❏ hair clips

❏ round brush

# Make Dreadlocks                                                    728

Dreadlocks, or dreads, are a cool hairstyle for some, a spiritual pursuit or political statement for others. If you have the right kind of hair, these steps will put a new twist into your locks.

## ◉ Steps

1   Consider that dreads work best on those with curly or very kinky hair. If you have thin, straight or wavy hair, you may want to give yourself a home perm with very thin rods. The perm will impart the needed texture.

2   Stop using conditioner a week to 10 days before you begin the process. Rinse your hair with a vinegar-and-water solution the day you plan to start making your dreads. This solution—about 1 tbsp. vinegar mixed with 1 quart water—will remove any residue or buildup that may impede the process.

3   Begin with dry hair. Take a portion of hair about 1 inch square at the roots. Twist the hair tightly.

4   Pin the rest of your hair back with hair clips or put it in a rubber band so you can concentrate on one portion at a time. Comb the section of twisted hair, beginning at the root and moving to the ends and then back to the scalp again. People with a great deal of texture in their hair might find that their hair stays in that tangled position after twisting and some combing, while those with less texture will have to comb quite a bit.

5   Add a dab of dread styling wax, beeswax or pomade to each section after combing, then retwist it. Wax will mold your dreads and help each lock stay twisted.

6   Secure the end of each dread with a rubber band, leaving some hair poking out. This step holds the twist and eventually gives your locks rounded ends.

7   Complete the twisting process on your entire head. Depending on your lifestyle or time frame, you might twist a few portions a day or your entire head in one sitting. Enlist the help of friends to get to the back parts of your head.

8   Twist, comb and wax on a regular basis to get your dreads to hold their shape. Remember that this hairstyle requires a lot of maintenance, so work on it while you watch TV, while you listen to music or whenever you find a free moment.

## ✱ Tips

Look for a fine-tooth metal comb or back comb. With the amount of combing you'll need to do, plastic combs may not hold up under the pressure.

Hair wax or beeswax helps secure your dreads, but it may also dry out your hair and scalp and attract dust and dirt. Look for styling waxes or pomades specifically made for dreads.

Wait a few weeks after the initial process before washing your hair.

Avoid towels, hair bands and bandanas made out of materials that shed: terry cloth, flannel or combed cotton. They will leave little particles embedded in your dreads.

## Things You'll Need

❏ 1 tbsp. vinegar

❏ hair clips or rubber bands

❏ fine-tooth metal comb or back comb

❏ dread styling wax, beeswax or pomade

9   Exercise patience. A full head of dreadlocks takes time and commitment. They will not appear overnight. In fact, it might take a few months until you're satisfied with your entire head.

## 729 | Conceal Hair Loss

Both men and women can be subject to hair loss. Although you can't do much to prevent it, you *can* take steps to hide it.

### ⊙ Steps

1   Consult with a physician or dermatologist before considering any method to conceal hair loss.

2   Think about wearing a hat or bandana, when appropriate, or even a toupee or hairpiece. You can get a hairpiece made to fit your remaining hair or bald head and wear it even during swimming and other athletic activities. However, in addition to the initial cost of the hairpiece, you often have to pay for a plan, which involves payments for maintaining hairpieces over the years.

3   Conceal thinning hair with hair weaves or extensions, available for people of all ethnicities. See your hairstylist for more information.

4   Try one of the medications that help to regrow hair. The two most popular—albeit expensive—products are minoxidil topical (Rogaine) and finasteride (Propecia). Results vary widely for Rogaine, which you apply to the scalp, and Propecia, which is an oral prescription medication.

5   Consider hair transplants. This surgical procedure takes healthy hair from one part of your head and transplants it to a bald area. Keep in mind that a licensed dermatologist experienced in this area must perform the procedure.

6   Investigate other forms of surgery, such as scalp reduction, which involves removing the bald part of your scalp and pulling the remaining portions together, and flap surgery, which involves pulling a receding hairline forward.

### ✱ Tips

Aside from the products mentioned, no creams, lotions, herbs or other over-the-counter products have been proved to increase hair growth or lessen hair loss.

Avoid hair transplants in the early stages of baldness—you may look unnatural if you lose more hair down the line.

### ⚠ Warning

Always follow your doctor's advice concerning medication and surgery. Inform your doctor about any medications you take regularly, and find out about side effects and interactions.

## 730 | Dye Away the Grays

If you're not ready to accept graying hair, consider coloring it to hang on to your natural shade.

### ⊙ Steps

1   Consult your hairstylist and discuss your plans to color your hair. Get suggestions for at-home products, natural vs. chemical treatments, and after-treatment hair care.

2   Consider how much of your hair is gray.

### ✱ Tip

Going to a salon is easier, but it costs a lot more than doing it yourself.

3   Use a semipermanent dye if your hair is close to 20 percent gray. Color will begin to fade after about 6 to 12 washings, so hair will require frequent recoloring if you shampoo daily.

4   Opt for longer-lasting semipermanent colors if you're up to 50 percent gray; they'll last for approximately 24 to 28 washes.

5   Use a permanent dye if most of your locks have made the change. To test the color, cut off strands of hair from the back of your neck to get a lock about 1/4 inch wide and an inch long, and bind one end with tape. Mix together a small amount of the hair-color solution according to the instructions and place the hair in it. Check the hair after the least amount of time recommended. Keep checking until it has reached the desired color, and then note how long this took.

6   Look for colors that closely match the natural shade of your hair. Consider a shade darker than your natural color if you're mostly gray, as the color may appear a shade lighter than indicated, and may fade in the sun. Touch up roots as needed, and dye again by the third month.

7   Begin your transition on a Saturday morning, if possible, so you have time to adjust to your new look before heading back to work, and so that co-workers won't notice an abrupt change as readily. Give yourself plenty of time to complete the process, as it may seem awkward at first.

8   Spread an old towel over the bathroom counter and put on an old T-shirt. Wearing fitted rubber gloves, begin your color process. Follow the directions exactly as indicated in the coloring kit.

9   Set the timer and enjoy a book or magazine while you wait. Rinse as indicated in the product instructions.

## ⚠ Warnings

Some color-enhancing products may irritate the scalp, so test new hair products by applying them to a small patch of skin on the back of your neck.

If you're pregnant, get your doctor's OK before proceeding with any hair-color treatment.

If you have applied henna to your hair, remember that you cannot perm it or use a chemical color over it.

Avoid chlorine and salt water for a few days after coloring your hair, since it may alter the color.

Avoid getting solution into your eyes at all costs. Rinse well with tepid water and consult a physician should this occur.

---

## Make Color Last Between Dye Jobs    731

Maintaining the color is an ongoing enterprise for people who dye their hair. Here's how to make your color last longer—and how to cover up those pesky roots.

### ◉ Steps

1   Opt for a color-boosting shampoo and conditioner every other day until you achieve the color you want, and then stop. Your salon will have good choices, or you can try a beauty specialty store, which may sell discounted products. Ask your hairstylist to recommend a brand.

2   Use a color-safe shampoo and conditioner when you wash your hair, once you've achieved the color you want with color-boosting shampoo and conditioner. You can buy all of these at beauty stores or drugstores.

3   Think about a hair sunscreen, which can protect your hair color from fading. Look for it in spray-on hair protectants.

4   Try smoothing your hair back with gel—this darkens the hair so colors blend together—and using a headband to conceal roots.

## ⚠ Warnings

Some color-enhancing products can irritate the scalp, so test all new hair products by applying them to a small patch of skin on the back of your neck.

If you're pregnant, get your doctor's OK before proceeding with any hair-color treatment.

Avoid chlorine and salt water for a few days after coloring your hair, since it may alter the color.

## 732  Trim a Mustache

There are many ways to groom a mustache. Decide how you want yours to look before following these instructions.

### ⊙ Steps

1  Wet your mustache slightly.

2  Use a fine-tooth mustache comb to brush the hair down.

3  Clip the hair on your mustache's outer edges with a pair of thin scissors. Remember to clip conservatively.

4  Snip across the bottom of the mustache.

5  Trim the body of the mustache to achieve the desired evenness and bushiness, and to clip errant hairs.

6  Touch up the top of the mustache with a razor until you have the desired line. If you have an unusual mustache, such as a pencil-thin or handlebar mustache, use more or less use of the razor as appropriate. Take care not to shave off the top of the mustache accidentally.

7  Comb again with the mustache comb.

### ✳ Tips

Work carefully. Clipping even a small amount of hair can change the appearance of a mustache greatly.

A beard trimmer is an excellent tool for reducing the bushiness.

For fancier styles, use mustache wax to shape or groom.

## 733  Trim the Back of Your Neck

You can solve one of life's pesky little problems with a few quick strokes of a razor.

### ⊙ Steps

1  Loosen your collar or remove your shirt.

2  If you're using an electric trimmer, set it on its closest setting and turn it on. If you're using a razor, apply a small amount of shaving cream to the back of your neck.

3  Begin trimming, using two mirrors if possible. Working in vertical lines, run the trimmer up the back of your neck from the base to the hairline. If you're using a razor, shave down in short strokes from the hairline to the base of the neck.

4  Even out the hairline as necessary.

5  Wipe off the shaving cream or brush off the clippings.

### ✳ Tips

Remember to shave all the way around to the area of the neck behind the ears.

Consider enlisting a friend to help you.

# Shave Your Face

Shaving makes a man look well groomed, and is also a terrific way for an older man to trim a few years off his age. Here's how to do it correctly using a razor blade.

## ⊙ Steps

1 Select a razor with a sharp blade; dull blades can cause nicks and cuts.

2 Wet your face with warm water. You may want to hold a hot washcloth to your face for a few moments to open the pores and soften the hair. This will also remove excess oil, which could interfere with the closeness of your shave.

3 Fill the sink basin halfway with water.

4 Make sure you have a sharp blade. Replace the used blade in your regular razor if it's dull.

5 Squirt a dollop of shaving cream or other lubricant into your hand and apply it to your beard with an upward circular motion. The amount you use may vary depending on the thickness of your beard, but you should cover the area uniformly. Or lather up shaving soap with a wet shaving brush and apply it liberally.

6 Shave downward, the way your whiskers grow, from your sideburns toward your jaw using long, even strokes. Apply light but firm pressure, pulling your skin taut before each stroke.

7 Rinse your razor with warm water after every stroke or two to keep it from getting clogged with hair.

8 Shave the area around your chin. Shave upward as necessary to make the area smooth. When shaving under your chin, pull the razor from your throat area toward your chin.

9 Shave your upper lip, keeping the skin tight by stretching your lip down over your front teeth.

10 Wash off any excess shaving cream and examine your face for straggling hairs. Check the edge of your jaw, around your ears, and near your lips and nostrils for missed hairs. Go back with the razor to shave anything you missed.

11 If you cut yourself, dab the wound with a styptic pencil. It will sting slightly, but the bleeding will stop. A touch of toilet tissue can also help. Apply some aloe to the wound after the bleeding has stopped.

12 Reapply the hot washcloth to help soothe your open pores if your skin is feeling irritated.

13 Drain and wash out the basin and rinse your face with cold water.

## ✱ Tips

An electric shaver does not give as close a shave as a razor blade. However, some men prefer electric shavers since no lathering is required.

Wait at least 15 to 20 minutes after you get up in the morning before you shave. This will allow any puffiness in your face to subside, making shaving easier.

Shave the areas of thickest growth (usually the chin and upper lip) last so your shaving lubricant has more time to soften the hair.

## ⚠ Warnings

Dull blades can irritate your skin and cause shaving mishaps.

Women should never shave facial hair, as it will grow back stubbly and not soft (see 736 "Get Rid of Unwanted Hair").

## Things You'll Need

❑ hot washcloth

❑ razor

❑ shaving cream or shaving soap

❑ styptic pencil

## 735 Shave Your Legs

Many women dread the return of summer, when their leg-shaving skills (or lack thereof) are put on display. Below are some helpful shaving tips to get you through the season nick-free.

### ◉ Steps

1 Shave in a warm shower or bath, if possible.

2 Wait a few minutes before starting to let the leg hair soften. If you take only showers, wait until the end of the shower to shave.

3 Sit on the ledge in your shower, if possible. If your shower has no place to sit, raise one leg against the wall of the shower and balance carefully.

4 Apply a small amount of shaving cream, rubbing it into a thick lather and spreading it over your leg. Avoid using soap in place of shaving cream, as it will dry out your skin.

5 Place the razor at the base of your ankle and pull gently up over your entire leg. If you experience severe razor burn, try shaving in the same direction as the hair growth. You may not get as clean a shave, but you'll avoid raising red bumps.

6 Rinse the blade between every stroke, and be sure to keep the razor wet while you're shaving.

7 Shave the entire leg until you've removed all the shaving cream.

8 Rinse.

9 Repeat for the other leg.

10 Pat dry and moisturize.

### ✳ Tip

Having your legs waxed at a salon is a nice alternative that also reduces overall hair growth. One drawback is that you'll have to wait for the hair to grow out before you can wax again—this can take 6 to 8 weeks. Expect to pay about $25 for a half-leg wax.

### ⚠ Warnings

Dull blades can cause razor burn on sensitive skin.

Shaving areas where bone is close to the skin surface, such as ankles and knees, can result in painful cuts and nicks. If you cut your leg while shaving, get out of the bath quickly, as the hot water will increase blood flow. Dab the wound lightly with a styptic pencil. It will sting slightly, but the bleeding will stop. A touch of toilet tissue can also do the trick.

## 736 Get Rid of Unwanted Hair

Sick to death of the mustache shadow under your ladylike nose? Want your legs to feel silky smooth for that special someone? You have options.

### ◉ Steps

1 Consider bleaching. Although this does not get rid of unwanted hair, it does lighten hair to a soft blond hue, rendering mustaches almost invisible. Some women also bleach the hair on their arms.

2 Try depilatories—cream-based products you apply on top of unwanted hair. Depilatories, popular for the bikini area, come with specific instructions for how long to leave the cream on. When you rinse away the depilatory, the unwanted hair should wash away with the cream. However, results vary widely.

3 Use that old standby—shaving. It's fast and easy, but the hair grows back quickly. Women should never shave a mustache, as it will grow back stubbly and not soft.

### ✳ Tips

Use sunscreen on skin you've treated with a depilatory cream.

Keep in mind that stubble cannot be waxed or sugared.

4   Consider plucking, which is effective for small patches of hair. Keep in mind that repeated tweezing of the same hairs over the years can damage the hair roots enough to result in permanent hair removal, so be careful when tweezing eyebrows—if styles change, you may not get your old brows back.

5   Evaluate waxing—especially popular for eyebrows and the bikini area. A mixture of hot oil, rosin and paraffin is spread over unwanted hair. Once the wax cools, it's ripped off, along with the unwanted hairs. Though this method can be uncomfortable, the advantage is that the hair doesn't return for several weeks.

6   Investigate sugaring, a technique devised by the ancient Egyptians that uses all-natural ingredients. A paste of sugar and water is applied over unwanted hair. When the sugar mix dries, it's yanked off, along with the hair. As with waxing, the advantage is that the hair doesn't return for several weeks; the discomfort is similar to that of pulling off a bandage with hair underneath.

7   Look into electrolysis, which involves removal of each hair with an electric current and a fine needle. You must continue electrolysis for several months or even years to remove all unwanted hair, and the process can be quite painful.

8   Investigate laser removal of unwanted hair. The light emitted from the laser vaporizes the pigment located in the hair follicles, destroying or disabling several hair follicles at a time. However, it may not result in permanent hair removal.

# Prevent Hangnails                                           737

When your nail cuticles become dry or rough, painful and unsightly hangnails often form. Pamper your nails to keep them healthy and free of hangnails.

## ◎ Steps

1   Give yourself regular manicures: Clean and trim your nails, brush your nails with a manicure brush, and push back cuticles with a cuticle stick. This removes excess skin that may later form hangnails.

2   Use a cuticle moisturizer as needed throughout the day to keep your nails and cuticles moisturized and strong. Try an exfoliating lotion if your skin is particularly dry or roughened.

3   Wear rubber gloves when washing dishes or doing housework. Hot water and various cleaning agents can dry out your hands and encourage hangnails. If possible, avoid soaking nails and cuticles in water, as this can weaken them.

4   Don canvas gloves when gardening or doing other tasks that can roughen and dry out your hands, causing cuticles and nails to crack.

5   Fight the urge to bite fingernails or hangnails. Such habits can aggravate the nail area and cause hangnails to bleed.

## ✳ Tips

If you have extremely dry or rough hands, try applying moisturizer at night, then donning cotton gloves when you sleep.

Cut hangnails as soon as you see them.

## Things You'll Need

❑ manicure scissors or nail clippers

❑ manicure brush

❑ cuticle stick

❑ cuticle moisturizer

❑ exfoliating lotion

❑ gloves (rubber, canvas, cotton)

## 738 Pluck Your Eyebrows

Tweezing your eyebrows is the most dramatic way to change your face without makeup or surgery. It can make your eyes look larger and give your face a clean, polished look.

### ◎ Steps

1 Sit near a window to get the best light.

2 Wash the area thoroughly so it's not oily.

3 Decide what shape you want for your eyebrows. Styles change: It may help to flip through fashion magazines for ideas.

4 Draw a brow line on your eyebrow with a brow pencil to serve as a guide. Follow the brow's natural line by conforming to the curve of your upper eyelid.

5 Pull the skin at the outer end of the eyebrow taut against the brow bone, and use the brow bone as an additional guide.

6 Use a pair of angled eyebrow tweezers to pluck the hairs below the brow; never shape your brow by plucking above it. Pluck only one hair at a time.

7 Start plucking in the middle of the eyebrow and pluck toward the outer end; then go back to the middle and pluck toward the nose. Your brows should extend a little beyond each corner of your eye.

8 Use a cotton ball or pad soaked in pure tea tree oil or witch hazel to soothe your plucked brows.

### ✳ Tips

Consider having your brows waxed once professionally to get exactly the shape you want. You can then pluck the strays as they grow in.

Habitual plucking may make some hairs stop growing permanently, so pluck with caution.

### Things You'll Need

❑ brow pencil

❑ eyebrow tweezers

❑ cotton balls or pads

❑ pure tea tree oil or witch hazel

## 739 Alleviate Puffy Eyes

Late nights, allergies, high salt intake or general stress can cause the unsightly phenomenon of puffy eyes. Try any or all of these remedies.

### ◎ Steps

1 Splash your entire face with the coldest water you can stand immediately after you wake up. Use either cold tap water or a mixture of cold water and ice cubes in a large bowl or tub. Splash your face for up to 5 minutes, if possible.

2 Prepare two tea bags by soaking them in water, wringing them out and chilling them in the refrigerator or freezer. Once they are chilled, lie down and place the bags on closed eyelids for 5 to 10 minutes.

3 Cut two slices off a cold cucumber, each approximately 1/2 inch thick. Place a slice on each eyelid for 5 minutes.

4 Drink lots of water. Puffy eyes often indicate water retention, which you can alleviate by drinking plenty of liquids; this flushes excess salt from your system.

5 Use an aloe-based eye-soothing gel or cream.

### ✳ Tip

Remove contact lenses each night before bed to avoid puffiness caused by lens irritation and drying.

### ⚠ Warnings

Don't use a hemorrhoid cream near the eye area—it's unsafe and won't diminish puffiness.

If the problem persists, see your doctor. You may be reacting to dust, pets, medication or other irritants, or you may have an underlying medical condition.

## Apply Makeup

Try to follow the same basic routine whenever you apply your makeup. Experiment to find out what works best for you.

### ◉ Steps

1 Wash your face and apply moisturizer (see 750 "Care for Dry Skin" or 751 "Care for Oily Skin" if your skin is dry or oily).

2 Apply a concealer that is one shade lighter than your foundation. Dot it on over any blemishes or under-eye circles and blend with your fingertips or a makeup sponge. If your concealer tends to cake, apply eye cream first.

3 Choose foundation that matches your skin tone exactly. Apply it in dots over the central part of your face, then blend it out with a makeup sponge or your fingertips until it covers your entire face (see 741 "Choose Foundation").

4 Use a loose or pressed powder to keep foundation and concealer on longer. Use pressed powder to touch up when you're away from home.

5 Do your eyebrows next. Use powdered eyebrow shadow on brows instead of pencil, which can often look unnatural. Apply it with a hard, slanted brush.

6 Choose three colors of eye shadow: light, medium and dark. Use the dark only to line your upper eyelid, in a fairly thin line along the upper lashes. Use the medium shade for the crease and the lightest shade for the area under the eyebrow. There are many variations on eye shadow application techniques (see 743 "Apply Eye Shadow" for more ideas).

7 Apply eyeliner. Use a cake eyeliner with a damp, thin liner brush, or an eyeliner pencil, and line the lower lid below the lashes. Line only the outer two-thirds of the lower lid, or all the way across if you're trying to achieve a darker look. Line all the way across the upper lid (just above the lash line and as close to the lashes as possible), or start the line where your lashes begin (see 744 "Apply Eyeliner").

8 Apply mascara to upper and lower lashes, in two thin coats to avoid clumpiness. Choose brown mascara if your coloring is fair; black or brown-black works well for darker coloring. Or try a colored mascara such as navy or plum for fun, but don't go too bright if you want to be taken seriously (see 745 "Apply Mascara").

9 Smile to find the apples of your cheeks, and apply blush to the apples or below, whichever you prefer. If you have to blend in blush, it's too bright.

10 Choose a lipstick color that's suited to your skin tone and that's perfect for your day look. You can mix colors and textures to suit your moods and your outfits (see 747 "Choose a Lipstick Color").

11 Line your lips *after* applying lipstick, not before. Avoid combining very dark lip liner and pale lipstick.

### ✱ Tips

Choose brighter or darker tones for a stronger look.

Clean makeup brushes by gently washing them in warm water and mild gel shampoo. Air-dry them overnight.

Don't skimp on makeup tools. High-quality tools make application easier and faster.

If you decide to curl your eyelashes, do this just before applying mascara—never after. Insert your eyelashes into the curler, squeeze just once, and hold for a few seconds.

### ⚠ Warning

Bacteria can grow in older cosmetics, which can lead to infections. Be on the safe side: Toss anything that's seems old, especially mascara, and avoid sharing products with others.

### Things You'll Need

❑ concealer

❑ foundation

❑ loose or pressed powder

❑ eyebrow shadow

❑ light, medium and dark eye shadow

❑ eyeliner

❑ mascara

❑ blush

❑ lipstick

❑ lip liner

## 741 | Choose Foundation

To even out your skin's appearance and create the illusion of flawless skin, head to the cosmetics counter. The right foundation can do wonders.

### ⊙ Steps

1   Consider your skin type. If you have oily skin, stick with an oil-free formula. If you have drier skin, select a creamier formula that offers moisturizing benefits.

2   Decide what type of look you'd like to achieve. Foundations can offer sheer to heavy coverage and finishes that range from satiny to matte.

3   Test the colors of your preferred formula on your jawline, which offers the truest facial coloring. Any foundation will look slightly darker in the bottle, so keep this in mind when assessing your options.

4   Blend in the foundation gently with a makeup sponge. The foundation should disappear into your skin. If you find you're between shades, blend two colors together, or keep looking for a brand that offers the perfect shade.

5   Bring a hand mirror along so you can view your options in natural light.

6   Look for yellow-toned foundation or tinted moisturizer if you're Caucasian or Asian; Hispanics should opt for foundation or tinted moisturizers with yellow-orange undertones. If you are African-American, it's a good idea to use light, medium and dark shades of foundation to allow for different gradations of color on different parts of your face.

7   Remember that you have plenty of options to choose from, so if you don't find a good color match, keep looking.

### ✱ Tips

For sheer, no-nonsense coverage, consider using a tinted moisturizer.

Look for the many extras some foundation formulas offer, such as sunscreen or ingredients that hide fine lines.

### Things You'll Need

❑ foundation

❑ makeup sponge

❑ hand mirror

## 742 | Conceal Freckles

If you're absolutely certain you don't love your unique distinguishing marks, experiment with these tips and techniques.

### ⊙ Steps

1   Try over-the-counter skin-bleaching agents to lighten your freckles, but know that you can't erase them entirely.

2   Apply tinted moisturizer or foundation, if you prefer light coverage, in a shade slightly darker than your natural skin tone to blend in and downplay your freckles.

3   Slather on sunblock with an SPF rating of 15 or higher every time you go outside, even in cloudy or overcast weather. As your skin tans, so do your freckles. Self-tanners will make your skin appear darker, but they will also darken your freckles.

4   Talk to a dermatologist if you want to try stronger measures intended to eliminate freckles. Ask about the pros and cons of acid or chemical peels, lasers and various bleaching agents available only by prescription.

### ✱ Tips

Protect your skin from sun to avoid a new crop of freckles. Freckles are inherited; limiting your sun exposure is the only way to prevent them. That's why you probably don't have any freckles on your derriere.

Learn the difference between moles and freckles, and keep an eye on the growth and shape of moles (see 806 "Examine a Mole"). Let your doctor know about any significant changes.

## Apply Eye Shadow `743`

Sweep a touch of shadow over your lids to accent your eyes. There are many good techniques for applying eye shadow; here's one that works well.

### ⊙ Steps

#### Application on Entire Lid

1  Prime the eyelids by dusting them with a small amount of loose powder.

2  Select a light base shadow. Using a shadow brush, sweep it across your entire lid, from brow to lash line.

3  Use a medium-toned shade to cover your lower lids.

4  Contour the crease of your eyelid with a dark shade, using a smaller eye shadow brush. This color can also work as an eyeliner (see the next section for instructions).

5  Blend shadow by stroking the lid gently with an eye shadow brush. Don't use your finger—you could wipe off the shadow entirely.

6  Use a cosmetic puff and a little pressed powder to tone down heavy shadow. Shake any excess powder off the puff, then press it gently on your lid.

#### Eye Shadow to Line the Eyes

1  Choose a medium or dark shadow color to line your eyes.

2  Use a small, flat, angled brush for the application.

3  Stroke the brush over the eye shadow.

4  Start at the inside edge of your upper lid. Angle the brush so that the longest tip follows the shorter end as the brush moves across your lash line. Bring the brush to the outer corner of the eye.

5  Create a more dramatic line by wetting the brush before stroking it through the shadow. Mist a small amount of water onto the brush, or dab it into a few drops of water and proceed with the line. The shadow may feel wet as you draw your line, but it will dry quickly.

### ✱ Tips

Before applying shadow with the brush, always tap any excess off the brush so you don't scatter loose powder on your face.

Apply eye shadow before putting on eyeliner and mascara.

### ⚠ Warnings

Don't share eye makeup or tools—you can unknowingly transfer eye infections such as pinkeye (conjunctivitis).

If you get shadow in your eyes, flush them gently with tepid water.

### Things You'll Need

❏ loose powder

❏ light, medium and dark eye shadow

❏ eye shadow brushes

❏ eyeliner brush

❏ cosmetic puff

❏ pressed powder

## Apply Eyeliner `744`

Shape and define your eyes with eyeliner after you've applied eye shadow and before applying mascara. Whether you choose a soft line or a dramatic stroke, eyeliner draws attention.

### ⊙ Steps

1  Choose an eyeliner appropriate for your eye color. Brown, navy and charcoal accent light eyes well, while brown and plum shades flatter brown eyes. Make sure your liner complements the color of your shadow.

### ✱ Tips

You may find eyeliner, particularly the liquid version, difficult and messy the first few times. Practice and have patience.

2  Consider the type of look you're after. Pencil eyeliner gives your eyes soft definition, while liquid versions offer precision and drama. You can also moisten dark eye shadow and apply it with a small, flat brush.

3  Prepare a cake liner or a dark eye shadow by applying a small amount of water to your brush. Or, if you're using a pencil eyeliner, ensure that you've sharpened the pencil adequately.

4  Move the wet brush gently through your cake liner or dark shadow. Hold the brush or pencil as you would hold a pen.

5  Tilt your head back slightly and bring your eyes to a half-open state. This creates a good angle for application, while allowing you to see what you're doing.

6  Draw a line across the upper lid just above the lashes, from the inside corner to the outside corner of the eye. If you're using liquid liner, allow it to dry before opening your eyes all the way, or the color may transfer into the crease of your eye.

7  If you used a brush or a pencil, soften the look by gently smudging the line with your brush, a cotton swab or your finger.

8  Line the lower lids. Moving from the outside edge inward, draw a line on the outer two-thirds of the lid or more, depending on the look you're going for. Your line should be slightly thicker at the outside corner, becoming thinner as it moves in toward your nose. Using your brush or pencil, lightly stroke the area. If using a liquid liner, apply it in one smooth stroke. Apply less color so your eyes don't appear raccoonlike.

Wash brushes regularly with makeup remover or a mild gel shampoo.

## ⚠ Warning

Lining the inside of the lower lid is not recommended—it may cause eye infections, and it greatly increases the risk of getting makeup in your eye.

## Things You'll Need

❑ eyeliner

❑ eyeliner brush

❑ cotton swabs

---

## 745 | Apply Mascara

Mascara—one of the most popular beauty items—defines and brings color to the lashes, and highlights and dramatizes eyes. Different formulas can enhance your lashes in different ways.

### ◉ Steps

1  Consider the types of mascara and select one appropriate for your lashes and the occasion. You have a choice of lengthening, thickening, long-wearing, conditioning and waterproof formulas, among others. For day, you might decide to add length, while a night on the town may require a long-wearing or thickening formula.

2  Select a color. If you have blond or red lashes, opt for brown mascara. Darker-lashed women can consider brown for a casual look, and black or brown-black for more pronounced or dramatic lashes.

3  Curl your lashes with an eyelash curler, if desired, and apply all other eye makeup prior to your mascara.

4  Remove the wand from the tube in one pull. Pumping the mascara will push air into the tube, potentially drying out the formula and introducing bacteria into it.

5  Begin with the underside of your upper lashes, moving the brush slowly upward toward the tips of your lashes. Always hold the wand parallel to

### ✳ Tips

Contact lens wearers should stick to waterproof mascara formulas, as they break down more slowly, minimizing the chance of any flakes getting into the eyes.

Always remove eye makeup thoroughly before going to bed. This will keep lashes healthier and prevent any mascara from getting into your eyes during the night.

Apply mascara after eye shadow and eyeliner.

your eyelid. Roll the brush slowly on the upward stroke to promote separation of the lashes.

6   Allow the first coat of mascara to dry before applying the second coat in the same manner.

7   Use an eyelash comb to separate the wet lashes. Also blot the lashes with tissue paper if necessary to remove excess mascara.

8   Use less mascara for the lower lashes. Begin where the lashes meet the rim of the lower eyelid, and gently stroke downward.

9   Remove any stray mascara around the eye with a cotton swab dipped in a small amount of eye makeup remover.

### Things You'll Need

❑ mascara

❑ eyelash curler

❑ eyelash comb

❑ cotton swabs

❑ eye makeup remover

---

# Use False Eyelashes                                    746

Go for glamour with false eyelashes. Whether you apply a few singles to create a subtle change or full lashes for optimal drama, practice first—this is a tricky maneuver.

### ◉ Steps

1   Decide what look you're seeking. A full set of false eyelashes adds high drama to your evening appearance or returns the eyelashes that may have disappeared due to illness. Little clumps of fake lashes on the outside corners of your eyes create a subtle, sophisticated glamour.

2   Choose a color that complements the occasion. For evening, stick to black (or dark brown if you have pale lashes), which adds drama without requiring mascara. In the daytime, go dark brown (light brown or blond if you have pale lashes) for a natural look.

3   Check their length. Full lashes should follow the natural line of your own lashes. Trim them with sharp scissors to accommodate your needs.

4   Begin with clean eyes, free of makeup or debris.

5   Hold the lashes in your hand and apply a very thin line of glue or adhesive along the base; let it sit for 1 minute. Begin with a minimal amount of glue, adding more if needed.

6   Look into a mirror, either on the wall or placed on a countertop. Apply the false lashes above your eyelashes, as close to your lash line as possible, following its natural curve.

7   Adjust the lashes with your fingertips, tweezers or a toothpick.

8   If you're using lash clumps, place them at the outside corners of your upper lashes (one or two per eye should suffice). Adjust their position with a toothpick, fingers or tweezers.

9   Apply eye makeup. You may find your new lashes dramatic enough without mascara, so take a good look in the mirror first.

10  Practice a few times before your debut. This is a challenging beauty trick to master, but a dress rehearsal should make for a smash opening.

### ✱ Tips

Remove false eyelashes before you go to bed, using a warm compress or makeup remover. Never pull the lashes from your lids, as you may pull your own lashes out or rip your skin.

After wearing full lashes, soak them in eyelash-cleaning solution until the next time you wear them.

### ⚠ Warning

Never apply glue directly to your eyelids; it may get into your eyes, or you may glue your eye shut.

### Things You'll Need

❑ false eyelashes

❑ eyelash glue or adhesive

❑ mirror

❑ tweezers or a toothpick

## 747 | Choose a Lipstick Color

Lipstick can be subtle, glamorous or flirty, adding the final touch to your day or evening makeup.

### ⊙ Steps

1  Choose a color that complements the natural shade of your lips and skin. Plums, wines and deep reds flatter a dark skin tone, while light-brown beiges with pink or orange undertones complement a lighter skin tone. Olive skin looks good with brownish reds, light browns and raisin shades of lipstick.

2  Keep colors lighter for daytime and darker for night. Matte and cream finishes offer a subtler daytime look, while a high-gloss finish adds glamour for evening. A sheer, natural-looking color with a little shine also works well for day.

3  Experiment. Head to your local department store and ask a makeup artist to test different shades on your lips. Whenever possible, check in natural light to see how the color really looks with your complexion.

4  Create your own shade by combining colors. If the shades you find don't completely satisfy you, mix your own color. The easiest way to do this is by applying each color to your lips with a lip brush, then blending with the brush on your lips.

5  Opt for a lip liner that is a shade darker than your lipstick and in the same color family.

6  Line lips *after* applying lipstick, not before. That way you won't end up with a dark circle of lip liner after your lipstick has worn off.

### ✳ Tips

Try a colored gloss or lip tint for a sheer hint of lip color.

Buy the colors that look good on you—not the ones that look good in the tube.

Deep or bold lip color complements light eye makeup, while light or nude lipstick flatters heavy eye makeup.

### Things You'll Need

❑ lipstick

❑ lip liner

## 748 | Apply Makeup to Achieve a Natural Look

This system of applying makeup for a natural look is fast and easy when you get the hang of it.

### ⊙ Steps

1  Understand that a "natural" look is one that uses colors that are right for your skin tone. How much you use, and where, depends on your personal style.

2  Make sure your concealer is yellow in tone since it mutes imperfections without adding color, giving your skin a natural look.

3  Apply foundation that matches your skin tone. The right foundation will seem to disappear on your face. If you are African-American, it's a good idea to have light, medium and dark shades of your foundation to allow for different gradations of color on different parts of your face.

4  Apply eye makeup in earthy tones—beige, brown, gold or plum for shadows and brown and charcoal gray for liner and mascara. Skip liner or shadow entirely if you want to keep makeup light.

5  Choose a blush color that is close to the color of your cheeks after you've exercised.

### ✳ Tips

Apply makeup in the order described in 740 "Apply Makeup," and remember to clean and moisturize your face first.

Choose brighter or darker tones for a stronger, more made-up look.

Intensify your natural makeup for evening. Instead of brown, for example, go for charcoal around the eyes. "Pop" blush with a brighter color over your usual one. Make lips brighter, darker or more shimmery.

6   Select lipstick that matches your skin tone. Try on colors when you are not wearing any other makeup. The lipstick color should not stand out too much.

7   Blend makeup well. For foundation, blend out to your hair and jawline with a makeup sponge until the foundation vanishes. Blend eye shadow by stroking your lid gently with a clean brush. Don't use your finger—you could wipe off shadow entirely

8   Make sure to check your makeup—particularly the foundation—in daylight before you go out because natural light helps you spot heavy, unnatural makeup application.

9   Enhance contrast between eyes and lips when intensifying natural makeup for the evening. For example, if you opt for a strong mouth, do softer eyes, or vice versa. You run the risk of looking overdone and unnatural if you opt for heavy makeup on both your eyes and mouth.

## Remove Makeup Thoroughly                                    749

Though you may be tempted to hop directly into bed after a long night, discipline yourself to remove makeup first so your skin can breathe and regenerate during the night.

### ◉ Steps

1   Pull your hair away from your face with a headband, if necessary, or secure it in a hair clip or ponytail holder.

2   Begin with your eye makeup. Moisten a cotton ball or pad with eye makeup remover and take off all traces of makeup by gently wiping each eye until the makeup dissolves.

3   Select a skin cleanser suitable for your skin type that can also remove makeup. Some soaps and cleansers don't thoroughly cleanse your skin of makeup. Check the packaging to see if the product is designed for makeup removal, or ask a makeup salesperson for advice.

4   Splash your face with lukewarm water, the best temperature for lathering up and facilitating the breakdown of makeup.

5   Place a dollop of cleanser in the center of one hand and rub your hands together to generate lather. Add water if necessary.

6   Apply the lather to your entire face and rub gently, concentrating on the places where you applied makeup.

7   Spend about a minute retracing your path to ensure that you've cleaned all areas.

8   Rinse your face multiple times to ensure the removal of the cleanser and makeup residue.

9   Pat your face dry with a towel.

**✱ Tip**

If your preferred skin cleanser does not break down makeup, wash your face first with a makeup remover that suits your skin type.

**⚠ Warning**

Avoid washing off eye makeup with cleanser, as it's too harsh and drying for this delicate area.

**Things You'll Need**

❏ headband, hair clip or ponytail holder

❏ cotton balls or pads

❏ skin cleanser

❏ eye makeup remover

❏ makeup remover

## 750 | Care for Dry Skin

Only a lucky few have "normal" skin; the rest of us have a dry, oily or combination variety. If dryness is your problem, read on.

### ◉ Steps

1 Remember the basics: Drink at least eight glasses of water a day to keep your skin well hydrated; eat a high-quality diet rich in fruits and vegetables; and limit sun exposure.

2 Wash your face no more than twice a day with a gentle cleanser formulated for dry skin. Washing more often can dry your skin.

3 Take short baths or showers and use warm rather than hot water. Try to limit showers and baths to one per day. Use soap only where you need it, such as on your underarms and groin.

4 Add a few teaspoons of olive oil or lavender-scented oil to your bath.

5 Pat your skin dry after washing. Avoid rubbing yourself dry with a towel, which can whisk away essential oils needed for moisture.

6 Apply moisturizer while your skin is still damp. Heed the advice of many experts in choosing a moisturizer—less is more when it comes to the ingredient list.

7 Understand that moisturizers contain barriers, which keep water on the skin, and water binders, which whisk moisture from the inner layer of skin to the top layer. Look for ingredients such as glycerin, alpha hydroxy acids, urea and lactic acids (binders), combined with petrolatum, lanolin or silicone derivatives (barriers). You have a choice of hundreds of products. A dermatologist or other skin care expert may be able to advise you on your specific needs, but trial and error will probably be your best bet in finding the product that's right for you.

8 Aim for a comfortable level of humidity in your home or office. Too much heat or too much air-conditioning can rob your skin of moisture.

### ✱ Tips

Consult an allergist to find out if an allergic reaction might be causing your dry skin.

Avoid caffeine and alcohol, which cause dehydration.

Steer clear of added fragrance, preservatives and botanicals, which may irritate already dry skin.

### ⚠ Warning

Check with a doctor if you have irritated, red or scaly skin. You could have a serious condition requiring medical treatment.

## 751 | Care for Oily Skin

Do you have overproductive sebaceous glands, which are responsible for oily skin? The following steps can minimize the negative effects.

### ◉ Steps

1 Stick with the basics: The experts suggest cleansing your face two or three times daily with good old soap and water. Pack a premoistened cleansing pad if you won't be around a water basin throughout the day.

2 Understand that dermatologists and aestheticians often disagree on which types of soaps or cleansers to use—but all agree that once you find a product that works well for your skin, you should continue using it.

3 Follow the recommendations of dermatologists and shower or bathe in tepid rather than steaming-hot water. Hot water can strip your skin of needed moisture, while cold water can shock your skin.

### ⚠ Warning

Constant breakouts may indicate that you have acne or another skin condition. Contact your dermatologist for medical advice and guidance.

4 Avoid using cleansers that tend to overdry skin. This paradoxically causes your skin to produce even more oil than usual.

5 Use only noncomedogenic moisturizers and sunscreen products—this means they're oil-free and won't clog pores.

6 Talk to your dermatologist about a class of drugs called retinoids, which reduce production in oil glands and shrink their size.

7 Keep in mind that oil glands are very sensitive—stimuli such as hormones, heat and (some say) fatty food can trigger them.

8 Remember that your efforts to keep your oily skin clear can only go so far, as some studies indicate that oily skin is hereditary.

## Treat Pimples 752

Although many people suffer from this condition only during the teenage years, pimples can occur throughout adulthood, depending on your hormonal activity, heredity and hygiene.

### ◉ Steps

1 Resist the urge to attack when these plugged sebaceous glands pop up. In other words, don't pop your pimples—this can cause infections and even scarring.

2 Keep in mind that a combination of hormonal activity, a buildup of bacteria and the shedding of dead skin cells causes pimples. Do what you can to prevent a breakout by establishing a skin-care routine appropriate for your skin type.

3 Have patience. It could take up to one month for a blemish to disappear completely. The less you poke at it, the better.

4 Buy an antibacterial, oil-free concealer that can blend the redness of the pimple into your own skin color. Green shades tend to offset redness the best. (This might not be an option for those who don't wear makeup.)

5 Try a facial mud mask. This may shrink a pimple.

6 Realize that despite the happy teens in the commercials, "zit zapping" solutions—medications you apply directly to pimples—don't do much more than dry out the top layer of skin covering the pimples. These medications don't provide a long-term cure.

7 If you are going to break the rules by "extracting the blemish"—aesthetician-speak for popping your pimple—wash your hands, then lightly squeeze the top of the pimple with a tissue or cotton swab. Clean the area thoroughly when you're done. If nothing happens, leave the pimple alone until it's ready to pop.

### ✱ Tip

If you're desperate (you get an unsightly blemish two days before your wedding, perhaps), consult a dermatologist about receiving a shot of cortisone to eliminate a pimple.

### ⚠ Warnings

Pimples can indicate the presence of acne, a chronic skin disease. If you have recurring pimples, talk to a dermatologist about acne medication. Your dermatologist may prescribe antibiotics, certain brands of birth control pills, or even Accutane for severe acne.

Consider carefully before using Accutane. Although this is the only truly long-term solution for severe acne, it can have serious side effects and is known to cause serious birth defects when taken during pregnancy. Sexually active women who use Accutane should use two forms of birth control.

## 753 | Brush Your Teeth

We do it every day without thinking too much, but here are some important points to remember when brushing your teeth.

### ◉ Steps

1   Squeeze some toothpaste onto a soft-bristled toothbrush. Your toothpaste should contain fluoride and bear the American Dental Association (ADA) seal.

2   Use short, back-and-forth brushing motions to clean the outside and inside surfaces of the teeth, as well as the chewing surfaces. Follow with up-and-down motions to clean the inside surfaces of the front teeth.

3   Brush along the gum line. This is extremely important, as gum disease starts here. Brush gently to avoid damaging your gums.

4   Make sure to brush your back molars, where bacteria like to hide.

5   Brush your tongue to remove bacteria that cause bad breath.

6   Spit out the toothpaste and rinse your mouth with water or mouthwash.

7   Try to floss at least once a day, since most adult cavities occur between teeth. The most important time to floss is before going to bed. Floss before or after you brush—either is fine. Guide the floss between the teeth and use it to gently rub the side of each tooth.

### ✳ Tips

Brush at least twice a day—or better yet, after each meal. Visit your dentist every six months to have your teeth cleaned.

Replace your toothbrush every three to four months, or sooner if the bristles become worn, splayed or frayed.

### Things You'll Need

❑ toothbrush

❑ toothpaste with fluoride

❑ dental floss

## 754 | Treat Bad Breath

The main cause of bad breath is a buildup of food particles in the mouth and the bacteria that result.

### ◉ Steps

1   Visit your dentist at least every six months for cleanings and checkups to keep your mouth free of plaque buildup and other problems that may lead to bad breath.

2   Watch your consumption of foods such as alcohol, coffee (both caffeinated and decaffeinated), dense proteins (such as those found in dairy and meat products), garlic and onions, and sugars. These are all bad-breath offenders.

3   Try to breathe through your nose. Breathing through your mouth can lead to having a dry mouth, which creates a breeding ground for odor-causing bacteria.

4   Keep a regular log of your eating habits and medications, as these can cause bad breath. Share the log with your dentist.

5   Brush your teeth and tongue twice a day to remove food particles and plaque, and floss between teeth once a day, preferably in the evening after you eat.

6   Try using a fluoride mouth rinse with antiseptic ingredients and a pleasant mint flavor. This helps to protect your teeth, and the flavor masks odor problems.

### ✳ Tips

Keep mints and gum on hand (or better yet, a toothbrush and toothpaste) for meals that include ingredients such as garlic and onions.

If bad breath persists, check with your dentist—this may indicate other health problems.

If you wear removable dentures, take them out at night and clean them before putting them in again.

### ⚠ Warning

Tobacco users often suffer from bad breath and other mouth-related problems.

7 Consider internal breath fresheners—such as over-the-counter pills you take before or after a meal to aid the prevention of malodorous breath—or go the natural route and munch on some parsley after a meal.

## Whiten Your Teeth 755

Tobacco, coffee, cavities, aging and drugs can stain teeth. Treatment for discolored teeth depends on the magnitude of the stain; remedies appear here in order of increasing intensity.

### ⊙ Steps

1 Brush and floss regularly to reduce or prevent stains.

2 Try whitening toothpastes. Though heavily advertised, these only partially whiten teeth and don't provide a complete remedy. Make sure the toothpaste has the American Dental Association (ADA) seal of approval and has been clinically proved to whiten teeth effectively. Very few whitening toothpastes have undergone any type of clinical trial, and ones that are too abrasive can damage teeth or make them very sensitive.

3 Get regular dental cleanings, which remove many food and tobacco stains. No amount of cleaning will remove the severe staining left by tetracycline or systemic disease because these pigments lie inside the tooth; you'll have to take more aggressive measures against these.

4 Consider the two options—in-office and at-home treatments—for bleaching your teeth. A dentist performs in-office treatments by coating the teeth with a bleaching agent, then using periodic flashes of light to activate the solution. Treatments last 30 to 60 minutes, and the complete procedure often requires several appointments. In at-home treatments, patients wear a mouth guard fitted with bleaching gel 2 hours a day for two weeks, depending on the severity of staining.

5 Think about getting veneers, which are custom-made shells bonded to the teeth with resins. This procedure often requires removing a small amount of tooth structure and is the most invasive—as well as the most expensive—treatment option.

### ✳ Tips

No bleaching method can permanently whiten teeth, and all require repeated treatments—especially if the factor that caused staining still exists.

All of the bleaching mechanisms described here can cause tooth sensitivity, usually temporary (lasting up to several weeks).

### ⚠ Warnings

Never try to remove or scrape off stains with your fingernails or other sharp objects.

The ADA and the U.S. Food and Drug Administration discourage use of over-the-counter bleaching kits, which can damage your gums.

## 756 Stock an Emergency Supply of Medicine and First Aid

When an injury occurs, having medical materials within easy reach can help minimize bleeding, swelling and trauma. That's why every home should possess a well-stocked first aid kit.

### ⊙ Steps

1 Buy a plastic storage container that is shoe box size or larger—an art-supplies container with big handles or a fishing-tackle box will work nicely. Think of this container as the "safe box" for your emergency supplies.

2 Gather materials necessary to treat cuts and lacerations: sterile plain and nonstick gauze pads in a variety of sizes, bandages, soft bandage wraps and a pair of latex gloves for the care of fresh bleeding wounds (caution: some people are allergic to latex).

3 Be sure to pack soap to clean wounds. Soap containing chlorhexidine makes a good antiseptic. If no family members are allergic to iodine, consider including products containing povidone-iodine, such as Betadine. Use Betadine swabs to clean difficult-to-reach areas and Betadine pads for small scrapes.

4 Include at least two sizes of bandage tape, and an elasticized wrap to hold gauze pads or other dressings in place.

5 Place analgesic/antihistamine cream in the kit.

6 Add a bottle of syrup of ipecac if you have children, so you can induce vomiting in case someone swallows poison. Do not use ipecac until you have confirmed the need with your doctor or a poison-control hot line.

7 Consider keeping an aqueous epinephrine solution kit (called an EpiPen or Ana-kit) in the box if anyone in the family is allergic to bees, wasps or yellow jackets. You will need a prescription for the kit. Review how to use the kit with everyone who might need to know.

8 Put a good pair of tweezers and a pair of sharp scissors in the kit. The tweezers are great for removing gravel from scraped knees, as well as splinters and glass bits. The sharp scissors can quickly cut away a pants leg from a lacerated thigh.

9 Include a bottle of sterile eye-irrigating solution.

10 Put a flashlight with fresh batteries in the kit, and be sure to check the batteries every few months. Good light is vital for detecting foreign bodies in the eyes, mouth and ears, and in assessing the depth and severity of wounds.

11 Keep a first aid manual inside the kit. Review the manual every six months so you'll remember what to do in an emergency.

12 Enroll in a CPR and a first aid class for optimal emergency preparedness. These are available at most community centers.

### ✳ Tip

Add a washcloth and towel (in a sterile plastic bag) to your kit when you travel. Most wounds can be cleaned effectively with soap and clean water, as long as the washcloth and towel are also clean.

### ⚠ Warnings

Inspect your kit once a year and replace expired medications.

Keep first aid kits in a cool, dark place, out of reach of children.

### Things You'll Need

☐ plastic storage container

☐ sterile plain gauze pads

☐ sterile nonstick gauze pads

☐ bandages and bandage tape

☐ soft bandage wrap and elasticized bandage wrap

☐ latex gloves

☐ Betadine swabs and pads

☐ soap with chlorhexidine

☐ analgesic/antihistamine cream

☐ syrup of ipecac

☐ epinephrine kit (EpiPen or Ana-kit)

☐ tweezers and sharp scissors

☐ sterile eye-irrigating solution

☐ flashlight and batteries

☐ first aid manual

## Avoid Poison Oak, Sumac and Ivy — 757

Poison oak, poison sumac and poison ivy can all cause a rash when their resin contacts the skin. The best prevention is to learn how to spot them and avoid them.

### ⊙ Steps

1 Learn to identify the habitats of these plants. Poison oak and poison ivy are often found below 5,000 feet in moist ravines, canyons and hilltops that don't get much sunlight. In general, poison oak grows in the western United States and poison ivy grows in the eastern half of the country. Poison sumac grows in moist and marshlike areas east of the Mississippi River.

2 Memorize the characteristics of these plants. The basic rule is "Leaves of three, let it be." Poison oak and ivy can be found as shrubs or vines, depending on geographic location; poison sumac is a shrub that grows in marshes and bogs.

3 Wear a pre-exposure skin conditioner on exposed parts of the body to minimize the effects in case of contact.

4 Wear long-sleeved shirts, long pants, socks and hiking boots to cover your skin when hiking in an area populated by poison oak, sumac or ivy.

5 Wash your hands and any exposed skin with soap and water immediately following contact, or use a special soap formulated to wash plant resins from skin and clothing. Such soaps are available in sporting-goods stores and outdoor-equipment stores.

6 Wash your clothes and shoelaces with a mild soap immediately following a hike in an area populated with poison oak, sumac or ivy, even if you don't believe you had any contact with the plants. Also shower, and wash your hair thoroughly.

7 Keep in mind that the entire plant (including the leafless stems during winter) carries the irritating oil.

### ✱ Tip

If you are hiking with your dog in an area inhabited by any of these plants, avoid contact with your pet until it has been bathed. Dogs are usually unaffected by the plants, but the oil sticks to their fur and can give you a rash.

### ⚠ Warning

Never burn poisonous plants. The oils are carried in the smoke, and it is dangerous to inhale. If you inhale the fumes from such a fire, seek medical care right away.

---

## Treat Poison Oak, Sumac and Ivy — 758

Millions of Americans each year suffer from contact dermatitis after exposure to poison oak, sumac or ivy. It normally takes at least three weeks for symptoms to completely disappear.

### ⊙ Steps

1 Immediately wash everything that might have touched the plant, including all clothing and tools, with a soap formulated to wash plant resins from skin and clothing. The oil can remain active for a long time on inanimate objects, but you may be able to take off the oil completely, or at least remove enough of it to reduce the impending rash.

2 Soothe the itching with a cool, wet washcloth.

3 Soak in a cool bath. Add colloidal oatmeal (approximately 5 cups) to cool water and soak for 15 to 30 minutes.

### ✱ Tip

Use a cotton ball to apply isopropyl alcohol to any skin that came in contact with the plant. The alcohol will deactivate the irritating oils if it is applied without delay.

### ⚠ Warning

Never burn poisonous plants. The oils are carried in the smoke,

4   Add a few drops of water to some baking soda to make a paste, which can dry it out, and apply it to your rash if the rash is oozing.

5   Avoid breaking the rash blisters. They can become infected if you do.

6   Opt for lotions containing calamine, alcohol and/or zinc acetate; these will dry the blisters and help speed healing. Cortisone lotions work well, too.

7   Avoid topical antihistamines; they are not as effective as oral ones and can cause a rash of their own in some people.

8   Leave the rash open to the air. That will help it heal.

9   See a doctor if the rash becomes infected, becomes very red and swollen, or does not appear to be improving after a few days of self-treatment, or if you have a question or concern. The doctor may prescribe an oral steroid or antihistamine to hurry along the healing process.

and it is dangerous to inhale. If you inhale the fumes from burning poisonous plants, seek medical care right away.

## Things You'll Need

- ☐ formulated soap
- ☐ washcloth
- ☐ baking soda or colloidal oatmeal
- ☐ anti-itch lotion

---

## 759 | Remove a Tick

Ticks are most active in the spring and summer and can be found almost everywhere in nature. Here's how to remove them correctly.

### ⊙ Steps

1   Check your naked body from head to toe for ticks—small black, brown, reddish or tan disklike arachnids (having eight legs), from the size of a pinhead to almost the size of a thumbtack. Pay special attention to the backs of your knees, your groin area and your torso.

2   Ask a friend or family member for help if you find a tick in a hard-to-reach spot.

3   Hold (or have the other person hold) a pair of tweezers in one hand and grasp the tick with the tweezers close to the surface of your skin. Also avoid grabbing the body of the tick with your fingers and trying to pull it out. This method may cause you to leave some parts of the tick under your skin and will also expose your hands to any disease the tick is carrying.

4   Gently but firmly pull the tick straight out, working for several seconds if necessary until it loosens and comes free. Occasionally, parts of the tick's mouth become separated from the rest of the tick; if they do, pull them out separately.

5   Dispose of the tick by throwing it into a fire or by squishing it using a tissue and then flushing it down the toilet. Don't smash it with your foot or your bare hands.

6   Clean the bite site thoroughly with soap and water or Betadine, and thoroughly wash your hands.

### ✱ Tips

You are not likely to get ticks from your pet, even if you are in close proximity. Ticks jump on you as you walk through or sit on grass or low-growing vegetation.

Ignore the old wives' tales that advocate using gasoline or nail polish to remove a tick, covering the tick with oil or holding burning matches up to the embedded tick. Although you may have some success with these methods, they are not recommended.

### ⚠ Warning

If you have removed a tick and later develop flulike symptoms, a strange rash or inexplicable pain in your joints, contact your doctor immediately. You may have Lyme disease or Rocky Mountain spotted fever.

### Things You'll Need

- ☐ tweezers
- ☐ soap or Betadine

## Help Prevent Altitude Sickness     **760**

When you rapidly ascend above 8,000 feet, you run the risk of suffering from an inability to adjust to the lower oxygen level.

### ⊙ Steps

1   Ascend slowly to give your body time to adjust gradually to the lower oxygen concentration in the air. A good rule of thumb when hiking is to ascend no more than 1,500 ft. per day, with plenty of rest in between.

2   Drink water as you climb, to maintain proper hydration.

3   Fill up on carbohydrates, with only enough proteins and fats to meet essential nutritional needs.

4   Take it easy when first reaching higher altitudes. Overexertion can make you more susceptible to acute mountain sickness.

5   Avoid alcohol and caffeine, which cause dehydration, and smoking and sedatives.

6   Ask your doctor about medication such as acetazolamide which can help your body acclimatize. Some research suggests that ginkgo biloba can help protect the body against altitude sickness.

### ✻ Tip

You'll know that you're drinking enough water if your urine is clear (not yellow) and copious.

### ⚠ Warning

If someone is showing signs of altitude illness—dizziness, apathy, loss of appetite, headache, confusion, lethargy, nausea, vomiting, or difficulties with breathing, walking or sleeping—descend until the symptoms subside. Seek medical attention if the symptoms fail to subside. Severe altitude illness can be fatal if left untreated.

---

## Help Prevent Heat-Related Illness     **761**

A summer day can be deadly to someone who is unable to cool down as a result of heat, dehydration or overexertion.

### ⊙ Steps

1   Identify climatic conditions in which heat-related illnesses are likely: temperatures of 90 degrees F or higher, and high relative humidity.

2   Get plenty of sleep and eat fruits and vegetables high in potassium to help your body adjust to the heat.

3   Keep cool: Stay out of the sun if you can; seek shade or air-conditioned buildings; wear sunscreen, a hat, sunglasses and baggy clothing that breathes well; schedule demanding activities for cooler parts of the day.

4   Limit physical exertion, especially if activity causes you to be soaked with sweat. If you're dripping with perspiration, this may be a sign that your sweat is not evaporating sufficiently to cool your skin.

5   If you can't avoid physical activities in the heat of day, allow your body to acclimatize by spending an hour or so doing physical activities in the heat over a period of 10 days. Increase the amount of time gradually to allow your body to adjust to the heat.

6   Stay hydrated. Drink a minimum of 3 quarts of fluid per day and increase this to 4 or 5 quarts if you will be exerting yourself. If you will be exercising vigorously or sweating a lot, water alone is not enough. You'll need a sports drink with electrolytes—about 1 quart for every hour of exercise.

7   Avoid amphetamines, antihistamines, anti-depressants or other drugs that affect your body's basic functions.

### ✻ Tips

Thirst is not a reliable indicator of heat stress. Follow the advice in step 6 and note that dark or scant urine indicates that your body needs more fluids.

Children, the elderly and people with endocrine or skin diseases are especially susceptible to heat-related illnesses.

### ⚠ Warning

If someone is exhibiting signs of a heat illness (muscle cramping, tiredness, a headache, dizziness, nausea or heavy perspiration), get him or her to a cooler place immediately. If a person exhibits vomiting, diarrhea, confusion or disorientation, hot and red or cool and clammy skin, elevated body temperature, an increased heart or respiratory rate, or seizures, seek medical help immediately. Heatstroke is potentially fatal.

## 762 | Prevent Frostbite

When it's cold enough (32 degrees F or below), skin can freeze, resulting in frostbite. Not only painful, frostbite can cause the loss of fingers and toes, or even limbs.

### ⊙ Steps

1   Recognize that by venturing out into the cold, you are risking frostbite. Wind and wetness will drain your body of heat—especially your frost-bite-prone extremities—with astonishing speed. Stay mindful of the risk.

2   Keep a close eye on the weather wherever you go into the wilderness, and adjust your plans as necessary to avoid the risk of frostbite. Frostbite can strike in any season, especially in the high country.

3   Bring along warm clothing when going outdoors: an inner wicking layer, a middle insulating layer and an outer wind- and water-resistant layer for both your upper and lower body. Be sure you also have gloves or mittens (mittens are better), a hat, and wool or thick fleece socks.

4   Make sure you have clothing that will not lose its insulating properties when wet. The primary offender is cotton; wool is much better, as are many kinds of synthetic fleece.

5   Stay hydrated. Dehydration is a predisposing condition for frostbite and hypothermia.

6   Eat plenty of food, especially carbohydrates, which are quick to digest and easy for your metabolism to turn into heat. Eat small amounts frequently rather than large amounts infrequently.

7   Set a reasonable pace when engaging in vigorous activities. Exhaustion can make treatment and even recognition of frostbite more difficult.

8   Stop and warm your feet or hands if they start to feel numb; this is an early warning of frostbite.

9   Turn back and seek shelter if the weather turns nasty, especially if you encounter snow, rain and/or strong winds.

### ✳ Tip

When layering your clothing, make sure each layer is roomier than the layer underneath to allow for some insulating air between layers.

### ⚠ Warnings

Avoid tight-fitting clothing—including footwear—that might impair circulation.

Avoid alcohol, which could contribute to dehydration and impair judgment, as well as caffeine and nicotine, which constrict blood vessels and therefore reduce the blood supply to extremities.

## 763 | Prevent Seasickness

The sea's repetitive motions can overstimulate the inner ear, causing nausea and vomiting. Here are some tried-and-true preventive measures.

### ⊙ Steps

1   Talk to your doctor about prescription medicines, or consider over-the-counter medication such as dimenhydrinate (Dramamine).

2   Try an anti-seasickness wristband, which stimulates the median nerve in your wrist, a well-known acupuncture point.

3   Try eating ginger 12 to 24 hours before your trip. Take it as a supplement, following directions on the package, or talk to a nutritionist at your local health food store. Some sources recommend putting powdered

### ✳ Tip

For many people, the most effective preventive medication is scopolamine, available by prescription and applied as a patch to the skin.

ginger into granola or sprinkling it on top of toast. Snacking on ginger-snaps several hours before your trip may also help.

4   Drink plenty of water before your trip. Good hydration helps prevent sea-sickness. But once on board, avoid foods and fluids until you're sure you won't get seasick. Avoid all alcoholic beverages; alcohol can not only add to your tipsy feeling but promote dehydration.

5   Eat oatmeal, crusty bread or bagels an hour before setting off. Some experts say that having food in your stomach can reduce seasickness.

6   Position yourself where the least motion is felt, usually in the center of the deck, and avoid going below deck, as the fumes and stuffy air will not help your nausea.

7   Suck on lemon drops—or your favorite hard candy—as soon as the boat begins moving. Besides tasting good, these tart treats may help to keep your nausea in check.

8   Take deep breaths and stare out into the distance. Focus on the horizon, not on waves or moving objects.

## Things You'll Need

- ❏ anti-seasickness medication
- ❏ anti-seasickness wristband
- ❏ ginger or gingersnaps
- ❏ lemon drops

# Stop a Nosebleed                                764

Nosebleeds are caused by broken blood vessels inside the nose and are especially common in children. They usually go away on their own but will stop more quickly with help.

## ⊙ Steps

1   Pinch your nose between your thumb and forefinger, and apply moder-ate pressure by squeezing against the nasal septum—the midsection of your nose—for 15 minutes.

2   Lean your head forward, not backward, so that the blood does not trick-le down your throat. This will prevent a feeling of gagging.

3   Breathe through your mouth.

4   Apply a cold, soft compress around your nose as you continue to pinch it between your fingers.

5   Once bleeding has stopped, elevate your head above your heart when you are lying in bed or on the couch. This helps alleviate nasal pressure.

6   Turn on a cool vaporizer to moisten mucus membranes, which will help prevent the nosebleed from recurring.

7   Apply a small amount of petroleum jelly to the inside of the nostrils to moisten the passages and prevent the nosebleed from recurring. Use your fingertip.

8   Avoid blowing your nose for 24 hours, and when you do blow it again, blow gently.

9   Avoid lifting heavy objects or engaging in other strenuous activities after a nosebleed. This can produce momentary surges in blood pressure that could cause the nose to bleed again.

## ✱ Tips

Anterior (in the front) nosebleeds are the everyday kind. Posterior (in the back) nosebleeds involve heavy bleeding from deep within the nose and are much more dif-ficult to stop. Posterior nose-bleeds occur most often in the elderly.

Keep your child's fingernails trimmed if she likes to poke around in her nose.

## ⚠ Warning

Seek medical care if your nose continues bleeding after 20 min-utes, if the bleeding worsens rather than improves, or if you have specific medical conditions or concerns.

## 765 | Care for Minor Cuts and Abrasions

Treating a cut right away lessens the chance of infection.

### ⊙ Steps

1 Wash your hands before and after tending a wound.

2 Rinse the wound with clean water. Flush out all dirt and debris.

3 Using clean gauze, put pressure on the wound to stop any bleeding.

4 Clean the area around the injury with soap and water or Betadine, but avoid getting any solution inside the wound.

5 Leave the wound open to the air unless there is a chance that you'll be exposing it to dirt or infection. In that case, bandage the wound loosely, allowing air to get in.

6 If the wound edges are open, use a butterfly bandage—a butterfly-shaped bandage that brings the edges of the wound together and reduces scarring—to close straight, clean, superficial wounds.

7 Call your doctor if you detect signs of infection, which include redness, warmth, redness up the arm, or oozing or drainage from the wound.

### ⚠ Warning

See a doctor if the wound is deep, won't stop bleeding or has edges that won't come together. Animal bites, human bites and deep wounds should be evaluated by a physician in case antibiotics are needed. Also see a doctor if the wound is very dirty and more than 10 years have elapsed since your last tetanus shot.

### Things You'll Need

- ☐ soap or Betadine
- ☐ gauze
- ☐ bandages

## 766 | Remove a Splinter

Splinters can cause pain, swelling and possibly infection if they're not removed promptly.

### ⊙ Steps

1 Try to "milk" out the splinter by gently squeezing your fingertips over or on each side of it. If this doesn't work, try the following steps.

2 If you're worried about causing pain, rub the splinter site with a numbing teething gel or ice before removing the splinter. Keep in mind, however, that chilling the area may cause the splinter to retract from the top of the skin and may make its removal more challenging.

3 Clean a needle, a pair of tweezers and a small pair of nail clippers with isopropyl alcohol or Betadine solution and let it air-dry. Be sure to swab the pinching surfaces of the tweezers and the cutting edges of the nail clippers.

4 Use soap and water, or Betadine, to wash the skin where the splinter has lodged.

5 With the tip of the needle, make a small hole in the skin above the splinter. Once you have access to the splinter, gently try to squeeze it through the hole. If necessary, increase the size of the hole with the needle. Use your tweezers to pull out the splinter as soon as you can get hold of it.

6 If you're not able to open a path for the splinter with the needle, use the nail clippers very carefully to cut away the skin above the splinter.

### ✳ Tips

Soak the infected area in warm water to soften the skin if you have trouble getting access to the splinter.

Most splinters eventually work themselves out on their own.

### ⚠ Warnings

Do not dig at a splinter for longer than 5 minutes. If you're unable to remove it within that time, leave it alone, or see a doctor if you feel you are at risk of infection. Too much poking and prodding will lead to tissue damage.

Be sure you are current on your tetanus vaccine. Once you've had your initial vaccine, you need to get a booster every 10 years. If a splinter comes in contact with dirt or animal dung before it

7   Wipe the site with isopropyl alcohol or Betadine when you've removed the splinter.

8   Apply an antibiotic ointment to the site.

punctures your skin, it could be carrying the bacterium that causes tetanus.

## Check a Wound for Infection                      767

Even cleaned and dressed wounds are by nature contaminated and may still become infected. Check daily for infection to minimize tissue damage and health risk.

### ⊙ Steps

1   Protect yourself. Scrub your hands thoroughly with soap and water, and put on latex gloves to prevent the spread of infectious disease.

2   Remove the bandage and dressing from the wound. Dispose of them immediately, handling them only with latex gloves or tweezers. The best means of disposal is burning, but wrapping them in plastic and throwing them away in the trash can is suitable for most situations.

3   Check the wound for any pus, swelling, redness or faint red lines radiating from the wound.

4   Feel the area surrounding the wound for any heat.

5   Ask the injured person if he or she has experienced any pain or chills.

6   Look for swelling or tenderness in the lymph nodes, located under the armpits, in the groin and neck areas, and behind the ears.

7   Take the person's temperature. Consider a temperature higher than 100 degrees F a possible sign of infection.

8   Contact a doctor immediately if you observe any fever, chills, swelling of the lymph nodes, or red lines radiating from the wound, or if you are in any doubt whatsoever.

9   Gently draw a circle with a pen around any reddening of the skin to help monitor whether the infection is spreading.

10  When you finish examining the wound, apply a fresh dressing and bandage the wound.

### ⚠ Warnings

If you see signs of infection or have questions or concerns, contact your doctor.

Infectious diseases such as AIDS and hepatitis are transmitted via the exchange of bodily fluids. Protect yourself by wearing latex gloves, and use responsible means of disposing of used bandages and gauze.

Tweezers and any implements used to check a wound should be disinfected by soaking in isopropyl alcohol immediately after use.

Some people are allergic to latex gloves. Use latex gloves only if you know you are not allergic to them.

## Soothe a Burnt Tongue                      768

That soup just smelled too good to wait for it to cool, didn't it? Now it's time to give your burnt tongue about 24 hours to heal.

### ⊙ Steps

1   Remember that the surfaces of your mouth and tongue are mucus membranes, and as such, they heal faster than other areas of your body. So even though your tongue may really hurt, be comforted in knowing that by tomorrow, the burn should be gone.

### ⚠ Warning

Contact a doctor if you have suffered a serious burn—blistering or severe pain—to your tongue.

2    Cool your tongue with a frozen dessert such as ice cream or sherbet. Let the treat linger on top of your tongue before you swallow it. For severe burns, frozen foods can be left on top of the tongue for 3 to 4 minutes, until the tongue becomes slightly numb and the pain is dulled.

3    Suck on an ice cube. Don't bite down on the cube, though, because it can crack your teeth.

4    Inhale air through your mouth, across and over your tongue. The cool breeze will help relieve some of the sting.

5    Suck on a cough drop containing phenol, which helps numb the tongue's surface.

6    Talk to your doctor about a prescription for lidocaine hydrochloride oral topical solution, 2 percent, to apply to your tongue. This will numb it and completely relieve your pain.

7    Avoid using mouthwash or harsh toothpaste until the burn heals.

8    Pass on oranges, pineapple and other acidic foods until your tongue stops hurting.

---

## 769  Treat Food Poisoning

**Symptoms of food poisoning may include vomiting, diarrhea, fever or cramping. They usually begin 3 to 36 hours after eating tainted food, and can last from 12 hours to several days.**

### ⊙ Steps

1    Consult your doctor if the symptoms are severe or if you have severe abdominal pain. You may be suffering from something more serious than food poisoning.

2    Sip clear fluids. Dehydration is the primary concern when experiencing vomiting or diarrhea.

3    Take small amounts of fluid frequently. Electrolyte replacements (such as sports drinks) are your best options. You can also sip flat ginger ale, which may help settle your stomach.

4    Suck on ice chips if nothing else stays down.

5    Introduce food slowly after vomiting stops.

6    Eat bland, easily digestible foods such as soda crackers if you are still having diarrhea. Bananas, applesauce, rice and toast are good.

7    Avoid milk, fatty foods, high fiber and caffeine for a few days until you are feeling better—these foods are harder to digest.

8    Limit your time in the sun, as this may dehydrate you further.

9    Gradually resume your normal diet once symptoms subside.

10   Contact your doctor if symptoms fail to subside in 24 hours.

###  Tip

You can use over-the-counter medications to control vomiting or diarrhea, but it is usually better not to use anything for at least the first 6 to 8 hours. The bacteria or virus causing the problem will pass from your body faster if you don't try to slow it down.

## ✓ 770 Recognize Signs of a Medical Emergency

Urgent medical attention is required for a number of medical conditions, including those whose common signs and symptoms are listed below. Call a physician or visit an emergency room immediately if any of these occur, even if you are not entirely sure that it is an emergency.

### Appendicitis

❑ Is the patient between the ages of 10 and 30? The condition is most common in this age group but can occur at any age.

❑ Is there pain and/or tenderness in the navel area that moves toward the lower right of the abdomen over the course of a few hours?

❑ Does the patient describe the pain as severe and sharp, and worsening with any movement?

❑ Is there a fever? This may be a sign of inflammation and infection, a possible sign of appendicitis.

❑ Is the patient experiencing signs of nausea, vomiting or loss of appetite?

❑ Did the patient take pain medications that may mask the symptoms of appendicitis?

### Anaphylactic shock

❑ Has the patient been exposed within the last 2 hours to a common allergen, such as an insect sting, nuts, peanuts, seeds, legumes, eggs or shellfish? A person may be allergic to any of these even if he or she has been exposed to them before without problems.

❑ Does the patient report tingling in the mouth and tongue and/or throbbing ears?

❑ Does the patient appear uneasy or agitated?

❑ Does the patient's skin appear flushed and feel itchy, and are hives appearing on the skin or swellings becoming evident on the eyes, lips or tongue?

❑ Is the patient sneezing, coughing, wheezing or having difficulty breathing?

❑ Is the patient vomiting or experiencing abdominal cramps or diarrhea?

### Heart attack

❑ Is there crushing pain, pressure or squeezing in the center of the chest that lasts for more than a few minutes?

❑ Does the pain spread to the jaw, neck, shoulders, back or arms (often the left arm)?

❑ Is there any nausea, sweating, dizziness or shortness of breath in combination with chest pain?

❑ Is the person over 50 and experiencing indigestion or heartburn that does not respond to over-the-counter medication?

❑ Is there a combination of these symptoms?

### Stroke

❑ Is there any numbness or weakness on one side of the body such as in one arm or leg, or on one side of the face?

❑ Is the person having problems such as difficulty speaking or a loss of speech altogether?

❑ Are there any vision problems such as double vision or loss of vision, especially if this occurs in just one eye?

❑ Is there any sign of sudden, severe, unexplained headaches, dizziness, loss of coordination or balance, or sudden falling without apparent cause?

checklist

## 771 | Choose a Doctor

Choosing the right physician for you and your family is an important decision, so research and investigate carefully.

### ⊙ Steps

1 Ask trusted family members, friends and co-workers to recommend a physician. Contact local hospitals, medical schools or medical societies for referrals.

2 Call several physicians as you search for one who best suits your needs.

3 Determine whether your insurance plan covers visits to that physician.

4 Make sure the physician is licensed by contacting your state medical licensing board for background information (including possible incidents of malpractice).

5 See if the physician is board certified, which indicates the successful completion of higher training and exams; call (800) 776-CERT.

6 Check the physician's hospital affiliations. Make sure you are satisfied with the hospitals' quality and reputation.

7 Find out if the physician belongs to a professional medical association.

8 Determine how accessible the physician is: Is the office near your home or job? Is it easy to get the appointment times you need?

9 Find out how you'd be able to get emergency care after hours.

10 Make sure the physician has a good bedside manner, is patient and compassionate, listens to your concerns, and explains medical issues clearly. Inquire whether phone or e-mail consultations are welcome.

11 Ask physicians how long they have been practicing and what sorts of continuing education they have pursued to stay current with new developments and research.

12 If you are looking for a surgeon to perform a specific procedure, ask the candidates how many times they have performed that procedure.

### ✳ Tips

HMOs, PPOs and other health care organizations can make it difficult to see the doctor or specialist of your choice. Read the fine print in your health care contract—this may be allowed under some circumstances. If it isn't, you may be able to persuade plan administrators to make an exception.

While good bedside manner is important, remember that it does not necessarily mean that a doctor has good medical skills. Nurses and other health care professionals can often recommend doctors who are both personable and competent.

## 772 | Know When to Call a Doctor if Your Child Is Sick

It's sometimes hard to know when your child needs a doctor. Here are some general guidelines to help you decide—but remember that if in doubt, it's always safest to call the doctor.

### ⊙ Steps

1 Take his temperature. High fevers can lead to seizures in children who are prone to them. If your child has a very high temperature (greater than 103 degrees F measured by an oral thermometer), is lethargic, is very irritable or refuses to eat, or if he doesn't respond to fever-reducing medication, contact a doctor.

### ✳ Tips

Put together a first aid kit with supplies you may need for your child (see 756 "Stock an Emergency Supply of Medicine and First Aid.")

**How to Do *(Just About)* Everything**

2 Check his breathing. If your child is having respiratory difficulties such as wheezing or rapid breathing, get him to a doctor immediately. This is especially important if your child is asthmatic.

3 Consider allergies. If your child has one or more severe food or environmental allergies, seek treatment immediately when you know or suspect that he has been exposed.

4 Go to a doctor if your child falls or bumps her head hard enough to lose consciousness—even a mild concussion can be dangerous. An inability to remember the events surrounding the injury may also indicate a concussion. Look for confusion and drowsiness as warning signs of more serious problems.

5 Talk to your child. If she is unresponsive or semiconscious, or has trouble focusing her eyes, get medical help immediately or call 911.

6 Seek help for cuts if you have trouble stopping the bleeding, or if the cut is deep and severe enough to require stitches.

7 Call the doctor if your child is vomiting frequently or has severe diarrhea. The doctor will be able to tell you how to monitor your child for dehydration, and will let you know whether to come in.

8 Call a poison-control hotline if you think your child has ingested anything toxic. The staff will be able to tell you what to do and whether the situation is a medical emergency.

9 Seek medical attention if your child complains of a severe headache, especially if it's accompanied by a stiff neck and a fever—these symptoms sometimes signal meningitis.

10 Whenever in doubt, call your doctor, or call 911 in an emergency. It's always better to be on the safe side.

Keep emergency numbers, including the number for a poison-control center (check your phone book), next to the phone.

### ⚠ Warnings

If your child is asthmatic, be sure to have a spare inhaler where you can find it immediately, as children often misplace inhalers.

If you think your child has taken poison, do not induce vomiting unless your doctor or the poison-control hot line tells you to.

If your child requires regular medication for any condition, always replace it well before it runs out or reaches its expiration date. This includes having an aqueous epinephrine kit if your child has a history of allergies and there is the possibility of a severe reaction that could lead to anaphylactic shock.

---

## Care for a Sinus Headache                                    773

A sinus headache is a symptom of inflamed, congested sinuses. To get rid of your headache, you must reduce the inflammation in your sinuses. Learning the cause will make it easier to treat.

### ⊙ Steps

1 Take acetaminophen, aspirin (if older than 18) or ibuprofen for pain relief.

2 Apply warm compresses to the site of your pain four times a day.

3 Call your doctor if the drainage from your nose is discolored. Clear or slightly white mucus is acceptable. Yellow, rust-colored or green drainage indicates a serious infection and is cause for concern.

4 Use extra pillows to elevate your head, which will allow your sinuses to drain.

5 Try using a nasal spray or a decongestant. Depending on the cause of your sinusitis, over-the-counter decongestants may offer some relief. Do not use nasal sprays for more than a few days because they can become addictive. If sinusitis persists, see a doctor.

6 Avoid allergens if you suspect your sinusitis is allergy-related.

### ✱ Tip

Blow your nose with your mouth slightly open and blow through both your nostrils. This helps to equalize the pressure in your sinuses. Avoid blowing too hard.

### ⚠ Warnings

Call your doctor if you have persistent fever, ringing in your ears, eye drainage or facial swelling associated with your sinus headache.

7   Stay away from cigarette smoke, which can aggravate sinuses.

8   Keep your distance from people with colds and flu. Your body is already compromised and fighting off an inflammatory process.

9   Eat properly to help increase your body's resistance to disease.

10  Get plenty of rest. Catnaps can do a lot to lessen the severity of a sinus headache. Stress and fatigue may aggravate it.

11  Try increasing the humidity in your room. Use a humidifier, or take a hot bath or shower. Boil a pot of water, take it off the stove, drape a towel over your head and the pot, and inhale the steam for 10 minutes, four times a day. Keep your face at least 18 inches away from the pot to avoid burning yourself.

12  Increase your fluid intake. This encourages your sinuses to drain by hydrating your body. Hot (noncaffeinated) tea is especially good because the steam loosens congestion in your sinuses.

Never take more than the suggested dosage of over-the-counter painkillers.

Do not give aspirin to children under 18 years of age.

---

## 774  Care for a Migraine

Migraine attacks can last for hours or days. Treatment for severe, chronic headaches begins by finding the cause, if possible. Don't accept unrelenting pain; treatments are available.

### ⊙ Steps

1   Talk to your doctor about your symptoms so he or she can make a proper diagnosis and rule out the possibility of an underlying disease. Look for signs of migraine such as throbbing pain, often on one side of the head, and nausea. These symptoms may be preceded by visual disturbances such as flickering lights.

2   Ask your doctor which type of prescription migraine medication is right for your type of headache. Many of these can effectively relieve a migraine if taken early on.

3   Lie in a darkened, quiet, odor-free room and apply cold compresses to the temples, eyes and eye sockets. This may curb a full-blown migraine.

4   Compress and release the artery running along the side of your temple with your fingers.

5   Quell the queasiness with a prescription antinausea medication. Consider antinausea suppositories.

6   Avoid any foods that might trigger a migraine. Common foods are hot dogs and preserved meats, shellfish, nuts, aged cheese, yogurt, alcohol (especially red wine), MSG, chocolate, artificial sweeteners and certain fruits. If you eat a food for the first time and get a migraine 2 hours later, it's probably best to stay away from this food.

7   Try drinking coffee. For some people suffering from caffeine withdrawal, caffeine helps relieve symptoms.

8   Ask your doctor if a preventive medication would be appropriate for you.

### ✱ Tips

These severe headaches can affect anyone, but most sufferers are women, and migraines often occur around the time of their menstrual periods.

The treatment of migraines is often accomplished through prescription drug therapy, which is relatively safe and effective. It's best to avoid narcotics, as addiction can be a problem.

### ⚠ Warning

Headaches that require medical attention include those that are of sudden onset or extremely painful, persistent or increasing in severity, increased by exertion or coughing, accompanied by fever or altered mental status, or unresponsive to treatment.

## Avoid a Hangover     `775`

The best way to avoid a hangover, of course, is never to drink at all. But if abstinence is not a part of your plans, check out these proven techniques.

### ⊙ Steps

1 Eat before you drink. Starchy carbohydrates such as bread and pasta will slow the absorption of alcohol.

2 Avoid very sweet drinks that disguise their alcohol content, and avoid mixing different types of alcohol.

3 Drink water in between alcoholic drinks to prevent dehydration.

4 Eat hearty food while you are drinking.

5 Drink another glass of water when you get home.

### ✳ Tip

If you get a really bad hangover, keep track of what you had to drink the night before and avoid it next time.

### ⚠ Warning

Avoid aspirin or ibuprofen if you have stomach ulcers or gastritis.

## Care for a Hangover     `776`

The headache, nausea, thirst and fatigue you feel are all symptoms of dehydration. Follow these steps to eliminate those symptoms and get back to feeling your best.

### ⊙ Steps

1 Drink water as soon as you get up in the morning to rehydrate yourself. If possible, have a sports drink. The electrolytes and nutrients in a sports drink can replenish your body's depleted reserves.

2 Drink even more water if you plan to have coffee. Caffeine is a mild diuretic and can contribute to dehydration.

3 Stick to liquids that are at room temperature. Drinks that are excessively hot or cold will be even more of a shock to your struggling stomach.

4 Take an over-the-counter pain reliever such as aspirin or ibuprofen to relieve a pounding headache or body aches.

5 Eat easily digestible foods when you're ready. Fresh fruit, toast and water-based soups are all easy on the stomach. Harder-to-digest foods such as eggs and milk can cause stomach problems.

6 Relax, rest or go back to bed. Allow some time for your body to feel positive effects from your treatments.

### ✳ Tip

Take preventive measures beforehand: Drink responsibly and in moderation. If you've drunk in excess and suspect you'll be hung over the next morning, drink a few glasses of water right before you go to bed.

### ⚠ Warnings

Do not take an acetaminophen-based painkiller to relieve symptoms. Combining acetaminophen and alcohol can damage your liver. Consider ibuprofen instead.

If you are an excessive drinker, use caution when taking any over-the-counter painkillers.

## 777 Care for a Sty

A sty is a bacterial infection that occurs inside an oil gland on your eyelid. Sties are usually benign and almost never cause damage to the eye or to vision.

### ☉ Steps

1  Wash your hands with soap and water before touching the eye area.

2  Soak a clean washcloth in warm or hot water.

3  Wring it out and place it directly on the affected eyelid. Make sure to keep the eye closed.

4  Keep the washcloth on the eyelid for about 10 minutes.

5  Repeat this three to four times a day for best results.

6  Continue the warm soaks until the sty comes to a head and drains.

7  Do not touch or squeeze the sty. This can cause the infection to spread.

8  See a doctor if the sty is still there after two days of self-care, if you have any eye pain, if the sty appears to be getting larger and spreading over the eyelid, or if you have questions or concerns.

### ✳ Tip

Most sties heal on their own. Antibiotics are usually only necessary if a sty is extremely large or does not respond to treatment. Occasionally, sties may need to be lanced and drained by a doctor. Do not attempt to do this on your own.

## 778 Care for Pinkeye

Conjunctivitis, or pinkeye, is an inflammation of the membrane that lines your eyeball and eyelid. It can be caused by a foreign body, an allergic reaction or a bacterial or viral infection.

### ☉ Steps

1  Determine if you have one or more of the following pinkeye symptoms: red, watery eyes; itching; sensitivity to light; or eye discharge that might be crusty around the eyelashes.

2  Wash your hands before touching the eye area.

3  Clean the eye area with a clean washcloth dampened with warm water.

4  Use a cool compress to relieve itching.

5  Wash any clothing, towels and bedding touched by the infected eye; bacterial and viral infections are very contagious.

6  Avoid wearing contact lenses until the infection clears up.

7  Note any yellow or greenish discharge from the eye. If this occurs or if only one eye is affected, it is more likely to be a bacterial infection than a viral infection or an allergy—consult your doctor for treatment.

### ✳ Tip

There is no over-the-counter medicine specifically for pinkeye. If the problem is caused by bacteria, you'll need to see a doctor for treatment. Viruses need to run their course. If the pinkeye is caused by an allergy, get rid of the allergen or see your doctor for allergy relief.

## Care for a Black Eye 779

A black eye is caused by bleeding under the skin around the eye, usually from a blow or other trauma. Take these steps to minimize the swelling and discomfort and to speed recovery.

### ⊙ Steps

1 Check the eyelid carefully for lacerations. If the lid has been cut, a doctor may need to repair it with a few fine sutures.

2 Place an ice pack or cold compress over the injury for 10 minutes every hour for the first day. Never put ice directly on your skin. Always use an ice pack or wrap a cloth around the ice. Ice helps constrict blood vessels and localize bleeding.

3 On the second and third days, apply a heating pad or warm, moist compresses to the injury for 10 to 20 minutes each hour or two. Heat applied 24 to 48 hours after the injury will help your body absorb the excess blood around delicate eye tissue.

4 Sleep with your head elevated on two pillows. This helps to reduce swelling of the eyelids.

5 Talk to your doctor about taking aspirin, ibuprofen or acetaminophen for discomfort if you are an adult. Children should not take aspirin.

6 Wear dark glasses, especially in well-lit areas, to reduce eyestrain as the black eye is healing.

### ✱ Tips

The eyeball, the bones around the eye and the eye muscles may all be affected by trauma to the eye.

Blood may drain into the eyelid, making it difficult to open. Blood may also drain into the cheek.

The tissue around the eye will remain bruised for two to three weeks.

See your doctor if your black eye causes you any special concerns.

### ⚠ Warning

If you experience double vision or any decrease in vision, see a doctor immediately.

## Care for a Toothache 780

Toothache symptoms include throbbing pain around a certain tooth, sensitivity to hot or cold, and discomfort when chewing. Causes vary from cavities and gum disease to cracked teeth and exposed roots.

### ⊙ Steps

1 Clean your mouth by rinsing it with warm water.

2 Floss gently around the sensitive tooth to dislodge any food particles.

3 Try placing an ice pack on your jaw to soothe the pain.

4 Use over-the-counter painkillers such as aspirin (for adults only) or ibuprofen to relieve the pain, or talk to a pharmacist about topical analgesic ointments.

5 Call your dentist if you have a fever or if the pain worsens, is recurrent or lasts for more than a few hours. Your dentist will ask you questions to determine the urgency of your need for treatment.

6 Prevent future toothaches with good oral hygiene. Brush twice a day with a fluoride toothpaste, floss once daily and see your dentist for checkups every six months.

### ✱ Tip

Some people find relief by chewing on cloves—if you can't find a clove, look for clove oil as the main ingredient in a pain reliever.

### ⚠ Warning

Never put aspirin or other painkillers directly on or around the sore tooth unless they are specifically designed to be used this way; some products can burn your mouth.

## 781 | Avoid a Cold

The common cold is caused by any one of more than 200 virus-es. Symptoms can include a fever, watery eyes, nasal conges-tion, a runny nose, sneezing, a sore throat and a cough.

### ⊙ Steps

1 Wash your hands often. Cold viruses can be transmitted by handshakes and by touching contaminated objects such as doorknobs.

2 Keep your hands away from your eyes, nose and mouth.

3 Avoid people who are coughing and/or sneezing.

4 Get plenty of rest to help strengthen your immune system.

5 Maintain a healthy diet and get an adequate amount of exercise.

6 Drink plenty of fluids.

7 Consider taking one 500mg tablet of vitamin C twice a day. Some scien-tists believe this can help boost your immune system, although there is no hard data to support this.

### ✳ Tips

Some studies have shown that the herbal supplement echinacea may be effective at fighting cold symptoms when taken during the first few days of illness—but not prior to exposure. However, there is no scientific data that supports the effectiveness of echinacea.

You may be more susceptible to colds when you are under stress, during your menstrual period, or when you are old—times when your immune system is weakened.

## 782 | Care for a Cold

The common cold is an upper respiratory infection involving the nose, throat and surrounding air passages. There is no quick cure, but these measures should help to hasten your recovery.

### ⊙ Steps

1 Eat chicken soup. It contains an amino acid called cysteine, which thins mucus and breaks up congestion. Plus, the steam from the soup helps open up air passages.

2 Gargle at the first sign of a scratchy throat with either mouthwash or 1/2 tsp. of salt dissolved in 8 oz. warm water.

3 Stay warm. Getting chilled compromises your immune system.

4 Take aspirin, acetaminophen or ibuprofen to reduce fever and inflamma-tion if you are an adult. Give children acetaminophen or ibuprofen. Determine the dose according to the child's age and weight.

5 Drink hot beverages and take hot showers. Steam helps open up nasal passages and reduces congestion.

6 Drink a lot of liquid, enough so that your urine turns clear. Yellow urine means your urine is fairly concentrated. Clear urine means your body is well-hydrated.

7 Use cough syrup sparingly. Coughing is one of the ways the body gets rid of mucus.

8 Suck on a throat lozenge for relief from a sore throat. Choose a menthol-, phenol- or benzocaine-based lozenge; these are the ones that will help to numb the throat. They also help open up nasal passages. Zinc lozenges may also be helpful.

### ✳ Tips

Antibiotics are effective only against bacteria, so they won't work against cold viruses.

Be careful not to overmedicate yourself with over-the-counter drugs. Some cough syrups have multiple ingredients that counter-act each other.

### ⚠ Warning

Contact a physician if your symp-toms become severe, if your fever fails to go down, if you have diffi-culty breathing, if you develop a serious cough, or if you have specific medical conditions or concerns.

9 Put an extra pillow under your head when you sleep to help your nasal passages drain.

10 Rest. If you have a bad cold, one of the best ways to treat it is to take a few days off and sleep.

---

## Prevent the Flu 783

Maintaining a healthy immune system is your best bet for avoiding the flu (short for influenza). Here are some simple ways to support your system through the flu season.

### ⊙ Steps

1 Avoid sharing drinking and eating utensils with people who are sick.

2 Wash your hands before eating—it really does help keep germs away.

3 Increase your vitamin C intake—which may boost your immune system—by eating ample amounts of fresh fruits and vegetables. Oranges, tomatoes and broccoli are good choices.

4 Drink at least eight glasses of water a day. Herbal teas and diluted fruit juices are good options for increasing your water intake.

5 Get enough sleep. Most people need at least 7 to 8 hours a night for optimal rest.

6 Manage your stress. Chronic stress can weaken the immune system.

7 Take a multivitamin every day to make sure you are getting enough vitamins and minerals.

8 Exercise regularly—it's been shown to reduce the occurrence of colds and flu.

### ✳ Tips

Vaccines (flu shots) are available and are particularly recommended for high-risk groups, such as those with immune disorders and anyone over the age of 50.

Some studies have shown that the herbal supplement echinacea may be effective at fighting flu symptoms when taken during the first few days of illness—but not prior to exposure. However, there is no scientific data that supports the effectiveness of echinacea.

Too much vitamin C can cause diarrhea and gastric discomfort. Avoid taking more than 500mg of vitamin C twice a day.

---

## Fight the Flu 784

Influenza can incubate in your body for up to three days. When it hits, be prepared.

### ⊙ Steps

1 See your doctor: There are effective prescription drugs that can treat a flu if taken within 48 hours of the onset of symptoms.

2 Sleep as much as you need to; let your body be your guide.

3 Stay hydrated by drinking plenty of water—at least eight glasses a day. If you don't feel like having plain water, add freshly squeezed lemon juice to water or drink diluted fruit juice.

4 If you are having nausea and/or vomiting, avoid solid foods until the vomiting stops and you are able to hold down clear fluids.

5 Start off with chicken or vegetable broth and dry crackers once you feel like eating. These are both easy to digest.

### ⚠ Warning

The flu is caused by a virus and cannot be cured with antibiotics. But if you are still sick three to five days after its onset, or if you become very sick very quickly, see a doctor. It's possible to have a bacterial infection along with a viral one, or to have an extremely virulent case of the flu.

6    Drink tea or herbal tea with honey. It is very soothing to a sore throat.

7    Take ibuprofen, aspirin or acetaminophen for fever, aches and pains if you are an adult. Give children acetaminophen or ibuprofen, not aspirin.

8    Use a humidifier or vaporizer if the air is dry. It will help break up mucus.

9    Choose an appropriate over-the-counter cough syrup based on your symptoms. Keep in mind that multiple-ingredient medications may contain ingredients that counteract each other.

---

## 785   Take a Temperature Orally

An oral thermometer is one of the best at-home diagnostic tools available. Use it any time you wonder if a family member is coming down with something.

### ⊙ Steps

1    Clean a glass thermometer with isopropyl alcohol before using it, then rinse or dip the tip in some cool water or wipe it with a tissue to remove the taste of the alcohol.

2    Shake down the thermometer, holding it firmly by the end opposite the metal bulb and snapping your wrist in a downward motion, until the mercury line is below 96.6 degrees F.

3    Slide the tip of the thermometer under one side of the tongue, well into the back of the mouth.

4    Close your lips around the thermometer—don't clench a glass thermometer with your teeth. Breathe through your nose, with mouth closed.

5    Leave the thermometer under your tongue for 3 full minutes, or as directed by the instructions on the original packaging.

6    Remove the thermometer and hold it under a bright light so you can see how high the mercury has risen. An arrow will indicate the point for a normal temperature reading, which is 98.6 degrees F.

### ✱ Tips

Use a thermometer specifically designed for taking an oral temperature. Do not use the same thermometer for oral and rectal temperatures. A rectal thermometer has an end that's more stout and stumpy.

For an oral temperature to be accurate, the person must not have had anything hot or cold to eat or drink for at least 10 minutes prior to inserting the thermometer in the mouth.

### ⚠ Warnings

Never heat a thermometer, either under hot water or by placing it on a hot surface.

Discard a broken thermometer immediately.

---

## 786   Help Reduce a Fever

A fever is a sign that your body is attempting to fight an infection. Help your body fight the fever in the following ways.

### ⊙ Steps

1    Get plenty of rest.

2    Drink plenty of fluids. Suck on an ice cube or flavored ice, or drink iced fruit juice or chilled clear broth.

3    Dress lightly and keep the room temperature between 70 and 74 degrees F. Use a blanket if you feel cold.

### ✱ Tips

A fever of 103 degrees F is not unusual in a young child. For adults, a fever higher than 101 degrees F or a fever that is greater than 101 degrees F at its onset is cause for medical attention.

4   Take anti-fever medicines only when necessary. For children under 18 years old, use acetaminophen or ibuprofen. For adults, use acetaminophen, aspirin or ibuprofen.

5   Give a child a lukewarm sponge bath for a temperature higher than 102 degrees F, but wait 30 minutes if you have given her acetaminophen. Wipe the child with a lukewarm washcloth or place her in a lukewarm tub for 20 minutes, then dry her thoroughly and check her temperature. If it is lower than 102 degrees F, don't continue with the lukewarm baths. If the child is shivering, warm up the water by a few degrees for the next bath.

6   Know your medications. Some drug allergies cause fevers. If you suspect that one of your prescription medications may be causing a fever, talk to your doctor or pharmacist.

7   Spread lip balm or petroleum jelly over the lips during the fever and for several days thereafter, since lips often crack and split during a fever.

Ice packs can be placed in the groin and armpit areas when an adult has a very high fever, but consult your doctor first.

## ⚠ Warnings

Call your doctor or emergency room if a high fever is accompanied by a stiff neck, difficulty breathing, confusion, lethargy, delirium or convulsions, or a cough with colored sputum.

Never use alcohol for a rubdown. The fumes are toxic, and alcohol is absorbed through the skin. Use lukewarm water.

---

# Relieve a Sore Throat                                787

Sore throats can be caused by bacteria or a virus and often accompany an illness such as a cold or flu. Most require no medical intervention and will go away in two or three days.

## ⊙ Steps

1   Consider the cause: a bug that's going around the office, enthusiastic cheering, or perhaps something more serious, such as strep throat. There are instant strep throat test strips that can tell you in less than 30 minutes if you have strep throat. Be aware, though, that these strips sometimes deliver false negatives.

2   Take an analgesic to reduce inflammation—aspirin, acetaminophen or ibuprofen for an adult, or acetaminophen or ibuprofen for children—as recommended by your doctor.

3   Suck on throat lozenges if you are an adult—especially those containing menthol, benzocaine or phenol, which numb the throat. Zinc lozenges may also be helpful. Children should suck on cough drops or hard candy.

4   Gargle with mint mouthwash or salt water (see 788 "Gargle").

5   Spray a throat spray containing numbing agents into the back of your throat, if you are an adult.

6   Brush your tongue. Sometimes, removing the buildup on your tongue can lessen the soreness in your throat.

7   Rinse your toothbrush in mouthwash between brushings to kill bacteria.

8   Drink ice-cold beverages. Try filling a glass half-full of crushed ice; then pour fruit juice over the ice. Let it sit for 10 minutes, insert a straw and suck slowly, letting the juice rest a minute on the back of your throat.

9   Add moisture to your environment with a humidifier or vaporizer, or sit in a steamy shower or bath.

10  Eat soft or liquid foods, especially sherbets and chicken broth.

11  Avoid cigarette smoke and other airborne irritants.

## ✳ Tip

Ask your pharmacist to recommend a good lozenge or throat spray.

## ⚠ Warnings

For a severe sore throat accompanied by fever, difficulty swallowing or breathing, a red rash, or coughing up of brown sputum, see your doctor or go to the emergency room immediately.

Contact a doctor if you have a sore throat that keeps you from being able to swallow.

Check young children for drooling. Drooling indicates trouble swallowing, which can lead to difficulty in breathing and requires immediate medical attention.

## 788 | Gargle

Gargling is a great way to kill bacteria in your mouth. It also helps to give you fresher breath.

### ⊙ Steps

1 Buy mint-flavored mouthwash, the flavor that's usually preferable for someone feeling ill. Opt for other flavors or salt water if you like.

2 Pour the mouthwash into a clean glass or paper cup. If you pour it into the cup attached to the top, you'll run the risk of contamination, especially if you share the bottle with others. If you prefer to gargle with salt water, dissolve ½ tsp. in 8 oz. of warm water.

3 Slide the mouthwash quickly over your tongue.

4 Throw your head back and stop the mouthwash right before it hits your epiglottis (the cartilaginous flap in the back of your throat). You'll know the mouthwash is resting in the right spot if you feel as if you're going to gag or swallow.

5 Make the mouthwash bubble and gurgle for at least 45 seconds. Pull your tongue back a little and blow air through your throat slowly. Be sure to keep your head way back, and remember to keep the mouthwash right in front of your epiglottis. That's where the germs are sitting, far back and out of sight. Try not to swallow any of the mouthwash.

6 Drop your head back down and spit the mouthwash out.

7 Repeat.

### ⚠ Warning

For children under 8, check with your pediatrician. Children who are too young to understand how to gargle should not be given mouthwash—there's a good chance they'll swallow it. Mouthwash isn't lethal, but don't let children swallow a lot of it.

## 789 | Blow Your Nose

It's best to follow a few basic guidelines for blowing your nose—especially when you're ill.

### ⊙ Steps

1 Use paper facial tissues instead of cloth handkerchiefs. Germs thrive in dark, moist environments. Wadded-up hankies are a perfect breeding ground for them.

2 Avoid blowing your nose too hard. Too much pressure will force infectious drainage into your ears and sinuses.

3 Press one finger over one nostril.

4 Blow gently through the open nostril.

5 Repeat on the opposite side.

6 Use tissues once, then throw them away.

7 Wash your hands. Germs will be on your fingers after you've handled your nose and your tissue. Don't spread the germs to other people or back to yourself.

### ✱ Tip

You'll feel most congested in the morning, after lying flat in bed all night. Wait to start blowing your nose until you've been sitting upright at least 5 or 10 minutes.

## Sneeze Properly                                          790

Sneezing on or near someone is perhaps one of the easiest ways to pass around a cold. Here's how to minimize the spread of germs when you sneeze.

### ⊙ Steps

1  Be prepared. If you have a cold, make sure you have lots of tissues.

2  Turn away from other people when you feel a sneeze coming on.

3  Use sturdy, fresh tissues to avoid getting the mucus on your hands.

4  If there are no tissues available, sneeze into your arm or elbow rather than your bare hands. This will help prevent the spread of germs.

5  Wash your hands after wiping or blowing your nose.

6  Avoid suppressing a sneeze. It can damage your ears.

7  Avoid holding your nose when you sneeze. That can also damage your ears.

**✳ Tip**

When you start to sneeze, don't hold it back. Let the air explode out into a tissue. Trying to suppress a powerful sneeze can cause your inner ears to pop or can spray bacteria into your sinuses and ears.

## Evaluate Your Sneeze                                     791

A reflex of the nasal passages, sneezing is one way the body rids itself of irritants. It's hard to know what a sneeze means, but there are some deductions you can make.

### ⊙ Steps

1  Evaluate the force of your sneeze. A weak sneeze indicates that a tiny bit of irritant may be tickling you. A strong sneeze means a big irritant.

2  Examine your tissue for discharge. Did you expel anything when you sneezed? If not, the sneeze was probably caused by an environmental irritant or bright light, which stimulates the optic nerve.

3  Look at the color and consistency of the discharge if you did expel. Green; yellow; rust-colored; or thick, globby nasal discharge indicates infection. Clear discharge can mean an allergy or the beginning of a cold or flu. Runny, watery discharge points to allergies or a cold draining.

4  Consider frequency. Repeated short, weak sneezes without significant discharge indicate allergies. Off-and-on sneezing, along with a handkerchief full of white or colored discharge, means you're fighting an infection.

5  Check the pollen and mold spore count. If those levels are high, your sneezes may be allergy induced.

6  Think back on what you did earlier in the day. Clean the house? Mow the grass? Paint furniture? Frequent sneezing after doing certain chores indicates allergies.

7  Check your temperature. A fever in the presence of frequent sneezing indicates an upper respiratory infection or flu.

8  Consider whether you might be pregnant. Unexplained sneezing has been associated with the hormonal changes in pregnancy.

**✳ Tip**

Sometimes people sneeze for no discernible reason. However, consistent sneezing, may be a sign of an allergic reaction to an unknown trigger.

## 792 | Ease a Cough

Coughing is a useful protective mechanism because it helps remove mucus and infectious agents from your respiratory system. Treatment that completely suppresses it could do more harm than good. Still, it's sometimes necessary to calm a cough, especially so you can sleep.

### ⊙ Steps

1   Determine the cause. Since a cough is not an illness but a symptom, it's important to figure out what is causing your cough in order to ease it.

2   Eliminate smoking. Many coughs are caused by irritants to the respiratory system such as cigarette smoke.

3   Remove chemical irritants you may be inhaling.

4   Use a vaporizer or humidifier. Moist air can help relieve a dry cough and break up thick mucus.

5   Drink plenty of liquids, especially clear fluids such as water. This will help relieve a dry throat and also liquefy mucus.

6   Sip hot liquids such as broth or tea. Tea with honey can soothe a tickle in the throat.

7   Use an antihistamine or an alternative method if your cough is caused by allergies.

8   Suck on lozenges, cough drops or other throat soothers.

9   Use a cough medicine containing guaifenesin if you have thick mucus that you cannot get up. Guaifenesin is an expectorant, which thins mucus and makes it easier to cough up and get out of your respiratory airways. Carefully follow label directions.

10  Decrease the activity of a cough with an antitussive cough medicine. An antitussive reduces the frequency of a cough. Use it only at night to help you sleep. It is important not to use antitussives around the clock because a cough helps clear your airways. Carefully follow label directions.

### ⚠ Warnings

See a doctor if your cough lasts for more than a week; if you are producing yellow, green, pink, blood tinged or rust-colored mucus; or if your cough is exhausting, persistent and/or accompanied by any of the following symptoms: a fever of 101 degrees F or higher, chest pains, wheezing, shortness of breath or weight loss.

Any smoker whose cough changes should contact a doctor. as this may be an early sign of lung cancer.

## 793 | Fight Allergies

The best way to fight allergies and their symptoms, including stuffy nose, watery eyes, sinus pressure or rashes, is to figure out the cause and avoid it as best you can.

### ⊙ Steps

1   Get tested for allergies by your doctor, or use the process of elimination to pinpoint your triggers. The most common allergens are pollen, mold, dust mites, animals, medications and certain foods.

2   Identify the allergen(s) as specifically as possible.

3   Keep your windows closed and stay indoors as much as you can if seasonal pollen is a problem. Consider a ventilation or filtration system for your home.

### ✳ Tip

Saline-solution nose spray can help loosen secretions. It is not a drug and can be used as often as needed. You can make your own by adding ¼ tsp. salt to 8 oz. warm water.

4   Seal your mattress, pillows and comforters in allergen-proof covers. Dust mites, a common allergen, live in bedding.

5   Sleep on a latex mattress (as long as you're not allergic to latex). Dust mites can't survive in latex mattresses.

6   Install a dehumidifier in your home if you live in a humid climate. Dust mites, mold and mildew all thrive in humid environments.

7   Use an exhaust fan in the bathroom or keep the window open.

8   Buy a vacuum cleaner with a HEPA filter and use it often.

9   Avoid wall-to-wall carpeting. It is virtually impossible to remove dust mites from carpeting.

10  Eliminate certain foods from your diet if you suspect they are causing allergy symptoms. Learn alternative cooking techniques if you are allergic to common foods such as wheat, corn or milk.

## ⚠ Warning

Read over-the-counter antihistamine labels carefully. Many make you drowsy. Avoid alcohol when taking them.

# Help Control Asthma Symptoms                                              794

Although there's no cure for asthma, there are many things you can do to manage your asthma and keep symptoms to a minimum. Avoiding triggers and modifying your lifestyle will help.

## ◉ Steps

1   Follow your doctor's medical advice, and don't discontinue your medications on your own. Undergo allergy tests as recommended by your doctor and comply with the follow-up treatment.

2   Keep a notebook and write down what you were doing right before you developed asthma symptoms, no matter how mild they were, each time they occur. Look for a pattern.

3   Stay away from any external trigger or allergy that your observations uncover or that tests reveal, whether that means dust that gets stirred up from cleaning, animal dander you're exposed to when riding a horse, or even your bedding if you find you can't breathe upon waking.

4   Avoid cigarette smoke, gasoline and paint fumes, perfume, aftershave, cold air, and pollution, including smoke from a wood stove or campfire. These are all irritants to someone with asthma.

5   Do your best to prevent colds. Stay away from anyone with an upper respiratory infection. Many patients say their symptoms started after a cold.

6   Control stress. Muscle tension and shallow breathing encourage asthma attacks. Practice relaxation techniques. Take yoga classes. Participate in activities that help you relax.

7   Drink a moderate amount of caffeinated coffee, tea or cola, unless otherwise ordered by your doctor. Caffeine, related to theophylline, is mildly therapeutic for asthma. However, too much caffeine can aggravate it.

8   Take prescribed asthma medication, both oral and inhalant, as recommended by your doctor. Bronchodilators and other drugs prescribed by your doctor relax smooth bronchial muscle tissue, decrease inflammation and help keep airways open.

## ✱ Tips

Get a flu shot if you have asthma.

Talk to your doctor about getting a peak flow meter, which can help you monitor your asthma.

For more information about asthma, including breathing exercises, call (800) 7-ASTHMA. Or call the American Lung Association at (800) LUNG-USA.

9   Exercise regularly per your doctor's recommendation. Proper use of prescription medication can decrease or eliminate asthma that is induced by exercise.

10  Learn how to breathe from your diaphragm and purse-lip breathe whenever your breathing feels labored, tight or fast, or when you feel stressed. To breathe from your diaphragm, lie down or sit in front of a mirror. Put one hand on your stomach, the other on your chest. Take a deep breath through your nose. Your stomach should rise under your hand each time you breathe; your chest should not rise. To purse-lip breathe, close your mouth and inhale through your nose. Purse your lips as if you're going to blow out a candle. Exhale slowly with as little force as possible. Your exhale should last twice as long as your inhale. Don't hold your breath between inhalation and exhalation.

## 795 | Reduce Snoring

**Snoring can be a real problem. Airway blockages that cause snoring often come from relaxed muscles in the back of the throat, or from stuffy nasal passages.**

### ◉ Steps

1   Don't drink alcohol before going to bed. It can increase muscle relaxation, which may make snoring more likely.

2   Avoid muscle relaxants and sleeping pills.

3   Sew or tape a tennis ball to the back of your pajamas or T-shirt. Snorers are more likely to snore when lying on their backs. The ball will make this position uncomfortable and force you to roll over onto your side.

4   To prevent snoring while lying on your back, elevate your upper body 30 degrees using a foam wedge.

5   Talk to your doctor about taking an antihistamine if your snoring is caused by a cold or allergy.

6   Give up smoking. Experts believe cigarette smoking disturbs sleep and increases the likelihood of snoring.

7   Lose weight; this helps reduce the size of the palate.

8   Offer your partner earplugs if your snoring keeps him or her awake.

9   See a dentist for information about an anti-snoring dental device, which prevents the lower jaw from falling back while you're sleeping.

10  Talk to an ear, nose and throat specialist for possible surgery or treatment. There are a variety of techniques that can help reduce snoring.

### ⚠ Warning

Heavy snoring can be a symptom of sleep apnea, a sleep disorder that has been linked to serious health problems. If you snore heavily and often feel drowsy or fatigued despite sleeping all night, consult a doctor.

## Care for Swimmer's Ear                                      796

When water gets in the ear, it can carry bacteria or a fungus and cause an outer-ear infection. Swimmer's ear usually clears up after a few days, with medication.

### ⊙ Steps

1   To help clear up a mild infection, use a mixture of equal parts isopropyl alcohol and white vinegar in the ear canal after swimming or showering. Tip your head to one side so the affected ear faces the ceiling, place a few drops of the mixture in your ear using a medicine dropper, then tip your head the other way to let the mixture drain out.

2   Take aspirin (adults only), ibuprofen or acetaminophen every 4 to 6 hours for any symptoms of a mild infection, such as discomfort or fever.

3   Apply mild heat, using a hot water bottle or a heating pad, to help reduce any pain.

4   Contact your doctor if your condition doesn't improve in 24 hours, the glands in your neck become swollen, your ears begin to drain a milky fluid, or you experience dizziness or ringing in your ears.

### ✳ Tips

Symptoms include itching, discomfort and swelling of the outer ear canal, which is usually tender to the touch.

During the healing process, keep water out of your ears. Clean them by wrapping your finger in a soft cloth and gently wiping the outer ear area. Avoid using instruments or cotton swabs to remove earwax.

### ⚠ Warning

Don't put any drops in your ear if you suspect a perforated eardrum.

---

## Get Rid of Hiccups                                          797

The cause and function of these abrupt diaphragmatic contractions have always baffled medical practitioners, but a few home remedies can help get rid of them.

### ⊙ Steps

1   Swallow 1 tsp. white table sugar, dry. A study found that this stopped hiccups immediately in 19 out of 20 people. Repeat up to three more times at 2-minute intervals if necessary.

2   Gulp down a glass of water if the sugar doesn't work.

3   Eat a piece of dry bread slowly.

4   Breathe in and out of a paper bag. Do not use a plastic bag under any circumstances, and don't do this longer than 1 minute.

5   Gargle with water (see 788 "Gargle").

6   Repeat the above steps until your hiccups stop.

### ✳ Tip

Hiccups can be brought on by eating too fast and subsequently swallowing a lot of air, or by drinking too much alcohol.

### ⚠ Warning

See a doctor if you have severe pain, if your hiccups last longer than a day (or 3 hours in the case of a small child), or if they started after you took a prescription medication.

## 798 | Reduce Excess Gas

**Although it can be annoying and embarrassing, excess gas usually doesn't indicate a serious medical condition.**

### ⊙ Steps

1 Slow down when you eat. The more slowly you eat, the less air you will swallow along with your food.

2 Watch your intake of gas-producing foods such as beans, cabbage, onions, brussels sprouts, wheat and wheat bran.

3 Keep a list of your food intake and note when you have gas. If you notice that gas and certain foods seem to go together, cut down on or eliminate those foods from your diet.

4 Find out if you are lactose intolerant. If you are, milk and dairy products can cause gas as well as general stomach discomfort.

5 Take supplements to aid in lactose digestion if you are lactose intolerant but want to eat dairy products.

6 Introduce high-fiber foods into your diet gradually. A sudden change from a low-fiber diet to a high-fiber diet can cause excess gas.

7 Reduce your consumption of high-fat foods.

8 Avoid or cut down on the use of sugar substitutes. People can't absorb them, which can cause gas.

9 Talk to your pharmacist about using Beano food enzyme, an over-the-counter product that breaks down the sugars in beans that cause gas.

10 Add Japanese kombu, a sea vegetable, to the water when you cook beans to make them more digestible and neutralize their gas-producing effect. Some cooks also use the Mexican herb epazote for this purpose.

**✳ Tip**

If you are lactose intolerant, consider buying lactose-free milk.

## 799 | Treat Diarrhea

**Diarrhea is characterized by excess water in the stool and can be quite debilitating. The cause varies from tainted food or a virus to severe anxiety. These steps can help you cope.**

### ⊙ Steps

1 Rest to give your body time to recover.

2 Avoid milk products, because temporary lactose intolerance is common after an insult to the intestine.

3 Wash your hands after every bowel movement to reduce the chance of transmitting the pathogen to someone else.

4 Consider your diet. Some people believe bananas help to form stools in children. Some doctors recommend a "BRAT" diet: bananas, rice, apple sauce and toast. But use them sparingly and cautiously so as not to aggravate the problem.

**✳ Tip**

Check your medicines: Products containing magnesium may cause diarrhea.

**⚠ Warning**

The elderly and children can quickly become dehydrated, which can turn an intestinal illness into a systemic emergency. Replace fluids by drinking water, an electrolyte replacement drink or juice if tolerable.

5   Withhold food for 24 hours in moderate to severe cases, allowing only lukewarm clear liquids. As stools begin to form, slowly add soft foods.

6   Visit your doctor if the diarrhea is painful, is severe, contains blood or is accompanied by a high fever. Also, see or call a doctor immediately if you are taking antibiotic or prescription drugs.

7   Ask your pharmacist about any antidiarrheal medication you're considering to make sure that it does not interact with medications you are already taking.

## Treat Constipation                                           800

If you only move your bowels once every three or four days, feel bloated, or pass small, hard stools, you may be constipated. Changing some of your daily habits may help.

### ◎ Steps

1   Drink lots of liquid every day. Eight glasses of water is recommended. When the intestines lack proper hydration, stools can turn hard and dry and become much more difficult to pass.

2   Add several servings of fibrous whole grains, fruits (such as prunes or prune juice) and vegetables to your diet every day—or opt for a fiber supplement. Fiber adds bulk to the intestines and creates well-formed stools that are easier to pass.

3   Drink hot water, tea or coffee. Hot beverages, especially ones containing caffeine, may help stimulate the bowels.

4   Incorporate a regular exercise regimen into your lifestyle. Digestion is enhanced when the abdominal muscles are used. The contraction and relaxation of the muscles helps the intestines to more effectively move stools through the digestive tract. Aerobic exercise such as jogging, tennis and brisk walking are especially helpful.

5   Check the medication you're taking. Antacids (particularly those containing calcium) and iron supplements can cause constipation, as can some other over-the-counter and prescription drugs, especially pain relievers that contain narcotics.

6   Keep in mind that constipation can be caused by digestive disorders such as irritable bowel syndrome, colon cancer, colitis, Crohn's disease or diverticulitis. Stress, pregnancy and even a new routine can temporarily cause a slowdown in the bowels.

7   Take a laxative if constipation continues, but avoid regular usage.

8   If you have a fever, severe abdominal pain, continuous vomiting, prolonged bloating, very thin stools, blood in your stools or frequent bouts of constipation, see a doctor.

###  Tip

There is no evidence that constipation need occur with aging. If you do have a problem as you grow older, add more fiber, fluids and exercise to your daily regimen.

### ⚠ Warning

Use enemas with extreme caution. They are a temporary solution, and frequent use may lead to dependency. Never give an enema to a child unless ordered by your pediatrician.

## 801 | Care for Hemorrhoids

Hemorrhoids, or piles, develop when anal and rectal veins become swollen because of straining or prolonged sitting. They may cause inflammation, pain or rectal bleeding. Hemorrhoids can be internal, external or both.

### ⊙ Steps

1 Apply a cold compress directly on the hemorrhoid to help ease the pain.

2 Avoid straining when you have a bowel movement.

3 Wipe with moistened toilet paper, a baby wipe or a pad soaked with witch hazel after a bowel movement. Commercial hemorrhoid-relief pads are commonly soaked with witch hazel.

4 Clean the area well with warm water several times a day. A handheld showerhead or a bidet works well.

5 Soak in a hot bath every day. Avoid bath salts, which may be irritating.

6 Increase your fiber intake. Eat fresh vegetables, whole grains and beans. Fiber helps your regularity and forms stools that are large and soft, which makes them easier to pass.

7 Drink at least eight glasses of water a day. This will keep stools loose and easier to pass.

8 Get regular exercise. Walking three times a week, for 30 minutes each time, will aid your digestion and make moving your bowels less difficult.

9 When lifting heavy objects, use proper body mechanics to avoid putting excessive strain on the lower body. Avoid sitting or standing for long periods of time.

10 Use over-the-counter hemorrhoid medications as directed on a short-term basis. Those containing corticosteroids are especially helpful in reducing anal pain. Check with a pharmacist to make sure the medication does not cause problems with other medications you are taking.

### ✳ Tip

In very rare cases, hemorrhoids may need to be treated surgically, either through injection sclerotherapy (which causes the vein to shrink), rubber-band ligation or hemorrhoidectomy. Consult your doctor to find out more about these treatments.

### ⚠ Warnings

Never assume that rectal bleeding is caused by hemorrhoids. It could be caused by colon cancer.

Prolonged use of over-the-counter hemorrhoid medication can lead to inflammation and scarring of the rectal tissue.

## 802 | Care for a Bruise

A bruise occurs when blood vessels rupture from a blow. It usually disappears in three days to two weeks with no special care, but you can reduce the swelling, coloration and duration.

### ⊙ Steps

1 Rest the bruised area. This permits the blood to clot more quickly, which limits the spread of blood beneath the skin.

2 Apply a cold compress to the bruise—20 minutes on, 20 minutes off—as often as you can for the first day or two. The cold will constrict blood vessels and help keep the bruise from spreading. Never apply ice directly to the skin. Always use an ice pack or a cold compress.

### ✳ Tips

Once blood vessels under the skin rupture, the area swells and oxygen is cut off. When the hemoglobin has less oxygen, the blood turns blue—hence the black and blue color of a bruise. When hemoglobin begins to break down, the bruise looks yellowish-green.

**How to Do** *(Just About)* **Everything**

3   Avoid aspirin until the bruise has started to heal. Aspirin is an anticoagulant, which prevents blood from clotting as quickly. Blood that does not clot spreads more extensively underneath the skin.

4   Take acetaminophen for pain. This does not affect clotting.

5   Apply a warm, wet compress after the first 48 hours to reduce pain and swelling. Heat is recommended once the blood has stopped spreading around the bruise. Heat dilates blood vessels, which will help speed the sweeping away of blood cells from around the ruptured vessels.

It's best not to wrap a bruise; the bruise needs room to swell. Elastic bandages can cause constriction that slows healing.

## ⚠ Warning

See your doctor if you find yourself bruising for no apparent reason.

## Recognize the Signs of Arthritis                  803

The most common form of arthritis is osteoarthritis, a degeneration of the joints. Rheumatoid arthritis is an autoimmune disease in which joints become inflamed.

### ◉ Steps

1   Notice whether exercise causes an intensified ache in your joints. This is the first telltale sign of arthritis.

2   Take note if you experience stiffness in one or more joints in the morning that typically subsides after 15 to 30 minutes of movement. This may be an early sign.

3   Evaluate your afflicted joint for range of motion. Does the joint creak or cause you pain when you bend it to its normal limits? This may be a sign of arthritis.

4   Is your skin pulled taut over a joint due to swelling? Is the taut skin shiny? These symptoms are indicative of joint swelling due to either osteoarthritis or rheumatoid arthritis (though they can also be signs of gout or an infection).

5   Test your afflicted joint for temperature. For instance, test your right knee joint by placing one hand on your right knee and one on your left knee, and feel for a temperature difference between the two. Hot joints can be a sign of rheumatoid arthritis, gout or joint infection. Cold, bone-hard joints are apt to be a sign of osteoarthritis.

6   Notice whether the joint pain is associated with fever or noticeable swelling. These are signs of rheumatoid arthritis or joint infection.

7   Pay attention if your joints have a gritty sensation, such that they seem to crackle and make noise when moving. In osteoarthritis, irritated cartilage and bones rub together, making a grating sound.

8   Check the location of the painful joints—are they located symmetrically? For instance, if you have joint inflammation in some of the fingers of your right hand, do you feel joint pain in the corresponding fingers of your left hand? This is characteristic of rheumatoid arthritis.

9   Visit your doctor for advice and possible treatment if you suspect that you have arthritis.

### ✳ Tips

Researchers have recently discovered a faulty gene that causes one type of osteoarthritis. Obesity also predisposes a person to osteoarthritis. The causes of other types of osteoarthritis are unknown.

For more information about arthritis, which afflicts at least 20 million Americans, call the Arthritis Foundation at (800) 283-7800.

---

## 804 | Use Crutches

Using crutches often appears easier than it actually is. Get proper instruction from your doctor or physical therapist and remember the following pointers.

### ⊙ Steps

1 Make sure the crutches fit properly. Your shoulders should lean forward slightly and your wrists and elbows should be bent.

2 Check that the padding is not worn or torn.

3 Walk by placing both crutches in front of you. Shift your weight and your healthy leg forward.

4 Keep your steps small. They should be no longer than 1½ feet.

5 Rest as needed. Crutches can irritate your armpits.

6 Try not to lean on your crutches. Sit down or lean against a wall.

7 Avoid stairs whenever possible. Use ramps and elevators when available.

8 Call ahead when you're going to a new building or area, and find out about handicapped access. Try to avoid places where you will have to climb long staircases, or that have staircases without railings.

9 Move slowly, especially if you are climbing stairs. Don't hurry and risk further injury.

10 Opening a door takes a little bit of skill. Make sure the door will clear your feet when you open it. Support yourself on one crutch and open the door with the other hand. Hold both crutches as the door opens, and place the tip of one crutch against the door to keep it open. Then go through the door.

11 Use the crutches as prescribed. If they are really uncomfortable, you may not be using them properly or they may not be the right size.

### ⚠ Warning

Speak with your doctor or a physical therapist about the proper use of crutches, especially if you may be using them for a long time. They can be tricky to manipulate on stairs and in wet, icy or uneven conditions. Improper use can cause further injury.

---

## 805 | Protect Your Skin From the Sun

To minimize skin damage from the sun, follow these guidelines, based on the recommendations of the American Cancer Society and the Centers for Disease Control and Prevention.

### ⊙ Steps

1 Long-term exposure to the sun's ultraviolet (UV) rays can damage your skin. To protect it, stay out of the sun between 10 a.m. and 4 p.m., when the rays are at their strongest. And remember that clouds don't block UV rays.

2 Seek shade when you're outdoors.

3 Wear a hat, preferably with a 4-inch brim all around, to effectively cover your face, neck and ears.

### ✳ Tip

Some clothing manufacturers offer SPF ratings for clothing.

### ⚠ Warnings

Sunscreen is not recommended for children under 6 months old. Cover them with a hat, shirt and pants, and keep them in the shade.

---

4   Wear long sleeves and long pants, making sure they're made of tightly woven fabrics.

5   Use sunscreen with a sun protection factor (SPF) of at least 15 every day to help protect against incidental sun exposure; reapply it after swimming or sweating.

6   Keep in mind that a typical T-shirt has a lower SPF than the American Cancer Society recommends, so you'll still need to apply sunscreen to areas the T-shirt covers.

7   Be aware that ultraviolet rays generally reflect off water, sand, snow and any light-colored surface, such as concrete; be diligent in applying sunscreen when you're around these surfaces.

8   Remember that some ultraviolet radiation will penetrate water and windows, so you always need protection.

9   Avoid indoor sunlamps and tanning beds, since they can be more harmful to your skin than the sun.

Frequent sunburns or lifelong sun exposure can increase your risk of getting skin cancer and speed your skin's aging process. Protect your skin diligently.

## Things You'll Need

☐ brimmed hat

☐ long-sleeved shirt and pants

☐ sunscreen

---

## Examine a Mole                                    806

Keeping watch on moles can help you detect the early stages of the form of skin cancer known as melanoma. Here's what to look for as you examine yourself or someone else.

### ◉ Steps

1   Look for asymmetry. See whether the shape or color of one half of the mole does not match the other.

2   Note any irregular borders, such as blurred edges.

3   Examine the mole to see whether its color is no longer uniform.

4   Be alert to any increases in the size of your mole, especially if its diameter is greater than 6mm, which is about ¼ inch.

5   Check for any spread of pigment from your mole to the skin in the surrounding area.

6   Note any redness in your mole, as well as changes in the surface, such as crusting or oozing.

7   Be alert to any changes in the sensation of your mole, such as pain or itchiness.

8   If you discover any of the above changes or any other unusual characteristics in your mole, contact a dermatologist for an exam.

### ✱ Tips

Examine your body regularly to become familiar with the size, shape and color of your moles, blemishes and birthmarks. This can help you be alert to changes that might indicate melanoma growths.

Ask your doctor if you should have regular examinations by a dermatologist, especially if you spend a lot of time in the sun or have fair skin or a family history of skin cancer (see 813 "Keep on Top of Physical Exams"). The doctor can make a body map of your moles, blemishes and birthmarks, thereby tracking any unusual growth or changes.

## ✓ 807 Treat Bites and Stings

The great outdoors is filled with creatures that can inflict painful and harmful bites. If you've been bitten, apply first aid measures listed below and get medical attention. If a victim is unconscious or not breathing, apply standard first aid while someone in your party summons help. In all cases, see a doctor again if signs of infection appear.

### Snakebite

- Seek medical help immediately. Remain calm and lie quietly until you can see a doctor.

- Remove watches and jewelry in anticipation of swelling.

- Wash the area with soap and water and keep it below heart level.

- Wrap a bandage snugly several inches above (not on) the bite if the snake has bitten an arm or leg. Immobilize the area—use a splint if at all possible.

- Don't use a tourniquet, apply ice or heat, cut the wound or try to suck out the venom. Avoid alcohol and medications.

- Take small sips of water to maintain hydration if possible.

### Bee, wasp or hornet sting

- Go to the emergency room immediately if you receive a large number of stings or exhibit signs of severe reaction or anaphylactic shock (see 770 "Recognize Signs of a Medical Emergency").

- Remove the stinger (if any) by scraping a dull butter knife against your skin in the opposite direction of the stinger entry. If a dull edge is not available, use tweezers or your fingers.

- Wash the site with soap and water, then apply an ice pack for 10 to 15 minutes to reduce pain and swelling.

- Take a painkiller such as ibuprofen, or an antihistamine, for relief from pain and swelling. If you are allergic to insect stings, always carry an aqueous epinephrine (EpiPen or Ana-kit) kit.

### Brown recluse spider bite

- Note that people often aren't aware that a spider has bitten them until these signs and symptoms appear: stinging or pain at the site of the bite, a blister that will often grow in size and rupture, and possibly nausea, vomiting, fever and chills.

- Clean the bite with soap and water. Do not attempt to lance the bite or extract the venom.

- Apply an ice pack to the area of the bite.

- Take a painkiller, such as ibuprofen, to obtain some relief from the symptoms.

- If a blister forms, then pops, carefully clean and dress the wound to prevent infection.

- See a doctor immediately for treatment to minimize tissue damage.

### Scorpion sting

- Look for the signs and symptoms of a scorpion sting: burning pain, swelling or numbness at the site of the sting.

- Seek medical attention immediately to receive an antivenin and be monitored for signs and symptoms of severe poisoning: muscle spasms, stomach pain, convulsions, impaired vision or speech, nausea, vomiting, difficulty breathing, impaired circulation, or coma.

- Remain calm to slow circulation, and keep the wounded area below heart level.

- Clean the sting with soap and water (gently—it may be painful), then apply an ice pack to the site.

- Immobilize the stung extremity with a sling if possible.

reference

## Care for a Blister                                                  808

Friction, minor injuries, pressure and sunburn all can cause blisters. If you can prevent a blister from getting infected, it will usually go away within a few days.

### ◉ Steps

1   Clean the skin around the blister.

2   Place a doughnut-shaped piece of moleskin over the blister. This will keep pressure off it.

3   Try to avoid popping the blister unless it's in an especially awkward place, such as the bottom of your foot. The blister provides a sterile environment for the skin underneath. Breaking it makes the area more susceptible to infection.

4   If you need to pop the blister, use sterile implements, puncture it in a few places at its base and drain the fluid.

5   If you need to puncture it or if it breaks on its own, clean the area with soap and water or Betadine.

6   Avoid peeling any skin off the blister; this can lead to an infection and delay healing.

7   Cover the exposed blister with dry sterile gauze.

8   Change the gauze regularly and watch for signs of infection, such as pus or redness.

### ✳ Tips

Prevention is always the best remedy (see 907 "Avoid Getting Blisters While Hiking").

If an infection from a blister doesn't clear up quickly, your doctor may want to prescribe an antibiotic.

### Things You'll Need

❑ moleskin

❑ soap or Betadine

❑ gauze

---

## Care for a Boil                                                     809

A boil is a skin infection, most often caused by the bacteria *Staphylococcus aureus.* It gets into a hair follicle and pus forms, causing the surrounding skin to rise and swell.

### ◉ Steps

1   Avoid squeezing a boil, as this may spread the infection.

2   Allow the boil to come to a head and open on its own. Applying a warm compress two or three times a day will speed up this process.

3   Keep the area very clean, especially after the boil has begun to drain.

4   Apply a saline solution once the boil has opened. Mix 1 tsp. table salt with 1 c. hot water. Wet a washcloth in the solution and apply it to the boil. This can help dry it out and reduce the amount of pus.

### ⚠ Warning

Most boils will heal without help. See a doctor if the area becomes increasingly red and inflamed, if you have a fever, or if the boil does not go away after two weeks.

## 810 | Care for Canker Sores

These painful sores inside the mouth may be triggered by stress, injury, nutritional deficiencies, menstruation or genetic factors. They usually clear up in one to two weeks.

### ⊙ Steps

1 Avoid hot and spicy foods, which can irritate canker sores.

2 Brush your teeth with a soft-bristled toothbrush to lessen aggravation.

3 Apply crushed ice or an over-the-counter oral anesthetic to the sore to numb the pain.

4 Practice good oral hygiene. Rinse with mouthwash or salt water, and try brushing with a toothpaste free of sodium laurel sulfate, which has been implicated in aggravating canker sores.

5 Consult a doctor if sores persist longer than two weeks, recur more than two or three times a year, are extremely painful, or occur with other symptoms, such as fever, diarrhea or skin rash.

6 Talk to your doctor about treating the sores with oral or topical steroids or oral antibiotics.

### Things You'll Need

❏ soft-bristled toothbrush

❏ crushed ice or anesthetic

❏ mouthwash or salt water

❏ toothpaste without sodium laurel sulfate

## 811 | Treat Head Lice

Infestations of head lice—small insects whose eggs (nits) become attached to hair shafts—are extremely contagious and spread through shared clothing and personal contact.

### ⊙ Steps

1 Assess whether you or your child actually has lice. Symptoms include itching, swollen glands in the back of the neck, foul-smelling hair, and small, oval white or gray-white spots stuck to the hair shaft.

2 Check for live lice and nits. Work in strong light and section the hair. Use a fine-tooth comb (a pet flea comb works well) to find the insects and to comb them out if possible; or remove them using tweezers, your fingernails, or a piece of tape wrapped around your finger, sticky side up. Adult lice are reddish-brown; nits are white or clear and adhere to the hair shaft. They do not jump or fly.

3 Check everyone in the household. Lice are very contagious.

4 Wash all bedding, recently used towels and recently worn clothing in hot water, and dry them in a hot dryer. Soak all combs and brushes in hot water for at least 10 minutes.

5 Treat eyelashes and eyebrows with a thick layer of petroleum jelly. Apply twice a day for eight days. Never use any chemical treatment on eyelashes or eyebrows.

6 Try using olive oil or mayonnaise on the head. There is some evidence that it works by smothering the nits. Massage it into the hair and leave it

### ✳ Tips

If you don't have access to a washer and dryer, isolate the infected clothes and bedding in a garbage bag for two weeks. The lice will die in this time period.

Avoid sharing hats, bicycle helmets, combs, brushes and clothing with anyone who may have lice. If you have lice, do not allow anyone to use your personal items.

Manual removal with a comb is the safest and often the most effective method of controlling lice.

Your doctor can prescribe a shampoo or cream that will kill lice or nits.

in as long as possible. Manually comb out the nits after the olive oil or mayonnaise application.

7   Use a blow dryer, as heat can kill lice and nits. But exercise caution— avoid placing the dryer too close to the scalp.

8   Examine the hair daily to make sure that all nits and lice are gone. If you see more nits, it may mean that there are still lice in the hair or that rein-festation has occurred.

9   Report the presence of lice to your child's school so the staff or faculty can check for an outbreak. Children with a lice infection should be kept home from school. They can return after the lice have been removed or have been treated with a commercial product.

10  Check with your pharmacist to make sure that any product you plan to use does not contain lindane. The National Pediculosis Association strongly advises against using lindane because it has been associated with a number of serious medical conditions, including seizures and possibly cancer.

## ⚠ Warning

Speak with your doctor before using any chemical lice treat-ments if you are pregnant or nursing, or if you have allergies, asthma or other medical condi-tions. Never use a lice treatment on a baby unless directed by your doctor.

---

# Do a Breast Self-Exam                                                812

The cure for breast cancer remains unknown, but research indi-cates that early detection from annual mammograms and monthly self-exams can increase survival chances.

## ◉ Steps

1   Lie down on your back and place a pillow under your right shoulder to flatten your right breast.

2   Put your right arm behind your head.

3   Place your left hand on your right breast, and press firmly with the pads of three fingers.

4   Move your hand over the area in concentric circles (starting from the perimeter and closing in on the nipple). Be sure to include the armpit, since breast tissue extends into this area.

5   Put a pillow under your left shoulder and repeat steps 2 through 4 to check your left breast with your right hand.

6   Examine your breasts in front of a mirror. Carefully note any changes in their appearance.

7   Squeeze the nipples to check for discharge.

8   Contact your doctor right away if you find any lumps, swellings, dim-pling, skin irritations, distortions, scaliness, thickenings, discharge, unfamiliar retraction of the nipples or other changes.

9   Do self-exams on a regular basis—preferably every month, about a week after your period begins. Regularity is the key. With practice, you will know how your breasts normally feel, so you can detect changes easily.

## ✱ Tips

Apply powder, lotion or oil to your breasts to make it easier to move your fingers over the sur-face of your skin.

For the most thorough self-exam, ask your doctor or nurse-practi-tioner to teach you.

Most breast lumps are not can-cerous, but they should be checked by a doctor anyway. The maxim "Better safe than sorry" is especially true when dealing with breast cancer.

Women over 40 should get a mammogram every other year. Women over 50 should get one every year.

Risk of breast cancer increases with age (especially over 50 years), if first-degree relatives have had breast cancer, or if you have not given birth.

### ✓ 813 Keep on Top of Physical Exams

No matter how healthy you are (or think you are), it's a good idea to get regular check-ups. Many forms of cancer are more curable when they are detected early, and other conditions such as high blood pressure and high cholesterol can be caught before they cause life-threatening damage. Note that these are general recommendations. Everyone has specific needs and risks, depending on family and medical history and risk factors, so consult your doctor for specific advice.

| PROCEDURE | FREQUENCY | WHO SHOULD HAVE IT DONE |
|---|---|---|
| Blood cholesterol | Every five years | Everyone over 18 |
| Blood pressure | Once a year | Everyone over 21 |
| Breast exam by doctor | Once a year | Women over 40; women over 35 whose mothers or sisters have had breast cancer |
| Breast self-exam | Once a month | Women 20 and older |
| Dental exam | Every six months | Everyone |
| Electrocardiogram | Once | Anyone over 40 with greater risk of heart disease |
| Eye exam | Every one to two years | Everyone |
| Fecal occult-blood test | Once a year | Everyone over 50; anyone over 40 with ulcerative colitis or a relative who has had colon cancer |
| General physical | Once a year | Everyone |
| Glaucoma | Every three to five years<br>Every one to two years | Everyone 39 to 49<br>Everyone 50 and over; everyone of African ancestry; anyone who has had a serious eye injury in the past or who is taking steroid medication |
| Height and weight | Once a year | Everyone |
| Mammogram | Every other year<br>Once a year | Women over 40<br>Women over 50 |
| Osteoporosis (bone density) | At least once | Women in early menopause; men and women with multiple risk factors for osteoporosis |
| Pap smear | Once a year | All women after onset of sexual activity |
| Rectal exam | Once a year | Everyone over 50 |
| Skin cancer check | Once a year | Everyone, especially those at increased risk |
| Sigmoidoscopy | Every five years | Everyone over 50 |
| Testicular exam by doctor | Once a year | Men beginning in adolescence |
| Testicular self-exam | Once a month | Men beginning in adolescence |
| Tuberculin skin test | As needed | Anyone exposed to or at risk for tuberculosis |

chart

## Relieve Menstrual Cramps 814

Cramps are caused by the contraction of the uterus during menstruation and vary in intensity from mild to debilitating.

### ⊙ Steps

1 Reduce your consumption of salt, sugar and caffeine during the week before your period to prevent cramps or reduce their severity.

2 Increase your intake of calcium-rich foods such as milk, yogurt or leafy green vegetables.

3 Keep in mind that a high-potency B-complex vitamin may help if you're susceptible to menstrual cramps. Vitamin $B_6$ is especially important, but don't take more than 100mg per day.

4 Apply heat to your muscles when cramps occur. Take a hot bath or place a hot water bottle on your abdomen or lower back.

5 Get moving. Sitting or lying around may actually make you feel worse. Swimming and walking are good activities because they are gentle and not too stressful. Certain stretches and yoga positions will also help to relieve the pain.

6 Avoid standing for long periods if you have pain in your lower back.

7 Massage your lower back to relieve tension and pain.

8 Take ibuprofen or naproxen to help relieve cramps.

9 Take a break, breathe deeply and listen to soothing music.

### ✱ Tip

If you are interested in using herbs, homeopathy or other natural remedies, consult a naturopath or a doctor who practices natural medicine.

### ⚠ Warning

If you are in extreme pain, have an unusually heavy flow or notice big blood clots, or if you also have other symptoms such as vomiting and fainting, consult a doctor.

## Find Out if You Are Pregnant 815

Thankfully, we don't take the lives of rabbits anymore to determine the answer to this all-important, age-old question.

### ⊙ Steps

1 Calculate when your period is due. If you have a regular cycle and you keep track of it, a late period is one of the earliest signs of pregnancy.

2 Notice any other changes in your body. Are you extremely sleepy? Are your breasts tender? Are you moody? Though sometimes subtle, these changes can be clear indicators.

3 Buy a home pregnancy test at a pharmacy or grocery store, or online. Choose one with two tests per box so you can double-check your results.

4 Test after you miss a period, or 14 days after you think you conceived.

5 Read and follow the test instructions carefully. Some tell you to urinate in a cup; others say to urinate right on the test stick.

6 If the test is positive, make an appointment with your doctor to confirm with other tests and a physical exam.

7 Retest after a few days if the test is negative and you still suspect that you're pregnant.

### ✱ Tips

Do the test first thing in the morning, when hormone concentrations are highest.

Home tests claim to be 97 percent accurate. When there are mistakes, they're usually false negatives; false positives are very rare.

## 816 Deal With Morning Sickness

You will probably feel morning sickness for the first trimester, but it can happen throughout the day and can last throughout your pregnancy. These steps can ease the nausea.

### ⊙ Steps

1 Try not to let yourself get hungry; an empty stomach can increase nausea.

2 Keep a supply of bland crackers handy. Have some in the morning before you get out of bed to settle your stomach.

3 Avoid high-fat foods—especially fried foods—and stay away from spicy and acidic foods.

4 Eat foods high in B vitamins, which may reduce nausea.

5 Add a bit of ginger to your diet in the form of ginger ale, ginger tea or gingersnaps. Or use ginger in your recipes.

6 Experiment with natural remedies such as papaya enzyme, vitamin $B_6$ or an acupressure wristband.

7 Drink plenty of water between meals. Try sparkling water flavored with a slice of lemon.

8 Take your prenatal vitamins with food. Your nausea will increase if you take them on an empty stomach.

9 Avoid taking iron supplements in the first trimester unless you are anemic. Iron can be hard on your stomach.

10 Utilize the fleeting moments when you feel OK to eat healthful foods and get a little exercise.

### ✳ Tips

Nausea can be a sign that everything is going well with your pregnancy. Hormonal adjustment may be what makes you feel so sick.

For most women, nausea lessens or disappears in the second trimester.

### ⚠ Warnings

Call your doctor if the nausea becomes debilitating or if you are unable to hold down any food.

If you are suddenly getting sick in your second or third trimester and you weren't earlier, call your doctor.

If vomiting is accompanied by pain or fever, call your doctor immediately.

## 817 Cope With Menopause

If you're a woman around age 50 or have had an ovariectomy, you're most likely facing menopause. Although some women breeze through menopause, others experience mood changes, hot flashes, sweats or vaginal dryness.

### ⊙ Steps

1 Research as much as you can about menopause therapies, such as hormone replacement therapy, that reduce symptoms and delay changes brought on by the decline in estrogen and progesterone production. This will help you decide which, if any, are best suited for your needs.

2 Realize that you may have headaches, perhaps even an occasional migraine. Hormonal changes, especially decreases in estrogen levels, may cause vasoconstriction of the blood vessels in your forehead.

3 Understand that menopause lessens the amount of elastin and collagen in the skin. Use lotions and body oils liberally to keep thinning skin supple and hydrated and to reduce the appearance of wrinkles.

### ✳ Tips

Be aware that as female hormone production declines, you are at increased risk for heart disease and osteoporosis. Get a periodic bone-density test as well as cholesterol and blood-pressure screening.

Many women have had success with homeopathy and acupuncture as alternatives to estrogen replacement therapy. Discuss these and other options with your doctor.

Consider using hormone creams to relieve vaginal dryness.

**How to Do** *(Just About)* **Everything**

4 Prepare yourself for night sweats—hot flashes that occur when you are sleeping. They are more common than hot flashes during the day.

5 Get enough calcium. A woman going through menopause needs 1,200 to 1,500 mg of calcium a day, as does a postmenopausal woman on hormone replacement therapy. Women not on hormone replacement therapy need 1,500mg of calcium per day. Discuss this with your doctor. Remember that vitamin D (or exposure to sunshine) helps your body absorb calcium.

6 Eat a diet rich in fruits and vegetables, which contain an abundance of vitamins $B_6$ and $B_{12}$, folic acid and certain antioxidants. These can help women through menopause and ease the aging process.

7 Talk to your doctor about eating foods high in phytoestrogens—soy products, flaxseed and some legumes and whole-grain foods. Intestinal bacteria can transform these foods into substances that your body can use to offset menopause-related hormonal depletions.

### ⚠ Warnings

Some menopause therapies are controversial because of potential side effects. Consult your doctor to find out about the risks.

Too much calcium may cause constipation and kidney stones.

## Conduct a Testicular Self-Examination 818

Each year, 7,500 American men, mainly young, are diagnosed with testicular cancer. A monthly self-exam helps increase your chances of detecting a tumor and getting early treatment.

### ◉ Steps

1 After a warm shower or bath, grasp one testicle with both hands. Place your middle and index fingers underneath the testicle and your thumbs on top.

2 Roll the testicle between your thumbs and fingers, feeling for any abnormal lumps. An abnormal lump will feel like a hard pea. Don't mistake the epididymis, a ropelike structure on the back and top of each testicle, for an abnormal lump.

3 Check your other testicle in the same way.

4 See your doctor immediately if you feel any lumps.

5 Repeat the self-exam once a month or as instructed by your doctor.

### ✱ Tips

An abnormal lump may also be a sign of a noncancerous infection.

You may find that one testicle is slightly larger or hangs lower than the other. This is normal.

A testicular self-exam is not a substitute for a medical exam. Any male who has reached adolescence should have an annual testicular exam by a doctor as part of a normal checkup.

## Care for Jock Itch 819

Jock itch is caused by a fungus called *Tinea cruris* that infects skin on the groin, inner thighs and sometimes the buttocks.

### ◉ Steps

1 Apply an over-the-counter antifungal cream three times a day, or as directed in the product instructions, to get rid of the fungus. Treatment must continue for three to four weeks or the fungus will reappear.

2 For a severe or persistent infection, see your doctor and discuss the possibility of topical and/or oral anti-fungal medication.

### ⚠ Warning

Your symptoms should improve within 7 to 10 days of using antifungal creams. If they don't, see your doctor.

3   Apply an anti-fungal powder when chafing aggravates jock itch.

4   Wear a jock strap, or athletic supporter, to keep your genitals away from the rest of your skin.

5   Keep the groin area clean and dry. After showering and towel drying, consider carefully drying the area completely using a handheld hair dryer at a low setting.

6   Wear roomy cotton underwear—boxers are best.

7   Wear loose-fitting clothes.

8   Remove a wet bathing suit as soon as you are finished swimming.

9   Sleep naked to let the infected area air out.

---

## 820 | Treat Crabs

**Pubic lice, which resemble tiny crabs, lay their eggs, or nits, at the base of the hair shaft, and are usually spread by physical contact, shared towels and linens, or infested toilet seats.**

### ⊙ Steps

1   Treat the area with an insecticide solution formulated for pubic lice. You can purchase one over the counter or by prescription. Use according to the directions.

2   Wash In hot water all linens, bedding, towels and clothing that may have come in contact with the pubic lice. Dry them in a hot dryer.

3   Dry-clean infested items that cannot be machine washed.

4   Put non-machine-washable quilts and blankets inside a large trash bag and seal it tightly. Leave it sealed for at least 10 days. Pubic lice can survive for only 24 to 48 hours away from the body, but nits may take longer to hatch and then die.

5   Inform your sexual partner and anyone who has shared any bedding or towels with you. They will need to be treated.

### ✳ Tips

Shaving your pubic hair is not usually necessary, and that alone will not kill the pubic lice.

Crabs are annoying but are generally not dangerous, and are not carriers of other sexually transmitted diseases.

### ⚠ Warning

Avoid lotions containing lindane, and make sure any prescription you have received is not for a lindane-based product. Lindane has been associated with a number of serious medical conditions, including cancer and seizures.

---

## 821 | Treat Athlete's Foot

**Several over-the-counter remedies can help cure athlete's foot, which is a fungal infection. Once you have successfully treated it, be diligent in preventing its return.**

### ⊙ Steps

1   Apply a topical anti-fungal ointment two or three times a day. Reapply after showering and before going to bed. Continue for three to four weeks to avoid recurrence.

2   Dry carefully between each toe whenever your feet get wet. Consider using a hair dryer set on low to thoroughly dry your feet.

### ✳ Tip

You should begin to see improvement within 7 to 10 days of using over-the-counter anti-fungal creams. If not, see your doctor.

3   Place cotton balls between your toes at night if your feet perspire excessively when you sleep.

4   Avoid harsh soaps, especially deodorant soaps.

5   Sprinkle an anti-fungal powder into your socks and shoes whenever you plan to wear your shoes for several hours.

6   Pour a small amount of astringent onto a piece of gauze and wipe the crusty areas on your feet and between your toes. Then let the gauze sit on the crusty spots for a few minutes. The astringent will draw more moisture from your foot.

7   Wear open sandals or go barefoot as much as possible during the acute phase of athlete's foot.

8   Ask your doctor to help with athlete's foot that spreads or will not go away. Your doctor can prescribe topical or oral anti-fungal medication.

## Treat Corns                                                                     822

A corn is a callus—generally a pea-size bump—that may ache and be tender with pressure. Corns usually develop over bony prominences on the feet, especially toe joints.

### ⊙ Steps

1   Apply a lotion containing cocoa butter, vitamin E or lanolin to soften the corn. This may aid in diminishing the corn's size or eliminating it.

2   Use nonmedicated corn plasters on corns to protect painful spots on the toes when you're wearing shoes. Always remove plasters carefully, so as not to damage surrounding tissue, and never wear the same plaster longer than one day.

3   Soak the affected foot in warm water for a while to soften the corn, then run a pumice stone or stick or an emery board across the corn. Pumice helps to abrade away the horny callus surface.

4   As another option, consider applying a keratolytic agent to remove horny corn tissue, choosing either a 17 percent salicylic acid solution in collodion or 40 percent salicylic acid plasters. Remove the agent with warm water, and blot the foot dry. Apply a 5 percent or 10 percent salicylic acid ointment, then place an adhesive bandage over the corn. Repeat this once or twice a week until the corn becomes loose enough to be dislodged easily.

5   Use a corn pad. Its oval opening forces a corn to bulge into the hole and displaces pressure in the area. Horseshoe-shaped corn pads are the most effective, as they protect against external pressure without creating new pressure.

6   Wear shoes with plenty of toe room—enough space so that you can freely wiggle your toes around inside.

### ⚠ Warnings

If you detect any redness around the corn, stop using any corn medication until normal coloring returns.

If the corn looks too advanced for you to deal with on your own, consult a physician.

If you have certain medical conditions, such as diabetes or circulatory problems, consult a physician before self-treating foot problems. If you choose to treat yourself, you may develop ulcerations or other problems.

Never try to use a razor on a corn.

## 823 | Relieve Bunions

A bunion is a deformity and swelling at the base of the big toe. If a bunion is allowed to worsen, the big toe may eventually come to rest under the second toe.

### ⊙ Steps

1. Wear shoes with plenty of toe room. If your shoe is not shaped like a human foot, don't wear it.

2. Go barefoot as much as possible. This reduces pressure on the big toe.

3. Buy custom-made shoes if your physician advises it. Shoes can be designed to help properly position the big toe.

4. Ask your doctor about special bunion pads and dressings available by prescription to protect your toes from shoe pressure. You can also buy bunion pads at the drugstore.

5. Elevate your foot and ice your big toe if the bunion is red and sore. Put the ice on for 20 minutes, every hour, until the bunion feels less painful. Do not apply ice directly; always use an ice pack, ice bag or compress.

6. Ask a doctor about getting a steroid injection and local anesthetic in your bunion to reduce inflammation. This shot is occasionally given when the bunion is causing bursitis, which is the inflammation of the bursa, or saclike joint covering.

7. Ask your doctor to apply splints or digital orthotics to reposition your big toe. Orthotics are devices that act as aids in improving body mechanics.

8. Get a prescription for an orthotic that will correct your foot function.

9. Consult your doctor about bunion surgery to correct foot deformities.

### ✱ Tip

Women are much more likely than men to get bunions, due to narrow-toed shoe fashions.

### ⚠ Warnings

If you have certain medical conditions, such as diabetes or circulatory problems, consult a physician before self-treating foot problems.

If severe swelling, redness, heat or pain persist for two days, or if you see a break in the skin and feel feverish, contact a physician.

## 824 | Care for Ingrown Toenails

When the skin around your toenail turns red and swollen and starts causing pain, the nail has probably grown into your toe.

### ⊙ Steps

1. Add two capfuls of povidone-iodine (Betadine) solution to 2 quarts warm water and soak your foot for 10 minutes to soften the tissues and nail.

2. Soak your toe in warm water for 10 minutes each day for three days, or until the soreness is gone. After soaking, dry your foot gently and apply an adhesive bandage.

3. Insert a sliver of cotton (tear a small piece from a cotton ball) between the nail and the skin and leave it in for a few days. This will keep pressure from the nail off the toe. Remove the cotton as soon as the nail begins to grow out and away from the toe.

4. Wear loose shoes or go barefoot as much as possible while your toe is healing. Consider switching permanently to shoes with more toe room. Your goal is to eliminate any pressure around your toenail.

### ⚠ Warnings

If you have certain medical conditions, such as diabetes or circulatory problems, consult a physician before self-treating foot problems.

If severe swelling, redness, heat or pain persist for two days, or if you see a break in the skin and feel feverish, consult a physician.

Chronic ingrown toenails require a podiatrist's services.

5   Keep your nails trimmed straight across and not too short. If the nail is curved, it is more likely to grow under the skin.

6   See your podiatrist for chronic ingrown toenails. A podiatrist may manipulate and elevate the end of your nail to prevent pressure on soft toe tissue, or correct the problem surgically.

## Be an Organ Donor                                                825

If everyone arranged to be an organ donor, there would be enough organs for every person who needed a transplant. Donating an organ is easy.

### ⊙ Steps

1   Make sure your family and doctor understand that you want to donate your organs. If and when the time comes for your family to face these issues, you'll be unable to communicate your wishes to them, so it's important for them to know beforehand.

2   Call the Living Bank at (800) 528-2971. This is an organ-donation education center and national organ registry.

3   Request an organ-donor form, and fill it out.

4   Ask two witnesses to sign your donor form. The witnessed signatures make the donor form a legal and binding document.

5   Keep in mind that in many states you can sign up to be an organ donor when you renew your driver's license. However, a donor card is often more effective in making sure that hospital personnel know your wishes.

6   Understand that if you fill out an organ-donor form, you can always revoke it at a later date. Be sure to inform your family, too, if you change your mind.

**✱ Tip**

Signing a donor form or carrying a donor card will not in any way affect the medical treatment you receive. Donation is considered only after three or four separate EEGs have shown you to be brain-dead.

**⚠ Warning**

If you have a donor card but your family refuses to allow your organs to be donated, the hospital will follow the wishes of your family—even though your donor card is a legal document. So make sure your family understands what you want.

## Add Fruit to Your Diet                                            826

By adding fruit to your diet, you'll not only be gaining a rich source of nutrients, you'll also be enjoying some delicious flavors. Fruits are terrific sources of vitamins, minerals and fiber.

### ⊙ Steps

1   Make an instant breakfast by blending a frozen banana, a handful of frozen strawberries and a cup of milk.

2   Stir applesauce—or sliced or shredded apples—into a bowl of hot oatmeal in the morning.

3   Choose an orange instead of potato chips with lunch.

4   Add bananas to vanilla yogurt for an afternoon snack.

5   Try some less familiar fruits like guava, papaya, mangoes, star fruit, kumquats or unusual varieties of bananas.

**✱ Tips**

Citrus fruits, berries and melons are great sources of vitamin C.

Orange-colored fruits such as mangoes, apricots and papayas are plentiful sources of vitamin A and beta-carotene.

6   Keep dried dates, apricots or cranberries in your desk for snacks.

7   Create a fruit salsa out of diced mango, red onion, diced mild or hot chile peppers, and cilantro.

8   Serve fruit salad for dessert.

9   Aim for four or five servings of fruit every day. A serving of fruit is one medium piece (such as an apple or orange), 6 oz. of juice or $\frac{1}{2}$ c. canned fruit. Fruit juice counts toward your four or five servings, but try to choose whole fruit instead, since most juices are low in fiber.

## 827 | Add Vegetables to Your Diet

**Mom was right when she told you to eat your veggies. They are great sources of fiber, vitamins and minerals—not to mention the phytonutrients so highly touted in medical news today.**

### ⊙ Steps

1   Mix carrot juice into your breakfast orange juice.

2   Add chopped broccoli or grated zucchini to an omelette.

3   Toss sliced cucumbers with seasoned rice vinegar for an instant Asian-style salad.

4   Dip raw vegetables (cherry tomatoes, mushrooms, celery or carrots) into low-fat salad dressing or hummus.

5   Toss cooked, chilled corn kernels (fresh or frozen) into a green salad.

6   Experiment with unusual vegetables such as long beans or kohlrabi, broccoli rabe and Jerusalem artichokes (sunchokes).

7   Try Asian and Latin American vegetables, such as bok choy and long beans from China, edamame (young soybeans) and kabocha squash from Japan, and jicama, chayote and tomatillo from Mexico.

8   Spread tomato and onion salsa over grilled fish.

9   Sprinkle peeled, diced beets and carrots with salt, pepper and olive oil, then roast them at 425 degrees F for 30 minutes.

10  Mix chopped spinach, kale or other greens into spaghetti sauce.

11  Aim for four or five servings of vegetables a day. A serving is $\frac{1}{2}$ c. cooked vegetables (such as carrots or broccoli) or 1 c. raw salad vegetables (lettuce or spinach, for example). Vegetable juice counts, but try to choose the whole vegetable instead, since most juices are lower in fiber.

### ✳ Tips

Buy prewashed salad greens to reduce salad-preparation time.

Shop the supermarket salad bar for precut broccoli, cauliflower and other vegetables. Eat these raw or steamed.

## Gain Weight 828

Gaining weight may be a cinch for most people, but for those who don't put on pounds easily, it can be a real struggle. Here's how to bulk up while maintaining a healthful lifestyle.

### ⊙ Steps

1 Eat nutritious foods that are high in calories. Some examples are whole-grain breads, avocados, potatoes, kidney beans, lean red meat, poultry and fish.

2 Boost the caloric value of your meals using healthful additions. Add powdered milk to casseroles, add avocados and olives to sandwiches, add wheat germ to cereal, add chopped meat to pasta sauce, and so on.

3 Eat three meals a day and at least two snacks.

4 Increase your normal portion size. Take a second scoop of pasta, or add a banana to your oatmeal.

5 Choose higher-calorie foods when given a choice. For example, corn is higher in calories than green beans.

6 Relax—excessive fidgeting and restlessness can burn up a lot of calories.

7 Add weight lifting to your exercise program. It helps build muscle mass. Be aware, though, that this will speed up your metabolism, so you'll need to increase your calories even more.

8 Tally up your caloric intake, and compare it with the number of calories you're burning. You need to be taking in more than you use up, and you may need to ease up a little on your exercise program.

### ✱ Tips

If you cannot seem to put on any weight, you should have a doctor rule out any physical problems, such as hormonal imbalances.

Although it seems like a logical way to bulk up, avoid adding excess fat and sweets to your diet. Too much fat is bad for your health regardless of your weight, and filling up on junk food will keep you from getting all the nutrition you need from healthier foods. Eat fats and oils in moderation; they should account for no more than 30 percent of your total caloric intake.

### ⚠ Warning

Consult your doctor before beginning any weight-gain program.

## Lose Weight 829

Proper diet and exercise can aid in weight loss, as well as keep you healthy. The challenge is to follow through. Others have lost weight by following these simple guidelines—so can you.

### ⊙ Steps

1 Set small, realistic goals. Some good goals are to increase your exercise or activity by 10 minutes, or to cut down on unhealthy snacks or sodas in the afternoon.

2 Start a regular exercise program and stick with it. Aim for a minimum of 30 minutes, three or four times a week. You'll burn more calories and get fit faster if you exercise even more—30 to 60 minutes, five to seven times a week.

3 Sneak in extra exercise in addition to your regular program. Park at the far end of the parking lot and walk; take the stairs instead of the elevator.

4 Eat low-fat, high-fiber foods such as salads and vegetable pasta dishes.

5 Choose foods that you like. Learn to prepare healthful, low-calorie foods that taste good. Eating well doesn't have to mean eating dull foods.

### ✱ Tips

Lose weight with a friend, or join a support group.

Avoid vending machines by carrying around your own healthful snacks and leaving pocket change at home.

### ⚠ Warning

Consult your physician before beginning any weight-loss program.

6   Eat smaller, more frequent meals. Some experts believe that this way, your body starts to increase its metabolism so that calories are burned faster. Also, mini-meals can prevent overeating later on. Keep in mind that this may not work for everyone—and remember that snacking on potato chips or doughnuts is not going to shrink your waistline. Stick to healthful, low-calorie foods.

7   Drink a minimum of eight glasses of water per day—more if you are active. Water is critical for weight loss.

8   Plan ahead. Keep the fridge stocked with healthful food, and you'll be less likely to run out for high-calorie, high-fat junk food.

9   Keep a food diary. This will help you pinpoint where you can improve your eating habits.

10  Once you discover your favorite snack time, be sure to have plenty of healthful options available.

11  Make sure you've chosen an exercise program you enjoy, and don't rule out the unconventional—regular vigorous dancing is exercise, too. Consult a doctor to find an exercise program that is best for you if you are extremely overweight.

12  Lose weight gradually—you are more apt to keep it off. A safe amount is 1 to 1½ pounds per week.

---

## 830  Help Your Family Lose Weight

According to a recent study, people with a family history of obesity are up to 75 percent more likely to have weight problems. Stop the trend by organizing a family weight-loss plan.

### ◉ Steps

1   Take a trip to the grocery store together. Let everyone choose his or her favorite nutritious foods, and remind one another to avoid the aisles with the junk food.

2   Share low-fat recipes and healthy cooking tips, and put these to good use by preparing meals together.

3   Serve reasonably proportioned meals on individual plates. That is, bring to the table plates that are already full, as opposed to passing around dishes from which family members can help themselves.

4   Take a walk together after dinner.

5   Turn off that television set and computer and spend time together doing more active things—play some football, shoot some hoops, ride bicycles around the neighborhood.

6   Join a health club together—be sure to ask about family or group rates.

7   Indulge in your family's taste for adventure by planning the next vacation around an activity that requires movement, such as hiking, skiing, canoeing or whitewater rafting.

 **Tip**

When talking to your kids about losing weight, be sure to put the emphasis on being healthy and fit, not on looking slim. Instead of saying that it would be nice to look thin in the next school picture, remind them that a healthy diet and exercise will give them more energy and make them stronger.

⚠ **Warning**

Consult your physician before beginning any weight-loss program.

## Build Lean Body Mass                                                831

Chiseled abs, shapely legs, toned arms—these can be yours when you increase your lean body mass and decrease your body-fat percentage.

### ⊙ Steps

1   Get your body-fat percentage measured before making dietary or exercise changes; this way you'll be able to track your progress. There are many ways to measure body fat, including calipers (skin-fold pinching), underwater (hydrostatic) weighing, and bioelectrical impedance. Your doctor's office or your gym should be able to provide this service.

2   Strength-train to build lean body mass. Work the major muscle groups, including the quadriceps (thighs), hamstrings, gluteal muscles (buttocks), back, chest, shoulders, arms and abdominal muscles.

3   Realize there is no such thing as spot reducing. You can increase the strength and tone of a certain part of your body, but unless you shed your overall excess body fat, you won't be able to see the definition.

4   Expend more calories than you consume. Any activity, from mowing the lawn to vacuuming, burns calories and helps create a calorie deficit, resulting in fat loss. Losing fat will help reveal your hidden muscles.

5   Keep in mind that to lose 1 pound of fat, you have to create a calorie deficit of 3,500 calories. Reducing calorie consumption or increasing activity by 500 calories a day will result in 1 pound of fat loss per week.

6   Include cardiovascular training in your workout. Aerobic exercise will increase the number of calories you burn and enhance your endurance.

7   Consider working with a personal trainer to help you get started on an exercise regimen.

### ✳ Tips

Keep in mind the following body-fat percentage standards: For women, 17 to 20 percent is considered lean, 20 to 25 percent is normal, 26 to 30 percent is overfat and 30 percent or higher is obese. For men, 8 to 12 percent is considered lean, 13 to 19 percent is normal, 20 to 24 percent is overfat and 25 percent or higher is obese.

Strength training creates an afterburn effect, meaning that your metabolism continues to burn calories at a higher rate even after the exercise is over.

Dieting without strength training can leave you with a high body fat percentage. It's possible to appear thin but have a high percentage of body fat.

## Fit Exercise Into Your Busy Schedule                                 832

Make a commitment to exercise every day if you can. Try to get in at least 30 minutes of walking or more vigorous exercise.

### ⊙ Steps

1   Try walking, biking or skating to work. If this takes longer than your usual commute, plan ahead: Pack your briefcase and lay out your clothes the night before. Keep a change of clothes at work if need be.

2   If an alternate commute is impossible, get off the bus a little earlier and walk the rest of the way, park at the far end of the lot, or take the stairs instead of the elevator.

3   Make use of your lunch break. Play a quick game of racquetball, make a speedy gym visit, go for a jog or take a brisk walk (use some light hand weights for a bonus workout).

4   Stretch at your desk. This reduces muscle tension, gets your circulation moving and prepares you for more strenuous activity later.

### ✳ Tips

New moms can join an aerobics class specially designed for them and their babies. You can network with other moms, stay fit and keep an eye on the baby, who gets involved as part of your workout routine.

Exercise with a buddy—you can motivate one another.

Carry a notebook and keep a record of your activities and their duration. Increase your daily exercise as time goes on.

5  Do some chores. Mow the lawn or rake the leaves for 20 minutes. Housework burns calories, and you have to get the work done anyway.

6  Play games with your kids. Shoot some hoops, play some hopscotch or toss a ball.

---

## 833 | Exercise at Your Office

You may not want to turn your office into a gym, but there are exercises you can do at or near your desk to boost your energy level, relieve stress and burn calories.

### ⊙ Steps

1  Try some squats: Stand in front of your chair with your feet shoulder-width apart. Bend your knees as though you're sitting on the chair, keeping your weight on your heels. When your legs are parallel with the seat of the chair, slowly rise to your original standing position.

2  Hold up the wall with wall sits: Stand with your back touching the wall. Move your feet away from the wall so that the wall is supporting the weight of your back. Bend your knees so that your legs form a 90-degree angle. Hold as long as you can.

3  Pose like a warrior—with a lunge: With your arms by your sides, take a giant step forward with your right leg so your thigh is parallel with the floor. Pushing off the same leg, return to your starting position. Repeat with the left leg. (Traveling lunges are also an option if you have room—keep moving forward with each lunge.)

4  Try calf raises during a coffee break: Holding on to your desk or a file cabinet for balance, raise your heels off the floor, then lower them.

5  Peek into your neighbor's cubicle while you do toe raises: Sitting in your chair or standing, lift and lower your toes while keeping your heels on the ground, or walk around on the heels of your feet.

6  Burn those buns with a gluteal squeeze: While sitting or standing, squeeze the muscles of your rear end. Hold, then relax.

7  Get on the floor and do some crunches: Lying on your back with your knees bent, reach for your knees, hold for two counts, then return to the floor. No need to curl all the way up—stop when your abdominal muscles are fully contracted; your shoulders will be just a few inches off the floor.

8  Do some push-ups—standing upright and pushing against a wall with your hands a little wider than shoulder-width apart, or lying facedown on the ground.

9  Do some dips: Sitting on your chair, with the palms of your hands on your chair and feet on the floor, scoot your rear end off the end of the seat. Bend your elbows, lowering your body, then straighten your arms to return to the starting position.

10  Release tension with shoulder raises: Raise your shoulders up to your ears, hold, then relax.

### ⚠ Warning

Always consult your health care provider before beginning an exercise program.

### ❋ Tips

Doing squats will help protect your knees from future injuries. However, if you've had a knee injury in the past, check with your doctor about what exercises are appropriate for you, and go easy when trying any new exercises involving the knee.

If you're not familiar with strength-training exercises, seek the assistance of a certified personal trainer or physical therapist to get you started properly.

Always warm up or begin exercising gradually.

Perform enough repetitions of each exercise to feel fatigue in the muscles being worked.

It helps to have comfortable clothes on hand or to work for a company that observes a casual dress code.

### ⚠ Warnings

Use discretion in the workplace: Only do what's appropriate for your particular work environment.

If using a chair to perform exercises, be sure to choose a sturdy, supportive one without wheels.

## Stay Motivated to Exercise

You know you should exercise, but some days it's tough to get moving. Discover what motivates you, and use these strategies to develop and maintain an active lifestyle.

### ⊙ Steps

1 Determine an attainable goal, such as exercising twice during the week and once on weekends. Creating realistic goals will set you up for success. If your goal becomes too easy, you can always design a more ambitious one.

2 Devise rewards for achieving your goal. The reward can be a massage, a new workout outfit, a new CD, a session with a personal trainer or that hardcover novel you've had your eye on—whatever you really want.

3 Partner with a friend, co-worker or loved one—someone who will support you and your goals without sabotaging them.

4 Subscribe to a fitness magazine or online fitness newsletter. New tips and exercises can be inspirational and alleviate boredom.

5 Create a competition with co-workers or friends. For example, the team whose members exercise for 30 minutes, three times each week, for two months wins a prize.

6 Change into your workout clothes. Sometimes, just getting dressed is the biggest barrier.

7 Erase the concept that if you can't do at least 30 minutes you're wasting your time. Even in small doses, exercise burns calories, increases energy and improves your health.

8 Try a new sport or class. Adding variety, group support and competition can increase your likelihood of exercising.

9 Make a commitment to your dog or your neighbor's dog to go for a long walk at least twice each week.

10 Look for ways to incorporate activity into your day, even if you can't do your normal exercise routine. Take the stairs instead of the elevator, go bowling instead of to the movies, or use a push mower instead of a power mower.

11 Sign up for a race and send in the entry fee. Whatever your activity—running, biking, walking, swimming—there are hundreds of races offered all over the world. Pick a place you've always wanted to visit.

12 Join a gym or health club. For some, paying for a membership increases the likelihood of compliance. It also eliminates the bad-weather excuse.

### ✳ Tips

Exercise in the morning. Research shows that people who make exercise a priority first thing in the day are more likely to stick with it.

Every person goes through periods when it's very challenging to maintain an exercise program. Acknowledge it when it happens, recognize that it's just a brief period of time, and restart your program as soon as possible.

Choose things that motivate you—not what others want.

Remind yourself of the many health benefits of an exercise program.

## 835 | Ease Sore Muscles

You can always relieve sore, tight muscles with a massage, or by using sports creams or medications. Before spending money, though, try these simple remedies.

### ◉ Steps

1 Apply an ice pack for 20 minutes to any area that hurts. Repeat this every hour until the pain subsides.

2 Opt for heat if you have a chronic condition or continual episodes of pain. In these situations, heat can work better than ice (if you are not treating an acute injury). Try a heating pad, or a warm shower or bath.

3 Stretch the sore area gently to loosen up damaged muscles.

4 Walk 15 to 30 minutes at least once a day to increase circulation throughout your body. This will also help deliver much-needed oxygen to the sore muscles.

5 Drink a minimum of eight glasses (64 oz.) of water daily—more if you're active—to hydrate your body.

6 Avoid strenuous activity as long as you're in pain.

### ✱ Tips

Be sure to warm up before exercising and stretching.

An over-the-counter non-steroidal anti-inflammatory medication, such as ibuprofen, may also reduce muscle soreness.

Avoid exercising or stretching to the point of pain.

## 836 | Get a Massage

Massage has been touted as a panacea for everything from migraines to ulcers. Although the scientific proof is sparse, almost everyone agrees that a massage at the very least feels good.

### ◉ Steps

1 Avoid eating close to the time of your massage.

2 Relax. Give yourself plenty of time to get to your massage appointment.

3 Wear clothing that you can get out of easily. If you plan to keep your clothes on, wear something like loose shorts and a jogging bra for a woman or boxers for a man; these options make it easier for the massage therapist to work on you.

4 Tell the therapist if you have any health concerns, if you may be pregnant or if you have had any injuries.

5 Let the therapist know if there is any area where you do not wish to be touched, or if there is an area where you would like special work done.

6 Clear your thoughts. A massage is a time to relax, not to worry about work projects or your car payments.

7 Breathe normally. Don't hold your breath if a sensitive spot is being worked on.

8 Try not to contract your muscles. Your body needs to be relaxed and flexible to get the best results. Imagine you are a rag doll.

### ✱ Tips

Before booking a professional massage, make sure the therapist is trained and certified.

If you prefer a massage therapist of a certain sex, remember to register your request when you make your appointment.

Leave on some clothing if you are uncomfortable being nude. The key is to be comfortable.

9   Report any discomfort or problems during the massage. If you feel any pain, are cold, don't like the music, and so on, tell the therapist.

10  Rise slowly after the massage is over. Get off the table gradually. Take your time, and try to maintain your state of relaxation.

11  Drink a tall glass of water after your massage.

12  Avoid driving if you are feeling spaced out or light-headed. Wait a few minutes to get grounded.

## Give a Back Massage                                                837

Providing a little touch therapy for stress reduction is a wonderful and therapeutic gift in this era of 14-hour workdays, repetitive-stress injuries and weekend warriors.

### ⊙ Steps

1   Have the person receiving the massage lie on her belly on a firm, comfortable surface, such as a floor mat or firm bed. Make sure you can reach her whole back without straining your own.

2   Stand or kneel by her side. Place one hand on the lower back and one hand between the shoulder blades, over the heart.

3   Warm up the back by applying thumb pressure along both sides of the spine simultaneously: Start at the lower back and knead gently with your thumbs up to the neck area. This will also promote relaxation.

4   Use a smooth, delicate stroke (called "effleurage") to apply massage oil. In one long stroke, slide your palms down either side of the spine to the pelvis; scoop out around the hips and back up the sides to the shoulders. Maintain contact with the back. Glide your hands over the back to start a new area.

5   Continue up both sides of the neck to the base of the head.

6   Start at the spine and slide your palms in opposite directions outward to the sides of the back, starting with the lower back area and moving up to the shoulders.

7   Knead the fleshy muscular areas at the top of the shoulders, the mid-back area and the buttocks to loosen tight muscles and fascia (the connective tissue).

8   Use your thumbs or fingers to apply pressure to areas that feel hard or tight, often called knots.

9   Perform clockwise circular friction with your fingertips along the muscles that are close to the spine and around the shoulder blades.

10  Rotate the arms gently, one at a time, to loosen the shoulder joints and enhance blood flow.

### ✱ Tips

The many benefits of massage include relaxation, increased body awareness, improved circulation, and improved lymphatic drainage for release of toxins.

Massage oil is typically used to decrease the friction created on the skin and to prevent the pulling of hair. The less oil, the greater the friction and the deeper the pressure.

Incorporate effleurage throughout your massage as a connective stroke to move from one area to another, to soothe an area of localized deep tissue work or to make a transition to another stroke.

Use slow movements for a soothing or calming response and fast movements for a stimulating effect.

### ⚠ Warnings

Do not put any direct pressure on the spine.

Avoid any broken skin, blisters or areas of possible infection.

## 838 Meditate

Meditation can be calming, rejuvenating and restorative. When practiced regularly, it can aid in reducing stress, lowering blood pressure and increasing personal awareness.

⊙ **Steps**

1 Choose a tranquil location, free of distractions.

2 Decide whether you'd like to have soothing music in the background.

3 Select a comfortable chair or place to sit, and assume a sitting position with your spine relatively straight.

4 Close your eyes.

5 Breathe in, allowing your rib cage and belly to expand as you inhale.

6 Exhale slowly.

7 Concentrate on your breathing. Be aware of each breath and the feelings of deeper relaxation.

8 Allow thoughts and feelings to enter your mind. Acknowledge them, allow them to pass, and refocus on your breathing.

9 Open your eyes after you feel more relaxed and centered.

10 Begin with 5 to 10 minutes of meditation each day and increase to 20 minutes or more twice each day.

✳ **Tips**

There are many forms and variations of meditation. If one particular form doesn't work for you, try another.

Avoid meditating on a full stomach. The best time to meditate is just before eating.

Some studies have suggested meditation may decrease the risk of heart disease, possibly because the resulting stress relief may promote the body's self-repair system to thin the fatty buildup on artery walls. Still, meditating should never be used as a substitute for a healthful diet, exercise and proper medical care.

## 839 Fight Insomnia

Everyone has an occasional sleepless night. Life's daily stresses, major decisions and caffeine too late in the day all contribute to insomnia.

⊙ **Steps**

1 Use your bed for sleeping only. Try to refrain from catching up on work or just hanging out in bed.

2 Relax by listening to soft music or a meditation tape before bedtime. Do yoga or gentle stretching.

3 Take a hot bath. Keep the lights dim.

4 Use essential oils to help you relax. Add six to eight drops of lavender or marjoram to a bath, or put four drops of oil on your pillow.

5 Snack on foods high in tryptophan, an amino acid that can help you relax. These include turkey, bananas, figs, dates, milk and tuna.

6 Try an herbal sleep remedy to help induce sleepiness. Valerian, chamomile, catnip, lavender, lime flower, passionflower, hops or skull-cap can be taken in tea or capsule form. The hormone melatonin can be taken as a pill or a lozenge and may promote sleep as well. Keep in mind that further research is still needed to verify the effectiveness of these alternative remedies.

✳ **Tips**

Room temperature, noise and physical ailments all can contribute to sleeplessness.

Trying too hard to fall asleep can have the reverse effect: You'll stay awake. Distract yourself by doing something else instead.

7  Get out of bed if you can't sleep. Lying in bed sleepless will only make you feel more stressed.

8  Read or perform a light chore until you start feeling sleepy. Then try to go back to sleep—or if you're feeling stressed or agitated, try some relaxation techniques.

9  Return to bed once you're feeling sleepy and relaxed.

## Break a Bad Habit | 840

Habits such as biting your nails, downing large amounts of caffeine and even gossiping are automatic behaviors that can be changed with patience and persistence.

### ⊙ Steps

1  Decide how serious you are about breaking the habit. In addition to a strong commitment, you'll need time and energy to pay attention to your behavior so you can change it.

2  Keep track of the behavior. Keep a notepad or journal handy.

3  Write down when it happens (what the overall situation is when it occurs) and what you were thinking and feeling. Writing increases your awareness of when and why you have this habit.

4  Read and think about what you write down. What does this habit do for you? Is it a way to deal with feelings of boredom, anxiety, stress or anger?

5  Think of what you could do instead of the habit that would be a more positive way to deal with the feelings or situation that provoke it. Write down some simple alternative behaviors. Pick one you want to practice.

6  Try to catch yourself when you find yourself indulging in the habit, and stop yourself as soon as you can. Start the alternative behavior you decided you wanted to do instead.

7  Aim to do this once a week at first, then increase the number of times per week over time. The more you practice a new behavior, the more it becomes the new habit.

8  Get support from others by letting them know you are working on the habit and telling them what they can do to help.

### ✴ Tips

Be patient with yourself. Habits are so automatic and unconscious, you may not even realize you're engaging in the behavior until you're already doing it.

Be kind to yourself. Browbeating yourself is another bad habit to be broken.

## Quit Smoking | 841

You've probably heard all the reasons why—now check out the hows of quitting, based on the recommendations of the American Cancer Society.

### ⊙ Steps

1  Ask yourself why you want to stop smoking.

2  Write your answers on a piece of paper and carry it with you.

### ✴ Tips

Ask your doctor about nicotine products and other medications if you have tried unsuccessfully to quit in the past.

3   Whenever you feel like smoking, use your list to remind yourself of why you want to stop.

4   Fill out a "stop smoking contract." Sign it, and have a family member or friend sign it as a witness.

5   Throw away all your cigarettes, lighters and ashtrays.

6   Change your schedule to avoid circumstances in which you usually smoke. Walk around the block or chew gum when you would normally be smoking.

7   Put up no-smoking signs in your house, your work area and your car.

8   Prepare yourself to feel the urge to start smoking again. Here are four ways to deal with the urge to smoke: delaying, deep breathing, drinking water and doing something else.

9   Carry around "mouth toys"—candy, gum, straws, carrot sticks.

10  List the good things that have happened since you stopped smoking, and keep the list with you as an inspiration wherever you go. For example, you might note that your breath is fresher, you can climb the stairs without getting winded, and you've saved enough money to buy a new DVD player.

11  Reward yourself for quitting; for example, you could take the money you might have spent on cigarettes and buy yourself something nice.

Be prepared to persist despite a few relapses.

Planning meals, eating a healthful diet and staying active will help you maintain your weight.

Look for a support group or smoking-cessation class.

### ⚠ Warning

You may experience irritability, depression or a dry mouth due to nicotine withdrawal after you stop smoking. These symptoms should pass.

---

## 842 | Overcome a Phobia

Overcoming a phobia entails learning how to relax and calm yourself so that you can gradually face the feared object or situation and feel less afraid.

### ◉ Steps

1   Explore exactly what it is you are afraid of. Is there some underlying reason or past event that causes you to avoid an object or situation? Is there something you gain by avoiding it (besides avoiding the fear or anxiety)?

2   Learn how to relax and calm yourself. There are many ways to do this. Here is one method: Take a slow, deep breath into your belly to the count of six and then breathe out slowly to the count of six. Practice this daily for 5 minutes; increase over time to 20 minutes.

3   Make a list starting with the feared object or situation—for example, driving on freeways. Then, write down what object or situation would be slightly less anxiety-producing—for example, driving on small highways.

4   Continue making a list of items that are slightly less anxiety-producing than the previous item—for example, driving on big, busy streets, then driving on less congested streets, and so forth.

5   Get into a relaxed state using whatever method you have been practicing. Starting with the least anxiety-producing item on your list (the last item), imagine yourself in that situation as vividly as possible while continuing to breathe and stay relaxed.

### ✳ Tip

Since this is quite challenging, it is often helpful to go through these steps with a psychotherapist. A therapist can teach you how to relax, help you come up with ways to challenge negative thoughts, and help you feel safer as you face your phobia.

### ⚠ Warning

Seek professional help if your phobia is interfering with your daily life or causing you significant distress.

How to Do *(Just About)* Everything

6 Go on to the next item up. Visualize yourself in that situation while continuing to practice relaxation and calm yourself.

7 Work up the list, imagining yourself in each situation while continuing to practice remaining relaxed and calm. Only go to the next item when you can successfully stay calm imagining the previous item. If one of the items produces too much anxiety, stop the exercise and come back to it later. Start at the beginning of your list each time, and progress as far as you can. It may take you several sessions before you progress to the top of the list.

8 Write down all the thoughts you have when facing your phobia, such as "I'm going to die," "I'm going to have a heart attack" or "I can't breathe."

9 Write down alternative thoughts that would help you calm down, such as "I am not going to die," "I can breathe" or "I can relax."

10 In real life, put yourself in the least anxiety-producing situation on your list (the last item) and practice relaxing and calming yourself just as you imagined. Include telling yourself the alternative thoughts to help you calm down.

11 Work yourself up to your most feared situation or object (your phobia) while practicing being relaxed and calm.

---

# Stop Worrying 843

The keys to worrying less are to challenge your worrisome thoughts and to calm yourself physically and emotionally.

## ◉ Steps

1 Write down what you are worried about. Include your imagined worst-case scenarios.

2 Think about how you would handle your worst-case scenarios.

3 Decide what actions you could take that would change the situation and give you less to worry about. Then follow through on those actions.

4 Try to think logically about the worrisome thoughts that you feel you can't take any action on. Consider which of them are excessive or distorted and have very little basis in reality.

5 For each of these worrisome thoughts, write down an alternative way of looking at the problem that presents a rational challenge to your worries.

6 Try to catch yourself when you notice that you're becoming overwhelmed with worry. Stop and remind yourself of the alternative way to look at the situation.

7 Practice relaxation and stress-reduction techniques. One simple thing you can do to help quiet your mind and calm your emotions and body is to breathe in slowly and deeply to the count of six and breathe out slowly to the count of six. Do this for 5 minutes; gradually increase to 20 minutes over time.

8 Learn to accept what you cannot change or have no power to control in life. Read books dealing with worry, anxiety, acceptance and inner peace. Look in the psychology, self-help and spirituality sections of your bookstore or library.

## ✱ Tips

If you need to, get help from others in coming up with challenges to your worrisome thoughts. They can often present you with a different perspective on things.

Many people find spiritual teachings or belief in a higher power extremely helpful in decreasing worry and developing more trust in life.

## ⚠ Warning

Seek professional help if your worries are interfering with your daily functioning or causing you significant distress.

## 844 | Hit a Baseball

It's a deep fly ball…heading way, way back…to the wall and over. It is outta here! Oh, the sounds of baseball. Follow these steps to hit a baseball successfully.

### ⊙ Steps

1 Hold the bat as you would an ax. Right-handers, place your left hand near the knob at the end of the bat and your right hand above that. Left-handers, use the opposite placement.

2 Place the curve of the bat in the middle of your fingers, not in the palm of your hand, and grip the bat firmly. Gloves can help you avoid blisters and have a better grip.

3 Stand in the batter's box. Different locations relative to the mound provide advantages for various types of pitches. For example, standing toward the rear of the batter's box gives you slightly more time to react to a fastball.

4 Assume a comfortable and effective stance. Try various foot angles and positions until you find one that works for you. Slightly bend your knees and spread your legs wide enough to maintain balance, usually a little more than shoulder width apart.

5 Hold the bat near the top of the strike zone, with your hands at about the height of your armpits. Hold your arms slightly away from your body but not extended. Bend your knees.

6 Step toward the pitch as the ball leaves the pitcher's hand. Keep your head and upper torso steady, eyes focused on the ball, as you stride toward the ball with your lower body.

7 Keep your hands and shoulders still as you move toward the pitch.

8 Recognize the pitch, and then go after the ball. Keep your swing level and stay behind the ball, exploding into the pitch.

9 Complete the swing by pivoting forward and shifting your weight from your back foot to your front foot, bracing your front leg as your back foot turns.

10 Keep your elbows close to your body as the bat follows a compact circle through the strike zone. Try to watch the bat strike the ball, keeping your head steady and chin tucked in. Remember to follow through, swinging the bat completely around your upper torso—don't stop the swing when the bat hits the ball.

### ✳ Tips

Establish the right mentality before stepping up to the plate. A hitter needs not only quick reflexes and upper-body strength, but also guts to stand up to a smoking four-seam fastball.

Select a comfortable bat so that you stay controlled and balanced through the strike zone. Remember that a heavier bat will not miraculously transform you into a power hitter, and a light bat can go a long way to greater bat speed.

Follow your coach's advice about things like batting stance and grip.

### ⚠ Warning

Always wear a helmet when batting.

## 845 | Hit a Home Run

The difference between a hit and a home run can be found in the speed and strength behind the swing.

### ⊙ Steps

1 Hold the bat, step inside the batter's box and assume a comfortable stance (see 844 "Hit a Baseball").

### ✳ Tips

Get into a weight-training program to build strength.

2  Watch the ball as it leaves the pitcher's hand.

3  Stay inward on the ball. In other words, keep your body weight leaning in toward the plate.

4  Rotate your body instead of your head when you swing. As you swing, pivot on your back foot, transferring your weight steadily from back foot to front, and follow through with the bat. It should end up in the middle of your back. Remember that it's the speed of your swing and the muscle behind it that will send the ball over the fence.

Increase strength by hitting a miniature basketball off a tee.

Practice without a ball to develop your speed and the finer points of your technique. Try rapid swings with the bat to build up speed.

## Break In a Leather Baseball Glove                                846

Many baseball players will tell you that leather fielding gloves and mitts need a lot of tender loving care. Try the following for a great start in your relationship with your glove.

### ⊙ Steps

1  Use your glove often. Playing catch is the best way to break in a new baseball glove.

2  Rub the pocket linings of the glove with linseed oil, saddle soap or shaving cream.

3  Let the glove dry on its own if it gets wet—placing it near a heat source or using a hair dryer will cause the leather to crack.

4  Place a baseball in the glove's pocket when the glove is not in use, and wrap a rubber band tightly around the glove; this will gradually give it a catching shape.

### ✱ Tips

There are several creams designed to treat new leather gloves.

Follow the same steps for leather mitts used by first basemen and catchers.

### Things You'll Need

❑ saddle soap, linseed oil or shaving cream

## Throw a Curveball                                                847

One of the key components of a successful pitching repertoire is an effective curveball—a ball that moves away from or toward the batter as it crosses the plate.

### ⊙ Steps

1  Hide the ball in your glove.

2  Grip the ball with your middle and index fingers perpendicular to the seams at their widest point, with your thumb underneath the ball.

3  Spread your top fingers apart slightly and keep your ring finger and pinkie tucked into your palm.

4  Hold the ball firmly, applying pressure with your middle finger and thumb. Try not to let the ball rest in the palm of your hand, and keep your index finger relaxed.

5  Wind up into the pitch. Use the same pitching motion as in your other pitches so that the batter cannot predict a curveball.

6  Keep your wrist relaxed. After drawing back the pitch, hold your wrist so that the back of your hand points toward your body.

### ✱ Tips

You can also try gripping the ball between and along the seams. Spread your fingers apart slightly and press your middle finger into the ball. Go with the grip that allows you a comfortable release, the proper spin and maximum control.

Turn your wrist further to increase the ball's spin. You will lose some control but will gain more curve. Throw harder, and the pitch gains speed but loses some of the curving movement.

7   Roll your wrist downward and to the right (if you are right-handed) or to the left (if you're left-handed) immediately before releasing the pitch.

8   Release the pitch and follow through by bending your wrist. A right-hander should finish with the palm facing in toward the chest. The top of your thumb should be facing up.

9   Throw the ball between the batter and home plate if you're a left-handed pitcher facing a left-handed batter or if you're a right-handed pitcher facing a right-handed batter.

⚠ **Warning**

Throwing a curveball can cause serious and possibly permanent damage to your shoulder, elbow and wrist. For this reason, most managers and coaches advise that young players avoid this pitch until they reach physical maturity.

---

## 848 | Throw a Fastball

**Does your curveball just not curve? Then work on blowing a powerful fastball past unsuspecting hitters. They can't hit what they can't see.**

◉ **Steps**

1   Choose one of the following handgrips for a combination of comfortable release and maximum control.

2   Grip the ball perpendicular to the seams, at their widest point, with your middle and index fingers spread 1/2 inch apart. Your thumb lies perpendicular to the seams on the underside of the ball. With this grip, expect the pitch to rise as it makes its way to the catcher.

3   Alternatively, grip the ball with your middle and index fingers at the point where the seams are closest to each other. Your fingers should lie perpendicular to the seams. Expect the pitch to sink.

4   Hide the ball in your glove.

5   Wind up, and use this windup to gain power. Use the same motion you use with other pitches so that the batter has trouble predicting a fastball.

6   Release the ball from your fingertips to maintain control and gain spin.

7   Continue the motion of your arm after releasing the pitch, and follow through with your body. Allow your natural momentum to carry your body forward.

↟ ↟ ↟

✳ **Tips**

For increased backward rotation of the pitch, snap your wrist slightly as you release the ball— this sacrifices some speed but makes the pitch harder to hit.

As your control improves, adjust your grip to maximize speed without losing control.

⚠ **Warning**

Gripping the ball across the seams may cause blisters.

---

## 849 | Throw a Knuckleball

**When you've got this pitch under control, hitters have no idea when to swing. When it's out of control, though, even the pitcher doesn't know where the ball is going!**

◉ **Steps**

1   Grip the baseball by clenching the top of the ball with the tips of your index, middle and ring fingers just below the seams. Dig the tips of your fingers deep into the ball.

2   Place your thumb below the ball to give it support. Keep your pinkie off to the side.

↟ ↟ ↟ ↟ ↟

✳ **Tips**

An effective knuckleball moves in two or three different directions in flight.

Try a variation on the knuckleball grip by using just the index and middle fingers on the top of the ball. The ring finger joins the pinkie off to the side.

3  Go into your windup. Remember to pivot and shift your body weight from the back foot forward toward home plate.

4  Throw the ball toward home, but don't snap your wrist—keep it stable, eliminating as much spin as possible.

5  Follow through. Extend all fingers toward home plate as you release the pitch. Your feet should be parallel at the end of the pitch, and your throwing arm should come across the front of your body.

The slower the pitch, the more time the ball has to weave toward home plate.

## Throw a Slider                                                    850

As the ball approaches the plate, a slider seems like a fastball but suddenly trails off to one side, baffling hitters and making them slide right back into the dugout.

### ◉ Steps

1  Grip the baseball with your index and middle fingers across the seams at its widest point. Keep both fingers slightly toward the outside of the ball (off-center).

2  Place your thumb under the ball and keep the ring finger and pinkie off to the side. These two fingers should not make any real contact with the ball's surface.

3  Exert pressure on the ball with your thumb and middle finger.

4  Go into your windup. Remember to pivot and shift your body weight from the back foot forward toward home plate.

5  Keep your wrist loose as you release the ball, and try not to drive it forward with more than an adequate amount of force.

6  Throw the slider like a fastball, but "cut" through the ball with the middle finger. Keep your fingers on the top of the ball until the actual release. Try not to twist your wrist; instead, turn the ball with your fingers. The greater the angle created by turning the fingers, the wider the break on the slider.

7  Follow through. Your feet should be parallel at the end of the pitch, and your throwing arm should come across the front of your body.

8  Note that the pitch should break late in its flight in the opposite direction from a curveball. A left-handed pitcher's slider should break down and away from left-handed hitters, and down and in on right-handed hitters —vice versa for right-handed pitchers.

### ⚠ Warning

Throwing a slider can cause serious and possibly permanent damage to your shoulder, elbow and wrist. For this reason, most managers and coaches advise that young players avoid this pitch until they reach physical maturity.

## 851 | Shoot a Free Throw in Basketball

Free throws are crucial to a team's success. Making these unguarded shots 15 feet from the hoop separates the winners from the losers.

### ◎ Steps

1 Balance yourself at the free throw line. Keep your feet shoulder-width apart and parallel to one another.

2 Point both feet and square your upper body toward the basket. Position your feet just behind the line; move one of your feet back an inch or two, if that's comfortable.

3 Hold the ball by using the hand of your nonshooting arm to support and cradle it lightly. Place the middle three fingers of your shooting hand on the seams of the ball, with your thumb and palm acting as supports.

4 Keep your shooting forearm straight, and avoid tilting it to one side. Try to keep the arm that will be releasing the ball oriented toward the basket.

5 Aim for a target just above the rim, and try not to shoot the ball short. A good target is the backboard shooting square drawn above the rim.

6 Bend your knees. An accurate shot doesn't rely on arm strength; it uses leg strength to propel the shooter upward.

7 Shoot in one fluid motion, straightening your knees to strengthen the shot and your arm to provide aim. Release the ball with your fingertips. This allows you more control over your shot and a softer arc because of the backspin you create.

8 Follow through by bending your shooting hand forward, as though you're reaching for the rim.

### ✳ Tips

Practice, practice, practice.

Being comfortable with your shot can make a big difference. If you find a motion that helps, such as adding a little hop while shooting, use it.

Take your time at the line. Most players bounce the ball or spin it in their hands before setting up their free throws.

## 852 | Make a Layup

Making a layup (a close-range shot on the run) is one of the easiest ways to score points. These instructions describe a right-handed layup; reverse them if you're a lefty.

### ◎ Steps

1 Stand at the far right-hand edge of the free throw line.

2 Dribble the ball with your right hand.

3 Concentrate on the shooting square painted on the backboard. The upper-right corner is most important.

4 Approach the basket slowly, dribbling the ball.

5 Stop dribbling when you're 5 to 8 feet from the basket.

6 Pick up the ball while you're stepping with your right foot.

7 Take another step and plant your left foot, then jump off it.

8 Bring your right knee up toward your chest as you jump.

### ✳ Tips

Smoothness is the key. Pick up the ball, take your step, jump and shoot in one fluid motion.

If you have trouble running and banking the ball off the backboard, first practice shooting while standing 3 to 4 feet from the basket.

Practice both left- and right-handed layups. It will be more difficult with your weaker hand, but worth the effort come game time.

9   Aim for the upper-right corner of the box on the backboard.

10  Shoot the ball with your right hand.

11  Practice approaching the basket faster and faster until you're running toward it.

---

## Dunk a Basketball                                                      853

No play in sports rivals the slam-dunk for sheer athleticism and crowd-pleasing action. You got game to spring high enough and jam the ball through the hoop?

### ⦿ Steps

1   Have big hands, or stick to the two-handed dunk—dunking is much easier if you can palm the ball.

2   Be a good jumper. Even if you're 6-foot-6, you need to be able to jump.

3   Dribble toward the basket with speed.

4   Pick up the ball from your dribble 10 to 12 feet from the basket.

5   Take your allowed two steps.

6   Palm the ball with your dunking hand, or grasp it firmly with both hands.

7   Push up from your second step, toward the rim, jumping as high as you can.

8   Extend your arm with the ball toward the rim, or if you're using two hands, bring the ball back behind your head for additional style points.

9   Slam the ball through the basket. Do not hang from the rim unless there's a danger of landing on somebody.

10  Celebrate your dunk in a cool way as you run back to play defense—make it clear that this wasn't your first or, certainly, your last dunk.

### ✳ Tips

Approach the basket in a manner similar to a layup.

You need to be able to touch the rim easily before having any realistic expectation of dunking the ball.

Many baskets are now installed with a device that allows you to adjust the height. Lower the rim temporarily to get an idea of how it feels to dunk.

### ⚠ Warning

You may get up pretty high and can injure yourself if you lose control.

---

## Make a Jump Shot                                                      854

Don't allow tall defensive hotshots to steal your moment of glory. Get some spring in those legs and shoot right over them.

### ⦿ Steps

1   Bend your knees as you prepare to jump.

2   Spring straight up.

3   Bring the ball from your waist up to your face, then into shooting position as you jump (see 851 "Shoot a Free Throw in Basketball" for the correct shooting position).

4   Shoot the ball when you reach the top of your jump.

5   Follow through after you release the ball by bending your wrist forward in a slow wave.

### ✳ Tips

The arc of the ball from a jump shot tends to be flatter. You may have to compensate by aiming for the back of the rim instead of the front.

Use the backboard to bounce the ball off for more control of side-angle shots.

## 855 | Increase Your Vertical Leap

Strengthening your legs and their fast-twitch muscle fibers can add inches to your vertical jump. This can help your basketball, volleyball or football game tremendously.

### ⊙ Steps

#### The Program

1   Begin every workout by warming up your muscles and then doing extensive leg stretches. Because you'll be building muscle fibers that are used for explosive activities such as jumping, stretching is of the utmost importance.

2   Jump rope for its excellent cardiovascular conditioning. This step should never be skipped, as it will be an important contributor to your results.

3   Sprint. This builds muscle, which will add to your jumping ability.

4   Run stairs on your toes. Start by running up a flight, one step at a time. Walk down and run back up, taking two steps at a time. Repeat as many times as you can manage.

5   Do sets of elevated jumps (see the next section).

6   Do sets of explosive jumps (see the third section).

7   Do sets of double jumps (see the third section).

8   Rest your legs at least two days a week. Results will come from sustaining the exercise program, not performing it aggressively for a few weeks and then slacking off.

#### Elevated Jumps

1   Begin by placing a step bench or platform on the ground (many health clubs have a platform for just this purpose).

2   Stand on the platform, then jump backward onto the ground, concentrating on landing softly.

3   Jump back onto the platform immediately, with a bouncing motion.

4   Complete three sets of 10 repetitions. Be very careful when performing this exercise, as there is a potential for injury.

#### Explosive Leg Jumps and Double Jumps

1   Position yourself for an explosive leg jump by facing a secure platform and placing your right foot on it.

2   Jump as high as you can, concentrating on exploding off the right leg.

3   Scissor your legs once in the air, then land with your left foot on the platform and your right foot on the floor. Gather yourself and explode upward again, this time off the left foot.

4   Do three sets of 10 repetitions, resting for about 30 seconds to 1 minute between sets.

### ✳ Tips

Do sets of double jumps on a basketball court, standing under a hoop. Reach for the net on your explosive jumps.

It will take time for your body to adjust to these new exercises, and even more time to see results. Go slowly and work your way up. It's the safest way to guarantee results.

### ⚠ Warning

Some of these exercises, particularly stair runs and explosive leg jumps, can cause injury if not performed properly. Your knees, in particular, are especially susceptible. Make sure you thoroughly understand all instructions before attempting the exercises.

5  Execute a double jump by jumping as high as possible with both feet from a stationary position.

6  Jump again immediately upon landing, using less effort.

7  Repeat until you've accomplished three sets of 10 jumps each.

## Hit a Game-Winning Jumper at the Buzzer                856

It's deep in the fourth quarter and your team is trailing by a few points, but don't despair. As the final seconds tick down to zero, you and your team have one last shot at victory.

### ◉ Steps

1  Know how many points you want. Do you trail by one and need a short jumper to win? Or are you two or three behind and shooting from downtown? Can you tie at best?

2  Check the number of seconds remaining and burn it into your brain.

3  Understand that your opponents will, without a doubt, press full court.

4  Know that it takes 3 to 4 seconds to bring the ball down court with a reasonable amount of control. Reduce this time for every long pass you choose to make.

5  Inbound or pass off the rebound to one of your two best ball handlers.

6  Get the ball across half court as quickly as possible. Your opponents will defend well, but (fearing a foul) probably will not reach in or attempt to slap the ball away. Don't make a silly turnover in your haste.

7  Use a third teammate to help pick off defenders. Whatever you do, don't foul or set a moving screen.

8  Signal for a timeout, leaving at least a few seconds on the clock.

9  Decide who wants to take the shot. Choose someone who's stroking it, someone with the confidence of the moment, someone in the zone.

10  Inbound the ball to one of your guards, who should be in the point position (top of the key).

11  Have the guard kick the ball back. Sometimes a quick inbound and pass back will take the opponents by surprise.

12  Move within or just outside of the three-point line.

13  Plant, lock your eyes on the basket, jump ... picture a lotus flower ... and release the ball.

14  Hold your breath, listen to the buzzer and watch time stop.

15  See nothing but the swish of a net, and hug your teammates amid the crowd's deafening thunder.

### ✱ Tips

Consider using your best player as a decoy. If the defense runs a zone, have that player move inside. You may draw two players with him or her.

Some coaches don't believe in last-second timeouts, even while trailing their opponents. Consider the situation in which your team retains possession, you're down by one or two points, and more than 5 seconds remain on the clock. Run the ball and don't allow the defense time to adjust. Don't break your own momentum.

Don't charge your opponents hoping for a foul—you'll likely get called for an offensive foul.

## 857 | Steal the Ball

If you don't have possession of the basketball, there's one simple way to correct that: filch the ball from your opponent.

### ⊙ Steps

#### Steal From an Opponent Dribbling the Ball

1 Keep within an arm's length of the player.

2 Maintain a proper defensive posture with your feet shoulder-width apart.

3 Slide your feet as your opponent moves.

4 Concentrate on your opponent's dribbling habits. Does she only do it with her left hand? Does she like to dribble the ball between her legs?

5 Reach for the ball in a side-to-side motion as it's bouncing up from the floor. The ball has less momentum when it's returning to the hand.

6 Return to your defensive positioning if you don't make the steal.

#### Steal a Ball Passed to the Player You're Defending

1 Establish a defensive position where you can see your player and the ball. The distance between you and the player you're guarding will differ depending on the position of the ball.

2 Attempt to lure a bad pass by appearing to be out of position and paying no attention to the ball handler, keeping in mind that in reality you neither want to be out of position nor are ignoring the ball handler.

3 When the ball is passed to your player, reach for it with the arm that gives you the most extension between your player and the flight of the ball.

4 Knock the ball down to either yourself or a teammate.

### ✱ Tips

Try not to lunge for the ball.

Chest and overhead passes are easier to pick off than bounce passes.

You're more likely to be flushed out of position when attempting to steal a pass. Only gamble for the steal when the odds are in your favor.

If you knock the ball away from its intended target, you've done a good job even if you don't steal the ball.

The more comfortable you are looking out of the corner of your eye, the easier it is to steal a ball.

Referees have a tendency to call a foul if they see you reaching for the ball in a downward motion because you're more likely to make contact with the other player.

## 858 | Play One-on-One Half-Court Basketball

A ball, a hoop and an opponent are all you need to play one-on-one basketball. Work on your game, get great exercise and have fun.

### ⊙ Steps

1 Pick a scoring system for your game. Most recreational games award one point for normal shots and two points for shots made beyond the three-point line. Feel free to use conventional two- and three-point scoring if you prefer.

2 Set a winning score. One-on-one hoop games usually end at 11 points. Also common are 7-, 15- and 21-point games. Set a high winning score if you're using conventional scoring.

3 Next decide on possession. Winner's outs (or "make it and take it") gives you the ball back after you score. Loser's outs gives the ball to your opponent after you score.

### ✱ Tips

One-on-one basketball provides a chance to polish up your bread-and-butter moves, test new tricks and improve your individual game like no other game can.

Playing inside at the post position with your back to the basket, blowing by your opponent on the way to the hoop, and pulling up for a jump shot are effective ways to score in a one-on-one game.

4  Determine a clearing point: a spot where each player must take the ball after rebounding an opponent's missed shot. This establishes continuity by giving both players a chance to set up for the next play. The three-point line is almost always used as a clearing point.

5  Start the game once you've finished arguing over who gets the ball first (or be quiet and shoot a free throw to decide).

6  Call your own fouls as they occur. Agree on whether you want just defense to call fouls, or just offense (or anyone at all). Decide between shooting free throws and awarding possession to the player who has been fouled. Once it's decided, stick to the choice.

7  Run the ball back to the clearing point. Rematches give the losing player a chance at redemption, while providing the winner with opportunities for further gloating.

Agree on what kind of change of possession calls for the ball to be cleared: all changes, just shots that hit the backboard or rim, or some other action.

## Spin a Basketball on Your Finger                                     859

Remember Curly from the Harlem Globetrotters? This is the first step to emulating the smoothness and grace he showed while spinning the ball upon his long fingers.

### ⊙ Steps

1  Balance the ball on the pads of the five fingers of your dominant hand.

2  Stretch out your arm until the elbow is slightly bent.

3  Twist your wrist to the left if you're holding the ball with your right hand (the right if you're using your left hand). At the same time, bend your elbow 90 degrees, causing the ball to hop to your fingertips and spin on your middle finger.

4  Expect to lose contact with the ball for a split second when the ball gains its maximum spin velocity; concentrate on returning your middle finger to the ball's center when it drops down.

5  Continue to spin the ball by snapping your wrist and forearm together to the right (if you're using your right hand) or to the left (if you're using your left hand), then back again as in step 3.

### ✳ Tips

Snap your wrist more forcefully to achieve more spin. The more spin, the easier it is to balance the ball on your finger—it's the gyroscope effect.

For the split second that you're not in contact with the ball, don't let it get much farther than an inch or two from your hand.

## Play Beach Volleyball                                                 860

The same rules apply as in the indoor game—you've just got a ton of sand slowing you down.

### ⊙ Steps

1  Bring an all-weather, outdoor volleyball and a net system of regulation size to the beach.

2  Gather a minimum of four players (two per side).

3  Set up your court away from sunbathers, in an area where the ball will not continually roll into the water.

### ✳ Tips

The less advanced the partici-pants, the more players you'll need to cover the ground and have long rallies. It's tough to get around on sand.

4   Play games to 15 points, earning a point only when you win a rally where you serve.

5   Serve only once per turn and within the court lines (draw a line in the sand to mark these), or forfeit the ball to your opponents.

6   Hit the ball a maximum of three times before it must go over the net to your opponents.

7   Bump the ball to a setter, who sets the ball for the spiker, who spikes the ball over the net (see 861 "Bump a Volleyball," 862 "Set a Volleyball" and 863 "Spike a Volleyball"). Do this without grabbing the ball or allowing it to rest in your hands. The same person cannot contact the ball twice in a row unless the first touch is off a block at the net.

8   Avoid touching the net at all times or lose the ball, and possibly a point.

9   Rotate player positions clockwise whenever your team has won a change in possession (called a "sideout," it's when it's your turn to serve).

10  Play a set of three or five games. The team that wins the most games in the set is the winner.

Drink lots of water and wear plenty of sunscreen.

Try not to kick up too much sand if it's windy and there are people lying on the beach nearby.

## ⚠ Warning

The most important rule to enforce is keeping players away from the net—opposing players who land on, or crash into, each other at the net can cause serious injuries.

---

## 861 | Bump a Volleyball

A volleyball player's most important skill is bumping—passing a volleyball by bouncing it off his or her extended forearms.

### ◉ Steps

1   Remember that the first contact after a serve is normally the bump, which sets in motion the three-step volleyball offense of bump, set, spike (see 862 "Set a Volleyball" and 863 "Spike a Volleyball").

2   Anticipate the flight of the ball so that you can receive it in a stationary, athletic position with your knees bent, your weight forward on the balls of your feet, and your arms extended forward and down.

3   Hold your palms open and facing up, and then lay one hand on top of the other.

4   Fold your hands inward until your thumbs are side by side, pointing away from your body and slightly down. The knuckles of your fingers should be facing out.

5   Bring in your elbows and lock them so that your forearms are as close to touching as possible, creating a flat platform from your elbows to the tips of your thumbs.

6   Tilt your platform toward your target.

7   Allow the ball to bounce off your forearms (rather than swinging your arms at it).

### ✳ Tips

The two keys to good, consistent bumping are using your feet to get in proper position to meet the ball, and keeping your elbows locked so that the ball hits a flat surface.

Bump-pass the ball high and 2 to 3 feet from the net to a position where the setter can get to it easily.

If you're setting and are having a hard time with the traditional setting technique, or are dealing with a bad, low pass, use the bump to get the job done.

## Set a Volleyball                    862

A set—the act of snapping the ball upward with two hands to set up a spike—is the hardest of volleyball's fundamentals to master. Here's how to do it correctly.

### ⊙ Steps

1   Remember that the first contact when receiving a serve is usually a bump, or pass (see 861 "Bump a Volleyball"), to the setter (normally positioned near the net to the right of center court), so always anticipate receiving the ball if you've been designated as this player.

2   Intercept the pass at the net (if it's a good pass). Make contact with the ball about 1 foot over your head.

3   Hold your hands above your forehead with your thumbs and index fingers nearly touching, making a diamond shape, with the rest of your fingers spread open.

4   Bend your knees.

5   Push up with your legs and arms, snapping the ball upward with your hands in the direction in which you'd like it to go (as though you're Superman flying). Ideally, this causes the ball to "hang" in the air without rotating, resting at the peak of its flight in the perfect position for the hitter to hammer away.

### ✱ Tips

In general, set the ball 2 to 3 feet inside and above the net so the hitter can get it over the net without its being blocked.

When setting, you need to make enough contact to control the direction of your set without allowing the ball to come to rest (however momentarily), which is illegal and known as a "lift." You also must make contact with both hands simultaneously or risk getting called for a "double hit."

## Spike a Volleyball                    863

The spike—sending the ball forward and downward over the net by striking it overhead with an open hand—is a player's most powerful offensive weapon.

### ⊙ Steps

1   Position yourself three to four strides from the net.

2   Anticipate where the ball is going so you can jump and intercept it with the palm of your hitting hand at the extent of your reach, above and slightly forward of your head.

3   Explode to that interception point with your first step (your right foot, if you're right-handed), raising both hands in front of your torso.

4   Take two quick small steps (left, right) to gather your feet under you (with knees bent), while simultaneously swinging your arms behind you like a pendulum.

5   Swing your hands forward and up while jumping; this helps you rocket into the air and places you in proper hitting position.

6   Draw your right hand back behind your head as you rise, so your open palm faces the sky—like a waiter carrying a tray.

7   Point your left hand at the ball, as if you're lining it up in your gun sight (actually, you are).

### ✱ Tip

If you can't jump high enough to hit the ball when it's above the height of the net, you should spike farther away from the net whenever possible. You want to hit the ball forward and down as much as you can, not straight up so the opposing players have plenty of time to react to it. If you're tall and/or a good jumper, make contact as close to the net as you can (without reaching over it, which is illegal). If there are no blockers in the way, pummel it straight down.

8    Hammer the ball with your open right hand, snapping the wrist and swiveling your torso to put the maximum amount of topspin and velocity on it.

9    Accept the praise of your teammates if the opposing team can't keep the ball in play—you've just recorded a "kill."

## 864 | Play Touch Football

These rules for informal backyard touch football games are among countless variations. League rules are much more rigid and complex.

### ⊙ Steps

#### Establish Rules, Field and Positions

1    Find a large, grassy area to serve as your playing field.

2    Divide players evenly into two teams.

3    Have each team decide who will act as its quarterback, running backs, receivers and line players.

4    Set your playing field's boundaries. The playing field should be rectangular, with an end zone at each end. Anything outside the playing area is out of bounds.

5    Decide whether you'll play one-hand touch or two-hand touch (see Tips).

6    Choose a method of deciding a winner by limiting either playing time or points scored. For example, the winning team could be the one with the highest score at the end of an hour or the first team to score five points.

7    Determine if you'll be able to earn new first downs. Traditionally, teams have four tries, or downs, to gain at least 10 yards. If they do so, they start over with a new set of downs. Your field may not be long enough for this. These instructions describe a game without new first downs.

8    Flip a coin to decide which team will begin playing offense.

#### Play the Game

9    Place the ball in the middle of the field.

10   Take an allotted time for deciding offensive and defensive strategies.

11   Line up the teams on either side of the ball, parallel to the end zones and facing each other.

12   The offensive player in the center of the line (the "center") passes the ball to the quarterback between his legs.

13   While line players block the defensive line, the quarterback hands off the ball to a running back or passes the ball to a receiver, who then runs with the ball toward the opposite end zone while defensive players try to tag him or her.

14   Other offensive players try to keep defenders from tagging the ball carrier by blocking for him or her.

### ✳ Tips

The playing area's size will vary with available space, but each end zone should cover about one-twelfth of the total playing field.

In one-hand touch, defensive players must tag the ball carrier with one hand to end the play. In two-hand touch, defenders must tag with both hands simultaneously.

Slow runners should play on the line, while fast runners should serve as receivers. The quarterback should be a player with a good throwing arm.

The ball cannot be passed forward (toward the target end zone) from past the line of scrimmage (the line—parallel to the end zone—from which the ball was passed to the quarterback for the current down). A ball carrier may pass backward to another offensive runner, however, once he has passed the line of scrimmage.

15  Stop the play once the runner is tagged, drops the ball or runs out of bounds. This counts as a down.

16  Set down the ball where it was last in play, and repeat steps 9 through 14.

17  Switch possession of the ball if three more tags, drops or out-of-bounds runs occur (for a total of four downs) before the offensive team reaches the end zone with the ball. The defense then becomes the offense at the point where the ball was last in play. The new offense gets four attempts to move the ball toward the opposite end zone.

18  Also switch possession of the ball when a point is scored; the scoring team then takes the defensive position. Play begins again by setting the ball in the middle of the field and lining the teams up as before.

19  Continue the game in this fashion until the point or time limit is reached.

An alternative to touch football is flag football, which is similar except that plays end when the ball carrier's flag is pulled from her belt. The ball carrier may not guard her flag by covering it with a hand or slapping away the hand of a defense player.

## ⚠ Warning

It's easy to overdo it out there— take it easy, or be prepared for sore muscles in the morning.

---

# Throw a Football                                      865

Throwing a football poses a problem for many people because of the ball's size and unique shape. But with a little practice, you can throw like a pro. More or less.

## ◎ Steps

1  Grip the football by interlacing your fingers between the football's laces and seams.

2  Protect the ball by cradling it with two hands, and hold it just under your chin as you step back to throw.

3  Cock your throwing arm back with your elbow bent.

4  Extend your free arm in front of you for balance; point the arm and hand at your target.

5  Keep your shoulders level for a short pass (10 yards or less); dip the shoulder of your throwing arm for longer distances.

6  Snap your arm forward and follow through with your shoulders and hips as your weight shifts to your front foot.

7  Release the ball when your arm is slightly above your head and out to the side.

8  Add velocity and spiral to the ball by flicking your wrist and fingers just as you release it.

9  Finish with your index finger pointing forward and down, and with your palm facing the ground.

## ✽ Tips

Move your hand forward, if your hands are large enough, and hold the ball so that your pinkie finger is toward the front of the ball. Most NFL quarterbacks with big hands feel that holding the ball this way gives them more control and a tighter spiral.

Finish on your front foot. Unless you have a cannon for an arm, finishing when falling back will cause the ball to sail high in the air and beg to be intercepted.

To make throwing easier, buy a ball compatible with your age and size.

## ⚠ Warning

Warm up properly and begin with easy throws to avoid muscle strain.

## 866 | Kick a Football

A good, hard kickoff or punt gives your team the chance to bury the opposition deep on its side of the field, while a field goal can win the game.

### ⊙ Steps

#### Perform a Kickoff or Kick a Field Goal

1. Set up the football for a kickoff. Position the football on the tee almost perpendicular to the ground, but angled slightly toward you.

2. Set up a field goal attempt, if you are looking to score. Have the holder kneel on the opposite side of the ball from where you'll be running, and place the football with the laces forward (away from you) and the ball almost perpendicular to the ground, but angled slightly toward you, the kicker. The holder should place either his palm or the tips of his index and middle fingers on top of the ball, gently applying pressure to hold it in place.

3. Stand about 7 yards behind the tee and slightly off to one side. If you kick with your left foot, stand to the right. If you kick with your right foot, stand to the left.

4. Run toward the ball, starting with the foot you won't be kicking with.

5. Plant your nonkicking leg firmly about 1 foot to the side of the ball, your foot pointing in the direction in which you want the ball to go (between the goal posts, for example, or straight down the field for a kickoff).

6. Power through the ball with the instep of your kicking foot, making contact about one-third of the way above the ball's lower tip.

7. Follow through as much as your flexibility will allow.

#### Punt a Football

1. Stand 15 yards behind the line of scrimmage.

2. Catch the ball when the center snaps it to you.

3. Hold the ball out in front of you horizontally with the laces pointing up.

4. Take two steps forward, beginning with your kicking foot.

5. Drop the ball toward your kicking foot and kick the ball hard with the top of your foot.

6. Follow through with your kicking leg as high as your flexibility will allow. Some punters practically kiss their knee.

### ✳ Tips

Don't look where you want the ball to go—concentrate on the ball instead.

How much you stand to one side for the kickoff or field goal is a matter of personal preference and is something you develop through experimentation.

The steps for executing a kickoff and a field goal describe soccer-style kicking. An alternative, less popular, method is "toe punching," in which the kicker lines up about 8 yards directly behind the ball and kicks with the front of the foot rather than the instep.

## Catch a Football 867

While there are many different ways to catch a football pass, the general idea is to keep your arms and hands up and out in front of you.

### ⊙ Steps

1 Run to the area that is called for in the play and try to clear yourself of any defenders.

2 Turn back toward the line of scrimmage as you run. Look for the ball and move toward the quarterback.

3 Stand with your feet shoulder-width apart and your knees slightly bent.

4 Raise and outstretch your arms, leaving your elbows bent slightly and in front of your chest. Your hands should be at about head level.

5 Bring your hands together, touching the thumbs and index fingers. The space in between should resemble a spade on a playing card.

6 Catch the nose of the ball within that shape. Keep your hands soft when you contact the ball—pretend it's an egg.

7 Bring your arms in and cradle the ball when you run by placing one end in the crook of your elbow and clutching the other end with your hand, the nose of the ball between your first and middle fingers. Hold the ball tight against your body.

8 Turn back toward the end zone and continue running. Make sure to dodge tackles.

### ✱ Tips

If you're tackled while carrying the ball, fall onto the ball so that it's under you, or clutch it to your body so the defense doesn't recover it.

If you're catching a kickoff and an immediate tackle seems unavoidable, raise your hand to signal a fair catch and drop to one knee after catching the ball. This will prevent the possibility of a fumble (not to mention extreme bodily harm).

## Tackle in Football 868

A good tackle downs the ball carrier without any injuries. Good technique can take down any opponent, even one who's bigger, stronger and faster than you.

### ⊙ Steps

1 Identify your opponent. This will be the individual running furiously toward the end zone with a ball under her arm.

2 Run toward the ball carrier at full speed, keeping your head up at all times. Aim your face mask at the center of her chest or inside shoulder.

3 Run through the ball carrier, wrapping your arms around her waist.

4 Pull the ball carrier into you and drive her to the ground.

5 If you get up first after a successful tackle, offer a hand to help your opponent up and give an encouraging pat or slap as you run back to your team. This shows good sportsmanship and preserves the spirit of the game after an extremely aggressive act.

### ⚠ Warnings

Keep your head up and lead with your face mask when tackling—you don't want to lose sight of your opponent.

Follow your coach's specific instructions on tackling technique and game regulations.

Football is, obviously, a contact sport. Wear a helmet and all proper pads and gear.

## 869 | Head a Soccer Ball

Heading (hitting a soccer ball with your head) allows you to gain possession of the ball, pass, set up an attack, score goals and defensively clear the ball from the goal area.

### ⊙ Steps

1 Arch your back as the ball approaches, with your chin inward, neck firm and legs bent. Keep your arms out to your sides for balance and to fend off defenders.

2 Spread your feet apart, wider than shoulder width. Keep both feet on the ground (unless you need to jump to reach the ball).

3 Snap your upper body toward the ball from the waist. Drive your head and neck forward as you make contact. Keep your head and neck moving together instead of holding your neck still while your head moves.

4 Make contact with the ball squarely with your forehead. Keep your eyes open and on the ball, and keep your mouth closed. Avoid making contact with the top of your head.

5 Direct the ball down by making contact with your head slightly closer to the top of the ball.

6 Make contact slightly lower on the ball to send it upward.

7 Follow through by continuing to drive your head forward. The strength of the header comes from the waist.

### ✳ Tips

If you need to jump, make contact at the highest point of your jump.

When heading the ball to score a goal, direct the ball down to make it harder for the goalkeeper to save.

To clear the ball from your own goal area, direct the ball up and out.

### ⚠ Warning

Incorrect heading can lead to neck injury. Beginners should go slowly. Practice with a light ball, such as a beach ball or soft volleyball, and gradually move on to a regulation soccer ball.

## 870 | Chip a Soccer Ball

The shortest distance between you and your teammate may be a straight line, but defenders sometimes don't cooperate. So, send a flying ball that's easy for your teammate to get hold of.

### ⊙ Steps

1 Understand that a "chip" is when the soccer ball travels in a tall arc. Usually a quick kick is used to send the ball up and over a short distance, rather than in a long, soaring flight.

2 Approach the ball at a slight angle.

3 Place your nonkicking foot approximately 6 inches to the side of the ball and slightly behind it.

4 Take a back swing with your kicking leg, keeping in mind that a shorter back swing will allow you more control and better placement.

5 Angle your toe down—imagine your foot to be wedgelike—as you make contact with the ball below its center.

6 Lean your body back as you kick to increase the lift of the ball. The farther you lean back, the greater the ball's arc.

### ✳ Tips

A proper chip should have backspin, which makes it easy for your teammate to control. A ball spinning backward is less likely to run away from the receiver once contact is made.

Use a chip as a goal shot if you wish. If the goalkeeper has come out to cut down the angle of your shot, chipping the ball over his head is a good technique for scoring a goal.

Be comfortable chipping with both feet, and chipping dead balls as well as moving ones.

## Cross a Soccer Ball 871

When you're stuck with the ball out near the sideline, how do you get it back closer to the goal? The answer is a cross (a pass from the sideline to center field) to one of your teammates.

### ◉ Steps

1 Control the ball as you move down the wing (outside) of the field, eluding defenders along the way.

2 Glance to the middle of the field to see where your teammates are making runs.

3 Chip the ball to the area to which your teammates are moving (see 870 "Chip a Soccer Ball").

4 Pass the ball back to a teammate if you are approaching the goal line. Try to keep the ball low to the ground so your teammate can shoot more easily.

### ✳ Tip

If you're close to the goalkeeper, cross the ball back far enough that he or she cannot grab it, but keep it close enough to the goal so that a teammate is able to score from that position.

## Slide Tackle in Soccer 872

A soccer slide tackle is a sideways slide that attempts to knock the ball away from your opponent's feet. You use it as a last-ditch effort if your opponent is going to get past you.

### ◉ Steps

1 Commit yourself to the slide, deciding whether you'll simply be kicking the ball away or trying to gain possession.

2 Slide on one side of your body.

3 Lead with one leg. If you're sliding on your left side, lead with your right leg, extending your foot toward the ball, while the left leg is bent at a 90-degree angle.

4 Be sure to slide only leaning partway down on the side of your leg; sliding in a more upright position will allow you to spring up after the slide.

5 Make contact with the ball first. If you hit your opponent first, you'll be called for a foul.

6 Knock the ball a long way if you're sending it out of play, or tap it more gently if you're attempting to gain possession.

7 Using your left arm and left leg, quickly rise from the turf and be on your way.

### ✳ Tips

You'll discover that you're more comfortable sliding on a particular side of your body, but you should always practice using both sides.

It's a good idea to learn to slide tackle on a wet day, when the ground is soft.

### ⚠ Warnings

Bumps, scrapes and bruises are all likely when you use the slide tackle.

In addition to injury to yourself, you risk hurting your opponent with an ill-placed slide.

## 873 Throw a Soccer Ball Sidearm

For the goalkeeper who needs to get the ball to a teammate quickly, the sidearm throw is more accurate than kicking the ball, if the distance is not too great.

### ⊙ Steps

1 Cock the wrist of your throwing arm.

2 Turn your body and raise your nonthrowing arm to aim at your target.

3 Pull your throwing arm back and twist your waist as far as you can comfortably manage.

4 Take two or three steps forward.

5 Begin to unwind the ball horizontally before taking your last step.

6 Release the ball with your arm extended as you take your last step.

7 Follow through toward your target by continuing to swing your arm across your body.

### ✱ Tips

Twist your waist more or less, depending on how far you need to throw the ball.

After some practice, you'll be able to throw the ball 35 to 40 yards on the fly.

## 874 Protect Your Teeth in Youth Sports

A mouth guard can help save your teeth from injury. Here's how to choose one—and what to do if a tooth gets knocked out.

### ⊙ Steps

1 Speak to your dentist or orthodontist. Although mouth guards have been in use for several decades, organized football and ice hockey are the only sports that have mandatory mouth-protector rules.

2 Understand mouth guards. They are divided into three general types: hard custom-made (usually made by a dentist), soft custom-forming (the boil-and-bite types) and hard noncustom-made (the type usually attached to football helmets).

3 Choose the best to get the most effective protection. Studies have shown that all types of mouth guards are effective in reducing the number of dental injuries, although the hard custom guard has proved most effective. Anyone with braces should use this type.

4 If a permanent tooth is knocked out and gets dirty, gently rinse it with water, but do not handle the root.

5 Reposition the tooth in the socket, if possible. If replacing the tooth is not possible, store it in milk or saliva (spit into a small cup).

6 Get to the dentist as soon as possible if a tooth is knocked out or loose.

### ⚠ Warning

Do not try to replant a baby tooth, as it could damage the permanent tooth that's in formation.

## Get Fully Equipped for Ice Hockey | 875

Fast-moving pucks, cross-checking and body checks make injuries in hockey a very real concern. Protective equipment allows you to play the game more than once.

### ⊙ Steps

1 Start with the basics: a hockey stick, hockey skates, knee pads, a protective cup and jockstrap (for both sexes), a helmet with attached mouth guard, some hockey pucks and a pair of hockey gloves.

2 Add hockey socks, a garter belt, shoulder pads, elbow pads and (optionally) a neck protector. A huge hockey jersey will go over all of this.

3 Choose a form-fitting protective girdle with a covering nylon shell. This piece will protect you from mid-thigh up to your ribs. It's belted in place.

4 Put on your jockstrap with the cup and strap, and secure the garter belt around your waist. Make sure everything is snug but not too tight.

5 Put on your knee pads. Pull your hockey socks over them and secure your socks at the top with the garter belt.

6 Pull the girdle over your other equipment. Cover it with your nylon shell. Belt it in place.

7 Tie your skates tightly. The bottoms of your knee pads should come just to the tongues of your skates.

8 Use athletic tape to secure anything that feels as though it could slip. Skates and knee pads are the most common equipment to be taped in place.

9 Pull on your shoulder and elbow pads, and cover them with your hockey jersey. Put on your helmet, neck protector and gloves, and you're ready to play.

### ✳ Tips

It's a lot of gear, so you need to decide between mobility and greater protection if you have doubts about wearing all of it. At the very least, wear your helmet; males should also wear a jockstrap and cup.

All the equipment is adjustable. If it doesn't fit quite right the first time, try playing with the settings.

## Hit a Slap Shot in Hockey | 876

The slap shot—when the puck rises with bullet speed from the ice and shoots into the goal—is a difficult but powerful and dangerous offensive weapon.

### ⊙ Steps

1 Skate to within a reasonable shooting distance from the goal.

2 Position your body sideways to the net and in a normal passing stance: skates parallel, knees bent, back bent forward, stick extended, blade edge flat on the ice (or roller rink surface) and puck cradled in the center of the blade.

3 Grasp your stick with hands about a foot apart, then raise it up and straight back until your bottom hand is at shoulder level.

4 Keep your bottom arm straight.

5 Shift your weight to your back foot.

### ✳ Tips

The slap shot is good for dumping the puck in the upper corner of the net.

The height of the shot depends on the height of the follow-through.

A slap shot is inherently inaccurate. Practice in aiming is essential.

6   Raise your eyes and mark the desired target (an open edge of the goal, not an opponent's helmet).

7   Bring the stick aggressively forward by pushing strongly with the bottom hand.

8   Transfer your weight to your front foot.

9   Strike the puck on its bottom edge.

10  Follow through with the stick.

11  Adjust the stick's blade to control the height of the puck.

⚠ **Warning**

Because of its speed and upward trajectory, this shot is extremely dangerous. Always make sure other players are wearing all necessary protective gear, including a helmet with a full face mask.

---

## 877 | Hit a Forehand in Tennis

Are your forehand ground strokes not making it over the net? Add zip to this most common of tennis shots. These directions are for right-handers; reverse them for left-handers.

### ⊙ Steps

1   Position yourself just inside the court's baseline and near the center line.

2   Keep your feet shoulder-width apart.

3   Hold the racket at about waist level directly in front of you. Use the handshake grip, which works well for beginners. This grip is like shaking hands with the handle of your racket, while the string face is perpendicular to the court surface.

4   Bend your knees slightly. You should be able to feel some strain on the quadriceps muscles in your thighs.

5   As the ball is hit toward you, turn your shoulders to the right, pulling the racket back. Lower the racket head toward the playing surface. This should be done prior to the ball's crossing the net.

6   Pivot on your right foot. With your other foot, step forward and across your body. Plant your left foot at a 45-degree angle, pointed toward the right net post.

7   Stop your backswing when the racket head is slightly below waist level and your arm is extended and relaxed. The racket, and your arm, should be perpendicular to the net so your arm and racket are pointing directly toward the back of the court.

8   Before the ball reaches you, pause for a moment, holding the racket in the backswing position. Think, "Bounce, step, hit."

9   Begin your swing from a position below your waist. Swing through the ball, with the contact occurring in front of your net-side hip. Try to hit the ball on the sweet spot (middle area) of the racket. This gives you a solid forehand by maximizing the efficiency of the shot.

10  Finish the swing above the opposite shoulder. Think, "Start low, finish high."

11  Quickly get back into your original position for the next shot.

**✱ Tip**

Always pull the racket back as soon as the ball approaches your forehand side. Your backswing should come from the shoulders, not the arm.

⚠ **Warning**

Using a two-handed forehand is quite difficult. If you're a beginner, learn the one-handed approach for more control and power. Leave the two-handed technique for your backhand.

## Hit a Lob in Tennis   878

You hit a lob (a high, slow shot over and beyond your opponent) offensively to add surprise to your game, or when you have no alternative defensively.

### ⊙ Steps

1   Assume the ready position at or near the baseline.

2   Drop your racket head lower than you would for a normal forehand.

3   Attempt to get under the ball.

4   Hit the ball at a greater angle than you would use for a normal forehand. In other words, your racket path must be more vertical than with a standard forehand.

5   Hit the ball up over your opponent's head.

6   Finish with the racket head over your back shoulder.

7   Be aware that the height of the shot depends on whether it's an offensive lob (hit with topspin) or a defensive lob (hit with underspin).

### ✳ Tips

You can hit a lob on the run, with your weight on either the front or the back foot.

Practice with a partner by lobbing the ball over the net to each other, attempting to send the ball as deep into your partner's court as possible.

## Hit a Backhand Ground Stroke in Tennis   879

The backhand ground stroke (turning 180 degrees to hit on the opposite side of your racket) is an essential tennis skill. Reverse the following alignments if you're a southpaw.

### ⊙ Steps

1   Move from the ready position, pulling the racket across your body and back to the left-hand side before the ball crosses the net.

2   Keep your right hand loose on the grip.

3   Tuck the racket toward the inside of your body while dropping the racket head.

4   Step forward with your right foot as you dip your right shoulder to the front, toward the net.

5   Swing from low to high, making contact when the ball is in front of your right hip, and finish above your right shoulder.

6   Help your playing arm during the shot by pointing the racket at the ground just before contact, then use your nonplaying hand to grab the throat of the racket and pull upward after contact as you turn your shoulders.

### ✳ Tips

Take small steps to position yourself after getting to the ball.

Tightening your forearm can cause pain in the wrist and elbow. Let the racket head do the work for you.

## 880 | Hit a Slice Serve in Tennis

A slice serve is usually the first serve that tennis players learn. These instructions explain a serve for right-handed players; reverse them for left-handers.

### Steps

1 Stand 6 or 8 feet to the right (or left) of the center mark.

2 Assume the regular serve posture: standing sideways to the net, with your left foot pointing toward the right net post.

3 Keep your arms down and relaxed to begin.

4 Hold the racket at the throat with the nonhitting hand. Your hitting hand should be as loose as possible on the grip.

5 Shift about 80 percent of your body weight to the back leg to start.

6 Toss the ball with your left hand, which remains pointing at the ball in the air. Your right arm should be bent at 90 degrees, with the racket head pointing up at the sky.

7 Bend your knees and move your body up when beginning to swing at the ball. Think, "Toss, bend."

8 Shift your weight forward and swing the racket head aggressively up and over your right shoulder, then hit the ball out diagonally in front of you, to the left. This is similar to the motion of throwing a baseball.

9 Transfer your body weight, uncoiling your upper body, and thrust upward from the legs as you hit the ball.

10 Fold in your tossing arm quickly toward your ribs as your racket makes contact with the ball. The weight transfer carries the body forward onto the court.

11 Allow your feet to come off the ground or nearly off the ground.

**✴ Tip**

A consistent toss is essential for a consistent serve. Practice tossing the ball with your left arm. The ball should land one foot in front of you and in line with your right shoulder.

**⚠ Warning**

Swinging aggressively can lead to back, shoulder and elbow problems.

## 881 | Grip a Golf Club

Your grip can make the difference between a good golf shot and a poor one. These directions are for right-handers. Reverse them if you're left-handed.

### Steps

1 Hold the grip with your left hand at the top of the club.

2 Adjust your hand so your thumb is heading straight down the golf grip. The top of your thumb should be facing out away from your body and the club's shaft, while the remainder of your left hand wraps around it.

3 Look at your right palm and notice the small vertical crease near your wrist (this is the crease formed when your thumb folds inward). Grip the golf club with your right hand so that this crease rests on top of your left thumb. Your hands should fit perfectly and lock together in this formation.

**✴ Tips**

Players with large hands should use an overlapping grip, with the right pinkie resting between and on top of the left hand's forefinger and middle finger.

Players with smaller hands should use a 10-finger grip, with all fingers on the club like a baseball grip, without overlapping the hands.

4　Notice the V where the thumb and finger meet. That angle should be pointing to your right shoulder.

5　Make sure your right thumb is not running straight down the club, but instead slightly to the left of the top of the grip.

Hold the club lightly with both hands. The more relaxed your grip, the straighter and farther you'll hit the ball.

## Replace the Grip on a Golf Club　882

A worn grip can cause your hands to slip, leading to errant shots. The daily golfer should regrip clubs two or three times a year, the weekend golfer yearly.

### ⊙ Steps

1　Pull off the old grip. Use a utility knife to cut it off if necessary. Scrape off tape fragments with your fingers or a utility knife.

2　Put solvent on a rag and clean the shaft where the grip and tape used to be, then let the shaft dry for a minute.

3　Put the middle of the shaft in a vise shaft holder—a special vise adapter that is capable of holding a thin rod like a golf club. These can generally be found wherever vises are sold. Put this adapter, with your club secured inside, into the vise. Tighten the vise for a strong hold.

4　Measure where the new grip will fit: Take the new grip in one hand and hold it alongside the bare shaft of the golf club. Align the butt of the grip with the end of the shaft. With the other hand, make a pencil mark on the shaft where the opposite side of the grip ends—down toward the head of the club.

5　Strip a piece of double-sided tape from the roll (cellophane tape works fine) and place one end at your pencil mark. Gently smooth down the length as you stick the tape along the shaft to its butt end.

6　Trim the tape off the roll at the shaft's end, then carefully wrap your piece around the shaft, overlapping the tape's width as necessary.

7　Take the new grip (it will be a pliable, rubbery piece of tubing) and plug one end by placing a golf tee in the little hole at its butt. Now, pour some solvent inside the grip. (Window cleaner works well as a solvent.) Its purpose is to take the tackiness off the tape without dissolving it.

8　Place a finger or thumb over the open end of the grip, leave the tee-plug at the bottom, and shake the entire grip. This allows the solvent to spread throughout the interior of the grip.

9　Spray or pour additional solvent onto the taped portion of the shaft.

10　Pull the golf tee out of the end of the grip, then slide the grip onto the shaft, over the tape. The longer you wait, the harder it will be to slide the grip on. If it's hard to slide it on, use more solvent, either inside the grip or on the tape.

11　Remove the club from the vise shaft holder and vise.

12　Hold the club as if you were hitting a shot. Adjust the grip gently so that it's straight on the club, making sure that any pattern on the grip is not twisted around the shaft.

### ⚠ Warnings

When using a utility knife, cut away from your body.

If solvent gets into your mouth or eyes or on your skin, flush immediately with water.

### Things You'll Need

☐ golf club grip

☐ utility knife

☐ bench vise

☐ vise shaft holder

☐ double-sided tape

☐ solvent

13 Work your hands up and down the golf shaft, pressing the grip firmly against the club to seat the adhesive.

14 Let the grip dry for about 10 hours before using.

## 883 | Hit a Golf Ball

Hitting a golf ball is easy, but hitting the ball where you want it to go takes a lot of practice. These instructions were written with right-handed hitters in mind; reverse them for left-handers.

### ⊙ Steps

1 Stand behind the ball and pick out your target far up the fairway or driving range.

2 Grip the club properly (see 881 "Grip a Golf Club").

3 Stand facing the ball with both feet together, about three-quarters of an arm's length away from the ball. Your left shoulder will be toward the target, just as in baseball.

4 Take a tiny step toward your target (to the left) with your left foot, and take a normal step backward (away from the ball) with your right foot. Your feet should now be shoulder-width apart.

5 Place your hands in a position known as the forward press. Viewed from above, this moves your hands slightly to the left of the ball. This angles the club forward (viewed from behind you, the shaft is now tilted to the left), flattening its already angled hitting face.

6 Pull the club to your right (straight back from the golf ball) to the top of the backswing. The club should be parallel to the ground, and back over your shoulder.

7 Without pausing at the top of the backswing, immediately swing the golf club back down along the same path.

8 Keep your head down and strike the ball. Allow the club to follow through until it touches your back.

9 Watch the ball travel toward the target.

### ✻ Tips

Don't be afraid to hit down on the ball and create a divot (a chunk taken out of the turf). Many people only catch the top of the ball, causing it to skip off down the fairway; this is because they do not dig deep enough. Replace the divot after your shot.

Remember that the harder you hit down, the higher it will go.

### ⚠ Warnings

Swinging the club too hard and too fast may cause back pain from all the furious twisting motion.

Make sure nobody is standing close to you when you swing a golf club.

## 884 | Read a Putt

Reading a putt requires a player to look at the green from all directions to determine how hard to hit the ball, and to compensate for the slope and any errant breeze.

### ⊙ Steps

1 Stand halfway between your ball and the hole to get a better idea of the slope of the green. This will help determine how fast or slow the putt should be.

2 Walk directly behind the hole and look back at your ball.

### ✻ Tip

Think about your putt while other group members are putting, to speed up the play.

**How to Do** *(Just About)* Everything

3   Read the slope of the green and determine whether it is straight or angled more to the right or left.

4   Return to your ball and stand behind it. Read the slope of the green once more to see if it looks the same as it did from the other side of the hole.

5   Choose your putting path based on your study of the green.

6   Pick a spot on the green about 6 inches in front of your ball, along your chosen putting path. This spot can be a dark area of the green or a taller blade of grass.

7   Keep your eye on the spot and stand up. This tactic allows you to lock in your putting path even as your perspective changes.

8   Approach the golf ball and take a practice stroke, putting at the air between your feet and the ball.

9   Place the putter behind the ball and putt the ball into the hole.

**⚠ Warning**

Avoid stepping in other putting paths while reading your putt.

## Calculate Your Golf Handicap                         885

Your handicap measures how well you'd stand up to a scratch golfer on any given course and allows golfers of different abilities to compete fairly.

### ⊙ Steps

1   Take the scores from the last five rounds (18 holes each) you played.

2   For each of these scores look up the rating and slope for the course you played. This information is usually printed on the scorecard, although you can also get the rating and slope by calling the course.

3   Subtract the course rating from the score you earned on that course.

4   Multiply that number by 113. The resulting number is the differential.

5   Take the lowest of your five differentials and multiply it by 0.96, and you have your handicap.

**❋ Tips**

If you have seven or eight scores to use instead of five, average your two lowest differentials and then multiply by 0.96. If you have nine scores, average the three lowest differentials and multiply the result by 0.96.

Once you have 20 or more scores, use the most recent 20 scores and average the 10 lowest differentials; multiply the result by 0.96 to get your handicap.

## Begin a Running Program                              886

Running will improve your stamina, help you control your weight and improve your general health. Here's how to get started.

### ⊙ Steps

1   Jog before you run. Every running program, no matter what level, has some jogging.

2   Begin at a conversational pace—one that allows you to talk comfortably without being winded.

3   Mix running with walking, if necessary. As you progress, increase the amount of running and decrease the walking.

**❋ Tip**

Find a partner or group. This will strengthen your commitment to a running program.

4   Be patient with your initial aches and lack of stamina. Understand that although the heart and lungs grow strong quickly with exercise, muscles and joints take longer.

5   Increase your running time or distance by no more than 10 percent each week to minimize the risk of injuries.

6   Build up your running to at least 20 to 30 minutes three times a week, done at a moderate level of intensity. Studies have shown that this is a sufficient amount of exercise for basic cardiovascular fitness. Running more than this amount is done for reasons beyond basic fitness.

7   Use the first month to learn about yourself. Pay close attention to your body; learn to read its signals of fatigue and stress, and when you can push beyond them.

### ⚠ Warning

Get a physical and consult your physician about your basic health and fitness before beginning a running program.

## 887 | Run a Marathon

You've been training for months, and the big race is finally here. For peak performance, heed the following suggestions.

### ◎ Steps

1   Position yourself at the starting line according to your predicted pace.

2   Start slowly—this is the key to finishing in good form. Check your time at the 2-mile marker. If you're going faster than your target pace, slow down.

3   Avoid attacking hills too aggressively. You'll need to conserve energy for the rest of the course.

4   Drink water or sports drinks at every station, even if you don't think you're thirsty.

5   Resist the urge to pick up your pace between miles 4 and 10; stay relaxed, calm and focused. Breathe rhythmically and pretend this is a practice run.

6   Toward the middle and end of the race, pour water over your head at each station, in addition to drinking it.

7   Carry power gels or other sports foods, or get them at rest stations if offered; eat what has worked for you in your practice runs.

8   Try to maintain your pace during miles 10 through 20. If you've gone through the first 10 miles too quickly, don't try to keep up your pace. A common error is to run too fast for the first 20 miles.

9   Shake out your arms and change your form for a few strides to provide relief during miles 14 to 20.

10  Draw willpower from the runners around you—concentrate on passing them or following one.

11  Slow down and visualize the finish if you hit the wall at mile 20. Think in terms of how much time is left, and approach the remaining distance as a 10K race.

### ✱ Tip

Understand that there's no shame in walking and no shame in dropping out if you can't continue. Listen to your body.

### ⚠ Warnings

Never attempt a marathon without proper training; this event is incredibly hard on the body. A good training program will help prevent injury.

Do not attempt to run a marathon if you have sustained an injury during training.

12  Gather your remaining strength for a final push during the last 2 miles; use the sight of the finish line and the crowd's cheers to overcome fatigue and discouragement.

13  Stay loose as you approach the finish. Keep your knees up and your arms moving. Run hard at least 10 yards beyond the finish line, to keep yourself from slowing before you cross it.

14  Congratulate yourself—you deserve it!

## Cycle Up Hills                                                    888

Climbing hills on a bike can be quite daunting. Focus on your technique, however, and you can make it a lot less painful.

### ◉ Steps

1  Consider your equipment. Having toe clips, or clipless pedals, will make you much more efficient on hills. It also helps to have a clean drive train (your chain, sprockets and gears) and to make sure your tires are inflated to the proper pressure.

2  Be sure your seat is adjusted properly for your height. To check, sit on the seat with your right foot on the pedal. Turn the pedal to its lowest point. Your leg should now be almost fully extended.

3  Select the proper gear for the hill. Find a gear that allows you to maintain your proper spin. In cycling, "spin" is defined as your optimum rate of revolutions—the point between cranking your pedals too fast (not enough resistance) or too slow (too much resistance).

4  Watch the hill's grade and feel for subtle changes in the pedals' resistance. You may need to shift often to stay in the groove.

5  Stay relaxed. If you tense up, it will make getting up the hill all the more difficult. Keep your arms loose and don't hold the bars in a tight grip.

6  Sit back on the seat and pedal smoothly. Try not to favor one leg over the other.

7  Stand up on the pedals from time to time. This allows you to switch muscle groups and stretch out a bit.

8  Concentrate on exhaling. Breathe all the way out and let your lungs fill back up on their own.

9  Power over the crest of the hill. Many riders start to ease up before they get to the top. Keep the power turned on, and you will have a smoother transition into the flat or downhill.

### ⚠ Warning

Always wear a helmet when cycling.

## 889 | Change a Flat Tire on a Bike

Don't let a flat tire slow down your biking fun. Pack the proper lightweight tools and an extra tube, get savvy with your wheel workings, and get back on the trail.

### ◎ Steps

### Remove the Tire

1 Invert the bike and remove the bicycle wheel from the frame by flipping the quick-release lever or unscrewing the bolt. Release any remaining air from the tire.

2 Insert the thin end of a tire lever (a thin plastic wedge made for this purpose) between the tire and the rim.

3 Pull the lever down, and clip the hook end to the nearest spoke.

4 Move over two spokes, and repeat with a second tire lever.

5 Move over two more spokes, and repeat with a third lever.

6 Take the first lever out, move over two spokes from the third lever, and repeat.

7 Work around one side of the wheel in this way until one side of the tire is free.

8 When one side of the tire is completely off the rim, pull the other side off with your hands.

### Change the Inner Tube

9 Pull out the old tube with your hand and discard it, or save it to patch later.

10 Run a hand lightly over the inside of the tire to find the cause of the flat, and remove it.

11 With a bicycle pump, put one or two strokes of air into the new tube.

12 Put the new tube in the tire.

### Remount the Tire

13 Find the hole in the tire rim for the inflation valve; this is the piece of metal attached to the rubber tube into which air is pumped.

14 Push the valve through the hole in the rim, and pull the tire (with the tube inside it) over the wheel.

15 Working around the wheel with your fingers, push one side of the tire onto the rim. The tire's edge will seat itself along the inside edge of the wheel's rim.

16 Once one side of the tire is on the rim, check that the tube is not pinched between the edge of the tire and the rim. If it is, gently pull the tube out from the other side.

17 Turn the wheel around when one side is complete.

### ✻ Tips

Buy the right size tube: Mountain bike inner tubes are 26 inches in diameter, while road bike tubes are either 27 inches or 70cm.

Make sure your new inner tube has the correct kind of valve. There are two kinds: A Presta, or European, valve is long and skinny and is usually found on road bikes; a Shrader, or American, valve looks like a car tire's valve and is usually found on older bikes and on most mountain bikes.

After changing the tube, don't use the tire levers to pry the tire back on. This could pinch the tube and create a new hole.

Inflate the tire slowly, watching for inconsistencies in inflation that might identify kinks in the tube or other problems with your installation.

### ⚠ Warning

A nail or a piece of glass may be sticking through the tire, so proceed with caution.

### Things You'll Need

☐ 3 tire levers

☐ inner tube

☐ bike pump

18 Push the second side of the tire onto the rim with your thumbs. When the tire is nearly all on the rim, it will become taut and will require a last hard push with your thumbs.

19 Inflate the tire to its recommended pressure as printed on the side of the tire.

## Swim the Breaststroke

This can be a relaxing and gliding swim stroke, or it can be a quick, intense motion if you're racing. It's accomplished by a strong, froglike kick and pull, then a long glide.

### ⊙ Steps

1 Lie facedown in the water with your head bent back, above the surface.

2 Keep your legs close together and pull your knees up against your chest. At the same time, hold your palms together and against your chest, as if in prayer.

3 Take a deep breath, then dip your head below the surface so the crown points straight forward.

4 Kick out to the side and apart with your legs, spreading them wide; then quickly squeeze them together, straight out behind you. Try to imitate the way a frog kicks.

5 As you kick, extend your arms out in front of you, keeping your palms pressed together.

6 Glide for a moment, with arms extended like a spear in front, and toes pointed behind you.

7 Turn your palms outward and pull with both hands out and around in a circular motion, until your hands end up in their original position, together against your chest.

8 Use the thrust of the outward pull with your hands to pull your head up and out of the water to take a breath.

9 As you push your hands together into their original prayer position, pull your knees up into their original position against your chest.

10 As your head goes back down, your arms should be just beginning to plunge forward with the next kick.

**✻ Tip**

The glide is the most important aspect of this stroke. After the big kick, streamline your entire body as much as possible. Your shoulders should be almost against your ears. Glide, and then pull your head up and forward with your stroke.

## Swim the Freestyle Stroke

The freestyle is known as the fastest swim stroke. Often called the "crawl," it is one of the most common swimming styles.

### ⊙ Steps

1 Visualize a line running down the center of your body from your chin to your chest. This line is the axis upon which your whole body should pivot, and it should extend in the direction in which you are swimming.

**✻ Tips**

Stretch out your stroking arms fully without ever pausing from the windmill motion.

2   Keep your legs straight but not rigid, with your toes pointed behind you. Kick up and down using your entire leg, bending your knees only slightly. Continue kicking the entire time. Your kick should not make a big splash, but rather should just churn the surface of the water.

3   Move your arms in a windmill motion opposite each other. While one arm is extended completely out, the other should be all the way back, almost against the side of your body.

4   Cup your hands and pull your extended front arm through the water beneath your body.

5   Bend this arm at the elbow and draw your fingertips along the imaginary line down the center of your body.

6   Lift your other arm out of the water from behind you and move it all the way forward as the first arm is pulling beneath you. Bend at the elbow and drag your fingertips along the surface of the water—right pas   our ear—then penetrate the surface as you completely extend the arm.

7   Breathe on one side by turning your head to that side as the arm comes out of the water.

Remain horizontal in the water. A strong kick will keep your legs from sinking behind you.

As you pull your hands through the water, keep them cupped firmly but not rigidly. Fingers should be held just slightly apart.

---

## 892 | Stop on Inline Skates

There are two ways to stop or slow down on inline skates. Master both techniques before you take your skates out into the world.

### ◉ Steps

#### Heel Braking

1   Skate forward with moderate speed.

2   Transfer the majority of your weight onto the skate without the heel brake.

3   Keep the other skate on the ground, but lift up on the toe. This causes the heel brake to rub on the ground and slow you down to a stop. The more pressure you put on your heel brake, the faster you'll stop.

#### Dragging a Skate

1   Skate forward at a moderate speed.

2   Transfer the majority of your weight to your left skate.

3   Lift up your right skate and hold it perpendicular to your left, which you're riding on. The right heel should be behind and almost touching the left heel, so the two skates form an L shape.

4   Drag the wheels of your right skate against the ground. This scrapes the sides of the wheels but acts as your brake.

5   Push harder on the dragging wheels to slow down faster.

6   Avoid tilting your skate too far toward the ground or you'll scrape the side of the skate as well as the wheels.

### ✱ Tips

Dragging a skate is more functional than using the heel brake, but it also wears out your wheels faster. (This can be done with either skate; just reverse the directions above to drag your left skate.)

Many skaters prefer to remove the heel brake to improve the maneuverability of their skates, which is why the skate-dragging method of stopping evolved.

### ⚠ Warning

Always wear a helmet, wrist guards and knee pads when inline skating.

## Do an Ollie on a Skateboard — 893

So, you think you're ground-bound on four wheels? Flip your ride into the air—a move that's known as an "ollie"—and stay aloft upon it.

### ⊙ Steps

1 Stand on the board with your rear foot placed on the tail and your front foot between the middle of your board and the front bolts (see 922 "Determine if You're a Regular or Goofy Foot").

2 Place the ball of your rear foot on the tail of the board, with your foot positioned perpendicular to the board. When you push the tail down with that foot, the ball of your front foot should feel the pressure of the end of the board rising,

3 Place your front foot across the board, with the toe pointed slightly forward (at about a 20-degree angle to your other foot).

4 Practice pushing down as fast as you can with your back foot and putting all your weight on the tail. This is the initial motion of the trick.

5 Notice that the harder you push, the more your board wants to keep going up once the tail is on the ground. You will use that motion in the next step.

6 Strike the tail on the ground and jump off the board with your rear foot as you slide your front foot up the board (so your knee moves toward your chest).

7 Drag the side of your front foot up the board as you are jumping. This will cause the board to come up with your jump. Once both feet are in the air, the board will seem to stick to them.

8 Come back down and try to land with both feet back in their original position. Or, once you're comfortable, you can use the ollie to jump obstacles, land on rails and slide, or do a hundred other tricks.

### ✱ Tips

Get comfortable with the motions of this trick before actually rolling on the board. Once you feel comfortable with the basics, you will be able to adapt to moving and going up or down things.

The hardest part is the timing of when to push down on the tail, when to jump and how quickly to suck up your legs. The secret: It's all done at the same time. The faster you do it, the easier it becomes. Think about jumping off with one foot and sucking your legs up to your chest.

### ⚠ Warning

Because this trick requires a lot of jumping and landing, you risk injuring yourself and your board. Use caution.

## Choose a Martial Art — 894

Martial arts are highly regimented systems of techniques used for fighting and self-defense. Use these guidelines to find the one that's right for you.

### ⊙ Steps

1 Assess your physical condition. Do you have any limitations that might affect which martial arts style is right for you?

2 Consider whether you prefer a hard or soft style. Offensive techniques, such as punching and kicking, indicate a hard style, which tends to be physically intense. Defensive techniques, such as blocking and redirecting, indicate a soft style, which can be less physically challenging and well-suited to older students and those with physical limitations.

3 Think about your preferences for either striking or grappling techniques. Striking is attacking with fists, feet, elbows and knees. Grappling uses joint locks and throws to control an attacker.

### ✱ Tips

Talk to students of different styles and ask what kinds of injuries are common. For example, if knees tend to get injured in a certain style, and you have bad knees, try another style.

Choosing a teacher is often more important than choosing a particular style. Observe a class at several different dojos to get a feel for the master's teaching style—some are much more formal than others.

4   Bear in mind that karate—a style originating in China and developed in Japan—is a hard, striking style that includes training with a variety of martial-arts weapons.

5   Realize that tae kwon do, from Korea, is also a hard, striking style that teaches joint locks and vital-point striking.

6   Understand that kung fu (also known as wushu), a style from China, can be hard or soft, striking or grappling; more than 400 styles exist.

7   Be aware that jujitsu, from Japan, is a soft, grappling style that emphasizes using the least amount of force necessary to confront and defeat an opponent.

8   Realize that judo, a style that is also from Japan, is a soft, grappling art based on jujitsu; its purpose is to use a calm and serene mind to defeat an opponent.

9   Consider the fact that aikido, another style based on jujitsu, is a soft, grappling martial art suitable for older practitioners or those with physical limitations. Though there is a good deal of tumbling involved in aikido, this martial art teaches you to fall correctly and safely. It differs from jujitsu by using weapons such as the bokken (a wooden sword) and the jo stick.

10  Bear in mind that tai chi, a style from China, is a soft, defensive style that has strong philosophical principles, stressing harmony with nature and fellow humans.

11  Scan a martial arts encyclopedia (or try an Internet search engine) for a more detailed overview of martial arts styles.

12  Delve into history to understand how the different styles originated. For instance, high kicks in tae kwon do began as a way for foot soldiers to attack mounted soldiers. Jujitsu is an unarmed variation of Japanese samurai sword fighting. Does the legacy of any of the arts appeal to you more than others?

13  Watch practitioners from the various styles that interest you before making a choice. Many schools have an observation area so you can watch while a class is being taught. Ask permission first.

14  Review what you have learned and settle on the martial arts style that best suits your interests, preferences and physical abilities.

## 895  Make a Fist in Karate

Whether you're a boxer, a martial artist or a cardio-kickboxing enthusiast, knowing how to make a proper fist will lend power to your straight punch while keeping your hand safe.

### ⊙ Steps

1   Open your hand with your fingers extended and touching each other.

2   Separate the thumb from the other fingers.

3   Bend the four fingers inward and touch the tips to the top of your palm. Don't allow the little finger to separate from the other fingers.

### ✱ Tip

Practice punching a heavy bag to make sure your striking surface is the first two knuckles of the fist.

4   Bend your thumb and press it over your index finger. Don't allow your thumb to extend past your finger knuckles.

5   Keep your wrist straight.

6   Keep your fist closed but relaxed when making contact with a target.

⚠ **Warning**

If the tip of your thumb is above your knuckles, an opponent 's kick or punch may catch it. Many thumbs have been broken this way.

## Handle a Punch in Martial Arts | 896

Martial arts training stresses confidence and avoidance of panic in an attack. Here's a way to deal with physical contact without being unnerved by it.

◉ **Steps**

1   Accept physical contact as an essential part of your martial arts training. Sparring with safety gear will help you absorb an opponent's punches as you develop your skills and confidence.

2   Practice with a partner to learn how to handle a punch. Drill on how to dodge, parry (deflect), block and counterpunch. When you do get hit, you'll know how to recover.

3   Adjust your level of contact while practicing with a partner. Don't throw full-contact punches unless you're both wearing safety gear and have agreed to the escalation.

4   Remain as calm and detached as possible if you get hit. Don't panic. If you're relaxed, your body will absorb or deflect the force of the impact. Your quick recovery acts as a psychological counterpunch to the attacker.

5   Trust your skills in a real situation. Acknowledge the possibility of getting hit before the fight, and visualize the surprise of your attacker when you execute your counterpunch.

✻ **Tips**

Unlike trained fighters, most people throw weak and ineffective punches. They tend to throw a punch from the shoulder instead of using the power of the whole body by pivoting from the hips.

Remember, the principle behind self-defense is to defend oneself as quickly as possible without taking unnecessary chances.

⚠ **Warning**

Use caution. Physical contact in martial arts may result in injury.

## Paddle a Canoe | 897

Seemingly the simplest maneuver in canoeing, the forward paddle can take years to truly master. These instructions offer beginner guidelines for the canoer's most essential skill.

◉ **Steps**

1   Kneel or sit in the canoe facing forward at either the stern or the bow, if two people are paddling. If you're canoeing solo, sit or kneel just a little rear of the middle.

2   Hold the paddle with your inside hand on top and your water-side hand 2 to 3 feet down (wherever feels most comfortable) with knuckles facing out.

3   Insert the blade of the paddle completely into the water with the paddle blade at a right angle to the side of the canoe, at least 2 feet in front of you, or as far forward as you can reach without lunging your body forward.

✻ **Tips**

Bent-shaft paddles are more efficient for forward paddling than straight-shaft paddles because the bend allows you to pull the paddle back farther in the water before you begin pushing water up.

After learning to paddle, next focus on steering and turning.

4    Push your top hand forward and pull your bottom hand back, drawing the blade through the water. Keep the shaft of the paddle perpendicular to the water and the top of the paddle handle lower than eye level.

5    Pivot your shoulder to draw the blade straight back. Avoid following the curve of the canoe—the paddle's handle should always stay to your side, never crossing in front of your body.

6    Pull the blade back through the water as far as your hip—no farther. After the blade reaches this point, it's actually slowing the canoe down by pushing water up and hence pushing the canoe down in the water.

7    Lift the blade out of the water and turn the blade parallel to the water (this is especially important on windy days) to carry it forward to the starting position.

8    Reinsert the blade and stroke again.

**⚠ Warning**

Avoid lurching forward on each new paddle stroke. Not only is it bad for your back, but it also wears you out faster.

---

## 898 | Paddle a River Raft

**Paddling instead of rowing is a fun way to guide a raft through whitewater rapids. These instructions are for the typical inflatable eight-person raft.**

### ⊙ Steps

1    Position the paddlers evenly on both sides of the raft. Paddlers should kneel, sit on thwarts or straddle the buoyancy tubes when paddling.

2    Hold the paddle with the inside hand on the top of the paddle and the outside hand, knuckles facing out, gripping the paddle low on its stem.

3    Lean forward and insert the paddle into the water. Dip the blade completely beneath the surface. Keep the shaft of the paddle perpendicular to the water and the top of the paddle handle lower than eye level.

4    Straighten your top arm while pulling back on the paddle with your lower arm to draw it through the water. This is the standard forward paddle.

5    Reverse the forward motion to back paddle. Dip the blade and pull the upper arm back while extending your lower arm.

6    To turn the bow right, have the right side of the raft (from the paddler's perspective) paddle back while the left side paddles forward. Reverse this procedure to go left.

7    Reach out with the paddle, dip in deep and pull toward yourself to draw stroke, pulling the raft in the direction of your paddle stroke.

8    Dip the paddle in close to the raft and push away to pry stroke, or move the raft sideways away from the direction of your paddle stroke.

9    Communicate with your rafting team and work together.

**✳ Tip**

Paddling is all about teamwork. Pick a captain, the most experienced rafter, to call out directions so everyone can work together.

**⚠ Warning**

When rafting on a river, always provide personal flotation devices for everyone on board.

## Catch a Wave

The surf may be up, but you can't surf until you master this critical skill of catching and riding a wave.

### ⊙ Steps

1 Paddle out beyond the breaking waves, sit on your board facing out to sea and wait for a good wave.

2 Sit just behind the middle of your board, with the nose pointing slightly out of the water, so you can easily pivot in any direction to paddle for a wave.

3 When you see a good wave coming, swing your legs up behind you to lie down on your board, and paddle to position yourself near the peak, where the wave is highest and will break first. If you are too far out, the wave won't be ready to break, and if you are too close to shore, the wave will immediately break and thrash you.

4 After paddling into position, sit up on your board and spin it around until you point in the direction you want to go when the wave picks you up.

5 Lie down when a choice wave swells your way. Paddle in the direction the wave is moving so that it overtakes you just before it breaks.

6 Note which way the wave is breaking: from your left to the right, for example. Eventually, you'll be propelled toward the beach and will want to surf sideways away from the break.

7 Accelerate your paddling as the wave approaches, applying full power as the wave picks you up and propels you.

8 Don't stop paddling until you feel the wave completely propelling you and your board. Keep your weight as far over the nose of the board as you can without dipping it under the water.

9 Grab the rails (edges) of your board directly beneath your shoulders and push up when you are sure the wave is taking you.

10 Quickly pop up from the rails of your board, pushing the board down into the face of the wave and quickly pulling your legs up beneath you.

11 Put your left foot forward if you're regular-footed, or place your right foot forward if you're a goofy-foot (see 922 "Determine if You're a Regular or a Goofy Foot"). Your feet should be roughly perpendicular on the board, depending on your own comfort. Keep in mind that the positioning of your feet depends on the size and shape of your board, but the position should enable you to instantly turn and control your board.

12 Lean to your wave-side rail (in this case, the right side). You should now be zipping along, riding the perfect wave.

### ✳ Tips

Keep your eyes focused down the wave, especially as you pop to your feet. The second you lean your weight back, you'll lose the wave.

Different breaks and different types of waves have different tendencies.

Take mental notes on each wave you miss and make corrections. Then try again.

Lay your board on the sand and practice pushing up and popping to your feet. When you pop up, try to plant your feet in the riding position, so you won't have to make adjustments as you drop in. Be careful not to break your fins or get a bunch of sand in your wax, however.

### ⚠ Warning

Observe the rules of surfer right-of-way, allowing other surfers to catch the wave when appropriate. If you "drop in" (catch an already breaking wave) in front of another surfer, that person will, justifiably, get very angry with you.

## 900 | Bodyboard

A bodyboard (often called a boogie board) is shorter and wider than a surfboard and made of pliable foam-core rather than hardened fiberglass. It's all you need to ride the waves.

### ⊙ Steps

1 Lie belly-down on your bodyboard, and position yourself beyond the breaking waves. As a wave approaches, begin kicking toward the beach so that the wave propels you instead of breaking behind you. At this point, both hands should be on the front of the board.

2 Feel the wave begin to carry you along and determine whether you are going to ride to the right or to the left along the wave's face.

3 Reposition your hands so that, if you are going left, your right hand is on the rail (the side of the board) while your left hand remains on the front, or vice versa.

4 Pull your body up over the front of your board and arch your back so that your chest is over the front of the board and your head is held high.

5 Use your outside hand to pull up on the side of the board, causing the wave-side rail of the board to dig into the face of the wave. This will prevent you from sliding down the face of the wave.

6 Release the right rail to slide down the face, and dig in again to ride up. Going up and down the face helps you build speed and control.

7 Drag your swimming fins (which are a necessity for serious bodyboarding) if you wish to slow down, but otherwise hold them up out of the water.

### ⚠ Warning

Beginning bodyboarders eat a lot of sand. If you get tossed in the waves, hold your breath until the tumbling stops, then swim ashore to rest.

## 901 | Launch a Sailboard

Take that boom in your hand and harness the power of the wind. Skimming across the surface of the water with the wind in your face is exhilarating. Here's how to start.

### ⊙ Steps

1 Bring your board and rig (sail, boom and mast) to the water's edge and prepare for action by attaching the mast to the board, inserting the daggerboard (if you use one) and putting on your life vest. Wear a wet suit if the water is cold.

2 Carry the board and rig into the water as a single unit. If you are unable to carry it by yourself, ask someone for help. If you are on soft sand, you can hold the tail of the board (the end with the fin) and the mast and drag the board into the water.

3 Enter the water knee-deep, with the board floating completely in the water and the sail on the leeward (downwind) side of the board. The wind should be at your back.

4 Step up on the board, facing the rig, and place one foot on either side of the mast.

### ⚠ Warning

Always keep your rig on the leeward side of the board. Otherwise, the wind can catch it, flip the sail and mast, and smack you in the kisser.

5 Bend down and grasp the up-haul line. One end is attached to the boom, the other to where the mast enters the board. Hoist the rig by pulling up on the up-haul line.

6 Grab the boom with both hands.

7 Sheet in (pull the boom and sail in to catch wind), and you should be propelled forward immediately.

## Use a Snorkel 902

Using a snorkel properly will give you a clear vision of what's going on under the sea without having to breathe water.

### ⊙ Steps

1 Test your mask and snorkel together to determine fit and comfort.

2 Position the small rubber strap that attaches the snorkel to your mask so that the snorkel passes just above your left ear. (If you are using a special left-handed snorkel, it will be on your right.)

3 Take a deep breath, bite down on the mouthpiece and submerge your head in the water.

4 Exhale sharply once to clear any water that may be in the snorkel shaft. This is commonly called "blasting" or "purging."

5 Inhale gently at first in case there is any residual water. Blast a second time if needed, and continue to do so whenever water enters the snorkel.

6 Learn to move gently on the surface—rapid or abrupt movements can fill the snorkel with water.

7 Inhale and hold your breath, then dive to explore the underwater environment around you.

8 Ascend, make sure the snorkel end is above the surface, then purge to clear the tube of water.

9 Breathe cautiously to be sure the snorkel has cleared completely. If you don't have enough air left to purge, lift your head above the surface and take the snorkel out to breathe.

### ✱ Tips

When you're floating facedown in the water in a relaxed position, the snorkel should extend vertically above your head.

It's normal for snorkels to flood with water periodically because of wave action as you move about on the surface. Practice purging your snorkel until it becomes routine.

### ⚠ Warning

If your snorkel becomes flooded too frequently, it is probably positioned incorrectly on your head, or you are snorkeling in conditions that are too rough.

## Rig a Fishing Rod to Catch Trout 903

Somewhere in the depths of that hidden lake, river or stream are your elusive finned friends the trout. Ready your rod, fearless angler—we're going in.

### ⊙ Steps

1 Put your rod together—many are stored in two pieces that slide or screw together, like a professional billiards cue.

2 Attach a spinning reel, which consists of a spool of fishing line and a crank to reel it in.

### ✱ Tips

If you don't want to use a swivel, just tie any lures or hooks directly onto the end of your line.

If your line is too heavy or light while casting, remove or add clamp sinkers to adjust.

3   Decide what type of bait or lures to use. Trout especially love worms and salmon eggs.

4   Choose from the myriad lures available if you don't like handling squishy bait. Remember, if you settle on using a spinning lure (and you're not fishing in moving water), you'll need to be casting and reeling continually to make the darned thing work properly.

5   Use a swivel if you plan to switch lures or use snelled hooks (hooks pre-tied with fishing line). A swivel is a small metal gizmo with a hole at one end and a clasp at the other—and of course, a swivel in the center. Tie the end of your line to the hole, just as you would a fishhook (see 904 "Tie On a Fishhook").

6   Open the swivel's clasp and put on a snelled hook, which should have a loop at the end of its line. Close the clasp.

7   If you decide not to use a snelled hook, take a length of fishing line (about 1½ feet) and tie a loop at one end. To the other end, tie on a hook or lure.

8   Attach a clamp sinker (often called "shot weight") to the line beyond the swivel. This little ball of lead comes in many sizes and resembles a tiny Pac-Man (remember that popular video game?). Set the open mouth of the lead ball against your line, then clamp it closed with a pair of pliers. Good placement for sinkers is about 1 foot above the bait or lure.

9   Decide whether to use a bobber (a plastic floating ball, traditionally half red, half white) if you want to keep your bait above the lake or river bottom. (Don't use bobbers with spinning lures.)

10  Attach the bobber, leaving a length of line beyond it equal to the depth where you'd like your bait to rest: Simply squeeze the raised button, then watch the tiny metal hook appear in the button's center. Loop your line through the hook, and wrap it halfway around the bobber and through the opposite hook at the bottom. Release the button.

11  Make sure the air behind you is clear, and cast out over the open water to test your handiwork.

## ⚠ Warning

When attaching clamp sinkers, be sure to pinch hard enough so the shot closes completely and won't slip down the line as you cast.

## Things You'll Need

❏ rod

❏ spinning reel with line

❏ bait

❏ lures

❏ swivel

❏ snelled hooks

❏ clamp sinker

❏ pliers

❏ bobber

---

## 904  Tie On a Fishhook

It won't matter how many pounds your fishing line can withstand. If the hook knot is weak, you've got no fish. This simple knot looks like a tiny noose.

### ◎ Steps

1   Ready your fishing line on the rod with any appropriate weights, spinners and other tackle.

2   Grab the fishhook along its flat plane between the thumb and index finger of your left hand.

3   Take the end of the line with your right hand. Thread 1 inch of the line through the hook eye.

4   Bend back the end of the line.

## ✳ Tips

Keep the end of the line taut (both in your teeth and by pulling back on the main line) while pushing down the knot with your fingernails.

To ensure that the knot is tight, pull back on the main line while holding the hook, then push down the knot again. Repeat until pulling on the line does not loosen the knot.

5 Cross the end over the main line and pin the intersecting lines with your right index finger and thumb. The hook should be trapped inside a loop you've created.

6 Turn the hook about five times with your left hand to make a twist in the line.

7 Feed the end of the line through the loop near the hook eye. The loop should be small now that you've twisted it down.

8 Grab the end of the line with your teeth.

9 Pull gently until the line is taut.

10 Let go of the hook with your left hand and then grab the main line above the knot.

11 Let go of the line with your right hand and pinch it above the knot between your right thumbnail and the nail of your index finger.

12 Tighten the knot by pushing it down the line toward the hook eye with your fingernails while pulling on the short end with your teeth.

13 Bite or cut off the excess line.

Don't twist the hook too many times or there will be no hole left to feed the end through.

Be sure to tighten the knot before trimming the excess line. If you trim too close and too soon, you'll pull the knot free while trying to tighten it.

## Cast a Line in Fly-Fishing — 905

In fly-fishing, casting is a back-and-forth motion of the rod and line that allows you to place your fly where you'd like. It takes a good deal of practice to get just right. This is the basic cast.

### ◉ Steps

1 Let out 25 feet of line in front of you. Practice out of the water and with-out a fly on the line so that you won't have to worry about getting caught up in anything.

2 Grip your rod as if you were shaking hands with it. Set the rod's handle in your palm and close your fingers around it, keeping your thumb on top.

3 Face the direction that you want to cast, putting your weight on the balls of your feet. Keep your wrist still and stiff; don't allow it to bend. Your elbow, not your shoulder, should be your pivot point. Picture hammering a nail.

4 Think of the movement of your arm in casting as being like that of a clock's hands. If you view a fly fisherman from his or her left profile, the caster will move the rod between 11 o'clock on the forward cast and 1 o'clock on the back cast.

5 Hold the rod at 11 o'clock to begin. From the tip, the loose fly line should trace down the rod until you can grab it with your free hand. Hold and keep it above waist level.

6 Pull the rod back to 1 o'clock, release the line and wait there until the line straightens behind you. Now accelerate the rod forward to 11 o'clock and wait for the loop formed by the arcing line to straighten out.

7 Bring the fingers of your free hand toward the reel and grasp the line between your index finger and thumb.

### ✳ Tips

Consider learning how to cast on grass first. Working on concrete will ruin the protective coating on your line. If you want to practice on concrete, use a piece of junk line you don't mind ruining.

Add a piece of colored yarn to the end of your line when prac-ticing so you can see where your fly will end up without worrying about getting an actual hook snagged on the grass.

8   Pull in your outstretched line in 6-inch lengths so it forms a big excess loop right above the reel. You're not pulling more line off the reel or putting any back—you're simply gathering slack to ease the next cast. Pull in only as much as you need to place your cast.

9   To end casting, stop with the forward cast at 11 o'clock. All the slack you pulled in will sail out with your fly (when you have one on the line), which should land right on your target. Assuming, of course, that you've been practicing.

## 906 | Load a Backpack

A well-loaded pack takes less energy to carry than one that's off-balance. It's also much more comfortable.

### ◉ Steps

1   Assemble all food, water, clothing and other equipment you intend to carry.

2   Small items you won't need until you pitch camp can go inside empty spaces, such as the inside of your cooking pot, to take full advantage of space.

3   Load your sleeping bag at the bottom of your pack (if you have an internal-frame pack) or tie it below (if you have an external-frame pack). You won't need it before you pitch camp, and a sleeping bag is light for its volume.

4   Pack heavy items—food, stove, fuel and water—above the sleeping bag and next to your back. Be sure that objects don't protrude into your back.

5   Keep your water bottle separate for easy access.

6   Try to keep the weight evenly distributed from side to side within the pack so that it won't be lopsided when you carry it.

7   Fill the remaining volume with clothing. The items farthest from your back should be the lightest.

### ✻ Tips

Keep only the items you need handy in the pockets or top flap of the pack. Most packs don't close very well, and a large, unstable load in the top pocket can throw you off balance.

If your pack doesn't have a special outside pocket for your water bottle, tuck a bottle underneath the top flap on its side and right up against your back.

## 907 | Avoid Getting Blisters While Hiking

There's nothing like painful blisters to ruin your backcountry trip, but you can avoid them by taking these measures.

### ◉ Steps

1   Break in hiking shoes or boots well before your hike, wearing the same shoe-sock combination you will use on the trail.

2   Wrap your blister-prone spots with athletic tape or duct tape before you start hiking, if you know you're likely to have a problem. Put the tape directly on your skin; when you're done hiking, take off your boots and pull off the tape immediately. The heat and sweat from your feet will make it easier to remove.

### ✻ Tip

Many hikers use liner socks— thin socks that absorb sweat and heat away from your feet. Regular thicker socks are worn on top of these. The liners provide a protective layer for the outer socks to rub against.

3   Soak any developing hot spot (an area that is irritated from rubbing) in cold water or air-dry it until the spot cools.

4   Apply a patch or doughnut of moleskin to the hot spot or cover it with tape. Theories about the pros and cons of patches, doughnuts and tape vary. Experiment and find what works best for you.

5   Use foot powder and change into a dry pair of socks before you put your boots or shoes back on and continue hiking.

**Things You'll Need**

❑ athletic or duct tape

❑ moleskin

❑ foot powder

❑ dry socks

---

# Build a Campfire                                            908

Follow a few simple steps to start a fire that can bring you light, warmth and hot beans.

## ⊙ Steps

1   Make sure that local regulations allow campfires.

2   Situate your fire at least 10 feet away from tents, trees, roots and other flammable items if there's no fire ring available. Clear a space 24 to 32 inches across.

3   Don't make a ring of rocks if one isn't already there, and don't build against a boulder or other rocks. This will needlessly char the rocks without adding any significant containment to the fire.

4   Gather firewood and kindling if necessary, using only fallen branches. Note that many parks and wilderness areas even forbid gathering fallen material, which plays an important role in the ecosystem.

5   Build a small, loose pile of kindling, making sure to allow space for air to feed the fire. Include paper scraps, dry plant matter and other small, flammable items.

6   Construct a pyramid of dry twigs and small sticks around and above the kindling pile.

7   Light the kindling with a match.

8   Add increasingly larger sticks and then logs as the fire grows in strength, always leaving enough space between them for the fire to breathe.

**✳ Tip**

Use a gas stove instead of a campfire to cook food—it's easier to use, cleaner and better for the environment.

**⚠ Warning**

Never leave your fire unattended.

**Things You'll Need**

❑ firewood

❑ kindling

❑ matches

---

# Avoid an Encounter With a Bear                              909

Bears in the wilderness are usually more interested in finding food than attacking you. Preventing encounters is the best way to avoid trouble.

## ⊙ Steps

1   Learn and obey the rules and regulations of the wilderness and other areas where you hike and camp.

2   Get as much distance as you can between your eating/food-preparation area and your sleeping area, preferably with natural barriers such as rocks, trees and creeks in between.

**✳ Tips**

Grizzly bears are responsible for most bear-attack fatalities, while black bears are generally more interested in making a meal out of your food than out of you.

3 Keep your food in a bear-resistant container, which generally comes in the form of a locking metal cylinder.

4 Try to cook downwind from your sleeping area, and eat everything you cook. Do not burn your scraps—keep these and any other leftovers with your other food in the bear-resistant container, then pack them out when you leave.

5 Sleep in a tent. Do not allow any food odors to get inside your tent. Otherwise, bears might come into your tent looking for food—and find you.

6 Gather your group together as one mass and make a ruckus if a bear wanders into your campsite: wave arms, yell, bang pots together and throw rocks. The bear will probably mistake you for a larger, aggressive animal and retreat.

7 Hike in a large group and stay together.

8 Stay on the trail and hike during the middle of the day, when bears are least active.

9 Wear bells while hiking. If bells are too annoying, try talking, singing and clapping as you hike. The important thing is to make lots of noise so bears will know to avoid you.

10 Scan ahead with binoculars when hiking in bear country. If you spot a bear, change your course to avoid it—especially if you spot a mother with her cubs.

Most bear encounters are at short range and in the brush, rather than on a worn trail.

### ⚠ Warning

Of the few attacks that do occur, most involve a mother and her cubs. Always stay well clear of cubs—Mom may not be visible, but you can be sure she's not far away.

### Things You'll Need

❑ bear-resistant container

❑ tent

❑ bear bells

❑ binoculars

---

## 910 | Survive an Encounter With a Bear

Bear attacks are extremely rare, but it's best to be prepared. Almost all bear attacks involve encounters with mothers and their cubs. Never approach a bear cub.

### ◉ Steps

1 Remain calm if you spot a bear; avoid sudden movements.

2 Back away slowly, avoid eye contact, and speak to the bear in a calm, quiet voice. Running might trigger a chase response, and you're not going to outrun a bear.

3 Throw something onto the ground (for example, a camera) if the bear pursues you, as this may distract the bear and allow you to escape.

4 Keep your backpack on; it may protect your body if you're attacked.

5 Don't climb a tree. Black bears can climb trees, and trees found in grizzly country generally have weak trunks and lack low branches.

6 Drop to the ground in the fetal position with your hands behind your neck if attacked. Stay silent and don't move.

7 Roll with the bear's blows and return to your motionless fetal position.

8 Stay quiet and motionless for at least 20 minutes once the bear leaves. Bears will often watch from a distance and return at the first sign of movement.

### ✱ Tips

Black bears and grizzly bears are very different animals, with grizzlies being responsible for most bear-attack fatalities. Black bears are less likely to attack and more likely to go through your trash.

Some hikers who have been confronted by aggressive bears have reported success with pepper spray.

9 Fight back only as a last resort if the bear persists. You'll have the best luck fighting back against a black bear. If you can get to your feet, strike it in the eyes or on the snout as you slowly back away.

## Relieve Yourself in the Woods 911

Human waste is one of the biggest problems people import to the wilderness. Going's OK—it's where you go that's important.

### ⊙ Steps

1 Anticipate the need to go so you can select a good site before urgency overwhelms you.

2 Find a spot at least 200 feet from water and 200 feet from campsites, trails and other popular areas.

3 Once you find a spot, dig a hole at least 6 inches deep.

4 Drop your drawers, squat down over the hole and go.

5 Use smooth rocks, grass, leaves or even snow in place of toilet paper if you want to go with a no-trace camping strategy. If you use toilet paper, burn it or carry it out of the woods with the rest of your belongings.

6 Fill the hole back up and use leaves, pine needles or rocks to camouflage the site.

7 If you only need to urinate, do so on sand, mineral soil or exposed rock.

### ✱ Tip

Urine burns plants, and its odor attracts animals that will destroy the site digging for the salt.

### Things You'll Need

❑ camping trowel or shovel

❑ toilet paper

## Signal for Help in the Wilderness 912

If weather conditions get so poor that you lose your way, or if you get stranded and need help despite sunny skies, keep the following in mind.

### ⊙ Steps

1 Know that any series of three signals is a universal call of distress: Three whistle blasts or three gunshots, for instance, will alert others that you need help.

2 Understand that yelling is only effective if people are nearby. The human voice doesn't carry well, so save your vocal cords and strength.

3 Find a clearing or hilltop and start three signal fires, making sure to keep them under control. Place them in triangular form (a known signal for help) and space them 50 feet apart so that a plane can distinguish the pattern from overhead.

4 Use green and wet wood to send up ample smoke during daylight; use dry material at night to make a strong, roaring blaze.

5 Spread out three sets of brightly colored equipment—for example, a tent cloth, a tarp and a space blanket—in an open space to signal your distress. Again, put them in triangular form.

### Things You'll Need

❑ whistle

❑ waterproof matches

❑ mirror

6   Use brightly colored gear or dark brush or rocks to create three piles, or lay out an "SOS" or a big "X" on an open snowfield to signal aircraft rescuers in wintry conditions.

7   Use a mirror to flash a sunlight signal over long distances if you see a plane or people in the distance. (This technique won't work on cloudy days.)

## 913 | Climb Mount Everest

**Everest can mercilessly test even those who honor it. Whether you choose a packaged, guided expedition or trek with friends, there are several things to keep in mind.**

### ◉ Steps

1   Start training today. Take mountaineering courses that teach you about technique, equipment, routes and survival. Then begin a minimum of two to three years of regular practice climbs in high alpine terrain, including steep faces, rough rocks, night climbs, ice falls and snow climbs.

2   Get a complete physical checkup. You'll need healthy veins and arteries to pump lots of blood to your brain and muscles, as well as to warm your body. Keep your blood pressure and cholesterol down.

3   Raise the cash. You'll need plenty—even a low-budget trip will cost $25,000, with guided package trips soaring to as much as $60,000. Realize that $10,000 goes to permits alone; then add travel, food, equipment, oxygen, insurance and Sherpa fees. Consider approaching corporations for sponsorship deals to cover your expenses.

4   Plan a May expedition. The weather is most cooperative then (when it isn't a whiteout, blowing 100-mph winds, and 50 degrees below zero). Six months in advance, you'll need to file for permits and send copies of passports and climbing letters of recommendation for your team to the Nepal Ministry and Administration, as well as to a trekking agency to help you with transporting your gear. You'll also need to contract with Sherpas to aid you on your voyage. For more information, contact the Nepalese Embassies and Consulate Offices in Washington, D.C., or in Kathmandu, Nepal.

5   Pack a first aid kit, medications, satellite phone, walkie-talkies, laptop computer, padlocks for bags, tents, sleeping bags, mountaineering clothing, climbing equipment and ropes, water, food, trash bags, sunscreen, vision protection, oxygen bottles and anything else you can fit on a yak or on your back, or that you can hire a Sherpa to carry for you. Make sure you've tested all your gear in cold, severe conditions before you pack it.

6   Get yourself to Kathmandu, Nepal, where your expedition truly begins. You can fly a number of international carriers connecting through major airports; none of these flights will be direct or nonstop. Jet lag is guaranteed. Check in with the local authorities, pay your fees and organize your crew.

7   Trek from Lukla to Base Camp at 17,600 feet. Scale the Khumbu Icefall up to 19,500 feet. Rest at Camp I in the Valley of Silence. Push on to

### ✱ Tips

Climb with people you know and trust, and who have extensive experience.

Ask other climbers who have tackled Everest to recommend the most skilled and reliable Sherpas.

Drink lots of purified water to stay hydrated.

### ⚠ Warnings

Stay warm, or risk losing body parts.

Climbing Mount Everest puts you at risk of severe injury, disease and possibly death from avalanche, falling rocks, crevasse falls, exhaustion, dehydration, frostbite, pneumonia, dysentery, Khumbu cough, whiteout disorientation, hypothermia, high-altitude cerebral and pulmonary edema, and other hazards.

Be prepared to call off your summit attempt due to fatigue or poor weather conditions.

Camp II at 21,300 feet. Scale the Lhotse Face and climb to Camp III at 23,500 feet. Rest and acclimatize for the trip to Camp IV, which at 26,300 feet is the only camp located in the "death zone."

8   Charge the summit when you have a weather window. Start early in the morning, before sunrise, with extra down mittens and plenty of oxygen.

9   Sit atop the 29,028-foot summit and know that you are at the highest point on earth. And then mentally prepare for the descent—getting down is just as dangerous.

10  Pack out all of your empty oxygen bottles and trash to get back your $4,000 environmental deposit and leave the mountain with good karma.

## Spot Potential Avalanche Danger                                914

If you can identify the site of a recent or potential avalanche, you will reduce your chances of being caught in an extremely dangerous situation.

### ☉ Steps

1   Check the amount of recent snowfall. Heavy amounts of new snow increase the likelihood of an avalanche.

2   Pay attention to radical changes in temperature that may cause snow to melt, become heavier or change consistency. Layers of snow will settle and fracture where there is a major difference in consistency.

3   Stay away from steep slopes, where gravity will have a greater effect on the new snow.

4   Keep an eye out for fractures in the snow along the face of the slope.

5   Look in the chutes, in gullies and at the bottom of steep slopes for avalanche debris. You will see a marked difference in the snow—it looks like cottage cheese or boulders.

6   Watch the snow around you as you ski. If it comes loose and sloughs down the hill with you, then you are at risk of getting caught up in it.

**✳ Tip**

Point out areas of concern to your guide and others in your group.

**⚠ Warning**

Don't get cocky armed with this information—stay out of areas prone to avalanches.

## Walk on Snowshoes                                              915

For thousands of years, snowshoes have been used for winter transportation. Today they're more popular than ever, thanks to improvements in their technology.

### ☉ Steps

1   Dress appropriately for winter recreation.

2   Stretch your muscles for 10 to 15 minutes. Be sure to stretch at least the thighs, groin and calves.

3   Attach the snowshoes to your footwear snugly so your foot and snowshoe move as one.

**✳ Tips**

Packed trails and flat slopes are the best places to learn to snowshoe.

Look back at your tracks—they should look like a zipper line.

4  Keep your feet shoulder-width apart, as most snowshoes are wider than regular footwear.

5  Swing the striding foot sideways and forward, clearing your opposite ankle. Your foot will wing out in an arc pattern. Be sure to swing away from your body and far enough forward to clear the opposite snowshoe.

6  Land with the pressure focused on the ball of your foot.

7  Repeat with the opposite leg.

---

## 916 | Make a Snowplow Turn on Skis

Learning how to make a snowplow turn—also known as a wedge turn—is the first step to controlling your speed and direction on skis.

### ⊙ Steps

1  Spread your feet about shoulder-width apart.

2  Make sure your knees and ankles are slightly bent.

3  Point your toes in toward each other. This will force the tips of your skis to angle toward each other.

4  Keep your weight approximately even between both feet until you're ready to initiate a turn.

5  Increase pressure on the inside edge of the ski you want to turn. If you want to turn left, you put pressure on the right ski by pushing down with your right big toe.

6  Maintain your center of gravity above both skis.

7  Turn the ski with your legs, hips and feet, not your upper body.

8  Allow your shoulders to face down the slope. Your shoulders and upper body should not follow the turn of your skis.

9  Ease pressure off the ski edge as you finish the turn.

10  Prepare for the next turn.

### ❋ Tips

Control your speed by making bigger turns or by making a bigger snowplow shape with your skis.

Linking one turn with another allows the skier to progress down the slope in a fluid manner. Linking turns is the ultimate goal when learning the snowplow turn.

### ⚠ Warning

Skiing is an inherently dangerous activity that can result in serious injury or death. Seek proper training and equipment.

---

## 917 | Make a Stem-Christie Turn on Skis

After you've mastered the snowplow turn and you've become accustomed to more speed, the stem christie (also known as the wedge christie) is the next turn to learn.

### ⊙ Steps

1  Form a snowplow (see 916 "Make a Snowplow Turn on Skis") before you begin your turn.

2  Begin increasing pressure on the inside ski that you want to use to initiate the turn—the left ski if you're turning right, or the right ski if you're turning left.

### ❋ Tips

Look downhill the entire time, not at your skis.

The faster you're going, the easier it is to do a stem-christie turn.

**How to Do** *(Just About)* **Everything**

3   Turn right by pointing your left arm to your right ski tip while holding your arms out in front of you. Do the opposite to turn left.

4   Touch the pole to the ground (on the right, for example, to turn right) a bit in front of your body, and turn around the planted pole. Increase pressure on the inside edge of the ski you want to turn. If you want to turn right, you put pressure on the left ski by pushing down with your left big toe.

5   Allow the tail of your inside ski to slide down toward your outside ski as you finish the turn. This is known as matching or parallel skiing. This step is the goal of the stem-christie turn. As the hill becomes steeper and you start skiing faster, your skis will naturally want to come together through the turn.

6   Keep your hands up and in front of your body throughout the turn.

7   Finish your turn with your skis together.

As you become more comfortable with the stem christie, form your wedge later and later before the turn.

Increase pressure on your edges to make the turn more crisp.

# Start Out on Cross-Country Skis                918

The sport of cross-country skiing can take you to some of nature's most beautiful winter terrain. It is also one of the easier snow sports to learn.

## ◉ Steps

1   Pick an easy trail to start. Flat terrain with only an occasional hill is the most suitable for beginners.

2   Put on your skis by inserting the fronts of your boots into the bindings.

3   Stick your poles in the snow at your sides and slide your skis back and forth while remaining in a stationary position. This exercise gives you a feel for your equipment.

4   Put your hands through the pole straps.

5   Put one foot in front of the other, letting the skis slide as if you were walking across an ice-skating rink.

6   Plant your poles in a rhythmic manner, placing the left one in the snow at the end of a right-foot glide and vice versa.

7   Practice until you feel comfortable enough to increase your speed and gliding distance.

**✱ Tips**

Make certain that your boots are free of snow before stepping into your bindings.

Expect to fall a few times on your first excursions—it's all part of the fun of cross-country skiing.

## 919 | Carve a Turn on a Snowboard

Carving—linking a toe-side turn with a heel-side turn—is one of the most basic maneuvers in snowboarding and one of the most pleasant experiences on earth.

### ⊙ Steps

1   Start by making a toe-side turn. Do this by leaning forward slightly, lifting your heels, and turning your shoulders to the right. (Reverse these directions if you ride goofy foot; see 922 "Determine if You're a Regular or Goofy Foot.")

2   Straighten up as you come to the end of your toe turn; face your shoulders straight ahead and arch your back slightly. In this position, your board should be flat on the snow, with neither edge engaged.

3   Lean forward with your knees bent, keeping your body low and flexible.

4   Make a heel-side turn: Rotate your shoulders to the left while lifting your toes and leaning back slightly.

5   Straighten up as you come to the end of your heel-side turn, and face your shoulders downhill.

6   Start your second toe-side turn. Lean forward, keep your body low and flexible (with your knees bent), and rotate your shoulders to the toe side while lifting your heels slightly.

### ✳ Tips

As you get more advanced, you can stay lower, face your shoulders downhill more and go faster. You also won't need to consciously go flat in between edges—you'll make a smooth transition.

The transition between the heel turn and the toe turn is where people often catch an edge and fall. It helps to have your weight low and slightly forward on the board.

### ⚠ Warning

Snowboarding is an inherently dangerous activity that can result in serious injury or death. Seek proper training and equipment.

## 920 | Stop a Snowboard With Your Toes

Stopping is a basic skill you need when snowboarding, and being able to stop on either your toes or heels is essential.

### ⊙ Steps

1   Prepare for the toe-side stop as you would for a toe-side turn by lowering your weight and leaning forward, rotating your shoulders around to the uphill side of the slope, and straightening your back as the turn ends.

2   Continue rotating uphill until the board is perpendicular to the slope instead of letting the turn flatten out to make the transition into the heel turn.

3   Hold that position perpendicular to the slope with your heels up, and let the board sideslip to scrub off speed. The faster you're going, the more you'll need to sideslip before you stop.

4   Sideslip to a full stop.

### ✳ Tip

To avoid overrotating the tail and going backward down the slope, balance your weight evenly between your front and back legs. If you feel the tail of your board drop too far, put more weight on the back foot.

## Catch Air on a Snowboard

Here's the most basic way to get airborne on a snowboard—your first step toward flying the friendly skies.

### ⊙ Steps

1 Approach the bump you'll use to catch air. Keep your knees deeply bent and your upper body relaxed.

2 Compress as you reach the bump.

3 Spring up just before you reach the top of the bump.

4 Draw your legs up evenly as you leave the ground.

5 Keep your board pointed forward, level and directly underneath you.

6 Extend your legs (back foot first if you've caught big air) as you come back down.

7 Compress again when you return to earth to absorb the landing.

**✱ Tip**

Make sure you can see the landing area so you don't run into anyone.

## Determine if You're a Regular or Goofy Foot

In snowboarding, surfing and skateboarding, you're a "regular foot" if you keep your left foot forward, a "goofy foot" if you keep your right forward. Here are three ways to tell which you are.

### ⊙ Steps

1 Put forward whichever foot makes you feel the most balanced, controlled and relaxed in that position. Generally, this will be the same for you from one board sport to another.

2 Lie on your stomach on the ground as you would on a surfboard, putting your hands under your shoulders as if you were going to do a pushup. Spring into a surfing or riding stance. Try it first with your left foot forward and then with your right. Whichever stance feels better is probably the right one for you.

3 Have someone give you a surprise shove from behind. Not only will your friend likely enjoy this, but whichever foot you step forward with first to catch your balance is probably the foot that goes in front when you surf, skateboard or snowboard.

## 923 Buy a New Car

Choosing a car is an important decision that merits careful planning. You are likely to live with this vehicle for quite some time. These pointers will help you choose wisely.

### ◎ Steps

1 Decide what you intend to use the car for—daily commuting; recreation; weekends and evenings out; carrying things; towing a trailer; carrying more than one passenger; driving in the city, suburbs or country. Consider factors that are important to you, such as fuel efficiency, reliability and safety features.

2 Check into the resale value and repair history of past models in this car line, such as by consulting *Consumer Reports* magazine or its Web site (www.consumerreports.org).

3 Come up with a realistic budget, based on what you can afford (consider the monthly payment and cost of upkeep). If you're considering a trade-in, check the Kelley Blue Book value of your current vehicle. The Blue Book is a catalog of new- and used-car values, available at libraries, banks and online at www.kbb.com. Factor your car's trade-in value into your total budget.

4 Locate a town or an area near your home with several car dealerships; check Sunday newspaper advertisements and the yellow pages. Choose one or more dealerships to visit and set out early, preferably on a weekday; remember to bring your driver's license so you can test-drive. You can also shop online (see 924 "Shop for a Car Online").

5 Find a car that interests you and check the stickers on the window. The first (and sometimes only) one is the factory sticker, which lists the MSRP (Manufacturer's Suggested Retail Price), and the second is the dealer's sticker.

6 You'll see that the factory sticker lists the car's features and its fuel-efficiency rating—the number of miles per gallon expected for city and highway driving. The MSRP on this sticker includes the sum of the vehicle's base price, any additional options and the destination fee. The MSRP has a built-in profit for the dealer, often around 10 percent.

7 Understand that the second sticker, if there is one, reflects a higher price. This price is set by the retailer for options and services it has supplied apart from the factory. Examples include an undercoating (to protect the car's underside exterior), dealer prep (washing, waxing, interior cleaning), interior and exterior treatment (sealant for the interior, no-wax finish for the exterior) and extra items (specialty wheels, for example). The second sticker price may also include additional dealer profits.

8 Tell the sales representative that you'd like to have a look inside the car, or just hop in if it's unlocked. Adjust the seat and mirrors, and check leg room in each part of the car.

9 Ask to take a test drive. Start out on city streets and then head out to the highway. Pay attention to steering ease, turning radius, braking response and acceleration. Adjust the mirrors and radio while you're driving to test convenience.

### ✳ Tips

It is usually cheaper for dealers to order a standard options package than to order a customized set of options just for you. Thus, you may be able to get a better deal on a luxury package car than you would on a car with only a few options that you specially request.

When the manufacturer sells a car to a retailer, the price is set to include a limited amount of dealer prep, such as washing and interior cleaning. Ask your dealer what additional services have been provided to warrant the charge, which is often listed on the second sticker as "dealer prep."

Avoid setting your heart on one particular model or make. There are hundreds of excellent vehicles on the market, and becoming attached to one of them may make you less hardheaded in your bargaining.

Avoid being nasty to the salesperson. Express regret over your own limited means and admiration for the sales rep's efforts on your behalf, as appropriate.

Manufacturers often survey dealers' customer satisfaction rating and award bonuses to those who score consistently high. So be sure you're satisfied with your salesperson—don't be shy about asking him or her to show you everything you want to know about the vehicle.

### Things You'll Need

☐ *Consumer Reports* magazine

☐ Kelley Blue Book

10 Return to the dealership and thank the dealer. If you like the car, ask for a business card and say you will return later.

11 Head to the next dealership and investigate other car models as described above. Ask dealers which car most closely resembles the one you previously test-drove, providing the make and model and explaining which features you liked. Test a number of models until you decide on a car, and compare these prices with those at other dealerships.

12 Inquire about availability and delivery time, especially if you're interested in a popular model or want special features.

13 Factor the dealership and its sales staff into your choice. A dealership you can trust, especially one with a competent service center on site, is worth more than money in your long future with the vehicle. You can, of course, have your car serviced at any dealer authorized by your new car's warranty.

14 Start negotiations on polite and friendly terms. Comment on what you like about the car and ask questions. The intent is to make the seller comfortable.

15 Remember that the dealer's second sticker lists options, not require-ments, regardless of whether those services have already been provid-ed. Ask for the factory wheels back, for example, or order a car that has no undercoating.

16 Make your first offer. It should be lower than what you're willing to pay, but not an insulting figure. Use the MSRP as a reference, remembering that dealer profit (often around 10 percent) is built into this figure.

17 Allow the seller to make a counteroffer. If the price is too high, say you're not able to afford that and ask him to talk to his manager.

18 If the salesperson balks at your first offer, make a slightly higher one. Continue negotiating until you can agree on a price within your budget. If you can't agree on a price, seek out another dealer. You may be able to go back and get the first dealer to underbid the second dealer.

## Shop for a Car Online

924

Shopping for a new or used car online can reduce the hassle of working with dealerships and provide detailed information about a specific car before you leave for the showroom.

### ⊙ Steps

1 Form a general picture of what you're looking for. Consider how you'll be using the car, what you're willing to spend, and which factors are impor-tant to you, such as fuel efficiency, reliability and safety features.

2 Check into the resale value and repair history of past models in this car line, such as by consulting *Consumer Reports* magazine or its Web site (www.consumerreports.org).

3 Open your browser and type in the name of a manufacturer—for exam-ple, "www.ford.com" or "www.toyota.com"—or use a search engine if this doesn't produce what you're seeking.

 **Tips**

Once you decide on a car, you'll most likely be referred to a local dealer or seller, so you may not be able to find exactly what you're looking for. This is espe-cially true when shopping for a used car.

If you do shop online, make sure you test-drive the car before finalizing the purchase.

4   Enter requested information when prompted. Most manufacturers' Web sites have detailed information on models, including available options, photos and MSRP (Manufacturer's Suggested Retail Price).

5   Find Web sites containing ads for used cars, if new models are a bit out of your price range. For example, look in the business or automotive sections of popular search engines, or try search strings like "Internet car dealers" and "buy a car online."

6   Look for a site that offers detailed information about each of its used-car listings. Some automotive sites conduct inspections of used cars via independent mechanics—these are generally good places to shop. Look in the "about us" section of each site for information on its background and services.

7   Use the site's database to find reviews and ratings for specific cars by make, model and year. Then, visit independent sites (sites that do not sell cars and are unaffiliated with car companies and dealerships) to find reviews and technical information about various makes and models.

8   Understand that many sites, whether selling new or used cars, will only put you in contact with retailers or individual sellers, leaving you to finish the deal the old-fashioned way: person to person.

9   Realize that online car shopping is changing every day. There is an occasional site that may deliver a new or used car to your door, with the paperwork completed by the truck driver; these transactions are usually accompanied by a hefty delivery fee. More likely, if a site delivers, it will do so to a nearby "delivery center" in your area.

The degree of the site's involvement in the transaction depends on the site. Some sites function as simple classified-ad forums, while others take a more active role in car sales. Most sites act mainly as communication points between buyers and sellers, but be prepared to pay an extra fee if the site provides added services such as inspections and warranties. Or even (if you really don't want to leave the computer) delivery.

---

## 925 | Utilize the Lemon Law

If you've bought a new or used vehicle that gives you continual grief (but has a valid warranty), and you're making multiple repairs, your state's lemon laws may be able to help.

### ⊙ Steps

1   Remember that if you're stuck with a lemon, your complaint is with the manufacturer. Although your instinct may be to blame the car dealer, the dealer is just the middleman for the defective product.

2   Document your repairs, and be accurate with each problem. Obtain copies of all warranty repair orders from the dealer and keep notes of your reported problems and all conversations you have with service people, including the date, time and participants in these conversations.

3   Contact your state attorney general's office or conduct other research to determine the provisions of your state's lemon law. There are variations in each state's laws.

4   Determine whether your previous efforts to repair the problem satisfy the requirements of your state's lemon law. Most state laws allow the manufacturer three or four chances to repair the defect or defects.

5   Write to the manufacturer if problems persist. Explain how burdensome it is to continually repair the car, and how your trust in the product's reli-

### ✳ Tip

Your best defense against an uncooperative manufacturer is a thorough, specific and accurate service-record paper trail. This shows that you made the correct number of attempts to have the problems fixed, whether the defect was the same each time, or several different ones.

### ⚠ Warning

Most lemon laws allow an offset for the consumer's use of the vehicle when determining reimbursement amounts. That is, when refunding a buyer's money, the seller can deduct a certain percentage to account for the buyer's usage of the vehicle.

ability has been shattered. Ask for reimbursement of your related expenses (such as a rental car, if it was needed), or other compensation for your troubled experience. Your particular state's lemon law will prescribe methods for doing so.

6   State in your letter that you wish to exercise your right to a refund or replacement of the vehicle, if you would rather not keep the lemon. Specify which option you desire.

7   Consider hiring an attorney if the manufacturer is unresponsive. Find an attorney who specializes in lemon-law cases. Remember, though, that only some state lemon laws allow a consumer to recover attorneys' fees when suing a manufacturer.

## Understand a Car Lease      926

When you lease a car, you put little or no money down and can drop off the car after a few years without the hassle of selling it. Convenient, yes—but potentially complicated.

### ☉ Steps

1   Think of holding a lease as making payments on the amount that the car depreciates while you have it. That depreciation is figured by subtracting the car's projected value at the end of the lease (residual value) from the sticker price (Manufacturer's Suggested Retail Price, or MSRP). For example, if a vehicle with a sticker price of $20,000 has a projected value of $12,000 in four years, the depreciation is the difference, or $8,000. You'll be making payments on this $8,000.

2   Know the parameters of a closed-ended lease. These leases give you the option of purchasing the car at the end of the lease term, but also allow you to walk away without buying. Generally, the purchase price is determined before the lease is signed. Closed-ended leases offer the benefit of choice.

3   Understand that open-ended leases require you to buy the car at the end of the lease. The price is the projected value. These can get expensive if at the end of the lease the projected value of the vehicle is larger than the fair market value. Open-ended leases generally offer the advantage of lower monthly payments.

4   Read the lease agreement carefully and understand any restrictions. For example, some leases won't allow you to take the car out of the country.

5   Look under the section called Early Termination. This section explains what will happen if you decide you don't want the car anymore or if it's totaled in a wreck. You will be required to pay at least the remaining lease payments, a disposition fee and possibly other fees, depending on your lease. Be sure you understand these charges before you sign any papers.

6   Remember that your insurance company might not pay what is still owed on the car after an accident. That's because your car may have depreciated by an amount more than you've paid on the lease. Some leases offer gap insurance to cover the difference.

**✱ Tip**

Keep up on the scheduled maintenance and save the records. You don't want to invalidate the warranty or give the leasing company any reason to charge you extra when you return your car.

7   Read the section on wear and tear. It should describe in detail what the leasing company will accept as regular wear and tear and what is considered excessive wear, which will add more to your final payment.

8   Know your mileage limit (usually 12,000 to 15,000 miles a year). Keep your car under that limit or you'll pay up to 25 cents for every mile over it. This fee adds up quickly.

9   Find out if your monthly payments include the final disposition charge or if you'll have to pay that at the end. This charge covers transferring the car to the dealer and getting it ready to sell.

## 927 | Inspect a Used Car Before Buying

Some used-car buyers answer classified ads and approach these vehicles with great trepidation. Such anxiety is rarely justified, but careful inspection is wholly warranted.

### ◉ Steps

1   Look at the car's exterior. If the paint is new, ask when the car was painted. Beware of cheap new details like $100 paint jobs. They often distract from larger problems such as underlying rust.

2   Check bumpers and wheel wells for signs of rust, dents or body filler. Then search the rest of the vehicle for rust, remembering to scan the underside. Exterior rust may indicate more in unseen areas.

3   Inspect both sides of the car—as well as the front, rear and beneath—for any signs of more major body repair. Look for inconsistencies: Do the edges of the hood and door panels line up with the fenders and other side panels? Does the frame look aligned correctly? Such inconsistencies may be clues to previous wrecks.

4   Open the door. Check the interior for tears in upholstery, sun damage and general appearance.

5   Lift the hood. Look at the engine's overall cleanliness. Look for rust on the exhaust manifold and oil leaks around the valve cover and head gasket.

6   Check the oil on the dipstick by rubbing it against your thumb (make sure the engine is cool). If you feel small particles in the oil, the engine may be worn or have other problems.

7   Start up the engine. It should start immediately.

8   Take the car for a test drive. Check the brakes. They shouldn't squeal and should bring the car to a stop in a sufficiently short distance.

9   Test the transmission for slippage. Set the emergency brake, depress the clutch pedal and shift through the gears (if the car has a manual transmission). There shouldn't be any grinding sounds.

10  Check to make sure all of the lights (front and back) work, as well as the windshield wipers, turn signals and radio.

11  Ask to see a current smog certificate, if it's necessary in your state.

### ✳ Tips

As a final precaution, take the car to a mechanic, who should charge a reasonable fee to check over a used car. The seller should agree to this, but may require that you leave a deposit. If the seller won't let you take the car, offer to meet him or her at a mutually convenient garage.

If you give the seller a deposit in order to take the car to have it checked, make sure to write out an agreement stating that the deposit will be returned immediately if you decide not to buy the car.

If the vehicle's mileage appears unusually low, have a mechanic determine whether someone has tampered with the odometer. If so, the seller must refund any money you have paid and may be liable for punitive damages under federal and state odometer laws.

12 Ask to see a record of the car's maintenance. Look to see that the car had regular oil changes and checkups (maintenance schedules will vary by model). Also, inquire about additional work that has been done on the car and ask to see receipts.

## Buy a Used Car 928

If you're still interested in a used car after a careful inspection, it's time to negotiate. The best way to know what's a reasonable price is to learn about the car's condition and value.

### ◎ Steps

1 Check the Kelley Blue Book value for the model and year of the car and compare it with the asking price. The Blue Book is a catalog of car values, available at most libraries and banks, and online at www.kbb.com.

2 Make a fair offer that fits your budget. Avoid a figure that greatly undervalues the car.

3 If the offer is not accepted, ask for a counteroffer. If it is too high, point out any problems you noticed about the car.

4 Make a second offer. This should be the counteroffer minus the cost of fixing any problems with the car.

5 Continue until you reach an agreement or a stalemate.

6 Pay with a money order or a cashier's check.

7 Ask the seller to sign the title to transfer ownership to you. Federal law requires the seller to provide you with two documents: the title certificate of the vehicle and an odometer statement showing the car's mileage. Certain states may require smog certificates and other forms (call your department of motor vehicles to determine exactly what you'll need).

8 Note that in many states the seller is required to contact the motor-vehicles department to inform it of the transfer of ownership; it's your responsibility to change the registration.

### ✱ Tips

Try to pay a fair price but not be hard-nosed. It's sometimes a fine line.

If the seller agrees to supply a warranty for the car (which is not required by federal law), make sure it is in writing.

## Sell a Used Car 929

Regardless of what shape your vehicle's in, you can expect a good selling experience if you're straightforward and honest with prospective buyers.

### ◎ Steps

1 Check the car's Kelley Blue Book value. The Blue Book is a catalog of car values, available at libraries and banks, and online at www.kbb.com.

2 Look in the classified section of your local paper or a local auto-trader publication (usually distributed free at grocery stores and similar outlets) to compare the market value of similar cars.

### ✱ Tips

Allow the buyer to inspect your car through an independent mechanic. Be up-front about both major and minor defects— rust, a bad engine, failing brakes—and subtract the cost of repairs from your asking price. Agree to meet the prospective

3  Decide how far above or below that value you can fairly go. Consider factors such as the car's condition, mileage, aftermarket add-ons, exotic coloring and any repair work you've had done.

4  Wash and wax the car, empty the trunk, and fix any small problems with the interior—broken knobs, sticking windows, torn upholstery. Clean the interior thoroughly (see 934 "Wash a Car" and 935 "Wax a Car").

5  Gather all the service and repair records together. Make photocopies of the records to give to a prospective buyer. Take measures to see that the car's paperwork is in order, such as paying off any outstanding parking tickets and making sure the registration is current.

6  Contact your state's department of motor vehicles or authorized automobile club to find out if you're responsible for a smog certificate; this varies from state to state.

7  Advertise your car. Put up signs at your repair shop, local cafe or grocery store if any of them have a bulletin board. Place ads in local newspapers and other classified ad resources, and put a "For Sale" sign in the window of your car.

8  Seek out online classifieds and bulletin boards. Often bulletin boards have discussions for a particular make and model.

9  When a buyer shows interest, explain your reasons for selling the car. State the repairs you've had done and the gas mileage. Note any new parts, in particular.

10  Appear to be mulling over the buyer's first offer, even if it's higher than you had hoped.

11  Avoid making a counteroffer to an insultingly low offer. Politely decline and say you cannot accept anything so low. Counteroffer when the buyer gets closer to what you might accept. Continue until you agree on a fair price.

12  Accept cash, a cashier's check or a money order in payment for the car. Don't take a personal check unless you know the person very well.

13  Sign your car's title certificate to transfer ownership to the buyer. Federal law requires the seller to provide the buyer with two documents: the title certificate of the vehicle and an odometer statement showing the car's mileage. Certain states may require a smog certificate and other forms (call your department of motor vehicles to determine exactly what you'll need). Other documents, such as the car's warranty (if transferable) and service records, are not required but may be turned over to the buyer.

14  Note that in many states the seller is required to contact the department of motor vehicles to inform it of the transfer of ownership; it's the buyer's responsibility to change the registration.

15  Notify your insurance company once the car sells, and after you have transferred the title to the new owner. Tell the company to remove it from your policy.

buyer at a garage or accept a deposit of a few hundred dollars while the car is being inspected.

Write the buyer a receipt for the transaction, indicating that you are selling the vehicle "as is," to avoid future problems.

## ⚠ Warnings

Failing to inform the state motor-vehicles department of the change of ownership can set you up for hardship if the car's new owner is irresponsible.

Check with your insurance company to see if the prospective buyer is insured during a test drive. Always ride along during the test drive—thieves have been known to steal cars this way.

## Check Automatic Transmission Fluid    930

Check your car's automatic transmission fluid (ATF) every
month and whenever the transmission isn't shifting smoothly.

### ⊙ Steps

1  Park your car on level ground and start the engine, leaving the gear in
   neutral or park. Wait for the engine to warm up. Unless your owner's
   manual directs otherwise, allow the engine to continue running throughout this procedure.

2  Find the ATF dipstick, located at the back of the engine. The ATF dipstick is often shorter than the engine oil dipstick but otherwise looks
   similar. If you're lucky, it will be labeled.

3  Pull on the dipstick and completely remove it. It may be very long.

4  Wipe the dipstick with a rag, replace it in the engine, push it all the way
   in and remove it again.

5  Look at the dipstick's tip. Observe whether there are two different full
   markings: one for cold readings and one for warm readings. If so, read
   the one for "Warm." If the ATF does not come up to the line marked
   "Full," add ATF.

6  Add ATF (see Tips) into the hole that the dipstick came out of (yes, that
   little tiny hole). Use a funnel with a long, narrow neck. Add only a little at
   a time, and check the level with the dipstick after each time. It's easy to
   add ATF but fairly difficult to take it out if you add too much.

7  Put the dipstick all the way back in when you are done.

### ✳ Tips

There are two types of ATF:
Dexron (also called Mercron) and
Type F; your owner's manual
should list the type to use.

With some cars the engine
should not be running while you
check the fluid, so be sure to
consult your owner's manual.

### ⚠ Warning

ATF doesn't get used up, so if it's
low, that indicates a leak. Don't
ignore leaks or drive around with
low ATF—it can lead to expensive transmission repairs.

### Things You'll Need

❑ rags

❑ automatic transmission fluid

❑ funnel with a long, narrow neck

## Check Brake Fluid    931

While checking your car's fluid levels, be sure to add brake fluid
to the list. It's easy to do and only takes a moment.

### ⊙ Steps

1  Find the brake master cylinder. This is usually located under the hood on
   the driver's side of the car, toward the back of the engine compartment.
   Imagine where your brake pedal would end up if it went all the way
   through to the engine. The brake master cylinder is a small (about 6 by 2
   inches), rectangular piece of metal with a plastic reservoir and a rubber
   cap on top, and small metal tubes leading from it.

2  Check your manual if you aren't sure that you've found the master cylinder. The rubber cap will usually read "Use only DOT 3 or 4 brake fluid
   from a sealed container."

3  Note that on most newer-model cars the reservoir is translucent and you
   can see the fluid level without removing the cap. There will be a "Full"
   line—the brake fluid should be at this line.

4  In older cars (pre-1980) the brake master cylinder reservoir may be made
   entirely of metal so that you must take the top off to check the fluid

### ✳ Tip

If the brake master cylinder is
empty, the brake pedal will go to
the floor. If this is the case, you
will have to bleed the brakes in
addition to adding fluid: Time to
see your mechanic, who will flush
and refill the braking system.

### ⚠ Warning

Brake fluid is very toxic. Keep it
away from hands and eyes, and
avoid spilling it on the ground or
on your car's paint. Dispose of
empty containers carefully.

level. The top is held on by a metal clamp—use a screwdriver to pop off the clamp and lift the lid.

5 Add brake fluid to the Full line. Use the correct brake fluid for your car: Check the rubber cap and your owner's manual to find out what grade of brake fluid your car requires. Most cars use DOT (Department of Transportation) 3 or 4. If the reservoir has two parts, fill both halves.

## Things You'll Need

- ❏ screwdriver
- ❏ brake fluid
- ❏ rags

---

## 932 | Know if Your Car Has a Fluid Leak

Except for gasoline and windshield wiper solution, the fluids in your car shouldn't get used up or go anywhere. If you notice that any are low, there's a good possibility of a leak.

### ◎ Steps

1 Understand that the fluids you may have in your car are gasoline, oil, coolant, brake fluid, windshield washer fluid, gear oil, power steering fluid and automatic transmission fluid. All cars will have at least gas, oil and brake fluid. Air-cooled engines (like old VW bugs) do not have coolant. Your model of car may or may not have power steering or automatic transmission fluid.

2 Open the hood and visually inspect the engine and engine compartment. Many leaks are easily detectable with just a simple look.

3 Note that you don't need to know the name of the fluid that's leaking or the name of the part it's leaking from to be able to find a leak.

4 Inspect underneath the engine and the car with a flashlight. Look for wet areas or drips clinging to the underside of the vehicle's carriage.

5 If you don't see any signs of a leak, lay down a large piece of corrugated cardboard and park your car so that the engine sits over it. With a pen, mark the position of the wheels.

6 Remove the cardboard the following morning. Note the position of any drip marks relative to the wheel markings. This information will help your mechanic diagnose the problem.

### ✱ Tips

Green, sticky fluid is coolant. Bluish, watery liquid is windshield wiper fluid. Honey- or dark-colored, greasy fluid is engine oil. Honey- or dark-colored thick fluid with a chestnut smell is gear oil. Clear or yellowish liquid with a very slippery consistency is brake fluid. Slippery reddish fluid is automatic transmission or power steering fluid.

Gasoline will evaporate when it leaks out and may not leave any residue, but it's easy to smell.

### ⚠ Warning

Ignoring a leak, even if there are no noticeable symptoms, can leave you stranded and/or cost you more in repairs later.

---

## 933 | Change Your Motor Oil

Plan to change your motor oil every 3,000 miles or every three months. However, you may want to do it more often if you've been driving in very hot and/or dusty conditions.

### ◎ Steps

#### Getting Ready

1 Gather the necessary tools and materials. Consult your owner's manual or an automotive-parts specialist to find out the weight of oil and type of oil filter your car needs. If you go to an auto-parts store, first make a note of your car's year, make and model.

### ✱ Tip

Record the date and mileage after you change the oil so you will know when your car is due for another oil change. It helps to put a small sticker on your windshield to remind you.

---

**How to Do** *(Just About)* **Everything**

2  Run the car's engine for 10 minutes before you drain the oil. Warm oil drains faster than cold oil.

3  Park the car on a level surface, engage the parking brake and turn off the engine. If your car has a low ground clearance, raise it by driving it onto a ramp or by jacking it up and supporting it securely. You will need two jack stands to support the front of your car after jacking it up. Never get under a car that is supported only by a jack (see 946 "Jack Up a Car Safely").

4  Open the hood and place the new oil and funnel on top of the engine to ensure that you won't forget to add oil afterward (an expensive mistake that many do-it-yourselfers make).

## Draining the Oil and Changing the Oil Filter

5  Crawl under the car once it is securely supported. Remember to use two jack stands to support the car.

6  Locate the oil drain plug on the underside of the engine, usually near the front center of the car. Consult your owner's manual for the exact spot.

7  Place an oil drain pan under the plug and loosen the plug with a socket wrench. Remember: Turn the wrench counterclockwise to remove the plug. Use the right size wrench or socket—and avoid using an adjustable wrench—or you risk stripping the plug's threads and rounding the plug's hex head.

8  Carefully remove the plug by hand. Be prepared for the rush of warm oil. Wear rubber gloves to remove the plug if it's hot.

9  Let the oil drain into the pan. Hold on to the plug.

10  Reposition the pan, if necessary, to catch all the dripping oil.

11  Wipe off the drain plug and the plug opening with a rag when the oil finishes draining.

12  Reinstall the plug. Begin turning it by hand to prevent cross-threading.

13  Tighten the plug with your socket wrench; be careful not to over-tighten.

14  Locate the oil filter, which is usually on one side of the engine.

15  Position the oil pan underneath the filter to catch any remaining oil.

16  Use an adjustable oil filter wrench to unscrew the oil filter. Be careful when removing this, as it is full of oil.

17  Use a rag to wipe the area where the filter mounts to the engine. Make sure the rubber seal of the old filter is not stuck to the engine.

18  Open a new quart of oil and use some to lightly coat the rubber seal of the new filter.

19  Screw the new filter into place by hand. It's usually not necessary to tighten the oil filter with the oil filter wrench, but have the wrench ready in case your grip's not strong (or large) enough.

## Adding New Oil and Cleaning Up

20  Locate the oil filler cap on top of the engine. Remove it.

21  Place the funnel in the opening and pour in the new oil. Typically, you will use 4 to 5 quarts of oil. Check your owner's manual for the correct amount of oil.

## ⚠ Warnings

Handle hot automotive oil with extreme care.

Use extreme caution when jacking up the car. Make sure the jack stands are completely secure.

On some new vehicles, oil must be changed every three months or the warranty will be invalidated. Check your warranty carefully.

## Things You'll Need

❑ 2 jack stands

❑ 4 to 5 quarts motor oil

❑ small plastic funnel

❑ oil drain pan

❑ socket wrench with appropriate-size sockets

❑ rubber gloves

❑ rags

❑ adjustable oil filter wrench

❑ oil filter

❑ old plastic containers

22 Replace the cap when you're finished.

23 Run the engine for a minute, turn it off, then check the dipstick. Add more oil if necessary.

24 Check the area around the oil drain plug and the filter for leaks. Tighten the plug or oil filter if you find leakage.

25 Use rags and newspapers to wipe away excess oil.

26 Pour the used oil into a plastic container after it cools.

27 Dispose of the used oil and filters at authorized locations: Bring them to either a recycling center or an auto repair shop that can recycle for you. Don't pour oil down a drain.

## 934 | Wash a Car

**The key to a successful car washing is working from top to bottom and doing one side at a time.**

### ◎ Steps

1 Choose a shady spot, preferably away from trees that are dripping sap or dropping leaves.

2 Close all car doors and windows.

3 Put one capful of car soap into a bucket and fill it three-quarters of the way with warm water. Set the bucket aside.

4 Hose any excess dirt off the car, beginning at the roof and working down to the tires.

5 Lather a sponge or terry cloth rag in the bucket of soapy water and sponge the roof of the car. Spray off excess soap when the entire roof has been cleaned.

6 Repeat for all four sides of the car, washing one full side, including the windows, fenders and tires, and rinsing completely before going to the next side.

7 Give the car one final rinse with the hose to get rid of any water spots when all four sides have been washed and rinsed.

8 Take a chamois leather ("shammy") or towel and dry the car thoroughly by setting the towel flat against the car's surface and dragging it along to pick up any water spots. Start at the roof and work your way down to the tires.

9 Wash the windows with a rag soaked in plain water and dry them with a dry rag, or use window cleaner and pieces of wadded-up newspaper on both the inside and the outside of the windows.

10 Give any metal or chrome an extra rubdown to get rid of water spots.

11 Clean the interior if you have time (see 936 "Clean a Car's Interior").

### ✳ Tips

Wear old clothes for this task.

Soap dries fast. Wash one side at a time to keep the soap from drying on your car's paint. Otherwise, you'll have to rewash to get the dried soap off.

Wet and wring out your chamois leather before you dry; it will be more absorbent.

### Things You'll Need

❑ car soap

❑ large bucket

❑ sponge or terry cloth rags

❑ chamois leather or towel

❑ window cleaner and newspaper (optional)

## Wax a Car

Although nothing beats a professional car detailer with an electric buffer, following these steps every few months will protect your car's paint finish and keep it looking great.

### ⊙ Steps

1  Wash and dry your car thoroughly before waxing.

2  Know that some waxes contain abrasives, which can damage clear-coat and lacquer finishes, and may be harmful to dark-colored paint jobs. When in doubt, use a nonabrasive wax.

3  Park the car in a cool, shady spot. If you don't have access to a shady spot, wax one section at a time so the sun doesn't bake the wax onto your car. Avoid waxing if it's very hot or very cold outside.

4  Dip a damp wax sponge into the car wax, getting a half-dollar-size clump on your sponge.

5  Rub the wax onto the car using small circles. Avoid getting wax into seams and jambs—if this happens, use an old, very soft toothbrush to remove it.

6  Working on a section at a time, cover your car's entire surface, remembering the path you took. By the time you have finished, the wax will be ready to remove.

7  Using soft terry cloth towels (or, better yet, cloth diapers), wipe off the wax in the same order in which it was applied.

8  Shake out the towel or cloth as you work, in order to avoid wax buildup and streaking.

9  Leaning as close to the surface of your car as you can, look down the sides and across the front, back and roof to spot any residual wax.

10  Use a cloth diaper or a cheesecloth to polish the car's entire surface.

11  Wash your used towels, cloths and pads with liquid fabric softener to keep them from scratching your car the next time you use them.

### ✱ Tips

Professional car detailers differ on which car wax is best, but many agree that the more expensive carnauba wax is superior to the inexpensive varieties—it seals better, and is easier to apply and buff.

As a rule, the easier the wax is to work with, the more often you'll have to apply it.

Don't leave wax on your car for more than 2 hours or it will be very difficult to remove. Excess wax left on the car can damage the paint, especially if the car is exposed to direct sunlight.

### Things You'll Need

❑ car wax

❑ wax sponge

❑ soft toothbrush

❑ terry cloth towels or cloth diapers

❑ cheesecloth (optional)

## Clean a Car's Interior

You can cut down on the cost of a professional detailing by getting out the vacuum cleaner and a few household products.

### ⊙ Steps

1  Remove the floor mats from the car. Shake them to remove any debris sticking to them.

2  Using the hose attachment, vacuum all seat cushions, paying special attention to the crevices where cushions meet. Be sure to vacuum the bottom and back of the seats. Check beneath seats for coins and trash before vacuuming.

### ✱ Tips

Vacuum the seats first, then the floorboards.

Car-interior and vinyl protectants are made to protect against sun damage and cracking. Carefully read the instructions before use.

3   Vacuum the floor of the car, including the area beneath the seats, still using the hose attachment.

4   Vacuum the floor mats. When finished, give the mats a final shake to remove any remaining debris, then return them to the car.

5   If any fabric seat cushions or carpets are stained, use a damp towel to apply a small amount of carpet shampoo to the stain. Work the carpet shampoo into a light lather.

6   Sponge away the shampoo with a damp sponge and allow to air dry. Don't use carpet shampoo on leather.

7   Clean all the windows using a window cleaner and newspaper.

8   Vacuum or wipe debris from the dashboard and doors.

9   Spray a small amount of car-interior or vinyl protectant on a towel or rag. With the moistened rag, gently wipe the dashboard, door handles and all vinyl parts.

10  Allow to air dry.

### Things You'll Need

- ❏ vacuum cleaner
- ❏ carpet shampoo
- ❏ window cleaner and newspaper
- ❏ car-interior or vinyl protectants
- ❏ rags and towels

## 937 | Remove Bumper Stickers

**You bought a used car and inherited all sorts of fascinating bumper stickers. Here's how you can remove those pesky, sticky proclamations.**

### ⊙ Steps

1   Spray the sticker with a lubricant such as WD-40, and try to peel it off. If this doesn't work, proceed to step 2.

2   Soften the adhesive with heat from a blow dryer.

3   Start to peel off a corner of the sticker while continuing to apply heat, or gently scrape off the sticker with a rubber spatula or a putty knife with its metal blade wrapped in duct tape. Do not use a razor blade; it can scratch paint and bumpers.

4   Wipe the remains of the sticker away with a soft, lint-free rag dampened with rubbing alcohol.

5   Buff the bumper or panel with a polishing compound and a fresh coat of wax to complete the job.

### Things You'll Need

- ❏ lubricant
- ❏ blow dryer
- ❏ rubber spatula or putty knife (wrapped in duct tape)
- ❏ rubbing alcohol
- ❏ car polish
- ❏ rags

## Replace Windshield Wiper Blades `938`

Windshield wiper blades are usually packaged with the rubber wiper as well as its support structure. Follow these steps to replace this entire piece, referred to here as the "wiper blade."

### ⊙ Steps

1  Look up your vehicle's make and model in the reference books where wiper blades are sold. This reference will provide you with the correct model of blade to purchase.

2  Open the package containing the new windshield wiper blade. The package should include up to three or four different styles of blade attachment—the small plastic piece that secures the new blade to the wiper arm.

3  Examine the existing attachment (where the arm and the blade meet), then find a new one in your package that matches it.

4  Grasp the windshield wiper arm and pull up, away from the car. The blade and arm should now be sticking out perpendicular to the window.

5  Remove the windshield wiper blade from the arm at the attachment. There will usually be a small tab you can depress with a screwdriver that will allow you to pull the blade from the arm. Some attachments have a small metal bump and two tabs on either side; you depress the tabs and pull hard to remove the blade. Some just snap onto the blade.

6  Remove the old attachment from the wiper blade and replace it with the new one.

7  Install the blade onto the windshield wiper arm.

8  Test by turning on the wipers. If the blades slip, turn off the wipers and seat the attachments more firmly.

### ✱ Tips

Replace your wiper blades when they are no longer clearing the windshield efficiently under normal rainy conditions.

Changing wiper blades for the first time has been known to cause extreme frustration. Relax—when you've done it once, you'll be able to do it again in a matter of minutes.

### ⚠ Warning

Do not let the windshield wiper arm snap back against the windshield when there is no blade attached, for this can crack the windshield.

## Replace a Tail, Brake or Reverse Light `939`

Replacing a dead bulb on your car is almost as easy as replacing a light bulb at home. Perform this simple maintenance and avoid the hassle of receiving a citation for a missing brake light.

### ⊙ Steps

1  Determine how the bulb is accessed: On some models the lens (the red or white plastic part over the light) must be unscrewed from the outside, and on others the bulb is accessible only from inside the trunk. If there are no screws on the lens, you can assume that the bulb must be replaced from inside. Usually there will be a plastic cover that must be removed in order to access the bulb; there may be tabs, screws or small knobs that hold this plastic cover in place.

2  Unscrew the lens on the outside, or take off the plastic cover from inside the trunk, to reveal the bulb.

3  Unscrew the bulb. You'll have to push in and turn at the same time.

### ⚠ Warning

The police can stop you for burned-out bulbs and give you a "fix-it" ticket, whereby you have a certain amount of time to fix the light. Afterward, you must drive to the police station to prove you've fixed the light in order to have the ticket cleared (the police officer who issues the citation will explain exactly what you need to do). You'll still have to pay a processing fee of

4   Take the bulb with you to the store to help you find an exact duplicate.

5   Clean the connection with a wire brush and/or wipe it clean with a rag if there's any corrosion.

6   Screw the new bulb into the empty socket. Again, you'll have to push in and turn simultaneously. Line up the tiny raised bumps on the base of the bulb in order to screw it in.

7   Replace the lens or the plastic cover.

8   Test your work by stepping on the brakes and turning on the headlights while a friend watches the new bulb to make sure it lights up.

around $10 to $15, but you'll have to pay a much larger fine if you don't fix the light in time. It's easier just to replace the bulb as soon as you see it's burned out.

---

## 940 | Spend Less on Gas

With the high price of gasoline, why spend more than you have to? Here are a few simple tips to help you save money.

### ⊙ Steps

1   Check to make sure you're not carrying any extra weight or unneeded items in the trunk or backseat of your car.

2   Use cruise control (if you have it) on the highway.

3   Turn off the engine instead of idling when you plan to be waiting for more than 3 or 4 minutes.

4   Avoid jackrabbit starts and speeding from one stop sign to the next. Accelerate slowly.

5   Use only high-octane gasoline (the expensive one at the pump) if your engine is pinging. Pinging is a rattling-type noise from the engine, mostly heard on acceleration and when driving uphill.

6   Keep all the tires properly inflated. The recommended tire pressure is listed in the vehicle's manual, stamped on the side of the tire, and often on a sticker on the driver's-side doorjamb. When in doubt, 32 pounds per square inch (psi) is a good average until other sources can be consulted. Low air pressure will cause bad gas mileage.

7   Follow a maintenance schedule. Most cars need a tune-up every year or 30,000 miles, whichever comes first. Older cars need to be serviced more frequently. A car in need of a tune-up may exhibit poor gas mileage as a symptom.

8   Change the air filter every 15,000 miles.

9   Drive just 55 mph on the highway if traffic allows you to do this safely. The faster you drive, the more gas your car will use.

10  Shut off the air conditioner when you don't absolutely need it.

11  Keep the clutch properly adjusted. A slipping clutch uses extra fuel.

### ✳ Tip

Pay attention to how much gasoline your car is using. Some problems manifest only as poor gas mileage without any noticeable drivability symptoms. See your mechanic if you notice any big changes in gas mileage.

# ✓ 941 Maintain Your Car Regularly

You can greatly extend the life of your car if you keep up with the checks recommended by the automaker and your mechanic. Use this calendar as a guide. It assumes that you drive 15,000 miles a year; if you drive more miles or on rough and dusty roads, perform these checks and services more frequently.

### Once a month

- Check oil, coolant, brake fluid and power steering fluid levels.
- Check the clutch reservoir and add brake fluid if low.
- Check the automatic transmission fluid.
- Check the windshield washer fluid reservoir.
- Check the belts for proper tension, cracks and age.
- Check the hoses for leakage, cracks or other signs of age.
- Visually inspect the engine for any leaks.
- Look under the car for any indication of leaks from the engine.
- Check the tire pressure on all the tires.
- Check the tire pressure in the spare tire.
- Visually inspect the tires for uneven wear, nails or other sharp objects lodged in the tread.
- Check the dashlights for proper operation.
- Start the engine and listen with the hood up. After doing this a few times, you will learn what sounds "normal" for your car.

### Once a year (in fall)

- Schedule a 30,000-mile full service, if due.
- Flush the cooling system and replace the coolant.
- Replace the windshield wiper blades.
- Have the battery serviced and load-tested to check its ability to hold a charge. If it is more than 4½ years old, replace it.
- Check the tire pressure for all four tires and the spare.
- Check the lights, heater and defroster.
- Remind yourself to keep the gas tank as full as possible to prevent moisture from freezing in the gas lines.
- Get a brake check.
- Check the fluids under the hood and replenish as necessary. Change the oil and oil filter if it's been 3,000 miles since the last oil change.
- Assemble an emergency winter kit for the trunk: blanket, extra boots and gloves, ice scraper, small shovel, flashlight and kitty litter (for traction when stuck in snow).
- Replace the air filter.

### Every two years

- Replace the fuel filter.
- Change the spark plugs (unless they're platinum, in which case you have 30,000 more miles to go). Also replace spark plug wires as needed.
- Replace the distributor cap and rotor if your car has them.
- Change the points and condenser if your car was built before 1978.
- Check the ignition timing and adjust as needed.
- Adjust the valves as needed (unless your car has hydraulic valves). Replace the valve-cover gasket, especially if you see oil on top of your engine.
- Check the belts. Replace if worn.
- Adjust the clutch if you have a stick shift.
- Service the battery.
- Replace the PCV (positive crankcase ventilation) valve.

calendar

## 942 | Keep Your Battery Alive

A little maintenance will keep your battery charged through the cold months as well as the warmer ones.

### ⊙ Steps

1 Estimate the age of your battery. If it's more than four years old, replace it.

2 Ask your mechanic to perform a "load test" on your battery. This tests whether the battery is capable of generating sufficient charge on below-freezing days. If it fails the test, replace the battery.

3 Clean the battery terminals if they are encrusted with deposits. Use a wire brush dipped in baking soda and water to clean them of corrosion and ensure that the deposits do not block the flow of electrical current.

4 Check to make sure the water level in the battery hasn't dropped. You can do this on conventional batteries by popping off the plastic cover and checking to see that the water inside reaches the plastic filler necks. Add distilled water if necessary. Maintenance-free batteries, however, generally have an indicator light that goes black when the battery needs service; take these types to a mechanic for service.

5 Check the tightness of the battery cable ends. A loose battery connection can prevent your car from starting and acts just like a dead battery. If you can move the battery cable ends that are attached to the battery terminals at all, they are too loose.

6 Check that the battery is securely fastened in the battery tray. A loose battery that is allowed to shift around can cause damage if it is able to tip over under the hood. Excessive vibration will also shorten the life of your battery.

7 Consider investing in an engine or battery heater if you live in an especially cold climate; the heater can reduce the power that's needed to start your car.

### ✳ Tips

In severe cases, the battery may need to be recharged with a battery charger to bring it back to life.

Your car may not be starting because other components in the charging system are failing, or because of a bad starter motor.

### ⚠ Warnings

Recharging your battery improperly may fry it and other electrical accessories in your car, so it needs to be done slowly.

Keep open flames away from your battery—the chemicals inside it are combustible.

Battery acid is highly corrosive. When adding distilled water to the battery, take care that acid doesn't splatter on your skin or clothes.

### Things You'll Need

☐ baking soda

☐ wire brush

## 943 | Interpret Tire Wear

Tire wear can tell you what's going on with your car's steering, suspension and tire pressure. Regular checks can also help you prevent flat tires or a dangerous blowout.

### ⊙ Steps

1 Check your tires outdoors where the lighting is good. Visually inspect all four tires.

2 Remember that under normal driving conditions, all four tires should wear evenly.

3 Check for even tread wear by using a tread-depth gauge, which costs less than $20. The depth of the tread (the grooves in the tire) should be even on all parts of the tire. Another way to check for tire wear (although not as accurate) is to stick a penny into the grooves, with Lincoln's head

### ✳ Tips

On average, tires need to be replaced every 40,000 miles, but the exact mileage depends on the type of tire and car and what kind of driving you do.

Have an automotive professional examine your tires if you're not sure they need replacing. For an unbiased opinion, consider getting this done at a shop that does not sell tires.

pointing into the tire. If you can see the top of his head, it's time to buy new tires.

4 Let some air out of your tires if there is wear down the middle and not on the sides. It means there's too much air in them.

5 Add air to tires with wear on both the inside and outside edges, which means there's not enough air in them.

6 Bring your car to an alignment shop for a front-end or four-wheel alignment if your tires are worn on one side or the other.

7 Run your hand lightly over the tread surface of each tire. If the treads feel bumpy or scalloped, even if the tread is still deep, you may need new shock absorbers or struts. (Some cars have shocks, some have struts and some have a combination—struts in front, shocks in back.)

8 Check the tire pressure in all four tires and the spare tire at least once a month. The recommended tire pressure is listed in your vehicle's manual, stamped on the side of the tire, and often printed on a sticker on the driver's-side doorjamb. When in doubt, 32 pounds per square inch (psi) is a good average until other sources can be consulted.

Get a front-end or four-wheel alignment if you are in an accident, even just a fender bender. If anything is out of alignment, it will affect your tires' wear.

## ⚠ Warning

Driving on tires that are bald or badly worn greatly increases your chance of getting a flat or a blowout and is especially dangerous when the roads are wet or slick. Don't put off buying new tires when you need them—your safety is at stake!

## Things You'll Need

❑ tread-depth gauge

❑ tire-pressure gauge

---

## Buy Car Tires                                    944

Here's how to properly re-outfit your set of wheels.

### ◉ Steps

1 Think about how and where you drive. Tire engineers design product lines for specific results, such as a cushy ride, durability, sporty handling, or traction in rain and snow. But choosing one virtue usually means giving up a little of the others.

2 Consider an all-season tire. It's a reasonable compromise for most drivers—that's why automakers usually provide all-season tires as original equipment on new cars.

3 Know your current tire. In general, it's best to replace your tires with those of the same brand, design and size, all of which you'll find printed on your tires. Look for the "P" (passenger vehicle) followed by the tire's width in millimeters; its height, shown as a ratio of its actual height to its width; "R" for radial; and the last number, which is the diameter of the wheel the tire fits.

4 Decide where to buy your new tires. In addition to car dealerships, tire stores and gas stations, they can now also be bought at discount stores or ordered over the phone or the Internet. Prices and service vary, so shop around if you can.

5 Have a mechanic or tire dealer perform the installation. Special machines are needed to slip your new tires over the car's wheels.

6 Keep tire wear even by rotating your tires as the manufacturer suggests—new cars are sensitive to tires with differing degrees of wear. Keeping tire wear even means your tires will all need replacing at the same time, so monitor tread depth to help you budget ahead for the expense.

### ✽ Tip

If you buy your tires from a tire center, make sure the price quoted includes installation as well as wheel balancing. Also be aware that getting new tires doesn't necessarily mean that you need a wheel alignment, which some tire dealers will offer as part of a purchase package. Check the uniformity of wear on your current tires to judge for yourself (see 943 "Interpret Tire Wear").

## 945 | Change a Flat Tire

If you drive a car, you should know how to change a flat, whether or not you have a cell phone and roadside service.

### ⊙ Steps

1   Put the car in park in a level area and apply the parking brake. Place manual transmission cars in gear. Make sure you have pulled off the road. Turn the engine off and put on the hazard lights. You may want to open the hood to indicate to other drivers that you are stopped for repairs.

2   Place a wheel chock or a large rock behind (if facing uphill) or in front (if facing downhill) the diagonally opposing wheel to prevent the car from rolling. Do this even on a slight incline. Get out the spare, a lug nut wrench (tire iron) and the car jack.

3   Remove the hubcap, if necessary.

4   Loosen the lug nuts, which hold the wheel in place, before jacking up the car: Place one end of the lug nut wrench over a lug nut. Use a hollow pipe (about 2 feet in length) for leverage by slipping it over the end of the lug nut wrench. Turn the wrench counterclockwise to loosen the lug nut. Loosen the lug nuts in a star pattern—first loosen one a few turns, then loosen the one opposite. Work across the tire until all the lug nuts are loose and unscrewed slightly.

5   Carefully jack up the car (see 946 "Jack Up a Car Safely"). Check your owner's manual for the correct and safe place to put the jack. Jack the car up a little higher than is necessary to remove the old tire so there is room to put the new, full tire on.

6   Remove the lug nuts all the way and set them aside in a place where you won't lose them and they won't roll away. The flat tire should be hanging from the threaded studs now.

7   Remove the flat tire and set it aside.

8   Lift the new tire onto the wheel studs. If you're confused about which is the right way to put the new tire on, check for the valve where you add air—it always faces out.

9   Replace the lug nuts. Tighten them the same way you loosened them: Give each nut a few turns, first one, then the one opposite, working around the wheel in a star pattern. Try not to tighten adjacent nuts consecutively.

10   Slowly lower the jack and remove it.

11   Tighten the lug nuts again—as much as you can.

12   Put the hubcap back on.

### ✱ Tips

To avoid back strain, use your knees when pulling on the wrench and pipe. To avoid bruised knuckles, pull rather than push when removing lug nuts.

If a lug nut sticks, squirt lubricant around its base and wait a moment, then try again.

Check out all your tire-changing equipment at home before you need it on the road.

Many people's spares are flat. Check yours once a month. Temporary spares (the small ones marked with a "T") require 60 psi (pounds per square inch); regular-sized spares should be inflated to match the other four tires' psi.

### ⚠ Warnings

Cars can slip off jacks. Never get under a car with only a tire-changing jack holding it up—put a jack stand in place first.

Mind your hands when you remove a flat. Strands of steel sticking out of the back of a bald tire can cut you.

### Things You'll Need

❑ wheel chock

❑ spare tire

❑ lug nut wrench

❑ car jack

❑ hollow pipe

❑ lubricant

## Jack Up a Car Safely

Everyone should know how to use the jack that comes with the car. Try this at home so that if you ever get a flat, you won't have to learn by the side of the road.

### ⊙ Steps

1 Park the car on level ground and engage the parking brake. Leave manual transmission cars in first gear or reverse and put automatics in park.

2 Place a chock or a brick behind or in front of (depending on the road's incline) the wheel diagonally opposite one being jacked up.

3 Place the jack under the car's frame nearest the wheel to be jacked up. There's a thin lip that runs along the side of your car—this is where the jack should go. Your owner's manual will have a picture of the safest place to put the jack. Bumper jacks will attach to slots in the front or rear bumper (on older cars).

4 When the jack is in place, insert the handle according to the directions on the jack, and turn or ratchet the handle to make the jack rise. If it lowers or cannot turn, rotate the handle the other way, or flip the switch marked "R" and "L" (for "raise" and "lower").

5 Raise the jack high enough to either replace a flat tire or place the car on a jack stand (a sturdy temporary stand at a fixed height). If you're changing a flat, remember to leave extra room—the new tire will be full of air.

6 Lower the jack when you're finished. Be cautious and go slowly. If you've used a jack stand, before lowering the jack you will need to raise the car slightly to pull the stand from its place.

#### ✹ Tip
Make sure everyone is out of the car before jacking it up.

#### ⚠ Warnings
Never get under a car that's supported only by a jack. Use jack stands if the car will be off the ground for any length of time, if you plan to get underneath it, or if you'll be working on the car.

Don't jack up a car unless you're on a very firm surface. Soft shoulders or very hot, soft asphalt may not support the jack.

#### Things You'll Need
❏ wheel chock
❏ car jack
❏ jack stands

## Fix a Scratch on a Car

Small scratches can be fixed with touch-up paint. Larger ones may require the use of paint sprayers and professional help.

### ⊙ Steps

1 Determine whether your car's paint is enameled (see the Warning); if it isn't, proceed.

2 Obtain body compound and primer paint. Primer is usually in spray-can form, comes in several colors and is generally labeled for automobile use. It's best to pick a light primer color that your touch-up paint will cover easily in one coat.

3 Wash the scratch and surrounding area with a mild laundry detergent. This removes any wax or coatings that would otherwise affect the new paint you'll apply.

4 Sand along the scratch with fine-grained sandpaper, being sure to sand away any rust that has accumulated.

5 Blow away all dust from the sanding, or use a soft brush.

6 Use masking tape and newspaper to isolate the scratch, leaving about a half-inch of working room around the scratch.

#### ✹ Tip
If your car has a very long scratch—across the hood or along an entire door—it may look better if you have the entire panel repainted in a paint shop.

#### ⚠ Warning
Some newer-vehicle paint jobs are enameled and will not mix well with lacquer-based primer paint. It's always best to provide your car's VIN to an auto-parts store and seek advice before proceeding.

7   Using a putty knife, apply body compound to a scratch that cuts deep into the metal. The knife should be made of plastic to avoid adding more scratches.

8   Let the body compound harden according to label instructions.

9   Sand the body compound flat.

10  Blow or brush away all dust.

11  Spray a small amount of primer paint to cover the scratch. Let the area dry overnight.

12  Identify the touch-up paint color you need by first checking your vehicle identification number (VIN), which is stamped into a small metal plate located on the dashboard on the driver's side.

13  Provide this number to an auto-parts store or an online site selling small bottles of touch-up paint. The VIN describes your car right down to its particular shade of paint, so matching your color is a breeze.

14  Use the touch-up's applicator brush to paint the primed area.

15  Let dry overnight.

### Things You'll Need

☐ primer paint

☐ mild laundry detergent

☐ fine-grained sandpaper

☐ soft brush (optional)

☐ plastic putty knife

☐ body compound

☐ touch-up paint

## 948 | Find a Good Mechanic

Finding a car-repair shop is like choosing any other small business. Look for quality, value and service.

### ◎ Steps

1   Ask trusted friends for recommendations.

2   Talk to people who have cars similar to yours, if you are new to an area.

3   Make sure the mechanic you've chosen services your type of car. Look around the shop and see what kinds of cars are being worked on.

4   Call the Better Business Bureau to check whether the shop has any complaints on file.

5   Check whether the shop is accredited by the American Automobile Association (AAA).

6   Ask whether the shop's mechanics are certified by the National Institute for Automotive Service Excellence (ASE).

7   Check the warranty on the repair work before leaving the car at the shop. Six months is great; 90 days is good; 30 days is a little suspect. Find out whether the warranty covers both parts and labor.

8   Ask for a full explanation of what is going to be done to the car.

9   Find out what the shop's hours are. Will it be open when you get off work? Is the shop near the bus or train? Will you get a loaner while your car is being worked on?

### ✳ Tips

Don't wait until your car needs major repairs or a tow to find a good mechanic. Bring your car into the shop for small stuff like oil changes and brake checks to get a feel for the place and develop a relationship.

Don't choose a shop based solely on price. The least expensive repair shop might not be the best place to take your car. At the same time, the most expensive shop (usually the dealership) may not give you the best service or quality.

# Deal With a Bad Repair

A bad repair isn't always the result of ill intent. Sometimes it's just an honest mistake. Give the mechanic the benefit of the doubt, but stand your ground.

## ◉ Steps

1 Ask the mechanic for a list of what was fixed and how before you leave the garage.

2 Go on a test drive before paying for major repairs.

3 Check the warranty on the work before you leave. Find out if it covers both parts and labor. It should be for at least 90 days; six months is even better.

4 Bring the car back to the garage immediately if things are still not right after you leave.

5 Ask to speak to the same mechanic who worked on the car. Explain the problem calmly: "I just went a mile from the shop and the brakes are still squealing. Something is still wrong."

6 Offer to take a ride in the car with the mechanic.

7 Request new replacement parts if new parts have been installed. Ideally, you should ask for the old parts back before the job is started; if you ask afterward, they might not be available.

8 Ask to speak to the shop manager if the mechanic will not check the problem immediately.

9 Tell the shop manager, as specifically as you can, the problem with the car. Say that you need the car fixed immediately. Remain calm. Assume that the manager will right the problem. Tell him or her that you know the shop's reputation is on the line and are sure he or she will want to take care of this "comeback" (mechanics' lingo for a car not fixed properly) right away.

10 Inform the manager that you are canceling the repair payment if he or she has refused to admit the car immediately. Leave the shop.

11 Consider going to another shop for a second opinion. However, be aware that if you choose to go to another shop, the original shop may not honor the repair warranty, while the second shop may not want to deal with the problem if someone else has already done work on the car.

12 Contact the Better Business Bureau and/or the state agency that regulates auto repair in your state if your problem is still not resolved. (For example, in California the Bureau of Automotive Repair regulates all repair shops and will send out a mediator to help resolve disputes.) The state attorney general's office can direct you to the proper agency in your state.

## ✱ Tips

Describe the problem as precisely as you can. "The steering is still too loose" is better than "Something's still not right."

Getting angry will not get you what you want. Be reasonable, and the mechanic probably will be also.

Don't leave the garage until you get what you want or are convinced that you will never get what you want and must cancel your payment.

Any guarantee that has been made and advertised must be honored by the mechanic.

## ⚠ Warnings

Don't anger anyone who still has your car or keys.

In most states, a garage has the right to withhold your car until the repair charges are paid, especially if the charges are in dispute between the mechanic and the vehicle's owner.

# ✓ 950 Diagnose Car Trouble

If your car is giving you trouble, you may save time and money if you can accurately describe the problem to your mechanic. You may even be able to solve some problems yourself. Here is a guide to the signs of common automotive disorders.

checklist

## Brake problem

☐ Is the brake light on? Check the brake fluid.

☐ Is there a scraping or squealing noise that goes away when you step on the brake? The brake pads are worn.

☐ Do you hear a grinding, metal-against-metal sound when braking? Your brake pads or shoes are completely worn away.

☐ Does the brake pedal feel soft, or get harder and higher when you pump it? There may be air bubbles in the brake lines.

☐ Does the brake pedal slowly sink? You could need a new master cylinder.

☐ Does the car pull to one side when you brake? You may have insufficient hydraulic pressure, or one brake may be sticking.

## Manual transmission problem

☐ Can you feel more than about 1 inch of free play (or slack) when you first put your foot lightly on the clutch pedal? If so, your clutch needs adjusting.

☐ Does the engine sound like it's revving when you accelerate or start moving from a stop? The clutch may be worn.

☐ Does the clutch pedal feel stiff and require more force to depress it? You may need to replace the clutch cable.

☐ With the engine running in fourth gear, the hand brake set and the clutch pedal depressed, can you slowly let up on the clutch while stepping on the gas pedal? If you are able to completely release the clutch pedal without the engine stalling (or the car moving), you need a new clutch.

## Overheating car

☐ Is the coolant level low at the radiator overflow/plastic coolant reservoir tank? Add more coolant if necessary.

☐ When the engine is cold, uncap the radiator and look inside. Is it empty? If so, fill with antifreeze or water and replace the cap.

☐ Do you see greenish, slippery, sweet-smelling fluid around the radiator and under the car? Inspect the radiator and hoses for a coolant leak.

☐ Are the lower and upper radiator hoses securely clamped to the radiator and leak-free? If not, tighten and replace.

☐ Is a fan belt loose or an electric fan mal-functioning? Either can cause overheating.

☐ Is the water pump belt loose or the pump broken? These can cause overheating.

## Alignment problem

☐ Rest your hands very lightly on the steering wheel while driving. Does the car go in a straight line without drifting?

☐ If the car drifts, look for uneven tire wear. Is the tread worn unevenly on one side (inner or outer)? If so, you probably need an alignment adjustment. Is it worn straight down the middle? Over-inflation is the cause. Is there wear down both the inside and outside? The cause is underinflation. Add air to tires as needed. Test-drive again to see if the car still drifts.

☐ Pay special attention to your car's align-ment after an accident. Even a minor fender-bender can cause problems.

☐ Though most cars typically require only a front-wheel alignment, some cars require four-wheel alignment (front and back).

# Drive a Car With a Manual Transmission                951

Learning to drive a car with a manual transmission isn't easy for most people, but with practice it becomes second nature.

## ⊙ Steps

1  Look at the floorboard; you'll see three pedals. From left to right, they are: clutch, brake, gas.

2  Study the simple diagram on the top of the gearshift, which will show you where the gears are. In most new cars, this will look like a three-legged H. First, third and fifth gears are at the tops of the legs; second, fourth and reverse gears are at the bottoms. The crossbar of the H is neutral.

3  Make sure the parking brake is engaged and the car is on a flat surface in an area where you have plenty of room.

4  Press down on the clutch pedal and then move the gearshift into the neutral position.

5  Start the car.

6  Keeping the clutch pedal down, put the car into first gear by moving the gearshift to the top-left position.

7  Apply the foot brake and release the parking brake.

8  Release the foot brake when you're ready to start moving.

9  Begin to release the clutch pedal slowly; when you hear or feel the engine begin to slow down, slowly press down on the gas pedal as you continue to release the clutch. The car will start to move forward.

10  Accelerate until the car has reached about 3,000 rpm, then take your foot off the gas, press down on the clutch pedal, and pull the gearshift directly down through neutral to second gear. Be sure to pull the gearshift down until it can't go any farther.

11  Release the clutch pedal gently, simultaneously pressing down gently on the gas pedal.

12  Repeat the shifting process each time you hit 3,000 rpm until you're driving at the appropriate speed. (Third gear is up and to the right; fourth gear is all the way down from there; fifth gear is up to neutral, right and then up again.)

13  Downshift by releasing the gas pedal when you want to decrease your speed. Press down on the clutch and move the gearshift through neutral into the next-lower gear (move down only one gear at a time). Once you're in the lower gear, release the clutch slowly and brake as you do so.

14  Stop the car by downshifting to second gear and applying the brakes. Apply the clutch just before the car stops. Don't downshift into first.

15  Drive in reverse by following the same steps you would for starting in first gear. The reverse gear engages more quickly than first gear, however, so be sure to release the clutch slowly and begin to press the gas pedal as soon as the car begins to move.

## ✱ Tips

Find a patient and knowledge-able friend to accompany you on your first attempt at driving a stick-shift car, and drive to a large, empty parking lot where you can practice safely.

When you park your car, leave it in gear and set the parking brake. That way, it won't start rolling if you're parked on an incline, or when you put it in neutral to start it again.

You'll know you're in the right gear for your speed if the engine is running smoothly. If it's cough-ing and sputtering, shift to a lower gear. If the engine noise pitch is too high, shift to the next-higher gear.

## ⚠ Warning

Repeated jerking, stalling, grind-ing, lurching and similar mishaps can wear on the clutch assembly. Be kind to your car—ask for help if you're having difficulty learning.

## 952 | Parallel Park

Practice with no obstacles first, then with plenty of space between vehicles. Take it slowly and you'll develop the skill and confidence to parallel park.

### ⊙ Steps

1   Use your turn signal to indicate the direction of the parking spot.

2   If the space is not yet vacant but the car in it is about to leave, wait behind the spot.

3   When the space is vacant, pull ahead of it until you have pulled up beside the car parked in front of the space. Your rear bumper should be even with that car's rear bumper with about 2 feet of road between you.

4   Put the car in reverse. Begin to back up slowly; as soon as the car starts moving, turn the wheel as far as it will go toward the curb.

5   Back slowly into the space.

6   When the back of your car's front door is even with the rear bumper of the car beside you, begin turning the wheel away from the curb.

7   Continue turning the wheel away from the curb and backing slowly into the space.

8   Straighten out the wheel, then pull forward or back in the space as needed to center yourself between the cars in front of and behind you. Your car should be 6 to 8 inches from the curb when you are parked.

### ✳ Tips

Go slowly.

If you aren't sure whether you'll fit in the space, pull up beside it and size it up first.

If it's a tight fit, get a passenger or a pedestrian to guide you.

### ⚠ Warning

Many cities will issue a citation for vehicles parked more than 18 inches from the curb.

## 953 | Jump-Start a Car

Knowing how to jump-start a car with a dead battery can keep an inconvenience from becoming a crisis. If you are unsure about how to use jumper cables, ask for help.

### ⊙ Steps

1   Read your owner's manual, as it will describe any peculiarities involved in jump-starting your vehicle.

2   Pull a car with a charged battery next to the car with the dead battery, situating the two batteries as close together as you can without allowing the two cars to touch.

3   Turn off both engines, pull out the keys, put both cars in park (or in first gear if they have stick shifts), engage the emergency brakes and open the hoods.

4   Attach a red-handled/positive jumper cable clamp to the positive terminal (the one with the plus sign) of the charged battery.

5   Connect the other red-handled clamp to the positive terminal of the dead battery.

6   Attach the neighboring black/negative cable to the car with the dead battery. Clamp it somewhere where the current can ground out, such as

### ✳ Tip

Some new cars have special jump-start lugs for batteries that are otherwise inaccessible. Your owner's manual will describe these.

### ⚠ Warnings

The voltage from a car battery is dangerous whether or not the engine is running. Do not touch the metal ends of the jumper cables with your hands, nor touch them to each other.

Many people jump-start a battery from a car with the engine running. However, it is safer to shut the engines off.

How to Do *(Just About)* Everything

a bolt or bracket on the engine. You can also attach it to any metal, unpainted part of the vehicle's frame.

7 Ground the other black/negative cable on the charging car, as described in the previous step. Be careful, as a small spark may be produced.

8 Attempt to start the car that has the dead battery.

9 Readjust the red/positive clamp on the dead car if there is no response; try reclamping it to the terminal or turning it for a better connection. Keep trying to start the dead car.

10 Once the dead car is running, remove the clamps one at a time in reverse order.

11 Allow the jump-started car to run for half an hour in order to charge the battery. It will charge whether driving or idling.

Be sure to remove and attach clamps one at a time to reduce the risk of shock. One trick is to work with one hand behind your back so that you don't inadvertently clasp both clamps at the same time.

## Create an Emergency Road Kit                                954

Having an emergency road kit may mean the difference between sitting at the side of the highway waiting for a tow truck and being able to make your way to your destination.

### ⊙ Steps

1 Get a cardboard or plastic box to keep everything in so it doesn't roll around in the trunk.

2 Buy or cull together a first aid kit (see 756 "Stock an Emergency Supply of Medicine and First Aid").

3 Sign up with a roadside emergency service, such as the American Automobile Association.

4 Gather all the necessary equipment to change a tire: working jack, spare tire (fully inflated), lug nut wrench, pipe for leverage (see 945 "Change a Flat Tire"). Most of this should already be stored in its designated place in the car's trunk or hatchback, so leave them where they are to conserve room in your box.

5 Include a flashlight with fresh batteries and triangle reflectors (or flares).

6 Purchase all the necessary fluids: 2 quarts of oil, brake fluid, power-steering fluid (if applicable), automatic transmission fluid (if applicable), and a gallon each of water and antifreeze. Add rags and a funnel.

7 Add flat and Phillips-head screwdrivers, pliers, an adjustable wrench (only to be used in an emergency—adjustable wrenches can easily round bolt heads) and jumper cables (at least 8 feet long).

8 Toss in work gloves or latex gloves, duct tape, a blanket and spare fuses. If you have the room, go ahead and make yourself a disaster kit, too, including bottled drinking water, emergency food, matches, radio, walking shoes and extra clothing.

9 Consider some optional items: a Swiss Army knife, a good book, a credit card, a pillow, a bathing suit, tasty snacks, a beach chair, clean underwear.

### Things You'll Need

- ❑ box
- ❑ first aid kit
- ❑ jack
- ❑ spare tire
- ❑ lug nut wrench and pipe
- ❑ flashlight and batteries
- ❑ reflectors or flares
- ❑ fluids (such as oil and brake fluid)
- ❑ water
- ❑ rags and funnel
- ❑ screwdrivers, pliers and wrenches
- ❑ jumper cable
- ❑ gloves
- ❑ duct tape
- ❑ blanket
- ❑ spare fuses
- ❑ disaster kit

## 955 | Buckle Up a Small Child

Traffic accidents are a leading cause of death for children. Take extra care in choosing and installing a child safety seat, and follow these guidelines from the National Highway Traffic Safety Administration (NHTSA).

### ⊙ Steps

1 Be sure that your car has a seatbelt (lap belt and shoulder belt) for every child you will be transporting.

2 Read the instructions for your vehicle's seatbelt system, as well as those for child safety seats and booster seats, for proper installation and use.

3 Install a rear-facing infant seat in the back seat for children under 1 year old who weigh less than 20 lbs. Children of this age who weigh over 20 lbs should be secured in a seat approved for heavier infants.

4 Install a toddler seat for children who are at least 1 year old and weigh less than 40 pounds.

5 Set up a booster seat for children who are 4 to 8 years old and weigh between 35 and 80 pounds (or are at least 35 inches tall). A booster seat raises the child so that the vehicle's lap and shoulder belts will fit him or her snugly.

6 Children under 12, whether in a safety seat or not, should be put in the back seat of the vehicle and properly restrained, using both the lap belt and the shoulder belt.

7 Move the front seat as far away from the dashboard as possible if the car has no back seat, and restrain the child as appropriate to his or her weight, height and age.

8 Even after careful installation, check each time you buckle up to make sure that straps are not twisted, buckles are fully locked and your child is restrained securely.

### ✽ Tips

If your vehicle has only lap belts, you can have shoulder belts installed by a dealer or repair facility.

You can have airbag switches installed, which allow you to turn off airbags when you have children in the car. To have this done, you'll need to fill out an authorization form with the NHTSA.

### ⚠ Warnings

Children should be placed in the back seat away from air bags, which can cause injury or death.

If you are not sure what safety equipment to use for your child, consult your pediatrician.

### Things You'll Need

- ❑ rear-facing infant seat
- ❑ toddler seat
- ❑ booster seat

---

## 956 | Remove Ice From Your Windshield

You walk outside to discover a sheet of ice blanketing your windshield, and you're already late for work. Here's how to clear things up quickly and get on your way.

### ⊙ Steps

1 Start your car's engine.

2 Turn the heat level to high and the defroster fan level to low. This low setting is extremely important—you don't want to crack the windshield by heating it too quickly.

3 Apply a deicing solution to your windshield, using a spray bottle. Home remedies include the following mixtures: 50 percent water and 50 percent ethyl alcohol, or 50 percent water and 50 percent vinegar.

### ✽ Tip

Leave windshield wipers in midsweep when you park your car at night, and it'll be easier to remove ice the next day.

### ⚠ Warning

Don't use hot water to melt the ice—it can crack the glass.

4  Scrape the ice from your windshield, using shallow downward strokes to avoid scratching the glass. A plastic spatula or credit card can do the trick if you don't have an ice scraper.

5  Work your way to the center of the windshield. If the ice coating is particularly thick, start by scratching a small square in one corner and then work your way across the windshield.

**Things You'll Need**

❑ deicing solution (or ethyl alcohol or vinegar)

❑ ice scraper, plastic spatula or credit card

---

## Drive Safely in Winter Conditions
957

Winter driving can be tough on cars and their owners. Yet motorists can survive the most difficult circumstances by taking these measures.

⊙ **Steps**

1  Make certain your battery is holding an adequate charge, since batteries are less efficient—and engines more demanding—in cold conditions. Your mechanic can use a meter called a "load tester" to simulate the effects of cold-weather starting and determine whether the battery is adequately charged.

2  Be sure your tires are adequate for whatever climate you live in. For most regions, all-season tires with plenty of tread are adequate, but mountainous and northern places often call for snow or studded tires.

3  Make sure your tire chains are the right size and type for your tires. Mismatched chains can cause tire failure.

4  Regularly check tire pressure in frigid weather. Tires lose roughly 1 pound per square inch of pressure with each 10-degree temperature decline. Never reduce tire pressure in an effort to increase traction in snow, ice or mud.

5  Make sure your windshield wipers and defroster are in good repair and that your washer reservoir is filled with antifreeze washer fluid (not all washer fluid has antifreeze capability). Keep snow and ice from accumulating on windshields, windows, rear-view mirrors and headlights (see 956 "Remove Ice From Your Windshield").

6  Be sure your radiator contains an adequate mixture of water and antifreeze for utmost protection.

7  Although it's tempting to neglect a dirty vehicle because it'll probably rain or snow again anyway, road salt, slush, grime and the like are particularly brutal to your car's finish. To minimize rust and paint damage, regular washings and waxes are necessary. Full- or self-service car washes make the task much more tolerable in cold weather.

8  Brake, accelerate and turn slowly. Keep plenty of distance between cars. You never know when you will hit an icy spot.

9  Pump the brakes slowly and gently if your car lacks antilock brakes. If you start to skid, let up on the gas and the brake, then shift into neutral. If your rear wheels are skidding, turn smoothly in the direction you want to go. If the front wheels are skidding, avoid steering until the car slows enough for the tires to regain traction.

✳ Tip

Keeping your battery's terminals free of corrosion can augment its performance, and a load test by a certified mechanic will determine if it holds enough charge for winter starts.

⚠ **Warnings**

When road ice begins to melt, the thin layer of water on top can make it even more slippery than when conditions are colder.

Beware of dark patches on the road; these may be covered with "black ice" and are extremely slippery.

Do not warm up your car in a closed space. Carbon monoxide is odorless and can be fatal.

**Things You'll Need**

❑ strong battery

❑ proper tires

❑ tire gauge

❑ antifreeze washer fluid

❑ antifreeze

## 958 | Buy Cheap Airline Tickets

With a little forethought and some flexibility, you can reach your favorite destinations without breaking the bank.

### ⊙ Steps

1 Keep yourself updated on airfare wars by watching the news and reading the newspaper. Look for limited-time promotional fares from major airlines and airline companies just starting up.

2 Be flexible in scheduling your flight. Tuesdays, Wednesdays and Saturdays are typically the cheapest days to fly; late-night flights ("red-eyes"), very early morning flights and flights with at least one stop tend to be discounted as well.

3 Ask the airline if it offers travel packages to save money in other areas. For instance, is a rental car or hotel room available at a discount along with the airline ticket?

4 Find out whether the stated fare is the cheapest, and inquire about other options when speaking to the airline reservations clerk. If you're using the Internet, check more than one Web site and compare rates.

5 Inquire about standby fares if you're flying off-season. High season is a bad time to fly standby because most airlines overbook flights, making it difficult to find a spare seat.

6 Purchase tickets through consolidators, who buy blocks of tickets and sell them at a discount to help an airline fill up all available seats. Check the travel section of the newspaper under "Ticket Consolidators."

7 Book early. You can purchase advance-ticket discounts by reserving 21 days ahead; book even earlier for holiday flights, especially in November and December. Keep in mind that holiday "blackout periods" may prevent you from using frequent-flier miles.

8 Stay with the same airline during your entire trip to receive round-trip or connecting fare discounts.

### ✱ Tips

Note strict refund and exchange policies on tickets bought through name-your-price sites.

Once you've shopped around, consult a travel agent to find out if he or she can ferret out a cheaper ticket.

If you take at least two trips a year, you can get discounted fares by joining a travel club.

If you will be visiting different countries on the same trip, you can save by asking the agent to arrange open-jaw flights, in which you arrive in one city but depart from another.

Ask about student, senior and military discounts.

### ⚠ Warning

Consolidators may delay in delivering your tickets, don't allow refunds or exchanges, and don't take reservations. To protect yourself, purchase through a travel agent, pay by credit card, and consider buying travel-cancellation insurance.

## 959 | Make the Most of Your Frequent-Flier Miles

Flying can earn you frequent-flier miles, as can charging purchases on a credit card with an airline tie-in. After all that spending, don't waste those precious miles—learn the tricks to using them.

### ⊙ Steps

1 Choose one frequent-flier program and concentrate on maximizing your benefits within that program.

2 Know and use the frequent-flier program's partners, who may range from florists to telephone companies to hotels.

3 Consult the program's newsletter frequently for updates on new partners and promotions. If you don't receive the newsletter in the mail, call and request a subscription, or check online for newsletter postings.

### ✱ Tip

Purchase tickets using frequent-flier miles as early as possible—even a year in advance if you can. These tickets get snapped up quickly.

4　Keep track of your miles. Work toward attaining elite status if you are a high-frequency traveler, or a free trip if you are a leisure traveler.

5　Save your free miles for flights that are usually expensive.

6　Check your statements carefully, and keep your travel receipts in case the airline forgets to credit your account properly.

## Choose a Good Seat on an Airplane 960

Where should you sit on an airplane if you're prone to motion sickness? If you have a connecting flight? If you're traveling with kids? Ask an airline agent about reserving the right seat for you.

### ☉ Steps

1　Request bulkhead seats—those behind the dividing walls of a plane—or a seat by one of the emergency exits if you want more leg room.

2　Choose an aisle seat for easier access to the overhead storage compartment and lavatories, as well as for faster disembarking.

3　Consider sitting near the lavatories if you are traveling with children.

4　Opt for the back of the plane if you want to sprawl out; there are usually fewer people in the back.

5　Sit toward the front if you want to get off the plane faster, which could be important if you're trying to make a tight connection. The front of the plane also tends to be a quieter ride.

6　Choose a seat toward the wings, which are the stability point for the plane, if motion sickness is a potential problem.

7　Sit near the galleys if you want early snack, beverage or meal service.

### ✳ Tips

If you're traveling with a companion, reserve the aisle and window seat of a three-seat row. Because middle seats are the last to be sold, you have a good chance of having an extra seat.

Join a frequent-flier program to increase your chances of getting a good seat on the plane.

### ⚠ Warning

Exit-door seats must be filled by passengers willing and able to help people in an emergency situation and may not be available for reservation. Check with your airline agent.

## Choose a Cruise 961

Cruise lines, one of the fastest-growing segments of the travel industry, offer a wide variety of interesting destinations and activities for all ages.

### ☉ Steps

1　Deal with a cruise-only travel agent or an online agency that specializes in cruise vacations. They are more likely to have access to specials and cruise deals.

2　Decide where and when you want to cruise and the port you want to embark from. There are Caribbean and Asian sails nearly year-round. Alaskan cruises take place only in the summer, as do most cruises in Europe. Trips through the Panama Canal take place in spring and fall.

3　Decide who will be joining you on the cruise. Families have different needs and entertainment requirements than singles or couples.

### ✳ Tips

Be aware that port fees are often not included in advertised prices. They can add significantly to your cruise costs.

Budget for tips to shipboard waiters, room stewards and service personnel. Ships often have suggested amounts, depending on the length of the cruise.

4   Outline the activities that appeal to you: ports of call, shore excursions, onboard facilities and amenities.

5   Decide if you have a preference about ship size. Large ships have more entertainment choices, while small ships have a more personal approach to service.

6   Determine your budget. Cruise lines give discounts for early bookings. You can also affect your costs by altering cruise dates, the length of your cruise and the region you sail to.

7   Ask about the typical age group of those sailing on a particular line or ship. This can help you determine whether you'll be compatible with your fellow passengers.

8   Choose the level of formality you prefer. Some ships demand formal or business attire at certain dinners. Other ships cater to vacationers who want to wear only casual clothing.

Pack light. Getting on and off ships is not as easy as picking up your luggage at the airport.

Bring along toiletries, film and sunscreen. They can be quite expensive onboard.

## 962 | Rent a Houseboat

Houseboating is popular worldwide, with hundreds of rental locations in North America alone. Choose a destination and plan ahead for the perfect vacation on a lovely lake or river.

### ⊙ Steps

1   Check with local travel agencies, or do a search on the Internet, for a list of companies that rent houseboats across the United States and abroad.

2   Call a few of the rental companies listed in the area you're interested in visiting. Find out what services they offer and request an information packet. Most important, ask for references and check them before making your decision.

3   Choose family or friends to share the vacation with you, if desired. Most houseboats can accommodate a dozen or so people, so you will be saving money if you split the costs.

4   Decide how luxurious you want your accommodations to be. Houseboats can come with everything from VCRs and air conditioning to fully stocked kitchens and hot tubs.

5   Obtain a list of exactly what you need to bring. The rental company should give you this information in advance.

6   Submit a confirmation deposit once you have selected a rental company. This is usually around $300 to $500, and is refundable at the end of the trip as long as the boat is in good condition when you return it.

7   Expect to pay the full rental amount either one or two months before your trip, depending on the time of year and the company you choose.

### ✷ Tips

Not every outfit on the same body of water charges the same amount to rent a houseboat. Call around.

Although you don't need prior nautical experience, you may be nervous about steering or maneuvering a houseboat. Be sure the rental company provides enough instruction so that you feel confident.

Ask about seasonal price differences, if any. Choosing a vacation during the area's off-season may save you money.

### ⚠ Warning

Since houseboating is so popular, don't expect to drop in at the last minute and get what you want. Operators suggest making plans and reservations up to a year ahead of your vacation to guarantee availability.

## File for a U.S. Passport | 963

If you're going on a foreign trip, it's best to apply for your passport at least eight weeks before you plan to leave, to allow time for processing and any possible complications.

### ⊙ Steps

1. Pick up a passport application. To find your nearest passport agency, look in the government pages of the phone book under "Passport" or "Immigration." You can also apply for a passport at many courts, post offices and libraries.

2. Download an application from the State Department's Web site (www.travel.state.gov) if you cannot find one locally.

3. Get two passport pictures at a photography shop, usually for $10. Make sure the photos match the dimensions of the diagram on your form. Color or black-and-white is acceptable, but the picture must have a white background.

4. Fill out the passport application and attach photos where noted.

5. Take the completed application to the location where you obtained the form, with your birth certificate or other citizenship papers. Your birth certificate must be an original, not a copy. If you're renewing a passport issued within the past 15 years, you may be able to apply by mail. Check with a passport agency or the State Department Web site for details.

6. Provide a current address where you can receive mail.

7. Ask the passport officer for expedited service if you need the passport in less than eight weeks. Keep in mind that expedited service requires an additional fee and, in some cases, additional documentation.

8. Expect to wait six to eight weeks if expedited service is not requested.

### ✳ Tips

Get multiple application forms in case you make a mistake.

Carry a photocopy of your passport in a safe place; if you lose your passport, you'll be able to replace it more quickly.

Some foreign countries don't require a passport for entry. Check with your passport office or with the embassy of the country you plan to visit.

### ⚠ Warning

If your passport is more than 10 years old, you need a new one. Children under 16 need to renew every 5 years.

### Things You'll Need

❏ passport application

❏ passport photographs

❏ birth certificate or citizenship papers

## File for a Travel Visa | 964

Many foreign countries require a visa in addition to your passport. You can apply for a visa at the nearest consulate of each country you plan to visit.

### ⊙ Steps

1. Call the consulate of the first country you intend to visit and ask for immigration services. Most consulates are located in Washington, D.C., within area code 202; many major U.S. cities also have consular offices.

2. Ask if you need a tourist visa to visit this country.

3. Request an application by mail if a visa is required.

4. Fill out the application as soon as you receive it. Describe the estimated length and nature of your visit where indicated.

5. Make a copy of your application to keep for your records.

### ✳ Tip

You may need to send passport photos with your application. For long, multicountry trips, you may want to have 10 or more photos taken at once for convenience.

### ⚠ Warning

Leave plenty of time for your application to be processed, as complications are common.

6  Attach any required fee and photos, and return the original application to the consulate by mail or fax, as appropriate. Be sure to submit it early, since processing can take several weeks.

7  Keep your visa with your passport, when it arrives.

8  Repeat the application process for other countries as needed.

---

## 965 | Exchange Currency

When you're traveling abroad, banks and legal money changers offer the best rates when you need to exchange one currency for another.

### ⊙ Steps

1  Look in the business section of the local newspaper for the current exchange rates.

2  Find a legal money changer (an American Express Travel Service, for example) or bank, which offers better rates than an airport or hotel. If you withdraw money from an ATM, you'll receive the bank's exchange rate, but you may incur transaction fees.

3  Show the teller your passport.

4  Use your own calculator to ensure the accuracy of the exchange.

5  Sign the release form.

6  Count the money before you leave the desk, and take your time.

7  Get a receipt. Customs officials won't ask to see it, but it's always a good insurance policy to have one when you've exchanged money.

### ✱ Tips

Exchange a small amount of money before you leave for your trip so that you're not forced to exchange currency at the airport upon arrival.

When you use traveler's checks, a commission is taken out per check. Exchange larger denominations when possible.

Money changers often don't exchange coins, so spend your loose change before you leave.

### Things You'll Need

❑ calculator

❑ passport

---

## 966 | Prepare Your Car for a Road Trip

Whether you're headed for the mountains or the beach, it's crucial that your auto be in good working order. There's nothing worse than having a vacation ruined by car trouble.

### ⊙ Steps

1  Make an appointment with your mechanic at least a few weeks before your road trip to do a pretrip inspection. Bring a checklist of things to ask your mechanic to review.

2  Check all fluids.

3  Check belts and hoses.

4  Look for any leaks.

5  Check and fill all tires, including the spare tire, and make sure they're in good condition.

6  Perform a four-wheel brake check (if not done in the last six months).

### ✱ Tips

These steps are in addition to routine maintenance; see 941 "Maintain Your Car Regularly."

Don't wait until the day before you plan to leave to make any big repairs or get a tune-up.

Some garages sell a pretrip inspection service. Find out exactly what they check, or just give them this list, so you get your money's worth. A pretrip inspection like the one suggested here should take no more than 1 to 1½ hours.

7   Check the condition of the exhaust system.

8   Flush the cooling system (if not done in the last year).

9   Pressure-check the cooling system to inspect for leaks.

10  Load-test the battery to test its ability to hold a charge.

11  Check the alternator output to make sure that the charging system is working well.

12  Replace the spark plug wires if they are more than two years old.

### ⚠ Warning

More than half the cars that get towed into shops are there for repairs that could have been prevented by regular maintenance.

## Pack a Suitcase                                                    967

Packing a suitcase is a strategic exercise in maximizing space and minimizing wrinkles. You may already have a favorite packing system, but read on for more suggestions.

### ◉ Steps

#### Pack Clothing

1   Remember this order of operations: shirts on the bottom, then dresses (if applicable), then pants.

2   Stack tops, unfolded, by placing wrinkle-prone tops toward the bottom of a pile and less easily wrinkled ones toward the top.

3   Fold the sleeves in toward the shirts' torsos.

4   Fold the shirts in half from the bottom. You now have a rectangular bundle of shirts; place it in your suitcase.

5   Drape long dresses in the suitcase so that the ends hang over the sides.

6   Place pants and skirts on a flat surface; fold each in half lengthwise.

7   Stack pants and skirts on top of one another, with easily wrinkled ones on the bottom and sturdier ones, such as jeans, on top. Fold the stack over, so that its length is halved.

8   Place your stack of pants and skirts on top of the dresses, then fold the ends of the dresses over the pants and skirts.

#### Pack Accessories

1   Roll ties loosely.

2   Stuff socks in shoes. Pack underwear in mesh laundry bags or side pockets to save space.

3   Arrange each pair of shoes so that the heel of one aligns with the toe of the other.

4   Wrap pairs of shoes in separate plastic bags, and place them along the border of your suitcase.

5   Protect clothes from leaks by placing toiletries in a plastic bag.

6   Pack essential toiletries in a carry-on bag. Include your toothbrush, toothpaste, makeup, medication and other important items.

### ✳ Tips

Pack items snugly, leaving little room for them to shift. Consider surrounding them with a plastic dry-cleaning bag to minimize creases; use a garment bag for suits or dresses.

Pack an easily flattened extra bag, such as a lightweight duffel, for carrying purchases you make on your trip.

Label both the outside and inside of your suitcase with your name, address and phone number. Remove old baggage claim checks.

Travel light. Check with your airline regarding restrictions on size, weight and number of luggage pieces allowed.

### ⚠ Warning

Avoid packing money, jewelry, travel documents, medication, keys and other valuables in your suitcase. Carry these items with you.

## 968 | Avoid Overpacking

Moderation is key when packing for any trip. A good rule of thumb is to pack approximately half of what you initially think you're going to need.

### Steps

1   Know your itinerary. If you know about the dressy events, casual evenings and business days you have in store, you can plan accordingly and avoid bringing unnecessary outfits.

2   Research the weather at your destination. If summer days are notoriously dry, take a risk and skip the umbrella; if nighttime temperatures are known to plummet, pack layers for warmth.

3   Plan your clothes around one main coordinating color. Black and khaki are good, neutral "foundation" colors that you can dress up, dress down, add color to and accessorize for different events and different days. Consider bringing dark colors and prints that don't show dirt.

4   Choose clothes for lightness and washability. Select several light layers that pack down easily and dry quickly, should you need to do hotel-room washing on the fly. Avoid bulky items like sweaters and heavy coats if you can be comfortable in two to three interchangeable layers.

5   Pack a couple of favorite scarves or belts for variety.

6   Pack a fanny pack or small backpack for day trips. If you're planning to shop, pack a lightweight duffel bag.

7   Wear your bulkiest outfit while traveling to save space in your luggage.

 **Tips**

Even if traveling for several months, you should never need more than five or six days' worth of clothing.

Check with your airline regarding restrictions on size, weight and number of luggage pieces allowed. Most major U.S. airlines allow three pieces of luggage, two of which may be carried onboard.

For more comfortable traveling, each bag should weigh no more than 20 lbs. when fully packed.

## 969 | Travel Wrinkle-Free

To avoid looking wrinkled and crinkled while you're on the road, buy and pack clothes in fabrics that resist crumpling—or that at least look good even when they're a bit mussed.

### Steps

1   Buy fabrics in wool or silk. These natural fibers have some elasticity, which keeps them from crinkling.

2   Buy synthetic fabrics or clothes that contain blends of synthetic and natural fibers. These fibers make clothing less wrinkle-prone, more durable and easier to care for.

3   Opt for linen, which creases easily but "falls out" nicely and carries off the crumpled-casual look well.

4   Choose knits instead of weaves. Knitwear—which includes cable, ribbed, tricot and jersey knits—wrinkles less than woven fabrics.

5   Pack intelligently. Make use of flat suitcase pockets and special packing accessories that hold clothes in place, and don't overstuff your bags. Consider rolling knits, denims and linens to avoid harsh fold lines.

6   Unpack your bags upon arrival.

**Tips**

Synthetics include nylon, polyester, microfibers, spandex, acrylic and acetate.

Cotton, like linen, is a natural fiber that creases easily (although the crumpled cotton look isn't generally in vogue). If you arrive at your destination with a few creases, hang up the clothes in the hotel bathroom while you run a steamy shower—harsh wrinkles will fall out.

## ✓ 970 Pack for Your Destination

Besides your regular clothes and toiletries, you'll need to include articles appropriate to your particular vacation plans. Use the checklist below as your guide to four popular types of travel excursions.

### Beach

- ❏ bathing suit
- ❏ sandals
- ❏ sunscreen and lip balm
- ❏ aloe vera gel for potential burns
- ❏ hat with a wide brim to protect your face
- ❏ sunglasses with adequate UV protection
- ❏ large sheet or blanket, thin enough to fit into your beach bag
- ❏ refillable water bottle
- ❏ beach toys that fit easily into a bag, such as inflatable balls and Frisbees
- ❏ long-sleeved overshirt
- ❏ thin pair of long pants
- ❏ long dress for cover-up
- ❏ reading material

### Slopes

- ❏ thermals or undergarments made from polypropylene or a similar synthetic fiber
- ❏ turtlenecks and light sweaters
- ❏ heavy-duty ski parka
- ❏ thin fleece jacket
- ❏ ski hat
- ❏ waterproof pants
- ❏ goggles or sunglasses with adequate UV protection
- ❏ scarf or neck gaiter
- ❏ gloves or mittens
- ❏ earmuffs or headband
- ❏ sunblock and lip balm
- ❏ several pairs of wool and liner socks
- ❏ refillable water bottle

### Boat

- ❏ jacket
- ❏ rain poncho or foul-weather gear
- ❏ wool socks
- ❏ waterproof shoes with nonslip soles
- ❏ gloves
- ❏ hat
- ❏ sunglasses
- ❏ sunscreen and lip balm
- ❏ binoculars
- ❏ still or video camera in waterproof bag
- ❏ seasickness medication (check with your physician)
- ❏ life jackets
- ❏ navigation charts and guidebooks

### Ranch

- ❏ sports bra
- ❏ three or four pairs of jeans
- ❏ turtleneck or other warm shirt
- ❏ warm jacket
- ❏ vest
- ❏ raincoat
- ❏ broken-in boots
- ❏ belt
- ❏ hat
- ❏ leather gloves
- ❏ sunglasses
- ❏ sunscreen and lip balm
- ❏ pantyhose (to help prevent your thighs from chafing)

## 971 | Clean Clothes While Traveling

Most of us take clean clothes for granted—until we travel. The following steps will help you launder clothes efficiently while on the road.

### ⊙ Steps

1   Pick clothes for your trip that are easy to wash. Buy as many drip-dry garments as you can.

2   Buy a universal sink stopper and a mesh bag for laundry. Ten feet of string or a small elastic bungee cord make a clothesline for drying.

3   Fill the sink with water and put in your clothes.

4   Work up a lather using shampoo, bar soap or, in a pinch, laundry detergent, which requires more rinsing than the other two.

5   Wring out clothes. If there's a dry, clean towel in your room, roll it up with your hard-to-dry wet stuff to expedite the drying process. Twist or sit on the clothes while they're rolled.

6   Hang clothes near a vent, air-conditioning unit or window, or in sunlight.

7   Put any undried clothes in your mesh bag when checking out. In dry, warm weather, you can keep this bag exposed to the air while traveling.

### ✳ Tips

Keep your body clean with showers, antiperspirant and powder, and your clothes will stay cleaner on the inside.

You can get clothes professionally laundered almost anywhere in the world, but the cost varies greatly. Hotels charge the most.

### Things You'll Need

❑ sink stopper

❑ mesh laundry bag

❑ string or small elastic bungee cord

---

## 972 | Make a Hotel Reservation

Comfortable and convenient lodgings—whether in a large hotel or a small bed-and-breakfast—will make your trip more pleasant. Here's how to arrange for them without using a travel agent.

### ⊙ Steps

1   Buy a travel guide to your destination, especially if you're not familiar with the area. Read up on lodging options and neighborhoods where accommodations are plentiful.

2   Plan your arrival and departure dates. If possible, choose off-season dates when you may be able to save money on lodging.

3   Choose the neighborhood you want to stay in. This generally depends on where you will be doing business or on the recreational or cultural sights you want to see.

4   Find two or three hotels in your price range that appeal to you.

5   Call each hotel. Tell the guest-services operator the dates you will be lodging there and your room requirements, and ask for the room rate. Ask about family packages where kids stay for free or at a substantial discount, and about special deals that give you a discount on surrounding attractions.

6   Find out what other services are included in the room rate. Is a hot breakfast included? Afternoon tea?

### ✳ Tips

You can also request a lodging directory from the convention and visitors center or the chamber of commerce of the area you'll be visiting. Remember, though, that you may get more honest appraisals from an independent guidebook, from friends' recommendations or from various Web sites.

If you are arriving at a local airport, ask if the hotel provides free transportation from the airport to the hotel.

Ask about other extras that may be important to you: refrigerator, hair dryer, iron, workout room, on-site restaurant, swimming pool, VCR, movie rental, wheelchair accessibility, pet-friendly accommodations.

**How to Do (Just About) Everything**

7   Tell the operator about any discounts or bonuses that will apply to your room rate. These may include AAA or AARP discounts, corporate deals, frequent-flier miles and other affinity-group concessions. Be sure the adjustment will be reflected in the final room rate.

8   Compare room rates and services and book one of the hotels. Be sure to specify a smoking or nonsmoking room.

9   Reserve the room with your credit card. This will generally hold the room for you no matter what time you arrive.

⚠ **Warning**

Check the hotel's cancellation policy. These differ from hotel to hotel, but if you cancel without letting the hotel know within the specified time, you may have to pay for a night's lodging.

# Get a Hotel-Room Upgrade                                    973

Sometimes upgrading your hotel room is possible, and sometimes it's not. Your chances depend on a combination of the available space, your arrival time and luck.

✳ **Tip**

Friendliness and charm may help encourage a hotel clerk to go the extra mile for you.

⊙ **Steps**

1   Establish loyalty by always choosing the same hotel in cities you visit often. Being friendly with the front-desk staff never hurts.

2   Ask about freebies and other specials when you book your reservation. If you don't ask, you usually don't get.

3   Join frequent-visitor programs at the chain hotels you visit. Your points earn upgrades and free stays along with other perks.

4   Organize reunions, meetings or conventions at your favorite hotel. Lots of hotels say thanks with credit for upgrades or free nights, either at the time of the event or at a later date.

5   Trade airline frequent-flier points for upgrades at participating hotels. But weigh this option carefully—it's rarely the most cost-effective way to spend frequent-flier credits.

6   Be vocal. If the room you were assigned isn't satisfactory—unclean, noisy or lacking the view you were promised—ask for an upgrade.

7   Offer to be appeased. If the staff makes a mistake that causes a delay or distress—say they misplace your luggage or, in a worst-case scenario, fail to make your room safe—make it known that an upgrade will help you forget all about the bad experience.

8   Take a chance on luck. Once in a while, you'll be in the right place at the right time. Budget rooms sometimes get overbooked, and the lucky guest who gets bumped up to the executive floor could turn out to be you.

## 974 | Overcome Your Fear of Flying

Studies have found that millions of people have a fear of flying, despite the enormous odds against a mishap. There are several ways to conquer your fears and make air travel more endurable.

### ⊙ Steps

1 Accept that it is unlikely you can conquer your fear of flying without help.

2 Get counseling or join a group. Since fear of flying is such a common phobia, many excellent clinics are available to help you. Look in the yellow pages under "Clinics," "Mental Health Services" or "Psychologists."

3 Read a book. Countless books are devoted to overcoming the fear of flying. Most include instructions on special breathing and relaxation methods and other helpful techniques.

4 Buy a tape. Some fear-of-flying programs are on tape so you can listen to instructions for relaxation and breathing.

5 Have confidence that you can succeed. Even the most serious fears about flying can be conquered with proper treatment and hard work.

6 Ask your physician for a prescription drug to relax you when you must fly, if all else fails. Keep in mind, however, that most professionals believe you can conquer this fear without medication.

### ✱ Tip

Symptoms often associated with fear of flying include anxiety attacks, heart palpitations, dizziness, a feeling of suffocation, sweating, nausea and shaking. These are symptoms of anxiety and are not medically dangerous.

### ⚠ Warning

Avoid using alcohol as a way to relax yourself, as it may impair sleep and cause dehydration. Never drink alcohol if you are also taking tranquilizers or other prescription drugs.

## 975 | Prevent Jet Lag

Jet lag doesn't have to ruin the first few days of your trip abroad. A few simple tips will help keep it in check.

### ⊙ Steps

1 Start shifting your sleep-wake cycle to match that of your destination several days before departure, changing at the rate of one hour per day.

2 Begin adjusting to the time zone of your destination by resetting your watch at the beginning of your flight.

3 Sleep on the plane when it is nighttime at your destination. Earplugs, headphones and an eye mask can help diminish noise and light.

4 Stay awake on the plane when it is daytime at your destination. Read a thriller with the light on and the window shade open, or cruise the aisles.

5 Drink plenty of water. The air on planes is extremely dry, and dehydration can worsen the effects of jet lag.

6 Avoid alcohol and caffeine while flying. They increase dehydration.

7 Exercise as much as you can on the flight during waking hours: stretch, walk down the aisles and do leg lifts (see 978 "Exercise on a Plane").

### Things You'll Need

☐ earplugs

☐ headphones

☐ eye mask

## Treat Jet Lag     **976**

Flying across numerous time zones can affect travelers for days. Try the following tips to speed up the adjustment process.

### ⊙ Steps

**Daytime Arrival**

1 Reset your watch to local time if you haven't done so already.

2 Eat a protein-packed breakfast, such as an omelet, which will help you stay awake.

3 Soak up natural sunlight to cue your body that it is time to be awake. Or spend your first day in well-lighted places.

4 Get some exercise, but don't overdo it; a good option is a gentle walk outside during the day to get fresh air and keep your body moving.

5 Take a short nap if you are really weary, but do so before 2 p.m. and sleep for no longer than an hour.

6 Go to bed at a reasonable time. Even if you feel like dropping off at 5 p.m., try to hold out until at least 8 or 9 p.m. so that you won't wake up too early the next morning.

**Nighttime Arrival**

1 Eat a high-carbohydrate meal, such as pasta, to help make you drowsy.

2 Plan to go to bed at the local bedtime, even if you aren't sleepy.

3 Think about other ways to induce sleep: a hot bath with lavender oil, a cup of chamomile tea or a massage. Keep lights dim.

4 Avoid sleeping late, even if you did not sleep well.

### ✳ Tip

Make sure your hotel room is not too hot. You'll get the best night's sleep in a cool (but not cold) room.

### ⚠ Warnings

Avoid drinking alcohol to help you sleep. It will interfere with your body's natural sleep patterns. Also avoid drinking a lot of caffeinated beverages to keep yourself awake during the day. These will dehydrate you and make you more tired when they wear off.

Avoid driving, especially in an unfamiliar place, if you are overtired. If you must drive while fatigued, be very careful. Keep the window open and make frequent stops to keep sleepiness at bay.

## Kill Time in an Airport     **977**

Waiting long hours at an airport can be boring and frustrating. Why not improve your mood by seeking out the attractions the airport has to offer?

### ⊙ Steps

1 Dissolve stress and increase energy by exercising in the airport gym. A growing number of airports now contain full-scale workout areas.

2 Power-walk around the entire airport if there is no gym. Store luggage in terminal lockers, lace up the walking shoes and get the blood pumping.

3 Surf the Web and answer e-mail at an Internet kiosk to make the time fly. Keep in mind that you'll be charged for the time you spend online.

4 Purchase souvenirs and presents for friends and family at the airport's gift shops and retail stores.

5 Get a shoeshine. Many larger airports feature hallway shine specialists to buff and polish your shoes.

### ⚠ Warning

Keep your eye on a clock at all times, and check the departure screens regularly to ensure that you do not miss your flight.

6    Enjoy a drink in the airport bar if there is one. In U.S. airports, the day's big sporting event will probably be blaring on the television.

7    Bring a good book or a stack of your favorite magazines. Airport time can constitute some of the most peaceful reading time you will ever get.

---

## 978 | Exercise on a Plane

Combat poor circulation, swelling, sore joints and lethargy on cramped flights by doing a short exercise routine. At the very least, you'll entertain your fellow passengers.

### ⊙ Steps

1    Squeeze a tennis ball, a racquetball or even a pair of socks with your hands until they're tired.

2    Keep the balls of your feet planted and raise your legs using your calf muscles. If this is too easy, place your carry-on bag on your knees. Continue until tired.

3    Plant your heels firmly and raise your toes as high as possible. Hold for five seconds, and relax. Repeat until tired.

4    Place your hands on your armrests and raise your knees slowly (together is harder than one at a time) toward your chin. Lower them slowly. Repeat until tired.

5    Cross your legs. Rotate the dangling foot in as wide a circle as possible. Continue until tired.

6    Stretch your neck by keeping your chin close to your throat and tilting your head forward. Roll your head from one shoulder to the other, but avoid rotating it backward.

7    Flex your trapezius muscles by doing shoulder hunches. Lower your shoulders, and then raise them up toward your ears into a shrug. Hold for five seconds. Continue until tired.

8    Arch your torso gently backward and forward like a cat.

9    Flex your gluteus muscles and hold for as long as possible. Squeezing your rear like this may occasion strange glances, but these muscles are the biggest in the human body and need to be exercised, too.

### ✱ Tip

When aisles are relatively empty and the seatbelt sign is off, walk around, stretch and do lunges. To lunge, take a big step (about half your height) and gently lower yourself as far as you can while keeping the torso upright and back leg straight. Return to a standing position by stepping either forward with the rear foot or backward with the front foot. Repeat. Once you become skilled, you'll be able to work up a sweat (and an audience) lunging to the toilet and back.

---

## 979 | Eat Healthfully on a Plane

With a little foresight and know-how, you can actually get a healthful—and edible—meal in the sky.

### ⊙ Steps

1    Call your airline at least 24 hours before you fly and order a special-diet meal at no extra cost. Vegetarian, Hindu, kosher, low-salt and sugar-free options are usually available. A special-diet meal doesn't guarantee that the food will be good, but at least you'll get some special preparation.

### ✱ Tip

Culinary possibilities open up on long international flights with major carriers. Call in advance and ask what special meals are available—you may be pleasantly surprised.

2 Pack a meal, if you have the time. Bring food that travels well and that requires no cutting, cleanup or permanent containers. Steer clear of foods that will bother other passengers, such as items with too much crunch or odor.

3 Bring an energy bar or some other meal replacement in case the in-flight meal is a travesty or your flight is delayed.

4 Eat in the airport if you don't want to entrust your airline with your culinary fate. Large airports have the usual variety of fast-food franchises, so pick what you know to be the most healthful.

5 Follow any alcohol or caffeine consumption with plenty of water to avoid becoming dehydrated.

## ⚠ Warnings

Avoiding MSG is tricky. You can speak to your airline, but don't expect a promise that MSG will be absent from your food. Consider bringing your own meal if you are sensitive to MSG.

Be wary of vegetarian breakfasts if you want something filling— you might get just a banana or juice.

## Sleep on a Plane | 980

Sleeping through the night or even taking a power nap on a plane can be dicey. But with the proper preparations, a satisfactory snooze is possible for almost everyone.

### ⊙ Steps

1 Reserve your seat in advance. Window seats give you a wall to lean on, and your neighbor won't need to disturb you on the way to the lavatory.

2 Buy and pack in your carry-on bag the following: travel pillow and eye mask, earplugs, comfortable clothing, slippers and bottled water.

3 Make sure that your body will be tired for the flight: Before your departure, avoid sleeping in, napping or consuming caffeine, and try to get some exercise.

4 Snag a pillow and blanket as soon as you get on the plane. Remember, your seat is reserved, but blankets are not.

5 Scan the cabin for better seats once the flight is under way. A row of empty seats with movable armrests is the best situation for sleeping on a plane—aside from first class.

6 Adjust your seat for maximum comfort. If you can't put it back far enough, try putting a pillow or blanket behind your lower back to make you more reclined.

7 Ask what time the in-flight meal will be served. Falling asleep is easier on a full stomach.

8 Tell your neighbor that you plan to sleep. The purpose is twofold: He'll leave you alone, and he can discourage the flight attendants from disturbing you while you sleep.

### ✳ Tip

Most travel stores carry a variety of pillows designed for sleeping in an upright position. Budget travelers find the inflatable U-shaped vinyl pillows satisfactory and compact; a small buckwheat-filled pillow is a higher-end option.

### ⚠ Warning

Consult your physician before taking any variety of sleeping pill.

### Things You'll Need

❏ travel pillow

❏ eye mask

❏ earplugs

❏ bottled water

## ✓ 981 Use Essential Phrases in Foreign Languages

When you're in a country whose language you don't speak, a few key phrases can get you far. This table lists useful expressions in 15 foreign languages, along with the pronunciation (in parentheses) where helpful. For languages that do not use the Roman alphabet or have a standardized transliteration, only the pronunciation is listed.

| LANGUAGE | HELLO | GOOD-BYE | PLEASE | THANK YOU | I WOULD LIKE | DO YOU SPEAK ENGLISH? |
|---|---|---|---|---|---|---|
| Arabic | mar-ha-ba | ma'a el-sa-la-ma | min fad-lak | shoo kran | o-reed | Let ka-lam In-glee-zi? |
| Chinese (Mandarin) | ni hao | zai jian | qing (ching) | xie xie (shieh shieh) | wo yao (woh yau) | Ni hui jiang ying yu ma? |
| Danish | hej (high) | farvel (far-VEL) | vaer så venlig (vaer SA VEN-lee) | tak (tahk) | jeg vil gerne (yigh veel GEHR-nor) | Taler de engelsk? (TA-ler dee EHN-gerlsk?) |
| French | bonjour (bohn-ZHOOR) | au revoir (oh ruh-VWAR) | s'il vous plaît (see voo PLAY) | merci (mehr-SEE) | je voudrais (zhuh voo-DRAY) | Parlez-vous anglais? (PAHR-lay voo ahn-GLAY?) |
| German | guten tag (GOOT-en TAK) | auf wieder-sehen (owf VEED-uh-zain) | bitte (BIT-eh) | danke (DAHNK-eh) | Ich möchte (ikh MERKH-teh) | Sprechen Sie Englisch? (SHPREKH-en zee ENG-lish?) |
| Greek | kherete (KHE-re-te) | andio (an-DEE-o) | parakalo (pah-rah-kah-LOH) | efkhareesto (eff-kah-rees-TOH) | tha l'thela (thah EE-the-la) | Milate Agglika? (Me-LAH-teh eye-lee-KAH?) |
| Hebrew | sha-LOM | sha-LOM | ba-va-ka-SHA | to-DA | a-NEE row-TSEH (if you're male); a-NEE-row-TSAH (if you're female) | At-a me-da-BER Ang-LIT? (to a male); at me-da-BER-et Ang-LIT? (to a female) |
| Hindi | namaste (na-MAS-tay) | namaste (na-MAS-tay) | KRIP-ya | dhan-ya-VAAD | mai cha-HA-ta hoon (if you're male); mai cha-HA-ti hoon (if you're female) | K'ya ap koh ungrazi hay? (Kya aap ko an-GREE-zi aa-TI hai?) |
| Italian | ciao (CHOW) | ciao (CHOW) | per favore (pehr fa-VOR-ay) | grazie (GRATS-ee-uh) | vorrei (vohr-RAY) | Parla inglese? (PAHR-la een-GLAY-say?) |
| Japanese | konnichi wa | sayōnara | onegaishimasu | arigatō | kudasai | Eigo o hanashimasu ka? |
| Polish | dzień dobry (jane DOUGH-bray) | do widzenia (dough ve-ZEN-ya) | prosze (PRO-shoa) | dziekuje (jen-KU-yeow) | poprosze (po-PRO-shoa) | Czy mowisz po angielsku? (che MOVE-ish poe an-GELL-sku?) |
| Portuguese | olá (oh-LA) | adeus (ah-DAY-osh) | por favor (pore fah-VOR) | obrigado (oh-bree-GA-du) if you're male; obrigada (oh-bree-GA-dah) if you're female | eu queria (eu kree-a) | Fala ingés? (FA-la in-GLESH?) |
| Russian | preev-YET | duh svi-DAR-nya | pah-ZAHL-sta | spa-SEE-ba | ya khah-TYEL-bi | VWEE guh-vah-RYEE-tya Pahn-GLEE-ski? |
| Spanish | hola (OH-la) | adiós (ah-dee-OSE) | por favor (pore fah-VOR) | gracias (GRAH-see-ahs) | yo quisiera (yo kee-see-YARE-uh) | Habla inglés? (AH-bla een-GLACE?) |
| Swahili | JAM-bo | kwa-HE-ri | ta-fa-DHA-li | a-SAN-te | nin-ge-PEN-da | U-na-SE-ma kiin-ge-re-za? |

## Learn Key Foreign Phrases Without a Phrase Book 982

You don't need a phrase book to learn a few key words in the local language where you're traveling. A little effort will make your travel easier and your hosts feel appreciated.

### ⊙ Steps

1 Set a reasonable goal about what you would like to learn, and stick with it. This can be as simple as learning a few basic greetings, polite terms of address, or how to order your favorite dish in a restaurant.

2 Pay attention to how others greet one another or part from one another; learning proper greetings and good-byes will always engender goodwill.

3 Find yourself a few good "teachers"—a hotel clerk, a waiter in a restaurant, a taxi driver. This doesn't have to be someone you will spend a great deal of time with, just someone who appreciates your curiosity about the language and with whom you can comfortably interact about day-to-day needs.

4 Ask how to say a few words that will help introduce you to the language's sounds. You don't need a common language to do this; pointing and gesturing will do just fine. Learning how to say your teacher's name, the name of the town you're visiting, or the numbers one through five is a good place to start.

5 Jot down words as you learn them, making up your own phonetic system that will help you remember how they sound. Have your teacher pronounce the word while you write it down the way you think it sounds.

6 Repeat new words or phrases to your teacher immediately after she says them. Ask her to say the word again. Repeat it, making adjustments in your pronunciation as you notice differences.

7 Keep a running list of new words, and review it several times throughout the day. The key to learning vocabulary in a foreign language is review.

8 Try using your new words or phrases with locals other than your teacher. Ask them to repeat the words you have learned, so you can get used to hearing the ways other people pronounce them.

**✽ Tip**

Keep your sense of humor. Trying to speak a foreign language often feels silly, embarrassing or frustrating at first, but be persistent—the payoff is worth it.

---

## Avoid Traveler's Diarrhea 983

When visiting areas with poor sanitation, avoid traveler's diarrhea by taking extra precautions with water and food.

### ⊙ Steps

1 Consider the following safe to drink: commercially bottled water with an unbroken seal, canned or bottled carbonated drinks, beverages made with vigorously boiled water, and wine and beer in their original containers.

2 Check seals on water bottles carefully; if the seal has been tampered with, the bottle may have been refilled with tap water.

3 Wipe off the lip of any bottle or can before drinking or pouring from it.

**✽ Tips**

Traveler's diarrhea, which is usually caused by consuming feces-contaminated water or food, may clear up by itself. But if it is very watery and lasts for several days, or if you are vomiting and have a fever, seek medical care; it may be a sign of a more serious infection.

4  Consider nondisposable glasses and cups unsanitary; drink from original containers and use sanitary straws, or carry your own cups.

5  Boil untreated water to purify it. Use both a filter and iodine tablets if bottled or boiled water is not available.

6  Avoid ice, fruit juice and any drinks made with tap water, such as mixed drinks or lemonade.

7  Brush your teeth with bottled water, and make sure to rinse your toothbrush with bottled water. Try not to swallow water when taking a shower.

8  Avoid any foods that may be rinsed in water, including salads, raw fruits and raw vegetables. Also stay away from dairy products if there's a question about pasteurization.

9  Eat meat, poultry and fish only if they are well-cooked, and make sure that cooked food is served hot. Some fish from contaminated waters may be toxic even after cooking; if there is any doubt, do without.

If you choose to eat raw fruits and vegetables, peel them.

For boiling water, consider purchasing an immersion coil. If you are traveling to a foreign country, you may also need to purchase a plug adapter and current converter.

---

## 984 | Get Mail on the Road

Most foreign post offices will allow travelers to receive mail through general delivery; all it takes is a little planning.

### ⊙ Steps

1  Distribute envelopes to family and friends marked "Poste Restante" or "General Delivery," and addressed to the main post office in destination towns on your itinerary.

2  Provide family and friends with a copy of your itinerary and the dates by which they should send mail so that it gets to you in time.

3  Ask family and friends to send all correspondence to your destination towns at least two weeks prior to your arrival. This will help ensure that the mail arrives by the time you do.

4  Note the hours of the local post office. Many post offices in foreign countries close for a few hours in the middle of the afternoon.

5  Bring your passport with you when you go to the post office to collect your mail. You may have to check back every few days until your correspondence arrives.

### ✷ Tip

Look for American Express locations in the area. You can also have people send you mail there, provided that you hold an American Express card or traveler's checks.

---

## 985 | Get E-mail on the Road

E-mail is a worldwide amenity these days. A few simple steps will make communicating from afar as easy as a mouse click, even when you've left the laptop at home.

### ⊙ Steps

1  Sign up for a free Internet-based e-mail account.

2  Give family and friends your new address, to prevent a lonely inbox during your trip.

### ✷ Tip

Before your trip, scan your passport and e-mail it to yourself. If you lose your passport abroad, print it out from e-mail at an Internet station.

3   Write down your e-mail password, and keep it in a safe and accessible place. Better yet, just memorize it.

4   Enter the e-mail addresses of family and friends in your e-mail address book before you leave for your trip.

5   Mark all listings for Internet cafés, universities and libraries in your travel guide. Most of these locations will offer Internet service for a nominal fee. Internet cafés typically abound near tourist spots and youth hostels.

6   Check airports each time you arrive at a new destination for Internet-access kiosks.

### ⚠ Warning

Make sure that your e-mail environment is safe. Lurkers may try to access information about you by watching you type your password or by reading your e-mail messages over your shoulder. When you've finished checking your e-mail, be sure to log off the Web site.

## Pay Bills During an Extended Absence                    986

It's important to find someone who is organized and trustworthy to assist you in paying bills while you're away. Your credit rating depends on it.

### ◉ Steps

1   Call all credit-card companies, insurance companies and other creditors that bill you monthly. Have all bills forwarded to a trusted family member or friend during your absence.

2   Make a list for your family member or friend of all creditors who must be paid monthly.

3   Make sure that your checking account has sufficient funds. Write one check to each creditor for each month that you'll be out of town. Postdate all checks accordingly, and leave them with your temporary bill payer. Supply envelopes and postage as an extra courtesy.

4   Log all postdated checks in your checkbook register so that you can balance it later.

5   Call all creditors once you return to have your address reinstated.

### ✳ Tips

Ask that your temporary bill payer keep all bill receipts for your records.

If you don't have direct deposit at work, arrange for someone to deposit your paychecks during your absence.

### ⚠ Warning

Make sure that all checks are thoroughly filled out, except for the amount. Blank checks are an invitation for fraud.

## Travel Alone                                            987

Traveling alone can open you up to unique personal experiences in new places. Take full advantage of these opportunities while maintaining your safety.

### ◉ Steps

#### Get Comfortable on Your Own

1   Follow some of the routines you have at home: Drink a cup of coffee in the morning, take an afternoon jog, visit the market in the evening.

2   Create a temporary home, if you are staying more than a couple of days, by decorating your room with familiar objects, such as pictures, candles and flowers.

### ✳ Tips

Before your trip, get used to the idea of being alone. Go to the movies or dine out alone.

To deter male attention, a woman should consider wearing a ring on her left ring finger, whether married or not. A whistle on a chain around the neck is also a wise idea—and don't be afraid to make noise if you're in trouble.

3   Go to a restaurant and bring a book, journal or materials for writing letters. You might also bring a guidebook or map to help plan the next part of your trip.

4   Become a regular: Visit one shop consistently or have breakfast at the same café each morning, and get to know the people who work there. They can give you helpful advice about the area and, when you need it, provide assistance, which can be especially important in an emergency.

5   Meet other travelers through classes or tour groups. They can share travel tips with you and even become temporary travel companions.

## Practice Personal Safety

1   Consider learning basic self-defense. For instance, by striking the eyes, nose, throat, groin or knees, you can disable an assailant (see 894 "Choose a Martial Art").

2   Research your destination so you'll know what to expect in terms of attitudes toward foreigners and, if you're female, women.

3   Request a room that isn't on the ground floor, which can offer easy access through a window.

4   Avoid opening your door to people who are unknown to you or who do not identify themselves.

5   Become familiar with the people at your hotel's reception desk, and inform them of your comings and goings. Give them emergency numbers of family or friends.

6   Get to know the area where you'll be staying, and trust your intuition; avoid places that look risky.

7   Dress like a local resident, or at least try to look inconspicuous in your dress and behavior.

8   Walk with confidence. If you're feeling nervous, seek out a fellow traveler as a temporary companion or stay close to another pedestrian so that you don't appear to be alone.

9   Stay sober, or at least know your limits when drinking.

⚠ **Warnings**

Be somewhat cautious when meeting new people. Ask lots of questions and get to know people first before you tell them that you're traveling alone. You don't want to become a target for others to take advantage of you.

If you run into trouble in a foreign country, contact your country's embassy or the closest consulate as soon as possible.

If you are harassed, be clear and firm in your rebuff and get away from the harasser as quickly as possible. Seek out the police or other authorities if necessary.

---

## 988 | Choose a Traveling Companion

There's no single "right" way to travel—it depends on the individuals involved. What is certain is that two people with different expectations traveling together is a recipe for trouble.

⊙ **Steps**

1   Talk in great detail about goals and expectations for the trip before agreeing to travel with someone. Why are you going? What do you most want to get from the trip? What will you regret not having done? Be honest with the other person and encourage her to do the same.

2   Consider generating a set of questions to discuss with any potential traveling companion, or look for a questionnaire produced by a commercial outfitter or guidebook. Encourage your potential companion to create

 **Tip**

Be patient and persistent in looking for a companion. Better yet, make your trip a challenge to overcome any fear of being alone. Don't settle on someone only because you're afraid of traveling alone (see 987 "Travel Alone").

**How to Do** *(Just About)* **Everything**

her own list of questions—the topics that concern you both may themselves be revealing.

3   Discuss your budget in detail. Consider not just how much money you have for the trip, but also how and where you want to spend it.

4   Come up with a tentative itinerary that includes locations you plan to visit, length of stay in each place, expected travel times from one place to another, and time spent together and separately.

5   Talk about your respective travel styles. Determine whether each of you is a morning or night person, how much shopping you each like to do, how spontaneous you like to be, whether or not you smoke or drink, and how much you expect to immerse yourself in local culture.

6   Consider getting assistance from an organization that specializes in matching travel partners, if you don't know a family member or friend with whom you would be willing to travel. An Internet search on "partner travel" or "travel companion exchange" should get you pointed in the right direction.

## Take a Road Trip With a Baby                    989

Even very young babies can safely go on road trips—in fact, children are at their most "portable" during the first year of life. Here are some tips to help you take your baby on the road.

### ⊙ Steps

1   Plan frequent stops for nursing, feeding or diaper changing. Babies can get cramped and uncomfortable when they are in car seats for long periods of time.

2   Bring toys that you can attach to the car seat. Pacifier clips work well, even if your baby doesn't use a pacifier.

3   Try to travel during times when your baby is likely to be asleep. You can even travel at night, as long as the driver is well-rested and alert.

4   Pack some restful music—perhaps some soothing children's music—to help keep everyone calm even during fussy times.

5   Try to travel during the cooler parts of the day, and protect your child from heat and glare by bringing an adjustable sunshade that you can move to different windows as the sun moves.

6   Pack lots of plastic bags to hold dirty diapers, used baby wipes, soiled clothes or garbage.

7   Bring an insulated cooler if you're bottle-feeding, or take along canned, prepared single servings of formula to use while you're on the road.

### ✳ Tip
Keep an eye on your baby as you drive with a small adjustable mirror clipped on to your rear-view mirror.

### ⚠ Warning
Never take your baby out of his car seat in a moving vehicle.

### Things You'll Need
❑ infant car seat

❑ baby toys

❑ pacifier clips

❑ music tapes

❑ car sunshade

❑ plastic bags

❑ cooler

## 990 | Take a Road Trip With a Toddler

Taking a road trip with a restless toddler can be a challenge, but there are many ways to make the time go faster and keep everyone happy for at least most of the trip.

### ☉ Steps

1 Follow the seatbelt/car-seat rule: The car doesn't move until everyone is securely strapped in, and the car stops if anyone gets unstrapped.

2 If your child naps, try to travel during the time she is most likely to fall asleep. You can even travel at night, as long as the driver is well-rested and alert.

3 Make regular stops at rest areas or safe pullouts. Freeway rest areas often have a grassy area where kids can run and stretch their legs.

4 Pack cool drinks and healthful finger foods; avoid sticky or moist foods that can ruin your car's interior. Dry cereal and crackers, along with a spill-proof cup of milk, juice or water, can keep a toddler busy for a while.

5 Try to play car games that involve looking out of the window. This makes it less likely that your child will get carsick, and helps to distract her from the reality of being stuck in a car seat.

6 Bring a portable potty, and consider bringing along some pull-ups for extra insurance if your child is toilet training.

7 Pack a selection of quiet toys for the trip to keep the child busy without driving the adults crazy.

8 Bring lots of good sing-along children's music tapes, which will help everyone pass the time.

### ✱ Tips

Even if your car has tinted windows, an adjustable sunshade can help to keep your toddler cool and comfortable.

If your child tends to drop her cup, consider attaching it to her car seat with a pacifier clip or a short piece of string.

### ⚠ Warning

Give your child lots of fluids, as long car trips can be dehydrating.

### Things You'll Need

❑ car seat

❑ drinks and snacks

❑ portable potty or pull-ups (if applicable)

❑ toys

❑ children's music tapes

❑ car sunshade

## 991 | Fly With a Baby

Planning ahead can make a world of difference in maintaining your sanity when you're traveling the friendly skies with your adorable little one.

### ☉ Steps

1 Book a nonstop flight during off-peak hours, and hope for empty seats.

2 Book in advance, if possible, and select the seats you want. Where there are three-seated rows, you can often request a window seat and an aisle seat and then have one seat for your supplies.

3 Check with the airline about what you can bring on the plane. If the flight is not full, you can often bring an airline-approved car seat onboard even if you didn't buy an extra ticket. Also, most airlines will allow you to check a fold-up stroller at the gate.

4 Inquire about services and amenities when you book the flight. Does the airline provide a bassinet? Does it provide special food for babies?

### ✱ Tips

Do a diaper change in an airport bathroom before boarding.

Children under 2 fly for free but sit on your lap. Consider buying a ticket for your baby. It's safer to bring a child's car seat on board.

5 Consider taking a red-eye if it's a long flight. Although you may not get a good night's sleep, it may be easier for your baby to travel at night and avoid dramatic changes in routine.

6 Try to fly with another adult, who can offer an extra pair of hands and provide additional ideas for entertaining the baby.

7 Bring food, bottles and new toys as well as old favorites. Also bring an extra pair of baby clothes and plenty of diapers. Being stranded in a plane with a baby in wet clothes or diapers does not bode well for any-one on the plane.

8 Travel equipped with medical records and your pediatrician's phone number if your baby takes medication.

9 Preboard. If you're choosing seats, try to sit near other families. In addi-tion to the distraction other children can provide, another family may tolerate your child's temper tantrum better than most other travelers.

10 Offer your baby a bottle, cup or breast on the ascent and descent. Swallowing helps eliminate any discomfort from changing air pressure.

### ⚠ Warning

If your child has a cold or any upper-respiratory symptoms prior to the flight, check with a health-care provider about whether to fly at all.

### Things You'll Need

❑ food

❑ bottles

❑ baby toys

❑ change of baby clothes

❑ diapers

❑ medical records and pediatrician's phone number

---

# Fly With a Toddler | 992

You don't have to stay at home just because you have a toddler. It's possible to go anywhere you like—even on long airplane trips—with some careful preparation.

## ⊙ Steps

1 Schedule a night flight, if possible, so that your little one is likely to sleep for at least part of the time.

2 Pack a change of clothes, or dress your child in layers that can be easily removed in case of spills.

3 Consider the preboarding option for parents of young children. If your child is mellow and sleepy, it's a great idea, but if he's wide awake and excited, it might be better to delay boarding as long as possible.

4 Keep in mind that only certain car seats are airline-approved. Be prepared to check your car seat as baggage if necessary.

5 Bring a selection of healthful, nonperishable snacks and a drink in a spill-proof cup. In-flight food services aren't designed with hungry, impa-tient toddlers in mind.

6 Prepare a surprise pack of small new toys, picture books and other tiny treats. Bring them out one treat at a time, whenever your child begins to get restless.

7 Remember that antinausea medications are a good idea if your child has a sensitive stomach. They also cause drowsiness.

8 Bring a collapsible stroller or kid-carrier backpack to use in the airport, especially if you have a connecting flight to catch. If it doesn't fit in the overhead bins, an attendant will check it for you. Airports are big and can be very tiring for little feet.

### ✱ Tip

Do a diaper change in an airport bathroom before boarding.

### ⚠ Warning

Turbulence can be dangerous for people who aren't strapped in, and walking or running in the aisles can also be disruptive.

### Things You'll Need

❑ change of clothes

❑ car seat

❑ snacks and drinks

❑ spillproof cup

❑ books and toys

❑ collapsible stroller or kid-carrier backpack

## 993 | Quickly Childproof the Grandparents' House

Grandma and Grandpa's can be a worrisome place when break-able or dangerous objects are within your child's reach. Here are some quick ways to help make the house child-friendly.

### ☉ Steps

1 Call first. Remind Grandma and Grandpa to move treasured figurines out of reach of little hands, preferably before your child sees them and wants to play with them.

2 Pack safety items you may need, such as simple press-on outlet covers, twist-ties to secure blind cords, or removable edge/corner guards for tables and low shelves.

3 Quickly tour the area your child will be in, preferably on your hands and knees. This will allow you to see possible hazards from her level.

4 Check closets and drawers, and remove dangerous objects like pens, lighters and matches. Remember to look under beds as well.

5 Move houseplants out of reach. Not only can some be toxic, but they also provide a great opportunity for your child to make a mess or injure herself with a falling pot.

6 Make sure that bags or purses containing medication are out of reach. Grandparents often replace childproof caps with caps that are easier for them to remove.

7 Lower the toilet lid and close the bathroom door. You'll reduce the risk of drowning and eliminate the opportunity for your child to lock herself in the bathroom.

8 Ask if outside doors and doors to other rooms within the house can be closed, and ideally locked. This makes it much easier to keep track of your child if she tends to wander.

9 Bring toys and books from home, making your child less likely to get into other things.

10 Be cautious with pets that may not be used to children and their quick, unpredictable movements.

11 Supervise! There's no substitute for the watchful eye of an adult.

### ✱ Tip

If your child will be sleeping in a big bed, bring a portable guardrail, or pull a couple of high-backed chairs next to the bed so that she can't fall out.

### ⚠ Warnings

If your child has food allergies, remind grandparents ahead of time, and suggest a list of appropriate snacks. Allergy attacks are common when children eat unfamiliar foods.

Ask Grandma and Grandpa not to leave out bowls of nuts or candy, which could pose a choking hazard.

Watch out for dangling blind and curtain cords; ask if you can tie them out of reach with a twist-tie or piece of string.

### Things You'll Need

❑ outlet covers

❑ twist-ties

❑ removable edge/corner guards

## 994 | Time Your Trip to Rome

Nearly 2,000 years have passed since Rome was at the height of its power, but it still retains much of its grandeur.

### ☉ Steps

1 Aim for the spring or fall low seasons if you want to avoid crowds and high prices. Flights are cheaper, hotel rates drop about 25 percent, and attractions and restaurants aren't as busy. If you go during summer, prepare for higher prices and more tourists.

### ✱ Tips

Must-sees if you visit Rome are the Colosseum, the most famous building of Roman antiquity; St. Peter's Basilica (Basilica di San

2. Keep weather in mind. The average low in January is 40 degrees F and the average high in July is 82 degrees F. From mid-May until October there's always a risk that the heat and humidity will combine to make it unpleasant. In spring and autumn, pack a sweater and raincoat.

3. Experience diverse aspects of modern Roman culture—religion, music, food and sports—at the Festa di San Giuseppe in the Trionfale Quarter around March 19.

4. Visit during the major Christian holidays of Christmas and Easter if you want to view the elaborate Vatican festivities firsthand.

5. Eat and drink yourself silly at La Festa di Noiantri. In mid-July the restaurants of Trastevere (in Old Rome) spill out into the streets to create a giant party.

6. Avoid a visit during the second half of August, when many Romans leave for their vacations and the city practically shuts down.

Pietro); the Vatican and its museums; the Pantheon; the Spanish Steps; and the Roman Forum.

Amble through the Piazza del Campidoglio by night, and climb the steps to the Cordonata for the best view of the Roman Forum and Palatine Hill.

You can see the Pope say Mass on most Wednesdays at noon when he blesses the crowd in St. Peter's Square.

# Time Your Trip to Paris

**995**

What hasn't been said about Paris, one of the world's most romantic and cultured destinations? When to go depends largely on what you want to see and how much you're willing to pay.

## ⊙ Steps

1. Decide when you want to visit. Paris enjoys a temperate climate with steady precipitation. Winters, often gray and chilly, are a cheap time for flights and lodgings. January's average low is 32 degrees F; the average high in July is 76 degrees F.

2. Consider visiting in the spring or fall. During the summer, Paris has two strikes against it: Transatlantic flights cost more, and most tourist attractions are inundated by international sightseers.

3. Catch the concerts and exhibitions that spice up Paris during February. Many of the best theater, concert and opera venues are at the height of their season. Look for listings in *Pariscope* (a weekly events calendar) or in local newspapers.

4. If you are a sports enthusiast, check out the Paris Marathon in April, the French Open Tennis Championship from the end of May to mid-June, or the famed Tour de France bicycle race, which ends in Paris in late July. If you aren't into sports, you might avoid Paris at these times.

5. Ponder avant-garde and traditional culture during the Festival d'Automne, which presents music, dance and theater performances at various locations around the city during October, November and December.

**✳ Tip**

At any time of year, you won't want to miss major sights like the Louvre (Musée du Louvre), which houses da Vinci's "Mona Lisa" and a vast array of other masterpieces; Notre Dame, France's most famous church and architectural masterpiece; and the Eiffel Tower, a tall metal structure that has become Paris's international symbol.

**⚠ Warning**

Parisians have a reputation for being rude to tourists. Though some of this is exaggerated, don't be surprised if you have an unpleasant experience or two.

## ✓ 996 Tip for Service When Traveling

The word *tip*, which originated in England, was originally an acronym for the phrase "to insure promptness." Tipping is de rigueur in most of the world, but the methods and percentages vary. These guidelines are for the United States. In other countries, a service charge is often added to restaurant or hotel bills in lieu of gratuities. Consult your travel guidebook for information about local customs.

| | PROPER TIP | NOTES |
|---|---|---|
| **Airport skycap** | $1 per bag | Have a couple of dollar bills easily accessible. |
| **Bartender** | 15% of tab; $1 for one drink | Leave the tip on the bar if the barkeep is engaged. |
| **Bellhop** | $1 to $2 per bag | The money should be discreetly passed in a handshake or small exchange. |
| **Bus tour driver** | $1 to $2 per passenger per day | Pay $5 to $10 for longer tours. |
| **Bus tour guide** | $1 to $2 per passenger per day | Pay $5 to $10 for longer tours. |
| **Cab driver** | 15% to 20% of the fare | Tip more if your driver performs an extra duty such as acting as a tour guide or handling bags—or if the cabbie gets you there lickety-split on a heavy traffic day. |
| **Concierge** | $5 to $10 in a first-rate hotel | Tip for special services, such as making restaurant reservations or purchasing tickets. |
| **Cabin steward** | $3 per guest per day | Fares on some cruise lines include gratuities. |
| **Cruise ship waiter** | $3 per guest per day | Fares on some cruise lines include gratuities. |
| **Hotel maid** | $3 per night in an upscale hotel, $1 per night in other hotels | Leave cash on the dresser or desk rather than adding the tip to your hotel bill. Reward extra service, such as bringing more soap or towels, with an appropriate tip when service is rendered. |
| **Maitre d'** | No tip necessary unless he or she performs an unusual service, then tip $5 to $10 | If you're a regular patron of the restaurant, tip the maitre d' every few visits. Make the exchange seamless and discreet. |
| **Room-service waiter** | 15% of the overall bill, not including the tax; pay a minimum of $2 | Service charge may be added to the bill; add an extra gratuity if service is exceptional. |
| **Valet** | $2 to $3 upon taking or dropping off clothes or shoes, $2 for retrieving your car | If you have a lot of items going back and forth with the valet, tip a dollar or two more. |
| **Waiter** | 15% to 20% of the overall bill, minus the tax | Tip an additional 5% if the service is unusually good; less if the service is bad. For large parties, a service charge may be added to the bill; check before adding a tip. |

chart

## Time Your Trip to London                                       997

London may well be the most cosmopolitan of all cities. It is an exhilarating potpourri of the British Empire's old glory and the bustling diversity of the modern world.

### ⊙ Steps

1   Join in the national pastime of agonizing over the weather. Actually, compared to many climes, Britain's is temperate and mild for most of the year.

2   However, avoid winter, when days are short, gray, chilly and damp. The best weather occurs from April to September. The average January low is 36 degrees F; the average July high is 74 degrees F.

3   Treat your eyes and nose to the horticultural highlights of England's moist climate by visiting the Chelsea Flower Show in late May.

4   If you are a sports fan, time your trip to see the soccer FA Cup Final held at Wembley or the London Marathon, both of which are held in May. Or slip into town in late June, just in time to enjoy two weeks of tennis at Wimbledon.

5   Celebrate British royalty and the Queen's birthday with the Trooping the Colour Parade in June.

6   Select from a huge variety of concerts and other productions at the City of London Festival in June and July.

7   Shake your booty at the Notting Hill Carnival, usually held on the last Sunday and Monday of August. Live soul, rhythm and blues, and reggae music combine with Caribbean food in this neighborhood celebration, the largest of its kind in Europe.

### ✳ Tip

Be sure to visit the Tower of London, the British Museum, Hyde Park, Trafalgar Square, the Houses of Parliament (Including its clock tower with the famous bell known as Big Ben), and, of course, Westminster Abbey (where English monarchs have been crowned and buried for most of the past millennium).

### ⚠ Warnings

London is so big that taking the "tube" (subway) is a must. Beware: This complex system corresponds little to the streets above, sometimes causing confusion. But the classic map of the tube system, posted at all stations and available in pocket versions at ticket offices, makes it easier to figure out.

London's world-class sights attract world-class crowds in July and August.

## Time Your Trip to New York City                               998

What other city has the audacity to style itself "the capital of the world"? New York is a city of superlatives, a kaleidoscope of famous buildings, museums and colorful neighborhoods.

### ⊙ Steps

1   Remember that late spring and early fall bring the best weather to New York. Summers are often sweltering and humid, while snowfall and freezing temperatures are common during winter. The average July high is 84 degrees F; the average January low is 26 degrees F.

2   If food is your passion, don your pants with the elastic waistband in mid-May and eat your fill of exotic fare at the International Food Fair on Ninth Avenue.

3   Listen to the greatest musicians in jazz at the JVC Jazz Festival during the second half of June. About 300 artists play 40 venues in and around the city.

4   Celebrate the end of summer by joining the million-plus people who participate in the Caribbean Day parade on Labor Day, in Brooklyn.

### ✳ Tips

New York is in a perpetual state of tourist high season. You stand the best chance of finding lower hotel rates and airfares from January to March, although even during these months it's difficult.

To find out what cultural events are going on, check out listings in *The Village Voice* weekly newspaper or the weekly magazines *New York* or *The New Yorker.*

5   Catch the latest arrivals to the silver screen at the New York Film Festival, held at Lincoln Center from late September to early October.

6   Cheer on runners at the New York City Marathon in early November. It's the largest in the United States and one of the most prestigious events of its kind worldwide. Two million cheering spectators line the course, along with 40-plus musical bands.

7   If you can bear the cold weather, experience the holiday season New York–style by ice-skating in Rockefeller Plaza and by shopping among show-stopping window displays along Fifth Avenue and the designer boutiques along Madison Avenue.

8   Find out in advance about special exhibitions that may be coming to New York's world-class museums, which include the Metropolitan Museum of Art (the Met), the American Museum of Natural History, the Guggenheim Museum and the Museum of Modern Art (MOMA).

9   For good deals on tickets to Broadway and off-Broadway shows, stop by the TKTS (cut-price tickets) booth at the northern end of Times Square before afternoon or evening performances.

No matter when you visit, make sure to ascend the Empire State Building and the Statue of Liberty, which afford great views of New York City but require waiting in line. The World Trade Center also offers spectacular views. When you need to regain your sanity, take a daytime stroll in Central Park.

## ⚠ Warning

While recent years have definitely seen a decline in crime, visitors should nonetheless observe the precautions they would in any large city, keeping personal valuables well-secured and avoiding secluded or unsavory-seeming areas after dark.

## 999  Time Your Trip to San Francisco

**Scenic, colorful and tolerant, San Francisco offers something for everyone. Its location between the ocean and the bay makes the weather as unusual as the city itself.**

### ⊙ Steps

1   For the best weather, visit in May, September or October, but remember that gorgeous weather is possible any day of the year. The climate can change dramatically from moment to moment, and it even varies from neighborhood to neighborhood. June, July and August are often cold and foggy, suitable only if you're trying to escape from somewhere hot.

2   Take in the Chinese New Year Festival and Parade in late January or early February. The parade is one of the biggest nighttime illuminated processions in the country, and features floats, Chinese acrobats, a 200-foot-long dragon and lion dancers.

3   Check out the San Francisco Flower and Garden Show in mid-March to see how the visions of Bay Area landscapers reach fruition. Attend free seminars on various aspects of gardening.

4   Learn about Japanese culture—martial arts, tea ceremonies and singular food—at the Cherry Blossom Festival in late April.

5   If you are a film buff, don't miss the San Francisco International Film Festival, which runs from mid-April into early May. Well-respected throughout the world, the festival screens a variety of films, puts on gala opening and closing nights, and includes lots of fancy parties for attendees and stars.

6   Jog from San Francisco Bay across the city to the Pacific Ocean. The Bay to Breakers, on the third Sunday in May, is a race with so many thousands of eccentrics that it feels more like a parade.

### ✱ Tip

No matter what time of year you visit, make sure to take in a panoramic view of this spectacular city. Drive or walk up to Twin Peaks, a small double-tipped mountain sitting in the middle of San Francisco. Other good places from which to admire city views are the top of the Mark Hopkins Hotel on Nob Hill, Coit Tower in North Beach and the Golden Gate Bridge, which you can walk across.

7   Fly your rainbow in June, the month San Francisco's gay community celebrates its freedom. There's a film festival, Gay Pride Week and a Gay Freedom Day parade.

8   Hit the North Beach Festival in June if you are a big fan of Italian and/or Beat culture. You can hear everything from opera to poetry readings and feast upon some of the city's best Italian cuisine.

9   Attend the San Francisco Blues Festival in late September. Always extremely popular, and a San Francisco favorite for almost 30 years, the festival includes world-class blues headliners playing at Fort Mason's Great Meadow.

10  Take your favorite chocoholic to the Ghirardelli Square Chocolate Festival, held in early September at the landmark Fisherman's Wharf headquarters of the famed local chocolate company. Sample all kinds of yummy treats like chocolate cheesecake and chocolate-covered strawberries.

11  Check out the fun at Fleet Week, a salute to sailors and the sea held in early October. You can watch the parade of ships, see Blue Angels air shows, tour ships or mingle with sailors to your heart's content.

## ⚠ Warnings

Summer is the season when travelers might wish to avoid San Francisco. Attractions are overrun by tourists, prices are higher, and the weather is often cold and foggy.

Rainy weather and poor visibility can cause significant delays at San Francisco International Airport. Find out if your airline flies into Oakland Airport just across the bay, which is often a better alternative.

# Time Your Trip to Tokyo                    1000

**Tokyo is so built-up and energetic, it makes New York feel like a lazy Sunday in the suburbs. Despite this intensity the Japanese are hospitable and helpful to strangers. Crime is extremely rare.**

## ◎ Steps

1   Enjoy Tokyo's fairly temperate climate, which has four distinct seasons. Winter brings cold, sunny weather and the occasional snowfall. Spring and fall are usually pleasant. June and early July are often rainy. Summer is hot and humid. The average July high is 80 degrees F, and the average January low is 35 degrees F.

2   Visit during April to pack numerous cultural events into one trip. The Buddha's birthday is celebrated nationwide on April 8, and the cherry blossom season (Sakura Matsuri) is appreciated at parks around Tokyo the same month.

3   Take the train to the medieval capital of Kamakura for a spectacular festival honoring heroes of the Middle Ages; it's held at the Tsurugaoka Hachimangu Shrine on the second to the third Sunday in April. Head to Kanayama Shrine in the city of Kawasaki in mid-April for the Jibeta Matsuri, a festival and parade praising the wonders of fertility.

4   Watch nearly naked giants wrestle. Most sumo matches in Tokyo are held in January, May and September, although you can see them on TV almost year-round.

## ✳ Tip

No matter when you go to Tokyo, make sure to visit the grand old Tokyo National Museum to learn about all aspects of Japanese civilization through thousands of artifacts. Attend a performance of kabuki, ornate and easy-to-follow stage plays that have historically been the favorite form of entertainment in Japan. Asakusa (old Tokyo), the Tsukiji Fish Market and Roppongi, Tokyo's club district, are other popular destinations.

## ⚠ Warning

Tokyo is the world's most expensive destination, estimated to be at least 60 percent more costly than New York.

## 1001 Use eHow

eHow.com is the Web site where you can find out how to do just about everything—and purchase the products and services you need to do it. Here's how to get the most from our site.

### ⊙ Steps

1   Go online, type "www.ehow.com" in your browser's Web-address field and press Enter or Return. Welcome to our home page!

2   Search for a how-to (what we call an "eHow") by typing a question—such as "How do I water a lawn?"—in the search field at the top of the page. Click "Do it" to search our database of eHows.

3   Or browse through our eHow centers, such as Home & Garden. You'll find these listed on our home page, and you can also find them via color-coded navigation tabs that are visible on every page.

4   Read the eHow on the topic you've chosen. Note that some eHows also include video instructions.

5   As you're reading, check out tips contributed by other eHow users. (See "Ask Someone on a Date" or "Boil an Egg" for hundreds of enlightening examples.) If it's something you know how to do well, why not contribute your own tip?

6   Look for the handy shopping list that accompanies each eHow, and notice the featured books and tools. Just click on whatever you need to buy in order to get things done—or visit the eHow store. The products you choose to buy travel with you in a virtual shopping cart as you go through the site.

7   Probe further into the eHow universe by clicking on Related eHows. Or explore other Web sites associated with your topic by clicking on one or more Related Sites.

8   Share favorite eHows with friends and family using our E-mail to a Friend feature. You can send any eHow—with a special message of your own—to anyone you want.

9   While you're online, sign up for our award-winning newsletter and be kept in the loop on the latest eHow happenings.

10   Personalize your view of the eHow site by creating a My eHow page, which can contain your favorite eHows, important reminders and other goodies you choose.

11   Put information in the palm of your hand by downloading any eHow to your personal digital assistant—for instant reference wherever you need it.

12   Take advantage of the time you've freed up by using our site to do the things you love. Or try something new and different: Start a business, paddle a canoe, win a sand-castle competition, plan a salsa party, redecorate your living room—or any of thousands of other things—using eHow's step-by-step instructions.

### ✳ Tips

If you don't have the time or desire to do a task, we can still assist you in getting the job done. Look for the Who Can Help You With This section to find people and services that can help you complete just about any task.

Check out our site regularly for new and timely features. For example, our seasonal centers come to life at holiday time to help you enjoy the festivities in new and creative ways. And the eHow store will help make holiday shopping a breeze.

Share with us what you think of our site or this book. E-mail us directly at feedback@ehow.com.

### ⚠ Warning

eHow can be highly addictive. People come to our site to find out how to do one task and end up learning a lot of other things along the way. Visit eHow.com only if you're prepared to learn more—and do more—than you ever thought you could.

# Contributor Credits

eHow would like to thank all of the writers, consultants and experts who helped make this book possible, especially the following:

Allan Abbott, MD
Jill Adler, MD
Steve Adler, MD
Ankush Agarwal
David Algeo
Paul Auerbach, MD
Gloria Averbuch
Sam Ayoubpour
Steve Baker
Sally Ann Barnes
Patrick Barrett
Jonnie Basarich
Susan Batten, DMD
Shelly Bellamy
Bryant Benson
Quita Bingham
Grant Bixby
Richard Booth
Anita F. Bott
Julia Bourland
Renee Branski
Karen Bridgers
Mike Brigante
Bobbi Brown
Teresa Cameron
June Campbell
Sandy Carlson
Joyce Chan, RN
Paul Chartrand
Jo Ann Cichewicz
Danny Clark
Lon Clark
Daniel Collado, DDS
Paula Criss
Greg Crouch
Laurie Daniel
Stephanie Daniels
Justin Davidson
Gail Davis, RN, IBCLC
Sanna James Delmonico, MS, RD
Annette Doherty, MPT
Pat Doherty
Ivan Donohue
Antonia Ehlers
Rob Einaudi
Lisa Ellis
Catten Ely
Sherri Eng
Melanie Feinberg
Jim Finnerty
Gary Fluitt
Veronica Lorson Fowler
Pam Gelman
Sarah Golden

Jason Graff
Stephanie Green
Beth Haiken
Kim Haworth
Rob Heidger
David Henry
John Henshell
Maria Hess
Daria Hutchinson
Alan Isabelle
Lea Jacobson
Robert Janis
James Jenson
Allison Johnson
Robin Jones
Marie Kare
Angella Kay
Dong Ho Kim, DDS
Eugene Kim, MD
Jane Kim
Jack Kolodny
Bill Kramer
Carl LaFong
Angela LaVelle
Margie Levinson
Danielle Lewis
David Lignell
Cindy Lin
Karen Lipker
Kim Llauget
Kai Llauget-Kurnik
Zen McCann
Paul McGrath
Tim McNeil
Doug McPherson
William Merrimack
Julie Metzler
Ronald Bruce Meyer
Sonia Michaels
Ryan Modjeski
Mary Ann Mohanraj
Candace Murphy
Shannon Murphy
Theresa Musser, DVM
Nathan Meyers
Nellie Neal
Roxanne Nelson, RN
Ellie Newman
Nolo.com
Andrew Nunn
Deborah Oksenberg, MD
Ben Olsen
Derek O'Neil
Ricardo Ortega

Jennifer Overhulse-King
Jason Patent
Jeff Peacock
Eve Pearlman
Larry Peetz, DVM
Thomas Penberthy
Annette Pennock
Christine Perez
Craig Perfect
Colette Plum
Joe Putnam
Janine Queller
Nik Remer
Gail M. Rickards
Bethallyn Black Rogers
Michelle Rogers
Sumit Sablok
Matt Samelson
Scott Samelson
Fred Sandsmark
Susan Sawyer
Helene Schneider, MA, MFT
Barry Schwartz
Larry Seben
Brette Sember
Pamela Shaffer
Valerie Singer
Kristin Steele
Catherine Stone
John Swartzberg, MD, FACP
Suzanne Sweers
Elvis Terrier
Ted Thomaidis
Doug Tinker
Jeff Tinker
Ryan Tinker
Patrick Towle
Jacqueline Tresl, RN
Ray Vandermay
Joseph Vause
Regina Vause
Kate Vause-Miller
Mary Vinnedge
Ren Volpe
Sharon Wagner
Lance Walheim
Kevin Walsh
Vicki Webster
Susan Wiedmann
Thatcher Wine
Marty Wingate
Sharron Wood
Ileana Zapatero, MD
Morgan Zeitler

# Index

**How to Do** *(Just About)* **Everything**

# Index

# Index

## ACKNOWLEDGMENTS

I thank every person who has helped us create both a phenomenal company and our first book: our employees, investors, partners and clients, and most of all, the millions of eHow.com users.

On a personal note, my deepest, heartfelt gratitude to my mom; my husband, Jeff; my siblings, Noah and Erin; my mentors; and my dear friends for their endless enthusiasm, patience, honesty and loving support. With you, I can do just about everything!

And finally, thank you for reading our book. Please make sure to visit us soon at www.ehow.com.

Courtney Rosen